The Computer Glossary

The Computer Glossary

The Complete Illustrated Desk Reference

Fourth Edition

Alan Freedman

American Management Association

Library of Congress Cataloging-in-Publication Data

Freedman, Alan, 1942–
   The computer glossary: the complete illustrated desk reference/
Alan Freedman.–4th ed.
     p. cm.
   Rev. ed. of: The computer glossary for everyone. 3rd ed. © 1983.
   ISBN 0-8144-7709-7 (pbk.): $24.95
   1. Computers–Dictionaries. 2. Electronic data processing–Dictionaries.
   I. Freedman, Alan, 1942– The computer glossary for everyone. II. Title.
   QA76.15.F734 1988
   004′.03′21–dc 19   88-26235

Copyright © 1989
The Computer Language Company Inc.
Point Pleasant, Pennsylvania 18950-0265
(215) 297-8082

FOURTH EDITION

The fourth edition of *The Computer Glossary* is published by the AMACOM
Division of the American Management Association. The third edition was
published by Prentice-Hall, under ISBN 0-13-164483-1, and by The Computer
Language Company Inc., under ISBN 0-941878-02-3.

Printed in the United States of America.

10 9 8 7 6 5 4 3 2

To my Mother,
Who had the vision to send me
to *Automation School* in 1960.

ILLUSTRATIONS: Irma Lee Morrison, Eric Jon Nones & Joseph D. Russo
EDITORIAL/PRODUCTION: Irma Lee Morrison
COPY EDITING: Mary E. McCann

TYPESET BY: The Computer Language Company Inc.
PUBLISHING SOFTWARE: Ventura Publisher, Version 1.1
FONTS: Bitstream Fontware, Swiss 16 pt. & Goudy Old Style 10 pt.

How Systems Relate

The symbol on the cover of this book is the corporate logo of The Computer Language Company. It was derived from the following chart, which is used in Alan Freedman's *Computer Literacy* seminars. It depicts the interrelationship of systems within the computer industry from the manager's point of view.

The management system is the set of goals, objectives, strategies, tactics, plans and controls within an organization. The information system is the database and application programs that turn the raw data into the information required by management. The computer system is the machinery that automates the process. Understanding this relationship has helped thousands of non-technical people make sense out of this field.

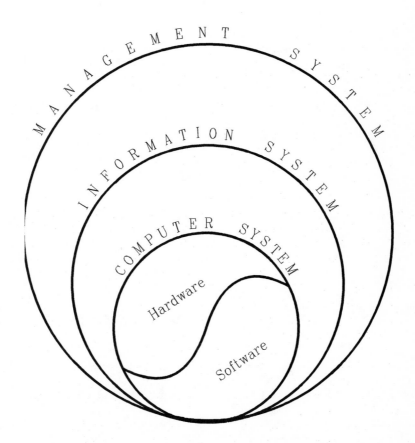

Contents

Acknowledgements xiii

Special Thanks xv

Introduction xvii

To the Business Manager xviii

To the Student xx

To the Personal Computer Buyer xxii

ALPHABETIC ENTRIES 3

NUMERIC ENTRIES 769

A Note From the Author

The purpose of *The Computer Glossary* is to provide a meaningful definition of every important computer term, be it a concept or a hardware or software product, old or new, for personal computers, minicomputers or mainframes. The degree of technical explanation chosen for each term is based on the term. General terms are explained for the lay person. Specific technical terms are explained with other technical terms. But, all the terms used in the definitions are defined in the book.

This edition is a departure from previous ones. It includes history about the hardware vendors; the companies that truly drive this industry, as well as many historical photos of the first computers and electronic devices. The old photos are not in the book for nostalgia; they are here to remind us of the extraordinary acceleration of the technology of our era. Virtually all of this has come about in little over a hundred years; since the harnessing of electricity. It should stop and give us pause as we race towards the newest and the fastest.

It is also the purpose of this book to make sense out of this industry in general. As impossible a task as that may be, I keep on trying with each edition. What started out over eight years ago as a 60-page, 300-term compendium for my seminars is now an 800-page, 3,500-term book for anyone interested in the high-tech world. In a sense, this book has become my life's work. And, for that, I am grateful, because I am truly interested in all the facets of this industry. I'm lucky to have had a wide variety of experience in this field, and I'm lucky to have expert professionals who are willing to help.

I hope you find reading this book enjoyable. If there are terms and products you feel should be included in the next edition, please let me know. In addition, if you can add facts and perspective to any of the terms in the book, I will be happy to hear from you.

Alan Freedman

The Computer Language Company Inc.
5521 State Park Road
Point Pleasant, Pennsylvania 18950-0265
(215) 297-8082

Acknowledgements

I would like to express my appreciation and thanks to each and every one of you for your technical assistance, reviews and help with this book.

PAUL T. BERGEVIN Information Representative, IBM Corporation
CHARLES L. BONZA Area General Manager, Hewlett-Packard Company
JEFFREY S. BURNETT Vice President, The Stepstone Corporation
PETER J. CHOATE Sales Manager, Solutions/Computer Bay
DR. ELIZABETH S. COBB Research Scientist, University of Utah
HENRY M. COHEN Manager Computer Systems, Rohm and Haas Company
JAGDISH R. DALAL Vice President, Unisys Networks
GARRY DAWSON Marketing Programs Manager, Hewlett-Packard Company
EMILIO DEL BUSTO Assistant Professor, New York University
STEPHEN C. DIASCRO, JR. Senior Computer Specialist, Tandy Corporation
THOM DREWKE President, Technical Directions, Inc.
THOMAS E. DUNN III Software Development Engineer, XyQuest, Inc.
MAX B. FETZER Vice President, Envirotronics, Ltd.
GEORGE C. FINLAY Senior Typographer, The Graphic Word
LYNN S. FRANKEL Sales Representative, The William Byrd Press
DR. GEORGE L. GERSTEIN School of Medicine, University of Pennsylvania
JUDI GOBEL Programmer, Hewlett-Packard Company
RICHARD W. GREENWOOD Staff Engineer (Retired), IBM Corporation
ROBERT A. GUSTAFSON Advisory Systems Engineer, IBM Corporation
DR. PHILIP HAYES Research Computer Scientist, Carnegie Mellon University
CHARLES H. IRBY Vice President, Metaphor Corporation
STEPHEN KALLIS Corporate Public Relations, Digital Equipment Corporation
SHRIPATHI KAMATH Software Engineer, Forth, Inc.
VERN LAUTNER Division Manager, American Management Association
WALTER A. LEVY President, Edgewood Computer Associates
MICHAEL A. LIND Director of Commercial Development, Optical Data, Inc.
HELENE OBACK-RUSSO Associate Professor, Long Island University
HOWARD J. POPOWITZ Vice President, Citicorp
C. WAYNE RATLIFF President, Ratliff Software Productions
MARK J. E. SHAPIRO Systems Engineer, Apple Computer, Inc.
STEPHEN SLADE Assistant Director, AI Project, Yale University
ELLEN W. SOKOL Partner, N. Dean Meyer & Associates Inc.
NADINE C. SPOTH Manager, Elxsi Corporation
JAMES R. STROH Vice President, LXD Inc.
JAMES F. SUTTER Vice President, Rockwell International
CARON R. WILLIAMS General Manager, Robo Systems Corporation
ROBERT F. WILLIAMS President, Cohasset Associates, Inc.

Special Thanks

JAMES J. FARRELL III Communications Manager, VLSI Technology, Inc.

I doubt if anyone alive understands chips better than Jim Farrell. The world of microelectronics is unbelievably complicated, and I have been unbelievably lucky to have his help. Thanks again, Jim.

KAREN E. FREEDMAN Manager, Kensington Microware

Karen Freedman made the ultimate sacrifice by loaning me her brand new Macintosh, which she had been eagerly awaiting for months. But, how could she refuse; I am her father. Thanks, Kiddo.

STEVEN M. GIBSON President, Gibson Research Corporation

Steve Gibson helped me clear up the mud of the IBM personal computer world like no other person could have. He knows the subject from the inside out. Thank you, Steve.

MARGARET A. HERRICK Principal, Margann Associates

What Margaret Herrick doesn't know about databases isn't worth knowing. I attended her database class over 14 years ago, and we've been debating the subject ever since. Thanks again, Margaret.

MARY E. McCANN Editor, The Boston Computer Society

Mary McCann has been editing my "Straight Talk" column for years, and, in so doing, she's helped me to become a better writer. She used her red pen extensively in editing this book. Thanks again, Mary.

LEONARD MIKOLAJCZAK President, DACOM

Len Mikolajczak is an expert in the maddening world of IBM communications. He knows as much about SNA as IBM does, and, more importantly, he can make more sense out of it. Thanks, Len.

IRMA LEE MORRISON Vice President, The Computer Language Co. Inc.

My wife and partner, Irma Lee Morrison, has not only worked long hours on the production of this book, but she has endured more on this project than anyone else... namely, me. Trying to make sense out of the most confusing field on earth isn't always conducive to cozy evenings in front of the fireplace. I couldn't have done this without her. Thanks, Irmalee. You're terrific.

DR. JOEL N. ORR Chairman, Orr Associates, Inc.

Joel Orr's exhaustive knowledge of CAD/CAM systems and his expertise in graphics is legendary. Joel graciously gave of his time whether he was in his office or on vacation. Thanks again, Joel.

JOSEPH D. RUSSO Designer/Illustrator

Joseph Russo provided the art direction for the book with an artistic eye that is uncanny. Only an expert can make a layout look simple. Thank you, Joseph. Your direction was superb, as always.

IRVING L. WIESELMAN President, Computer Printer Corporation

Irving Wieselman is an expert in the world of computer printers. His vast experience helped me wade through the rather arcane ways ink gets onto paper. Thanks again, Irv.

E. R. (GENE) YOST President, Black Box Corporation

Gene Yost provided me with entre to his very competent staff of communications specialists. Pat Flanigan, Mark Bennett, Mike Ramos, Larry Clark, Randy Morse and Bill Ihrig helped me in the areas of local area networks, modems and connectivity. Thank you, Gene.

Introduction

**THE COMPUTER GLOSSARY is not just a glossary...
It's a guide to Computer Literacy.**

Reading *The Computer Glossary* on a regular basis will help you keep up with the terminology, concepts and perspective necessary to interact with computer professionals effectively and get the most out of computers.

If you hear a term that is not in this book, it may be the trade name of a hardware product or software package. Find out what category it falls into, and then look it up. If a term is not in the book that you feel makes an important contribution to this industry, please let me know about it.

On the next six pages are overviews for the business manager, the student and the personal computer buyer. They will provide you with an outline to work your way through *The Computer Glossary* depending on your area of interest. The terms in the outline also serve as a springboard to other terms in the book. Every computer term that is used within the definition of another term is also defined in the book.

To the Business Manager

Learning some basic concepts and a little technical jargon can go a long way in helping you deal more effectively with computer professionals.

You should understand the system development cycle, which is the series of steps that transforms information requirements into working information systems. The systems analysis & design phase must be performed slowly and carefully. The functional specifications, which are the blueprints of the information system, must make sense to you. If they don't, there's no telling what you'll wind up with.

Prototyping the new system will lead to a better definition of requirements. If prototyping is not possible, then, once you have signed off on the design, the programming must be done as quickly as possible.

Be aware of the importance of well-designed user interfaces, the advantages of database management systems (for providing future flexibility) and the many problems with standards & compatibility.

When considering a new system, you should think about all the kinds of questions that you would ideally like to be able to ask it when it is running. The computer's ability to provide answers to ad hoc questions may provide its biggest payback. Decision support tools should be integrated into the information system design from the beginning. The most important step in systems design is looking at the entire problem at the beginning, no matter how small the first phase to be implemented may be.

If you're a manager of a small business, don't be fooled. Personal computers cost only a fraction of what computers used to cost; but, people cost as much or more. Custom-developed software that requires in-depth systems analysis & design costs just as much as it used to, if not more.

Computers are invaluable for business, but they're hardly magic. In order to ensure success with new systems, your thorough involvement with technical personnel in the design and implementation stages is crucial.

Perspective

management system
information system
computer system
system development cycle
information management

Technical people

systems analyst
application programmer
programmer analyst
systems programmer
operator

Application development

system development cycle
data administration
functional specifications
prototyping
documentation
database management system
standards & compatibility

Basic concepts

computer
byte
field
record
file
database
space/time

Software tools

query language
report writer
spreadsheet
decision support system
financial planning system

Additional subjects

office automation
graphics
communications
chip
artificial intelligence

To the Student

If you're planning a career in the information processing industry, you have many choices. If you're not, no matter which industry you choose to work in, a solid foundation of computer concepts will be extremely helpful in coping with it.

Within the computer industry, you can be involved at the electronics level as a computer designer or as a field service engineer. As an application programmer, you can work on solving problems in just about any field of endeavor. As a systems programmer, you can work as a technical consultant within a user organization, or you can design and develop system software for vendors. If the workings of business intrigue you, the fields of systems analysis and data administration are open to you. Sales and marketing of computer products also offer a wide variety of opportunities for people who enjoy the high-tech world.

Take some time to learn and understand the differences between the computer sciences and the information sciences. In theory, they are distinct fields; each with different objectives and disciplines. In practice, they are thoroughly intertwined, and the casual observer cannot often perceive their differences.

The flow chart on the opposite page provides a textbook-like curriculum for learning about computers. Also read the introductions *To the Business Manager* and *To the Personal Computer Buyer* on the previous and next pages.

Basics

hardware
software
data
computer
analog
digital
binary
byte
peripheral
magnetic recording
printer
monitor
modem
operating sytem
bus
space/time
chip
standards & compatibility

Programming

programming language
procedural language
non-procedural language
source language
machine language
assembly language
compiler
interpreter

Application development

data administration
information system
data element
field
record
file
database
database management system
data dictionary
functional specifications
systems analysis & design
system development cycle
decision support system

Office automation

office automation
word processing
electronic mail
teleconferencing

Graphics

graphics
paint program
drawing program
wireframe modeling
surface modeling
solids modeling

Communications

communications
OSI
tp monitor
front end processor
network architecture
local area network
digital PABX

Advanced programming

address modes
relocatable code
base/displacement
reentrant code
multitasking
multithreading

Advanced concepts

virtual memory
RISC
multiprocessing
computer architecture
pipeline processing
memory protection

To the Personal Computer Buyer

All personal computers are not equal. Before you purchase one, you must first know what you want to do with it. A particular computer may be great for graphics, but terrible for word procssing, and vice versa.

The hardest thing to evaluate is the software. Each type of software package has its own set of evaluation criteria. What makes one spreadsheet better than another has nothing to do with what makes one word processing package better than another. Unless you're relying on the judgment of someone you implicitly trust, you should "test drive" programs from three different vendors before making a decision.

Choosing hardware is easier. If you plan on exchanging files of data (not just mail) with other people, compatibility is the key issue. If not, the kind of software you want to use will make the decision for you. Once the hardware brand has been selected, the right model can be chosen based upon your disk and memory requirements. Hard disk capacity determines how many different programs and how much data is available to you at all times. Memory capacity determines how many different things you can do at the same time.

Unless cost is absolutely critical, don't get a system without a hard disk. It's not worth the headaches. But, when you have a hard disk, make backup copies often!

Remember. The moment you purchase a personal computer, whether it's for home or business, you have purchased a set of standards. Make your decision carefully.

Hardware

computer
memory
magnetic disk
modem
keyboard
operating system
IBM personal computer
Macintosh
Amiga
MEGA
Apple II

Software

word processing
database management system
spreadsheet
business graphics
communications program

Information basics

byte
field
record
file
database
space/time

Additional subjects

graphics
communications
chip
standards & compatibility

ABC

(Atanasoff-Berry Computer) The ABC was the first digital calculating machine that used vacuum tubes. It was started in 1939 and completed in 1942 by John Atanasoff, a professor at Iowa State University, and his assistant, Clifford Berry, a graduate student. Although the machine was specialized for differential equations, it embodied the memory, arithmetic unit and input facilities of future computers.

ABC COMPUTER
(Courtesy Charles Babbage Institute, University of Minnesota)

Since John Mauchly, cobuilder of the ENIAC in 1946, visited Atanasoff in 1940 and corresponded with him, he was considered to be influenced by

Atanasoff. In 1973, Honeywell challenged Mauchly's patents, now belonging to Sperry Univac, which had purchased Eckert and Mauchly's company years earlier, and the patents were judged invalid.

Eckert and Mauchly are still considered the creators of the first working electronic digital computer, but Atanasoff and the ABC are acknowledged as strong contributors.

abend

(ABnormal END) An *abend*, also called a *crash* or *bomb*, occurs when the computer is presented with instructions or data it can't recognize. An abend is the result of erroneous software logic or hardware failure.

When the abend occurs, if the program is running in a personal computer under a single-task (one program at a time) operating system, such as MS-DOS, the computer freezes up and has to be rebooted. Multitasking operating systems will halt only the offending program and allow the remaining programs to continue. See *protected mode*.

If you consider what goes on inside a computer, you might wonder why it doesn't crash more often. A large mainframe's memory can contain 288 million storage cells (bits). Some of the cells are in a charged state, some are uncharged. Within every second, millions of these cells change their state from uncharged to charged and vice versa. If one of those cells is unable to hold its charge, and that cell happens to be where operating system instructions are stored, the entire computer could come "crashing" to a halt. Makes you want to have another computer standing by just in case, doesn't it?

Ability PLUS

Ability PLUS is an integrated software package from Migent, Inc., that runs on IBM compatible pcs. Ability PLUS combines word processing, database management, spreadsheet, business graphics and communications in a single package. Ability PLUS also provides a way of creating a computer slide show of the output.

absolute address

An *absolute address*, or *machine address*, is the explicit identification of a peripheral device, of a location within the peripheral device or of a location in memory. For example, disk drive no. 2, sector no. 23 and byte no. 1,744,432 are absolute addresses. The absolute address is the machine identification built into the hardware. The computer must be given absolute addresses to reference its memory and peripherals. See also *base address* and *relative address*.

absolute vector

In computer graphics, an *absolute vector* is a vector with end points designated in absolute coordinates. Contrast with *relative vector*.

AC

(Alternating Current) AC is an electric current whose direction is periodically reversed and is the common form of electricity generated and transmitted to our homes and offices. Within the United States, the AC standard is 60 cycles (reversals) per second; in Europe, it's 50 cycles. All electronic digital systems use DC (direct current) within their circuits and have built-in power supplies that convert the AC into DC.

acceptance test

An *acceptance test*, usually performed by the end user of the system, determines if the system is working according to the specifications in the contract.

access

Access is used as a verb and refers to storing data on and retrieving data from a disk or other peripheral device. See *access arm* and *access method*.

access arm

An *access arm* is a mechanical arm that moves the *read/write head* across the surface of a disk. The access arm is similar to a tone arm on a phonograph turntable that moves the stylus across the record surface. The access arm is directed by instructions in the operating system to move the read/write head to a specific track on the disk. Then, the rotation of the disk positions the read/write head over the required sector, the unit of storage that is read and written as a whole.

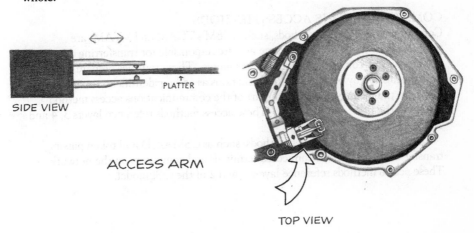

SIDE VIEW   PLATTER

ACCESS ARM

TOP VIEW

access charge

An *access charge* is a charge imposed by a communications service or telephone company for the use of its network.

access code

(1) An *access code* is an identification number and/or password used to gain access into a computer system.

(2) An *access code* is a number used as a prefix to a calling number in order to gain access to a particular telephone service.

access method

Access methods are software routines which are part of the operating system or network control program that perform the actual storing and retrieving or transmitting and receiving of data. Access methods are also responsible for detecting a bad transfer of data caused by hardware or network malfunction (read or write error, line error) and correcting it if possible.

TAPE ACCESS METHODS
With tapes, the *sequential* access method is always used for storing data, which places the next block of data after the previous one.

DISK ACCESS METHODS
For disks, the *indexed* access method is most frequently used for keeping track of individual records that must be retrieved quickly. The index serves as a table of contents to each record in the file. The sequential method is also used for disks when retrieval of individual records is not required. An *indexed sequential* (ISAM) method keeps the index in sequential order but also provides the location of each record for fast retrieval. For fastest retrieval, the *direct* access method may be used, which uses a formula to convert the record's identifying field, such as account number, into a physical storage address.

COMMUNICATIONS ACCESS METHODS
Communications access methods, such as IBM's TCAM and VTAM, are programs that reside in a mainframe and are responisble for transferring data between a host computer and remote terminals. These routines prepare the data for transmission by performing such functions as adding identification, or header, blocks to the messages. A counterpart of the communications access method resides in the front end processor. These access methods reference layers 3, 4 and 5 of the OSI model.

Local area network access methods, such as CSMA/CD and token passing, transfer data to and from connected terminals and computers on the network. These access methods reference layers 1 and 2 of the OSI model.

access time

Memory *access time* is how fast a character in memory can be transferred to or from the processor. Fast RAM chips for personal computers range from 50 to 80 nanoseconds. Disk access time is an average of how fast the access arm can position the read/write head over the requested track. Fast hard disks for personal computers range from 12 to 28 milliseconds. Disk access times are the common performance measurement for disk drives, but total performance is also influenced by channel speed, interleaving design and caching.

account number

An *account number* is a number assigned to an employee, customer, vendor or product for identification purposes. Numbers are typically used for identification rather than names, because names are problematic due to misspellings and possible valid duplications.

    Although an account number may contain only numeric digits, it is often stored as a character, or alphanumeric, field in a record, since it used only for matching purposes and not for calculation. When stored as character data, parts of the account number can be searched independently. For example, the account number might be broken up into components that refer to location, such as state or territory, and the records could be selected based on these criteria.

accounting machine

An *accounting machine* refers to any of a variety of older office machines that are used to perform calculations and prepare records or ledgers, such as for billing or payroll. Punched card accounting machines were used to summarize and print totals of numeric data in a deck of punched cards.

ACK

(ACKnowledgment code) In communications, the ACK is a code sent from a receiving station to a transmitting station to acknowledge that it is ready to accept data. It is also used to acknowlege the error-free receipt of transmitted data. Contrast with *NAK*, which is a negative acknowledgment.

ACM

(Association for Computing Machinery) ACM is a membership organization, founded in 1947, with over 73,000 computer professionals. Its objective is to advance the arts and sciences of information processing. In addition to special awards and publications, ACM also maintains special interest groups (SIGs) in the computer field. For more information, contact ACM, 11 West 42nd Street, New York, NY 10036, (212) 869-7440.

acoustic coupler

An *acoustic coupler* is a hardware device that connects a terminal or personal computer to the handset (mouthpiece and receiver) of a standard telephone. The acoustic coupler contains a foam bed shaped to allow the handset to be placed into it. The acoustic coupler may also contain the modem, which is necessary to convert the digital pulses from the computer into the audio frequencies required by the telephone system.

ACOUSTIC COUPLER

ACTOR

ACTOR is an object-oriented programming language from The Whitewater Group that runs on IBM compatible pcs. ACTOR runs under Microsoft Windows and has a Pascal-like syntax to ease the transition for programmers from traditional languages to object-oriented languages.

A-D converter

See *analog to digital converter.*

Ada

Ada is a high-level programming language developed as a standard for the Department of Defense of the United States. Ada was designed as a common language for both business applications, such as inventory control, and embedded applications, such as guidance systems built into rockets. Ada is a Pascal-based language that is very large and comprehensive.

Ada was named after August Ada Byron (1815-1852), Countess of Lovelace and daughter of the English poet, Lord Byron. August Ada Byron was a mathematician and colleague and friend of Charles Babbage, who was developing a stored program calculator known as the Analytical Engine. Some of her programming notes for the machine have survived, giving her the distinction of being the first documented programmer in the world.

ADABAS

ADABAS is a database management system from Software AG of North America that runs on IBM mainframes and Digital Equipment's VAX series. ADABAS is an inverted file system with relational capabilities and includes a fourth-generation language called "NATURAL," which provides interactive processing and application development. An optional text module called "Text Retrieval System" (TRS) provides text processing capabilities, and the ADANET option provides distributed database functions.

ADAPSO

(Association of Data Processing Service Organizations) ADAPSO is a membership organization, founded in 1960, that is primarily composed of timesharing service organizations. ADAPSO is involved in improving management methods and defining standards of performance for computer services. ADAPSO is also concerned with governmental regulations as they affect the computer services field. For more information, contact ADAPSO, 1300 North 17th Street, Arlington, VA 22209, (703) 522-5055.

adapter

(1) An *adapter* is a device that allows one system to connect and work with another.

(2) *Adapter* often refers to the display adapter, or video display board, for a personal computer, which controls the display screens. See *video display board*.

ADC

See *analog to digital converter*.

adder

An *adder* is an elementary electronic circuit that adds the bits of two numbers together.

address

An *address* is the number of a particular memory or peripheral storage location. Every byte of memory and every sector on a disk have their own unique address just like a post office box. After a program has been written, it is converted (assembled, compiled) into machine language that references the actual addresses in the computer.

address bus

An *address bus* is an internal channel from the processor to memory across which the addresses of data are transmitted. The number of lines (wires) in the address bus determine the amount of memory that can be directly addressed as each line carries one bit of the address. For example, the Intel 8086/8088 processors have 20 address bus lines and can address up to 1,048,576 bytes of memory. The Motorola 68020 has 32 address lines and can address over four billion bytes of memory.

Various swapping and switching techniques can be added to the hardware that allow a computer to use more memory than is directly addressable by its address bus. See *EMS*.

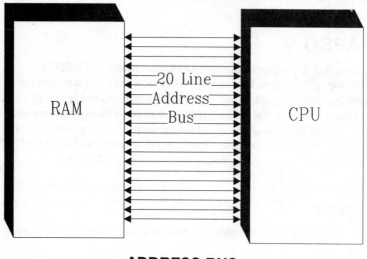

ADDRESS BUS

address mode

The *address mode* is how a machine instruction refers to memory and peripheral devices. An *indexed address* is modified by the contents of an index register before execution. An *indirect address* points to another address. Ultimately, in order to do any actual processing, the instruction must derive *real*, or *absolute addresses* where the required data is located.

address register

An *address register* is a high-speed memory circuit that holds the addresses of data to be processed or of the next instruction to be executed.

address space

The *address space* is the total amount of memory that can be used by a program. The address space may refer to the physical limitation of memory, or, if virtual memory is used, to the virtual limit of memory, which includes physical memory and disk storage. For example, the Intel 80386 CPU can address 64 trillion bytes of virtual memory.

address translation

Address translation is the transforming of one address into another. For example, assemblers and compilers translate symbolic addresses into machine addresses. Virtual memory systems translate a virtual address into a real address when the instruction or data is actually needed.

addressable cursor

An *addressable cursor* is a cursor on a display screen that can be programmed to move to any row or column of characters or bits on the screen.

ADF

(**A**pplication **D**evelopment **F**acility) *ADF* is a programmer-oriented application generator from IBM that runs on IBM mainframes under the IMS database management system.

ADP

(**A**utomatic **D**ata **P**rocessing) *ADP* is synonymous with data processing (DP), electronic data processing (EDP) and information processing.

ADP, Inc.

ADP, Inc. is a nationwide computer services organization that offers international communications services.

ADROIT

ADROIT is an authoring language from Applied Data Research (ADR) for creating computer-based training packages that run on IBM compatible pcs. ADROIT is a full-featured program that is used to create courseware that displays text and graphics and also controls audio and video playback devices.

ADRS

(**A** **D**epartmental **R**eporting **S**ystem) *ADRS* is a report writer from IBM that runs on IBM mainframes.

Advanced-Program-to-Program-Communications

See *LU 6.2*.

AdvanceNet

AdvanceNet is a network strategy from Hewlett-Packard that incorporates the Open System Interconnection (OSI) and IBM SNA network architectures. In 1983, HP was the frist major vendor to make a commitment to the OSI standard. AdvanceNet also supports MAP, Starlan 10, Ethernet and X.25 packet switching networks.

AFIPS

(American Federation of Information Processing Societies Inc.) *AFIPS* is a membership organization, founded in 1961, with over 250,000 professionals. AFIPS serves as a national voice for the computer industry seeking to advance knowledge in the information processing sciences. For more information, contact AFIPS, 1899 Preston White Drive, Reston, VA 22091, (703) 620-8900.

AI

See *artificial intelligence*.

AIX

(Advanced Interactive eXecutive) *AIX* is a version of the UNIX operating system from IBM that runs on 80386-based PS/2 and RT personal computers and IBM's 370 mainframe series, which includes the 9370, 4381 and 3090 series. AIX is based on AT&T's UNIX System V with Berkeley extensions.

ALC

(Assembly Language Coding) *ALC* is a generic term for IBM mainframe assembly languages.

ALGOL

(ALGOrithmic Language) *ALGOL* is a high-level compiler language that was developed as an international language for the expression of algorithms between people, as well as between people and machines. Introduced in the early 1960s, ALGOL achieved more acceptance in Europe than in the United States.

algorithm

An *algorithm* is a formula for solving a problem. An algorithm is a set of steps in a very specific order, such as a mathematical formula or the instructions in a program. Except for artificial intelligence programs, most software programs are algorithmic programs.

alias

(1) An *alias* is an alternate name used for identification, such as for naming a field or a file.

(2) An *alias* is a phony signal that is created under certain conditions when digitizing voice.

aliasing

In computer graphics, *aliasing* refers to the stair-stepped appearance of diagonal lines. See *anti-aliasing*.

All-In-1

All-In-1 is office systems software from Digital Equipment Corporation that runs on its VAX series of computers. All in 1 provides a menu to all of Digital's office systems programs, including word processing, appointment calendars and electronic mail systems.

alpha test

An *alpha test* is the first test of newly developed hardware or software in a laboratory setting. The next step is *beta testing* with actual users.

alphageometric

See *alphamosaic*.

alphamosaic

In computer graphics, *alphamosaic* is a display technique for very-low-resolution images. Images are created from elementary graphics characters which, like alphabetic letters and numeric digits, are designed as part of the character set.

alphanumeric

Alphanumeric refers to data that contains alphabetic letters mixed with numbers, such as a name and address. Alphanumeric data, which is also called a *string*, cannot be calculated.

Altair 8800

The *Altair 8800* was a microcomputer kit introduced in late 1974 from Micro Instrumentation and Telemetry Systems (MITS) that sold for $400 and used an Intel 8080 microprocessor. In 1975, it was packaged with MBASIC, Microsoft's BASIC interpreter written by Paul Allen and Bill Gates. Although microprocessor-based

(Courtesy The Computer Museum, Boston)

kits from other vendors were advertised and sold a few months before the Altair 8800, an estimated 10,000 Altairs were sold. Hence, the Altair 8800 was the first signficantly successful microcomputer, if not "the" first microcomputer.

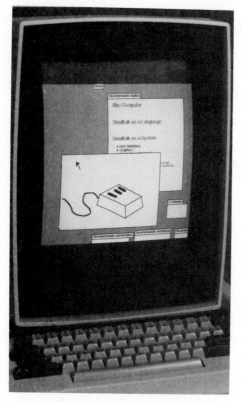

ALTO COMPUTER

(Courtesy Xerox Corporation)

Alto

The *Alto* was the personal computer from Xerox that pioneered the mouse/icon operating environment. Developed at Xerox's Palo Alto Research Center, the Alto was the forerunner of Xerox's own Star workstation, introduced in 1981, and was the inspiration for Apple's Lisa and Macintosh personal computers.

It was designed in 1973 with 128K of memory and a bit-mapped screen with 608x808 pixels. It used a 2.5 megabyte removable hard disk and could attach to the Ethernet network. By 1979, nearly 1,000 Altos were in use.

ALU

(Arithmetic Logic Unit) The *ALU* is the high-speed circuit in the CPU that does the actual calculating and comparing.

Numbers are transferred from memory into the ALU for adding, subtracting, multiplying and dividing, the results of which are transferred back into memory. Alphanumeric data is sent from memory into the ALU for comparing. The results of the comparison are tested by GOTO instructions. For example, IF ITEMA EQUALS ITEMB GOTO UPDATE ROUTINE.

AM

(Amplitude Modulation) In communications, AM is a transmission technique that modulates (merges) the data signal into a fixed carrier frequency by raising and lowering the amplitude (strength) of the carrier wave. Contrast with *frequency modulation* (FM) and *phase modulation*, which are the two other major techniques for transmitting a signal by modulating a carrier.

Amdahl Corporation

Amdahl Corporation was founded in 1970 by Gene Amdahl, chief architect of the IBM System/360. Amdahl's purpose was to compete directly with IBM by providing an IBM compatible mainframe with better cost/performance. Five years later, Amdahl installed its first product, the 470/V6 computer.

Although not the first to make an IBM compatible mainframe, Amdahl's advanced engineering and innovation helped it succeed where others failed. In 1984, Amdahl announced its "Multiple Domain Feature," which allows a single processor to function under multiple operating environments. One CPU can provide a production environment for regular users while also providing a test environment for a new operating system for systems and application programmers.

Gene Amdahl left the company he founded to form Trilogy in 1979. He is currently heading up Andor Corporation, a new venture that is making IBM compatible mainframes to compete at the lower end of the spectrum.

DR. GENE M. AMDAHL

(Courtesy Dr. Gene M. Amdahl)

Dr. Amdahl is standing beside the computer he designed in 1950. The Wisconsin Integrally Synchronized Computer (W.I.S.C.) was constructed in 1952. The picture was taken in 1975.

American Bell

American Bell was the name used by AT&T right after the breakup of the Bell telephone companies on January 1, 1984. Later that year, they were ordered by the Federal Court to drop the use of the Bell name.

American National Standards Institute

See *ANSI*.

Amiga

Amiga is a series of personal computers from Commodore Business Machines International. Amiga computers run under the AmigaDOS multitasking operating system that features a window-oriented user interface called "Workbench." The Amiga 500 is geared for home use and includes built-in speech synthesis, four-voice stereo sound and color graphics with 4,096 colors. The Amiga 2000 is designed for office applications, including CAD and desktop publishing. The 2000 includes optional IBM PC compatibility and video generation capabilities for processing NTSC video.

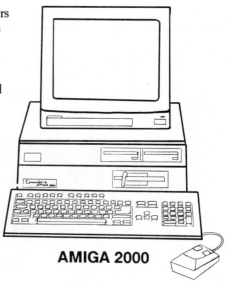

AMIGA 2000

AMIGAS II

(Advanced Meteorological Image and Graphics Analysis System) *AMIGAS II* is a meteorological software package that runs on Control Data's CYBER computers. AMIGAS II can access multiple databases, analyze the data and create products in response to meteorologist/forecaster requests.

amp

(AMPere) An *amp* is a unit of electrical current that is used to measure the quantity or amount of electricity in a circuit. *Volts* measure the force or pressure behind the current. *Watts* are a total measurement of power derived from multiplying amps times volts.

amplitude

Amplitude is the strength or volume of a signal, which is usually measured in decibels.

amplitude modulation

See AM.

analog

Analog means analogous to real-world events. *Analog* devices monitor conditions, such as movement, temperature and sound, and convert them into an analogous representation. For example, an analog watch represents the planet's rotation with the rotating hands on the watch face. Telephones turn voice vibrations into electrical vibrations of the same shape. Analog implies continuous operation and is contrasted with *digital*, which is broken up into numbers.

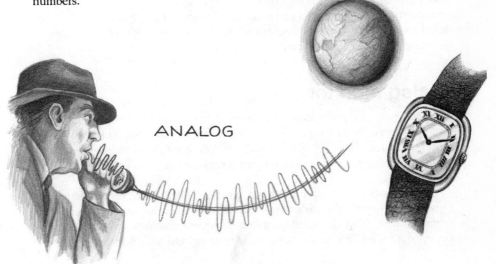

ANALOG

Advantages and Disadvantages
Of Analog Techniques

Traditionally, audio and video recording has been analog. Sound, which is continuously varying air vibrations, has been converted into continuously variable electrical vibrations. Video cameras scan their viewing area a line at a time and convert the infinitely varying intensities of light into a infinitely varying electrical signal representing that light.

The ability to capture the subtle nature of the real world is the single advantage of analog techniques. However, modern electronic equipment, no matter how advanced, cannot copy analog signals perfectly. Third and fourth generations of audio and video recordings show marked signs of deterioration.

By converting analog signals into digital, the original audio or video data can be preserved indefinitely and copied over and over again without deterioration. The continuously varying analog signals are measured, and those measurements, once recorded in digital form, can be stored and transmitted without loss of integrity due to the inherent accuracy of digital methods.

The key to conversion is the amount of digital data that is created from the analog signal. The more often samples are taken, and the further the sample is broken down, the more the digital encoding reflects the original signal. See CD.

analog channel

In communications, an *analog channel* is a channel that carries voice or video in analog form as a varying range of electrical frequencies. Contrast with *digital channel*, which requires that all information has been converted into binary coded signals.

analog computer

An *analog computer* is a computer that accepts and processes infinitely varying signals, such as voltage fluctuations or frequencies. For example, a thermostat is the simplest analog computer. A continuously varying change in temperature causes a metal bar to bend correspondingly. Although complex analog computers are built for special purposes, most computers are *digital*. Today, digital computers can generally equal the speed of analog computers while also providing programming flexibility.

analog monitor

An *analog monitor* is a television-like display screen that accepts video signals and transfers them a line at a time to the screen surface. Analog monitors come synchronized for television signals as well as for some range of computer displays. Multisync analog monitors match up with the widest variety of computer display standards.

Analog monitors accept separate red, green and blue (RGB) signals, which is a higher quality signal than the composite television signal that mixes all three colors together. If synchronized for television, analog monitors may also accept the standard NTSC composite signal as do most modern television sets.

Analog versus Digital Monitors

All tube-type monitors are fundamentally analog devices that are capable of "painting" an infinite number of colors or shades on the screen. Since the computer is digital, a conversion from digital to analog must be performed. When analog monitors are used, the video display board in the computer does the conversion. The display board can be replaced with a more advanced board that provides greater subtleties of color within the same signal, and the same analog monitor can still be used.

When digital monitors are used, the display board sends out digital signals that the monitor must know how to convert. Hence, digital monitors are tied to a precise digital display standard. A change in display board requires a change in monitor.

analog to digital converter

Analog to digital converters (A-D converters) convert the continuously varying analog signals from instruments that monitor such conditions as movement, temperature, sound and air quality, into binary coded form for the computer. Analog to digital converters may be a single circuit on a chip. See *modem* and *codec*.

ANALOG IN   DIGITAL OUT

A-D CONVERTER

analysis

See *systems analysis & design*.

analyst

See *systems analyst*.

Analytical Engine

The *Analytical Engine* was a conceptually sophisticated calculator that was designed by the British scientist, Charles Babbage (1791-1871). Started in the mid 1820s, Babbage worked on the machine throughout his life. Although it was never entirely completed due to lack of funds and constant redesign, it represented a major advance for its era and incorporated the basic principles of the stored program computer. His close friend, Lady Lovelace (August Ada Byron), daughter of the poet Lord Byron, worked with him for several years and was his liaison to the outside world explaining the machine's concepts and programmable aspects to the public and press. Because of her association with Babbage and the Analytical Engine, the Ada programming language was named after her.

ANALYTICAL ENGINE
(Courtesy Charles Babbage Institute, University of Minnesota)

AND, OR & NOT

AND, OR & NOT are the fundamental operations of Boolean logic. *AND* requires that both inputs (a and b) be present (true) in order to generate output. *OR* requires that either one of two inputs (a or b) be true in order to generate output. *NOT* is an inverter; the output is always the opposite state of the input. See *Boolean search, chip* and *gate.*

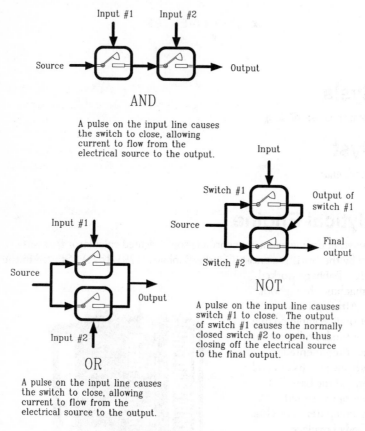

AND

A pulse on the input line causes the switch to close, allowing current to flow from the electrical source to the output.

NOT

A pulse on the input line causes switch #1 to close. The output of switch #1 causes the normally closed switch #2 to open, thus closing off the electrical source to the final output.

OR

A pulse on the input line causes the switch to close, allowing current to flow from the electrical source to the output.

BOOLEAN LOGIC

angstrom

An *angstrom* is a unit of measurement approximately equivalent to a 25 millionth of an inch. Angstroms are used to measure the elements in electronic components on a chip.

anode

In electronics, an *anode* is the positively charged receiver of electrons that flow from the negatively charged *cathode*.

anomaly

An *anomaly*, which means inconsistent, contradictory or abnormal, is a favorite word among some computer people when complex systems produce output from time to time that is unexplicable.

ANSI

(American National Standards Institute) ANSI is a membership organization, founded in 1918, that is devoted to the development of American industry standards. ANSI also coordinates and manages American participation in the International Standards Organization (ISO) and the International Electrotechnical Commission (IEC). Through ANSI, American business and industry is able to influence international standards that affect trade. ANSI has over 1,300 members.

Standards pertaining to the computer industry relate to data and communication codes and to programming and data management languages. For example, ANSI COBOL (also called ANS COBOL) is the ANSI-endorsed version of the COBOL programming language. Any vendors stating that their COBOL compilers are ANSI standard must conform to the language standards (reserved words, syntax, rules) as set forth by ANSI.

For more information, contact ANSI, 1430 Broadway, New York, NY 10018, (212) 354-3300.

ANSI compatible

ANSI compatible refers to a standard defined by the American National Standards Institute (ANSI).

answer only modem

An *answer only modem* is a modem that is capable of answering a call, but not initiating one.

anti-aliasing

In computer graphics, *anti-aliasing* is a category of techniques that is used to smooth the jagged appearance of diagonal lines. On the following page is an example of *dithering*. The pixels that surround the edges of the line are filled in with varying shades of gray in order to blend the sharp edge into the background. See *dithering*.

Magnified
view of
individual
pixels.

Picture
shows top
right side of
lid handle.

With Anti-aliasing

Without Anti-aliasing

THE "UTAH TEAPOT" WITH AND WITHOUT ANTI-ALIASING

(Photos courtesy Computer Sciences Department, University of Utah)

ANVIL

ANVIL is a family of CADD/CAM software packages from Manufacturing and Consulting Services, Inc. ANVIL-1000MD is a 2 1/2-dimensional CADD system for mechanical engineering that runs on 80286 machines. ANVIL-5000pc is a mainframe CADD/CAM package that has been restructured to run on 80386 machines. It produces 3-D wireframe models and provides optional surface modeling and numerical control modules. ANVIL-5000 is a 3-D CADD/CAM system for mechanical engineering that runs on major workstations, superminis and mainframes. It integrates drafting, wireframe, surface and solids modeling, geometric analysis, finite-element mesh and 3-axis and 5-axis numerical control using the same data structure and interface for all functions.

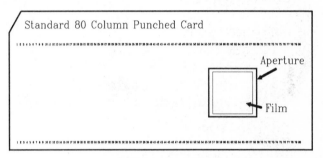

aperture card

An *aperture card* is a punched card that holds a frame of microfilm.

APERTURE CARD

API

(**A**pplication **P**rogram **I**nterface) An *API* is a language used between programs. For example, application programs must communicate with the operating system, database management system and other control programs. An API is made up of a set of codes and commands used to interrupt the computer, get the attention of the other program and pass messages back and forth between them.

PROGRAMS TALK TO EACH OTHER!

APL

(A Programming Language) *APL* is a high-level, interactive scientific programming language noted for its brevity and matrix generation capabilities. Developed by Kenneth Iverson in the mid 1960s, APL is often used to develop mathematical models. APL is primarily used on IBM mainframes and PCs, although versions have been developed for other computers. APL is typically an interpretive language, but compilers are also available.

APL uses a unique set of character symbols and requires that the computer be capable of displaying and printing these characters. Adding special software and/or changing ROM chips is required to customize a personal computer for APL usage. Although APL is a very advanced programming language, the requirement for custom symbols may have kept it from becoming widespread.

The following APL programming example converts fahrenheit to centigrade:

```
[0] CONVERT
[1] 'Enter fahrenheit
[2] fahr ←☐
[3] cent ← 5 × (fahr-32) ÷ 9
[4] 'Centigrade is ', (⍕cent)
```

APPC

(Advanced-Program-to-Program-Communications) See *LU 6.2*.

append

Append refers to adding data to the end of an existing structure. For example, in dBASE, the APPEND command starts the data entry mode and allows users to add records to the end of the file. In dBASE programming, APPEND BLANK creates a new blank record at the end of the file.

Apple Computer

Apple Computer is one of the computer industry's most fabled success stories. Founded in a garage by Steve Wozniak and Steve Jobs and guided by Mike Markkula, Apple Computer blazed the trails for the personal computer industry. Ironically, none of the original founders is with the company today, and Jobs' exit from the company has become legend. For the whole story, read John Sculley's book, "Odyssey," published by Harper & Row.

In 1976, Wozniak and Jobs formed the Apple Computer Company on April Fool's Day and soon after introduced the Apple I at the Homebrew Computer Club in Palo Alto, California. By the end of the year, 10 retail stores in the country were selling Apple I's.

In 1977, Apple, now incorporated, introduced the Apple II, a fully-assembled personal computer with 4K of memory at a price of $1,298. In 1979, the Apple II+ was introduced with 48K of memory.

The Apple II was the industry's first open-architecture system, which encouraged third party vendors to build plug-in circuit boards to enhance its capability. This philosophy, combined with the fact that it was the first personal computer providing sound and color graphics, caused the Apple II family to become the most widely used computer for education in both the home and classroom. Due primarily to the VisiCalc spreadsheet, Apple IIs found their way into many large and small companies as well.

APPLE I

In January 1983, Apple introduced the Lisa, a personal computer with integrated application programs. It's high price and slow speed kept it from succeeding, but its baby brother, the Macintosh, introduced a year later, has been a major success. The Mac provides a consistent way of working with a computer that has become extremely popular. Apple's new advertising theme of "a computer for the rest of us" highlights the Macintosh's ease of use. Because of the Mac's excellent graphics, it was immediately successful as a low-cost desktop publishing and CAD system. But, its closed architecture (reversing the Apple II's philosophy), sluggish performance, small 9" screen and penchant for mouse-driven applications

STEVE JOBS

MIKE MARKKULA

kept the Mac from making significant inroads into the corporate market. In early 1987, Apple introduced the Mac SE, an expandable machine, and the Mac II, a much faster computer that once again embraces open architecture. The Mac II also provides color graphics on a full 12" screen and finally provides Apple with the opportunity of competing in the high-performance workstation market.

STEVE WOZNIAK

(All photos on this page courtesy Apple Computer, Inc.)

Apple II

The *Apple II* is a family of personal computers from Apple Computer that has become widely used for education, business and entertainment in the home as well as the classroom. There is a huge variety of software packages available for the series, and, except for the Apple IIc, there is a large number of plug-in boards that enhance its capabilities.

The Apple II machines use the 6502 family of microprocessors and include a version of the BASIC programming language (AppleSoft BASIC), which is built into a ROM chip and is always available to the user. The Apple IIs run under Apple's DOS or ProDOS operating systems, or under CP/M if a Z80 microprocessor board is installed in the machine.

APPLE II, II+

Introduced in April 1977, the Apple II was an 8-bit computer that came with 4K of memory and was designed for use with a TV set and an audio cassette tape recorder. By mid 1978, the Apple II floppy disk was available. In June 1979, the Apple II+ was introduced with 48K of memory and an improved auto-start ROM for easier startup and screen editing.

APPLE IIe

Introduced in January 1983, the Apple IIe is an upgraded model of the Apple II+ that provides an enhanced keyboard (four cursor keys instead of two) and increases memory from 48K to 64K and optionally 128K.

APPLE IIe

APPLE IIc

Introduced in April 1984, the Apple IIc is a portable version of the Apple II series. Unlike other Apple II models, the Apple IIc is not designed for expandability; however, it is software compatible with most of the Apple II series.

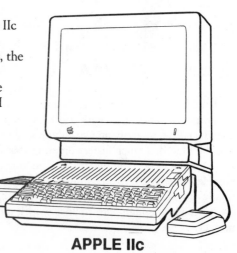

APPLE IIc

APPLE IIGS

Introduced in September 1986, the Apple IIGS is a 16-bit version of the Apple II series that runs most software up to 2.8 times as fast internally, and features enhanced color graphics and sound (the "GS"). The GS can drive an RGB analog monitor and display up to 256 on-screen colors, and it can generate up to 15 separate and simultaneous sounds.

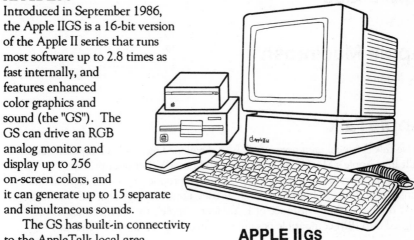

APPLE IIGS

The GS has built-in connectivity to the AppleTalk local area network through one of its serial ports. The GS will accept most plug-in boards designed for the Apple II series, but requires software written for the GS in order to activate its enhanced graphics and sound capabilities.

APPLE III

Introduced in September 1980, the Apple III was an enhanced model of the Apple II that was intended for business use. The Apple III was not 100% compatible with the Apple II and was not widely used.

MODEL	CPU# (Size)	CLOCK SPEED (MHz)	BUS SIZE	RAM (Bytes)	FLOPPY DISK (Bytes)	HARD DISK (Bytes)	SCREEN RES.	OS
II, II+	6502 8 bits	1.0	8 bits	48-64K	5.25" 143K	**	280x192 6 colors	DOS ProDOS Pascal CP/M*
IIe, IIc	6502 8 bits	1.0	8 bits	64-128K	5.25" 143K	**	280x192 6 colors	
IIGS	65C816 16 bits	2.8	8 bits	512K-8M	5.25" 143K 3.5" 400-800K	20M	320x200 256 cols.	

APPLE II SPECIFICATIONS
* CP/M requires third party Z80 processor board
** Hard disks available from third party vendors

Apple key

The *Apple key* is a key on an Apple computer's keyboard that is pressed in conjunction with another key to perform a command. The Apple key is also called a "command" key.

Apple Lisa

See *Lisa*.

Apple Macintosh

See *Macintosh*.

AppleTalk

AppleTalk is a local area network (LAN) developed by Apple Computer that is built into Apple's Macintosh computers and LaserWriter laser printers. AppleTalk, introduced in January 1985, uses a proprietary access method and transmits at 230,400 bits per second. It uses a bus topology that can connect up to 32 devices within a distance of 1,000 feet. AppleTalk boards that can be plugged into IBM compatible pcs are available from third party vendors.

AppleWorks

AppleWorks is an integrated software package from Apple Computer that runs on the Apple II personal computers. AppleWorks, introduced in November 1983, combines word processing, file management, spreadsheet, business graphics and communications in a single package.

application

An *application* is any specific use of the computer. For example, payroll, inventory and accounts receivable are typical business applications. Word processing, spreadsheets and business graphics are also called applications. The term is often used synonymously with program. Contrast with *operating system*.

application developer

An *application developer* is an individual that develops a business application and usually performs the duties of a systems analyst and application programmer.

application development language

Same as *programming language*.

application development system

An *application development system* is a programming language and associated utility programs that allow for the creation, development and running of application programs. A database management system, including query languages and report writers, may also be part of this system.

application generator

An *application generator* is a software program that generates application programs from descriptions of the problem rather than from detailed programming. Application generators are one or more levels higher than the programming language, whose source code they generate, but still require the user to input basic mathematical expressions in order to state complex processing on their business data. For example, a complicated pricing routine will require that the pricing algorithms be stated just as they would in any programming language, if, in fact, the application generator will even allow them.

application layer

In communications, the *application layer* is the interaction at the user or application program level. It is the highest layer within the protocol hierarchy. See *OSI model*.

application note

Application notes are usually short lists of instructions and recommendations from the vendor or manufacturer that are provided in addition to the normal reference manuals accompanying the product.

application package

An *application package* is a software package from a software vendor that is created for a specific purpose, function or industry.

application processor

Application processor refers to the computer that is processing data in contrast with the computers that are handling control functions, such as front end processors or database machines.

application program

Any program that processes business data is an *application program*, such as a data entry, update, query or report program. Contrast with *systems program*, such as an operating system or network control program. Also contrast with *utility program*, such as a copy or sort program.

application program interface

See *API*.

application program library

The *application program library* is the collection of application programs used by an organization.

application programmer

Most programmers are *application programmers*, since they design and write application programs that process data for the organization. Contrast with *systems programmer*.

Apollo Computer

Apollo Computer is a leading supplier of high-performance workstations for technical and business applications. Founded in 1980, Apollo pioneered the concept of networked workstations. In 1982, it introduced its first color workstation. In 1987, it introduced its Network Computing System (NCS), which allows users to develop and run programs across networks of computers from various suppliers. Apollo's Domain Series workstations are used in a wide range of industries including aerospace, automotive and electronics.

APRIL

(**AP**plication Rational Interface Logic) *APRIL* is a logic chip from IBM that employs neural network techniques that make it capable of learning from its environment.

APT

(Automatic Programmed Tools) *APT* is a high-level programming language used to generate instructions for automated factory machines (numerical control machines).

arbitration

Arbitration is the set of rules for allocating machine resources, such as memory or peripheral devices, to more than one user or program.

architecture

See *computer architecture* and *network architecture*.

archival storage

Archival storage is backup or long-term storage of data in machine readable form.

ARCNET

ARCNET is a local area network developed by Datapoint Corporation that interconnects a wide variety of personal computers and workstations via coaxial cable. Twisted wire pairs and fiber optic versions are also available. It uses the token passing access method and transmits at 2.5 megabits per second. ARCNET is a distributed star topology that interconnects up to 255 computers.

Introduced in 1968, ARCNET was the first local area network technology. With adapters, ARCNET can connect to most other mainframe and minicomputer networks as well.

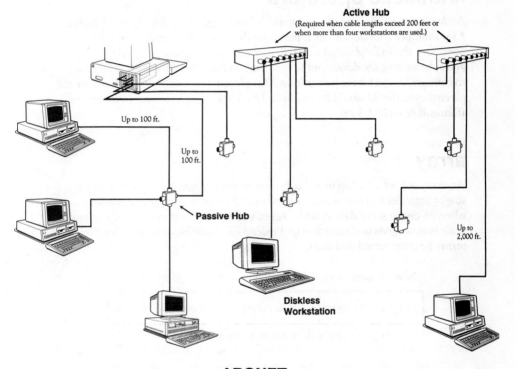

ARCNET

(Courtesy Black Box Corporation)

arg

See *argument*.

argument

In programming, an *argument* is a value that is passed between programs, subroutines or functions. Arguments are independent items, or variables, that contain data or codes. When an argument is used to customize a program for a user, it is typically called a *parameter*.

arithmetic expression

See *expression*.

arithmetic logic unit

See *ALU*.

arithmetic operators

Arithmetic operators used in programming languages are + for add, - for subtract, * for multiply, / for divide. In expressions that contain several arithmetic operators, the multiplications and divisions are performed first, then the additions and subtractions are done. In the following formula, which converts fahrenheit to centigrade, the **fahrenheit minus 32** is placed into parentheses. Without the parentheses, the 32 would be multiplied by 5, resulting in an incorrect answer: **(fahrenheit - 32) * 5 / 9**

array

An *array* is a set of adjacent fields in a program that may be treated as a single row of data elements or as a matrix (rows and columns) of data. Arrays are used when an entire set of data must be kept in memory for instant access, such as price lists, weights and measures and calendars. Most programming languages let arrays be constructed and used.

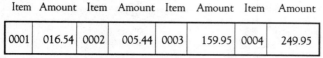

Price list in one-dimensional array

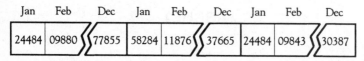

Sales figures for various years in two-dimensional array

ARRAYS

array element

An *array element* is one item in an array.

array processor

An *array processor* is either a stand-alone computer or a hardware attachment to an existing computer that performs multiple operations simultaneously on data in matrix (array) form. Certain problems, such as fluid dynamics or rotation of 3-D objects, are solved by calculations in matrices. Table lookup functions may also be adapted to array processors, since multiple lookups can be performed simultaneously. See *vector processor* and *math coprocessor*.

artificial intelligence (AI)

Artificial intelligence refers to a broad range of computer applications that resemble human intelligence and behavior. For example, machines or robots with sensory capabilities that recognize sound, pictures and textures fall under artificial intelligence. So do voice recognition, natural language understanding and foreign language translation.

Expert systems are one of the major categories of artificial intelligence. They contain a base of knowledge about an area of expertise and are used to assist us in performing such tasks as medical diagnosis, equipment repair, scheduling and financial planning.

One of the most significant benefits of artificial intelligence will be in voice recognition and natural language understanding. After the turn of the century, you should be able to walk up to any computer and ask it a question. When that occurs, everything we now know and think about a computer will change. Future operating systems will ask you what help you need and automatically call in the appropriate applications, also created with artificial intelligence techniques, to aid you in solving your problem.

As with all buzzwords in this industry, artificial intelligence will be abused as it will refer to all variety of advanced products. However, the "acid test" of an AI system was defined years ago by the English computer pioneer, Alan Turing, who said, "A machine has artificial intelligence when there is no discernible difference between the conversation generated by the machine and that of an intelligent person."

Note: The term *intelligence* by itself refers to processing capability. Therefore, every computer is "intelligent,"

"SHAKEY" THE ROBOT
(Courtesy The Computer Museum, Boston)

Developed in 1969 by the Stanford Research Institute, Shakey was the first fully-mobile robot with artificial intelligence. Shakey is seven feet tall and was named after its shakey actions.

since it can follow instructions in a program. Artificial intelligence implies human-like intelligence.

AS

(Application System) *AS* is a fourth-generation language from IBM that runs on IBM mainframes under the MVS operating system. AS was originally designed for non-computer people and includes commands for planning, budgeting and graphics. However, a programmer can also produce complex application programs. AS also provides a computer conferencing capability.

ASCII

(American Standard Code for Information Interchange) *ASCII*, pronounced "ask-ee," is a binary code for data that is used extensively in communications, in most minicomputers and in all personal computers.

ASCII was originally a 7-bit code allowing 128 possible character combinations, the first 32 of which are used for communications and printing control purposes. Since today's common unit of storage is an 8-bit byte and ASCII is only 7 bits, the extra bit has been used as a parity bit or for a variety of different symbols. For example, the IBM personal computer uses the additional 128 characters, called *extended ASCII*, for lines, borders, foreign languages and special graphics symbols.

ASCII file

An *ASCII file* is a data or text file that contains only characters coded from the standard ASCII character set (characters 0 through 127 in the ASCII chart). Text files, such as word processing documents, batch files and source language programs, are usually ASCII files as they contain only letters, digits and common symbols such as commas and semicolons.

However, the upper half of the ASCII code is not the same in all computers, and any files that contain characters from 128 to 255 may not display or convert properly by another ASCII program. Database files are usually not ASCII files, since they contain numbers in binary or floating point form or control codes in binary form that may be coincidentally the same as any ASCII character.

The ASCII file can be used as a common denominator for data conversion. For example, if program A can't convert its data to the format of program B, but both programs can input and output ASCII files, the conversion may be possible. However, dates, floating point and binary numbers and other types of data may still cause conversion problems.

ASCII protocol

An *ASCII protocol* refers to the simplest form of transmitting ASCII data and implies little or no error checking. Each character can be transmitted with a parity bit in order to provide some degree of error checking, but important data, such as numbers, and complex files, such as source and machine language programs, should be transmitted with a more sophisticated protocol.

STANDARD ASCII
The first 32 characters (0-31) are control codes

EXTENDED ASCII
(IBM and compatible pcs)

0	NUL	Null
1	SOH	Start of heading
2	STX	Start of text
3	ETX	End of text
4	EOT	End of transmit
5	ENQ	Enquiry
6	ACK	Acknowledge
7	BEL	Audible bell
8	BS	Backspace
9	HT	Horizontal tab
10	LF	Line feed
11	VT	Vertical tab
12	FF	Form feed
13	CR	Carriage return
14	SO	Shift out
15	SI	Shift in
16	DLE	Data link escape
17	DC1	Device control 1
18	DC2	Device control 2
19	DC3	Device control 3
20	DC4	Device control 4
21	NAK	Neg. acknowledge
22	SYN	Synchronous idle
23	ETB	End trans. block
24	CAN	Cancel
25	EM	End of medium
26	SUB	Substitution
27	ESC	Escape
28	FS	Figures shift
29	GS	Group separator
30	RS	Record separator
31	US	Unit separator
32	SP	Blank space (Space bar)

Code	Char		Code	Char
33	!		81	Q
34	"		82	R
35	#		83	S
36	$		84	T
37	%		85	U
38	&		86	V
39	'		87	W
40	(		88	X
41	)		89	Y
42	*		90	Z
43	+		91	[
44	,		92	\
45	–		93	]
46	.		94	^
47	/		95	_
48	0		96	`
49	1		97	a
50	2		98	b
51	3		99	c
52	4		100	d
53	5		101	e
54	6		102	f
55	7		103	g
56	8		104	h
57	9		105	i
58	:		106	j
59	;		107	k
60	<		108	l
61	=		109	m
62	>		110	n
63	?		111	o
64	@		112	p
65	A		113	q
66	B		114	r
67	C		115	s
68	D		116	t
69	E		117	u
70	F		118	v
71	G		119	w
72	H		120	x
73	I		121	y
74	J		122	z
75	K		123	{
76	L		124		
77	M		125	}
78	N		126	~
79	O		127	▓
80	P			

Code	Char		Code	Char		Code	Char
128	Ç		174	«		220	▄
129	ü		175	»		221	▌
130	é		176	░		222	▐
131	â		177	▒		223	▀
132	ä		178	▓		224	α
133	à		179	│		225	β
134	å		180	┤		226	Γ
135	ç		181	╡		227	π
136	ê		182	╢		228	Σ
137	ë		183	╖		229	σ
138	è		184	╕		230	μ
139	ï		185	╣		231	τ
140	î		186	║		232	Φ
141	ì		187	╗		233	Θ
142	Ä		188	╝		234	Ω
143	Å		189	╜		235	δ
144	É		190	╛		236	∞
145	æ		191	┐		237	φ
146	Æ		192	└		238	ε
147	ô		193	┴		239	∩
148	ö		194	┬		240	≡
149	ò		195	├		241	±
150	û		196	─		242	≥
151	ù		197	┼		243	≤
152	ÿ		198	╞		244	⌠
153	Ö		199	╟		245	⌡
154	Ü		200	╚		246	÷
155	¢		201	╔		247	≈
156	£		202	╩		248	°
157	¥		203	╦		249	•
158	₧		204	╠		250	·
159	ƒ		205	═		251	√
160	á		206	╬		252	η²
161	í		207	╧		253	²
162	ó		208	╨		254	▪
163	ú		209	╤		255	
164	ñ		210	╥			
165	Ñ		211	╙			
166	ª		212	╘			
167	º		213	╒			
168	¿		214	╓			
169	⌐		215	╫			
170	¬		216	╪			
171	½		217	┘			
172	¼		218	┌			
173	¡		219	█			
174			220				
175			221				

ASCII CODE

ASIC

(Application Specific Integrated Circuit) *ASICs* are customized chips that are designed by choosing circuits from a library of predesigned circuits. ASIC design is much faster than designing a chip from scratch, and changes can be made to the chip far more easily. An ASIC chip is faster than a computer on a chip with its instructions in ROM (read only memory), since there are no instructions that have to be executed.

ASM

(Association for Systems Managment) ASM is an international membership organization, founded in 1947, with over 10,000 administrative executives and specialists in information systems. ASM sponsors conferences in all phases of administrative systems and management and serves business, education, government and the military. For more information, contact ASM, 24587 Bagley Road, Cleveland, OH 44138, (216) 243-6900.

aspect ratio

In computer graphics, the *aspect ratio* is the ratio of the horizontal to vertical size of the frame used to hold an image. It is an important specification for maintaining accuracy when transferring images from the screen to the printer and to other systems.

assembler

An *assembler* is a software program that translates assembly language into machine language. Contrast with *compiler*, which is used to translate a high-level language, such as COBOL or C, into assembly language first and then into machine language.

assembly language

Assembly language is a programming language that is one step away from machine language. Each assembly language statement is translated into one machine instruction by the assembler program. To program in assembly language, you have to be well versed in the computer's architecture. Unless well documented, assembly language programs can be extremely difficult to maintain.

Assembly languages are hardware dependent; there is a different assembly language for each CPU series, and their language statements are quite different as is evident in the examples that follow this definition.

In the past, systems software (operating systems, database managers, etc.) was written in assembly language to maximize the machine's performance. Today, C has become the language of choice for systems software, because, like assembly language, it can manipulate the bits at the machine level, and, unlike assembly language, a C program can be compiled into machine language for all CPUs from micro to mainframe.

The terms assembly language and machine language are often used synonymously due to their one-to-one relationship; however, they are not the same. The assembly language statement is a symbolic, or mnemonic, representation of the instruction and the data. For example, the assembly language statement, MULT HOURSWORKED,HOURLYRATE is translated

INTEL 8086 (IBM compatible pc)

```
cseg     segment  para public 'CODE'                shl      bx,1
         assume   cs:cseg,ds:cseg                    add      bx,ax
start:                                               jmp      llp
         jmp      start1                    llr:     mov      dx,offset cseg:crlf
msgstr   db       'Enter farenheit '                 mov      ah,9
crlf     db       13,10,'$'                          int      21h
nine     dw       9                                  mov      ax,bx
five     dw       5                                  ret
outstr   db       'Centigrade is $'         putval:  xor      bx,bx
start1:  push     ds                                 push     bx
         push     cs                                 mov      bx,10
         pop      ds                        llg:     xor      dx,dx
         mov      dx,offset cseg:msgstr              div      bx
         mov      ah,9                               add      dx,'0'
         int      21h                                push     dx
sloop:                                               test     ax,ax
cent:    call     getnumb                            jne      llg
         test     ax,ax                     bloop:   pop      dx
         je       exit                               test     dx,dx
         push     ax                                 je       endx
         mov      dx,offset cseg:outstr              mov      ah,6
         mov      ah,9                               int      21h
         int      21h                                jmp      bloop
         pop      ax                        endx:    ret
         sub      ax,32                     cseg     ends
         jns      c1                                 end      start
         push     ax
         mov      dl,'-'
         mov      ah,6
         int      21h
         pop      ax
         neg      ax
c1:      mul      five
         div      nine
         call     putval
         mov      dx,offset cseg:crlf
         mov      ah,9
         int      21h                       ### HEWLETT-PACKARD HP 3000
         jmp      sloop
exit:    pop      ds                        begin
         mov      ah,4ch                    intrinsic  read,print,binary,ascii;
         int      21h                       array buffer(0:17);
getnumb:                                    array string(0:3);
         xor      bx,bx                      byte array b'string(*) = string;
llp:     mov      dl,0ffh                    integer ftemp, ctemp, len;
         mov      ah,1                         move buffer:= "Enter fahrenheit ";
         int      21h                          print (buffer,-30,%320);
         cmp      al,0dh                       len:=read (string,-4);
         je       llr                          ftemp:= binary(b'string,len);
         sub      al,'0'                       ctemp:= (ftemp-32) * 5 / 9;
         jb       llr                          len:= ascii(ctemp,10,b'string);
         cmp      al,'9'                        move buffer:= "Centigrade is ";
         ja       llr                          move buffer(14):= string,(-len);
         xor      ah,ah                        print (buffer,-32,%0);
         shl      bx,1                      end
         add      ax,bx
         shl      bx,1
```

ASSEMBLY LANGUAGE

Assembly languages are quite different between mainframes, minis and micros as you can see in the examples above. It takes 16 lines of assembly language code to accept a fahrenheit number and convert it into centigrade on an HP 3000 minicomputer, but it takes 83 lines to do it in Intel 8086 assembly language for an IBM compatible pc.

into a machine instruction that stipulates the actual memory addresses, such as, MULTIPLY the contents of locations 23400-23402 with the contents of locations 45678-45683. The actual machine instruction is coded in binary and might look like this: 10010101010010111010101010101001.

assignment statement

In programming, an *assignment statement* places a value into a variable. For example, COUNTER = 0 creates a variable named counter and fills it with zeros. The "variablename = value" syntax is common among programming langauges.

associative storage

Associative storage is a technique for storing data and instantly recognizing it by its content. Using specially designed circuits, the data key is matched against all the stored keys at the same time. With this technique, there is no need to keep track of addresses.

asymetrical modem

An *asymetrical modem* is a full-duplex modem that transmits data in one direction at one speed and simultaneously in the other direction at another speed.

asynchronous

(1) *Asynchronous* refers to a series of events that take place which are not synchronized one after the other. For example, the time interval between event A and B is the not the same as B and C.

(2) In IBM's SNA environment, *asynchronous* means independent events rather than concurrent events. For example, if one user sends mail to a party who is not online and available, the ability to store and forward the mail at a later time is considered asynchronous.

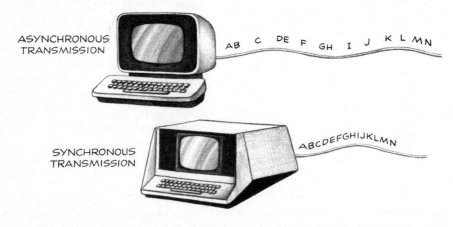

asynchronous communications

Asynchronous communications is the transmission of a single character at a time. It is also called start/stop transmission because each character is treated as a unit, with a start bit signalling the character bits that follow, and one or more bits that signal the end of the character transmitted.

Asynchronous communications is the common method of transmission between portable timesharing terminals and mainframes, between dumb terminals and minicomputers and between microcomputers. Contrast with *synchronous communications*, in which characters are transmitted in groups.

AS/400

(Application System/400) The AS/400, also known by its code name "Silverlake," is a series of minicomputers from IBM that supersedes and advances the performance of both the System/36 series and the System/38 series. Introduced in June 1988, the AS/400 runs both System/36 and System/38 applications. System/36 programs run in the AS/400 in "System/36 mode" after they have been recompiled. System/38 programs run intact in "System/38 mode." After recompilation, System/38 programs will run in native AS/400 mode, which takes advantage of all of the systems resources.

The AS/400 is designed to serve in a variety of networking configurations. It can function as a host or intermediate node to other AS/400s and System/3x machines, as a remote system to System/370-controlled networks and as a network server to IBM personal computers. The AS/400 is the first IBM series to offer such a wide range of connectivity options in its initial introduction.

IBM AT

AT

(Advanced Technology) The *AT*, introduced in August 1984, is an Intel 80286-based personal computer from IBM. It is the most advanced machine in IBM's first-generation PC line. With it, IBM introduced a 1.2 megabyte floppy disk drive and a new keyboard that corrected the key placement flaws in the original PC keyboard.

ATs and compatible machines have become the major workhorses in many companies for the last half of the 1980s. They run from four to seven times as fast as the original 8088-based PCs, and a great deal of new software has been written with this in mind.

Although the 80286 can intrinsically provide multitasking and can address up to 16 megabytes of memory, most ATs run under Microsoft's single user DOS operating system that cannot directly address more than one megabyte. In order to increase the utility of the machine, users have to migrate to Microsoft's OS/2 operating system or add a windowing environment to DOS, such as DESQview or Windows, all of which allow users to keep several applications open at the same time and quickly switch back and forth between them.

As application programs and operating systems are becoming larger and more complicated, the AT class machine (80286 processor) is quickly becoming the minimum standard for responsive performance in the IBM compatible pc world.

AT bus

The *AT bus* is a 16-bit interface used in the IBM PC AT. The term is used to refer to the first-generation bus in contrast with the Micro Channel bus of the IBM PS/2 series.

AT class

An *AT class* machine is a personal computer that uses the Intel 80286 microprocessor. AT class implies a computer that is 100% compatible with the IBM AT personal computer; however, that is not always the case.

AT keyboard

The *AT keyboard* is an 84-key keyboard that was provided by IBM with the PC AT personal computer and is used extensively with IBM compatible pcs. The AT keyboard corrected the improper design of the return key and left shift keys that were on the original PC keyboard. However, the backspace key was shortened, making it harder to reach for fast touch typists.

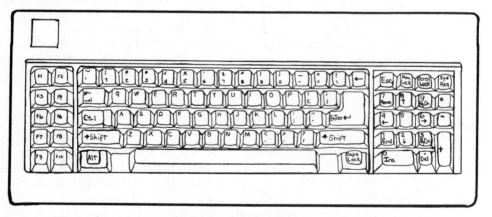

AT KEYBOARD

ATM

(Automatic Teller Machine) *ATMs* are special-purpose banking terminals that allow users to make deposits and withdrawals. ATMs can be stand-alone units or online to a central computer system. ATMs are activated by inserting a magnetic card (cash card or credit card) in the machine that contains the user's identification number.

ATM

atom

In list processing languages, such as LISP, an *atom* is a single element in a list.

atomic operation

An *atomic operation* is an operation that cannot be divided. It cannot be broken up into parts that can be performed by different processors.

AT&T

(American Telephone & Telegraph) *AT&T*, once the largest corporation in America, is today the largest long distance communications carrier in the country. Relieved of its operating telephone companies on January 1, 1984, by Federal court order, AT&T has gone through a traumatic change from the world's largest monopoly to a competitive enterprise.

Its initial venture into personal computing with its 6300 series of IBM compatible pcs has been modest, but AT&T's resources, including the famous Bell Labs, where the transistor and laser were invented, are formidable. In addition, AT&T has been making powerful telephone switching computers for years.

Being the last to enter the computer world is a distinct advantage. There is no customer base to be compatible with and the standards have been set, at least, for a while. As the technology gets cheaper and more powerful, AT&T could come in at any level: micro, mini or mainframe, and carve out a niche.

attached processor

An *attached processor* is an additional CPU connected to the primary CPU in a multiprocessing environment. The attached processor operates as an extension of the primary CPU and shares the system software and peripheral devices.

attenuation

Attenuation is the decreasing of power of a transmitted signal.

attribute

(1) In relational database management, an *attribute* is a field within a record.

(2) In computer graphics, an *attribute* is a characteristic that displays normal characters differently, such as boldface, underline, reverse image (black on white/white on black) and blinking.

(3) In printing, an *attribute* is a characteristic that changes normal fonts to print differently, such as underline or boldface.

audio

Audio is the range of frequencies (vibrations) that can be heard by the human ear. Although human voice is confined to a smaller range, the human ear can perceive approximately from a low bass end of 15 Hertz to a high treble of 20,000 Hertz (cycles, or vibrations, per second). Audio frequencies look like rippling waves when viewed electronically on a display screen.

Traditional audio devices, such as radios, phonographs, and tape recorders are analog devices because they handle the sound waves in an analogous form. Radios maintain the audio signal as a vibration from antenna to speaker. The phonograph record holds the vibration carved into its plastic surface. An audio tape records the sound waves as patterns of magnetic waves on the surface of the tape. Audio signals are processed in a digital computer by converting the analog signal into a digital code using various techniques, such as pulse code modulation.

audio response

Audio response is verbal output from a computer system usually made up of piecing prerecorded human voice segments together or is generated by synthesized speech techniques.

audit

A data processing *audit* is an examination of systems, programming and datacenter procedures in order to determine the efficiency of all computer-related operations.

audit software

Audit software refers to specialized programs that perform a variety of audit functions, such as sampling databases and generating confirmation letters to mail to customers. Audit software can highlight exceptions to categories of data and alert the examiner to possible error. Audit software may provide a high-level, non-procedural language that lets the auditor describe the computer and data environment without detailed programming.

audit trail

An *audit trail* is a record of transactions in an information system. Audit trails provide a means of identification and verification of the activity of an information system. The simplest audit trail is the transaction itself; for example, if a person's salary is increased, the transaction, which includes the date, amount of raise and authorizing manager, becomes an audit trail for future inquiries.

A more elaborate audit trail can be created when the system is being verified for accuracy; for example, samples of processing results can be recorded at various stages. Transaction item counts and hash totals are also used to verify that all input has been processed through the system.

authorization code

An *authorization code* is an indentification number or password that is used to gain access to a local or remote computer system.

auto bypass

Auto bypass is the ability to bypass a terminal or other device in a network if it fails, allowing the remaining devices connected farther down the path to continue functioning.

auto dial/auto answer

Auto dial/auto answer is an integral feature of the modem. The auto dial part opens the telephone line and dials the telephone of the receiving computer to establish connection. The auto answer part receives the telephone ring and accepts the call to establish connection.

AutoCAD

AutoCAD is a full-featured computer-aided design program from AutoDesk that runs on IBM compatible pcs, the VAX series, UNIX workstations and the Macintosh. It was originally developed for first-generation personal computers using the CP/M operating system. AutoCAD set the standard for personal computer CAD packages, since it was the first major CAD program available. Many software packages import and export graphics files in AutoCAD format.

autocoder

Autocoder is an IBM assembly language for 1960s-vintage 1400 and 7000 series computers.

AUTODIN

(**AUTO**matic **DI**gital Network) *AUTODIN* is the worldwide communications network of the U. S. Defense Communications System.

AUTOEXEC.BAT

(**AUTO**matic **EXEC**ute **BAT**ch file) *AUTOEXEC.BAT* is a Microsoft DOS file that, if present on disk, is executed immediately when the computer is started (booted). The file contains DOS instructions that can initialize operating system settings, load RAM resident programs and/or automatically call in a specific application program. The equivalent file in OS/2 is the *STARTUP.CMD* file; however, in OS/2, the AUTOEXEC.BAT file is also executed when the computer is switched to DOS mode (real mode).

automata theory

Automata theory relates the operations and applications of automatic machines to concepts of human behavior.

automated office

See *office automation*.

automatic data processing

Same as *data processing*.

automatic teller machine

See *ATM*.

automation

Automation implies the replacement of manual operations by computerized methods. Office automation refers to the integration of clerical tasks such as typing and filing. Factory automation refers to computer-driven assembly lines and warehouses. The term is used loosely to describe almost any task performed by machines rather than people.

A VISION OF AUTOMATION
(Artist Unknown, Circa 1895)
(Courtesy Charles and Gabrielle Hurst)

autostart routine

An *autostart routine* is a set of instructions that is built into the computer and is activated when the computer is turned on. Instructions in the routine perform diagnostic tests, such as checking the computer's memory, and then cause the operating system to be loaded. Control is then passed to the operating system.

A/UX

A/UX is a version of the UNIX operating system from Apple Computer that runs on the Macintosh II. A/UX is based on AT&T's UNIX System V with Berkeley extensions.

auxiliary memory

(1) *Auxiliary memory* is a high-speed memory bank that is used in large-scale mainframes and supercomputers. It is not directly addressable by the CPU as is main memory, and data is transferred to and from main memory and auxiliary memory over a high-speed channel.

(2) Same as *auxiliary storage*.

auxiliary storage

Auxiliary storage devices are external storage devices, such as disks and tapes.

back end processor

Same as *database machine*.

background

The *background* refers to processing that is taking place in the computer that is not interactive and visible on screen. See *foreground/background*.

background ink

In optical character recognition, *background ink* is a highly reflective ink that is used to print the parts of the form that are not going to be detected or recognized by the scanner.

background noise

Background noise is any extraneous, low-level signal that has crept into a line, channel or circuit.

backing storage

Backing storage is any external peripheral storage, such as disk or tape. Same as *secondary storage* or *auxiliary storage*.

backplane

Backplane refers to the back side of a panel that contains wires or printed circuits for interconnecting a series of plug-in printed circuit boards on the other side. It is the same as a *motherboard* that contains only sockets.

backspace

(1) In word processing, pressing the *backspace* key moves the cursor one character column to the left, deleting the character that was displayed in that position. A backspace code will also move the printer one character column to the left.

(2) In magnetic tape units, a *backspace* instruction moves the tape to the previous block.

backup

Backup refers to additional resources for emergency purposes. Backup disks and tapes are copies of the latest files and databases. A backup computer is an additional CPU or complete second computer system that can be used if the main system goes down. Backup power refers to a UPS (uninterruptible power supply), an auxiliary power system that is called upon if electrical power fails.

Making backup copies of data is a discipline that most personal computer users learn the hard way. All the data stored on a hard disk can be lost!

backup & recovery

Backup & recovery is a combination of manual and machine procedures that can restore lost data in the event of hardware or software failure. Routine backup of files, databases and programs, and system logs that keep track of the computer's operations are all part of a backup & recovery program. See *checkpoint/restart*.

Backus-Naur form

Backus-Naur form, also known as Backus normal form, was developed in 1959 by John Backus and Peter Naur. It was the first metalanguage (language used to describe a language) to define programming languages.

bad sector

A *bad sector* is a segment of disk storage that cannot be read or written due to a physical flaw in the disk. Bad sectors on hard disks are marked by the operating system and ignored. If data is recorded in a sector that becomes bad, it is usually not recoverable by normal means. Special hardware and software must be used to recover valuable data in bad sectors.

BAK file

(BAcKup file) In Microsoft DOS and OS/2, *BAK* is a commonly used file extension for backup files that is typically the previous version of a word processing document or data file.

BAL

(1) (Basic Assembly Language) *BAL* is the assembly language for the IBM 370/3000/4000 mainframe series.

(2) (Branch And Link) A *BAL* instruction is used to transfer control to another subroutine in the program.

balun

(BALanced UNbalanced) In communications, a *balun* is a device that connects a balanced line to an unbalanced line, for example, a twisted wire pair to a coaxial cable. A balanced line is one in which both wires are electrically equal. In an unbalanced line, such as a coaxial cable, one line has different physical properties than the other.

BALUN

(Courtesy Black Box Corporation)

This balun connects a coaxial cable with twisted pair wires.

band

(1) In communications, a *band* is a range of frequencies that are used for transmitting a signal. A band can be identified by the difference between its lower and upper limits as well as by its actual lower and upper limits, for example, "a 10 megaHertz band in the 100 to 110 megaHertz range."

(2) On disks and drums, a *band* is a contiguous group of tracks that are treated as a unit.

(3) A *band* is the printing element in a band printer.

band pass filter

In electronics, a *band pass filter* prohibits all but a specific range of frequencies to pass through it.

band printer

A *band printer* is a line printer that uses a metal band, or loop, of type characters as its printing mechanism. The band spins horizontally around a set of hammers. When the desired character is in front of the selected print position, the corresponding hammer hits the paper into the ribbon and onto the character in the band.

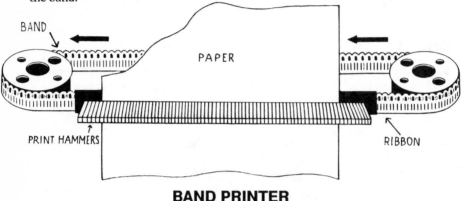

BAND PRINTER

bandwidth

Bandwidth is the transmission capacity of a computer or communications channel. Pure digital transmission is measured in bits or bytes per second. When digital data is converted to frequencies for transmission over carrier-based networks, bandwidth is still stated in bits or bytes per second. However, when frequencies are used as the transmission signal rather than on/off pulses, bandwidth may also be measured in cycles per second, or Hertz, the bandwidth being the difference between the lowest and highest frequencies transmitted. In this case, the frequency will be equal to or greater than the bits per second.

bank

A *bank* is an arrangement of identical hardware components.

bank switching

Bank switching is the engaging and disengaging of electronic circuits. Bank switching is used when the design of a system prohibits all circuits from being addressed or activated at the same time requiring that one unit be turned on while the others are turned off.

bar chart

A *bar chart* is a graphical representation of information in the form of bars. See *business graphics*.

bar code

Bar code is a specialized code used for fast identification of items with an optical scanner. The actual coding of the bars is the width of the bar, not the height. The extended height allows tolerance for the recognition system. See *UPS* (universal product code).

BAR CODE

barrel printer

Same as *drum printer*.

base

(1) In numbering systems, the *base*, also called the *radix*, is the number that determines the value of each digit position. For example, in a base 10 (decimal) system, each position is worth 10 times the value of the position on the right. In base 2 (binary), each position is worth twice as much as the position on its right.

(2) In a bipolar transistor, the *base* is the triggering line that toggles the switch. Same as *gate* in a metal oxide semiconductor (MOS) transistor.

base address

The *base address* is the location in memory where the beginning of a program is stored. The relative address from the instruction in the program is added to the base address to derive the absolute address. See *base/displacement*.

baseband transmission

Baseband transmission is a technique for transmitting digital data at up to approximately 10 megabits per second. Using low frequency transmission over twisted pair or coaxial cable, baseband transmission distance is usually limited to within a couple of miles. Contrast with *broadband transmisssion*, which can transmit analog as well as digital data over greater distances.

base/displacement

Base/displacement is a technique that allows a program to be stored and run from any location in memory. The addresses in the machine language program are relative only to the beginning of the program. As the program is running, the hardware adds the relative addresses to the base address (where the beginning of the program is currently stored) and derives the absolute addresses.

BASIC

(Beginners All purpose Symbolic Instruction Code) *BASIC*, developed by John Kemeny and Thomas Kurtz in the mid 1960s at Dartmouth College, is a programming language used for solving mathematical and business problems. Although originally developed as an interactive time-sharing language on large mainframes, BASIC has become widely used on all sizes of computers, including pocket computers. There are countless varieties of BASIC dialects used today.

BASIC is available in both compiler and interpreter form, the latter being more popular and easier to use, especially for the first-time programmer. In interpreter form, the language is conversational and can be used as a desktop calculator. In addition, it is easy to debug a program, since lines of code can be tested one at a time.

BASIC is considered one of the easiest programming languages to learn. For simple problems, BASIC programs can be written "on the fly" at the keyboard. However, BASIC is not a structured language, such as Pascal, dBASE or C, and there's no inherent documentation built into the language as there is in COBOL. As a result, it's easy to write spaghetti code and wind up with a program that's difficult to decipher later.

The following BASIC programming example converts fahrenheit to centigrade:

```
10 INPUT "Enter fahrenheit "; FAHR
20 PRINT "Centigrade is ", (FAHR-32) * 5 / 9
```

BASIC in ROM

BASIC in ROM refers to a BASIC interpreter that has been stored in a read only memory chip within the computer and is available to the user at all times.

BAT file

(BATch file) In Microsoft DOS and OS/2, a *BAT* file is a set of operating system commands that is executed as if each command were interactively entered one at a time. BAT files must have a BAT extension and can be created by any word processing program. The contents of the BAT file are executed by entering the name of the file at the DOS prompt (A:, C:). The following two-line BAT file changes the current directory to DATABASE and calls in the dBASE program. See *AUTOEXEC.BAT*.

```
cd \database
dbase
```

batch

A *batch* is any collection of items. A batch program or batch job refers to a batch processing program that processes an entire set of data until finished, such as a report or sort program. Batch data entry is the keyboarding of a group of source documents. Remote batch transmission refers to sending data in bulk over a network. Batch operations are also called offline operations. Contrast with *online, interactive* and *transaction processing.*

batch job

A *batch job* is a non-interactive program that is run in the computer, such as a listing or sort.

batch processing

Batch processing is the processing of a group of transactions at one time. Transactions are collected and processed against the master files (master files updated) at the end of the day or some other time period. Contrast with *transaction processing,* in which each transaction updates the master file at the time it is entered into the computer system.

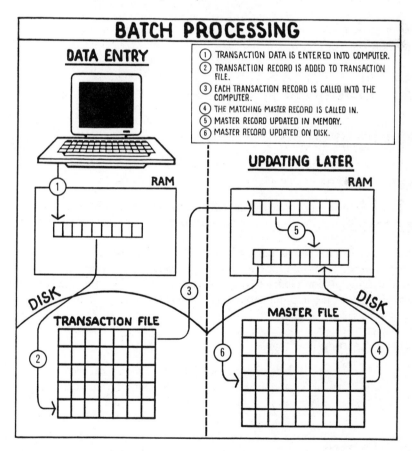

Batch Processing versus Transaction Processing

Information systems are usually combinations of batch processing and transaction processing. For example, in a typical order processing system, transaction processing takes place during the day whereby inventory files are immediately updated when the order is entered into the computer. Picking lists might be generated on the spot in the warehouse.

At the end of the day or week, the batch processing programs turn the orders into printed invoices and also produce the reports required by management.

batch session

A *batch session* is the transmission of an entire file, the updating of a master file from a transaction file, a sort or the printing of a report. Contrast with *interactive session*, which implies a conversational, question and answer session.

batch stream

A *batch stream* is a collection of batch processing programs that are scheduled to run in the computer.

batch system

Same as *batch processing* system.

batch terminal

A *batch terminal* is a terminal that is set up for transmitting or receiving blocks of data, such as a card reader or printer.

batch total

A *batch total* is the sum of a particular field in a number of records that is used as a control total to ensure that all data has been entered into the computer. For example, if entirely numeric, the account number on a batch of source documents could be used as a control total. The account numbers are summed manually before entry into the computer and then by the computer after data entry. If the totals don't match, the source documents in the batch are hand checked against the computer data.

baudot code

Developed in the late 19th century by Emile Baudot, the *baudot code*, pronounced "baw-doh," was one of the first standards for international telegraphy. Baudot code uses five bits to make up a character.

baud rate

(1) *Baud rate* is the transmission speed of a communications channel. Baud rate is commonly used to represent bits per second. For example, 4,800 baud is 4,800 bits per second of data transfer. In typical personal computer transmission

(asynchronous), 10 bits are used for each character, thus, 4,800 baud is equivalent to 480 characters, or bytes, of data per second.

(2) *Baud rate* is technically the switching speed of a line. It is the number of changes in the electrical state of the line per second. Baud rate is equivalent to bits per second at low speeds, for example, 300 baud. At higher speeds, the number of bits per second is greater than the baud rate, because one baud can be made to represent more than one bit.

BBS

(Bulletin Board System) See *bulletin board.*

BCD

(Binary Coded Decimal) *BCD* is the storage of numbers in a computer where each decimal digit is converted into binary and is stored in a single character or byte. For example, a 12-digit number would require 12 bytes of storage (96 bits). See *EBCDIC* and *packed decimal.* Contrast with *binary numbers,* in which the entire decimal number is converted into a binary number that is stored in a fixed amount of storage space from eight bits up to about 60 bits in length.

The following example illustrates the storage of the number 260 in both BCD and binary forms:

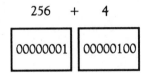

256   +   4

The number "260" coded in binary

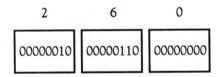

2   6   0

The number "260" coded in binary coded decimal

BCS

See *Boston Computer Society.*

BDOS error

See *read error* and *write error.*

bead

(1) In programming, a *bead* is a small subroutine. A sequence of beads that are strung together is called a *thread*.

(2) A *bead* is the insulator surrounding the inner wire of a coaxial cable.

BEL

See *bell character*.

bell character

A *bell character* is a control code that is used to sound an audible bell or tone in order to alert the user of the computer. It is character 7 in the ASCII code.

Bell compatible

In communications, *Bell compatible* refers to a modem that is compatible with modems, or data sets, originally introduced by the Bell Telephone System.

Bell Labs

Bell Labs, or more formally *Bell Laboratories*, is the research and development center of AT&T and is one of the most well known scientific laboratories in the world.

Bell System

The *Bell System* refers to the entire AT&T organization that included the Bell Telephone Companies before January 1, 1984. By federal court order, on January 1, 1984, AT&T divested itself of its 23 operating companies, which became seven independent regional telephone companies known as the Bell Operating Companies, or BOCs (Ameritech, Bell Atlantic, BellSouth, Nynex, Pacific Telesis, Southwestern Bell and US West). Bell Labs, AT&T's famous research and development center, was renamed AT&T Bell Labs, and Western Electric, its manufacturing division, was renamed AT&T Technologies.

ALEXANDER GRAHAM BELL

(Courtesy AT&T)

Bell 103, Bell 113

Bell 103 is an AT&T standard for 300 bits per second asynchronous, full-duplex modems with originate/answer capability. *Bell 113* provides originate or answer capability, but not both.

Bell 201

Bell 201B is an AT&T standard for 2,400 bits per second synchronous, full-duplex modems. Bell 201B was originally designed for public telephone network applications and later for leased line applications. Bell 201C was designed for half-duplex operation over public telephone network applications.

Bell 202

Bell 202 is an AT&T standard for 1,800 bits per second asynchronous, four-wire, full-duplex modems as well as 1,200 bits per second two-wire, half-duplex modems.

Bell 208

Bell 208 is an AT&T standard for 4,800 bits per second synchronous transmission. Bell 208A was designed for leased line applications. Bell 208B was designed for public telephone network applications.

Bell 209

Bell 209 is an AT&T standard for 9,600 bits per second synchronous modems using four-wire leased lines.

Bell 212, Bell 212A

Bell 212 is an AT&T standard for 300 and 1,200 bits per second asynchronous, full-duplex modems.

benchmark

A *benchmark* is a test of performance of a computer or peripheral device. The best benchmark is when the actual set of application programs and data files that the organization will use are used in the test. Running benchmarks on a single user personal computer is reasonably effective; however, obtaining meaningful results from a benchmark of a multiuser system is a complicated task. Unless your end user environment can be duplicated exactly, the benchmark will be of little value. It may be far more effective to find a user organization with a similar computer system and processing environment and simply monitor the operation. See *Linpack, Dhrystones, Whetstones* and *Khornerstones*.

Bernoulli Box

The *Bernoulli Box* is a removable disk system from Iomega Corporation that connects to personal computers through a small computer systems interface (SCSI). The Bernoulli Box was introduced in 1983 with 10 megabytes of storage on a high-capacity 8" floppy disk cartridge. Storage was increased to 20 megabytes per cartridge in 1985, and, in 1987, the Bernoulli Box II introduced 20 megabytes of storage on a 5 1/4" disk.

The name comes from the 18th century Swiss scientist, Daniel Bernoulli, whose principle of fluid dynamics is demonstrated in the disk mechanism. When the floppy disk is spun at high speed, it "bends up" and maintains a thin band of air between it and the read/write head. Unlike a hard disk in which the read/write head flies over a rigid disk, the floppy disk in the Bernoulli Box flies up to a rigid read/write head. In the event of a power failure, a hard disk has to retract the read/write head to prevent a recording failure or a head crash, whereas the floppy disk in the Bernoulli Box automatically bends down.

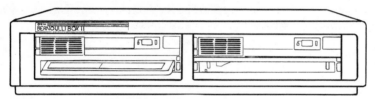

BERNOULLI BOX II

Beta

Beta, developed by Sony, was the first home videocassette format. The Beta standard records video signals in traditional analog form on a 1/2" cassette, which provides a higher quality image than the VHS format later developed by Sony's competitors. "Beta Hi-fi" is a subsequent standard that records an additional audio track in high fidelity, but is compatible with older Beta VCRs. "SuperBeta" is a format that provides a minor improvement in the visual image, but is still compatible with all Beta machines.

beta test

A *beta test* of hardware or software is a test performed by users under normal operating conditions. Contrast with *alpha test*, which is a first-time inhouse test of the product.

betaware

Betaware is software that is still in beta test, but has been provided to a large number of users in advance of the formal release.

Bezier curves

In computer graphics, *Bezier curves* are a type of analytical curve that obey certain conditions at their end points so that they can be continuously connected. Analytical curves are curves that can be described with mathematical equations.

bidirectional printer

A *bidirectional printer* prints in both forward and backward motions. By holding two lines of data from the computer in the printer's buffer, it can print the second line from right to left without having to return to the left side.

bifurcate

Bifurcate is to divide into two.

Big Blue

Big Blue is slang for the International Business Machines Corporation and was coined because of IBM's blue covers on most of its earlier model mainframes.

bill of materials

A *bill of materials* is a list of components that make up a system. For example, a bill of materials for a house would include all the cement block, lumber, shingles, doors, windows, plumbing, electric, heating, air conditioning and so on. Each subassembly also contains a bill of materials, for example, the heating system is made up of the furnace, ducts, thermostat, etc.

The first hierarchical databases were developed for automating bills of materials for manufacturing organizations in the early 1960s.

bill of materials explosion

A *bill of materials explosion* is the breaking apart of each assembly or subassembly into its component parts.

billion

A *billion* is one thousand times one million. In computer specifications, a billion is represented by *giga*; for example, one gigabyte is one billion bytes. One billionth is represented by *nano*; for example, one nanosecond is one billionth of a second.

binary

Binary means "two" and is the fundamental principle behind the design and function of digital computers. All input to the computer is converted into binary numbers made up of the two digits 0 and 1, called bits (from the words BInary digiTS). For example, when you press the "A" key on your personal computer, the keyboard generates and transmits the number 01000001 to the computer's memory as a series of pulses. The 1 bits are transmitted as pulses of electricity (high voltage); the 0 bits are transmitted as no pulses (low voltage). The 1s and 0s are stored as a series of charges (and no charges) in the cells of the computer's memory. On magnetic disk and tape, the bits are stored as positively and negatively charged spots. We see the real characters because the display screens and printers convert the binary numbers into the visual characters we understand.

The electronic circuits that process these binary numbers are themselves binary in concept. They are made up of on/off switches (transistors) that are electrically opened and closed. The current flowing through one switch effects the operation of another switch, and so on. These switches open and close in nanoseconds and picoseconds (billionths and trillionths of a second). To understand more about these circuits, see *Boolean circuit*.

A computer's capability to do work is based on its storage (memory and disk) capacity and internal transmission speed. Greater storage capacities are achieved by making the memory cell or magnetic spot smaller. Faster transmission rates are achieved by shortening the time it takes to open and close the switch and developing circuit paths that can handle the increased speeds. In order to improve the performance of a computer, we simply continue to refine the binary concept.

How Binary Numbers Work

Binary numbers are not difficult. You can even have "math phobia" and still understand how the binary system works. Binary numbers work with only the digits 0 and 1 instead of the digits 0 through 9 as in our decimal numbering system.

For example, in decimal, when you add 9 and 1, you get 10. But, if you break down the steps to get to 10, you find that by adding 9 and 1, what you get first is a result of 0 and a carry of 1. The carry of 1 is moved over and added to the digits in the next position on the left. Since, in this case, there are no other digits in that position, the carry of 1 becomes part of the answer.

$$\begin{array}{r} 9 \\ + 1 \\ \hline 10 \end{array}$$

The following example adds 1 ten times in succession in both binary and decimal. Note that the binary method has more carries than the decimal method. In binary, 1 and 1 are 0 with a carry of 1.

Binary	Decimal
0	0
+ 1	+ 1
1	1
+ 1	+ 1
10	2
+ 1	+ 1
11	3
+ 1	+ 1
100	4
+ 1	+ 1
101	5
+ 1	+ 1
110	6
+ 1	+ 1
111	7
+ 1	+ 1
1000	8
+ 1	+ 1
1001	9
+ 1	+ 1
1010	10

10,000,000	1,000,000	100,000	10,000	1,000	100	10	1

Value of each position in the decimal system

128	64	32	16	8	4	2	1

Value of each position in the binary system

binary chop

Same as *binary search*.

binary code

Binary code is a coding system made up of binary digits.

binary coded decimal

See *BCD*.

binary field

A *binary field* is a field that contains binary numbers. It may refer only to the storage of binary numbers for calculation purposes, or it may refer to a field that is capable of holding any information format including data, text, graphics images, voice and video.

binary file

A *binary file* is a software program in machine language form (object code) that can be directly executed by the computer. When files are referred to as binary files, it's usually to distinguish them from plain text files (ASCII files). When transmitting binary files between computers, low-level ASCII, or teletype, protocols cannot be used, since they can't handle all the combinations in an 8-bit byte that are possible in binary files. An error checking protocol that handles the full eight bits is required.

binary format

(1) *Binary format* refers to numbers stored in pure binary form in contrast with *binary coded decimal* form.

(2) *Binary format* refers to any information representation stored in a binary coded form, such as data, text, images, voice and video. See *binary file* and *binary field*.

binary notation

Binary notation is the use of binary numbers to represent values.

binary numbers

Binary numbers are numbers that are stored in pure binary form. Within the eight binary digits (bits) of a single byte, the values 0 to 255 can be stored. The 16 bits of two bytes can hold values from 0 to 65,535. Within three bytes, the values 0 to 16,777,215. Contrast with *binary coded decimal* numbers in which each decimal digit occupies one byte of storage. In decimal form, the maximum value in three bytes is 999.

binary search

A *binary search* is a technique for quickly locating an item of data in a sequential list of items. The desired key is compared to the data in the middle of the list. The half that contains the data is then compared in the middle, and so on, either until the key is located or until a small enough group is isolated to be sequentially searched.

binary synchronous transmission

See *bisync*.

binary tree

A *binary tree* is a data structure in which each node contains one parent and no more than two children.

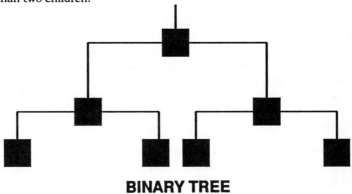

BINARY TREE

bind

(1) *Bind* is to assign a machine address to a logical or symbolic reference or address.

(2) *Bind* is to assign a type or value to a variable or parameter. See *binding time*.

(3) *Bind* is to link modules together. See *link editor*.

binding time

(1) In program compilation, *binding time* is the point in time when symbolic references to data are converted into physical machine addresses.

(2) In programming languages, *binding time* is the point in time when a variable is assigned its type (integer, string, etc.). Traditional compilers and assemblers provide early binding and assign types in the compilation phase. Object-oriented languages, such as LISP and Smalltalk-80, provide late binding and assign types at run time when the variable receives a value from the keyboard or other source.

bionic

A *bionic* device is any machine that is patterned after principles found in humans or in nature, for example, robots. Bionic also refers to artificial devices implanted into humans replacing or extending normal human functions.

BIOS

(Basic Input Output System) A *BIOS* is a set of routines that contain the detailed instructions for activating the peripheral devices connected to the computer.

In IBM personal computers, the BIOS resides in a read only memory (ROM) chip and accepts requests for input and output from both the operating system and the application programs. Since many popular software packages send requests to the BIOS directly, all compatible computers must also have a compatible BIOS. The "autostart" routine in the BIOS is responsible for testing memory upon startup and preparing the computer for operation. It searches for BIOS components that are located on the plug-in boards and sets up pointers in main memory to access them. The BIOS in a compatible machine must set up the computer in precisely the same manner.

bipolar

Bipolar is a category of microelectronic circuit design. The first transistor and the first integrated circuit were designed using the bipolar technique, which derives its name from the use of both positive and negative charges at the same time within the body of the transistor. Integrated circuits (chips) employ the bipolar design when fast speeds are required. The most common variety of bipolar chip is called *TTL* (transistor transistor logic). *ECL* (emitter coupled logic) and *I2L* (integrated injection logic) are also part of the bipolar family. Bipolar and *MOS* (metal oxide semiconductor) are the two major categories of chip design. See *chip*.

bipolar transmission

In communications, *bipolar transmission*, also known as "polar transmission," is a technique for sending digital data that alternates between negative and positive states.

biquinary code

Biquinary code stands for "two-five" code, and is a system for storing the decimal digits 0 through 9 in a four-bit binary number. The three low-order digits hold the decimal numbers 0 through 4 in traditional binary form, but the high-order fourth digit has a value of zero when it is a 0 and a value of five when it is a 1. Thus, the decimal digit nine is represented as 1100, and the decimal digit five is represented as 1000.

bistable circuit

Same as *flip-flop*.

bisync

(BInary SYNChronous) *Bisync* is a major category of synchronous communications protocols used extensively in mainframe networks. Bisync communications require that both sending and receiving devices are synchronized before transmission of data is started. Then the bit patterns of each data character are sent in one contiguous stream. Contrast with *asynchronous* transmission, in which each data character is preceded and followed by one or more bits signalling the start and stop of each character.

bisynchronous

See *bisync*.

bit

(BInary digiT) A *bit* is single digit in a binary number (1 or 0). Within the computer, a bit is physically a memory cell (made up of transistors or one transistor and a capacitor), a magnetic spot on disk or tape or a pulse of high or low voltage travelling through a circuit. Conceptually, a bit can be thought of as a light bulb; either on or off.

Groups of bits make up storage units in the computer, called characters, bytes, or words, which are manipulated as a group. The most common storage unit is the byte, which is made up of eight bits and is equivalent to one alphanumeric character. See *space/time*.

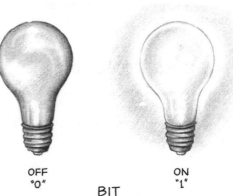

OFF
"0"

BIT

ON
"1"

bit density

The *bit density* is the number of bits that can be stored within a given physical area.

bit flipping

Same as *bit manipulation*.

bit manipulation

Bit manipulation is the processing of individual bits within a byte. Processing at the bit level is typically required in low-level programming of control programs and graphics operations.

bit map

(1) In computer graphics, a *bit map* is the area in the computer's memory that represents the video image. For monochrome screens, one bit in the bit map represents one pixel on screen. For gray scale or color screens, several bits in the bit map represent one pixel or group of pixels on the screen.

(2) *Bit map* refers to any binary representation in which each bit or set of bits corresponds to some object or condition.

bit mapped font

A *bit mapped font* is a complete set of dot patterns for each letter and digit in a particular font. Each font size requires an entirely different set of dot patterns. Contrast with *outline fonts*, which are a set of patterns for a font design that, through the use of an algorithm, can be sized (scaled) to the user's requirements.

bit mapped graphics

Bit mapped graphics refers to the raster graphics method for generating images. Contrast with *vector graphics* and *character graphics*.

bit-oriented protocol

A *bit-oriented protocol* is a communications protocol that uses individual bits within the byte as control codes. IBM's SDLC is an example of a bit-oriented protocol. Contrast with *byte-oriented protocol*, which uses control codes made up of full bytes.

bit parallel

Bit parallel is the transmission of several bits at the same time, each bit travelling over a different wire or line in the cable.

bit pattern

A *bit pattern* is a specific layout of binary digits.

bit rate

Bit rate is the transmission speed of binary coded data. Same as *data rate*.

bit serial

Bit serial is the transmission of one bit after the other on a single line or wire.

bit slice processor

A *bit slice processor* is a logic chip that is used as an elementary building block for the computer designer. Bit slice processors usually come in 4-bit increments and are strung together to make larger processors (8 bit, 12 bit, etc.).

bit stream

A *bit stream* is the transmission of binary signals.

bit stuffing

In communications, *bit stuffing* is the adding of bits to a transmitted message in order to round out a fixed frame or to break up a pattern of data bits that could be misconstrued for control codes.

bit twiddler

A *bit twiddler* is an individual who likes to program or work with computers. See *hacker*.

bitblt

(bit **BL**ock **T**ransfer) In computer graphics, *bitblt* is a hardware feature that moves a rectangular block of bits from main memory into display memory at high speed. Bitblt technology improves the performance of computers used in realtime animation and modeling on screen.

bits per inch

See *BPI*.

bits per second

See *BPS*.

BIX

(Byte Information eXchange) *BIX* is an online database of computer knowledge available from BYTE magazine. BIX is designed to help users fix problems and obtain information about specific hardware and software products.

Black Apple

The *Black Apple* is an Apple II+ personal computer that was made for Bell and Howell to be sold with one of its instructional training packages. It is black instead of beige and has additional audio jacks and volume controls that allow for the mixing of external audio sources.

black box

A *black box* is specialized hardware that converts one code into another, for example, from one communications protocol to another. A black box is a transparent solution for interconnecting incompatible hardware and/or software and should not require changes to the existing systems. Originally custom-made items, black boxes have become standard off-the-shelf products today.

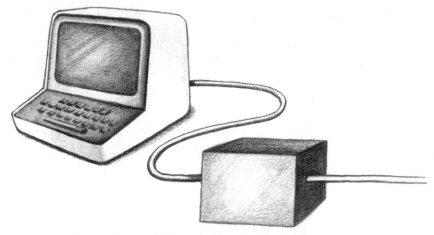

BLACK BOX

Black Box Corporation

The *Black Box Corporation* is an organization that specializes in data communications, computer connectivity products and local area network (LAN) equipment. It offers a wide variety of unique, hard-to-find products as well as expert services for customizing solutions to interconnection problems.

blank character

A *blank character* is a space character such as ASCII 32. A blank character is entered into the computer when the space bar is pressed on the keyboard. Contrast with *null character* (ASCII 0), which appears as a blank, but is considered a control code that has no value, not even a blank value.

blip

A *blip* is a mark, line or spot on a medium, such as microfilm, that is optically sensed and used for timing or counting purposes.

block

(1) On magnetic disk and tape, a *block* is a group of records that is stored and transferred as a single unit.

(2) In communications, a *block* is a contiguous group of bits or characters that is transmitted as a unit.

(3) In word processing, a *block* is a contiguous group of text characters that has been marked for moving, copying, saving or some other operation.

block diagram

A *block diagram* is a chart that contains squares and rectangles connected with arrows to depict hardware and software components and their interconnections. For program flow charts, information system flow charts, circuit diagrams and communications networks, more elaborate graphical representations are usually used.

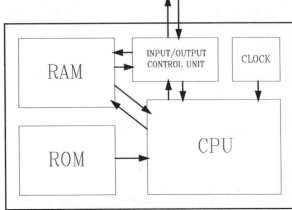

BLOCK DIAGRAM OF A COMPUTER

blocking factor

The *blocking factor* is the number of records in a block.

blow

Blow is to write code or data into a programmable read only memory (PROM) chip. Setting the binary code permanently into these kinds of chips actually means blowing the fuses of the bits that are to be 0s and leaving the bits alone that are to be 1s.

blow up

Same as *crash*, *bomb* or *abend*.

BNC connector

A *BNC connector* is used to connect coaxial cable to various audio, video and communications devices. See *plugs & sockets*.

board

Same as *printed circuit board*.

board level

A *board level* device refers to components available on a printed circuit board instead of in a cabinet or finished housing. Board level computers and controllers are designed for the custom builder of electronic systems.

BOC

(Bell Operating Company) A *BOC* is one of the 22 telephone companies that was formerly part of AT&T and is now part of one of the seven regional Bell telephone companies.

BOF

(Beginning Of File) *BOF* is the status of a file when it is first opened or when an instruction or command has reset the file pointer.

boilerplate

In word processing, *boilerplate* is any common phrase or expression that is used over again. Boilerplate phrases are stored on disk and are copied into the document as needed.

boldface

Boldface is a printed type font that is darker and heavier than normal type. **For example, this sentence is printed in boldface type.**

boldface attribute

A *boldface attribute* is the ability of a display screen or printer to automatically create a bold, dark character.

boldface font

A *boldface font* is a set of type characters that are darker and heavier than normal type. In a boldface font, all the characters have been designed as bold characters. Contrast with *boldface attribute*, in which all characters in a normal type font can be turned into boldface.

bomb

Same as *abend* and *crash*.

BOMP

(Bill Of Materials Processor) *BOMP* was one of the first database management systems used for bill of materials explosions in the early 1960s from IBM. A subsequent version, called DBOMP, was used in manufacturing organizations during the 1970s.

Boolean expression

A *Boolean expression* is a statement using Boolean operators that expresses a condition which is either true or false.

Boolean logic

Boolean logic, developed by the English mathematician George Boole in the mid 19th century, is considered the "mathematics of logic." Its rules and operations govern logical functions (true/false) rather than numbers. As add, subtract, multiply and divide are the primary operations of arithmetic, AND, OR and NOT are the primary operations of Boolean logic.

The integrated circuits in computers are wired together in patterns of Boolean logic. To understand how it works, you can simulate the flow of electricity through a half-adder circuit, a common circuit that adds one bit to another. To do this, you must understand the four possible results you can get when you add one bit to another. They are:

Carry bits

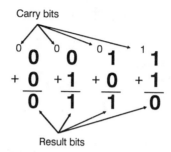

Result bits

In a digital circuit, a 1 is represented as a high voltage, and a 0 is represented as a low voltage. The circuit is wired together according to the following rules:

(1) AND accepts two inputs and generates one output. It requires that both inputs be 1 in order to produce output (1).

(2) OR accepts two inputs and generates one output. It only requires one input to be 1 in order to produce output (1).

(3) NOT reverses the input. If a 1 comes in, a 0 comes out; if a 0 comes in, a 1 comes out.

The inputs to the following example are a 1 (high voltage) and a 0 (low voltage). A line represents the 1. No line represents a 0. See if you can determine why the half-adder circuit below correctly generates a result bit of 1 and a carry of 0:

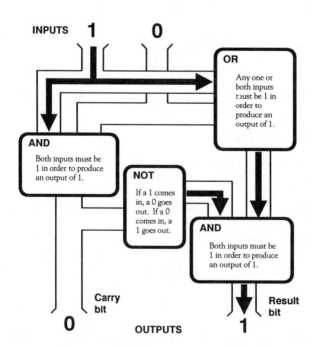

Try This!

Try simulating the flow of current through the following circuits yourself.

(a) Start with the two inputs. If the bit is a 0, draw nothing. If the bit is a 1, draw a line through the circuit path to the first OR and AND gates.

(b) Determine the output of the first AND and draw a line (or nothing) to the NOT and also to the carry bit.

(c) Determine the outputs of the OR and the NOT and draw lines (or nothing) to the second AND gate.

(d) Determine the output of the second AND and draw a line (or nothing) to the result bit.

Your outputs should be a result of 1 and a carry of 0 for the first circuit and a result of 0 and a carry of 1 for the second. If they're not, reread the rules for AND, OR and NOT above, and retrace your steps.

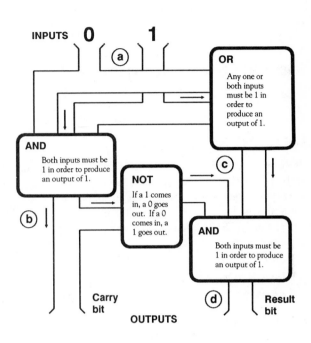

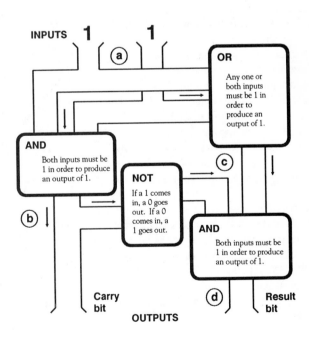

Boolean operator

A *Boolean operator* is one of the Boolean logic operators such as AND, OR and NOT.

Boolean query language

See *Boolean search*.

Boolean search

A *Boolean search* is a search for specific data. It implies that any condition can be searched for using the Boolean operators AND, OR and NOT. For example, the English language request: "Search for all the Spanish and French speaking employees who have MBAs and don't work in Sales." turns into the following query in the dBASE command language:

```
list for degree = "MBA" .and.
(language = "Spanish" .or. language =
"French") .and. .not. department = "Sales"
```

boot, bootstrap

Boot means start the computer. It comes from "bootstrap," since bootstraps help you get your boots on; booting the computer helps it get its first instructions. In personal computers, there's a small bootstrap routine in a ROM chip that is automatically executed when the computer is turned on or reset. The bootstrap routine searches for the operating system, loads it and then passes control over to it. In large computers, the bootstrap procedure may require a more elaborate sequence of button pushing and keyboard input.

A cold boot is when the computer is first turned on. A warm boot is when the computer is already on and is being reset. With personal computers using single-tasking operating systems, it is usually necessary to reset the computer after it crashes.

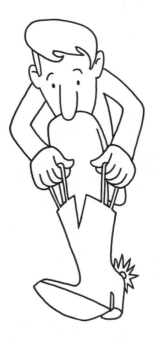

BOOTSTRAP

Boston Computer Society (The)

Founded in 1977 by Jonathan Rotenberg, *The Boston Computer Society* is a nonprofit educational organization for users of personal computers. With over 27,000 members, The Boston Computer Society is the largest personal computer association in the world. Members receive over 100 services, including membership in all user and special interest groups, a subscription to a variety of publications, access to the BCS Resource Center, discounts, telephone referrals, public-domain software and shareware and electronic services. For more information, contact The Boston Computer Society, One Center Plaza, Boston, MA 02108, (617) 367-8080.

BPI

(Bits Per Inch) *BPI* measures the number of bits stored in a linear inch of a track on a recording surface, such as on a disk or tape.

BPS

(Bits Per Second) *BPS* measures the speed of data transfer.

breadboard

A *breadboard* is a development board for building electronic prototypes or one-of-a-kind electronic systems. It's a thin plastic board full of holes used to hold the electronic components (transistors, chips, etc.) that are then wired together.

BREADBOARD
(Courtesy 3M Company)

branch

(1) A *branch* directs the computer to go elsewhere in the program. Same as *goto* or *jump*. Branch may also refer to the sequence of instructions executed as a result of the branch instruction.

(2) A *branch* is a connection between two blocks in a flowchart or two nodes in a network.

break

Break is to temporarily or permanently stop executing, printing or transmitting.

break key

A *break key* on a keyboard is used to stop the execution of the current program or transmission.

breakout box

A *breakout box* is a device that is connected into a multiline cable and provides terminal connections for testing the signals in a transmission. Breakout boxes may also have a small light for each line that glows when a signal is transmitted over that line.

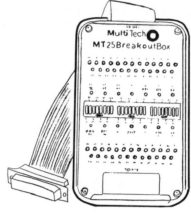

BREAKOUT BOX

bridge

(1) *Bridge* is to purposefully or inadvertently cross from one circuit, channel or element over to another.

(2) In communications, a *bridge* is a device that connects two networks of the same type together. Contrast with *gateway*, which interconnects two different types of networks. See *router* and *brouter*.

bridgeware

Bridgeware is hardware or software that converts data or translates programs from one format into another.

British Telecom

British Telecom is the division of the British Post Office that manages telecommunications throughout Great Britain and Northern Ireland.

broadband transmission

Broadband transmission is a technique for transmitting large amounts of data, voice and video over long distances. Using high frequency transmission over coaxial cable or optical fibers, broadband transmission requires modems for connecting terminals and computers to the network. Using frequency division multiplexing, just like cable TV transmission, many different signals (sets of data) can be transmitted simultaneously. Each signal is modulated onto a separate frequency just like the video picture of a TV station is modulated onto that stations' channel frequency.

Contrast with *baseband transmission*, which transmits at lower speeds over shorter distances and uses time division multiplexing (intersperses data) over a single channel path.

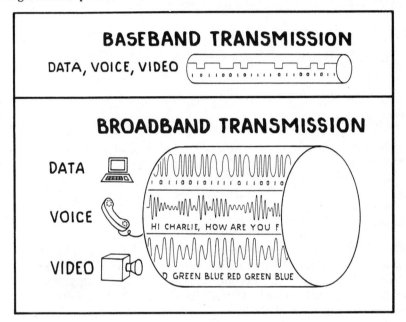

broadcast

Broadcast is to disseminate information to several recipients simultaneously.

Brooklyn Bridge (The)

The Brooklyn Bridge is a file transfer program from White Crane Systems, Inc., that runs on IBM compatible pcs. One computer is designated the master, the other the slave. The user at the master computer can manipulate the disks on the slave computer using common DOS functions, such as COPY and DEL.

brouter

In communications, a *brouter* is a device that performs functions of both a bridge and a router. Like a bridge, the brouter functions at the data link level (layer 2) and remains independent of higher protocols, but like a router, it manages multiple lines and routes messages accordingly.

browse

(1) In database and file management programs, the *browse* mode lets a user display and possibly edit a data file just like text in a word processing document. Browse commands let the user scroll through the data horizontally by field and vertically by row or screenful.

(2) In object-oriented programming languages, *browse* lets the programmer display and edit the class hierarchy of the objects.

BSC

(Binary Synchronous Communications) See *bisync*.

BTAM

(Basic Telecommunications Access Method) *BTAM* is an IBM communications program that is used in bisynch, non-SNA mainframe networks. Application programs must interface directly with the BTAM access method.

B-tree

(Balanced-tree) A *B-tree* is an organization technique for creating indexes that keep track of stored data. A B-tree index stores the data keys in a hierarchy that continually keeps itself in balance in order to keep access time to all data to a minimum. All the nodes in the hierarchy maintain a similar number of keys. As items are inserted and deleted in the index, the B-tree realigns its hierarchical structure to keep the nodes balanced and the search paths uniform.

   A version of the B-tree, called B+-tree, maintains a hierarchy of indexes while also linking the data sequentially. B+-trees allow for direct access and fast sequential access to data. IBM's commonly used VSAM access method uses the B+-tree organization method.

bubble

A *bubble* is a bit in bubble memory or a symbol in a bubble chart.

bubble chart

A *bubble chart* uses bubble-like symbols and is often used to depict data flow diagrams.

bubble memory

Bubble memory is a technology that combines both semiconductor and magnetic recording methods to create a solid state storage device. Like disk and tape, bubble memory holds its contents without power and is about as fast as a slow hard disk. It's used in equipment designed for rugged, heavy duty applications.

Conceptually, bubble memory can be thought of as a stationary disk whose bits spin instead of the disk. Bubble memory units are only a couple of square inches in size and contain a thin film magnetic recording layer. The bits, called bubbles because of their globular shape, are electromagnetically generated in circular strings inside this layer. In order to read or write the bubbles, the strings of bubbles are made to rotate past the equivalent of a read/write head in a disk or tape drive.

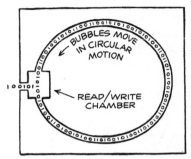

CONCEPTUAL PICTURE OF A
TRACK OF BUBBLE MEMORY

bubble sort

A *bubble sort* is a multiple-pass sorting technique that starts by sequencing the first two items, then the second with the third, then the third with the fourth and so on until the end of the set has been reached. The process is repeated until all items are in the correct sequence.

bucket

In programming, a *bucket* is another term for a memory variable. It's just a place to store something.

buffer

A *buffer* is memory reserved to hold something temporarily. In a program, buffers are reserved areas of RAM that hold data while it's being processed. A buffer may be physically a specified part of the computer's general memory pool (RAM) as declared by the program, or it may be special memory set aside for a single purpose. For example, a bidirectional printer has a buffer that holds at least two lines of data so that it can print alternate lines from right to left instead of having to go back to the left margin. See *print buffer*.

buffer pool

A *buffer pool* is an area of memory reserved for buffers.

bug

A *bug* is any error in hardware or software. A bug usually refers to a recurring and permanent error, whereas a glitch refers to a temporary malfunction. The term goes back to the 1940s when a moth was found squashed between the points of an electromechanical relay in one of the earliest computers.

bulk storage

Bulk storage refers to large amounts of internal main memory or external disk or tape storage.

bulletin board

Bulletin boards are computer systems that function as centralized information sources and message switching systems for a particular interest group. Users dial up the bulletin board, review and leave messages for other users as well as communicate to other users attached to the system at the same time.

BUNCH

See *The BUNCH.*

bundled/unbundled

A *bundled* system is a complete package of hardware and software for a single price. *Unbundled* systems have separate prices for each component.

bunny suit

A *bunny suit* refers to the protective clothing worn by an individual that works in a clean room. The bunny suit keeps human bacteria from infecting the chip fabrication process.

BUNNY SUIT
(Coutesy Hewlett-Packard)

burn in

Burn in is to test an electronic system by keeping it running for a specified length of time. When a new computer system is purchased, the customer may ask the vendor to burn it in for a few days in order to uncover any weak components that will generally fail when first used.

burst mode

Burst mode is an alternate method of high-speed transmission in a communications or computer channel. Burst mode implies that due to certain conditions, the system can send a "burst" of data at higher speed for some period of time. For example, a multiplexor channel may suspend tranmission of several streams of data and send one high-speed data transmission utilizing the entire bandwidth.

burster

A *burster* is a mechanical device that separates continuous paper forms into cut sheets. A burster can be attached to the end of a collator, which separates multipart forms into single parts.

bus

A *bus* is a common channel, or pathway, between hardware devices either internally between components in a computer, or externally between terminals and computers in a communications network.

When bus architecture is used in a computer, the processor(s), memory banks and peripheral control units are all interconnected through the bus. The bus is divided into two channels, one to select where data is located (address bus), and the other to transfer the data (data bus). When you plug in a printed circuit board into your personal computer, you're plugging into the bus.

When bus architecture is used in a communications network, all terminals and computers are connected to a common channel that is made of twisted wire pairs, coaxial cable or optical fibers.

COMPUTER BUS

bus extender

A *bus extender* is a device that allows additional printed circuit boards to be plugged into a bus. It is a separate cabinet that contains a number of slots and a cable that plugs into one of the free slots of the original bus. It usually contains its own power supply to ensure reliable operation of all the additional circuits that will be added.

bus mouse

A *bus mouse* is a mouse that plugs into a printed circuit board that is inserted into the computer's bus. Contrast with *serial mouse*, which comes with a cable that plugs into the computer's serial port. A bus mouse takes up one expansion slot, whereas the serial mouse takes up one serial port. The choice depends on the number of devices you plan on connecting to each type of socket.

business analyst

A *business analyst* is an individual who analyzes the operations of a department or functional unit with the purpose of developing a general systems solution to the problem that may or may not require automation. Solutions are primarily changes in operational procedures, including reallocation of human and machine resources. While a new or revised information system may be the solution to the problem, that is not the major thrust. The business analyst can provide valuable insights into an operation for an information systems analyst.

business graphics

Business graphics are numeric data represented in graphic form. While line graphs, bar charts and pie charts are the common forms of business graphics, there are many additional graphic representations available. Although some people think effectively in numbers, most people think in pictures. By transforming numerical data into graphic form, patterns of business activity can be viewed and related more quickly. When business graphics are printed on clear acetates, they can be placed one on top of the other to reveal relationships and irregularities.

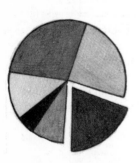
PIE CHART

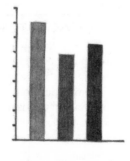
BAR CHART

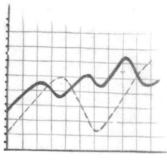
GRAPH

business information system

See *information system*.

business machine

A *business machine* is any office machine, such as a typewriter or calculator, that is used in clerical and accounting functions. The term has always excluded automated systems, teletypewriters, terminals and computers; however, as times change, the term will embrace all mechanical, electromechanical and electronic devices used in a business or office.

by modem

By modem implies the transmission of data over the dial-up telephone system. A modem converts the digital pulses of the computer into audio tones the telephone lines can handle, and vice versa.

bypass

In communications, a *bypass* is the avoidance of the local telephone company for transmission of voice and data signals. Bypass is accomplished by using satellite and microwave systems, for example.

byte

A *byte* is the common unit of computer storage from personal computers to mainframes. A byte holds the equivalent of a single character, such as the letter A, a dollar sign or decimal point. With regard to numbers, in *decimal* mode, a byte holds a single digit from 0 to 9. In *packed decimal* mode, one byte holds two numeric digits. In *binary* mode, a byte can hold a number from 0 to 255, two bytes from 0 to 65535, and so on. See *binary numbers*.

The primary specifications of hardware are rated in bytes; for example, a 20-megabyte disk holds 20 million characters of instructions and data. A one-megabyte memory allows one million characters of instructions and data to be stored internally for processing.

With database files and word processing documents, the size of the file in bytes is slightly larger than the actual number of characters stored in it. Word processing files contain embedded codes for layout and print settings (margins, tabs, underline, boldface), therefore, a 100,000-byte word processing document implies slightly less than 100,000 characters of text. A page of text takes up from 2,000 to 4,000 bytes. Database files contain codes that describe the structure of the records. A 100,000-byte database file implies slightly less than 100,000 characters of data.

Unlike data and text, a 100,000 byte graphics file is not indicative of the size or nature of the image contained in it. There are various graphics standards used, and the higher the quality of the image, the more bytes are needed to represent it. A low-resolution graphics file can take as little as 8,000 bytes, while an ultra-high resolution file can take 4 million bytes, even though both images may appear on the same physical screen size. See *graphics*.

A byte is made up of eight binary digits, or *bits*. An additional ninth bit is also used for creating a parity bit for error checking.

byte addressable

Byte addressable refers to a computer that can address each byte of memory independently of the others. Contrast with *word addressable*, which breaks down the memory into word lengths of typically two or more bytes in length.

byte-oriented protocol

A *byte-oriented protocol* is a communications protocol which uses control codes that are made up of full bytes. The bisynchronous protocols used by IBM and other vendors are examples of byte-oriented protocols. Contrast with *bit-oriented protocol*, which uses individual bits within a byte as control codes.

B2500, 3500, 5000

The *B2500* and *B3500* are families of small to medium-scale mainframes from Burroughs Corporation that were introduced starting in 1966. Now part of Unisys, the successors to these machines are named the "V Series." The *B5000*, introduced in 1961 by Burroughs, was the first in a family of medium to large-scale mainframes that took on many successive designations such as the B5500, B5900 and B7900. This line of computer systems is now called the "A Series" by Unisys. Burroughs mainframes gained a reputation early on for their advanced virtual memory capabilities.

C

C is a high-level programming language originally developed by Bell Laboratories. C is a high-level compiler language that is also able to manipulate the computer at a low level like assembly language. During the last half of the 1980s, C has become the language of choice for developing complex systems software such as operating systems and database management systems.

Since C is a high-level language; it can be compiled into machine languages for almost all computers. For example, the UNIX operating system, written in C, runs in a wide variety of personal computers, minicomputers and mainframes.

C is programmed as a series of functions (small subroutines that perform a task) that call each other for processing. The main body of the program is even a function always named "main." C functions are very flexible, allowing programmers to choose functions from the standard library that comes with the compiler, to use third party functions from other C suppliers, or to develop their own functions.

Compared to other high-level programming languages, such as BASIC and Pascal, C appears complicated. Its unusual appearance is due to its extreme flexibility.

The following C example converts fahrenheit to centigrade using standard library functions:

```
main()
{
 float fahr;
 printf("Enter fahrenheit ");
 scanf("%f", &fahr);
 printf("\nCentigrade is %f", (fahr-32)*5/9);
}
```

C: drive

In Microsoft DOS and OS/2 operating systems, the C: *drive* is the common designation for the primary hard disk.

cable

A *cable* is a flexible metal or glass wire or group of wires that are separated and insulated from each other by a material such as plastic or rubber.

cable matcher

Same as *gender changer*.

cabletext

Cabletext is a videotex service that uses coaxial cable. See *videotex*.

cache memory

Cache memory, pronounced "cash" memory, is a reserved section of main memory (RAM) or a special bank of high-speed memory that is used to improve computer performance. A main memory cache is used to hold instructions and data that are transferred to and from a disk. When the disk is read, a large block of data is copied into the cache. If subsequent requests for disk data can be satisfied with data in the cache, a slower disk access is not required. If the cache is used for writing disks, data is queued up in the cache memory and written to the disk in larger blocks. Some cache systems attempt to anticipate future data requirements by transferring data from disk into the cache that has not been formally requested.

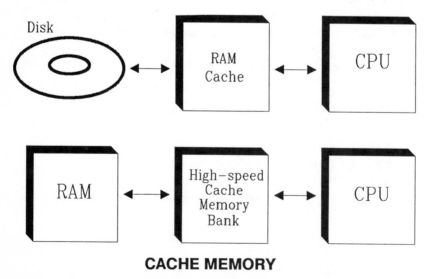

CACHE MEMORY

High-speed memory caches are independent memory banks that act as buffers between lower speed main memory and the CPU. Blocks of instructions and data are copied into the cache and instruction execution and data updating are performed in the higher-speed cache memory.

caching

See *cache memory*.

CAD

(Computer Aided Design) *CAD* is the use of computers for designing myriads of consumer and industrial products from toys to airplanes. CAD systems are specialized workstations or high-performance personal computers that employ CAD software packages and input devices such as graphic tablets and scanners. CAD systems allow graphic images to be drawn or entered and manipulated in an infinite variety of ways. CAD drawings provide the input into computer-aided manufacturing (CAM) systems for complete electronic design and fabrication (CAD/CAM).

CAD software is available for generic use or for specialized uses, such as architectural, electrical and mechanical design. CAD software may also be highly specialized for creating products such as printed circuit boards and integrated circuits.

CAD systems are often turnkey systems which are put together by vendors that may develop or integrate software into standard or optimized hardware. Except in a few cases, CAD systems rely extensively on graphics. See *graphics, CADD*, and *CAE*.

CAD/CAM

(Computer-Aided Design/Computer-Aided Manufacturing) *CAD/CAM* is the integration of computer-aided design with computer controlled manufacturing. CAD/CAM implies that the products designed in the CAD system are direct input into the CAM system. For example, after a machine part is designed in a CAD system, its electronic image is transferred to a numerical control (NC) programming language, which then generates the machine instructions to control the machine that fabricates the part.

CADD

(Computer-Aided Design and Drafting) *CADD* systems are CAD systems with additional features for the drafting function, such as dimensioning (size annotations on standard engineering drawings) as well as text (description and notes) entry.

CADKEY

CADKEY is a fully integrated 2-D drafting and 3-D design system for IBM compatible pcs. In addition to the ability to design machine accurate geometric models, CADKEY offers the user a total design solution with solids creation and built-in DXF and IGES translators. Two hundred manufacturing systems link to CADKEY through its advanced programming language (CADL), including those for numerical control, stress analysis and desktop publishing.

CAE

(Computer-Aided Engineering) CAE refers to software which analyzes designs that have been created in the computer or that have been created elsewhere and entered into the computer. Different kinds of engineering analyses can be performed, such as structural analysis and electronic circuit analysis.

CAI

(Computer-Assisted Instruction) CAI applications are designed for teaching all varieties of subjects to young and old alike. Any combination of graphics, voice response, and touch-sensitive screens may be used to enhance the interactive dialogue between student and machine. CAI takes many forms, from hand-held devices used for exercises in spelling and mathematics to sophisticated courseware developed for personal computers.

Because computers have infinite patience with a student, they make excellent teachers. In addition, the computer can tailor the curriculum to the student's ability to absorb the material. In the future, CAI, combined with artificial intelligence techniques, will prove to be an effective educational assistant for human teachers.

CAL

(1) (Computer-Assisted Learning) Same as CAI.

(2) (Conversational Algebraic Langauge) CAL is a timesharing language that was developed by the University of California.

calculator

A *calculator* is a machine that provides arithmetic capabilities. A calculator accepts input from a keypad and displays results on a readout or paper tape. Unlike a computer, a calculator cannot handle alphabetic data and generally provides limited formatting capabilities for displaying or printing the output.

call

(1) In programming, a *call* is a statement in the program that references an independent subroutine or program. The call is turned into an actual branch

instruction by the assembler, compiler or interpreter. The routine that is called is responsible for setting up the return address to go back to the calling program after it has finished processing.

(2) In communications, a *call* is the action taken by the transmitting station to establish a connection with the receiving station in a dial-up network.

call by reference

In programming, a *call by reference* is a call to a subroutine that passes addresses of the parameters used in the subroutine.

call by value

In programming, a *call by value* is a call to a subroutine that passes the actual data of the parameters used in the subroutine.

called routine

In programming, a *called routine* is a program subroutine that performs a task and is accessed by a call or branch instruction in the program.

calling program

In programming, a *calling program* is a program that initiates a call to another program.

calling routine

In programming, a *calling routine* is a program subroutine that initiates a call to another program routine.

CAM

(1) (Computer-Aided Manufacturing) CAM is an extensive category of automated manufacturing systems and techniques, including numerical control, process control, robotics and materials requirements planning (MRP).

(2) (Content Addressable Memory) Same as *associative storage*.

candela

A *candela* is a unit of measurement of the intensity of light. An ordinary wax candle generates one candela. The flow of light, or rate of emission, is measured in *lumens*. The same wax candle generates 13 lumens.

canned program

A *canned program* is any software package that can be purchased "off-the-shelf" and implies a fixed solution to a problem. Canned programs for typical business applications, such as inventory control, invoicing and accounts payable, should be analyzed very carefully as they provide a fixed set of solutions that usually cannot be changed all that much. However, any application program that has its own programming language or macro language, such as a database management system or spreadsheet, can provide the flexibility necessary to adapt to changing requirements.

canned routine

A *canned routine* is a program subroutine that is prewritten and performs a specific processing task.

canonical synthesis

In database management, *canonical synthesis* is the process of designing a model of the database without redundant data items. A canonical model, or schema, is independent of the hardware and software that will process the data.

capacitor

A *capacitor* is an electronic component that holds a charge. Capacitors are available in varying sizes for use in electronic power supplies. They are also built into chips as the cells, or bits, of dynamic memories (DRAMs).

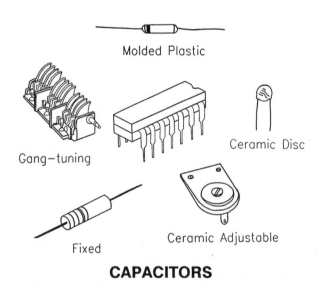

Molded Plastic

Gang—tuning

Ceramic Disc

Fixed

Ceramic Adjustable

CAPACITORS

capstan

On magnetic tape drives, a *capstan* is a motorized cylinder that traps the tape against a free-wheeling roller and moves it at a regulated speed.

CAR

(Computer-Assisted Retrieval) CAR systems use the computer to keep track of text documents or data records stored outside of the computer on paper or on microform. The computer maintains an index of the stored items and is used to derive the location of a requested item. The user must manually retrieve the item from the location indicated by the computer, which may be on a shelf, in a bin, or on a particular microform.

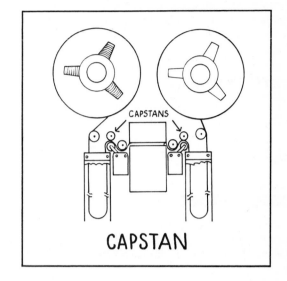

CAPSTAN

card

See *printed circuit board, magnetic card, punched card* and *HyperCard*.

card cage

A *card cage* is a cabinet or metal frame that holds printed circuit cards.

card column

A *card column* is a vertical space that is used to represent a single character of data by the combination of holes punched in it. The common IBM punched card contains 80 card columns.

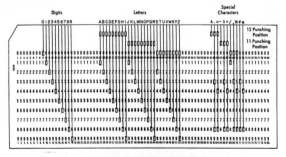

CARD COLUMN

(Courtesy IBM)

card image

A *card image* is an exact representation of punched cards on magnetic tape or disk in which each hole in the punched card is represented by a bit in the magnetic medium.

card punch

(1) A *card punch* is a peripheral device connected to the computer that punches holes into cards at rates of approximately 100 to 300 cards per minute.

(2) A *card punch* is another term for a keypunch machine.

card reader

(1) A *card reader* is a peripheral device that reads punched cards at a rate of approximately 500 to 2,000 cards per minute. The punched card code is detected by patterns of light streaming through the holes in the card as they pass by.

(2) A *card reader* is a peripheral device that reads the magnetic stripes on the back of a credit card.

cardinal number

A *cardinal number* is a number that expresses how much or how many of something. Contrast with *ordinal number*, which expresses a sequence. In the expression, "record number 43 has 7 fields," 43 is the ordinal number, and 7 is the cardinal number.

caret

A *caret* is the small, up-pointing symbol (^) typically found over the "6" key on the top row of the keyboard. It is used to represent various things, such as a decimal point in a number as well as the control key on the keyboard. For example, ^Y means hold the control key down and press the Y key.

carriage

A *carriage* is the part of a printer or typewriter that controls the feeding of paper forms. In a non-Selectric typewriter, the carriage is the part that moves from side to side.

carriage return

See *return key*.

carrier

In communications, a *carrier* is an alternating current that vibrates at a fixed frequency and is used to establish a boundary, or envelope, in which a signal is transmitted. Carriers are commonly used in radio transmission (AM, FM, TV, microwave, satellite, etc.) in order to differentiate one transmitting station from another. For example, an FM radio station's channel number is actually its carrier, or carrier frequency. The FM station merges its audio broadcast (the data signal) into this carrier frequency and transmits the entire signal over the airwaves. At the receiving end, the FM tuner latches onto the carrier frequency and filters out the audio signal, which is amplified and sent to the speaker.

Carriers are used in network transmission in order to transmit several signals simultaneously through a wire or cable. For example, several voice, data and video signals can travel over the same line as long as each one resides within its own carrier vibrating at a different set of frequencies.

carrier based

Carrier based refers to a transmission system that generates a fixed frequency, or carrier, to contain the data being transmitted.

carrier frequency

A *carrier frequency* is a unique frequency that is used to "carry" data within its boundaries. The carrier frequency is measured in cycles per second, or Hertz. See *frequency division multiplexing*.

Carterfone decision

The *Carterfone decision*, made in 1968 by the U. S. Federal Communications Commission, permitted users to connect their own telephone equipment to the public telephone system for the first time.

cartridge

A *cartridge* is a self-contained, removable storage module that contains disks, magnetic tape or memory chips. Cartridges are inserted into slots in the drive, printer or computer.

TAPE CARTRIDGE

cartridge font

A *cartridge font* is a set of characters for one or more typefaces that is contained in a removable module which is plugged into a slot in the printer. The fonts are stored in a read only memory (ROM) chip within the cartridge. Contrast with *soft font* and *internal font*.

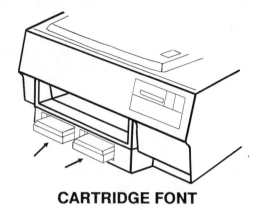

CARTRIDGE FONT

CASE

(Computer Aided Software Engineering or Computer Aided Systems Engineering) CASE refers to the use of software packages that aid in developing all phases of an information system including analysis, design and programming. For example, data dictionaries and diagramming programs aid in the analysis and design phases, while application generators can speed up the programming phase. CASE tools provide automated methods for designing and documenting traditional structured programming techniques. The ultimate goal of CASE is to provide a language for describing the overall system that is sufficient to generate all the necessary programs.

CASE ENVIRONMENT (THE)

(The Cincom Advanced Software Engineering Environment) *THE CASE ENVIRONMENT* is a unified set of software tools from Cincom Systems, Inc., that runs on IBM mainframes and pcs, Digital minicomputers and other hardware. It combines Cincom's MANTIS application development language with software from Index Technology, D. Appleton Company and Aion Corporation in order to support all phases of application development, including planning and analysis, project management, development, implementation and documentation.

case sensitive

Case sensitive refers to the distinguishing of lower case letters from upper case letters. If a language is case sensitive, "abc" will be treated differently than "ABC."

case statement

In programming, a *case statement* is a variation of the if-then-else statement that is used when several ifs are required in a row.

cash memory

See *cache memory*.

cassette

A *cassette* is a self-contained, removable storage module that contains a supply reel of magnetic tape and a takeup reel.

TAPE CASSETTE

catalog

A *catalog* is a directory of disk files or a directory of files for a specific application. It may also refer to any map, list or directory of storage space used by the computer.

cathode

In electronics, a *cathode* is a device that emits electrons. Electrons flow from the negatively charged cathode to the positively charged *anode*.

cathode ray tube

See CRT.

CATV

(Community Antenna TV) CATV was the original name for cable TV where a single antenna, placed at the highest location within the community, would pick up TV signals for the residents of the community. CATV refers to cable TV or to the types of coaxial cable used for cable TV.

CB

(Citizen's Band) CB is a frequency band for radio transmission in the 27 Mhz range that is reserved for public use. The use of CB does not require a license as does amateur radio.

CBEMA

(Computer and Business Equipment Manufacturers Association) CBEMA is a professional membership organization, founded in 1916, composed of computer vendors and business equipment manufacturers and suppliers. With over 40 members, CBEMA is concerned with the development of standards for data processing and business equipment both in the United States and abroad. For more information, contact CBEMA, 311 First Street, N.W., Washington, DC 20001, (202) 737-8888.

CBT

(Computer Based Training) CBT is the use of the computer for training and instruction. CBT programs are called *courseware* and provide interactive training sessions for all variety of disciplines. CBT uses graphics extensively, and media such as CD ROM and interactive videodiscs may also be employed. CBT courseware is developed with authoring languages, such as Adroit and PILOT, which are designed for creating interactive question and answer sessions. Sophisticated CBT systems may use specially designed terminals with touch screens and other interfacing methods, such as the PLATO system from Control Data Corporation.

CBX

(Computerized Branch eXchange) CBX may refer to a PABX controlled by a computer or to a digital PABX.

CCD

(Charge Coupled Device) A CCD is an electronic memory made of a special type of metal oxide semiconductor (MOS) transistor which can store patterns of charges in a sequential fashion. CCDs are used in TV and in optical scanning devices since they can be charged by light as well as by electricity.

CCIA

(Computer and Communications Industry Association) CCIA is a membership organization composed of mainframe, peripheral and data communications vendors, software houses, service bureaus, leasing companies and equipment repair organizations. With over 60 members, CCIA represents interests of members in domestic and foreign trade. Working with the National Bureau of Standards, it keeps members advised of regulatory reform and policy. For more information, contact CCIA, 666 11th Street, N.W., Washington, DC 20001, (202) 783-0070.

CCIS

(Common Channel Interoffice Signaling) CCIS is a digital communications technique that transmits voice and control signals over separate channels. The separate channels are provided by time division multiplexing the signals over the same physical line.

CCITT

(Consultative Committee for International Telephony and Telegraphy) The CCITT is one of four permanent organs of the International Telecommunications Union (ITU), headquartered in Geneva, Switzerland. The ITU, founded in 1865, is an international organization with over 150 member countries. CCITT sets international communications standards.

CCP

(Certificate in Computer Programming) The CCP is a certificate awarded for successful completion of an examination in computer programming, offered by the Institute of Certification of Computer Professionals (ICCP).

CD

(Compact Disc) A CD is an audio disc that contains up to 72 minutes of high-fidelity stereo sound. A CD, which is 4 3/4" in diameter, is like a miniature phonograph record; however, only one side of the CD contains recorded material and there's no disc flipping. In a CD, the individual selections are numbered and can be programmed to play back in any sequence. Unlike phonograph records in which the disc platter contains "carved sound," the CD is recorded in digital form as a series of tiny pits that are covered with a clear, protective layer of plastic. Instead of a needle vibrating in the grooves, a laser in the CD player bounces light onto the pits and picks up the on/off reflections as binary code.

Sound is converted into digital code by sampling the sound waves 44,056 times per second and converting each sample into a 16-bit number. It requires almost a million and a half bits of storage for each second of stereo high-fidelity sound. The reason digital sound is so clear is that the numbers are turned back into sound electronically. There's no tape hiss or needle pops and clicks to contend with. In addition, the CD can hold a wider range of volume (dynamic range) than a phonograph record providing more realism in the recorded material. A soft whisper can be interrupted by a loud cannon explosion, and the difference between the softest and loudest sound (at the same volume level) is greater than a phonograph record can handle. The needle would literally jump out of the groove.

The CD is the forerunner of the CD ROM, which is used to store static data, and the CD-I standard, which holds audio, data, still video pictures and animated graphics.

The compact disc was introduced in the United States in 1983, and by 1986, sales of CDs and CD players exceeded sales for LP phonograph records and turntables.

CD audio

Same as CD and DAD.

CDC

See *Control Data Corporation*.

CD-I

(Compact Disc-Interactive) *CD-I* is a compact disc standard that includes CD audio (music compact discs), static data (CD ROM), still video pictures and animated graphics. The CD-I format holds up to 552 megabytes of data and provides multiple levels of audio and video formats. For example, up to 72 minutes of high-fidelity stereo sound can be recorded just like a CD audio disc, but up to 19 hours of sound can be recorded in a lower fidelity like that of an AM radio broadcast. Developed by Philips International and Sony, the CD-I format is envisioned for home use with CD-I players set up to connect to a standard television set. During 1989, CD-I players and discs, which feature interactive games, education and home reference materials, will be available.

The CD-I format is also available for personal computers, allowing business users access to large text and picture databases.

Although CD ROM provides the standard digital recording scheme, CD-I provides an operating system standard, as well as proprietary hardware standards for compressing the data even further in order to display high-quality video images. CD-I can currently display only half-screen video images due to the bandwidth limitation of the CD ROM standard. In the future, full-screen images will become available. However, as we enter the 1990s, CD technology is barely out of the cradle.

CDP

(Certificate in Data Processing) The *CDP* is a certificate awarded for successful completion of an examination in hardware, software, systems analysis and programming, management and accounting, offered by the Institute of Certification of Computer Professionals (ICCP).

CD ROM

(Compact Disc Read Only Memory) A *CD ROM* is a computer storage disk in the same physical form as a CD audio disc (music compact disc). CD ROMs can hold approximately 550 megabytes of digital data. CD ROMs are used for such things as encyclopedias and catalogs, but will eventually become a major force in interactive education and training as the interactive CD standards and players become popular. See *CD-I*.

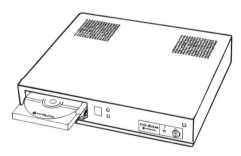

CD ROM

A CD ROM drive may look very similar to a compact disc (CD) player.

Ceefax

Ceefax is a teletext service of the British Broadcasting Corporation.

cell

(1) A *cell* is an elementary unit of storage for data (bit) or power (battery).

(2) A *cell* is the basic data structure in a spreadsheet. It is the intersection of a row and column.

centimeter

A *centimeter* is one hundredth of a meter or approximately 4/10ths of an inch (0.39 inch).

central office

A *central office* is a telephone switching system that interconnects subscribers' telephone lines to each other and to intra and intercity trunk lines.

central processing unit

See *CPU*.

central processor

Same as *CPU*.

centralized processing

Centralized processing is processing performed in one or more computers in a single, centralized location. It implies that all terminals throughout the organization are connected to the computer(s) located within a single datacenter. Contrast with *distributed processing* in which processing is performed in several locations with communications between all the computers. Also contrast with *decentralized processing* in which processing is performed in separate locations without connectivity between them.

CENTREX

CENTREX is a service provided by a local telephone company that offers direct inward dialing from any telephone extension to any other as well as direct dialing to outside lines. The switching equipment resides in the telephone company's facilities.

Centronics parallel interface

The *Centronics parallel interface* is a standard for connecting printers and other peripheral devices to a computer. It defines the plug, socket and electrical signals that are used for controlling the transmission of data. Unlike a serial interface, a parallel interface uses eight wires for the transmission of a full byte of data at one time.

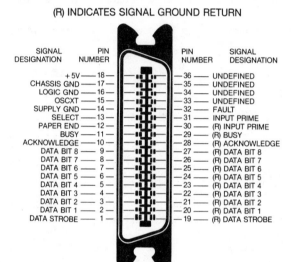

(R) INDICATES SIGNAL GROUND RETURN

SIGNAL DESIGNATION	PIN NUMBER		PIN NUMBER	SIGNAL DESIGNATION
+ 5V	18		36	UNDEFINED
CHASSIS GND	17		35	UNDEFINED
LOGIC GND	16		34	UNDEFINED
OSCXT	15		33	UNDEFINED
SUPPLY GND	14		32	FAULT
SELECT	13		31	INPUT PRIME
PAPER END	12		30	(R) INPUT PRIME
BUSY	11		29	(R) BUSY
ACKNOWLEDGE	10		28	(R) ACKNOWLEDGE
DATA BIT 8	9		27	(R) DATA BIT 8
DATA BIT 7	8		26	(R) DATA BIT 7
DATA BIT 6	7		25	(R) DATA BIT 6
DATA BIT 5	6		24	(R) DATA BIT 5
DATA BIT 4	5		23	(R) DATA BIT 4
DATA BIT 3	4		22	(R) DATA BIT 3
DATA BIT 2	3		21	(R) DATA BIT 2
DATA BIT 1	2		20	(R) DATA BIT 1
DATA STROBE	1		19	(R) DATA STROBE

CENTRONICS PARALLEL INTERFACE

(Courtesy Black Box Corporation)

CEO

(Comprehensive Electronic Office) CEO is integrated office software from Data General Corporation that was introduced in 1981. It includes word processing, electronic mail, spreadsheet, business graphics and desktop accessory tools, such as an appointment calendar and phone list.

CGA

(Color/Graphics Adapter) CGA is a video display board from IBM that is available as a plug-in board for IBM PC and compatible personal computers. CGA generates low-resolution text and graphics and was the first graphics standard for the IBM PC. CGA has been superseded by the EGA and VGA standards.

CGA's text mode provides 25 lines of 80 columns in up to eight colors and uses an 8x8-dot cell for each character. Its graphics mode provides 320x200 pixels in up to four colors from a palette of 16. A medium-resolution graphics mode provides 640x200 pixels in two colors. CGA requires a digital RGB "Color Display" monitor.

CGI

(Computer Graphics Interface) CGI is a standard format for writing graphics drivers. A graphics driver is the set of instructions that activates a graphics device, such as a screen, printer or plotter. The CGI standard also includes the GDI and VDI standards.

CGM

(Computer Graphics Metafile) CGM is a standard graphics format that is used for interchanging graphics images. CGM stores images primarily in vector graphics format, but provides a raster format as well. Earlier GDM and VDM formats have been merged into the CGM standard.

chad

A *chad* is the piece of paper that is punched out on a punched card, on a paper tape or on the borders of continuous forms. A chadded form is when the holes are cut completely through. A chadless form is when the chads are still attached to one edge of the hole.

chain printer

A *chain printer* is a line printer that uses character typefaces linked together in a chain as its printing mechanism. The chain spins horizontally around a set of hammers. When the desired character is in front of the selected print position, the corresponding hammer hits the paper into the ribbon and onto the character in the chain.

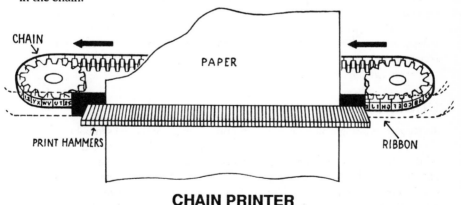

CHAIN PRINTER

chained list

A *chained list* is a group of items in which each item contains the location of the next item in sequence.

chaining

Chaining is the linking of items or records to form a chain. Each link in the chain points to the next item.

change file

A *change file* is a file of transactions that is used to update a master file.

channel

(1) In computers, a *channel* is a high-speed metal or optical fiber pathway between the computer and the control units of the peripheral devices. Channels imply independent transmission paths built into medium and large-scale computers in which multiple channels can transfer data concurrently with each other and with other processing. In a personal computer, the main channel is called the *bus*.

(2) In communications, a *channel* is any pathway between two computers or between a terminal and a computer. It may refer to only the physical media, such as twisted wire pairs, coaxial cable and optical fibers, or it may refer to a specific carrier frequency (subchannel) within a larger channel or wireless medium. See *carrier*.

channel program

In a large-scale computer, a *channel program* is a set of instructions that is executed by a high-speed peripheral channel. The instruction in the program initiates the input/output operation and indicates where the channel program resides. The channel follows the instructions in the channel program independently, allowing other operations to take place within the computer concurrently.

character

A *character* is a single alphabetic letter, numeric digit, or special symbol such as a decimal point or comma. A character is equivalent to a byte; for example, 50,000 characters of memory is the same as 50,000 bytes of memory. A character may also be invisible, such as a blank space or null character. Control characters, such as line feeds, carriage returns and escape codes may be non-printable characters as well.

character cell

A *character cell* is a matrix of dots that is used to form a single character on a display screen or printer. For example, an 8x16- character cell is made up of 16 horizontal rows containing eight dots each. Character cells are displayed and printed contiguously; therefore the design of each character within the cell must include surrounding blank space.

character generator

(1) In display screens and readouts, a *character generator* is the circuitry that converts a data code (ASCII, EBCDIC, etc.) into the pattern of dots that appears on the screen.

(2) In video production, a *character generator* is a device which creates text characters that are superimposed onto video frames.

(3) A *character generator* is any hardware device or software program that generates text characters for display on screen.

character graphics

Character graphics are a set of special symbols that are strung together just like letters of the alphabet to create graphics. For example, some of the character graphics of the IBM personal computer are used to print rules and lines, bar charts and other simple graphics as in the chart below.

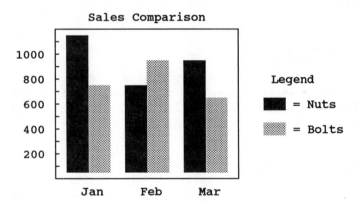

character mode

Character mode refers to displaying only text and not graphics.

character-oriented protocol

See *byte-oriented protocol*.

character printer

A *character printer* prints one character at a time, such as a daisy wheel or dot matrix printer. See *printer*.

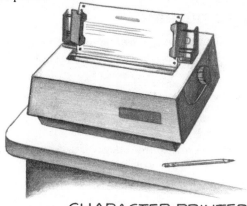

CHARACTER PRINTER

character recognition

Character recognition is the ability of a machine to recognize printed text. See OCR and MICR.

character set

A *character set* is a complete collection of unique symbols and codes that are used for a particular purpose. For example, the ASCII character set contains 128 codes and characters numbered from 0 to 127. The character set of the English language contains 26 unique symbols from A to Z.

character string

A *character string* is a group of alphanumeric characters. Contrast with *numeric* data, which are numbers used in calculations.

character terminal

A *character terminal* is a display screen without graphics capability.

characteristic

In logarithms and floating point arithmetic, the *characteristic* is the number that indicates where the decimal point is placed.

characters per second

See *CPS*.

charge coupled device

See *CCD*.

check bits

Check bits are bits that are used for error checking purposes. The bits hold a number which has been calculated from a segment of data that has been transmitted or stored. See *parity check*, *check sum* and CRC.

check digit

A *check digit* is a digit that is used to ensure that account numbers are correctly entered into the computer. Check digits are added to account numbers before the numbers are actually assigned and used. Using a special formula, the check digit is calculated from the original account number and is added to and maintained as part of the number at all times, usually as the last digit of the number. When the account number is keyed into the computer, a check digit validation routine in the data entry program recalculates the check digit and compares it to the check digit entered. If the digits in the account number were accidentally transposed or the number was incorrectly entered, the calculated check digit will not be the same as the entered check digit, resulting in an error condition.

check sum

A *check sum* is the total of a group of data items or segment of data that is used for error checking purposes. Both numeric and alphabetic fields can be used in calculating a check sum, since the binary content of the data can be added. Just as a *check digit* tests the accuracy of a single number, a check sum serves to test an entire set of data which has been transmitted or stored. Check sums can detect single bit errors and some multiple bit errors.

checkpoint/restart

Checkpoint/restart is a method of recovering from a system failure. A *checkpoint* is a copy of the computer's memory that is periodically saved on disk along with the current register settings (last instruction executed, etc.). In the event of a power failure, or hardware or software failure, the last checkpoint serves as a recovery point. When the problem has been fixed, the *restart* program copies the last checkpoint into memory, resets all the hardware registers and starts the computer from that point. In a communications environment, messages sitting in memory after the last checkpoint was taken until the power failure occurred will still be lost.

child

In database management, a *child* is data that is dependent on its parent. See *parent-child*.

Chinese binary

Chinese binary is an arrangment of binary digits in a vertical column on a punched card in which each punched hole represents one bit of a number.

chip

A *chip* is a miniaturized electronic circuit. Chips are approximately 1/16th to 1/2 inch square and about 1/30th of an inch thick. They hold from a few dozen to several million electronic components (transistors, resistors, etc.). The terms *chip*, *integrated circuit* and *microelectronic* are synonymous.

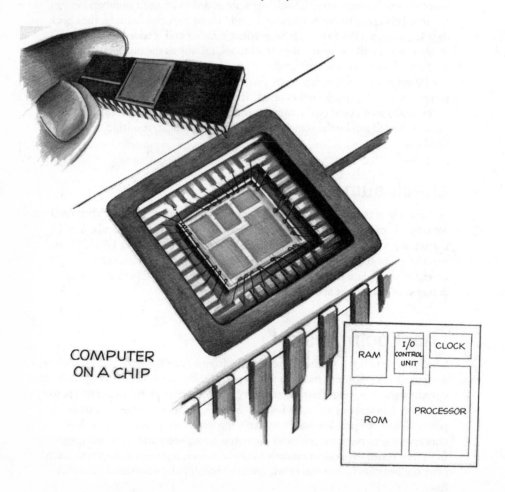

COMPUTER
ON A CHIP

| RAM | I/O CONTROL UNIT | CLOCK |
| ROM | PROCESSOR | |

Types of Chips by Function

LOGIC CHIP

A single chip can perform some or all of the functions of a processor. A microprocessor is an entire processor on a single chip. Desktop and portable computers use one or more microprocessors while larger computers may employ several types of microprocessors as well as hundreds or thousands of specialized logic chips.

MEMORY CHIP

Random access memory (RAM) chips contain from a couple of hundred thousand to several million storage cells (bits). RAM chips are the computer's internal working storage and require constant power to keep their bits charged. Firmware chips, such as ROMs, PROMs, EPROMs, and EEPROMs are permanent memory chips that hold their content without power.

COMPUTER ON A CHIP

A single chip can contain the processor, RAM, ROM, an input/output control unit, and a timing clock. A computer on a chip is used in myriads of consumer and industrial products.

ANALOG/DIGITAL CONVERTER

A single chip can perform the conversion between analog and digital signals, for example, a codec in a telephone.

SPECIAL PURPOSE CHIP

Chips used for low-cost, consumer items, such as digital watches and calculators, may be designed from the ground up to obtain the most economical product. Chips for higher-cost products, such as video game computers, may be designed from scratch as well. Today, application specific integrated circuits (ASIC chips) can be quickly created for any special purpose.

LOGIC ARRAY AND GATE ARRAY

These types of chips contain logic gates which have not been tied together. A final set of steps applies the top metal layer onto the chip stringing the logic gates together into the pattern required by the customer. This method eliminates much of the design and fabrication time for producing a chip.

BIT SLICE PROCESSOR

Bit slice chips contain elementary electronic circuits that serve as building blocks for the computer architect. They are used to custom-build a processor for specialized purposes.

How the Chip Came About

REVOLUTION

In late 1947, the semiconductor industry was born at AT&T's Bell Laboratories with the invention of the *transistor* by John Bardeen, Walter Braittain and William Schockley. The transistor, fabricated from solid materials that could change their electrical conductivity, would eventually replace all the bulky, hot,

DRS. BARDEEN, SHOCKLEY & BRATTAIN (1947)

(Coutesy AT&T)

glass vacuum tubes used as electronic amplifiers in radio and television and used as on/off switches in computers. By the late 1950s, the giant first-generation computers were giving way to smaller, faster and more reliable transistorized machines.

EVOLUTION

The original transistors were discrete components; that is, each one was a separate unit soldered onto a printed circuit board to interconnect with other transistors, resistors and diodes. Since hundreds of transistors were fabricated on one round silicon wafer and cut apart only to be reconnected again, the idea of building them in the final pattern to begin with was an evolutionary one. In the late 1950s, Jack Kilby of Texas Instruments and Robert Noyce of Fairchild Semiconductor created the *integrated circuit*, a set of interconnected transistors on a single chip.

Since then, the number of transistors that have been microminiaturized onto a single chip has increased exponentially, from only a handful in the early 1960s to millions in the

**VACUUM TUBE TO TRANSISTOR
TO INTEGRATED CIRCUIT**

(Coutesy AT&T)

late 1980s. Today, the physical space occupied by a million transistors takes up no more space than one of the first transistors.

A byproduct of miniaturization is speed. The shorter the distance a pulse has to travel, the faster it gets there. The smaller the components making up the transistor, the faster the transistor switches. Switch times of transistors are measured in billionths and trillionths of a second (nanoseconds and picoseconds). And if that seems fast, a Josephson junction superconductor transistor has been able to switch in 50 quadrillionths of a second (femtoseconds).

LOGIC AND MEMORY
In first and second-generation computers, a computer's internal storage, or main memory, was made of such materials as tubes filled with liquid mercury, magnetic drums and magnetic cores. As integrated circuits began to flourish in the 1960s, breakthroughs in design allowed memories to also be made of semiconductor materials. Thus, logic circuits, the "brains" of the computer, and memory circuits, its internal workspace, were moving along the same path of microminiaturization and fabrication. By the end of the 1970s, it was not only possible to put an entire processor on a single chip, but it was possible to put a processor, working memory (RAM), permanent memory (ROM), a control unit for handling input and output and a timing clock all on the same chip. Within 25 years, the transistor on a chip grew into the computer on a chip. When the awesome UNIVAC I, which was so big you could literally walk into it, was introduced in 1951, who would have believed that an equivalent amount of electronics would later be built into a child's stuffed bear?

MORE EVOLUTION
Just as integrated circuits eliminated cutting apart the transistors only to be reconnected again, eventually *wafer scale integration* will eliminate cutting apart whole chips only to be reconnected again. In time, instead of adding more circuits across the surface, the circuits will be built in overlapping layers. Within the next 10 to 15 years, it is conceivable that the electronics in today's multi-million-dollar supercomputer can be built within a cube one inch square!

The Making of a Chip

Computer circuits are pathways carrying electrical pulses from one point to another. The pulses flow through on/off switches, called *transistors*, which open or close when electrically activated. The current flowing through one switch effects the opening or closing of another and so on. Small clusters of transistors form *logic gates*, which are the building blocks and rules behind all this magic, and a specific combination of logic gates make up a circuit. To trace your way through a digital circuit, see *Boolean logic*.

FROM LOGIC TO PLUMBING
Today, the majority of circuits being used have already been designed and reside in circuit libraries on a computer's disk. A computer designer merely has to pick and choose ready-made modules from a menu. But they all had to be invented at one point, and new circuits still have to go through an elaborate process to convert logical patterns on paper into an equivalent maze of plumbing on the chip.

convert logical patterns on paper into an equivalent maze of plumbing on the chip.

Today, computers help make computers. The logical design is entered into the computer and converted into transistors, diodes and resistors. Then the combination of electronic components is turned into a plumber's nightmare that is displayed for human inspection. After corrections have been made, the completed circuits are transferred to specialized machinery that create lithographic plates made out of glass, called *photomasks*. The photomasks are the actual size of the wafer and contain as many copies of the design of the chip as will fit on the wafer. The transistors are built by creating subterranean layers in the silicon, and a different photomask is created to isolate each layer to be worked on. With each layer, the same part of every transistor on every chip is constructed at the same time.

REVIEWING THE "PLUMBING"

(Courtesy Elxsi Corporation)

CHIPS ARE JUST ROCKS

The base material of a chip is usually silicon, although materials such as sapphire and gallium arsenide are also used. Silicon is found in an unpure state in quartz rocks and is purified in a molten state. It is then chemically combined (doped) with other materials to alter its electrical properties. The result is a salami-like silicon crystal from three to five inches in diameter that is either positively charged (p-type) or negatively charged (n-type). *Wafers*, about 1/30th of an inch thick, are cut from this "crystal salami."

BUILDING THE LAYERS

Circuit building starts out by adhering a layer of insulation (silicon dioxide) on the wafer's surface. The insulation is coated with film and exposed to light through the first photomask, thus hardening the film and insulation below it. The unhardened areas are etched away exposing the silicon base below. By shooting a gas under heat and pressure into the exposed silicon, a process called *diffusion*, a sublayer with different electrical properties is created beneath the surface.

Through multiple stages of masking, etching, and diffusion, the sublayers on the chip are created. The final stage lays the top metal layer (usually aluminum), which interconnects the transistors to each other and to the outside world.

Each chip is tested on the wafer, and bad chips are marked for elimination. The chips are sliced out of the wafer, and the good ones are placed into a spiderlike package, called a *DIP* (dual in-line package). The chip is connected to the DIP with tiny wires, then sealed and tested as a completed unit. Depending on the complexity of the chip, the number of chips that make it through to the end can be less than the number that fail.

The chip-making business is an extremely precise one.

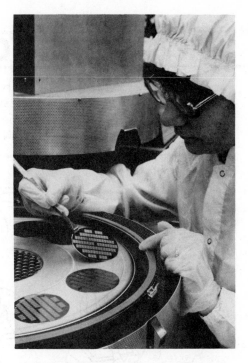

INSPECTING WAFERS
(Coutesy AT&T)

Many operations are performed in a "clean room," since particles in the air could mix with the microscopic mixtures being created and easily render a chip or wafer worthless.

THE FUTURE

In order to miniaturize the elements of a transistor still further, the photomasks have to be made with x-rays or other beams which are narrower than light. Eventually, the circuit patterns will be etched directly onto the chip eliminating the entire photographic masking process.

During the 1990s, it will be commonplace to build several million transistors on a single chip. However, when wafer scale integration becomes a reality, a single wafer could hold 100 megabytes of memory, and a quantum reduction in the cost of circuitry would occur. When superconductor transistors become a reality, there will be a gigantic leap in performance. Should both technologies become production realities at the same time, watch out!

THE TEST FLOOR
(Courtesy VLSI Technologies, Inc.)

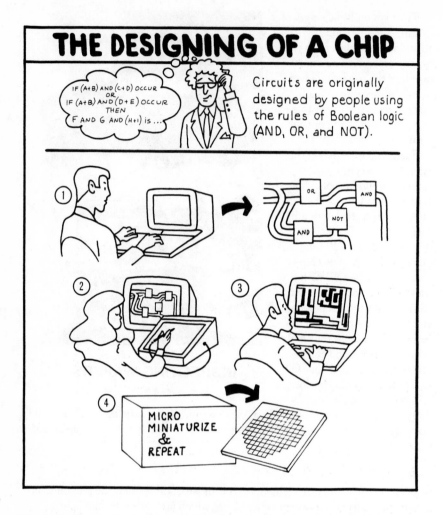

(1) All fundamental circuits are designed by people using the rules of Boolean logic. After they have been designed, they reside in disk libraries in the computer system waiting to be selected by the designer.

(2) The chip designer selects the appropriate circuits from the library and the computer generates the physical circuit paths that resemble a "plumber's nightmare."

(3) The "plumbing" is refined by a designer.

(4) The final results are further inspected to ensure that all the components are aligned properly.

(5) The "plumbing" is turned into several photomasks that will transfer the design of the elements of every transistor onto the chip.

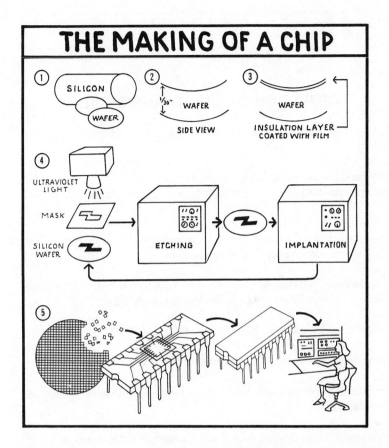

THE MAKING OF A CHIP

(1 and 2) Silicon, the raw material of chips, is refined from quartz rocks and purified. It is fabricated into salami-like ingots from three to five inches in diameter. The ingots are sliced into wafers approximately 1/30th of an inch thick.

(3) The wafer is covered with an oxide insulation layer and then coated with film.

(4) A design is transferred onto the wafer by exposing it to ultraviolet light through a mask. Wherever light strikes the film, the film is hardened along with the insulation layer beneath it. The wafer is subjected to an acid that etches out the unhardened insulation layer exposing the silicon below. The next step is an implantation process that forces chemicals into the exposed silicon under pressure, creating electrically altered elements below the surface.

Through a series of masking, etching and implantation steps, each element for every transistor is created at the same time. Millions of transistors are created together, one step at a time.

(5) The finished wafer is tested, and the bad chips are marked for disposal. The wafer is sliced into chips, and the good ones are placed into their final spider-like package. Tiny wires bond the chip to the package's "feet." Each chip is then tested individually. The number of chips that make it through to the very end can be less than the number that don't.

FORMATION OF ONE TRANSISTOR

The following steps are performed on every transistor in every chip in the wafer at the same time.

(1) The film and insulation layer are hardened after exposure to light. The dark area is the exposed, hardened part; the light area is the unexposed, unhardened part.

(2) The wafer is subjected to acid, and the acid etches out the unhardened film and insulation area exposing the silicon beneath it.

(3) Chemicals, under pressure, are implanted into the silicon creating a sublayer element that is electrically altered from the rest of the silicon.

(4) The wafer is recovered with insulation and film.

(5) The next design is transferred by photomask onto the wafer.

(6) A new hole is opened up, and chemicals are implanted to create an element within the sublayer.

(7) "The patient is sewed up once more," and another design is transferred onto the wafer.

(8) The third element is created by the same etching and implantation processes.

(9) The final stage is to tunnel through the insulation again and adhere the aluminum pathways that carry the current to and from the transistor.

Line A is the triggering line. The signal that activates the transistor comes over this line. Line B has a constant source of electricity. When a pulse comes in on line A, the middle sublayer becomes electrically conductive (the switch is closed) allowing current to travel from B to C.

FORMATION OF ONE TRANSISTOR

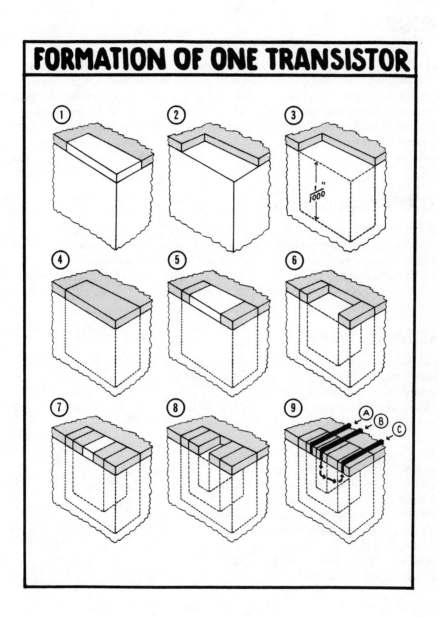

chip card

See *smart card*.

CICS

(Customer Information Control System) CICS, sometimes pronounced "kicks," is a TP monitor from IBM that adds online capabilities to IBM's batch-oriented operating systems running in medium to large-scale mainframes.

CICS lets programmers develop screens for their interactive applications, and it transmits the required screens to the appropriate user terminals. It also provides password security as well as transaction logging for backup and recovery. CICS creates a journal of activity that can be evaluated for analyzing the performance of a CICS session.

CICS programmer

A CICS *programmer* is an individual who designs and writes CICS code for controlling applications in a CICS environment. Application programmers utilize CICS by placing commands into their BAL (Basic Assembly Language), COBOL, PL/I and RPG-II programs. Screen formats, terminal routing and other control information must be coded in the CICS language.

CIM

(1) (Computer-Integrated Manufacturing) CIM integrates the office and accounting functions with the automated factory systems in a manufacturing organization. Systems for point of sale, billing, machine tool scheduling as well as ordering supplies are all part of a CIM system.

(2) (Computer Input Microfilm) CIM refers to reading microfilm and converting the characters into a data code such as ASCII or EBCDIC for input into the computer. However, CIM was never widely developed. Today, microfilm images are scanned into computers and displayed as bit mapped graphic images, but there's no recognition of the actual text characters.

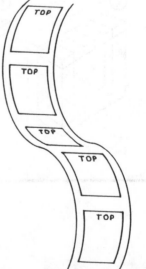

cine-oriented image

In microfilm, a *cine-oriented image* is a film image that is perpendicular to the outer, long edge just like movie film. Contrast with *comic-strip oriented image*.

CINE-ORIENTED IMAGE

CIO

(Chief Information Officer) A *CIO* is an executive officer in charge of all the information processing departments within an organization.

ciphertext

Ciphertext is data that has been coded (enciphered, encrypted, encoded) for security purposes.

circuit

(1) A *circuit* is a set of electronic components that perform a particular function in an electronic system.

(2) A *circuit* is a communications channel.

circuit analyzer

(1) A *circuit analyzer* is a device that tests the validity of an electronic circuit.

(2) In communications, a *circuit analyzer* is the same as a *data line monitor*.

circuit board

Same as *printed circuit board*.

circuit breaker

A *circuit breaker* is a protective device that opens a circuit upon sensing an overload of current. The difference between a circuit breaker and a *fuse* is that the circuit breaker can be reset closed again.

circuit card

Same as *printed circuit board*.

circuit switching

Circuit switching is the physical connecting of two communications channels together. Circuit switching is used to switch analog communications channels, in which the actual physical contact must be maintained from the sending station to the receiving station.

CISC

(Complex Instruction Set Computer) *CISC*, pronounced "sisk," refers to computers that have large sets of instructions. Contemporary CISC machines can have from two to three hundred built-in instructions that they can execute. Contrast with *RISC* (reduced instruction set computer) computers, which have far fewer instructions, for example, only a couple of dozen.

In CISC computers, more work is done in the hardware. In RISC machines, more work is done in the software, which means assemblers and compilers have to generate more code to accomplish the same thing. The complexity of a CICS machine makes it harder to microminiaturize onto a single chip. In addition, the richness of the instruction set also slows down many of the simpler instructions. Depending on the kind of application running, CISC machines can run considerably slower than RISC machines. See *RISC*.

cladding

Cladding is a plastic or glass sheathing that is fused to and surrounds the core of an optical fiber. The cladding keeps the light waves inside the core and adds strength to it. The cladding is covered with a protective outer jacket.

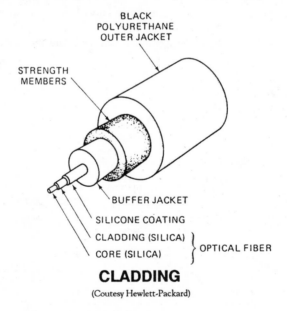

CLADDING
(Coutesy Hewlett-Packard)

Clarion Professional Developer

Clarion Professional Developer is a self-contained application development system from Clarion Software that runs on IBM compatible pcs. It includes a Pascal-like programming language, two compilers and a number of menu-driven utilities for creating screens and reports. Clarion uses its own database management system, but has an optional module that works with dBASE files directly. It also includes an application generator, called "Designer," that allows for the creation of complex multi-file applications.

clean room

A *clean room* is a room that is highly filtered in order to keep out impurities. People working in a clean room wear protective clothing ("bunny suits") and masks that make them look like oversized rabbits.

clear memory

To *clear memory* is to reset all RAM memory and hardware registers to their blank or non-value position. Rebooting the computer may or may not clear memory, but turning the computer off and on again ensures that all memory is cleared. A reset button on the computer will usually clear all memory as well.

click, double click

Click is to select an object with a mouse. Click refers to pressing the mouse button after having moved the mouse to point to an on-screen icon. *Double click* refers to pressing the mouse button twice in rapid succession. If the user presses the buttons too slowly, the system will perceive it as two separate clicks and not as a double click. This time interval can usually be adjusted within the program in order to adjust to a user's personal rate of movement.

client/server

In a communications network, the *client* is the requesting machine and the *server* is the supplying machine.

clip art

Clip art is a set of graphics images that is used to illustrate word processing and desktop publishing documents. Clip art is available in various graphics file formats and is typically specialized for different purposes, such as business, sales and medical.

CLIP ART

(Courtesy Marketing Graphics Inc.)

Clipboard

The *Clipboard* is a reserved segment of memory used to hold data that has been copied from one text, data or graphics document in order to insert it into another.

Clipper

(1) *Clipper* is a dBASE compiler from Nantucket Systems. Clipper translates programs written in the dBASE III PLUS language into executable machine language programs that run by themselves. dBASE III PLUS, from Ashton-Tate, is an interpretive language that requires that the dBASE program reside in the computer in order to run a dBASE application program. Clipper does not support all of the interactive dBASE commands, but does contains features that are not found in dBASE III PLUS.

(2) *Clipper* is a 32-bit RISC microprocessor from Intergraph Corporation.

clipping

Clipping is the cutting off of the outer edges or boundaries of a word, signal or image. See *scissoring*.

clock

A *clock* is an internal timing device. The different varieties of clocks are:

CPU CLOCK
The CPU clock uses a quartz crystal to generate a uniform electrical frequency (vibrations) that governs the computer's machine cycles and is used to create the digital pulses. See *clock speed*.

REALTIME CLOCK
The realtime clock is a time-of-day clock that keeps track of regular hours, minutes and seconds and makes this data available to the programs running in the computer.

TIMESHARING CLOCK
The timesharing clock is a timer set to interrupt the CPU at regular intervals in order to provide equal time to all the users of the computer.

COMMUNICATIONS CLOCK
In a synchronous communications device, the clock maintains the uniform transmission of data between the sending and receiving terminals and computers.

clock/calendar

A *clock/calendar* is an internal time clock and month-and-year calendar that is kept continuously active with a battery backup system when the computer is turned off. The readout from the clock/calendar allows software to be programmed to schedule and remind users of appointments, to determine the age of a transaction or event and to automatically activate computer tasks at specified times.

clock pulse

A *clock pulse* is a signal that is used to synchonize the operations of an electronic system. Clock pulses are continuous, precisely spaced changes in voltage. See *clock speed*.

clock speed

The *clock speed* is the internal heartbeat of a computer and governs the speed of the processor. The clock circuit uses the fixed vibrations generated from a quartz crystal to deliver a steady stream of pulses to the processor. A faster clock will speed up all processing operations provided the rest of the circuits in the computer can handle the increased speed. For example, the same processor running at 20 megahertz (million cycles per second) is twice as fast internally as one running at 10 megahertz.

clone

Technically, a *clone* is an identical copy of some device. With regard to personal computers, a clone is a compatible computer that is capable of running the same software as the original machine. It does not imply that the machine looks exactly the same as the original. And, although clones imply 100% operational compatibility with the original, that is not always the case.

closed architecture

A *closed architecture* is a system in which the detailed, technical specifications for it are not made available to the public. Contrast with *open architecture*, in which third parties are encouraged to build add-on products to enhance the performance of the system.

closed shop

A *closed shop* is a computing environment in which only data processing staff is allowed access to the computer. Contrast with *open shop*, which allows users to run their own programs.

closed system

A *closed system* is a system that does not accept interconnection to foreign terminals or devices. Contrast with *open system*, which allows a wide variety of foreign equipment to be attached.

cluster

(1) A *cluster* is a terminal control unit along with its associated terminals. See *cluster controller*.

(2) A *cluster* is a group of disk sectors that is treated as a single entity. See *lost cluster*.

(3) A *cluster* is a group of related items.

cluster controller

A *cluster controller* is a control unit that manages several peripheral devices, such as terminals or disk drives.

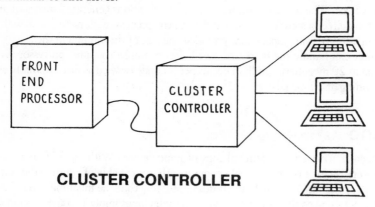

CLUSTER CONTROLLER

CMOS

(Complementary Metal Oxide Semiconductor) Pronounced "see-moss," CMOS integrated circuits are widely used for processors (logic chips) and memories. The CMOS technique uses a PMOS and NMOS transistor connected in a complementary fashion, which results in using less power to operate. CMOS chips are especially valuable in portable, battery-operated devices.

CMS

(Conversational Monitor System) CMS is a system program that provides online, interactive capability in the VM operating system, one of the two major IBM mainframe operating systems (the other is MVS). CMS is used for both timesharing and interactive program development.

CMY

(Cyan, Magenta, Yellow) CMY refers to the color mixing system used to print colors. See *colors* and *RGB*.

coax

Coax is an abbreviation for coaxial cable.

coaxial cable

Coaxial cable is a connecting cable used extensively in audio, video and communications applications. There are many varieties of coaxial cable, but their construction is similar. An insulated wire runs through the middle of the cable. A second wire surrounds the insulation of the inner wire like a sheath, which is constructed of either a solid or mesh metal. The outer insulation wraps the second wire. Coaxial cable has a greater transmission capacity (bandwidth) than standard twisted pair telephone wires.

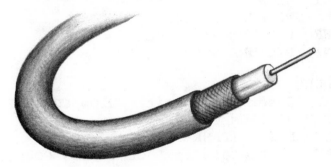

COAXIAL CABLE

COBOL

(COmmon Business Oriented Language) *COBOL* is a high-level business programming language used extensively on mainframes and minicomputers. COBOL, a compiled language, was one of the first high-level programming languages developed. Formally adopted in 1960, it stemmed from a language called Flowmatic in the mid 1950s.

COBOL is a wordy language, usually requiring more writing than other programming languages. As a result, it provides automatic documentation for the person trying to change or maintain another programmer's COBOL program. COBOL is structured into the following four divisions:

Division name	Contains
IDENTIFICATION	Program identification
ENVIRONMENT	Source and object computers identified.
DATA	Buffers, constants and work areas.
PROCEDURE	The processing (program logic).

See the COBOL example on the following page.

The folllowing COBOL example accepts a fahrenheit number and converts it to centigrade. To keep the example simple, it performs the operation on the main console of the computer rather than a user terminal.

```
IDENTIFICATION DIVISION.
PROGRAM-ID.   EXAMPLE.

ENVIRONMENT DIVISION.
CONFIGURATION SECTION.
SOURCE-COMPUTER.    IBM-370.
OBJECT-COMPUTER.    IBM-370.

DATA DIVISION.
WORKING-STORAGE SECTION.
77 FAHR   PICTURE 999.
77 CENT   PICTURE 999.

PROCEDURE DIVISION.
DISPLAY 'Enter fahrenheit ' UPON CONSOLE.
ACCEPT FAHR FROM CONSOLE.
COMPUTE CENT = (FAHR- 32) * 5 / 9.
DISPLAY 'Centigrade is ' CENT UPON CONSOLE.
GOBACK.
```

CODASYL

(COnference on DAta SYstems Languages) CODASYL is an organization devoted to the development of languages. Founded in 1959, CODASYL is made up of individuals and institutions that contribute effort and expense toward designing and developing techniques and languages to assist in data systems analysis, design and implementation. For example, COBOL is a product of CODASYL. For more information, contact CODASYL, c/o Jan Prokop, 29 Hartwell Avenue, Lexington, MA 02173, (617) 863-5100.

code

(1) A *code* is a set of symbols or abbreviations used to represent data. For example, a parts code is an abbreviated name of a specific product, type or category.

(2) Source *code* is the same as source language, the language a program is written in. The complexity of a program is often stated in lines of code.

(3) Machine *code* is the same as machine language.

(4) Digital *code*, or data *code*, is a binary code for representing data in the computer, such as ASCII and EBCDIC.

codec

(COder-DECoder) A *codec* is an electronic circuit that converts human voice into digital code using techniques such as pulse code modulation and delta modulation. The codec also converts the digital voice back into sound waves. A codec is an analog to digital and digital to analog converter. Codec chips are used in digital telephones.

coder

(1) A *coder* is an individual who writes the lines of codes of a program in which the logic has been designed by another programmer. A coder is typically a junior, or trainee, programmer.

(2) A *coder* is an individual who codes data.

coding

See *coder*.

COGO

(COordinate GeOmetry) COGO is a programming language for solving civil engineering problems.

cold boot

A *cold boot* refers to turning the power on and booting the computer. Contrast with *warm boot*, which is when the computer is rebooted after it has been running.

collator

(1) A *collator* is a punched card machine that merges two decks of cards into one or more stacks.

(2) A *collator* is a utility program that merges records from two or more files into one file.

collector

A *collector* is the output side of a bipolar transistor. Same as *drain* in a metal oxide semiconductor (MOS) transistor.

Color/Graphics Adapter

See CGA.

color graphics

Color graphics is the ability to display graphic images in colors.

colors

Colors are the human perception of the different wavelengths of light. It is possible to create almost all visible colors using two systems of primary colors. Transmitted colors use red, green and blue, and reflected colors use cyan (light blue), magenta (purplish-red) and yellow. Color CRTs use clusters of red, green and blue phosphor dots, and color printers use cyan, magenta and yellow inks. See *RGB*.

column

A *column* is a vertical set of data or components. Contrast with *row*, which is a horizontal set of data or components.

COM

(Computer Output Microfilm) COM refers to machines that create microfilm or microfiche directly from computer-generated output. Input to the the COM unit is the same as data sent to a printer. It's already formatted into rows and columns with page headers, numbers and so forth.

Using traditional camera methods that take a picture of an image generated on a CRT, or by using lasers that write images directly, COM units create a film image of each page of the report. Additional graphics, such as lines and company logos, may be added by the COM unit. COM units can be stand-alone devices or online to the computer.

COM file

In Microsoft DOS and OS/2 operating systems, a COM *file* is a machine language program that can be loaded and executed in the computer. COM files are designed to work only in specific memory locations. Contrast with *EXE file*, which can be relocated anywhere in memory.

REPORT COLUMNS

Columns
of
text
on a
character-based
display
screen.

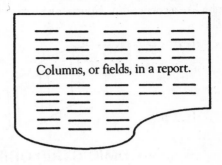

Columns, or fields, in a report.

COLUMNS OF PIXELS

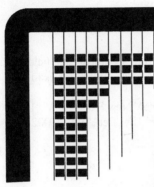

Columns
of dots
in a
graphics
system.
(Raster graphics
or
dot matrix).

MAGAZINE COLUMNS

TABBED COLUMNS

EXPENSES	Planned	Actual
Rent	2,300.00	2,300.00
Electric	450.00	562.23
Gas	100.00	87.46
Water	50.00	43.23
Phone	1100.00	1457.99
Salaries	12,330.00	12,765.32
Auto	1200.00	1,371.09
Garage	225.00	225.00
Entertainment	1500.00	1,093.44
Travel	2500.00	2,788.40
Fees	6000.00	2850.00
Commissions	22,000.00	17,844.34
Advertising	5000.00	7,488.21
Miscellaneous	5000.00	2,389.20
TOTAL	59,755.00	53,265.91

NAME	STREET	BALANCE
Jones, Jennifer A.	10 West Main Ave.	0000208.49
Russo, George C.	23 East Benton St.	0000107.49
Morrison, Emil T.	1240 Parkway East	0001005.77
Fernandez, Joseph R.	39 Gate Drive	0003484.49

Columns of data
cells in a spreadsheet
or fields in a
database.

COLUMNS

comic-strip oriented mode

In microfilm, *comic-strip oriented mode* is a film image that runs the length of the film like a comic strip. Contrast with *cine-oriented image* which is like a movie film.

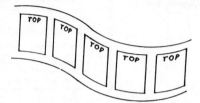

COMIC-STRIP ORIENTED IMAGE

comma delimited

Comma delimited is a record layout that separates each field of data with a comma and usually surrounds character data with quotes, for example:

"Karen Morris","10 Hemlock Drive","New Hope","PA","18950"
"Keith Schiller","348 East 88 Ave.","Syosset","NY","10024"

command

A *command* is an action statement or order to the computer. Commands are language statements which are part of any software package that offers choices and accepts user input.

Commands can be in the form of English-like statements (command-driven), or they can be a series of options in a menu (menu-driven).

command-driven

Command-driven refers to a program that accepts typed-in command words and statements from the user in order to do work. Contrast with *menu-driven* program, which lets the user pick from a list of options.

Command-driven programs are harder to learn, but usually offer more features and capabilities than a menu-driven program. Once learned, command-driven programs are usually much faster to use, because the user doesn't have to wade through levels of menus to do routine tasks.

command language

A *command language* is a special-purpose language that accepts a limited number of commands, such as a query language, job control language (JCL) or command processor. Contrast with *programming language*, which accepts a full range of input, output and processing statements that can solve a wide variety of problems.

command interpreter

Same as *command processor*.

command processor

A *command processor* is a system program that accepts a limited number of user commands and converts them into the machine commands required by the operating system.

command shell

Same as *command processor*.

COMMAND.COM

COMMAND.COM is a command processor for Microsoft's DOS operating system and Microsoft's OS/2 operating system running in compatibility, or real, mode. COMMAND.COM creates the user interface by displaying the screen prompts, accepting the typed-in commands and executing them. Other command processors, or shell programs, can be substituted for COMMAND.COM in order to provide a different way of commanding the operating system.

comment

In programming, a *comment* is a descriptive statement that is used for documentation purposes only and has no effect on the processing.

Commodore 64, 128

The *Commodore 64*, introduced in 1982 by Commodore Business Machines International, is a very popular home computer. The restyled 64C model provides 64K of RAM, color graphics with up to 16 colors and three independent tone generators, each with nine octaves. A 350K 5 1/4" floppy disk and a one megabyte 3 1/2" microfloppy disk is available for the 64C.

COMMODORE 128

The *Commodore 128*, introduced in 1986, provides 128K of RAM, expandable to 640K, and runs both Commodore 64 and Commodore 128 software. With the addition of Commodore's CP/M board, the Commodore 128 will run CP/M software, such as WordStar and dBASE II. In 1987, Commodore introduced the *128D*, an enhanced model with a built-in disk drive and detached keyboard. By the end of the 1980s, well over 10 million units of the 64 and 128 models will have been installed worldwide.

Commodore's Amiga series is a more powerful family of personal computers that offers increased performance and enhanced graphics.

common carrier

A *common carrier* is a government regulated organization which provides telecommunications services for public use, such as AT&T, the telephone companies, ITT, MCI and Western Union.

communications

Communications refers to the transfer of information from one computer to another. Communications is a major technology that requires special expertise in both the network and related hardware and software that controls it.

There are some overlapping and synonymous terms for this field. *Data communications* refers to data and text communications. *Telecommunications* refers to all forms of communications, including voice and video. *Teleprocessing* is an old IBM term for data communications/data processing. In this book, the term *communications* is used to refer to all forms of transmission over a network.

The Protocol

The way communications systems "talk to" each other is defined in a set of standards called *protocols*. Protocols work in a hierarchy starting at the top with the user's program and ending at the bottom with the physical plugs and sockets and electrical signals. To get an understanding of this hierarchy, see *OSI*, the Open Systems Interconnection international reference model.

Personal Computer Communications

Personal computer communications takes on several forms.

(1) Data can be transferred between two geographically distant personal computers by using modems, the dial-up telephone system and a communications program in each computer.

(2) Data can be transferred between two side-by-side computers by hooking up a cable (null modem cable) from one computer's serial port to the other computer's serial port.

(3) Personal computers can act like a remote terminal to a minicomputer or mainframe. For example, DCA's IRMAboard plugs into a personal computer

and turns it into an IBM 3278 or 3279 terminal, the common interactive terminal connected to IBM mainframes.

(4) Personal computers can be part of a local area network, in which databases and other files, as well as printers, can be shared among many users. If the local area network interconnects with a minicomputer or mainframe network, then personal computers can communicate with larger computers.

Minicomputer Communications

Minicomputer communications systems control as many as several hundred terminals connected to a single computer system. They support a variety of low-speed dial-up terminals and high-speed local terminals. With larger minicomputers, the communications processing is handled in separate machines, called *communications controllers*.

Since minicomputers were originally designed with communications in mind, it is usually more straightforward than with mainframes. The communications programs and operating systems are often designed as an integrated system providing a more coherent approach from the start.

Minicomputers can interconnect with a mainframe by emulating a mainframe terminal, in which case, the mainframe thinks it's talking to just another user terminal. Minicomputers can hook up directly with some local area networks, or they can interconnect with the use of a gateway, which converts the protocols.

Mainframe Communications

Mainframe communications systems can control several thousands of remote terminals connected to one mainframe complex. They support a variety of low-speed dial-up terminals and high-speed local terminals.

Large mainframes use separate machines, called *communications controllers* or *front end processors*, to handle the communications processing. The controllers and front end processors take the data from the mainframes and package it for transmission over the network. They also strip the codes from the incoming messages and send pure data to the mainframes for processing.

Mainframes set the standards for communications. It's usually up to the mini and micro vendors to provide compatibility with the mainframe systems.

Analog vs Digital Communications

The most common form of long-distance communications in the world has been the telephone system, which, up until a few years ago, transmitted only voice frequencies. This transmission technique, known as *analog* communications, has been error prone, because the electronic frequencies get garbled together with unwanted, extraneous signals (noise) that invade the line for a variety of reasons.

In analog telephone networks, amplifiers are located in the line every few miles to maintain a strong signal. Their job is simply to boost the incoming signal, but they can't distinguish between a meaningful signal and garble. Thus, tiny drops of interference creeping into the line keep getting louder and louder as the signal is boosted hundreds of times. In a noisy line, by the time the receiving person or machine gets the signal, it may be impossible to decipher it.

In a *digital* network, only binary code is transmitted. In other words, only two distinct frequencies or only two distinct voltages will ever be sent over the line. Therefore, instead of amplifiers, repeaters are used, which analyze the incoming signal and regenerate a brand new outgoing signal. Any noise that invades the line will get only as far as the next repeater and be filtered out.

That's the secret to digital transmission. When only bits (0s and 1s) need to be analyzed, there's a good chance the data bits can be distinguished from the garble.

THE FIRST ANALOG COMMUNICATIONS (1876)

(Courtesy AT&T)

"Mr. Watson, come here. I want you."

Communications and Computers

In very large organizations, the data communications department has been separate and distinct from the telecommunications department. Data communications concerned itself with the data processing terminals, and telecommunications managed the telephones. As telephone systems become all digital, and as office automation dictates that terminals become as pervasive as the telephone, the authority and control over the two technologies will become a political issue.

Communications Act of 1934

The *Communications Act of 1934* established the Federal Communications Commission (FCC) that regulates all interstate and foreign telecommunications. Its mission is to provide high quality services at reasonable costs to everyone in the United States on a nondiscriminatory basis.

communications channel

Also called a *circuit* or *line*, a *communications channel* is a pathway over which data is transferred between remote devices. It may refer to the entire physical medium, such as a public or private telephone line, optical fiber, coaxial cable or twisted wire pair, or, it may refer to the specific carrier frequency transmitted within the medium, such as in a microwave or satellite channel or in a broadband local area network.

communications controller

A *communications controller* is a peripheral control unit that connects several communications lines to a computer and performs the actual transmitting and receiving as well as various message coding and decoding activities. Communications controllers are typically nonprogrammable units designed for specific protocols and communications tasks. Contrast with *front end processor*, which is a more sophisticated version of the communications controller and can be programmed for a variety of protocols and network conditions.

communications network

A *communications network* is a number of communications channels that interconnect terminals and computers. All hardware and software used to link the channels together and support the communications within the network are part of the communications network.

communications program

A *communications program* is software that transmits data to and receives data from local and remote terminals or between computers. In a mainframe, it is a complex set of programs (also called *access methods* and *network control programs*) that reside both in the computer and in the front end processor and can handle thousands of online users. Minicomputer communications programs are capable of handling several hundred users.

Personal computer communications programs usually handle only one line and typically include several file transfer protocols that provide error checking to ensure against loss of data. If the communications program in the second personal computer does not support the same protocol, both machines can communicate via a straight ASCII protocol without error checking. However, without error checking, characters can be lost in transmission over noisy telephone lines.

communications protocol

A *communications protocol* is a set of hardware and software standards for transmitting data between terminals and computers. See *OSI*.

communications satellite

A *communications satellite* is a radio relay station in orbit 22,300 miles above the equator. It travels at the same rate of speed as the earth (geosynchronous), so that it appears stationary to us. Communications satellites contain many communications channels that receive analog and digital signals from earth stations. Digital signals are transmitted within a carrier frequency.

The signals are amplified and transmitted back to earth, covering either a small geographical area (spot beam) or almost a third of the earth's surface. In the latter case, private data is often encrypted to prevent eavesdropping.

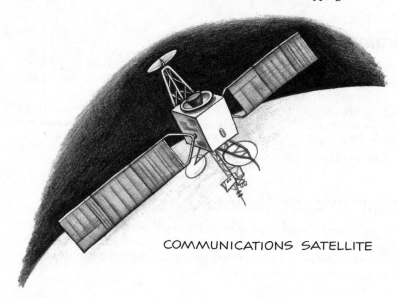

COMMUNICATIONS SATELLITE

Communications Satellite Corporation

See *COMSAT*.

communications server

Same as *gateway*.

compact disc

See *CD*.

COMPACT II

COMPACT II is a high-level numerical control programming language used to generate instructions for numerical control (machine tool) devices.

compandor

(COMpressor/exPANDOR) A *compandor* is used to improve the signal for AM radio (voice) transmission. The compandor raises the amplitude (volume) of weak signals and lowers the amplitude of strong signals on outgoing transmission. On incoming transmission, the compandor reverses the operation and restore the signal to its original form.

Compaq

Compaq is a manufacturer of personal computers that was the first company to sucessfully clone the IBM PC. In 1983, its first year in business, Compaq achieved sales of 111 million dollars, an all-time first in American business. The original Compaq was a transportable version of the IBM PC simply known as the "Compaq" computer. Subsequent desktop models using the Intel 8086 and 80286 chips use the "Deskpro" designation. In 1986, Compaq introduced the "Compaq 386," the first machine to use Intel's 80386 microprocessor, which has set a standard for the industry.

COMPAQ 386

Compaq has become well known for its rugged and reliable personal computers and has become an industry leader in a few short years.

comparator

A *comparator* is a device that compares two quantities and determines their equality.

compare

Comparing is a major processing capability of the computer. By comparing one set of data with another, the computer can locate, analyze, select, reorder and make decisions. At the fundamental level, the compare capability is all the computer can do to determine an outcome. After comparing, the computer can indicate whether the data were equal, unequal or which set was greater or less than the other. Using the Boolean operators AND, OR and NOT, the program can direct the computer to compare multiple conditions and determine their outcome. For example, "if age is greater than 65 AND income is less than $15,000," then perform some operation as a result. See *computer (The 3 C's)*.

compatibility

See *standards & compatibility*.

compatibility mode

Compatibility mode is a special feature of a computer or operating system that allows it to run programs written for a different system. The compatibility mode is usually built into the hardware, but may also require special software. Compatiblity modes can also be created entirely in software. Programs are usually slower when running in compatiblity mode.

compilation

A *compilation* is the compiling of a program. See *compiler*.

compile time

Compile time is the time it takes to translate a program from source language into machine language. The link editing time may also be included in the compile time.

compiler

A *compiler* is a software program that translates a programming language into machine language, the language the computer understands. High-level programming languages, such as COBOL and C, are compiler languages.

Contrast with *interpretive* languages, such as BASIC, which are translated at the time they are running. Compiled programs run faster than interpreted programs, because the entire program has been translated into machine language before the program is run.

A compiler usually generates assembly language first, since assembly language has a one-to-one relationship with the machine. The assembly language is then assembled into machine language.

The following example compiles program statements into machine language:

Source code	Machine language	Actual machine code
IF COUNTER = 10	Compare 34434 38479	10010011100101010101
GOTO DONE	If = go to 45881	10010100101000101100
ELSE		
GOTO REPEAT	Goto 23990	10010010101000100101
ENDIF		

compiler language

A *compiler language* is a high-level programming language that is translated into machine language before the program is executed. Contrast with *interpretive language*, which is maintained in its original form and translated a line at a time when it is running.

compiler program

Same as *compiler*.

complement

A *complement* is a number that is derived by subtracting a number from a constant or, for binary numbers, by reversing all the digits and adding 1. Complement numbers are used in digital circuits, because it's faster to do subtraction by adding complement numbers than by performing a true subtraction operation.

The binary complement of a number is created by changing all 1s to 0s and all 0s to 1s and adding 1. When adding complement numbers the carry from the most significant (high-order) position is eliminated. The following example subtracts 5 from 8. The 5 in binary (0101) is first changed to 1010, then 1 is added, deriving the 1011 complement. The 1011 is then added to the 1000 (8).

Decimal Subtraction	Binary Equivalent	Subtraction by Adding the complement
8	1000	1000
5	0101	1011
3		0011

component

A *component* is one element of a larger system. A hardware component can be a device as small as a transistor or as large as a disk drive as long as it is part of a larger system. Software components are routines or modules within a larger system.

composite video

Composite video is the video-only (no audio) portion of the standard NTSC color television signal used in the United States. Some personal computers, such as the Apple II series, have composite video output that connects directly to the video input of a color television set using a common RCA phono cable.

In a composite video signal, the red, green and blue signals have been mixed together. The resulting on-screen images are not as crisp as an RGB video signal in which the red, green and blue signals are transmitted separately.

compression

See *data compression*.

compressor

(1) A *compressor* is a device that diminishes the range between the strongest and weakest transmission signals. See *compandor*.

(2) A *compressor* is a routine or program that compresses data. See *data compression*.

CompuServe

CompuServe is an information utility that provides a wide variety of information and services, including bulletin boards, online conferencing, business news, sports and weather, financial transactions, electronic mail, travel and entertainment data as well as online editions of computer publications.

compute

Compute is to perform mathematical operations; however, a computer's computing is called *processing*, and it entails more than just arithmetic calculations. See *computer (The 3 C's)*.

compute bound

Same as *processor bound*.

computer

A *computer* is a general-purpose machine that processes data according to a set of instructions that are fed into it. The computer itself and all the equipment attached to it are called *hardware*. The instructions that tell it what to do are called *software*. A set of instructions that perform a particular task is called a program, or *software program*. The instructions in the program direct the computer to input, process and output as follows:

Input/Output

The computer can selectively retrieve data into its electronic circuits, called *main memory* or *RAM*, from any peripheral device (terminal, disk drive, tape drive or communications line) connected to it. After processing the data internally, the computer can send a copy of the results from its main memory out to any peripheral device. The more memory it has, the more programs and data a computer can take in and work on at the same time.

Storage

By outputting data onto a magnetic disk or tape, the computer is able to store data permanently and retrieve it when necessary. A computer's size is based on how much disk storage it has. The more disk, the more data is immediately available to the computer.

Processing (The 3 C's*)

Once the data has been stored in the computer's memory, the computer can process it by (1) calculating, (2) comparing and (3) copying.

CALCULATE
The computer can perform any mathematical operation on data by adding, subtracting, multiplying and dividing one set of data with another.

COMPARE
The computer can analyze and evaluate data by matching it with sets of known data that are included in the program.

COPY
The computer can move data around to create any kind of report or listing in any order.

Using **calculation**, **comparing** and **copying**, the computer can accomplish all forms of data processing. For example, the computer sorts records into a new order by **comparing** two records at a time and **copying** the record with the lower value in front of the record with the higher value.

The computer locates the desired customer record out of a file of thousands of records by **comparing** the requested account number with each account number in an index of account numbers until it finds a match.

In word processing, inserting new text into existing text is accomplished by **copying** the characters over one memory location (byte) for each new character that is inserted. Deleting text is accomplished by **copying** the remaining characters on top of the characters to be deleted.

The dBASE query statement: SUM SALARY FOR TITLE = "NURSE" causes the computer to **compare** the title field in each record for NURSE and then add (**calculate**) the salary field into a counter for each match.

Remember The 3 C's*

If you wonder whether the computer can solve your problem, think of the 3 C's. Identify your data on a piece of paper, and think of the paper as the computer's internal, electronic memory. If you can solve your problem by using any combination of **calculating**, **comparing** and **copying**, the computer do it too.

(***The 3 C's** is a service mark of The Computer Language Company Inc.)

The 3 C's®

CALCULATE

In the update example on the opposite page, the extended price is calculated on a group of line items in an order. A line item record is read from the disk and written into memory. The number in the quantity field is multiplied by the number in the price field, and the result is written into the extended price field. The record is then read from memory and written back on the disk. The program gets the next record and repeats the process until it reaches the end of file.

COMPARE

In the search example on the opposite page, ARIZONA records are being selected. Records are read from the disk and written into memory. The STATE field in the record is compared with the search data "AZ." If they are equal, the record is selected, in which case it is written to another disk file or it is formatted for the printer. The program then goes back and inputs the next record until the end of file is encountered.

COPY

In the sort example on the opposite page, data is input into memory and compared. If an item is out of sequence (lower when it should be higher, or vice versa), it is copied into its correct order. By copying, data can be placed into any desired sequence; for example, from low to high order (A to Z) or from high to low order (Z to A). Data can be copied into one sequence within another. For example, sales totals can be sorted into high-low order by amount within low-high order by state. The main list would be in natural alphabetic order by state, but within each state, the list would be highest sales to lowest sales.

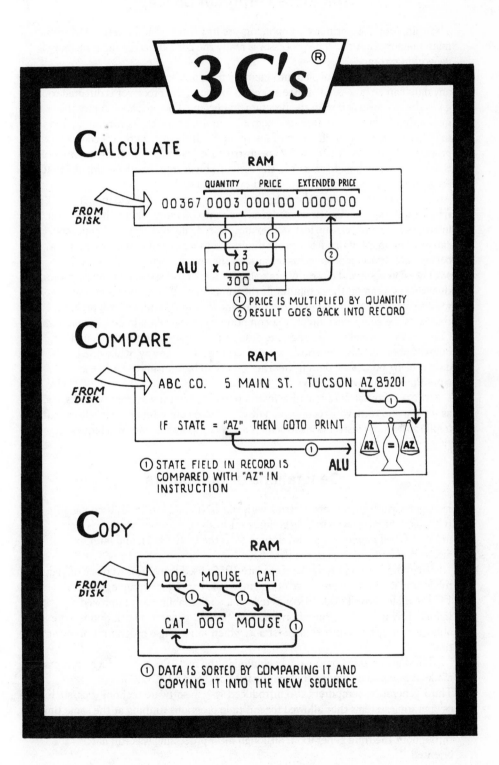

3C's ®

CALCULATE

RAM

FROM DISK

QUANTITY PRICE EXTENDED PRICE

00367 0003 000100 000000

ALU x 100 / 3 / 300

① PRICE IS MULTIPLIED BY QUANTITY
② RESULT GOES BACK INTO RECORD

COMPARE

RAM

FROM DISK

ABC CO.   5 MAIN ST.   TUCSON AZ 85201

IF STATE = "AZ" THEN GOTO PRINT

ALU AZ = AZ

① STATE FIELD IN RECORD IS
COMPARED WITH "AZ" IN
INSTRUCTION

COPY

RAM

FROM DISK

DOG   MOUSE   CAT

CAT   DOG   MOUSE

① DATA IS SORTED BY COMPARING IT AND
COPYING IT INTO THE NEW SEQUENCE

The Stored Program Concept

The computer's two primary components are its processor and internal electronic main memory (RAM). The processor is really the computer, the main memory is its working storage.

The program is first copied into memory from a disk, tape or other source before any data can be processed. Once stored in memory, the processor is directed to go to the first instruction in the program and begin. The processor copies the instruction from memory into its electronic circuit, called the control unit, and matches it against its built-in set of instructions. If the instruction is coded properly, the processor carries out the instruction (executes it). If the instruction is not a valid machine instruction, the computer will stop the processing for that program, otherwise known as an abend (abnormal end).

The processor executes the program by keeping track of where in memory it got the last instruction. The processor goes back into memory and fetches the next instruction, and so on, one instruction at a time, again and again. Computers can execute instructions from many thousands to many millions of instructions per second. It accomplishes this because of the speed at which electronic switches can open and close. We take advantage of this speed by running more than one program in the computer at the same time. While one program is waiting for input from one user, the operating system (master control program that runs the computer) directs the computer to process data in another program. Computers, especially large ones, are designed to allow multiple inputs and outputs to occur simultaneously with processing. In that way, while one user's data is being processed, data from other users can be transmitted into the computer to be processed next.

It takes thousands of machine instructions to perform very routine tasks, such as storing and retrieving records on a disk. A large computer could easily execute a million or more instructions to search for and display the data you requested.

Generations of Computers

First-generation computers, starting with the UNIVAC I in 1951, used vacuum tubes as their primary switching component in the processor. Memories were made of liquid mercury delay lines, such as in the UNIVAC I, and later on magnetic drums, such as in the IBM 650.

Second-generation systems in the late 1950s used transistors in place of vacuum tubes, and memories were made of magnetizable cores, for example, the IBM 1401 and Honeywell 800. Size was reduced, and reliability was improved significantly in second-generation systems. Second-generation computers were almost entirely batch processing systems, which ran a single program running at a time.

Third-generation computers, beginning in the mid 1960s, introduced processors made of integrated circuits, such as the IBM 360 and CDC 6400. Third-generation computers also introduced system software technologies, such as operating systems that allowed for multiple programs running at the same time and database management systems. Online systems were widely developed throughout the third generation, although most processing was still batch oriented.

Starting in the middle to late 1970s, the fourth generation brought us computers made entirely of chips containing large numbers of electronic components. It brought us the microprocessor, which spawned the personal computer. The fourth generation embraces integration of small and large computers together in a distributed processing/office automation environment. Fourth-generation query languages, report writers, spreadsheets and other software packages brought the non-computer person squarely in contact with computers.

The fifth generation ought to become formalized by the early 1990s. VLSI and eventually SLSI technologies will put current-day mainframes on everyone's desk. Fiber optics, optical disks and technologies now in the research labs, will be used to construct fifth-generation computer systems. Artificial intelligence techniques will be incorporated into many applications, and by the turn of the century, a computer will be able to converse somewhat intelligently with its users.

Computers Come in Many Sizes

Computers can be as small as a chip or as large as a truck. The difference between them is in the amount of work they can perform within the same time frame. A computer's power is based on many factors, including its word size and the speed of its CPU, memory and peripherals. The following list is a rough guide to the cost of a complete computer system:

Computer system type (Bits show word size)	Approximate retail cost In 1989 U. S. dollars
Computer on a chip (4, 8, 16-bit)	$2 - 75 (chip only)
Microprocessor (4, 8, 16, 32-bit)	$5 - 250 (chip only)
Personal computer (8, 16, 32-bit)	$500 - 10,000
Supermicro or Micromini (16, 32-bit)	$5,000 - 25,000
Minicomputer (16, 32-bit)	$15,000 - 250,000
Supermini or Micromainframe (32-bit)	$200,000 - 750,000
Mini-supercomputer (64-bit)	$100,000 - 750,000
Mainframe (32-bit)	$150,000 - 3,000,000
Supercomputer (64-bit)	$1,000,000 - 15,000,000

computer-aided design

See *CAD*.

computer-aided engineering

See *CAE*.

computer-aided instruction

See *CAI*.

computer-aided manufacturing

See CAM.

computer architecture

A *computer architecture* is the design of a computer system. It is based on the type of programs that will run in it and the number of different programs that are expected to run at the same time. The design will determine how the computer will service the concurrent activities (via interrupts, parallel processing, etc.), the amount of memory required (size of address bus) and the size of the internal channels or bus that transfer data and instructions back and forth.

Providing a foundation for the execution of all the functions in the computer is the design of its native language instruction set. Computers can be built with a set of instructions fixed into its circuits, or with instructions in *microcode*, a read only memory that can be enhanced and modified more easily.

A major design criterion is the tradeoff between hardware and software functions. Since the first computers, more and more complicated instructions have been built into the computer resulting in instruction sets containing hundreds of instructions. A recent trend, called *RISC*, is returning to simpler instruction sets that can be built more economically and that can run faster than their complicated instruction set (CISC) counterpart.

Non-stop, or fault tolerant, operation may be a design objective that will influence the construction of every component in the computer. Specialized machines, like array processors and database machines, require different architectures than standard computers in order to facilitate faster processing.

In time, more system software functions (operating system, database management system, etc.) will be moved out of software and be built into the hardware circuits for improved performance.

A computer's architecture and resulting machine language set the standard for all peripheral devices that connect to it and all software that runs in it for years to follow.

computer-assisted instruction

See CAI.

computer-assisted learning

See CAI.

computer-based training

See CBT.

computer center

Same as *datacenter*.

computer designer

A *computer designer* is an individual who designs the electronic structure of a computer.

computer graphics

See *graphics*.

computer input microfilm

See CIM.

computer integrated manufacturing

See CIM.

computer language

Computer language is technically the machine language that only the computer understands; however, the term is used to refer to any programming language, command language or way to "talk to" the computer.

computer literacy

Computer literacy is an understanding of computers and information systems, which includes a working vocabulary about computer and information system components, the fundamental principles of computer processing and a perspective for how non-technical people can take advantage of the world of computer technology.

Computer literacy does not deal with how the computer works (digital circuits), but does imply knowledge of how the computer does its work (inputs, processes, outputs). It also includes a basic understanding of systems analysis & design, application programming, systems programming and datacenter operations.

To be computer literate in management, an individual must be able to define information requirements effectively and have an understanding of what the primary decision support tools, such as query languages, report writers, spreadsheets and financial planning systems, can accomplish. To be truly computer literate, one must understand "standards & compatibility" in this book.

computer on a chip

A *computer on a chip* is a single chip that contains the processor, RAM, ROM, clock and I/O control unit. Computers on a chip are used for myriads of applications from automobiles to toys.

computer output microfilm

See COM.

computer power

Computer power is the effective capacity of a computer to do work. Computer power can be expressed in MIPS rate (millions of instructions per second), clock speed (10Mhz, 15Mhz, etc.) and in word or bus size, (8-bit, 16-bit, 32-bit). However, as in automobile specifications, such as number of cylinders or valves and horsepower, any individual specification is only a rough guideline.

The net throughput of a computer system is how long it takes to get the job done. Benchmarks are only valid for the class of program being tested. Another test program with a different mix of calculations or disk accesses will produce different results in the same computer system.

A software package may be called "powerful" too, which is due to its many features and capabilities.

computer readable

Same as *machine readable*.

computer science

Computer science is the field of computer hardware and software. It includes systems analysis & design, application and system software design and programming and datacenter operations.

Computer science may touch on, but does not delve into information sciences, the study of information and its uses. This is the most serious failing in our country's educational system with regard to teaching computer technology, especially in the elementary and high school grades. The emphasis is usually on learning a programming language or making a personal computer work with minimal or no study of the data and information required by a typical business.

Instead of only learning BASIC on a personal computer, which is fine for solving algorithmic problems, students should be introduced to database management systems in order to learn about transaction and master files, audit trails and the nature of an organization's information systems.

computer services organization

A *computer services organization* is an organization that offers data processing, software and/or professional computing services. It can be a service bureau that provides timesharing and batch processing services, a software house, VAR (value added reseller) or consulting firm. See *service bureau*.

computer system

The *computer system* is made up of the CPU, all the peripheral devices connected to it and its operating system. Computer systems fall into ranges called *microcomputers* (personal computers), *minicomputers* and *mainframes*, roughly small, medium and large. Computer systems are sized for the total user workload, which is primarily based on the following criteria:

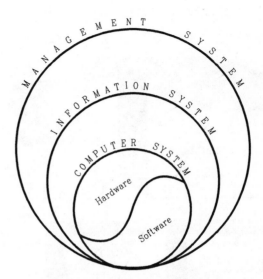

HOW SYSTEMS RELATE

(1) The number of terminals required.

(2) The amount and nature of work that must be performed simultaneously by users at each terminal. Interactive processing, such as questions and answers and filling in forms, is light work. Batch processing (long searches or printing an entire report) is heavy work. Computer-aided design, engineering, and scientific applications require fast mathematical processing.

(3) The amount of online disk storage necessary to hold the data. A single computer system has a maximum amount of memory and a maximum number of peripherals that can be connected to it.

Computer System Architecture

Following are the major components of a computer system and their significance:

Component	Significance
Machine language	Compatibility with future hardware/software
Operating system	Performance and compatibility with future hardware/software
Clock speed (MIPS rate)	Performance
Number of terminals	Number of concurrent users that can be served
Memory capacity	Performance
Online disk capacity	Amount of available information at all times
Communications	Access to other networks and computers
Programming languages	Compatibility with future hardware
Fail-safe design	Reliability

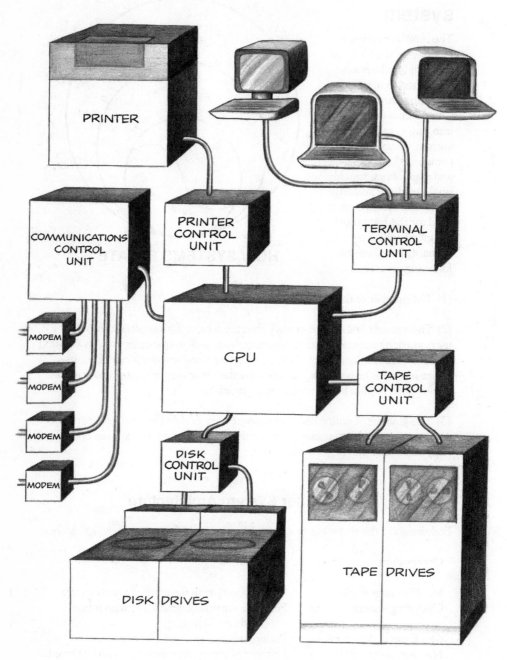

COMPUTER SYSTEM

COMSAT

(COMmunications SATellite Corporation) COMSAT, created by an act of Congress in 1962, is a private organization that launches and operates communications satellites. In 1965, COMSAT launched the "Early Bird," the first commercial satellite to retransmit signals from a fixed position in space (geosynchronous orbit).

COMSAT provides satellite capacity to international carriers such as AT&T, MCI, RCA and others. COMSAT owns part of the International Telecommunications Satellite Corporation (INTELSAT) and is also part owner of the International Maritime Satellite Corporation (INMARSAT), which provides communications to and from ships and offshore rigs.

"EARLY BIRD"

(Courtesy COMSAT)

concatenation

Concatenation is linking together various data structures; for example, concatenating files is combining two or more files together. If city and state are fixed length fields in a record, in order to print CHICAGO, IL instead of CHICAGO   IL, the fields have to be concatenated with a "blank squash." In speech synthesis, units of speech called phonemes (k, sh, ch, etc.) are concatenated to produce meaningful sounds.

concentrator

In communications, a *concentrator* joins several communications channels into a single one. A concentrator is similar to a multiplexor, except that it does not spread the signals back out again on the other end. The receiving computer performs that function.

conceptual view

See *view*.

Concurrent CP/M

See CP/M.

concurrent operation

See *multitasking, multiprocessing* and *parallel processing.*

Concurrent PC-DOS

Concurrent PC-DOS is a multitasking operating system from Digital Research that runs on IBM compatible pcs. It runs up to four programs simultaneously.

conditional branch

In programming, a *conditional branch* is a computer instruction that directs the computer to another part of the program based on the results of a compare. For example, the GOTO instruction is the conditional branch in the following simulated assembly language statements:

    COMPARE FIELDA with FIELDB
    GOTO MATCHROUTINE if EQUAL.

conditional statement

In programming, a *conditional statement* is a language statement, such as an IF THEN ELSE or CASE statement, which tests a condition and branches to a subroutine based on the results of that test.

conditioning

Conditioning is fine tuning a private telephone line to optimize data transmission.

conductor

A *conductor* is a material that can carry electrical current. Contrast with *insulator*, which will impede the flow of current.

CONFIG.SYS

CONFIG.SYS is a file of instructions for Microsoft's DOS and OS/2 operating systems that is executed when the computer is booted or rebooted. It allows the operating system to be customized to the user's environment. For example, when new peripheral devices, such as disks, mice or graphics tablets, are added to the computer, the instructions for activating it are contained in a program called a *device driver* that comes with the new hardware. The device drivers must be copied onto the hard disk, or system disk if floppies are used, and the names of all device driver files must be included in the CONFIG.SYS file so that the operating system can reference them. If a RAM disk is installed, which emulates a disk drive in memory, its device driver must be specified in the CONFIG.SYS file.

Device drivers have an SYS extension and the command line to add a device driver to the system is **DEVICE=drivername**. For example, to add a driver named NEWDISK.SYS to the system, the line **DEVICE=NEWDISK.SYS** would be added to the CONFIG.SYS file.

configuration

A *configuration* is a particular system of interrelated components, such as a computer system or communications network.

connect time

Connect time is the time a user at a terminal is logged-on to a computer system. See *service bureau*.

connector

(1) A *connector* is any cable or wire that links two devices together. See *plugs & sockets*.

(2) In database management, a *connector* is a link or pointer between two data structures.

(3) In flowcharting, a *connector* is a symbol that is used to break a sequence and resume the sequence elsewhere. It is usually a small circle with a number or some other identification written in it.

console

A *console* is another term for display terminal. It may refer to the terminal used by the computer operator or systems programmer to control the operation of a large computer.

constant

In programming, a *constant* is any data with fixed values that is part of the program itself. A number used as a minimum value or maximum value or any data used to look (compare) for data in the database are examples of constants. Words or phrases in a program, which will be displayed or printed as messages or headlines, are also constants.

constant ratio code

A *constant ratio code* is a code that always contains the same ratio of 0s to 1s.

consultant

A *consultant* is a specialist who is either part of an internal technical staff or who works for a consulting firm. Consultants can act as advisors, or they can perform detailed systems analysis & design functions. They can help users formulate their information requirements and produce a generalized or detailed set of specifications from which hardware or software vendors can respond. Consultants are often used as project advisors throughout the entire system development cycle.

contact

A *contact* is a metal strip in a switch or socket that touches a corresponding metal strip in order to close the switch or connector and allow current to pass. Contacts are often made of precious metals to avoid corrosion.

content addressed storage

See *associative storage*.

contention

Contention is the condition that arises when two devices attempt to use a single resource, such as a channel, network or time period. *Contention resolution* is the process of resolving which device gains access first. See *CSMA/CD*.

context sensitive help

Context sensitive help refers to a help screen in a program that provides specific instructions about the mode or status the user is currently in. It also provides instructions for handling a particular error condition that has just occurred.

contextual search

A *contextual search* is a search for records or documents based upon the text contained in them as opposed to searching on key field or by file name.

contiguous

Contiguous is adjacent, consecutive or touching. Sequential data does not imply contiguous data; for example, records in a sequential files are often scattered throughout the disk, since the operating system uses all available space on the disk when storing data.

continuity check

A *continuity check* is a test of a line, channel or circuit to determine if the pathway exists from beginning to end and can transmit signals.

continuous carrier

In communications, a *continous carrier* is a carrier frequency that is transmitted even when data is not being sent over the line.

continuous forms

Continuous forms are paper forms that are manufactured as a continuous series of sheets joined together with perforated edges and borders containing sprocket holes along the left and right sides. The continuous forms are moved through the printer by a tractor feed mechanism that grabs the paper at the holes. After printing, forms are separated manually or by a bursting machine.

control ball

Same as *track ball*.

control block

A *control block* is segment of disk or memory that contains a group of codes used for identification and control purposes.

control break

(1) A *control break* is a change of data category which is used to trigger a subtotal in a report or listing. For example, if data is subtotalled by state, when NJ changes to NM, a control break takes place.

(2) A *control break* is the suspension of a computer operation that is sometimes accomplished by pressing the CTRL and BREAK keys simultaneously.

control character

A *control character* is a special character that triggers some action on a display screen or printer. For example, a LINE FEED character moves the cursor to the next line on the screen or the printer mechanism to the next line on the paper.

control code

A *control code* is one or more control characters used for control purposes.

Control Data Corporation

Control Data Corporation, founded in 1957, was one of the first major computer companies in the country. Bill Norris was its first president and the guiding force behind the dramatic growth of the company. Control Data's first computer, the 1604, was introduced in 1957 and delivered to the U. S. Navy Bureau of Ships. Since then, it has been heavily involved with governmental agencies.

In its first year of operation, Control Data acquired Cedar Engineering, a peripherals manufacturer, launching it into the data storage products business.

In 1968, Arbitron was acquired, a computer-based audience measurement service that has contributed to the company's financial success ever since. Also in that year, Control Data filed an antitrust suit against IBM, which resulted in its acquisition of The Service Bureau Corporation from IBM in 1972.

WILLIAM C. NORRIS
(Courtesy Control Data)

Control Data has always specialized in high-speed, large-scale mainframes that have been used extensively in scientific environments as well as in large commercial establishments, including timesharing service bureaus. Over the past 30 years, its computer series has evolved into a complete product line from high-speed CYBER workstations and mainframes to ETA10 supercomputers.

Control Data computers are used in a wide variety of applications and are noted for their extreme reliability. They have controlled more than 300,000 hours of space flight without holding up a launch, and the Ticketron system holds the wagering industry record for reliability having gone 393 days without downtime.

control field

Same as *key field*.

control key

The *control key* is a special key on the keyboard which, like the shift key, is depressed with some other key. It is used to command the computer. For example, Control U, might turn on the Underline mode in a word processing program. Control N might return you to Normal mode. The effect of the control key is determined by the application program running in the

computer. The control key, abbreviated CTRL or CTL, works like the Alt key or the open and closed Apple keys on Apple keyboards.

control program

A *control program* is a software program that controls the running of the application programs in the computer. It includes such system software as the operating system, database management system and network control programs. Contrast with *application program*, which performs the business processing for the organization.

control total

Same as *hash total*.

control unit

(1) Within the processor, the *control unit* is the circuitry that performs primary computer functions. It locates, analyzes and executes each instruction in the program.

(2) Within the computer, a *control unit*, also called a *controller*, is a hardware device that controls peripheral activities such as a disk or display terminal. Upon signals from the CPU, it performs the physical data transfers between memory and the peripheral device. In single chip computers, an elementary control unit is included on the chip that accepts input from a keyboard and displays output on a small readout or display screen. In personal computers, control units are usually printed circuit boards that can be plugged in. In larger computers, control units can be one or more printed circuit boards within the computer's cabinet, or they can be housed in stand-alone cabinetry.

control variable

In programming, a *control variable* is a variable that controls the number of iterations of a process. Its value is incremented or decremented with each iteration, and it is compared to a constant or another variable to test the end of the process or loop.

controller

Same as *control unit*.

conventional programming

Conventional programming is the use of procedural languages, which are the traditional assembly languages and high-level programming languages, such as FORTRAN, COBOL and BASIC. Conventional programming requires that programmers state all repetitive processing sequences (loops) and test for their conclusion (end of loop, end of file, etc.).

Programs that do not require conventional programming in order to be used are non-procedural languages, such as application generators, query languages, report writers and spreadsheets.

conversational

Conversational is an interactive dialogue between the user and the computer and implies a question and answer type of session.

conversion

(1) *Data conversion* is the changing of physical media, such as from tape to disk, or the changing of data from one file or database format to another. Data conversion may also require code conversion from ASCII to EBCDIC or vice versa.

(2) *Program conversion* is the changing of the programming source language from one dialect to another, or the changing of the programs to work with a different operating system or database management system.

(3) *Computer system conversion* is the changing of the computer model and peripheral devices.

(4) *Information system conversion* requires both data conversion and either program conversion or the installation of newly purchased or created application programs.

converter

(1) A *converter* is a device that changes one set of codes, modes, sequences or frequencies to a different set. For example, an analog to digital converter converts analog signals to digital signals.

(2) A *converter* changes electrical currents from 60 Hz to 50 Hz, or vice versa, or from AC to DC, or vice versa.

cooperative processing

Cooperative processing is the sharing of the workload among two or more computers such as a mainframe and a personal computer.

coordinate

A *coordinate* is the intersection of two or more planes. For example, end points in 2-D vector graphics, cells in a spreadsheet and bits in memory are all identified by the intersection of a row and column.

coprocessor

Coprocessors are additional processors used to speed up operations by handling some of the workload of the main processor (CPU). For example, a math coprocessor option in a personal computer increases the computational speed of the system and is often used in CAD applications requiring large amounts of recalculation in order to display a revised image.

copy

Copy refers to making a duplicate of the original. In digital electronics, all copies of data and programs are the same as the original, since a digital copy is 100% identical to the original or any other copy. The text in this book takes up a million and a half characters, or 13.5 million binary digits. During writing, editing and desktop publishing this book, the text was copied hundreds of times, causing billions of pulses (bits) to be transmitted between disk and memory. However, just to show that things aren't all that perfect, at least a half dozen characters became garbled at one time or another! Perhaps, we'll have to settle for 99.9999% instead of 100%.

copy buster

A *copy buster* is a program that bypasses the copy protection scheme in a software program and allows normal, unprotected copies to be made .

copy protection

Copy protection is the resistance to unauthorized copying of software. In the mainframe and minicomputer worlds, copy protection has not been a major issue since vendor support provided to registered customers is usually vital in these environments, and there is little advantage in obtaining a free copy of an application program.

The personal computer world is another story. It's tempting to copy a program from a friend for only the cost of a floppy disk. Although copy protection has been implemented using various techniques, for every technique implemented, there's a copy buster program that overrides the copy protection scheme.

Copy protection methods make it very difficult for hard disk users to move programs from one part of the disk to another. For this reason, by the late 1980s, most copy protection has been removed from personal computer software. As personal computer software becomes more complicated, vendor support is often just as necessary as it is with the larger computers.

core

A *core* is a round magnetic doughnut that represents one bit in a core storage system. A computer's main memory used to be referred to as core.

core storage

Core storage is a non-volatile memory that holds magnetic charges in tiny ferrite cores about a 16th of an inch in diameter. The direction of the magnetic flux determines whether it is a 1 or 0. Invented by Dr. An Wang in 1948, core storage was used extensively in the 1950s and 1960s. Since it holds its content without power, it is still used in specialized applications; for example, in the military and in space vehicles.

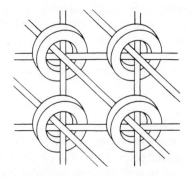

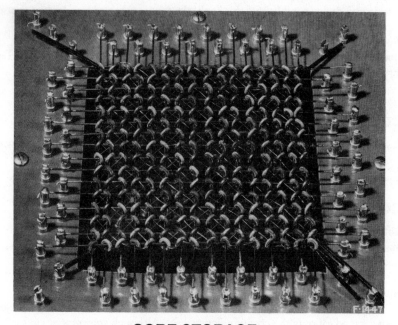

CORE STORAGE

(Courtesy The MITRE Corporation Archives)

In 1952, this core plane held 256 bits of memory for the Whirlwind I Computer. Today, a single RAM chip holds one million bits of memory.

Core System

The *Core System* was the first proposed standard for computer graphics. It was developed by the Graphics Standards Planning Committee of SIGGRAPH and was used in the late 1970s and early 1980s. The major objectives of the Core System were portability of programs from one computer system to another and the separation of modeling graphics from viewing graphics. Almost all features of the Core System were incorporated into the ANSI-endorsed Graphical Kernel System (GKS) standards.

co-resident

Co-resident refers to a program or module that resides in memory along with other programs.

Corporation for Open Systems

The *Corporation for Open Systems*, founded in 1986, is a not for profit, international research and development consortium dedicated to assuring acceptance of an open network architecture in world markets. It is made up of some 65 information technology manufacturers and user organizations that provide development, service, and support of systems that conform to international standards, which includes the Open System Interconnection (OSI) and Integrated Services Digital Network (ISDN).

For more information, contact Corporation for Open Systems International, 1750 Old Meadow Road, Suite 400, McLean, VA 22102, (703) 883-2700.

corruption

Corruption is the altering of data or programs due to hardware failure or erroneous software logic.

COS

See *Corporation for Open Systems*.

cost/benefits analysis

A *cost/benefits analysis* is a study that projects the costs and benefits of the development of an information system. Costs include people and machine resources during the system development cycle as well as operational costs when the system is developed. On-going costs include payroll and utilities to run the computer, hardware and system software maintentance, application program maintenance, storage media and paper supplies.

Tangible benefits can be derived by estimating the cost savings of both human and machine resources to run the new system versus the old system. Intangible benefits, such as improved customer service and employee relations or more effective competition in the marketplace may ultimately provide larger payback than the tangible benefits, yet are the hardest to justify. Justification for intangible benefits relies heavily on expert management judgment.

counter

(1) In programming, a *counter* is a variable reserved for keeping track of some activity. The programming language determines the number of counters (variables) that are available to a programmer. When writing a program, counters can be made up and used to keep track of anything that must be counted.

(2) In electronics, a *counter* is a circuit that counts pulses and generates an output after a specfied number has been counted.

courseware

Courseware is educational software. Computer programs that are used for education and training are often referred to as courseware rather than software.

CP

(Central Processor) See *processor* and *CPU*.

CPE

(Customer Premises Equipment) CPE refers to all the communications equipment that resides on the customer's premises.

CPF

(Control Program Facility) CPF is the operating system for IBM's System/38 minicomputer series. CPF also includes an integrated relational database management system that is part of the overall System/38 architecture.

CP/M

(Control Program for Microprocessors) CP/M was the first operating system that ran on a variety of personal computers. Created by Gary Kildall, founder of Digital Research Corporation, CP/M had its heyday in the late 1970s and early 1980s. CP/M was a single user operating system written for the 8080 and Z80 microprocessors.

CP/M was a very simplistic program that didn't give early users much confidence in computers; nevertheless, it helped spawn the personal computer revolution by offering a standard that could be used by any hardware vendor who wanted to make a personal computer. In all the rush to make personal computers available, the industry never got together on a standard disk or video format for the CP/M world. Some offered graphics, some didn't. Software packages had to include multiple video drivers, much as word processing packages have to include multiple printer drivers today. Worse yet, floppy disks weren't interchangeable, requiring software distributors to carry dozens of different formats. This chaos helped IBM to take control of the personal computer world almost overnight.

The MS-DOS operating system used in IBM compatible pcs was modeled after CP/M. Apparently, Digital Research had the opportunity to be IBM's operating system supplier, but was somewhat indifferent about it. This now-legendary story is why IBM went to Microsoft instead.

CP/M and CP/M-80 are synonymous. CP/M-86 is CP/M for the 8086/8088 microprocessors. Concurrent CP/M and Concurrent CP/M-86 are multitasking versions of CP/M. MP/M is the multiuser version of Concurrent CP/M.

CPM

(Critical Path Method) CPM is a project management planning and control technique implemented on computers. The critical path is the series of activities and tasks in the project that have no built-in slack time. Any task in the critical path that takes longer than expected will lengthen the total time of the project.

CPS

(Characters Per Second) CPS measures the speed of a serial printer or the speed of a data transfer between hardware devices or over a communications channel. CPS is equivalent to bytes per second.

CPU

(Central Processing Unit) The CPU, also called the *central processor*, or simply *processor*, is the computing part of the computer. It is made up of the control unit and arithmetic/logic unit. The control unit extracts the instructions out of

THE CPU OF THE DATAMATIC 1000
(Courtesy Honeywell Inc.)

The arithmetic logic unit (ALU) and control unit in the picture made up the CPU in Honeywell's DATAMATIC 1000 in 1957. Today, the equivalent amount of processing power is built into a single chip, and, the space of the actual circuitry takes up a quarter of a square inch and is 1/1000th of an inch thick.

memory and executes them. The arithmetic/logic unit performs the arithmetic calculations and comparisons.

A minicomputer CPU is contained on from one to several printed circuit boards. A mainframe CPU is contained on many printed circuit boards. In a personal computer, the CPU is contained on a single chip, called a *microprocessor*.

The CPU, clock and main memory together make up a computer. A complete computer system requires the addition of control units, input, output and storage devices and an operating system before any application programs can be run.

In normal usage, the terms CPU and processor imply the use of main memory. For example, the sentence "data is sent to the CPU and then processed," automatically implies memory since the data has to be stored in memory in order to be processed.

CPU bound

Same as *process bound*.

CPU time

CPU time is the amount of time it takes for the CPU to execute a set of instructions and explicitly excludes the waiting time for input and output to occur. The CPU time is always less than the total duration of time for a data processing job to be completed from start to finish.

CRAM

(Card Random Access Memory) CRAM units, developed by NCR in the 1960s, were a direct access mass storage device that used removable cartridges filled with magnetic cards. In order to read or write data, a card was pulled out of the cartridge and wrapped around a rotating drum.

crash

A *crash* is an unplanned program termination due to a hardware or software failure. A software failure occurs when the program logic gets confused and starts processing non-data or looks for instructions that aren't there. A hardware failure occurs when an electronic circuit fails to operate correctly. See *head crash*.

Cray Research, Inc.

Cray Research, Inc. was founded in 1972 by Seymour Cray, who, through his work at ERA, Remington Rand, UNIVAC and Control Data, had become a leading designer of large-scale computers. In 1976, Cray Research shipped its first CRAY-1 computer system to Los Alamos National Laboratory. It was a 75 megaHertz, 64-bit computer with a peak speed of over 160 megaflops (million floating point operations per second), establishing it as the world's fastest scalar processor while also providing an effective implementation of vector processing.

In 1977, Cray Research released its first operating system and FORTRAN compiler.

In 1982, Cray introduced the CRAY X-MP, a family of supercomputers that has become the mainstay product line. X-MP machines come in up to four-processor configurations with 64 million words (512 megabytes) of high-speed ECL bipolar main memory and up to four billion bytes of auxiliary memory, which can be used as a disk cache. Data can be transferred from auxiliary memory to main memory as fast as two billion bytes per second. The X-MP models calculate in the range of 500 megaflops under normal operation with peaks around 1.4 gigaflops (billion floating point operations per second).

In 1985, came the CRAY-2, a four-processor system with 256 million words (two gigabytes) of memory that was up to 12 times faster than the CRAY-1. The CRAY-2's circuits are immersed in a liquid coolant. In 1988, Cray introduced the eight-processor Y-MP. This 165 megaHertz, 64-bit, 20 million dollar computer can calculate well into the gigaflop range under normal operations.

SEYMOUR CRAY
(Courtesy Cray Research, Inc.)

Needless to say, Seymour Cray has always been interested in building fast computers.

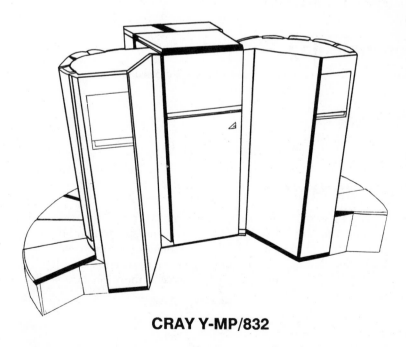

CRAY Y-MP/832

CRC

(Cyclical Redundancy Checking) CRC is an error checking technique used to ensure the accuracy of transmitting digital code over a communications channel. The transmitted messages are divided into predetermined lengths which, used as dividends, are divided by a fixed divisor. The remainder of the calculation is appended onto and sent with the message. At the receiving end, the computer recalculates the remainder. If it doesn't match the transmitted remainder, an error is detected.

cross assembler/compiler

A *cross assembler* or *cross compiler* is a translator program that generates machine language for a foreign computer. They are used to develop programs for computers on a chip or microprocessors used in specialized applications, which are either too small or are incapable of handling the development software.

cross tabulate

Cross tabulate is to analyze and summarize data. For example, cross tabulation is used to summarize the details in a database file into totals in a spreadsheet.

crossfoot

Crossfoot is a numerical error checking technique that compares the sum of the columns with the sum of the rows.

crosshatching

In computer graphics, *crosshatching* is a pattern of crossed lines.

crosstalk

Crosstalk is interference from an adjacent channel.

Crosstalk Mark 4

Crosstalk Mark 4 is a communications program from Microstuf, Inc., that runs on IBM compatible pcs. Version 1.01 handles transmission speeds from 110 to 115,200 bits per second, emulates 12 different terminals, supports seven protocols and can allow up to 15 concurrent communications sessions. It provides a user definable menu system and also accepts the original Crosstalk command language.

Crosstalk XVI

Crosstalk XVI is a communications program from Microstuf, Inc., that runs on IBM compatible pcs. Crosstalk XVI is a 16-bit version of the original Crosstalk that was developed for first-generation 8-bit CP/M personal computers.

CRT

(Cathode Ray Tube) A CRT is the vacuum tube used as a display screen in a video terminal or television set. CRT is used synonymously with terminal, which includes the keyboard.

crunch

Crunch is to process data.

cryogenics

Cryogenics is the use of materials that operate at very cold temperatures. See *superconductor*.

cryptography

Cryptography is the conversion of data into a secret code for security purposes. Same as *encryption*.

crystal

A *crystal* is a solid material containing a uniform arrangement of molecules. See *quartz crystal*.

CSMA/CD

(Carrier Sense Multiple Access/Collision Detection) CSMA/CD is a baseband communications access method that uses a collision-detection technique. When a device wants to gain access onto the network, it checks to see if the network is free. If it isn't, it waits a random amount of time before retrying. If the network is free and two devices attempt to gain access at exactly the same time, they both back off to avoid a collision and each wait a random amount of time before retrying.

CSP

(Cross System Product) CSP is an application generator from IBM that runs in a variety of IBM mainframes and minicomputers. CSP/AD (application development) programs provide the interactive development part of CSP, while

CSP/AE (application execution) programs are required to run an application created and generated in CSP/AD.

CSV

(Comma Separated Value) Same as *comma delimited*.

CTL, CTRL

See *control key*.

current

(1) *Current* refers to present activities or the latest version or model.

(2) *Current* is the flow of electrons within a wire or circuit and is measured in amperes (amps).

current directory

The *current directory* is the disk directory the system is presently working in. Unless otherwise specified, all commands to the operating system imply the current directory.

cursor

(1) A *cursor* is a blinking character on a display screen that indicates where the next keystroke will appear when typed in on the keyboard.

(2) A *cursor* is a pen-like or puck-like device used with a graphics tablet for drawing and pointing. As the tablet cursor is moved across the tablet, the screen cursor moves correspondingly. Often mistakenly called a mouse, the cursor was the original graphics device from which the mouse concept was conceived. The tablet cursor functions differently than a mouse in that it makes contact with absolute coordinates on the tablet it's moved on. A mouse is a relative device; it takes its bearings from any starting point on the desktop it's moved on.

cursor keys

The *cursor keys* are the keys that control the cursor on the screen, which are made up of the four directional arrow keys (up, down, left and right), home, end, page up and page down keys. In addition to cursor keys, a graphics cursor or mouse also moves the cursor on screen.

On older terminals and first-generation personal computers, such as the Apple II+, there may be only left and right or no cursor keys at all. In these cases, pressing the control key along with a letter key will move the cursor depending on the software used.

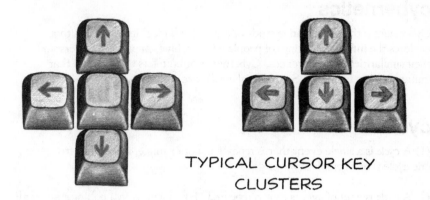

TYPICAL CURSOR KEY
CLUSTERS

customized software

Customized software is software that is designed and programmed for a particular customer, in contrast with software packages that are available off-the-shelf for a particular industry, such as insurance of banking. Software packages, such as spreadsheets and database management systems, although canned, off-the-shelf packages themselves, are designed to create customized solutions to a user's problem as well.

CUT emulation

(Control Unit Terminal emulation) *CUT emulation* is the technique used to allow a personal computer to emulate a mainframe terminal, such as the IBM 3270 series.

cut & paste

Cut & paste moves a block of text from one part of the document to another or from one file to another. The operation is performed by marking the block of text either by pointing to both the beginning and end of the text and pressing a keyboard or mouse key, or by pressing specific keystrokes to mark the entire segment instantly. The movement is accomplished by moving the cursor to the new location and selecting a menu command or by pressing certain keys.

CYBER

CYBER is a trade name for a wide range of computers from Control Data Corporation that includes models from high-speed workstations to supercomputers.

cybernetics

Cybernetics is the comparative study of organic and machine processes that explores the internal workings of people and machines in order to understand their similarities and differences. Cybernetics often refers to machines that imitate human behavior. See *artificial intelligence* and *robots*.

cycle

(1) A *cycle* is a single event that is repeated. For example, in a carrier frequency, one cycle is one complete wave.

(2) A *cycle* is a set of events that is repeated. For example, in a polling system, all of the attached terminals are tested in one cycle. See *machine cycle* and *memory cycle*.

cycle stealing

Cycle stealing is a CPU design technique that periodically "grabs" machine cycles from the main processor usually by some peripheral control unit, such as a DMA (direct memory access) device. In this way, processing and peripheral operations can be performed concurrently or with some degree of overlap.

cycle time

Cycle time is the time interval between the start of one cycle and the start of the next cycle.

cycles per second

The number of *cycles per second* is measured in Hertz. For example, 1,000 Hertz is equivalent to 1,000 cycles per second.

cyclical redundancy checking

See CRC.

Cycolor

Cycolor is a printing process from Mead Imaging that prints full tonal images like photographs. It uses a special film that is coated with light-sensitive microcapsules, called "cyliths," that contain leuco dyes. The film is exposed to the color image that is being printed, resulting in a latent image of hard and soft cyliths. The latent image donor film is transferred onto a special Cycolor paper by being squeezed together through pressure rollers, thus releasing the dyes from the film onto the paper. The paper is then briefly heated, and the result is a full-color image that resembles a photograph.

cylinder

A *cylinder* is the aggregate of all the tracks that physically reside in the same location on every disk surface. If there's only one disk platter, such as with a floppy disk, a cylinder comprises the top and bottom track with the same track number. On multiple-platter hard disks, the cylinder is the sum total of space on every track with the same track number on every disk surface.

For fast access to sequentially stored data, the operating system fills up a cylinder first before moving to the next track number. In that way, the access arm remains stationary until all the tracks in the cylinder have been read or written.

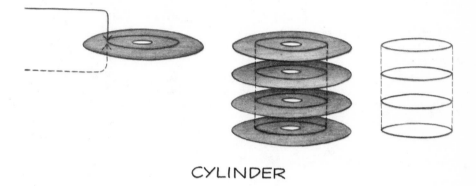

CYLINDER

D

DA

See *data administrator*.

DAC

See *digital to analog converter*.

DAD

(1) (Database Action Diagram) A *DAD* describes the processing performed on data in a database.

(2) (Digital Audio Disc) *DAD* technology records sound in digital form on an optical disk (compact disc). See *CD*.

daisy chain

A *daisy chain* is an arrangement of devices connected in series, or one after the other. Any signals transmitted to the devices go to the first device and from the first to the second and so on.

daisy wheel

A *daisy wheel* is a print mechanism used to produce letter quality (like a typewriter) printing. The daisy wheel contains the character images on the end of spokes of a plastic or metal hub. The wheel is spun around until the required character is under the print hammer. Then the hammer hits the character image into a ribbon onto the paper. The entire daisy wheel mechanism is then moved over to the next character location on the paper. Each daisy wheel contains a particular type font. Changing fonts requires changing the daisy wheel.

Daisy wheel printers come in a variety of speeds from very slow (10-15 characters per second) to moderately fast (45-75 characters per second).

DAISY WHEEL

damping

Damping is a technique for stabilizing an electronic or mechanical device by eliminating unwanted or excessive oscillations.

Dan Bricklin's Demo II Program

Dan Bricklin's Demo II Program is a program for building software prototypes, demonstrations and tutorials from Peter Norton Computing, Inc., that runs on IBM compatible pcs. It is a tool for the software designer and developer to create prototypes of a user interface before actually writing the program. A complete interactive session can be simulated. Demo II can be used to create sequential slide shows on screen and to create computer based training (CBT) sessions. Demo II contains a complete programming language and is the successor to the original Dan Bricklin's Demo Program.

Darlingon circuit

In electronics, a *Darlington circuit* is a an amplification circuit that uses two transistors coupled together.

DASD

(Direct Access Storage Device) Pronounced "dazdee," a *DASD* is any peripheral device that is directly addressable, such as a disk or drum.

DAT

(Digital Audio Tape) *DAT* is a digital technology that records sound on tape. Like compact disc (CD), DAT provides an extremely high-quality audio recording. The advantage of DAT over compact discs is that it is an erasable medium, whereas current compact discs are a read-only medium. In time, erasable optical discs will replace all tape media, since disks offer the advantage of quick access to any part of the medium.

data

(1) Technically, *data* are raw facts and figures, such as orders and payments, which are processed into *information*, such as balance due and quantity on hand. However, in common usage, both data and information are used synonymously.

The amount of data kept online in the computer system versus the amount of information is always a tradeoff. Data can be processed into different forms of information, but it takes time to sort and summarize thousands of transactions. Online, up-to-date summaries (information) can provide answers to questions immediately.

A common misconception is that software is also data. Software is not data to the computer. Software programs contain instructions that are executed, or run, by the computer, not processed by the computer.

(2) *Data* refers to any form of information whether on paper or in electronic form. In electronic form, data refers to data fields, records, files and databases, word processing documents, raster and vector graphics images and digitally-encoded voice and video.

(3) *Data* may refer strictly to data items in traditional files and databases in contrast with text files (word processing), graphics, voice and video files.

(4) *Data* is the plural form of datum; however, datum is rarely used, and although "data are" is grammatically correct, "data is" is the more common usage.

data acquisition

(1) *Data acquisition* is the automatic collection of data from sensors and readers into the computer in a factory, laboratory, medical or scientific environment.

(2) *Data acquisition* is the gathering of source data for data entry into the computer.

data administration

Data administration is a function within an organization that manages data. It analyzes, classifies and maintains all the data and data relationships. Data administration coordinates the development of data models and data dictionaries, which, combined with transaction volume, are the raw materials for database design.

Database administration often falls within the jurisdiction of data administration; however, data administration functions provide the overall management of data as an organizational resource. Database administration is the technical design and management of the database.

Data Is Complex

The flow of data/information within an organization is complex since the same data is viewed differently as it moves from one department to the other. For example: A customer places an order. That order becomes a commission and quota fulfillment for sales, a demographic statistic for marketing, an order to keep track of in the order processing department, an effect on cash flow projection for financial officers, picking schedules for the warehouse, and production scheduling for manufacturing. Users have their own view of this data and have different requirements for interrogating and updating it. Operations people need detail, management needs summaries. The resulting database design must take all these factors into consideration.

data administrator

A *data administrator* is an individual who coordinates activities within the data administration department. Contrast with *database administrator*, which is an individual who designs and manages the actual database structures.

data attribute

See *attribute*.

data bank

A *data bank* is any electronic depository of data.

data bus

A *data bus* is an internal pathway across which data is transferred to and from the processor. Controllers for peripheral devices, such as monitors and disks, are printed circuit boards that plug into the computer's data bus.

data carrier

(1) A *data carrier* is a medium such as a disk or tape that can hold machine readable data.

(2) In communications, a *data carrier* is a carrier frequency into which data is modulated (merged) for transmission in a network.

DATA CARTRIDGE

data cartridge

A *data cartridge* is a removable storage module containing magnetic tape.

Data Cell

A *Data Cell* was an earlier direct access storage device from IBM that used strips of tape stored in cartridges. In order to read or write the tape, the tape was selected out of the cartridge and wrapped around a rotating drum. Data Cells from IBM, RACE units from RCA and CRAM units from NCR were the first attempts at large-volume direct access storage devices back in the 1960s. As magnetic disks increased in storage capacity, all of these devices, which were very slow and error prone, have become obsolete.

data code

(1) A *data code* is any coding system applied to data, for example, a set of codes that represents regions, classes, products and status.

(2) A *data code* is a digital coding system applied to data for input into the computer, such as ASCII and EBCDIC.

data collection

Data collection is the act of acquiring source documents for the data entry department. Data collection comes under the jurisdiction of the data control or data entry department. Contrast with *data acquisition*, which implies the automatic collection of data from sensors and instruments in a laboratory, medical or scientific environment. Data collection may also refer to data acquisition.

data compaction

See *data compression*.

data compression

Data compression is the coding of data to save storage space or transmission time. Although data is already coded in digital form once it's in the computer, it can be coded further. For example, when data is stored in fixed length fields, in which the same number of bytes is reserved for each item of data in every record, a lot of space is wasted. By analyzing actual data content, strings of blanks can be replaced with a code that represents them, but takes up less space. When data is stored in compressed form and then called back into the computer, it must be decoded before it's processed.

data communications

Same as *communications*.

data control department

A *data control department* is responsible for the collection of data for input into a computer's batch processing operations as well as the dissemination of the finished reports. The data entry department may be under the jursidiction of the data control department or vice versa.

data declaration

Same as *data definition (1)*.

data definition

(1) In programming, *data definition* is the part of the program that includes the defining of data constants and data formats, such as fields, records and arrays.

(2) In file or database management systems, *data definition* is the process of describing the record structure to the program.

data description language

See *DDL*.

data dictionary

A *data dictionary* is a database about data and databases. It holds the name, type, range of values, source, and authorization for access for each data element in the organization's files and databases. It also indicates which application programs use that data so that when a change in a data structure is contemplated, a list of the affected programs can be generated.

The data dictionary may be a stand-alone information system used for management and documentation purposes, or it may be an integral part of the database management system where it's used to actually control its operation. Data integrity and accuracy is better insured in the latter case.

data division

The *data division* is the part of a COBOL program in which the data files and record layouts are defined.

data element

A *data element* is the fundamental data structure in a data processing system. Any unit of data defined for processing is a data element, for example: ACCOUNT NUMBER, NAME, ADDRESS and CITY. The definition of a data element comprises its size (in characters) and data type (alphanumeric, numeric only, true/false, date, etc.). A specific set of values or range of values may also be part of the definition.

Technically, a data element is a logical definition of data, whereas a field is the physical unit of storage in a record. For example, the data element ACCOUNT NUMBER, which exists only once, is stored in the ACCOUNT NUMBER field in the customer record, as well as the ACCOUNT NUMBER field in the order records.

Data element, data item, field and *variable* all describe the same unit of data and are used interchangeably.

data encryption standard

See DES.

data entry

Data entry is the act of entering data into the computer, which also includes optical scanning and voice recognition as well as keyboard entry.

When transactions are entered after the fact (batch data entry) and are just stacks of source documents to the data entry operator, the data entry process is error prone. Since scribbled letters or digits on the form may be entered as a best guess, it's often necessary to enter, print and review the entries manually or enter the data twice and compare the entries. In data entry operations, in which the operator is taking the order or information in person or over the phone, there's interaction and involvement with the transaction. If operators are trained properly to review and repeat the information, the interactive data entry process is very accurate.

data entry department

The *data entry department* is the part of the datacenter where the data entry terminals and operators are located.

data entry operator

A *data entry operator* is an individual who enters data into the computer via a keyboard or other input device, such as an optical scanner or card reader.

data entry program

The *data entry program* is an application program that accepts data from the keyboard or other input device and stores it in the computer system. The data entry program may also be part of a larger application program that also provides updating, querying and reporting.

The data entry program is important, because it establishes the data in the database and it should test for all possible input errors. These tests are called edit checks or validity checks and typically compare the input to ranges of data stored in the program. All key fields, such as account numbers, should be checked for validity so that when the transaction is matched against a master file for updating, there will be a match.

Most high-level programming languages provide data entry functions, such as range checking and table lookups so that tedious programming is not necessary. Database management systems also provide data entry validation so that databases can be set up properly for interactive use. See *check digit* and *intelligent database*.

data file

A *data file* is a collection of data records. Contrast with *word processing file*, which contains words, and contrast with *graphics file*, which contains line segments or dots.

data flow

(1) In computers, *data flow* is the path of data from original source document through data entry all the way to final reports. Data may change its format and sequence as it moves from program to program.

(2) In communications, *data flow* is the path taken by a data message from its origination to its destination and includes all nodes through which the data travels.

data flow diagram

The *data flow diagram* depicts the movement of data within an organization by describing the data and the manual and machine processing performed on the data.

data format

Same as *file format*.

Data General

Data General Corporation was founded in 1968 by Edson D. de Castro, who after 20 years, continues to head the company.

In 1969, Data General introduced the Nova, the first 16-bit minicomputer designed with four accumulators in its central processor, a leading technology at the time. During its early years, the company was successful in the scientific, academic and OEM markets. With its Comprehensive Electronic Office (CEO)

EDSON D. de CASTRO
(Courtesy Data General)

software in the early 1980s, Data General gained entry into the commercial marketplace.

Data General's computer offerings range from a 12-pound portable, the DG/One, to the 32-bit family of ECLIPSE minicomputers. Throughout the 1990s, Data General will provide UNIX-based systems using Motorola 88000 CPUs.

data independence

Data independence is a primary concept of database management that allows the database to be structurally changed (categories of data added and deleted) with minimal disruption to existing systems.

Data independence separates the data from the processing. The detailed knowledge of each record layout is not required in each application program. Therefore, when the record layout is changed (fields added, deleted or change in size), fewer programs are affected, and ideally none are affected.

The following illustration shows an application program (in machine language form) that does not use a database management system (DBMS) and thus has no data independence. Buffer space is reserved in the program for the entire record, fields A through K, regardless of how much of that data is actually processed by the program. (For an explanation of the graphical representation used in the following three illustrations, see *program*.)

The following illustration shows a traditional application program, such as BASIC, Pascal or C, that does use a DBMS for its data. The application program provides space for only the data it processes; in this case only fields D, G and K. As long as fields D, G and K aren't affected, this program will not have to change due to structural modifications to other parts of the record.

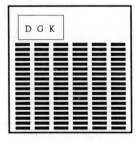

The following illustration shows a program that uses a DBMS and is written in the DBMS's own programming language. In this case, the program provides no space for the data. The buffer space is made available (dynamically created) within the DBMS itself when the program is running. If the record structure is changed, there is nothing to change within the application programs. This environment is the most flexible for responding to an organization's changing information requirements.

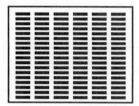

data integrity

Data integrity is the preservation of data and implies the process of keeping the database from accidental erase or adulteration.

data item

Same as *data element*.

data library

The *data library* is the part of the datacenter where disks and tapes are catalogued and stored. Data library personnel determine when disks and tapes must be cleaned and replaced or reused.

DATA LIBRARY

data line

A *data line* is an individual circuit, or line, that carries data within a computer or communications channel.

data line monitor

In communications, a *data line monitor* is a test instrument that analyzes the signals and timing of a communications line. It either visually displays the patterns or stores the activity for further analysis.

data link

In communications, a *data link* is the physical interconnection between two points. It may also refer to the modems, protocols and all required hardware and software to perform the transmission. See *OSI*.

data link escape

In communications, a *data link escape* is a control character that indicates that the following character is not data, but a control code.

data management

Data management refers to several levels of managing data. From bottom to top, they are:

(1) *Data management* is the part of the operating system that manages the physical storage and retrieval of data on a disk or other storage device. See *access method*.

(2) *Data management* is software that allows for the creation, storage, retrieval and manipulation of files interactively at a terminal or personal computer. See *file manager* and *database management system*.

(3) *Data management* is a function that manages data as an organizational resource. See *data administration*.

(4) *Data management* is the management of all data and information within an organization and includes data administration, the standards for defining data and the way in which people perceive and use it in their day-to-day tasks.

data management system

See *database management system*.

data manipulation

Data manipulation is the act of processing data.

data manipulation language

A *data manipulation language* is a database language that is used within an application program written in a programming language such as COBOL or C, to request data from a database managment system.

data model

A *data model* is a description of the organization of a database.

data module

A *data module* is a sealed, removable storage module containing magnetic disks and their associated access arms and read/write heads.

data name

A *data name* is a name assigned to an item of data, such as a field or variable.

data network

A *data network* is a communications network that transmits data. See *communications*.

Data Physician

Data Physician is a virus detection program from Digital Dispatch, Inc., that runs on IBM compatible pcs. Data Physician is designed to detect a virus that may attach itself to selected programs, and it is capable of removing certain viruses that have been discovered.

data processing

Data processing is the capturing, storing, updating and retrieving of data and information. The term may refer to the entire computer industry, to only datacenter operations, or to only data processing activities, in contrast with word processing and other office automation functions.

data processor

(1) A *data processor* is a computer that is processing data, and the term would be used to differentiate it from another computer that is performing other tasks, such as controlling a network.

(2) A *data processor* is an individual who works in the data processing field.

data rate

The *data rate* is the measurement of the speed of data transmission within a computer or communications network.

data resource management

Same as *data administration*.

data set

(1) In data management, a *data set* is a data file or collection of interrelated data.

(2) In communications, a *data set* is the name for a modem as originally defined by AT&T.

data signal

A *data signal* is the actual representation of data as it travels over a line or channel, which is physically either electricity or light. The signal travels either as on/off pulses or as waves (alternating current) of a specific frequency.

data sink

A *data sink* is a device or part of the computer that receives data.

data source

A *data source* is a device or part of the computer in which data is originated.

data stream

A *data stream* is a block of data or a continuous flow of data from one place to another.

data structure

A *data structure* is how the data is physically laid out, for example, the fields in a record.

data switch

A *data switch* is a manual or automatic switch box that routes one line to another. It is used, for example, to connect multiple printers to one computer or to connect multiple computers to one printer. An manual data switch requires the user to select the appropriate line by turning a dial or pressing a button. An

automatic data switch tests for
signals on the lines and performs
the switching automatically.

data system

Same as *information system*.

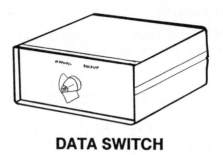

DATA SWITCH

data tablet

Same as *digitizer tablet*.

data transfer

Data transfer is the movement of data within the computer system. Typically,
data is said to be transferred within the computer, but it is *transmitted* over a
communications network. A transfer is technically a copy function since the
data is not automatically erased at the source.

data transfer rate

Same as *data rate*.

data transmission

Data transmission is the same as data communications. See *communications*.

data type

A *data type* is the characteristic of the data being stored; for example, numeric,
alphanumeric (character), dates and logical (true/false) data types are typical.
Each programming language allows for the creation of a different number of data
types. When data is assigned a particular type, it can only be manipulated
according to the rules of the type. For example, alphanumeric data cannot be
calculated, and the digits within numeric data cannot be separated. When date
data types are calculated, they result in a correct date; for example, January 30 +
12 = February 11.

database

(1) A *database* is a collection of interrelated files that is created and managed by
a database management system (DBMS).

(2) A *database* is any collection of data that is electronically stored.

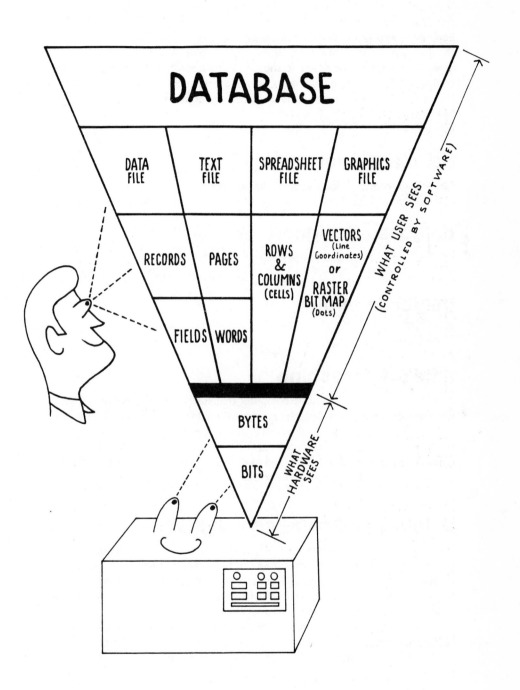

database administrator

The *database administrator* is an individual who is responsible for the physical design and management of the database and for the evaluation, selection and implementation of the database management system. In smaller organizations, the data administrator and database administrator are often one in the same; however, when they are different, the database administrator's function is more technical. The database administrator would implement the database software that meets the requirements outlined by the organization's data administrator and systems analysts.

database analyst

See *data administrator* and *database administrator*.

database designer

See *data administrator* and *database administrator*.

database engine

Same as *database manager*.

database machine

A *database machine* is a separate computer that stores and retrieves data from the database. It is a specially designed machine for database access that is coupled to the main computer(s) by a high-speed channel. Contrast with *database server*, which is a computer in a local area network that manages the database. The database machine is "tightly" coupled to the main CPU, whereas the database server is "loosely" coupled in the network.

database management system

A *database management system* (DBMS) is an extremely complex set of software programs that controls the organization, storage and retrieval of data (fields, records and files) in a database. It also controls the security and integrity of the database. The DBMS accepts requests for data from the application program and instructs the operating system to transfer the appropriate data.

When a DBMS is used, information systems can be changed much more easily as the organization's information requirements change. New categories of data can be added to the database without disruption to the existing system.

Major Features of a DBMS

DATA SECURITY AND INTEGRITY
Data security prevents unauthorized users from viewing or updating the database. Using passwords, users are allowed access to the entire database or subsets of the database, called *subschemas* (pronounced "sub-skeema"). For example, an employee database can contain all the data about an individual employee, but one group of users may be authorized to view only payroll data, while others are allowed access to only work history and medical data.

The DBMS can maintain the integrity of the database by not allowing more than one user to update the same record at the same time. The DBMS can keep duplicate records out of the database; for example, no two customers with the same customer numbers (key fields) can be entered into the database.

INTERACTIVE QUERY
Query languages and report writers allow users to interactively interrogate the database and analyze its data.

INTERACTIVE DATA ENTRY AND UPDATING
If the DBMS provides a way to interactively enter and update the database, as well as interrogate it, this capability allows for managing personal databases. However, it does not automatically leave an audit trail of actions and does not provide the kinds of controls necessary in a multiuser organization. These controls are only available when a set of application programs are customized for each data entry and updating function.
This is one of the most common misconceptions about database management systems that are used in personal computers. Thoroughly comprehensive and sophisticated business systems can be developed in dBASE, Paradox and other DBMSs; however, they are created by experienced programmers using the DBMS's own programming language. That is not the same as users who create and manage personal files that are not part of the mainstream company system.

DATA INDEPENDENCE
When a DBMS is used, the detailed knowledge of the physical organization of the data does not have to be built into every application program. The application program asks the DBMS for data by field name; for example, a coded representation of "give me customer name and balance due" would be sent to the DBMS. Without a DBMS, the programmer must reserve space for the full structure of the record in the program.). Any change in data structure requires changes in all the applications programs. See *data independence*.

Database Design

A business information system is made up of subjects (customers, employees, vendors, etc.) and activities (orders, payments, purchases, etc.). Database design is the process of deciding how to organize this data into record types and how the record types will relate to each other. The DBMS that is chosen is the one that can mirror the organization's data structure properly and process the transaction volume efficiently.

Organizations may use one kind of DBMS for daily transaction processing and then move the detail onto another computer that uses another DBMS better suited for random inquiries and analysis. Overall systems design decisions are performed by data administrators and systems analysts. Detailed database design is performed by database administrators.

Hierarchical, Network and Relational Databases

Hierarchical, network and relational databases are the three most commonly advertised methods of organizing data. A database management system may provide one, two or all three methods. Inverted lists and other methods are also used.

The structure that best suits an organization depends on the organization's particular requirements, the volume of daily transactions and the estimated number of ad hoc inquiries that will be made.

Hierarchical databases link records together like an organization chart, and a record type can be owned by only one owner. In the following example, orders are owned by only customer. Hierarchical structures were widely used in the first mainframe database management systems. However, due to their restrictions, they often cannot be used to relate structures that exist in the real world.

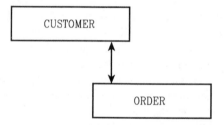

In network database structures, a record type can have multiple owners. In the order processing example below, orders are owned by both customers and products, since that's the way they relate in the business.

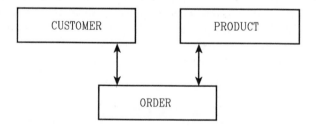

Relational databases don't link records together physically, but the design of the records must provide a common field, such as account number, to allow for matching. Quite often, the fields used for matching are indexed in order to speed up the process. In the following example, customers, orders and products are linked by comparing data fields and/or indexes when information from more than one record type is needed. This method is the most flexible for ad hoc inquiries, but may be too slow for heavy transaction processing environments. Although relational database is often considered a new concept, database management systems have traditionally provided relational capability with their hierarchical or network designs.

| CUSTOMER | ORDER | PRODUCT |

Intelligent Databases

All DBMSs provide some data validation; for example, they will reject invalid dates entered into date fields, alphabetic data entered into money fields. But the real processing is left up to the application programs.

Intelligent databases provide more validation; for example, table lookups will reject incorrect spelling or coding of items. There's no limit to the amount of processing that can be placed into an intelligent database as long as the process is a standardized function for that data. For example, the correct sales tax can be computed by the database and applied to all orders for the customer based on the customer's billing address.

When the validation process is left up to the individual application program, one program can allow one set of codes to be entered into a field, while another program can allow a totally different, and erroneous, set of codes. Data integrity is best served when there's one controlling source for the validation of data.

Mainframe databases have increasingly become more intelligent, and personal computer database systems are rapidly following suit. In time, all database management systems will be "intelligent."

Database Machines

Database machines are specially designed computers that hold the actual databases and run only the DBMS and related software. Connected to one or more mainframes via a high-speed channel, database machines are used in large volume transaction processing environments. Database machines have a large number of DBMS functions built into the hardware and also provide special techniques for accessing the disks containing the databases, such as using multiple processors concurrently for high-speed searches.

Future Databases

The world of information is made up of data, text, pictures and voice. Many DBMSs manage text as well as data, but very few manage both with equal proficiency. Throughout the 1990s, as storage capacities continue to increase, DBMSs will begin to integrate all forms of information. Eventually, it will be common for a database to handle data, text, graphics, voice and video with the same ease as today's systems handle data. When this happens, the office of the future will have finally arrived!

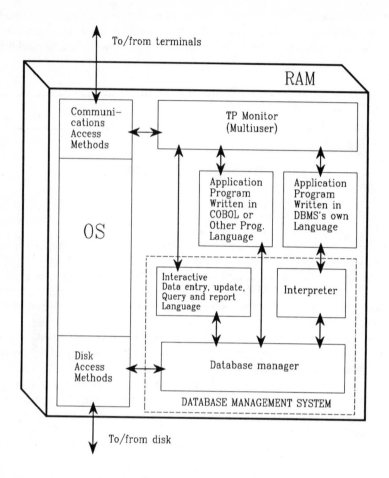

To/from terminals

RAM

Communi-
cations
Access
Methods

TP Monitor
(Multiuser)

OS

Application
Program
Written in
COBOL or
Other Prog.
Language

Application
Program
Written in
DBMS's own
Language

Interactive
Data entry, update,
Query and report
Language

Interpreter

Disk
Access
Methods

Database manager

DATABASE MANAGEMENT SYSTEM

To/from disk

database manager

A *database manager* is the part of the database management system (DBMS) that handles the organization, storage and retrieval of the data. A database manager may work with traditional programming languages, such as COBOL and BASIC, or may work only with its proprietary programming language. The terms database manager and database management system are used interchangeably.

A database manager links two or more files together and is the foundation for developing routine business systems. Contrast with file manager, which works with only one file at a time and is typically used interactively on a personal computer for managing personal, independent files, such as name and address lists.

database server

A *database server* is a stand-alone computer in a local area network that holds and manages the database. It implies that database management functions, such as locating the actual record being requested, is performed in the server computer. Contrast with *file server*, which acts as a remote disk drive and requires that large parts of the database, for example, entire indexes, be transmitted to the user's computer where the real database management tasks are performed.

First-generation personal computer database software was not designed for a network; thus, modified versions of the software released by the vendors employed the file server concept. Second-generation products, designed for local area networks, perform the management tasks in the server where they should be done, and consequently are turning the file server into a database server.

datacenter

The *datacenter* is the computer operations department wherein the computers are physically located and managed. The data library is the part of the datacenter where disk packs and tape reels containing master copies of all the programs and backup copies of all the data are stored. An input/output control section is often part of a large datacenter, which accepts all work from user departments and distributes all outputs from the computers throughout the organization.

The data entry and systems programming (technical support) departments often come under the jurisdiction of the datacenter.

DATACENTER

datacom

(DATA COMmunications) See *communications*.

DataPhone

DataPhone is an AT&T trade name for various devices, such as modems and multiplexors, as well as transmission services.

DataPhone Digital Service

DataPhone Digital Service is a private line service from AT&T that provides digital transmission rates from 2.4 to 56 kilobits per second.

datum

Datum is singular for the word data, for example, "one datum." However, datum is rarely used, and *data*, its plural form, is commonly used to refer to both datum and data.

daughter board

A *daughter board* is a small printed circuit board that is attached to or plugs into a removable printed circuit board.

dazdee

See *DASD*.

dB

See *decibel*.

DB

See *database*.

DBA

See *database administrator*.

dBASE

C. WAYNE RATLIFF
(Courtesy Ratliff Software Productions)

dBASE is a relational database management system from Ashton-Tate that runs on IBM compatible pcs. The original dBASE II runs also on CP/M personal computers. dBASE was the first comprehensive database system available for personal computers. dBASE, originally named "Vulcan," was created by Wayne Ratliff to manage a company football pool. It was modeled after JPLDIS, the database managment system at Jet Propulsion Labs in Los Angeles. Renamed dBASE II, after George Tate and Hal Lashley formed Ashton-Tate to market it, dBASE became a huge success within a couple of years. dBASE is the most widely used personal computer database system, and its programming language and file formats have become industry standards.

dBASE provides a Pascal-like programming language and a fourth-generation language for interactively creating, editing and interrogating database files.

The following dBASE programming language example converts fahrenheit to centigrade:

```
INPUT "Enter fahrenheit  " TO FAHR
? "Centigrade is ", (FAHR - 32) * 5 / 9
```

The following dBASE fourth-generation language example opens the product file and displays records with "green" items:

```
use products
list for color ='GREEN'
```

dBASE II
Introduced in 1981, dBASE II is the original command-driven dBASE and runs on CP/M and IBM compatible pcs. dBASE II data formats and programs must be converted in order to run under dBASE III, and vice versa.

dBASE III & dBASE III PLUS
Introduced in 1984, dBASE III is a major upgrade of dBASE II that runs only on IBM compatible pcs. It handles larger databases, includes a "memo" field for text and has more programming commands and functions. dBASE III added a menu mode for its interactive commands called the "Assistant."

Introduced in 1986, dBASE III PLUS is an upgrade of dBASE III, which provides a number of new features, including the ability to create and keep queries and relational views of the database. The "Assistant" menus are entirely redesigned.

dBASE IV
Introduced in 1988, dBASE IV is a major upgrade of dBASE III PLUS. It provides a query by example method for asking questions as well as an SQL language interface. Its report and forms generation screens as well as its "Assistant" menus are entirely redesigned. Many new commands and features are added to the programming language, including arrays and windows.

dBASE Mac

dBASE Mac is a relational database management system from Ashton-Tate that runs on the Macintosh personal computer. dBASE Mac is visually oriented following in the Macintosh's graphics tradition. For example, it provides its own drawing functions that allow graphics to be created for screens and reports. Relational links and other database functions are created by linking fields on screen using the mouse as a pointer. Programming is accomplished by selecting from menu options that aid the programmer in constructing lines of code.

dBASE Mac is not compatible with traditional dBASE file formats or the dBASE programming language; however, it can convert dBASE II and dBASE III data files into the dBASE Mac file format.

DB/DC

(Database/Data Communications) *DB/DC* refers to software that performs database and data communications functions.

DBF file

A *DBF file* is a dBASE database file extension. For example, a file named ACCOUNTS.DBF can be identified as a dBASE file. All dBASE files use the same extension, even though dBASE II files cannot be read directly by programs written in dBASE III and subsequent versions.

DBMS

See *database management system.*

DBOMP

(DataBase Organization and Maintenance Processor) *DBOMP* is a database management system that was derived from the earlier BOMP version developed by IBM.

DBS

(Direct Broadcast Satellite) A *DBS* is a one-way broadcast service direct from a satellite to a user's dish (antenna). DBSs are used to deliver private information or television services without having to wire or rewire a geographical area.

dBXL

dBXL is a dBASE interpreter from WordTech Systems. dBXL performs almost all of the tasks of dBASE III PLUS. It accepts the standard dBASE language and also features a menu option that lets you run the program without having to know any commands.

DB2

(DataBase 2) *DB2* is a relational database management system from IBM that runs on large mainframes. DB2 is a full-featured and very powerful database system that has become IBM's major DBMS product. DB2 uses the SQL language interface.

DB-9, DB-15, DB-25, DB-37, DB-50

DB-9, DB-15, DB-25, DB-37 and *DB-50* refer to plugs and sockets with 9, 15, 25, 37 and 50 pins respectively. These connectors are used to hook up a wide variety of communications and computer devices. The DB refers to the physical structure of the connector and does not deal with the purpose for each of the pins in it.

DB-9 connectors are commonly used for RS-232 and video interfaces, and the DB-25 is widely used for RS-232. The DB-25 is also used on the computer end of the parallel printer cable for IBM compatible pcs (the printer end is the Centronics 36-pin connector).

A high-density DB-15 connector is used in the PS/2 series, which places 15 pins into the same shell as the DB-9 connector.

DB-25 PLUG AND SOCKET

DC

(1) (Direct Current) *DC* is electrical current that travels in one direction and is used within most electronic circuits in a computer. Contrast with *alternating current* (AC), which is available at the standard wall outlet. AC is converted into DC by the power supply in the computer.

(2) (Data Communications) *DC* is an acronym for data communications; for example, a DC/DB product handles both data communications and database management.

DCA

(1) (Document Content Architecture) *DCA* is a set of file formats from IBM for files that contain alphanumeric data, such as word processing documents. DCA Revisable Form refers to a document format that can be modified. DCA Final Form refers to a document format that cannot be changed.

(2) (Distributed Communications Architecture) *DCA* is a set of rules and protocols that govern Unisys communications networks.

(3) (Digital Communications Associates, Inc.) *DCA* is the manufacturer of communications products that includes the IRMAboard, a terminal emulator for micro to mainframe transmission.

DCE

(Data Communications Equipment or Data Circuit-terminating Equipment) A *DCE* is a communications device that is typically a modem. It establishes, maintains and terminates transmission over a communications line and may also convert the signals from the terminal or computer (DTE) for transmission over the channel.

DDBMS

See *distributed database management system*.

DDCMP

(Digital Data Communications Message Protocol) *DDCMP* is a synchronous communications protocol from Digital Equipment Corporation that is the primary data link component in its DECnet communications architecture.

DDE

(Dynamic Data Exchange) *DDE* is the message protocol in Microsoft Windows that allows application programs to request and exchange data automatically. A program in one window can query another program in another window using the DDE protocol.

DDL

(1) (Data Description Language) A *DDL* is a language used to define data and their relationships to other data. It is used to create files, databases and data dictionaries.

(2) (Document Description Language) *DDL* is a printer control language from Imagen that runs on the HP LaserJet series of laser printers.

DDM

(Distributed Data Management) *DDM* is a software program in an IBM SNA environment that allows users to access data in remote databases within the network. DDM works with IBM's LU 6.2 session to provide peer-to-peer communications and file sharing.

DDP

(Distributed Data Processing) See *distributed processing*.

DDS

See *Dataphone digital service*.

deadlock

See *deadly embrace*.

deadly embrace

A *deadly embrace* is when two elements in a process are each waiting for the other to respond. A deadly embrace can occur in a local area network when two users request the same record or file from a database and the system is not programmed properly.

deallocate

Deallocate is to release a computer resource that is currently assigned to a program or user, such as memory or a peripheral device.

deblock

Deblock is to separate records from a block.

debug

To *debug* hardware or software is to correct it. Debugging software means finding the errors in the program logic. Debugging hardware means finding the errors in circuit design.

debugger

A *debugger* is a program that aids in debugging a program. It provides ways of stopping the program or capturing various system data at prescribed times. The debugger may be able to jump directly to the line in the source program that created the problem.

DEC

(Digital Equipment Corporation) *DEC* is a registered trademark of Digital Equipment Corporation and is commonly used to refer to the company and its equipment.

decay

Decay is the reduction of strength of a signal or charge.

decentralized processing

Decentralized processing is two or more computer systems in different physical locations. Although data may be transmitted between the computers at the end of the day or some other time period, decentralized processing implies limited daily communications. Contrast with distributed processing where routine communications between the computers is part of the daily routine.

decibel (dB)

A *decibel* is a ratio of power or voltage that is used to measure loudness or strength, such as the signal strength of a transmission or the loudness of a machine. A decibel is a relative measurement that is derived from an initial and final level or from a reference and observed level.

decimal

Decimal is the numbering system universally used between humans. Decimal means 10, and each digit in a decimal number can hold up to 10 before the value is carried over to the next position on the left. Computers use the *binary* system instead of the decimal system because each digit position holds only one of two values. It is easier to design elementary electronic systems that must be in one of two states rather than in one of ten states.

decision box

A *decision box* is a diamond-shaped symbol that is used to document a decision point in a flowchart. The decision, which is based on a compare, is written in the decision box, and the results of the decision branch off from the points in the box.

decision instruction

In programming, a *decision instruction* is an instruction that compares one set of data with another and branches to a different part of the program depending on the results of the compare.

decision making

Decision making is making choices, and determining how much decision making should be automated is a critical systems analysis & design function. The proper balance of human and machine decision making is often the key to success.

The analysis of the processing steps performed by an intelligent and intuitive human worker requires considerable experience and talent. If an improper analysis of human decision making is undertaken, too much decision making may be prematurely placed into the machine. Decision making performed by computers often tends to get buried in documentation that is rarely reviewed, and may even become a mystery to the organization.

From a programming point of view, decision making can be performed in two ways: (1) algorithmic - A precise set of rules and conditions that never change, or, (2) heuristic - A set of rules that may change over time (self-modify) as conditions occur. Heuristic techniques are employed in the development of artificial intelligence systems, which are designed to imitate a human's thinking capabilities.

decision support system (DSS)

A DSS is an integrated management information and planning system that provides users with the ability to (1) interrogate its computer systems for information on an ad hoc basis, (2) analyze the information in various ways, and (3) predict the impact of decisions before they are made.

Database management systems allow users to select data and derive information for reporting and analysis purposes. Spreadsheets and modeling programs provide both analysis and "what if?" planning capabilities. However, any single application program that supports a manager's decision making is not a DSS. A DSS is an integrated set of programs that share the same data and information. For example, a comprehensive DSS would even include industry data obtained from external sources that is integrated and used for historical and statistical purposes.

An integrated DSS will directly impact the management decision-making process and can change the way decisions are made within an organization. The DSS is an integral part of an information systems implemenation within an organization and often turns out to be its most cost beneficial component.

decision table

A *decision table* is a list of decisions and their criteria. Decision tables are designed in a matrix format that list criteria (inputs) and the results (outputs) of all the possible combinations of these criteria. A decision table can be placed into a program to direct its processing. By changing the decision table, the program's processing is changed accordingly.

OUTPUTS

INPUTS	APPROVE LOAN	DENY LOAN	SEE LOAN OFFICER	SEE LOAN OFFICER
SAME JOB OVER 5 YRS	YES	NO	NO	YES
OWNS CAR	YES	NO	YES	NO
OWNS HOME	YES	NO	YES	NO
IN DEBT	NO	YES	NO	NO

DECISION TABLE

decision tree

A *decision tree* is a
graphical representation of all of the alternatives in a decision making process.

deck

(1) A *deck* is the part of a magnetic tape unit that holds and moves the reels of tape.

(2) A *deck* is a set of punched cards.

declaration

In programming, a *declaration* is an instruction or statement that defines data, procedures and resources to be used, but does not create an executable processing instruction.

DECmate

DECmate is a family of computer systems from Digital Equipment Corporation that are specialized for word processing. Introduced in 1981, the DECmates use Digital's PDP-8 architecture.

DECnet

DECnet is a communications architecture and series of related hardware and software products from Digital Equipment Corporation. DECnet supports both Ethernet-style local area networks as well as wide area networks using baseband and broadband, private and/or public communications channels. It provides interconnection of PDP and VAX minicomputers, Rainbow and VAXmate personal computers as well as IBM compatible pcs and Macintoshes. DECnet is built into the VMS operating system for the VAX line.

In DECnet philosophy, a node must be an intelligent processing machine and not simply a terminal as in other systems.

decoder

A *decoder* is any hardware device or software program that converts a coded signal back into its orignal form.

decollator

A *decollator* separates multiple-part paper forms into separate parts while removing the carbon paper. Decollating is done after the forms have been printed.

decrement

Decrement is to subtract a number from another number. Decrementing a counter means to subtract 1 or some other number from its current value.

DECstation

DECstation is a small computer system from Digital Equipment Corporation that was introduced in 1978. DECstations are used for word processing and general purpose computing.

DECsystem

DECsystem is a series of mainframes from Digital Equipment Corporation. DECsystems were introduced from 1974 through 1980 and were the successor to the 36-bit PDP-10 computers.

DECtalk

DECtalk is a voice synthesizing system from Digital Equipment Corporation that accepts serial ASCII text from any computer system and converts it into audible speech. It is used in Touch-tone telephone response systems as well as for voice-output for visually handicapped users.

dedicated channel

In communications, a *dedicated channel* is a line or circuit that is used exclusively for one purpose. Same as *leased line* or *private line*.

dedicated service

A *dedicated service* is a service that is not shared by other users or organizations.

defacto standard

A *defacto standard* is a format or language that is widely used and copied, but has not been officially sanctioned by a standards organization, such as the American National Standards Institute (ANSI). Defacto standards often eventually become official standards.

default

A *default* is a standard setting or action taken by hardware or software if the user has not specified otherwise. For example, defaults in word processing programs define the margins, tabs, page length and lines per inch, all of which can be reset by the user.

degausser

A *degausser* is a demagnetizer that erases the contents of magnetic storage media, such as magnetic tape. The contents of the tape are erased without removing the tape from the reel. A degausser is also used to demagnetize the read/write heads of a magnetic tape or disk unit.

DEL key

(DELete key) The *DEL key* is a common keyboard key used to delete the character under the cursor on the screen. In word processing programs, it is often used in combination with the shift, control and alt keys to delete various text segments, such as words, lines and sentences.

delay line

A *delay line* is a communications or electronic circuit that has a built-in delay. Acoustic delay lines were used to create some of the earliest computer memories; for example, in the UNIVAC I, tubes of liquid mercury were used. The electrical pulses were changed to pressures that caused the bits to ripple much more slowly through the mercury from one end to the other. They were then changed back into electrical pulses and reintroduced into the mercury again in a continuous loop. During the electrical stage, the bits were sent into the arithmetic and logic circuits for processing.

delete

(1) In data management, *delete* is to remove a record from the file or erase the entire data file from the disk.

(2) In word processing, *delete* is to erase some amount of text from the document or erase the document from the disk.

(3) In computer graphics, *delete* is to erase an area or one or more objects from the image or to erase the entire image file from the disk.

(4) In spreadsheets, *delete* is to remove one or more rows or columns from the spreadsheet or to erase the spreadsheet file from the disk.

delimiter

A *delimiter* is any character or combination of characters used to separate one item or set of data from another. For example, in comma delimited records, a comma is used to separate each field of data.

delta modulation

Delta modulation is a technique that is used to sample voice waves and convert them into digital code. Delta modulation typically samples the wave 32,000 times per second, but generates only one bit per sample. Contrast with *PCM* (pulse code modulation), which samples the wave 8,000 times per second, but generates eight bits for each sample.

DEMA

(Data Entry Management Association) *DEMA* is a professional organization devoted to the advancement of data entry management personnel. DEMA, organized in 1976, sponsors educational courses and conferences for data entry managers. For more information, contact DEMA at 101 Merritt 7 Corporate Park, Norwalk, CT 06851, (203) 846-3777.

demand paging

Demand paging is the copying of a program page from disk into memory when required by the program.

demand processing

Demand processing is the processing of transactions as they are entered into the computer system. Same as transaction processing and real time processing.

Demo Program

See *Dan Bricklin's Demo Program*.

demodulate

Demodulate is to reconvert a modulated signal back into its original form by filtering the data out of the carrier frequency.

demultiplex

Demultiplex is to reconvert a transmission that contains several intermixed signals back into their original and separate signals.

dense binary code

Dense binary code is a binary code that uses all possible bit patterns of the storage unit in contast with one that may have unused binary patterns.

departmental computing

Departmental computing is the processing of a department's data with its own computer system. See *distributed processing*.

dependent segment

In database management, a *dependent segment* is data that depends on data in a higher level for its full meaning.

dequeue

Dequeue, pronounced "d-q," is to remove items from a queue in order to process or transmit them.

DES

(Data Encryption Standard) The DES is a standardized (National Bureau of Standards) encryption technique that allows binary code to be scrambled into an undetectable stream of bits for transmission over a public network. The DES uses a binary number, offering more than 72 quadrillion combinations, as the key for encryption. The number, which can be randomly chosen for each transmission, is used as a pattern to convert the bits at both ends of the transmission.

descenders

Descenders are the parts of the lower case characters g, j, p, q and y that fall below the line. Sometimes these characters are displayed and printed with shortened descenders in order to fit into a smaller character cell, making them difficult to read.

descending sort

A *descending sort* is the arranging of data records from high to low sequence (Z to A, 9 to 0).

descriptor

A *descriptor* is a word used to identify a document in an information retrieval system that is indexed for fast searching.

deserialize

Deserialize is to convert a serial stream of bits into parallel streams of bits.

Designer

(1) *Designer* is a drawing program from Micrografx, Inc., that runs on IBM compatible pcs and is compatible with Microsoft Windows. It is a full-featured graphics design program that creates illustrations in up to 64 layers and provides almost all of the drawing tools of the PostScript programs that run on the Macintosh. Designer is used for sophisticated illustrations as well as computer-aided design (CAD) drawings. Designer creates its own proprietary DRW file format and also supports PIC files that are compatible with other Micrografx products.

(2) *Designer* is an application generator that is part of the Clarion Professional Developer application development system.

desk checking

Desk checking is the manual testing of the logic of a program.

Deskpro

Deskpro is the model designation of a series of desktop personal computers from Compaq Computer.

desktop

The *desktop* refers to an on-screen representation of a user's desktop in icon/mouse-oriented operating environments. See *Macintosh user interface*.

desktop accessory software

Desktop accessory software provides a series of useful functions that simulate the kinds of office accessories you would have on your desktop, such as a calculator, notepad and appointment calendar. Desktop accessory programs are typically RAM resident so that they are immediately available to the user.

desktop application

See *desktop accessory software*.

desktop computer

Desktop computer is another term for personal computer or microcomputer.

desktop organizer

See *desktop accessory software*.

desktop publishing

Desktop publishing is using a personal computer to produce high-quality printed output that is camera ready for the printer. It requires a desktop publishing software package and a personal computer with a graphics-based monitor that can display one or two full pages at the same time. In order to produce printed output directly from the system, a laser printer is required; however, the 300 dot-per-inch output of a desktop laser printer is fine for text and line art, but is not suitable for shaded drawings and photographs. Today, many typesetting systems, which can generate 1,200 dots per inch and more, accept formatted output directly from popular desktop publishing programs.

The key feature of desktop publishing is that it merges text and graphics and displays it on screen in *wysiwyg* (what you see is what you get) style before it's printed. It flows the text around the graphics, and the sophistication with which it performs the task varies from program to program. Text and graphics may be created in the desktop publishing program, but very few of them have full-featured word processing and graphics capability. Typically, the initial creation of the work is done in traditional word processing, CAD, drawing and paint programs and then copied into the publishing system. Desktop publishing programs accept many common text and graphics formats directly.

Desktop publishing programs provide the ultimate in page layout capabilities, including a multitude of different type fonts, magazine style columns, rules and borders and page numbering in a variety of styles.

Since desktop publishing has brought the cost of professional page makeup systems down to the personal computer level, it is often thought of as "the" way to produce inhouse high-quality newsletters and brochures. However, the professional appearance of printed material comes from graphics layout experience. Desktop publishing is no substitute for a graphics designer who knows which fonts to use and how to lay out the page in an artistic manner. The software will not do it for you.

In addition, extensive amounts of desktop publishing require workstation-level machines in order to provide respectable performance. Computers with CPU performance in the Motorola 68020 or Intel 80386 category are quite necessary for large, routine jobs that mix a lot of graphics with the text.

DESQview

DESQview is a multitasking and windowing environment from Quarterdeck Office Systems that runs on IBM compatible pcs under Microsoft's DOS operating system. DESQview allows users to keep multiple applications in memory and switch back and forth between them. Each application program can take up the full screen or several programs can be viewed on screen at once. Data can be also be copied or moved from one application into another. The significant feature of DESQview is that programs do not have to be modified in order to use it.

destructive memory

Destructive memory is a memory that loses its content when it is read, requiring that the circuitry regenerate the bits after the read operation.

detail file

Same as *transaction file*.

developer's toolkit

A *developer's toolkit* is a set of program subroutines that are used to support the writing of an application program in a particular programming language or operating system environment.

development cycle

See *system development cycle*.

development system

A *development system* is the computer and software that allows a programmer to create a program. The term may also refer to only the hardware or only the software.

development tool

A *development tool* is hardware or software that assists in the creation of electronic machines or software programs. See *developer's toolkit*.

device

A *device* is any electronic or electromechanical machine or component, from as small as a transistor to as large as a peripheral unit, such as a magnetic tape or disk drive. Device always refers to hardware. Device driver refers to the software that activates the hardware.

device adapter

Same as *interface adapter*.

device address

See *address*.

device control character

In communications, a *device control character* is a special code that activates some function on a terminal. In ASCII code, character #17 through 20 are four device control characters.

device dependent

Device dependent is a program that is written to directly address the hardware at the machine level.

device driver

A *device driver* is a software routine in an operating system that commands a peripheral device. Drivers contain the knowledge about the unique properties of their devices, for example, the number of sectors per disk track or the number of lines of resolution on the screen. The operating system requires a device driver for every peripheral device attached to it.

When the operating system gets a request from an application program for input or output, it sends that request to the appropriate device driver to handle it. The device driver may use elementary routines within the operating system to activate the hardware, such as the BIOS in IBM compatible pcs, or it may activate the hardware directly. See *driver*.

device independent

Device independent refers to keeping the detailed instructions for activating a peripheral device in the operating system and explicitly out of the application programs. With device independence, an application program can run in many different computer systems, each using different kinds of devices. See *device driver*.

device name

A *device name* is a name assigned to a hardware device that represents its physical address. For example, LPT1 is a device name.

DFT emulation

(Distributed Function Terminal emulation) *DFT* is a feature of OS/2 Extended Edition that allows the IBM personal computer user to interact with more than one application program in the mainframe at the same time. It also allows the mainframe to display more flexible (dot addressable) graphics on the OS/2 screen.

DG

See *Data General*.

Dhrystones

Dhrystones is a benchmark program that tests a general mix of instructions. The results of the program are expressed in Dhrystones per second, which is the number of times the program can be executed in one second. Contrast with *Whetstones*, which tests floating point operations.

DIA

(Document Interchange Architecture) *DIA* is a format standard used in IBM's SNA networks that is used to exchange documents from dissimilar machines within an LU 6.2 session. DIA acts as an envelope to hold the document and does not set any standards for the content of the document, such as layout settings or graphics standards. DIA is typically used in an office automation environment.

Diablo emulation

Diablo emulation is a printer feature that allows the printer to be activated with the same set of codes and commands as the Diablo letter quality printers.

diacritical

A *diacritical* is a mark added to a letter of the alphabet that changes its pronunciation, such as the Spanish tilde (wavy line over an N) or the French cedilla (small hook under a C).

diagnostics

(1) *Diagnostics* are software programs that test the operational capability of hardware components, such as memory and disk drives. In personal computers, diagnostics are often permanently stored in a ROM (read only memory) chip and are automatically activated when the computer is started.

(2) *Diagnostics* are error messages in a programmer's source listing.

dialog box

A *dialog box* is a small window that is displayed on screen to highlight some action or to request an answer to a question.

dial-up telephone system

The *dial-up telephone system* is the switched telephone network that is regulated by national governments and is administered in the United States by various common carriers, such as AT&T, MCI, GTE, Sprint, the Bell Telephone companies and a host of other independent companies. By attaching a modem to a computer, data can be converted into audio frequencies that can be transmitted over the network just like voice.

diazo film

In micrographics, *diazo film* is used to make copies of microfilm or microfiche. To make copies, diazo film is exposed to the original film under ultraviolet light and when developed, creates a copy with the same polarity as the original. Negative originals make negative copies, positive originals make positive copies. Diazo copies come in several colors, typically blue, blue-black and purple.

dibit

A *dibit*, which stands for "two bit," is any one of the four patterns obtainable from two consecutive bits: 00, 01, 10 and 11. Using a technique called phase modulation, each two bits of data is modulated onto a carrier as a different shift in the phase of the wave.

DIBOL

(DIgital coBOL) *DIBOL* is a version of the COBOL programming language from Digital Equipment Corporation that runs on its PDP and VAX series of computers.

dice

See *die*.

dichotomizing search

Same as *binary search*.

die

A *die* is the formal term for the square of silicon containing the integrated circuit when it is cut out of the wafer. The more popular term is chip, because the die looks like a chip. The plural of die is *dice*.

dielectric

A *dielectric* is an insulator, such as glass, rubber or plastic. Dielectric materials can be made to hold an electrostatic charge, but current cannot flow through them.

DIF

(1) (Data Interchange Format) *DIF* is a standard file format for spreadsheet and other data that are structured in row and column form. Originally developed by Software Arts, creator of VisiCalc, the first spreadsheet program, DIF is now under the jurisdiction of Lotus Development Corporation.

(2) (Display Information Facility) *DIF* is a program from IBM that runs on the System/38 minicomputer. It lets users build customized programs for online access to their data.

(3) (Document Interchange Format) *DIF* is a document interchange standard developed by the U. S. Navy in 1982.

Difference Engine

The *Difference Engine* was a mechanical computational device designed and constructed in the early 1820s by the British scientist, Charles Babbage (1791-1871). The British government provided some of the funds for the machine, making it one of the first subsidized high-technology projects of 19th century Europe. Babbage's machine was not totally original. The concept of using rods and wheels was taken from earlier attempts at calculating devices.

The Difference Engine was designed to add numbers up to six decimal places and perform these computations more accurately than with existing methods. However, the machine was only partially completed. In the course of building it, Babbage realized he could develop something much better from scratch, and in the early 1830s, he turned his attention to his next design, the Analytical Engine. It, too, was never completed, but was much more sophisticated than the Difference Engine and incorporated many of the concepts of today's general-purpose computer.

DIFFERENCE ENGINE
(Courtesy Smithsonian Institution)

Differential Analyzer

The *Differential Analyzer* was an analog computational device that was built to solve differential equations at the Massachusetts Institute of Technology by Professor Vannevar Bush during the 1930s. Less than a dozen of these machines were built, but they were known for their effectiveness in calculating ballistics tables during World War II. The machine took up an entire room and was programmed, with screwdriver and wrench, by replacing its camshaftlike gears.

DIFFERENTIAL ANALYZER
(Courtesy The MIT Museum)
Your basic hand-held programmable calculator of the 1930s.

diffusion

Diffusion is a semiconductor manufacturing process that infuses tiny quantities of impurities into a base material, such as silicon, to change its electrical characteristics.

digit

A *digit* is a single character in a numbering system. In the decimal system, the digits are 0 through 9. In the binary system, the digits are 0 and 1.

digital

Digital has always meant using numbers and originally came from the word digit, or finger, since the numbering system was based on the ten fingers of both hands. Today, digital is used synonymously for binary coded numbers or for any digital microelectronic device. In other words, digital has become synonymous with "computer."

digital camera

A *digital camera* is a video camera that records its images in digital form. Unlike traditional analog TV cameras that convert light intensities into infinitely variable signals, digital cameras convert light intensities into discrete numbers.

A digital camera breaks down the picture image into a fixed number of dots called pixels (picture elements), tests each pixel for light intensity and converts the intensity into a number. In a color digital camera, three numbers, representing the amount of red, green and blue in the pixel, are created and stored.

digital channel

In communications, a *digital channel* is a transmission path that handles only digital signals. All voice and video signals have to be converted from their analog form into digital in order to be carried over a digital channel. Contrast with *analog channel*, which handles voice and video as infinitely varying frequencies.

digital computer

A *digital computer* is a computer that accepts and processes data that has been converted into discrete binary numbers. Almost all computers are digital. Contrast with *analog computer*, which processes data made up of continuously varying voltages.

Digital Data Service

Digital Data Service is a nationwide digital transmission service from the Bell System that is leased to customers on a private line basis.

Digital Equipment Corporation

Digital Equipment Corporation, commonly known as DEC, was founded in 1957 by Kenneth Olson, who after 30 years is still the head of the company. Digital pioneered the minicomputer business with its PDP computers starting in 1959 and later with its VAX series in 1977.

Digital's early successes were in the scientific, process control and academic

KENNETH H. OLSON
(Courtesy Digital)

communities; however, after the VAX series was announced, Digital gained a strong foothold in commercial data processing environments. The VAX series has evolved into a complete line of compatible computers from desktop micro to mainframe and uses the same VMS operating system in all of its models. The VAX machines caused Digital to achieve substantial growth throughout the 1980s.

Over the years, Digital has been widely recognized for its high-quality computer systems.

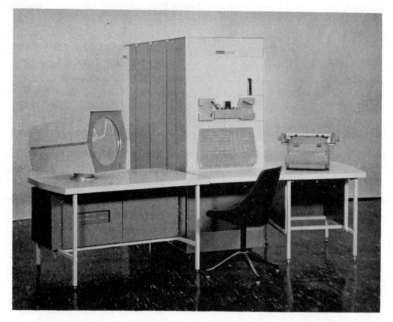

THE PDP-1, DIGITAL'S FIRST COMPUTER
(Courtesy Digital)

digital monitor

A *digital monitor* is a video display unit that accepts a digital signal from the computer. The majority of digital monitors use the same CRT (cathode ray tube) technology that is found in a television and must convert the digital signals to analog internally in order to illuminate the screen. For the differences between analog and digital monitors, see *analog monitors*.

digital PABX

(digital **P**rivate **A**utomatic **B**ranch **E**xchange) A *digital PABX* is a telephone switching system that handles both voice and data. Both telephones and data terminals are connected to a digital PABX network.

A digital PABX may be an analog PABX that has been adapted for data requiring modems for each data device, or it may be an all-digital switching device that requires that the telephones generate digital voice signals. Some digital PABXs offer both analog and digital options.

While performing all the functions of a computerized PABX, such as least cost routing (determining the most economical service to place a call with), a digital PABX may also perform functions, such as protocol conversion between different computers and terminals as well as word processing format conversion between different word processors.

Digital PABXs can serve as a local area network or may connect to a local area network. They can also serve as a gateway between a local area network and an external network, providing the necessary protocol conversion. The terms digital PABX and *digital PBX* are used synonymously.

SWITCHBOARD (1915)
(Courtesy AT&T)

Hardly automatic, and by no means digital, this switchboard was sophisticated technology for its time.

digital radio

Digital radio is the microwave transmission of digital data through the air. In order to transmit voice in a digital radio system, it must first be digitized (sampled and turned into digital code).

digital recording

See *magnetic tape & disk*.

digital signal processing

Digital signal processing is a category of techniques that analyze signals generated from a wide range of sources, such as human voice, weather satellites, earthquake monitors and nuclear tests. Digital signal processing converts the signals into digital form and breaks apart the signal using various algorithms such as the fast Fourier transform. Once a signal has been reduced to numbers, its components can be isolated and analyzed more readily than in analog form. Digital signal processing is used in such fields as biomedicine, sonar, radar, seismology and speech and data communictions.

digital termination service

See *DTS*.

digitize

Digitize is to convert an image or signal into digital code for input into the computer. Digitizing is tracing a picture on a graphics tablet, scanning an image or converting camera images into the computer. Three dimensional objects can be digitized by a device which uses a mechanical arm that is moved on and around the object. Sound, temperature and movement are also said to be digitized when they are analyzed and converted into digital code.

digitizer tablet

A *digitizer tablet* is a graphics input device that functions like a drawing tablet. It can be used for sketching new images or tracing old ones, selecting from menus or simply for moving the cursor around on the screen, all of which can be provided within a single program.

The user makes contact with the digitizer tablet with a device called a cursor, which is a pen-like or puck-like instrument that is connected to the tablet by a wire. For sketching, the user draws with the tablet cursor and the screen cursor "draws" a corresponding image. For tracing an existing image, the screen cursor is often not required. The tablet picks up the drawing as a series of x-y coordinates (vector graphics), either as a continuous stream of coordinates, or as end points.

Menu selection is accomplished by a tablet overlay or by a screen display. The tablet cursor selects an item by making contact with it on the overlay, or by controlling the screen cursor.

DIGITIZER TABLET

dimension

A *dimension* is one axis in an array. In programming, a dimension statement defines the array and sets up the number of elements within the dimensions.

dimensioning

In CAD programs, *dimensioning* is the management and display of the measurements of an object. There are various dimensioning, or drafting, standards which determine such things as tolerances, sizes of arrowheads and orientation on the paper.

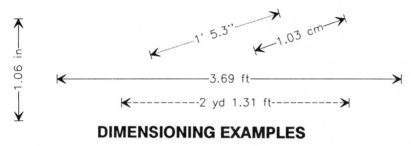

DIMENSIONING EXAMPLES

DIN connector

A *DIN connector* is a plug and socket that is used to connect a wide variety of devices. For example, the keyboard on most IBM compatible pcs uses a DIN connector. See *plugs & sockets*.

diode

A *diode* is an electronic component that primarily acts as a one-way valve. As a discrete component or built into a chip, diodes are used for a wide variety of functions. Diodes are a key element in changing AC into DC. They are used as temperature sensors, light sensors and light

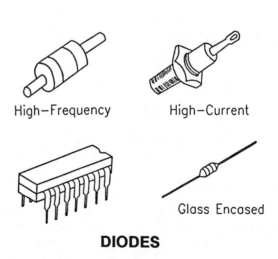

High–Frequency   High–Current

Glass Encased

DIODES

emitters (LEDs). In communications, they're used to remove both analog and digital signals from carriers and to modulate signals onto carriers. In digital logic, they're used as one-way valves and as switches similar to transistors.

DIP

(Dual In-line Package) A *DIP* is a housing that is commonly used to hold a chip. Tiny wires bond the chip to metal pins that wind their way down into the spider-like feet that are inserted into sockets on the printed circuit board.

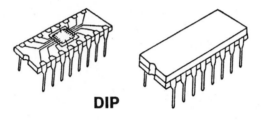

DIP

DIP switch

(Dual In-line Package switch) A *DIP switch* is a series of tiny toggle switches that are built onto a housing, called a *DIP*, which is commonly used to mount a chip on a printed circuit board. DIP switches are used to set many different conditions such as assigning baud rate or port number. Although originally designed for the technician, users are often required to set DIP switches when they install or change a peripheral device in their personal computers.

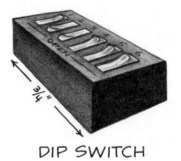

DIP SWITCH

DIR

(DIRectory) *DIR* is a CP/M and Microsoft DOS and OS/2 operating system command that lists the file names on the disk. Unless otherwise specified, DIR lists the files in the current working directory.

direct access

Direct access is the ability to go directly to a specific storage location without having go through what's in front of it. Memories (RAMs, ROMs, PROMs) and disks are the major direct access devices. Memories hold data in sequentially numbered bytes, and disks hold data in sequentially numbered sectors. Access methods are software routines that keep track of data on a disk. Assemblers, compilers and interpreters are programming language translators that keep track of data stored in memory.

direct access method

The *direct access method* is a technique for determining the location of data on a disk by formulating the storage address from an identifying key in the record, such as account number. Using an algorithm, the account number is turned into the actual track and sector address where the data is stored. This is much faster than comparing hundreds or even thousands of entries in an index, however, a lot of disk space is wasted if the account numbers are not reasonably consecutive in number.

direct access storage device

See *DASD*.

direct address method

Same as *direct access method*.

direct current

See *DC*.

direct memory access

See *DMA*

direct read after write

See *DRAW*.

direct view storage tube

See *DVST*.

directory

A *directory* is an index to the location of files on a disk. In personal computers, directories are used to catalog files for different purposes. Usually, the programs and data for a single application, such as word processing or spreadsheets, are kept in a single directory. Directories create the illusion of file drawers on the disk, even though the physical files are scattered all over the disk.

disable

Disable is to prevent some action from occurring. Disabled means turned off, rather than broken. Contrast with *enable*, which turns something on.

disc

Disc is an alternate spelling for disk.

discrete

Discrete refers to any component or device that is separate and distinct and is treated as a singular unit.

discrete component

A *discrete component* is an elementary electronic component that is constructed as a single unit. Before integrated circuits (chips), all electronic components, such as transistors, resistors, diodes and capacitors, were discrete components. Discrete components are still used in conjunction with integrated circuits, either to augment them or because a particular type of electronic component requires more electrical power than can be handled in a microminiaturized circuit.

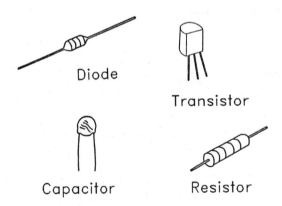

Diode

Transistor

Capacitor

Resistor

DISCRETE COMPONENTS

discretionary hyphen

In word processing, a *discretionary hyphen* is a code used to identify where a word will break if it's too long to fit at the end of a line. A discretionary hyphen gives the user the choice of splitting the word rather than adhering to the rules for hyphenation in the software. If the word does not require hyphenation, the discretionary hyphen is ignored.

dish

A *dish* is a dish-shaped antenna that receives signals from a satellite. Earth stations, which are transmitters as well as receivers, are also dish-shaped.

disk

A *disk* is a direct access storage device. See *magnetic disk & tape*.

disk cartridge

A *disk cartridge* is a removable disk module that contains a single hard disk platter or a floppy disk.

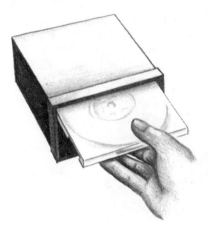

DISK CARTRIDGES

disk crash

See *head crash*.

disk drive

A *disk drive* is a peripheral storage device that holds, spins, reads and writes magnetic or optical disks. The disk drive may be a receptacle for disk cartridges or disk packs, or it may contain non-removable disk platters like most hard disks in personal computers.

disk file

A *disk file* is any set of instructions or data that is recorded, cataloged and treated as a single unit on a disk. Source language programs, machine language programs, spreadsheets, data files, text documents, graphics files and batch files are examples of disk files.

disk memory

Disk memory is the same as disk storage. Memory terminology is confusing since the computer's internal memory, or RAM, doesn't "remember" after the power is turned off, but disks and tapes do hold their content until purposefully erased. In this book, disks and tapes are referred to as storage devices, not memory devices.

disk operating system

See *DOS*.

disk pack

A *disk pack* is a removable hard disk module that contains several hard disk platters mounted on a central spindle. When outside of the disk drive, the disk pack is held in a plastic container that keeps the disk platters dust free. Before insertion, the bottom of the disk pack is removed. After inserting the disk pack into the disk drive, the rest of the housing is released for removal.

DISK PACKS

disk unit

Same as *disk drive*.

diskette

Same as *floppy disk*.

diskless workstation

A *diskless workstation* is a computer in a network that does not have any local disk storage. All programs and data are retrieved from the network's file server.

DISOSS

(DIStributed Office Support System) *DISOSS* is a centralized document distribution and filing application from IBM that runs in an IBM mainframe under the MVS operating system. DISOSS's counterpart in the VM environment is called "PROFS." DISOSS allows for electronic mail and the exchange of documents between a variety of IBM office devices, including Displaywriter word processors, personal computers, 8100 and 5520 computers.

dispatcher

Same as *scheduler*.

dispersed intelligence

Same as *distributed intelligence*.

displacement

Displacement is the distance from a starting point. For example, in a machine language program, the displacement is the distance an instruction is located from the beginning of the program. When the instruction is executed, the displacement is added to the *base*, which is the current memory location the program starts at.

display

(1) *Display* is to show text and graphics on a video or flat panel screen.

(2) A *display* is a screen, or monitor.

display adapter

Same as *video display board*.

display attribute

See *attribute*.

display board

Same as *video display board*.

display card

Same as *video display board*.

display cycle

In computer graphics, a *display cycle* is the series of operations required to display an image.

display device

A *display device* is a video monitor or flat panel display screen. The term may also include the video display board (controller board) that generates the signals for the monitor.

display element

(1) In graphics, a *display element* is a basic graphic arts component, such as background, foreground, text or graphics image.

(2) In computer graphics, a *display element* sometimes refers to a graphics primitive, such as a dot, line or circle.

display entity

In computer graphics, a *display entity* is a collection of display elements that can be manipulated as a unit.

display frame

In computer graphics, a *display frame* is a single frame in a series of animation frames.

display list

In computer graphics, a *display list* is a collection of vectors that make up the image stored in vector graphics format.

Display PostScript

Display PostScript is a display language from Adobe Corporation that provides a translation from elementary commands in an application program to graphics and text elements on screen. Display PostScript is the screen counterpart of the PostScript printer language and is designed for inclusion in an operating system to provide a standard (device independent) display language.

display screen

A *display screen* is a surface area upon which text and graphics are temporarily made to appear for display purposes. It is typically a cathode ray tube (CRT), but flat panel technologies are rapidly advancing.

display terminal

A *display terminal* is a terminal with a display screen typically using the same cathode ray tube (CRT) technology as a television set. Same as *terminal, video display unit, video display terminal,* CRT, *monitor* and *console.*

DisplayWrite

DisplayWrite is a word processing program from IBM that runs on IBM compatible pcs. DisplayWrite is the personal computer version of the DisplayWriter word processing system that was first introduced in 1980 by IBM.

distributed data processing

See *distributed processing.*

distributed database

A *distributed database* is a database that is physically stored in two or more computer systems. Although geographically dispersed, a distributed database system manages and controls the entire database as a single collection of data. If redundant data is stored in separate databases due to performance requirements, updates to one set of data will automatically update the additional sets in a timely manner. Distributed database implies that redundancy will be managed and controlled.

distributed database management system

A *distributed database management system* is a DBMS that can manage distributed databases.

distributed function

Distributed function is the distribution of processing functions throughout the organization.

distributed intelligence

Distributed intelligence is the placing of processing capability in terminals and other peripheral devices. Intelligent terminals (terminals with built-in CPUs) can be used in a system to handle screen layouts, data entry validation and other pre-processing steps. Intelligence placed into peripheral devices, such as disk drives, can also relieve the central computer system from many routine tasks.

distributed logic

See *distributed intelligence*.

distributed processing

Distributed processing is a system of computers connected together by a communications network. The term is loosely used to refer to any computers with communications between them. However, in true distributed processing, each computer system is chosen to handle its local workload, and the network has been designed to support the system as a whole.

Contrast with *decentralized processing*, in which different computers each process a separate workload without communications between them. Also contrast with *centralized processing*, in which one or more computer systems are located in one facility and handle the entire workload.

dithering

In computer graphics, *dithering* is the creation of additional colors and shades from an existing palette. In monochrome displays, textures of grays are created by varying the density and patterns of the dots. In color displays, colors and textures are created by mixing and varying the dots of existing colors. Dithering is used to create a wide variety of patterns for use as backgrounds, fills and shading, as well as for creating halftones for printing. It is also used in anti-aliasing in order to make jagged lines appear smoother on screen.

divestiture

Divestiture often refers to the breakup of AT&T, which divested itself of its operating telephone companies on January 1, 1984.

DL/1

(Data Language 1) *DL/1* is the database manipulation language used in IBM's IMS database management system.

DMA

(Direct Memory Access) *DMA* is a specialized microprocessor that transfers data from memory to memory directly without using the main processor, although it may periodically steal cycles from it. The DMA technique moves data faster than by passing it through the processor.

do loop

A *do loop* is a primary high-level programming language structure that repeats a series of instructions a certain number of times. A do loop tests the comparison of two or more values. In a DO WHILE loop, if the comparison is true, the program steps within the loop are executed. When the comparison is false, the steps are bypassed. In a DO UNTIL loop, if the comparison is true, all the steps in the loop are bypassed. When the comparison is false, the steps are executed. The following DO WHILE loop in dBASE prints the numbers 1 through 10 and then stops.

```
COUNTER = 0
DO WHILE COUNTER <> 10
 COUNTER = COUNTER + 1
 ? COUNTER
ENDDO
```

do nothing instruction

A *do nothing instruction* is a computer instruction that performs no other operation than to take up space. It is used for future insertion of a machine instruction. Same as NOP (no op) instruction.

document

(1) A *document* is any paper form that has been filled in.

(2) A *document* is a word processing text file.

(3) In the Macintosh, a *document* is any text, data or graphics file that is created in the computer. In this book, document refers only to text files.

document handling

Document handling is a procedure for transporting and handling paper documents for data entry into scanning machines.

document mark

In micrographics, a *document mark* is a small optical blip on each frame on a roll of microfilm that is used to automatically count the frames.

document processing

Document processing is the processing of text documents, such as in word processing, but also includes indexing methods for text retrieval based on document content.

documentation

Documentation is the narrative and graphical description of a system. Documentation for an information system includes:

OPERATING PROCEDURES
(1) Instructions for turning the system on and getting the programs initiated (loaded).
(2) Instructions for obtaining source documents for data entry.
(3) Instructions for entering data at the terminal, which includes a picture of each screen layout the user will encounter.
(4) A description of error messages that can occur and the alternative methods for handling them.
(5) A description of the defaults taken in the programs and the   instructions for changing them.
(6) Instructions for distributing the computer's output, which includes sample pages for each type of report.

SYSTEM DOCUMENTATION
(1) Data dictionary - Description of the files and databases.
(2) System flow chart - Description of the data as it flows from source document to report.
(3) Application program documentation - Description of the inputs, processing and outputs for each data entry, query, update and report program in the system.

TECHNICAL DOCUMENTATION
(1) File structures and access methods
(2) Program flow charts
(3) Program source code listings
(4) Machine procedures (JCL)

The quantity and quality of programming documentation is difficult to determine for non-technical people. It depends on the programming language used as well as the conventions established in the programming department.

docuterm

A *docuterm* is a word or phrase in a text document that is used to identify the contents of the document.

domain

(1) In database management, the *domain* is all possible values contained in a particular field for every record in the file.

(2) In communications, a *domain* is all the resources that are under control of a computer system.

(3) In bubble memory, a *domain* is a bubble, or bit.

dominant carrier

A *dominant carrier* is a telecommunications services provider that has control over a large segment of a particular market.

dopant

A *dopant* is an element that is diffused into pure silicon in order to alter its electrical characteristics.

doping

Doping is the altering of the electrical conductivity of a semiconductor material, such as silicon, by chemically combining it with foreign elements. Doping results in either an excess of electrons (N-type or N-channel) or a lack of electrons (P-type or P-channel) in the silicon.

DOS

(Disk Operating System) *DOS* (pronounced "doss") may refer to any computer operating system from microcomputer to mainframe. However, for personal computers, it usually refers to the operating system used in IBM compatible pcs, known as DOS, PC-DOS or MS-DOS. It may also refer to the DOS used in the Apple II personal computer series.

With regard to IBM mainframes, it usually refers to the DOS/VSE operating system, a contemporary version of an earlier IBM operating system, which used to be pronounced "dee-o-ess."

DOS box

The DOS box is the DOS compatibility mode in OS/2.

DOS prompt

A *DOS prompt* is a set of characters that is displayed on screen to indicate that the operating system is ready to accept a command from the user. The DOS prompt for a hard disk in Microsoft's DOS or OS/2 operating systems is **C:** or **C:**.

DOS/VSE

(Disk Operating System/Virtual Storage Extended) *DOS/VSE* is a multiuser, multitasking, virtual memory operating system from IBM that typically runs on IBM's 43xx series of medium-scale mainframes.

dot

A *dot* is a tiny round, rectangular or square spot that is one element in a matrix, which is used to display or print a graphics or text image. See *dot matrix*.

dot addressable

Dot addressable is the ability to program each individual dot on a video display, dot matrix printer or laser printer.

dot chart

Same as *scatter diagram*.

dot matrix

Dot matrix is a technique that uses patterns of tiny dots to form character and graphic images on video terminals and printers. Display screens use a matrix (set of rows and columns) of dots just like television sets. Serial printers use one or two columns of dot hammers that are moved across the paper. Laser printers "paint" dots of light a line at a time onto a light-sensitive photographic drum.

The more dots per square inch, the higher the resolution of the characters and graphics.

dot matrix printer

A *dot matrix* printer is a printer that forms images out of dots. The common desktop dot matrix printer that is connected to a personal computer uses one or two columns of dot hammers that are moved serially across the paper. The more dot hammers used, the higher the resolution of the printed image. 24-pin dot matrix printers can produce typewriter-like output.

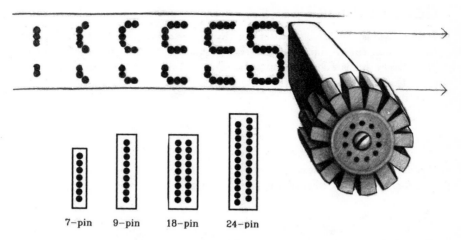

SERIAL DOT MATRIX PIN CONFIGURATIONS

7–pin   9–pin   18–pin   24–pin

dot pitch

Dot pitch is the width of a dot in a dot matrix. The smaller the dot, the sharper the image. For display screens, dot pitch is expressed in millimeters; for example, a .28 dot pitch is 28/100ths of a millimeter. With laser printers, the individual dot pitch is typically not expressed. For example, in a 300 dpi (dots per inch) printer, each dot is 1/300th of an inch.

double buffering

Double buffering is a software technique that uses two buffers to speed up data retrieval. For input operations, data in one buffer (reserved memory) is being processed, while the second buffer is used to input the next set of data. For output, data is being output from one buffer, while the next set of data is being formatted (prepared for output) in the other buffer. Double buffering requires that the hardware handle concurrent operations.

double click

See *click*.

double-dabble

Double-dabble is a method for converting binary numbers into decimal numbers by doubling the highest order (leftmost) bit, adding the next lower order bit, doubling the sum and repeating the process until the sum contains the lowest order bit.

double density disk

A *double density disk* is a disk with twice the storage capacity of the previous model. The next step up is *high density*. For example, in IBM compatible pcs, the 360K floppy disk is a double density disk, but the 1.2M floppy is a high density disk. The 720K microfloppy (3 1/2" disk) is double density, and the 1.44M microfloppy is high density.

double precision

Double precision is the use of two computer words instead of one to hold a number used for calculations, thus allowing twice as large a number for more arithmetic precision.

double punch

A *double punch* is more than one punched hole within a single column of a punched card.

double sided disk

A *double sided disk* is a floppy disk that is written (recorded) on both of its sides.

double strike

In printing, *double strike* is to print each character twice in order to darken the image.

down

When a computer fails to operate, it is *down*. Although usually due to an electronic or mechanical failure in the hardware, a computer can also be down due to a problem in the system software, such as the operating system or database management system. A communications channel is also down when it is unable to transfer data.

down link

A *down link* is the communications channel from a satellite to an earth station.

download

Download is to transmit data from a central computer to a remote computer or from a file server to a personal computer. Download typically implies the transmission of an entire file, such as an application program or a word processing document, rather than a single record. Contrast with *upload*.

downtime

Downtime is the time during which a computer is not functioning due to hardware or system software failure. That's when you truly understand how important it is to have reliable hardware.

downward compatible

Downward compatible refers to software that will run without modification on smaller or earlier models of a computer system. Contrast with *upward compatible*, which is software that will run on larger or later models of a computer system.

DP

See *data processing*.

DPMA

(Data Processing Management Association) *DPMA* is a membership organization, founded in 1951, with over 40,000 directors and managers of data processing installations, programmers, systems analysts and research specialists. The *DPMA* is the founder of the Certificate in Data Processing (CDP) examination program, now administrated by an international organization. It also offers many professional educational programs and seminars, in addition to sponsoring student organizations around the country interested in data processing. For more information, contact DPMA, 505 Busse Highway, Park Ridge, IL 60068, (312) 825-8124.

DPS

DPS is a series of Honeywell Bull minicomputers.

Drafix

Drafix 1 Plus and *Drafix 3-D Modeler* are 2-D and 3-D computer-aided design packages respectively from Foresight Resources Corporation that run on IBM compatible pcs and the Atari ST. Drafix features a unique user interface that provides constant on-screen information during drawing. Drafix combines professional-level features, such as curve fitting, multiple fonts and isometric slant.

drag

In computer graphics, *drag* refers to moving an image on screen in which its complete movement is visible from its starting location to its destination. The movement may be activated with a stylus, mouse or keyboard keys.

drain

A *drain* is the output side, or receiving side of the bridge, in a field effect transistor (MOS transistor). When the *gate* is charged, current flows from the *source* to the drain. Same as *collector* in a bipolar transistor.

DRAM

See *dynamic RAM*.

DRAW

(Direct Read After Write) The *DRAW* method reads the data right after it has been written to immediately check for errors in the recording process.

drawing program

A *drawing program* is a graphics software package that allows the user to design and illustrate an endless variety of products and objects. Drawing programs maintain an image in vector graphics format, which means that all the elements of the graphic object can be easily isolated and manipulated individually. Drawing programs and computer-aided design (CAD) programs are similar; however, drawing programs usually provide a large number of special effects for fancy illustration purposes, while CAD programs provide ultra-precise dimensioning and positioning of each graphic element in order that the objects can be transferred to other systems for engineering analysis and manufacturing. CAD programs are also specialized for different categories, such as architectural and mechanical design. Contrast with *paint program*, which maintains images in raster format. See *graphics*.

DRDBMS

(Distributed Relational DataBase Management System) A *DRDBMS* is a relational database management system that manages distributed databases. See *distributed database management system*.

drift

A *drift* is a change in frequency or time synchronization of a signal that occurs slowly.

drive

(1) A *drive* is an electromechanical device that spins disks and tapes at a specified speed. Drive also refers to the entire peripheral unit such as *disk drive* or *tape drive*.

(2) *Drive* is to provide power and signals to a device. For example, "this control unit can drive up to 15 terminals."

driver

(1) A *driver*, or *device driver*, is a program routine that contains the machine codes necessary to control the operation of a peripheral device. For example, a printer driver contains the instructions necessary to print boldface and underline, change fonts and eject the paper. A disk driver contains the instructions to store and retrieve data on a particular type of disk.

Drivers are required for each unique display screen, mouse, graphics tablet, disk, tape and printer used. Drivers normally come with the operating system, but, with personal computers, there is such a proliferation of hardware enhancements that the operating system does not support every device on the market. In these cases, drivers are supplied by the maker of the new device or by the vendor of the application software. For example, word processing packages come with printer drivers for many popular printers. Graphics programs and desktop publishing programs come with drivers for popular tablets and printers. Before using a new hardware device or running a new software package, users must install the appropriate driver in their computer.

(2) A *driver* is a device that provides signals or electrical current to activate a transmission line or display screen. See *line driver*.

drop in

A *drop in* is the recognition of a 1 bit on a magnetic medium that was not intentionally recorded there. It may be due to a defect in the recording surface or to a malfunction in the transfer process.

drop out

(1) On magnetic media, a *drop out* is a recorded bit that has lost its strength due to a defect in the recording surface or a malfunction of the recording process.

(2) In data transmission, a *drop out* is a momentary loss of signal that is due to a malfunction in the system or excessive noise.

drum

See *magnetic drum*.

drum plotter

A *drum plotter* is a graphics plotter that wraps the paper around a drum. It uses pens for plotting, and the drum turns to produce one direction of the plot. See *plotter*.

drum printer

A *drum printer* is a line printer that uses formed character images around a cylindrical drum as its printing mechanism. There is a band of characters for each print position. When the desired character for the selected print position has rotated around to the hammer line, the hammer hits the paper from behind and pushes it into the ribbon and onto the character.

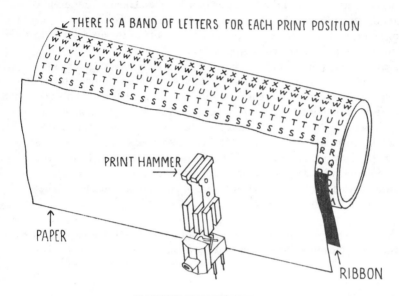

DRUM PRINTER

dry plasma etching

Dry plasma etching is a method for inscribing a pattern on a wafer by shooting hot ions through a mask to evaporate the silicon dioxide insulation layer. Dry plasma etching replaces the wet processing method that uses film and acid for developing the pattern.

drystone

See *Dhrystone*.

DSA

(Distributed Systems Architecture) *DSA* is a set of rules and protocols that govern Honeywell Bull communications networks.

DSS

See *decision support system*.

DTE

(Data Terminating Equipment) A *DTE* is a communications device that is typically a terminal or computer. It is the source or destination of signals on a communications network.

DTS

(Digital Termination Service) *DTS* is a digital communications service provided directly to the user's premises.

dual in-line package

See *DIP*.

dumb terminal

A *dumb terminal* is a display terminal without processing capability. Dumb terminals are asynchronous communications terminals that are entirely dependent on the main computer for processing. Contrast with *intelligent terminal*, which has processing capability. Also contrast with *smart terminal*, which has built-in display features, such as underline, boldface and blinking characters.

dump

A *dump* is an unformatted printout of data or instructions. A disk or tape dump is not easily recognized without a record layout that describes the organization of the data. See *memory dump*.

duplex channel

A *duplex channel* is a pathway that allows transmission in both directions at the same time. Same as *full-duplex*.

duplexed system

A *duplexed system* is two systems that are functionally identical to each other. They both may perform the same functions, or one system may be in standby mode, ready to take over if the other one fails.

duplicate key

A *duplicate key* is a record that contains the same identification data as another record in the file. Duplicate keys may or may not be permitted in the database. For example, account numbers are often the primary key in a file and cannot be duplicated, since no two customers or employees should be assigned the same account number. Dates may be a secondary key in a file and are naturally and often duplicated as there are many transactions for the same date.

Dvorak keyboard

A *Dvorak keyboard* is a keyboard with a different alphabet layout than the keyboard that is universally used. The original typewriter keyboard, called a *qwerty* keyboard (q,w,e,r,t and y are the first letters on the top row), was designed for mechanical typewriters in the late 1800s. The qwerty keyboard layout was chosen to actually slow down the typist in order to prevent the type slugs from jamming.

In the 1930s, August Dvorak, professor of Education at the University of Washington, and his brother-in-law, William Dealey, conceived a new keyboard that would considerably speed up typing. The Dvorak keyboard is designed so that 70% of all the words are typed on the home row, compared to only 32% with the qwerty keyboard. In addition, more words are typed using both hands than with the qwerty method. In an eight-hour day, an average qwerty typist's fingers travel 16 miles, while a Dvorak typist's fingers travel only one mile.

The Dvorak keyboard is built into the Apple IIc and IIGS and can be switched easily. With a keyboard, or macro, processor, virtually any personal computer can be set up with the Dvorak layout.

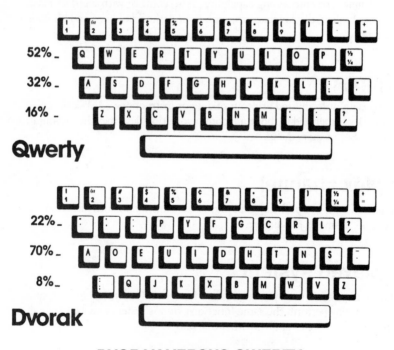

DVORAK VERSUS QWERTY
(Courtesy Dvorak International Federation)

In the Dvorak keyboard, 70% of the keystrokes are made on the home row compared to 32% with the qwerty keyboard.

May 12, 1936   A. DVORAK ET AL   2.040,248

TYPEWRITER KEYBOARD

Filed May 21, 1932

THE ORIGINAL DVORAK KEYBOARD

(Courtesy Dvorak International Federation)

DVST

(Direct View Storage Tube) A *DVST* is a graphics terminal that maintains the image on screen without continuous refreshing from the computer. Any changes to the image require that the entire screen be erased and redrawn from scratch. This design is contrary to the common display technique that constantly refreshes the screen many times each second whether the image is changed or not. DVST is an earlier technology that is no longer manufactured.

DXF

DXF is a 2-D graphics file format developed by AutoDesk for the AutoCAD system. Many CAD systems import and export the DXF format for graphics interchange.

dyadic

Dyadic means two and refers to operations in which two components are used or work together; for example, dyadic processors are two computers working in a multiprocessing environment.

dye polymer recording

Dye polymer recording refers to a category of optical recording techniques that use dyed plastic layers as the recording medium. For example, in certain write once read many (WORM) devices, a single dye polymer layer is used as the recording surface.

Dye polymer recording for erasable optical disks uses a recording surface of two dyed plastic layers. The top layer is called the retention layer and the bottom layer is the expansion layer. A 1 bit is created (written) by shining a laser beam through the top retention layer and into the bottom expansion layer, which heats the area and causes it to expand into the retention layer to form a bump. The bumps in the retention layer are the actual bits that are read by the unit. In order to erase a bit, a laser with a different wavelength is used to strike the retention layer, and the bump subsides. See *optical disk*.

dynamic

Dynamic refers to operations that are performed on the spot, while the program is running. In the expression, "the buffers are dynamically created," dynamic implies that the space is not fixed or reserved beforehand.

dynamic address translation

In a virtual memory system, *dynamic address translation* is the ability to determine what the real address is at the time of execution.

dynamic RAM

Dynamic RAM is the most common type of electronic memory used in computers today. Dynamic RAM (DRAM) architecture usually uses one transistor and a capacitor (tiny storage tank) that holds a charge to represent a 1 bit. The capacitors must be energized hundreds of times per second in order to maintain the correct charges. Contrast with *static RAM*, which is usually faster and does not require constant refreshing. Unlike firmware chips, such as ROMs and PROMs, both varieties of RAM lose their content when the power is turned off.

dynamic range

The *dynamic range* is a range of signals from the weakest to the strongest.

Eagle

Eagle is a database application language from Migent, Inc., that runs on IBM compatible pcs under the Emerald Bay database engine. Introduced in 1988, and developed by Wayne Ratliff, creator of dBASE II, Eagle is an advanced programming language that can handle text as well as data. Eagle comes in both interpreter and compiler form and includes a report writer and forms generator as well as a database administrator that maintains the data dictionary and security functions.

EAM

(Electronic Accounting Machine) EAM is another term for unit record equipment, the punched card tabulating machines that were the first data processing machines.

EAM ROOM (1952)
(Courtesy IBM)

early binding

See *binding time*.

EAROM

(Electrically Alterable Read Only Memory) Same as *EEPROM*.

earth station

An *earth station* is a transmitting and receiving station for satellite communications. An earth station's antenna is shaped like a dish, which is used for microwave transmission to and from the satellite.

EARTH STATION

easy to learn, easy to use

Easy to learn refers to software that is logically designed and capable of being used right away. Easy to learn is not hard to figure out. If you can make the program work right away, it's easy to learn. Easy to learn programs have help screens that really help you figure out what to do.

Easy to learn implies easy to use right away, but it does not imply easy to use after you're thoroughly familiar with it. The very simple menus that coddled you in the beginning are the ones that become tiresome and time consuming when you use the program day in and day out. The best programs let you record the menu selections you make so that you can play them back automatically. This is called writing or recording a *script* or *macro*.

EasyCAD 2

EasyCAD 2 is a computer-aided design (CAD) program from Evolution Computing that runs on IBM compatible pcs. It's a full-featured CAD program that is well-designed and is known for its ease of use. EasyCAD users can migrate to the more sophisticated FastCAD, which looks almost identical on screen, but provides multiple windows and is designed for high-speed CAD operations.

EBCDIC

(Extended Binary Coded Decimal Interchange Code) Pronounced "eb-suh-dick," EBCDIC is a binary code for representing data developed by IBM as part of its System/360 series of mainfames in 1964. It is built into all IBM and compatible mainframes, most IBM minicomputers and other mainframes. EBCDIC is an 8-bit code allowing 256 possible character combinations. EBCDIC stores one alphanumeric character or two decimal digits within a single byte.

EBCDIC and ASCII are the two codes most widely used to represent data.

e-beam

See *electron beam*.

ECF

(Enhanced Connectivity Facilities) ECF is an application program from IBM that allows users of personal computers to query and download data from IBM mainframes as well as issue mainframe commands. ECF connects to the Server-Requestor Programming Interface (SRPI) protocol and is planned to link to the Advanced Program-to-Program Communications (APPC) protocol.

echo check

In communications, *echo check* is an error checking method that retransmits the data back to the sending device for comparison with the original.

echo suppressor

An *echo suppressor* is a device on a telephone line that blocks the listening side while one person is talking in order to eliminate echos. When there's no constant signal (speech) for about a tenth of a second, the echo supressor releases the block.

echoplex

In communications, *echoplex* is a transmission technique in which the sending terminal does not display the data being keyed in. Instead, the data is transmitted to the receiving station, which then retransmits it back to the sending terminal for display.

ECL

(Emitter-Coupled Logic) ECL is a type of microelectronic circuit design that is noted for its extremely fast switching speeds. ECL is a variety of bipolar transistor.

ECLIPSE

ECLIPSE is a series of 32-bit minicomputers from Data General Corporation. The development of the initial 32-bit ECLIPSE MV/Family superminicomputer, the MV/8000, was the subject of Tracy Kidders' best selling book, "Soul of a New Machine." The ECLIPSE line, running under the AOS/VS operating system, ranges from a single board processor up to dual-processor configurations that can handle over 500 terminals.

ECMA

(European Computer Manufacturer's Association) *ECMA*, headquartered in Geneva, Switzerland, is the European counterpart of CBEMA (Computer and Business Equipment Manufacturer's Association) in the United States.

edge connector

An *edge connector* is a row of etched lines on the edge of a printed circuit board, which is inserted into a slot for interconnection with a motherboard or some other printed circuit board.

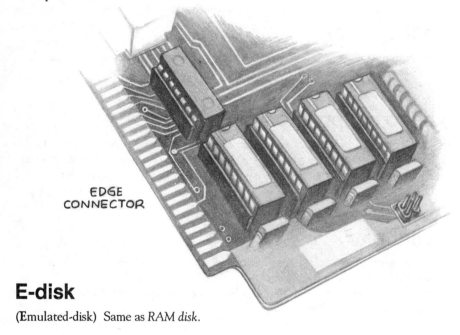

EDGE
CONNECTOR

E-disk

(Emulated-disk) Same as *RAM disk*.

EDI

(Electronic Data Interchange) *EDI* is the electronic communication of transactions, such as orders, confirmations and invoices, between organizations. For example, instead of printing purchase orders, stuffing them into envelopes and mailing them, EDI provides instant transfer of information as well as confirmation from one company to another. Independent service organizations provide EDI services that enable users to interconnect with another organization's network regardless of type of equipment used.

edit check

An *edit check*, or edit test, is a program instruction or subroutine that tests for valid input in a data entry program.

edit instruction

An *edit instruction* is usually a hardware instruction, but may also be implemented in software, which inserts decimal points, commas and dollar signs, etc., into a field of data for display or printing purposes.

edit key

The *edit key* is a particular keyboard key used by a word processing or database program that allows the user to enter the edit mode in order to change or replace existing text or data.

edit mode

An *edit mode* is the ability to change existing text or data. Some word processing programs require that you change into edit mode in order to add or replace existing text. Database management programs also provide edit modes for updating existing data.

edit program

(1) An *edit* program is a data entry program that validates user input and stores the newly created records in the file.

(2) An *edit* program is an update program that allows users to change data that already exists in a file.

editor

See *text editor* and *linkage editor*.

EDLIN

EDLIN is an elementary text editor that is part of Microsoft's DOS operating system. With EDLIN, users can create and modify simple batch files.

EDP

(Electronic Data Processing) *EDP* was the first acronym used to identify the electronic computing field.

E-drive

(Emulated-drive) Same as *RAM disk*.

EDSAC

(Electronic Delay Storage Automatic Calculator) The *EDSAC*, developed by Maurice Wilkes at Cambridge University in England and completed in 1949, was one of the first stored program computers and one of the first to use binary digits. Its memory was 512 36-bit words of liquid mercury delay lines, and its input and output were provided by paper tape. The EDSAC could do about 700 additions per second and 200 multiplications per second. It was in routine use at the university until 1958.

EDSAC
(Courtesy Science Museum, London)

education

Education is the teaching of concepts that relate to a subject. Education about computers includes information about computer systems and information systems. Contrast with *training*, which provides detailed instruction about the use of a particular product.

edutainment

Edutainment is educational materials that are inherently entertaining. As interactive media, such as CD-I, become accepted for consumer use, quality edutainment will become a critical factor in the success of educational discs.

EEMS

(Enhanced Expanded Memory Specification) *EEMS* is an enhanced version of the EMS standard. See *EMS*.

E/EMS

(Enhanced/Expanded Memory Specification) *E/EMS* is the designation for a group of plug-in memory boards for IBM compatible pcs that conform to the Expanded Memory Specification and the Enhanced Expanded Memory Specification.

EEPROM

(Electrically Erasable Programmable Read Only Memory) An *EEPROM* is a non-volatile storage chip that holds its content until erased. Since the computer can erase it internally and then write data into it again, it functions like a RAM chip; however it is slower and considerably more expensive than RAM. EEPROMs are used in terminals and devices that must maintain up-to-date data without power. For example, a price list could be stored in EEPROM chips in a point-of-sale cash register terminal and be maintained even though the unit is turned off at night. When a price changes, the chip can be updated from the central computer.

EFT

(Electronic Funds Transfer) *EFT* is the exchange of money via communications and refers to any financial transaction that originates at a terminal and transfers a sum of money from one account to another.

EGA

(Enhanced Graphics Adapter) *EGA* is a video display board from IBM that is available as a plug-in board for IBM PC and compatible personal computers.

EGA generates medium-resolution color text and graphics. Its text mode provides 25 lines of 80 columns in up to 16 colors and uses an 8x14 dot cell for each character. Its graphics mode provides 640x350 pixels in up to 16 colors from a palette of 64.

The EGA has previous modes built in; thus, software written for the MDA and CGA display standards will run on the EGA. The EGA requires a digital RGB "Enhanced Color Display" or equivalent monitor.

EIA

(Electronic Industries Association) *EIA* is a membership organization, founded in 1924, that includes manufacturers of electronic parts and systems. With over 1,200 members, EIA sponsors electronic shows and seminars and gives many awards for outstanding contributions to the electronics industry. The EIA sets electrical and electronic interface standards, such as the EIA RS-232-C interface. For more information, contact EIA, 2001 I Street, N.W., Washington, DC 20006, (202) 457-4900.

EIS

(Executive Information System) An *EIS* is an information system for managers that consolidates and summarizes ongoing transactions within the organization. An EIS should be able to provide management with all the information it requires at all times from external as well as internal sources.

EISA

(Extended Industry Standard Architecture) Pronounced "eesa," *EISA* is a bus standard for IBM compatible pcs that extends the AT bus architecture to 32 bits and allows more than one CPU to easily share the bus (multiprocessing). EISA was announced in late 1988 as a counter to IBM's more advanced Micro Channel in its PS/2 series. Existing PC and AT boards, which cannot plug into the Micro Channel, can plug into an EISA slot.

electricity

Electricity is the natural energy found in all matter. In order to harness it, excess electron particles are "borrowed" from atoms in the earth. The electrons, which we call "negatively charged," have an inclination to restore themselves and naturally flow back to earth, which is why the ground is the receiving side of a circuit. The speed of electricity is the same as the speed of light (approx. 186,000 miles per second). In a wire, it is slowed due to the resistance in the material.

The flow of electrons in a circuit is measured by its pressure, or force, in *volts* and by the size of current (thickness of the wire) in *amperes*, or *amps*. The total amount of energy is computed in *watts* by multiplying volts times amps.

Although we seem to know a lot about electricity and have been able to put it to a never-ending variety of uses, we only know how it works. We don't know, and most likely never will know, why.

electrode

An *electrode* is a device that emits or controls the flow of electricity.

electroluminescent display

Electroluminescent display is a flat panel display screen that contains a powdered or thin film phosphor layer sandwiched between an x-axis and a y-axis panel. An individual dot (pixel) is selectable by charging an x-wire on one panel and a y-wire on the other. When the x-y coordinate is charged, the phosphor in that vicinity emits visible light. Phosphors are typically amber in color, but green is also used. In the 1990s, color electroluminescent displays will become available.

For portable applications, electroluminescent displays are rugged, light weight alternatives to cathode ray tubes (CRTs). They use small amounts of power and also provide a wide viewing angle.

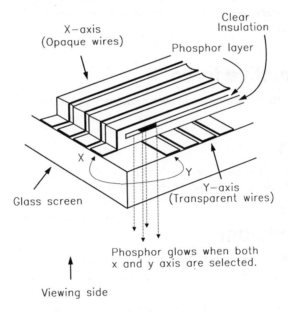

ELECTROLUMINESCENT SCREEN

(Courtesy Planar Systems, Inc.)

electromagnet

An *electromagnet* is a magnet that is energized by electricity. A coil of wire is wrapped around an iron core, and when current flows in the wire, the core generates an energy called magnetic *flux*.

electromagnetic radiation

Electromagnetic radiation is the energy transmitted through the air by a radio transmitter. By converting electrical energy into magnetic energy, we are able to control and direct it more accurately for wireless transmission.

All radiating energy in the universe is classified as electromagnetic radiation, which includes gamma rays, x-rays, ultraviolet light, visible light, infrared light and radar.

electromagnetic spectrum

The *electromagnetic spectrum* refers to the entire range of electromagnetic radiation.

electromechanical

Electromechanical refers to systems that use electricity to run moving parts. Disk drives, printers and motors are examples of electromechanical devices. Electromechanical systems are difficult to design, since metal and plastic parts eventually wear and break down.

electromotive force

Electromotive force is the pressure in an electric circuit that is measured in *volts*.

electron

An *electron* is an elementary particle that circles the nucleus of an atom. Electrons are considered to be negatively charged particles.

electron beam

An *electron beam* is a stream of electrons, or electricity, that is directed towards a receiving object.

electron gun

An *electron gun* is a device which creates a fine beam of electrons that is focused on a phosphor screen in a cathode ray tube (CRT).

electron tube

Same as *vacuum tube*.

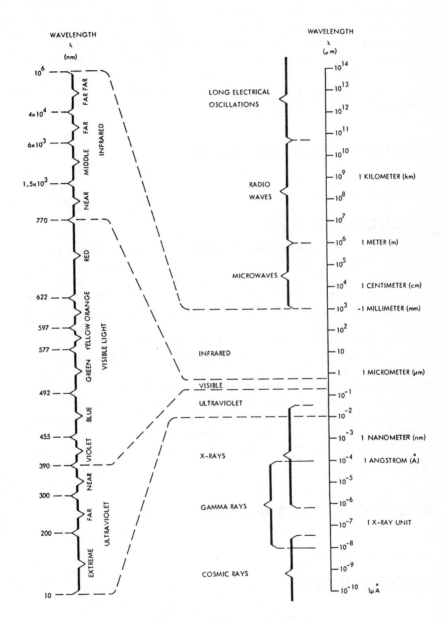

ELECTROMAGNETIC SPECTRUM

(Courtesy RCA)

electronic

Electronic is the use of electricity in intelligence-bearing devices, such as telephones, radios, televisions, instrumentation, analog and digital computers and telecommunications. Electricity, which is used as raw power for heating, lighting and motors, is considered electrical, and not electronic. Although coined before, the magazine "Electronics" (first published April 1930) brought the term to popularity. The subheading of the magazine then read: Electron Tubes - Their Radio, Audio, Visio and Industrial Applications. The word electronic was derived from the use of the electron tube, or vacuum tube, which was originally used as an amplifier of electronic signals.

electronic bulletin board

See *bulletin board*.

electronic circuit

An *electronic circuit* is an integrated series of electronic components that perform a function. Electronic circuits are pathways through which electricity is directed in a prescribed pattern to accomplish some task. Electronic circuits used in digital computers deal with discrete on/off pulses (bits). Electronic circuits used in analog computers or devices, such as radio and television, deal with electrical vibrations (frequencies).

A digital circuit can be conceptualized as a mass of plumbing where the circuit pathways are the water pipes, the transistors are the valves and the electricity is the water. Imagine opening a valve, and the water that passes through it and down a pipe will eventually reach a second valve, causing it to turn on, allowing water in another pipe to flow through the second valve, which will reach another valve, and so on. A resistor could be viewed as a large pipe that narrows into a pipe with a smaller diameter, a capacitor as a storage tank, and a diode as a one-way valve, allowing water to flow in only one direction. See *chip* and *Boolean logic*.

electronic funds transfer

See *EFT*.

electronic mail

Electronic mail is the transmission of letters, messages and memos over a communications network. The backbone of an electronic mail system is a communications network that connects remote terminals to a central system or a local area network that interconnects personal computers. Users can send mail to a single recipient or they can broadcast it to any number of selected users on the system. The method for receiving mail depends on the sophistication of the system. When multitasking personal computers and workstations are used, mail can be delivered to users while they are working on something else. Otherwise, users have to interrogate their mailboxes (disk space) in a central system or file server. More sophisticated systems will prompt users if they haven't responded to certain memos after some period of time.

Electronic mail programs often come with local area network software or are add-on options. Or, they are independent programs designed to work with a particular network environment.

A simple form of electronic mail is the use of facsimile (fax) terminals in remote locations, which use the public telephone network for transmission. The advantage of facsimile is that any form of information printed on paper can be transmitted.

Electronic Message Service

See *EMS (2)*.

electronic messaging

Same as *electronic mail*.

electronic printer

An *electronic printer* is a printer that uses electronics to control the printing mechanism. The term refers to a variety of computer printers, including laser printers and line printers.

electronic publishing

Electronic publishing is the providing of information in electronic form to readers or subscribers of the service. See *information utility* and *videotex*.

electronic spreadsheet

See *spreadsheet*.

electronic switching system

See *ESS*.

electronic typewriter

See *memory typewriter* and *word processing*.

electrophotographic

Electrophotographic is the printing technique that is used in laser printers and copy machines. A negative image made of dots of light is painted onto a photosensitive drum or belt that has been electrically charged. The light comes from a laser, a row of light emitting diodes (LEDs) or liquid crystal shutters that function as gates.

Wherever light is applied, the drum becomes uncharged. A toner (dry ink) is applied to the drum and it adheres to the charged areas of the drum. The drum transfers the toner to the paper, and pressure and heat fuse the toner and paper permanently.

Some electrophotographic systems use a positive approach in which the toner is attracted to the laser-produced latent image.

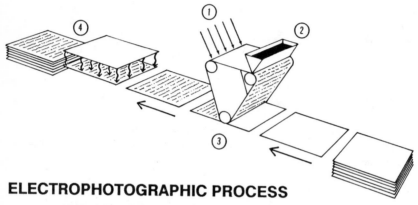

ELECTROPHOTOGRAPHIC PROCESS

(1) The belt (or drum) is charged.
(2) Dry ink (toner) is adhered to the charged areas.
(3) The toner is transferred onto the paper.
(4) The toner is fused to the paper.

electrosensitive printer

An *electrosensitive printer* is a dot matrix printer that burns away dots on the outer silver coating of a special black paper.

electrostatic

Electrostatic refers to electrical charges that are stationary. There is no electrical current flowing in an electrostatic charge.

electrostatic plotter

An *electrostatic plotter* is a plotter that uses a special paper that is charged as it passes by a line of electrodes. Toner is then applied to the charged paper.

electrostatic printer

Same as *electrostatic plotter*.

elegant program

An *elegant program* is a program that is simple in design, uses the least amount of memory and runs fast.

elite

Elite is a typeface that prints 12 characters per linear inch.

em

In typography, an *em* is a unit of measure equal to the width of the capital letter M in a particular font.

E-mail

See *electronic mail*.

embedded command

In word processing, an *embedded command* is a code inserted within the text document that is used to instruct the printer to change its printing characteristics, such as to change fonts, print underline and boldface. The embedded commands may be partially or totally invisible on the display screen unless revealed with a special command. At print time, the embedded commands are converted into the actual machine codes needed to activate the printer.

These embedded commands are typically incompatible from one word processing system to the other.

embedded system

An *embedded system* is a specialized computer that is used as a control function within the device it's controlling, for example, in avionics, rockets and space vehicles. An embedded system implies custom-programmed software that usually integrates system software and application software functions.

Emerald Bay

Emerald Bay is a database engine from Migent, Inc., that runs on IBM compatible pcs. Introduced in 1988 and written by Wayne Ratliff, creator of dBASE II, Emerald Bay was designed as a central database management system for local area network use. Although it can be used on a single computer, it was designed to serve multiple users from a network file server. Emerald Bay is an advanced database product which provides a binary field that can store all forms of information, including text, graphics images and voice (virtually anything that can be digitized). It is designed to be interfaced with many different language products, or "surfaces," as coined by Mr. Ratliff. The interfaces announced by Migent at the time of introduction are Eagle, a database application language, an interface for the C language and Summit, a utility program that lets Lotus users access Emerald Bay for their 1-2-3 spreadsheets.

emitter

The *emitter* is the source of current in a bipolar transistor. Same as *source* in a metal oxide semiconductor (MOS) transistor.

emitter-coupled logic

See *ECL*.

EMM

(Expanded Memory Manager) An EMM is a software routine that handles the expanded memory in an IBM compatible pc. In an 80386 model, the EMM can simulate expanded memory in normal extended memory without requiring special EMS (expanded memory) boards. See *EMS*.

EMS

(1) (Expanded Memory Specification) *EMS* is a technique for going beyond the standard memory limitation in IBM compatible pcs when Microsoft's DOS operating system is used. EMS increases the amount of memory DOS applications can work with from one to 32 megabytes.

In 8086 and 80286 machines (IBM XT, AT and compatibles), EMS is achieved by plugging an EMS memory board, such as Intel's Above Board, into the computer. In 80386 machines, EMS can be simulated in normal (extended) memory with a memory manager program, such as Quarterdeck's Expanded Memory Manager (QEMM-386) and Microsoft Windows/386.

In order for a single program to take advantage of EMS, such as a memory-based spreadsheet, it must be written to the EMS standard, and many DOS software packages have been modified accordingly. The extra memory can be utilized for normal DOS programs when memory managers and windowing environments are used with DOS. They allow multiple programs to be placed in memory at one time and let users instantly switch back and forth between them.

An EMS board tricks the operating system by swapping segments of high-end memory back and forth into the lower memory (below one megabyte) that DOS can physically handle.

In 1984, Lotus, Intel and Microsoft introduced the EMS technique, which increased memory from one to eight megabytes. Later, AST, Quadram and Ashton-Tate introduced a superset of EMS, called *EEMS* (Enhanced Expanded Memory Spec) in order to increase performance and flexibility. For example,

AST's Rampage 286 (EMS board) supports EEMS. In 1987, Lotus, Intel and Microsoft introduced EMS Version 4.0, which increases memory to 32 megabytes and incorporates both previous standards.

Note: Expanded memory is not extended memory. Extended memory is normal, additional memory beyond one megabyte, which has always been available on 80286 and 80386 machines even though DOS and DOS programs can't use it.

(2) (Electronic Message Service) EMS is a portion of the radio spectrum that has been assigned to electronic messaging over digital satellite circuits.

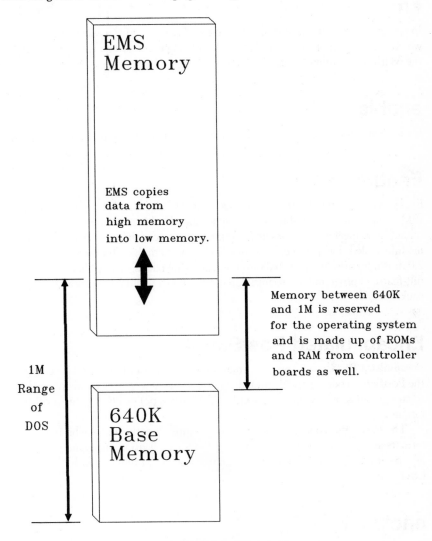

EXPANDED MEMORY

emulator

An *emulator* is a device that is built to work like another. A computer can be designed to emulate another computer and execute the same software that was written to run in that machine. A terminal can be designed to emulate various communications protocols and hook into different networks. The emulator itself can be hardware, software or both.

en

In typography, an *en* is a unit of measure equal to one half the width of an em, which is the width of a capital M in the font being used. An en is also typically the width of one numeric digit.

enable

Enable is to turn on. Contrast with *disable*, which is to turn off.

Enable

Enable is an integrated software package from The Software Group that runs on IBM compatible pcs. Enable provides relational database, word processing, spreadsheet, business graphics and communications capabilities. An additional module, called "Perspective," provides 3D business graphics, but as of Version 2.0, it is not entirely integrated into the rest of the package. Enable is a full-featured program with sophisticated capabilities rivaling many stand-alone packages.

Encapsulated PostScript

Encapsulated PostScript is the file format for the PostScript language. It contains the PostScript code for the document as well as preview images in bit-mapped (raster graphics) representation in either TIFF (IBM pc) or PICT (Macintosh) formats.

The PostScript code drives a PostScript printer directly, and the bit map formats allow the image to be manipulated in an application program. In Microsoft DOS and OS/2 files, Encapsulated PostScript files use an EPS extension.

encipher

Encipher is to encode data for security purposes. See *encryption*.

encode

(1) *Encode* is to assign a code to represent data, such as a parts code.

(2) Same as *encipher* or *encrypt*.

encryption

Encryption is the encoding of data for security purposes by converting the standard data code into a proprietary code before transmission over a network. The encrypted data must be decoded at the receiving station. See *DES*.

end key

The *end key* is a keyboard key that is used for cursor movement. It is used to move the cursor to the bottom of the screen or to the end of a list or file. It may also be used to move the cursor to the next word or field.

end points

In vector graphics, the *end points* are the two ends of a line (vector). In 2-D graphics, each end point is typically made up of two numbers representing coordinates on two planes (x and y). In 3-D, each end point is typically made up of three numbers representing coordinates on three planes (x, y and z).

end user

An *end user* is a user of the computer's output. With personal computers, end users are also the computer's operator, as well as the systems analyst and data administrator. When it comes to making the whole thing work, they sometimes function as systems programmers.

endless loop

An *endless loop* is a program loop that never ends. Loops are a basic programming structure that repeat a set of instructions until a condition changes. If by error, the condition never changes, the computer will always repeat the same steps. An endless loop can be intentional, for example, a series of ads on screen in a storefront that are designed to go 24 hours a day.

endnote

See *footnote*.

engine

(1) *Engine* is another term for a processor, such as a CPU or graphics processor. Like any engine, the faster it is, the quicker the job gets done.

(2) *Engine* sometimes refers to system software; for example, a database engine.

Enhanced Graphics Adapter

See *EGA*.

Enhanced Keyboard

The *Enhanced Keyboard* is a 101-key keyboard from IBM that supersedes the PC and AT keyboards. There are two more function keys (F11 and F12) on the Enhanced keyboard, and all the function keys are in a row across the top of the keyboard instead of along the left side. Since there are millions of keyboards with the original function key layout, it is now impossible for a software vendor to design the function keys intelligently. The keys that are easy to reach on one keyboard are difficult to reach on the other, and vice versa.

The enhanced keyboard has a separate cursor key cluster that is located between the original numeric/cursor combination keypad and the letter keys. The escape key is relocated from the right side to the left side. Additional control and alt keys have been added to the right side of the keyboard, but the original control key has been moved down to a more awkward location for touch typists. The delete key has been duplicated in a new cluster above the cursor keys, but it is still in a location that makes it easy to delete text inadvertently. The backspace key, which was shortened in the AT keyboard, has been restored to its original length, making it easier to reach.

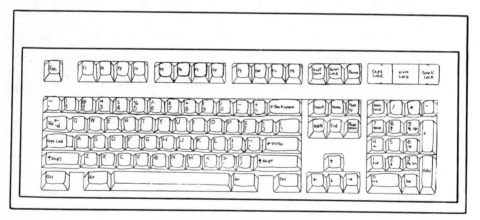

ENHANCED KEYBOARD

enhancement

An *enhancement* is any improvement made to a software package or hardware device.

ENIAC

(Electronic Numerical Integrator And Calculator) The *ENIAC* was the first operational electronic digital computer and used almost 18,000 vacuum tubes for its internal construction. Developed for the U. S. Army by John Presper Eckert, Jr., and John William Mauchly at the Moore School of Electrical Engineering, University of Pennsylvania, it was completed in 1946. Taking up 1,800 square feet of floor space, the decimal-based ENIAC performed approximately 5,000 additions per second. ENIAC was the forerunner of all the subsequent machines that led up to the creation of the UNIVAC I, the first computer that was built in quantity.

ENIAC

(Courtesy The Moore School of Electrical Engineering, University of Pennsylvania)

enquiry character

In communications, an *enquiry character* is a control character that requests a response from the receiving station.

enter key

The *enter key*, also called the *return key*, is the key on a computer keyboard that is pressed to end a line of input. It is similar to the carriage return key on a typewriter; however, in word processing, its function differs slightly from that of a typewriter. See *return key*.

Enterprise System Architecture

See *ESA/370* and *MVS/ESA*.

entity

In database management, an *entity* is a record. An *entity type* is a particular kind of file, for example, a customer, employee or product file.

entry

An *entry* is the input of an item or set of items at a terminal. See *data entry*.

entry point

In programming, an *entry point* is the starting point of the instructions in a subroutine.

envelope

(1) An *envelope* is a range of frequencies for a particular operation.

(2) An *envelope* is a group of bits or items that is packaged and treated as a single unit.

environment

The *environment* is the computer system that application programs are running in, which includes the computer hardware and system software (operating system, data communications and database systems). It can also include the programming language used. The term often refers only to the operating system; for example, "This program is running in a UNIX environment."

EOF

(End Of File) In programming, when a sequential file is being searched, the program must test for *EOF*. The physical EOF designation is a special code written (recorded) on the storage medium.

epitaxial layer

In chip making, an *epitaxial layer* is a semiconductor layer that is created on top of the silicon base rather than below it. See *molecular beam epitaxy*.

EPROM

(Erasable Programmable Read Only Memory) An *EPROM* is a reusable PROM chip that holds its content until erased by being exposed to ultraviolet light. A special device called a PROM programmer is used to program them (write data into them) and reprogram them.

EPS, EPSF

See *Encapsulated PostScript Format*.

EQ

(EQual to) See *relational operators*.

equalization

In communications, *equalization* is a category of techniques that are used to reduce or eliminate transmission distortion in a line, typically a leased telephone line.

equation

An *equation* is an arithmetic expression that equates one set of conditions to another set. For example, $A = B + C$ is an equation. In a programming language, assignment statements take the form of an equation. $A = B + C$ would assign the sum of B and C to the variable A.

erase

See *delete*.

erase head

In a magnetic tape drive, the *erase head* erases the tape before a new block of data is recorded.

Eratosthenes's Sieve

See *Sieve of Eratosthenes*.

ergonomics

Ergonomics is the science of people-machine relationships. An ergonomically designed product implies that the device blends smoothly with a person's body or actions. "Egonomically designed" is a term that, like "user friendly," has been used too often and refers to almost any improvement over the competition or previous models.

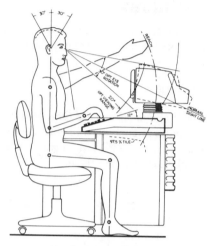

ERGONOMICS
(Courtesy Hewlett-Packard)

Erlang

An *Erlang* is a unit of traffic use that is used to specify the total capacity or average use of a telephone system. One Erlang is equivalent to the continuous usage of a telephone line. Traffic in Erlangs is the sum of the holding times of all lines divided by the period of measurement.

error checking

(1) *Error checking* is the testing for accurate transmission of data over a communications network or internally within the computer system. See *parity checking* and CRC.

(2) For data entry error checking, see *validity checking* and *edit checking*.

error detection & correction

See *error checking, validity checking* and *edit checking*.

error handling

Error handling is the way a software program responds to errors. Poorly written programs may just hang up the computer when the wrong data is entered or a system error occurs, such as a disk error. The measurement of quality in error handling is the degree to which the system informs the user of such error conditions and provides alternatives for continuing. This is an important part of the design of any software package.

error rate

The *error rate* is a measurement of the effectiveness of a communications channel. It is the ratio of the number of erroneous units of data, usually bits, to the total number of units of data transmitted.

ESA/370

(Enterprise System Architecture/370) *ESA/370* is a mainframe upgrade from IBM that increases the performance of its 4381 and 3090 medium to large-scale mainframes. Introduced in 1988, ESA/370 provides a number of performance enhancements, including a dramatic increase in virtual memory capability. See *MVS/ESA*.

ESC

See *escape character* and *escape key*.

escape character

An *escape character* is character 27 in the ASCII data code. It is often used in conjunction with other characters, to command a peripheral device, such as a display screen or printer. For example, an escape character, followed by the code &l10, sets the HP LaserJet printer to landscape mode.

escape key

The *escape key* is a keyboard key that is used in a variety of software packages. It's typically used to exit a mode or routine, but it also may be used to call up a routine or command sequence.

ESDI

(Enhanced Small Device Interface) The *ESDI* is a hardware standard for connecting disk and tape drives to computers. ESDI standards allow for the transfer of data from approximately one to three megabytes per second and can manage disk drives with up to one gigabyte of storage.

ESS

(1) (Electronic Switching System) An ESS is a large scale computer system manufactured by AT&T and is used by the common carriers to switch telephone conversations in a central office.

(2) (Executive Support System) See EIS.

Ethernet

Ethernet is a local area network developed by Xerox, Digital and Intel that interconnects personal computers via coaxial cable. It uses the CSMA/CD access method and transmits at 10 megabits per second. Ethernet uses a bus topology that can connect up to 1,024 personal computers and workstations within each main branch. Ethernet has evolved into the IEEE 802.3 standard.

The following example shows an Ethernet system running with a variety of network operating systems.

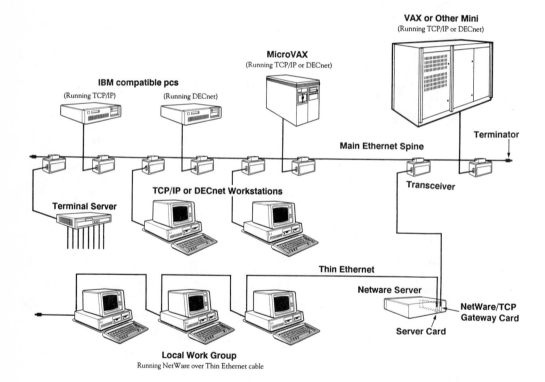

ETHERNET
(Courtesy Black Box Corporation)

This sample Ethernet installation uses TCP/IP, DECnet and NetWare Protocols)

E-time

See *execution time*.

even parity

See *parity*.

Excel

Excel is a spreadsheet program from Microsoft that runs on Macintosh and IBM compatible pcs. Excel is a full-featured program that can link many spreadsheets together for consolidation of data. Excel provides a wide variety of business graphics and charts and takes full advantage of a laser printer for making elaborate reports and presentation materials.

exception report

An *exception report* is a listing of abnormal items or items that fall outside of a specified range.

exclusive NOR

See *NOR*.

exclusive OR

See *OR*.

EXE file

In Microsoft's DOS and OS/2 operating systems, an *EXE file* is a machine language program that can be loaded and executed in the computer. EXE files are designed as relocatable files and can reside in any memory locations. Contrast with *COM file*, which is designed to work only in specific memory locations.

executable form

Executable form is a program in machine language ready to be executed in the computer.

executable program

An *executable program* is a program that is capable of being run in the computer.

execute

Execute is to carry out the instructions in a program. When a program is running in the computer, it is being executed.

execution time

The *execution time*, or *E-time*, is the time in which a single instruction is executed and makes up the last half of the instruction cycle.

executive

Same as *operating system*.

executive information system

See *EIS*.

exit

(1) *Exit* refers to getting out of what you're currently in. An exit option in a menu means to leave the mode or program you're currently working in. It's good practice to get into the habit of exiting a program before turning the computer off. Some programs don't close all the files properly until the exit is issued.

(2) In programming, *exit* refers to getting out of the loop, routine or function that the computer is currently in.

expanded memory

See *EMS*.

expanded memory manager

See *EMM*.

expander board

See *expansion board*.

expansion board

An *expansion board* increases the hardware capacity of a computer by expanding the number of printed circuit boards that can be plugged into it. The expansion board plugs into one of the existing expansion slots and connects to a box that contains several additional slots.

expansion slot

An *expansion slot* is a receptacle inside a computer or other electronic system that is used to plug in printed circuit boards. The number of expansion slots determines the amount of future expansion that is possible within the existing system. In a personal computer, the expansion slots are connected to the computer's bus.

ExperLogo

ExperLogo is a version of the Logo programming language from ExperTelligence that runs on the Macintosh personal computer. Although Logo is modeled after the LISP programming language, ExperLogo contains more functions similar to LISP than most versions of Logo.

expert system

An *expert system* is an artificial intelligence application that uses a knowledge base of human expertise to aid in solving problems. The degree of problem solving is based on the quality of the data and rules obtained from the human expert. Expert systems are designed to perform at a human expert level. In practice, they will perform both well below and well above that of an individual expert.

The expert system derives its answers by running the knowledge base through an inference engine, a software program that interacts with the user and processes the results from the rules and data in the knowledge base.

Expert systems are used in applications, such as medical diagnosis, equipment repair, investment analysis, financial, estate and insurance planning, route scheduling for delivery vehicles, contract bidding, counseling for self-service customers, production control and training.

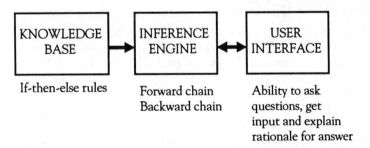

EXPERT SYSTEM

exponent

An *exponent* is a number written above the line and to the right of a number that indicates the power of a number, or how many zeros there are in a number. For example 10^3 indicates three zeros, or thousands, thus the number 467,000 can be stated as 467×10^3. On a display screen or printout, the same number is expressed as 467E3. In floating point arithmetic, the exponent raises the mantissa to a specified power.

exponential growth

Exponential growth implies extremely fast growth. On a chart, the line would curve up dramatically rather than be a straight line. Contrast with *linear growth*, which is an even growth pattern.

exponential smoothing

Exponential smoothing is technique used in forecasting.

expression

In programming, an *expression* is a written statement that describes a set of variables, data fields and/or constants that are combined with arithmetic, relational and/or logical operators. Like a mathematical equation, each item is evaluated individually and then combined in order to derive an answer. For example, **VALUE 2 * COST** and **PRODUCT = "HAT" AND COLOR = "GRAY"** are expressions.

extended ASCII

Extended ASCII is the last half of the ASCII code (characters 128 through 255). See *ASCII*.

Extended Edition

The *Extended Edition* is a version of the OS/2 operating system from IBM that includes communications and database management capabilities. The "Communications Manager" has built-in protocols (LU 6.2 and X.25) that allow it to interconnect with IBM mainframes. The "Database Manager" is built around IBM's SQL database language and is designed to facilitate file transfers between PS/2s and mainframes and to coexist in a distributed database environment. The Extended Edition takes full advantage of the PS/2's Micro Channel by being able to transfer data to and from a mainframe while performing other operations in a local mode.

extended maintenance

Extended maintenance is on-call service that is ordered for periods in addition to the primary period of maintenance.

extended memory

In 80286 and 80386-based IBM compatible pcs, *extended memory* is normal memory above one megabyte. Contrast with *expanded memory*, which is memory in this range that has been specialized to work with the limitation of Microsoft's DOS operating system and applications. In 80386-based machines, extended memory can be made to simulate expanded memory with memory management programs, such as Quarterdeck's QEMM or Windows/386. Many add-in memory boards can be set up as either extended memory or expanded memory. See *EMS*.

extensible language

An *extensible language* is a programming language that can be expanded by the user by adding such things as new control structures, statements or data types.

extension

An *extension* is a category name that is added to files created under Microsoft's DOS and OS/2 operating systems. All programs and most data files use standard extensions. However, many word processing text files do not, in which case users can set up their own filing system by creating extension names. When extensions are used, they are connected to the file name with a dot, for example, ANSI.SYS and SALES.DBF. The following are commonly used extensions:

Extension	Type of file	Software
EXE	Executable program	Compilers and assemblers
ASM	Source program	Intel Assembly language
BAK	Backup version	Common
BAS	Source program	BASIC
BAT	Batch	DOS and OS/2
C	Source program	C
CAP	Captions	Ventura Publisher
CGM	Graphics	Common vector & raster format
CHP	Chapter	Ventura Publisher
CIF	Chapter information	Ventura Publisher
COB	Source program	COBOL
COM	Executable program	Compilers and assemblers
DB	Database	Paradox
DBF	Database	dBASE
DBT	Text	dBASE
DCA	Text	IBM
DOC	Document	Multimate, Microsoft Word
DXF	Graphics	AutoCAD common
DWG	Graphics	AutoCAD proprietary
EPS	Graphics/Text	Encapsulated Postscript
EXE	Executable program	Compilers and assemblers
GEM	Graphics	GEM draw format (vector)
HPG	Graphics	Hewlett-Packard (vector)
IMG	Graphics	GEM paint format (raster)

NDX	Index	dBASE
OBJ	Object module	Compilers and assemblers
OVL	Executable program	Compilers and assemblers
PCT	Graphics	Macintosh
PCX	Graphics	PC Paintbrush
PDV	Printer driver	PC Paintbrush
PIC	Graphics	Lotus 1-2-3
PIC	Graphics	Micrografx products
PIF	Program information	Microsoft Windows
PRD	Printer driver	Microsoft Word
PRN	Printer driver	XyWrite
PRS	Printer driver	WordPerfect
PRG	Source program	dBASE
SLD	Graphics	AutoCAD slide format
STY	Style sheet	Ventura publisher
SYS	System	DOS and OS/2
TIF	Graphics	Common vector format
TMP	Temporary	Common
TXT	ASCII Text	Common
WK1	Spreadsheet	Lotus 1-2-3 Version 2
WKS	Spreadsheet	Lotus 1-2-3 Version 1a
XLS	Spreadsheet	Excel
$$$	Temporary	Common

extent

An *extent* is contiguous space on a disk reserved for a file or application.

external interrupt

An *external interrupt* is an interrupt caused by an external source such as the computer operator, external sensor or monitoring device, or another computer.

external reference

In programming, an *external reference* is a call, or branch, to a separate independent program or routine.

external sort

An *external sort* is a sort that uses disk or tape as temporary workspace during the resequencing process.

external storage

External storage is peripheral storage that is external to the CPU, such as disk and tape.

F connector

An *F connector* is a plug and socket for coaxial cable that is typically used for television. It is used to connect a television or video cassette recorder (VCR) to an antenna or cable source, or to interconnect a VCR with a TV. See *phone connector, phono connector* and *plugs & sockets*.

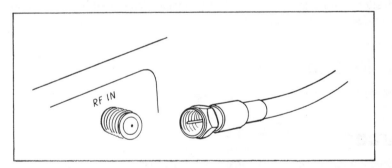

F CONNECTOR

facilities management

Facilities management is the management of an organization's own computer installation by an outside organization. All operations including systems, programming and the datacenter can be performed by the facilities management organization on the user's premises.

facsimile

See *fax*.

factorial

A *factorial* is the total number of possible sequences that can exist with a fixed set of items. For example, with three items, there are six possible arrangements: 1 2 3, 1 3 2, 2 3 1, 2 1 3, 3 1 2 and 3 2 1. The factorial is derived by continuously multiplying the number of items by the next lowest number until 1 is reached, for example, 3 x 2 x 1.

fail safe

Fail safe is failure proof operation. See *fault tolerant*.

fail soft

Fail soft is the ability to fail with minimum destruction. Fail soft systems detect failures, and although they can't correct them, they provide for less destructive failure. For example, a disk drive can be built so that when power fails, the heads are automatically brought to a safe home position.

FAMOS

(Floating Gate Avalanche-injection Metal Oxide Semiconductor) *FAMOS* is a fabrication technology for making EPROM memory chips that hold their content until erased with ultraviolet light.

fan-fold paper

Same as *continous forms*.

Farad

A *Farad* is a unit of electrical charge that is used to measure the storage capacity of a capacitor. In microelectronics, measurements are usually in microfarads or picofarads.

Fast

Fast is an asynchronous communications protocol for personal computers that is used on error-free lines to transmit files as quickly as possible. Error checking is done after the entire file has been transmitted.

fast Fourier transforms

Fast Fourier transforms are a class of algorithms used in digital signal processing that break down complex signals into their elementary components.

FastCAD

FastCAD is a computer-aided design (CAD) package from Evolution Computing that runs on IBM compatible pcs. FastCAD is a full-featured and sophisticated CAD package that is designed for high-speed work. FastCAD runs only in pcs with math coprocessors. FastCAD is also known for its well designed user interface. Less sophisticated users can start out with EasyCAD 2, FastCAD's baby brother.

FAT

(**F**ile **A**llocation **T**able) A *FAT* is a map of disk space in Microsoft's DOS and OS/2 operating systems that keeps track of current used, unused and damaged sectors. The FAT is replicated twice on each disk volume. The directory, which contains file ID, such as name, extension and date of last update, points to the FAT, which contains the actual sector locations for the file.

fatal error

A *fatal error* is an error condition that prohibits continued processing by the program. A fatal error can occur if a program encounters a disk read error while reading in additional parts of the program. Fatal errors are often the results of anomalies in large and complicated programs. If an expected condition within a particular function of the program is not found, a fatal error can occur. Often, a number indicating the kind of error is displayed, and the program stops. Restarting the program may correct the situation, but in early releases of software, fatal errors may be just that.

FatBits

FatBits is the mode in Apple's MacPaint program that lets a user edit a pixel at a time. FatBits is an option in the "Goodies" menu.

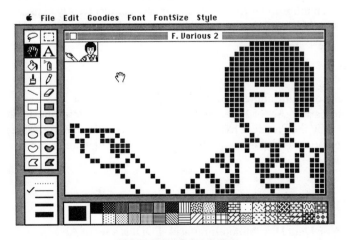

FAT BITS MODE

Note the actual size picture in the upper left hand side of the screen.

father file

See *grandfather, father, son.*

fault tolerant

Fault tolerant is continous operation in the event of failure. Fault tolerant computer systems can be created using two or more conventional computer systems that duplicate all the processing, or having one system stand by if the other fails. Fault tolerant computer systems can be built from the ground up, such as Tandem, Stratus and Sequoia computers, which offer commercially available redundant processors. Such systems have several processors, control units and peripheral units combined into a modular integrated system and are widely used in financial applications, such as for stock market transactions and online banking functions.

Total fault tolerant operation also requires backup power in the event of power failure from the electric utility. It may also imply duplication of systems in physically disparate locations in the event of natural catastrophe or premeditated attacks of vandalism.

fax

(FACSimile) *Fax*, or *facsimile*, is the communication of a printed page between remote locations. Fax terminals scan a paper form and convert its image into an analog code for transmission over private lines or the public dial-up telephone system. The receiving terminal reconverts the codes into images and prints a "facsimile" of the original page.

Fax printed circuit boards, plugged into a personal computer, can send copies of text files or a copy of the current display screen to a remote fax terminal. Fax transmissions can be received as well.

Fax machines are grouped into four classifications based on transmission speed. Groups 1 and 2 transmit a single page in six and three minutes respectively and were the standards used throughout the 1970s. Group 3 transmits one page in less than a minute and is the most common standard currently in use. Higher-speed Group 4 machines will become widely used during the 1990s.

FCC

(Federal Communications Commission) Created under the U. S. Communications Act of 1934, the FCC is a board of commissioners that is appointed by the President to regulate all interstate telecommunications services and international telecommunications services that originate within the United States.

FDDI

(Fiber optic Data Distribution Interface) *FDDI* is a set of ANSI standards for fiber optic local area networks. FDDI networks transmit at 100 megabits per second, ten times faster than Ethernet networks. At this speed, large volumes of high-resolution graphics can be handled as well as voice and video in realtime.

FDM

(Frequency Division Multiplexing) *FDM* is a communications transmission method that is widely used to transmit multiple signals over a single channel. Each signal transmitted (data, voice, etc.) is modulated (mixed) onto a carrier of a different frequency. The multiple signals actually travel simultaneously over the channel. Contrast with *TDM* (time division multiplexing) wherein the signals are digital and the bits from each signal are interleaved. See *carrier* and *broadband*.

FEA

(Finite Element Analysis) *FEA* is a mathematical technique that is used to analyze the stress on complex physical structures. The total structure is broken down into a series of substructures, called "finite elements." The finite elements and their interrelationships are converted into equation form and analyzed by solving thousands of equations. Graphics-based FEA software can display the model on screen as it is being built and, after analysis, display the object's reactions under load conditions. Models created in popular CAD packages, such as AutoCAD, can be input into the FEA software.

FEA has typically been done on large computers due to the large amounts of calculations necessary. With the advent of high-performance workstations and personal computers, FEA is being performed on small and medium-size structures in desktop computers.

feasibility study

A *feasibility study* is a preliminary analysis of an information system or computer system. It determines if a proposed problem can be solved by the installation of an information system and/or computer system. The operational (can it work in the environment?), economical (cost/benefits analysis) and technical (can it be built?) aspects are part of a feasibility study. The results of a feasibility study should provide sufficient data for a go/no-go decision.

Felix

Felix is a unique pointing and drawing device from Lightgate that is available for IBM compatible and Macintosh personal computers. Felix provides absolute positioning like a graphics tablet, rather than relative positioning like a mouse. For example, when you move the small lever (its stylus equivalent) to the upper left side of its 1 1/2" square field of movement, the cursor is in the upper left side of the screen. In normal mode, Felix covers the entire screen, but it has a precision mode that covers only a small portion of the screen for detailed drawing.

female connector

A *female connector* is a receptacle into which the male counterpart of the connector is plugged.

femtosecond

A *femtosecond* is one quadrillionth of a second. See *space/time*.

FEP

See *front end processor*.

ferromagnetic

Ferromagnetic is the capability of a material, such as iron and nickel, to be highly magnetized.

FET

(Field Effect Transistor) An *FET* is the type of transistor used in MOS (metal oxide semiconductor) integrated circuits.

fetch

Fetch is to locate the next instruction in memory for execution by the CPU.

FF

See *form feed*.

Fibonacci numbers

Fibonacci numbers are a series of integers (whole numbers) in which each number is the sum of the two preceding numbers. This series of numbers is implemented in various search and sort programs to speed up the processing.

fiche

Same as *microfiche*.

field

A *field* is the physical unit of data in a record. Name, address, city, state, zip and amount due are examples of fields in a record. A field is one or more bytes in size, and the collection of fields make up a record. A field also defines a unit of data on a source document, video screen or report.

Since the field is the smallest meaningful unit of data that can be defined and manipulated, it's really the common denominator between the user and the computer. When you interactively query and manipulate your databases at a terminal using such programs as query languages, report writers and database management systems, you identify and reference your data by field name.

Technically, a field is the physical unit of storage, whereas a data element or data item refers to the data generally (logically). For example, it is correct to say, "These data elements are stored in these fields." However, the terms *field, data element, data item* and *variable* all refer to the same unit of data.

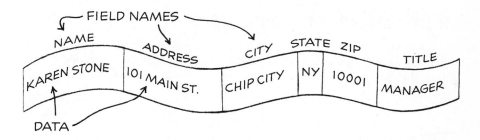

FIELDS IN A RECORD

field effect transistor

See *FET*.

field engineer

A *field engineer* is an individual responsible for hardware installation, maintentance and repair. Field engineers are service personnel who are trained in electromechanical engineering and digital electronics.

field separator

A *field separator* is a character that is used to mark the separation of fields in a record. See *comma delimited*.

field service representative

Same as *field engineer*.

field squeeze

In a mail merge operation, a *field squeeze* eliminates extra blank spaces in a data field so that it prints correctly within the text of the letter.

FIFO

(First In-First Out) *FIFO* is a storage method that retrieves the item stored for the longest time. Contrast with *LIFO* (last in-first out), which retrieves the item most recently stored.

fifth-generation computers

Fifth-generation computers are the next generation of computer systems that are designed around artificial intelligence methods and applications. Appearing in the mid 1990s, these systems will represent the next quantum leap in computer technology.

file

(1) In data management, a *file* is a collection of related records.

(2) In word processing, a *file* is a single text document.

(3) In computer graphics, a *file* is a set of image descriptors for one picture, either in televisionlike format (raster graphics) or in line format (vector graphics).

(4) In programming, the source program and machine language program are stored as individual *files*.

(5) In computer operations, a *file* is any collection of data that is treated as a single unit on a peripheral device, such as all of the examples in items 1 through 4 above.

file and record locking

File and record locking are techniques for managing data in a multiple user environment. File locking prevents users from gaining access to a data, text or image file. Record locking prohibits access to a single record within a data file. File and record locking are usually initiated on a first-come, first-served basis. Whoever gets there first locks out the others from the data until they're finished updating it.

file extension

See *extension*.

file format

A *file format* is the specification for the structure of a file. There are hundreds of proprietary formats for database files, word processing files and graphics files that have become standardized and used for data interchange. For example, in the IBM compatible pc world, dBASE, R:BASE, WordPerfect, WordStar, PC Paintbrush and GEM Paint all have proprietary methods for laying out the data in the file. See *record layout*.

file layout

Same as *record layout*.

file maintenance

File maintenance is the periodic updating of master files. For example, adding and deleting employees and customers, making name and address changes and changing the prices in a product file. It does not pertain to an organization's daily transaction processing and batch processing (order processing, billing, etc.).

File maintenance also refers to disk maintenance, which is the periodic reorganization of a computer system's disks. Data that has been continuously updated becomes physically fragmented over the disk space and requires regrouping. Personal computer users with hard disks should run an optimizing program on their computer every so often (weekly, monthly) to maintain their disks.

file manager

A *file manager* is a data management software package that provides some of the features of a database management system, but works with only single files. Often erroneously called database managers, file managers provide the ability to create, enter, change, query and produce reports on only one file at a time. They have no relational capabilty and usually don't include a programming language for application development.

file name

A *file name* is a name assigned by the user or programmer that is used to identify a file.

file protect ring

A *file protect ring* is a plastic ring inserted into a reel of magnetic tape to prevent it from being erased.

file protection

File protection is the prevention of accidental erasing of a disk or tape. Physical file protection is provided on the storage medium itself by turning a switch, pressing a slide lever or covering a notch. In these cases, recording of new data is prohibited even if the software directs the computer to do so.

To protect a floppy disk, do the following. On 3 1/2" disks, push the slide lever on the bottom, back side of the disk toward the edge of the disk uncovering a hole through the disk. On 5 1/4" disks, cover the notch on the side of a disk with a stick-on label. On 8" disks, remove the stick-on label covering the notch on the side.

On 1/2" tape reels, protection is provided by removing a plastic ring in the center of the reel, "no ring-no write."

Logical file protection is provided by the operating system, which can designate a single file as read only. This method allows both regular (read/write) and read only files to be stored on the same disk medium. In addition, files can often be designated as "hidden" files, which means that they are invisible to most software programs.

file server

A *file server* is a computer in a local area network that stores the programs and data files shared by the users connected to the network. A file server acts like a remote disk drive to the users in the network. A file server is also called a *network server*.

file specification

A *file specification* is a designated path for locating a file on a disk. It includes the disk drive, name of directory and name of file. For example, in Microsoft's DOS and OS/2 operating systems, `C:\WORDSTAR\BOOKS\CHAPTER1` is a file specification for the file CHAPTER1 in the BOOKS subdirectory of the WORDSTAR directory on drive C.

file system

(1) A *file system* is a method for cataloging files in a computer system; for example, a hierarchical file system as is used in Microsoft's DOS and OS/2 operating systems.

(2) A *file system* is a data processing application that manages individual files and provides its own programming for relating them. A file system implies that a database management system is not used to perform any of these tasks.

film recorder

A *film recorder* is a device that takes a 35mm slide picture from a graphics file, which has been created in a CAD, paint or business graphics package. Film recorders generate much higher resolution than traditional display screens. Typical resolutions are 2,000 lines and go up to 4,000 lines. The device usually works by recreating the image on a built-in CRT that shines through a color wheel onto the film in a standard 35mm camera. Some units provide optional Polaroid camera backs for instant previewing. Film recorders can be connected to personal computers by plugging in a special controller board that is cabled to the film recorder.

filter

(1) A *filter* is a pattern or mask through which only selected data is passed. For example, in dBASE, `set filter to file region4`, passes all data through the matching conditions specified in the query file REGION4.

(2) A *filter* is a process that changes data, such as a sort program.

financial planning language

A *financial planning language* is a language used to create data models and command a financial planning system.

financial planning system

A *financial planning system* is a financial modeling software package that aids the financial planner and manager in examining and evaluating many alternatives before making final decisions. Financial planning systems allow for the creation of a data model, which is a series of data elements in equation form, for example, `gross profit = gross sales - cost of goods sold`. Different values can be plugged into the data elements, and the impact of various options can be assessed (what if?).

Financial planning systems are a step above spreadsheets by providing additional analysis tools. For example, sensitivity analysis lets you assign a range of values to a data element. When calculations cause the data to exceed the range, the errors are highlighted. Another feature is goal seeking, which provides automatic calculations to achieve an objective. For example, by entering a goal, such as `gross margin = 50%`, as well as the minimums and maximums of the various inputs, the program will calculate an optimum mix of inputs to achieve the goal (output).

Finder, MultiFinder

Finder and *MultiFinder* are components of the Macintosh's operating system that manage the desktop. They keep track of all the icons on the desktop and control the Clipboard and Scrapbook. They also let you copy files from one disk to another.

Finder is the single tasking version, and MultiFinder is the multitasking version. With Mulifinder, two or more application programs can be opened at one time.

fingerprint reader

A *fingerprint reader* is a specialized scanner that is used to identify an individual for security purposes. To enroll a user in the system, the user's fingerprint is initially scanned by the reader. Access to a computer system or other restricted area is then granted when the user's fingerprint matches the stored sample. A personal identification number (PIN) may also be captured and stored with the fingerprint sample.

FINGERPRINT READER

(Courtesy Identix Inc.)

finite element analysis

See *FEA*.

firmware

Firmware is a category of memory chips that hold their content when the power is turned off. ROMs, PROMS, EPROMS and EEPROMS are examples of firmware and are used in a wide variety of applications from hand-held toys to the largest computer systems. Firmware is "hard software."

first-generation computer

First-generation computers used vacuum tubes as switching elements, for example, the UNIVAC I, which was commercially available in 1951.

fixed disk

A *fixed disk* is a non-removable disk system such as is found in most personal computers. Using a copy program, programs and data are copied from a floppy disk onto the fixed disk. Same as *hard disk*.

fixed head disk

A *fixed head disk* is a direct access storage device, such as a disk or drum, that has a read/write head for each storage track. Since there is no mechanical action required to move the read/write head, access times are significantly improved.

fixed length fields

Fixed length fields are fields that contain the exact same number of bytes in each record. For example, a 25-byte name field will always take 25 bytes on the disk even when a short name is stored in it. Fixed length fields are easier to program, but waste a lot of disk space and also restrict the design of the file. For example, description and comments fields are always a dilemma. Should 30 bytes be reserved, 100 or 200? 200 bytes allows about 40 words in the field, but requires that 200 bytes be reserved for each record in the file. 30 bytes allows a half dozen words, which may not be enough. Although much more complicated to program, variable length fields, where the field is only as large as the data stored in it, is the superior method for storing data.

fixed length record

A *fixed length record* is a data record that contains fixed length fields.

fixed point

Fixed point is a method for storing and calculating numbers where the decimal point is always in the same location. Contrast with floating point, which allows for variations in decimal point location.

flag

(1) In communications, a *flag* is a code in the transmitted message which indicates that the following characters are not data, rather they are some kind of control code or command.

(2) In programming, a *flag* is a status indicator that may be built into hardware or programmed in software. Flags are usually no larger than a bit or a byte and hold on/off, true/false conditions.

Flash-Up Windows

Flash-Up Windows is a programming utility from Software Bottling Company that runs on IBM compatible pcs. It creates scrollable light-bar menus and help screens that pop up on screen as required. Flash-Up Windows works with standard programming languages, such as BASIC and dBASE.

flat file

A *flat file* is a data file that does not physically interconnect with or point to other files. Any relationships between two flat files are purely logical, for example, matching account numbers. Flat files may refer to data created by a text editor or file manager, or it may refer to non-interconnected files for use in a relational database manager.

flat panel display

A *flat panel display* is a thin display screen that uses any of a number of technologies, such as liquid crystal (LCD), electroluminscent or plasma. Flat panel displays are used in laptop computers in order to keep the overall size and weight of the machine to a minimum. In time, flat panel displays will supersede the cathode ray tube (CRT) screens that are so widely used today.

flatbed plotter

A *flatbed plotter* is a graphics plotter that draws onto sheets of paper that have been placed into a bed. The size of the bed determines the maximum size sheet that can be drawn.

flexible disk

Same as *floppy disk* and *diskette*.

flicker

Flicker refers to an image that does not appear to be stable on screen.

flip-flop

A *flip-flop* is an electronic circuit that alternates between one state and another. When current is applied, it changes from its current state to the opposite state (0 to 1, 1 to 0). Made of several transistors, a flip-flop is used in the design of static memories and hardware registers.

flippy-floppy

A *flippy-floppy* is a 5 1/4" floppy disk that is used in a single sided disk drive, but is recorded on both sides. A second write protect notch is punched into the floppy disk so that the disk can be flipped over and inserted upside down.

floating point

Floating point is a method for storing and calculating numbers where the decimal points don't line up as in fixed point numbers. The significant digits (no zeros on the right) are stored as a unit called the mantissa, and the location of the decimal point is stored in a separate unit called the exponent. Floating point methods are used for calculating a large range of numbers quickly.

Floating point operations can be implemented in hardware with math coprocessor circuits, or they can be done in software. They can also be performed in a separate floating point processor that is connected to the main processor via a channel.

MANTISSA	EXPONENT		ACTUAL VALUE
6508	0	=	6508
6508	1	=	65080
6508	-1	=	650.8

FLOATING POINT

floating point processor

A *floating point processor* is an arithmetic unit that is designed to perform floating point operations. It may be a coprocessor chip in a personal computer, a CPU designed with built-in floating point capabilities or a separate machine, often called an *array processor*, which is connected to the main computer.

floppy disk

A *floppy disk* is a removable storage medium used with many varieties of computers and word processing systems. The storage medium itself is a single round disk of flexible, tape-like material that is housed in a square envelope or cartridge. Like magnetic tape, floppy disks can be recorded, erased and reused over and over again. Some floppy disks are recorded only on one side (*single sided*); however, most of them are recorded on both sides (*double sided*).

FLOPPY DISK DRIVE

The original floppy disk was developed by IBM and is housed in an 8" square envelope that holds from 100,000 to 500,000 bytes.

Minifloppy disks are second-generation disks developed by Shugart and are commonly used in personal computers. The disk is housed in a 5 1/4" square envelope and holds from 100,000 to 1,200,000 bytes of data.

Microfloppy disks are the third generation of floppies and were developed by Sony. Microfloppies are very popular due to their compactness, ruggedness and large storage capacities. The disk itself is housed in a rigid 3 1/2" square cartridge and holds from 400,000 to 2,000,000 bytes of data.

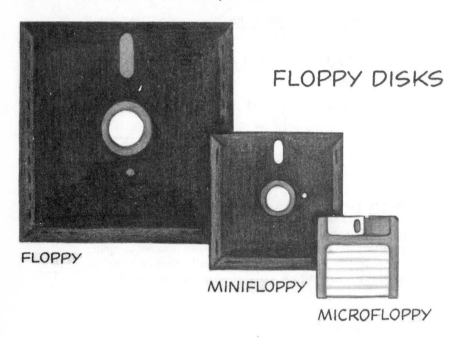

FLOPPY DISKS

FLOPPY

MINIFLOPPY

MICROFLOPPY

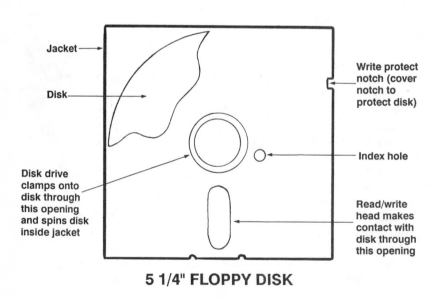

Jacket

Disk

Write protect notch (cover notch to protect disk)

Disk drive clamps onto disk through this opening and spins disk inside jacket

Index hole

Read/write head makes contact with disk through this opening

5 1/4" FLOPPY DISK

A floppy disk, fresh out of the box, is blank. The disk drive it is used in determines its storage capacity. Most floppy disks are *soft sectored* disks, which requires that they be run once through a *format* program to lay out the recording segments, called *sectors*, on the disk surface. Although the physical disk may look the same, a microfloppy formatted in an IBM compatible pc drive will not work in a Macintosh.

All floppies are vulnerable to mishandling, extremes in temperature and magnetic influences; however, the 8" and 5 1/4" disks are more fragile than the microfloppy disks as is indicated in the following chart:

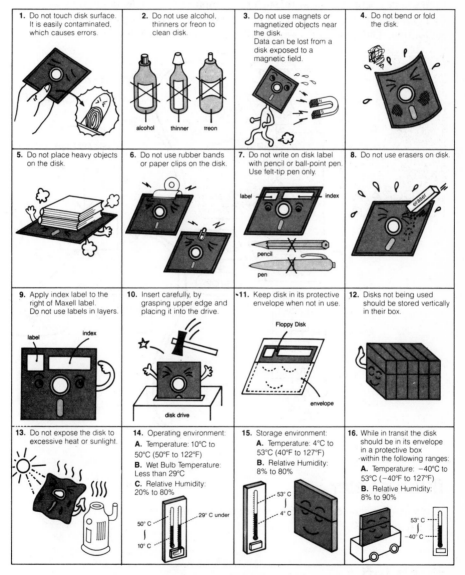

FLOPPY DISK HANDLING AND STORAGE

(Courtesy Maxell Corporation)

FLOPS

(**FLO**ating point operations **P**er **S**econd) *FLOPS* measures the speed that floating point calculations can be performed in a computer; for example, 100 megaflops is 100 million floating point operations per second.

flow chart

A *flow chart* is a graphical representation of the sequence of operations in an information system or program. Information system flow charts show how data from source documents flows through the computer to final distribution to users. Program flow charts show the sequence of instructions in a single program or subroutine. Different symbols are used to draw each type of flow chart.

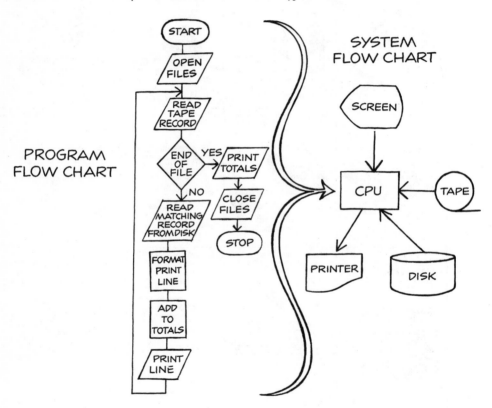

flush center

In typography, *flush center* refers to centering text uniformly between the left and right margins.

flush left

In typography, *flush left* is the alignment of all text uniformly to the left margin. All text is typically set flush left.

flush right

In typography, *flush right* is the alignment of all text uniformly to the right while
maintaining a ragged left margin.   For example,
all lines following the first line
in this definition
are set as flush right.

flux

Flux is the energy field generated by a magnet.

FM

(1) (Frequency Modulation) In communications, FM is a transmission technique
that modulates (merges) a data signal into a fixed carrier frequency by modifying
the carrier frequency. Contrast with *amplitude modulation* (AM) and *phase
modulation*, which are the two other major techniques for modulating a carrier.

(2) (Frequency Modulation) On magnetic media, FM is a recording technique
that places a clock bit onto the medium along with each data bit. FM is a
low-density method for recording data and has been superseded by MFM
(modified frequency modulation) and RLL (run length limited) techniques,
which eliminate more of the clock bits.

FOCUS

FOCUS is a database management system from Information Builders, Inc., that
runs on IBM mainframes, VAX series, Wang VS series and IBM compatible pcs.
FOCUS provides relational, hierarchical and network data structures and can
access a variety of databases, including standard IBM mainframe files, DB2, IMS,
IDMS and others. It includes a fourth-generation language and a variety of
decision support facilities, including financial planning and statistical analyses
capabilities.

folder

In the Macintosh, a *folder* is a file
folder that holds several
documents. The Macintosh's
hierarchical file system lets you
create folders and store any
documents within them. A folder
is analogous to a DOS subdirectory
in IBM compatible pcs. In the
Macintosh, a document is any text,
data or graphics file that is created
in the computer.

MACINTOSH FOLDERS

In the Macintosh desktop, folders are
represented by tiny pictures (icons) with
captions. The Glossary folder is currently
selected.

folio

In typography, a *folio* is a printed page number in contrast with the physical page number. For example, in this book, folio no. 3 is actually the 27th physical page in the book. See *pagination*.

font

A *font* is a set of characters of a particular design and size. For example, the text you're reading is 10 point Goudy Old Style. The definition headers are 16 point Helvetica Bold. In daisy wheel printers, fonts are changed by changing the daisy wheel. In dot matrix printers, the fonts are usually built in and can be selected by software or a switch on the control panel. In laser printers, some fonts are built in, and the rest are either downloaded from the computer or plugged into the printer in the form of cartridges containing ROM chips.

There are several characteristics that make up a font. For example, in order to select a font in the Hewlett-Packard LaserJet printer, codes are sent to the printer that indicate the following characteristics of the font:

Code	Characteristic
Typeface	Primary design (Courier, Times Roman, etc.)
Orientation	Portrait or landscape orientation
Symbol set	Country or special characters
Spacing	Proportional or fixed spacing (horizontal widths)
Pitch	Number of characters per inch if fixed spacing
Point size	Height of characters
Style	Upright (normal) or italic characters
Stroke weight	Light, medium or bold appearance

Font Structures

Fonts are designed either as bit mapped images or as outlines. Bit mapped images are the dot patterns for every character within each point size. For example, the fonts that are downloaded into the HP LaserJet printers are bit mapped fonts.

Outline fonts are general patterns for each character. The outlines are turned into dot patterns by a program called a *font generator*. In a PostScript printer, a set of base fonts and the routine to scale (size) them reside in the printer. Additional outline fonts can be downloaded and scaled in the printer before they are printed.

font cartridge

See *cartridge font*.

font compiler

Same as *font generator*.

font generator

A *font generator* converts an outline font into the precise patterns of dots required for a particular size of font.

Fontware

Fontware is a font generation system from Bitstream Inc., that runs on IBM compatible pcs. Fontware includes a library of typefaces that come in outline form and a font generator program that converts the outlines into bit mapped fonts from 6 to 99 points. Each typeface package includes four weights of the selected typeface, for example, normal, italic, bold and bold italic. Using the font generator, the user selects the weights and point sizes and the program scales the outlines into the required fonts that are stored on disk for future use.

footer

In a document or report, a *footer* is common text that appears at the bottom of every page. The footer may also contain the page number.

footnote

In word processing, a *footnote* is text that appears at the bottom of a page which adds explanation to the text within the page. For example, footnotes are often used to give credit to the source of a particular statement. When footnotes are accumulated and printed at the end of a chapter, they are called *endnotes*.

footprint

A *footprint* is the physical amount of space that is covered by an object. For example, a computer's footprint is the number of square inches of desk or floor surface it occupies. A satellite's footprint is the geographic area on earth that is covered by its downlink transmission.

for-next statement

A *for-next statement* is a high-level programming language structure that repeats a series of instructions a finite number of times. It differs from a do while or do until loop in that do loops repeat the instructions until a condition is no longer true. The FOR-NEXT STATEMENT specifies the exact number of times the steps between the FOR and the NEXT will be repeated. The following example in the BASIC programming language prints "Hello" 10 times:

```
FOR X = 1 to 10
PRINT "Hello"
NEXT X
```

foreground/background

Foreground/background is an operating system prioritizing method in multitasking computer systems. Programs running in the foreground have highest priority, whereas programs running in the background have lowest priority. For example, online users at terminals are usually given the foreground, and batch processing activities, such as long sorts and updates, are given the background. If, at any time, the batch processing activities are given the higher priority, terminal response times will slow down.

In a personal computer, the foreground program is the one the user is currently working with, and the background program could be a communications program that is ready and available to accept a message from another computer.

form feed

A *form feed* is a code that is sent to the printer to advance the paper to the top of the next page. It is character 12 in the ASCII character set. The form feed button on the printer will also do the same thing.

format

(1) *Format* refers to the physical structure of an item.

(2) A screen *format* is the layout of fields on the screen.

(3) A report *format* is the layout of the printed page including print columns, page headers and footers. See *layout setting*.

(4) A record *format* is the layout of fields within the record.

(5) A file or database *format* is the layout of fields and records within a data file, layout codes within a word processing document or display lists (vector) or bit maps (raster) within a graphics file. It also includes the structure of header data, or identification data, that is typically affixed to the beginning of the file.

(6) A disk *format* is the layout of the storage units of a disk. Before data can be recorded (written) on a disk, a format program must be used to break up the disk into recording segments, called *sectors*. The format program records the sector numbers on the disk which are used to identify the sectors from then on.

formula

(1) A *formula* is an arithmetic expression that solves a problem. For example, (fahrenheit - 32) * 5 / 9 is the formula for converting fahrenheit to centigrade.

(2) In spreadsheets, a *formula* identifies how the data in a specific number of cells is to be calculated. For example, +**C3*D8** means that the contents of cell C3 are to be multipled by the contents of cell D8 and the results are to be placed where the formula is located.

FORTH

(**FO**u**RTH**-generation language) *FORTH* is a high-level programming language created by Charles Moore in the late 1960s as a tool for the programmer who wants direct control of the computer. FORTH is quite different from other programming languages. Its syntax resembles the LISP language, and it uses reverse polish notation for calculations. FORTH is noted for its extensibility, which means its language can be expanded by the programmer.

FORTH is both a compiler and interpreter. The source program is compiled first and then executed by its operating system/interpreter. FORTH is used extensively in process control applications in which tight control over the operation is necessary. The data acquired from instruments and sensors must be handled quickly in these kinds of real-time environments. FORTH is also used in arcade game programming as well as robotics and other artificial intelligence applications. The following polyFORTH example converts fahrenheit to centirgrade:

```
: CONV ( n) 32 - 5 9 * / . ." Centigrade is" ;
: USER_INPUT  ." Enter fahrenheit " CONV ;
```

Since FORTH handles only integers in order to obtain the highest speed for realtime operations, the above example would not handle decimal places. The example below, in which the 5 and the 9 are multiplied by 20, would add two more decimal places:

```
: CONV ( n) 32 - 100 180 * / . ." Centigrade is"
: USER_INPUT  ." Enter fahrenheit " CONV ;
```

FORTRAN

(**FOR**mula **TRAN**slator) *FORTRAN*, developed in 1954 by IBM, was the first high-level programming language and compiler developed for computers. It was originally designed to express mathematical formulas, and although it is used occasionally for business applications, it is still the most widely used language for scientific, engineering and mathematical problems.

The following example accepts a fahrenheit number and converts it into centigrade:

```
WRITE(6,*) 'Enter fahrenheit '
READ(5,*) XFAHR
XCENT = (XFAHR - 32) * 5 / 9
WRITE(6,*) 'Centigrade is ',XCENT
STOP
END
```

Fortune 500

The following computer and electronics companies represent 300 billion dollars worth of sales for 1987. The figures are from the April 1988 Fortune 500 listings and are reprinted with permission of Fortune Magazine. Office equipment companies are included in the first list under computers. The rank is their position in the Fortune 500 list, which includes all industries.

COMPUTERS Rank	Company	Sales (millions)	Profit (millions)	Employees (thousands)
4	IBM	54,217	5,258	389
36	Unisys	9,713	578	93
38	Digital Equipment	9,389	1,137	111
49	Hewlett-Packard	8,090	644	82
74	NCR	5,641	419	62
125	Control Data	3,367	19	35
146	Wang Laboratories	2,837	(71)	30
152	Apple Computer	2,661	217	7
175	Pitney Bowes	2,251	199	29
231	Amdahl	1,505	146	8
271	Data General	1,274	(127)	16
278	Gould	1,233	(96)	10
282	Compaq Computer	1,224	136	4
318	Tandem Computers	1,035	106	7
334	Prime Computer	961	65	9
360	Telex	822	77	8
379	Storage Technology	750	26	9
397	Cray Research	687	147	4
409	Intergraph	641	70	6
440	Xidex	573	(45)	7
446	Computervision	564	19	5
454	Apollo Computer	554	22	4
456	SCI Systems	553	16	7
463	Sun Microsystems	538	36	4
484	Atari	493	57	4
	TOTAL	111,573	9,059	949

ELECTRONICS Rank	Company	Sales (millions)	Profit (millions)	Employees (thousands)
6	General Electric	39,315	2,915	302
8	AT&T	33,598	2,044	303
33	Westinghouse Elec.	10,679	739	112
45	ITT	8,551	1,018	120
53	Raytheon	7,659	445	77
61	TRW	6,821	243	78
62	Motorola	6,707	308	98

ELECTRONICS		Sales	Profit	Employees
Rank	Company	(millions)		(thousands)
63	Honeywell	6,679	254	79
67	Emerson Electric	6,170	467	69
75	Texas Instruments	5,595	309	78
86	North American Phillips	4,847	(18)	50
96	Litton Industries	4,420	138	54
105	Whirlpool	4,179	192	30
110	Eaton	4,054	201	36
118	Cooper Industries	3,586	174	43
128	Combustion Engineering	3,301	57	28
134	Teledyne	3,217	377	44
151	Johnson Controls	2,677	90	27
170	Zenith Electronics	2,363	(19)	35
171	AMP	2,318	250	22
187	Harris	2,079	85	24
199	Maytag	1,909	153	13
200	Intel	1,907	248	19
202	Singer	1,903	26	28
204	National Semiconductor	1,868	(25)	29
234	Square D	1,484	110	20
244	Chicago Pacific	1,412	35	22
245	Reliance Electric	1,408	4	17
250	Allegheny International	1,390	(451)	13
261	National Service Ind.	1,327	76	19
281	E-Systems	1,227	60	16
328	Advanced Micro Devices	997	(48)	18
329	Champion Spark Plug	996	19	9
332	Varian Associates	983	21	12
335	Seagate Technology	958	140	15
340	General Instrument	947	(80)	16
341	Raychem	944	74	10
396	Loral	690	57	7
407	Pittway	649	32	8
412	Bairnco	630	28	5
419	Magnetek	609	5	13
437	Hubbell	581	63	5
459	M/A-Com	543	(35)	7
483	Scientific Atlanta	495	24	3
495	Sprague Technologies	470	4	8
499	Western Digital	462	48	3
	TOTAL	195,603	10,855	2,046

fourth-generation computer

A *fourth-generation computer* is a computer that is made up almost entirely of chips with limited amounts of discrete components. We are currently in the fourth generation.

fourth-generation language

A *fourth-generation language* is a computer language that commands the computer at a higher level than traditional high-level programming languages. For example, in dBASE, the command **LIST** starts listing records in a database file from the beginning to the end of the file. In traditional second and third-generation programming languages, all the instructions necessary to bring in each record, test for end of file, place each item of data on screen and go back and repeat the operation would have to be coded.

First-generation languages are the machine languages themselves; second-generation languages are machine dependent assembly languages; and third-generation languages are high-level programming languages, such as FORTRAN, COBOL, BASIC, Pascal, and C. Although many languages, such as dBASE, are called fourth-generation languages, they are, in fact, a mixture of third and fourth generations. The dBASE example in the previous paragraph is a fourth-generation language command, but routine application programs written in the dBASE programming language use third-generation language techniques.

Query language and report writers are also fourth-generation languages. Any computer language with English-like commands that don't require traditional input-process-output logic fall into this category.

FoxBASE+

FoxBASE+ is a dBASE III PLUS compatible database management system from Fox Software, Inc., that runs on IBM compatible pcs and the Macintosh. FoxBASE+ provides both interpreter and compiler versions of the language and is known for its speed. It is extremely compatible with dBASE III PLUS and also provides enhancements not found in the dBASE programming language.

FoxBASE+/Mac for the Macintosh conforms to the traditional dBASE language and allows existing dBASE programs, written for the IBM compatible pc world, to run in the Mac.

fragmentation

Fragmentation is the uneven distribution of data on a disk. As files are updated, they become less contiguous on the disk. When data is added, the operating system stores it in the available free space. As a result, parts of the file wind up in disparate areas of the disk, causing additional arm movement when the file is sequentially read. A disk maintenance, or optimizer, program is used to reorder the files in a contiguous manner.

FRAM

(Ferromagnetic RAM) *FRAM* is a memory technology that records microscopic bits on a magnetic surface. The advantage of FRAM memory is that, like disk and tape, the bits are non-volatile and remain permanent until intentionally changed.

frame

(1) In computer graphics, a *frame* is often used to designate the storage space for one screenful of data.

(2) In communications, a *frame* is a group of bits that make up an elementary block of data for transmission by certain communications protocols.

(3) In artificial intelligence, a *frame* is a data structure that holds a general description of an object. The description is derived from basic concepts and experience.

frame buffer

In computer graphics, a *frame buffer* is a separate memory component that holds a graphic image. Frame buffers may have one plane of memory for each bit in the pixel. For example, if eight bits are used to represent one pixel, there are eight separate memory planes.

frame grabber

A *frame grabber* is a device used to combine video images with computer graphics. The frame grabber accepts standard television video signals and, upon command of the user, digitizes the current image.

Framework

Framework is an integrated software package from Ashton-Tate that runs on IBM compatible pcs. It provides database management, word processing, spreadsheet, communications and business graphics capability in a single package. Framework also contains its own programming language called Fred.

Fred

Fred is the programming language used in the Framework software package.

free-form language

A *free-form language* is a programming or command language that can be written or entered without regard to precise spacing between words and without having to rigidly place statements at predefined columns.

FreeHand

FreeHand is a drawing program from Aldus Corporation that runs on Macintosh computers. It is an extremely powerful graphics program that combines a wide range of drawing tools with special effects. FreeHand requires a PostScript printer for its output.

freeware

Freeware is software that is provided at no cost.

Freeway Advanced

Freeway Advanced is a communications program from Kortek, Inc., that runs on IBM compatible pcs. Version 1.0 handles transmission speeds from 75 to 115,200 bits per second, emulates three different terminals and supports six protocols. Freeway Advanced is a menu-driven program with an optional command line for entering Crosstalk XVI commands.

frequency

In electronics and communications, the *frequency* is the number of oscillations, or vibrations, that are in an alternating current within one second. See *carrier*.

frequency division multiplexing

See *FDM*.

frequency modulation

See *FM*.

frequency shift keying

In communications, *frequency shift keying* is a simple modulation technique that merges binary data into a carrier frequency. It usually creates only two changes in the frequency, one for the 0 bit and another for the 1 bit.

Friendly Finder

Friendly Finder is a searching program from Proximity Technology that enables users to find names without entering the exact spelling. It runs on IBM compatible pcs and works on ASCII and dBASE files directly. Friendly Finder can be run as a stand-alone program or can be RAM resident (TSR) with other programs.

front end processor

A *front end processor* is a communications computer. It connects to the communications channels on one end and the main computer on the other.

Software in the front end processor directs the transmitting and receiving of messages according to the protocol used in the network. It detects and corrects transmission errors and assembles and disassembles messages. A front end processor is sometimes synonymous with a communications control unit, although the latter is usually not as flexible as a front end processor.

FSK

See *frequency shift keying*.

FTAM

(File Transfer Access and Management) FTAM is a standard communications protocol for the transfer of files between systems of different vendors.

FUD factor

(Fear Uncertainty Doubt factor) The *FUD factor* is a marketing strategey that instills caution in the minds of the buyer regarding the use of a competitive product. The larger company typically uses the FUD factor when competing with a smaller company by creating doubt about the smaller company's ability to compete, or survive and service its products. The FUD factor is often employed more by implication than by facts. However, if the larger company has developed a reputation for being late or for inferior products, the smaller company can also use the FUD factor in its marketing strategy.

full-duplex

In communications, *full-duplex* transmission is the transmitting and receiving of data simultaneously. In pure digital networks, this is achieved with two pairs of wires. In analog networks or in digital networks using analog frequencies, full-duplex transmission is achieved by dividing the bandwidth of the line into two frequencies, one for sending and one for receiving.

full-featured

Full-featured refers to software that provides capabilities and functions comparable to the most advanced programs of the same category that are available.

full project life cycle

Full project life cycle refers to a project from its inception to its completion.

full-screen

Full-screen operations display data across the entire video display screen. Contrast with *teletype* mode, in which data is displayed a line at a time at the bottom of the screen. Programming languages usually allow both display methods to be used. The full-screen method requires that the programmer state the exact row and column positions for each field of data.

fully populated

Fully populated refers to a printed circuit board which contains the maximum number of chips that can be plugged into it.

function

In programming, a *function* is a routine, or set of instructions, that performs a particular task. When the program passes control to a function, the function performs the task and returns control to the instruction following the calling instruction. The function may perform a stand-alone task, such as initializing a set of variables, or it may accept values (arguments) from the calling instruction, process them and pass the results back when finished.

High-level programming languages usually provide a set of standard functions as well as let progrmmers define their own functions. For example, in dBASE, there are over 70 standard functions that do things such as testing for end of file, converting data and removing leading and trailing blanks. Programmers can also create their own functions, called "procedures." In C, the entire language is built upon functions; some that are part of the original compiler, some that may be purchased from third party vendors and others that are user created. C's extraordinary flexibility is due to this structure.

When used in programming, the term function is very specific. However, function is also used as normal English to describe any functional entity or component, such as the data entry function.

function keys

Function keys are an extra set of keys on a computer keyboard that are used to command the computer. Dedicated word processing systems use function keys that are specially labeled for their purpose. On personal computers, function keys are numbered, and their purpose depends on the software program that is running. For example, IBM's original PC and AT keyboards have 10 function keys (F1 - F10) in a cluster on the left side of the keyboard. Keys F11 and F12 were added on IBM's subsequent "Enhanced" keyboard, and all 12 keys were placed horizontally across the top of the keyboard.

Function keys can be programmed to work by themselves or in conjunction with the control, alt and shift keys. Software packages come with thin plastic templates that fit around the function keys to identify their purpose in the program.

SPECIAL-PURPOSE FUNCTION KEYS

GENERAL-PURPOSE FUNCTION KEYS

function library

A *function library* is a collection of program routines. See *function*.

functional specifications

Functional specifications are the blueprints for the design of an information system. They provide documentation for the database, human and machine procedures, and all the input, processing and output details for each data entry, query, update and report program in the system.

fuse

(1) A *fuse* is a protective device that is designed to melt or "blow" when a specified amount of current is passed through it. Programmable read only memory (PROM) chips are created as a series of fuses that are selectively "blown" in order to create the binary patterns in the chip.

(2) *Fuse* is to bond together.

G

G

(Gigabyte) See *space/time*.

gain

Gain is the amount of increase that an amplifier provides on the output side of the circuit.

gallium arsenide

Gallium arsenide (GaAs) is an alloy of gallium and arsenic compound that is used as the base material for chips. It is several times faster than silicon.

gang punch

Gang punch is to punch an identical set of holes into a deck of punched cards.

gap

(1) A *gap* is the space between blocks of data on a magnetic tape.

(2) A *gap* is the space in a read/write head over which magnetic flux (energy) flows causing the underlying magnetic tape or disk surface to become magnetized in the corresponding direction.

gapless

Gapless refers to magnetic tape that is recorded in a continuous stream without interblock gaps.

garbage collection

Garbage collection is a routine that searches memory for program segments or data that are no longer active in order to reclaim that space for new instructions or data.

garbage in, garbage out

Garbage in, garbage out means that invalid data entered into the computer produces invalid output. The data entry process is a critical one, and all possible tests should be made on data that is input into the system. More appropriate than garbage in, garbage out is "garbage in, gospel out," since people have a tendency to believe what is printed from a computer.

gas discharge display

See *plasma display*.

gate

(1) A *gate* is one of the AND, OR and NOT Boolean logic gates that ties transistors together. See *Boolean logic* and *gate array*.

(2) A *gate* is the trigger that toggles the switch in a metal oxide semiconductor (MOS) transistor.

gate array

A *gate array* is a chip that is manufactured with a series of logic gates that have not been tied together. A customized chip is obtained by adhering the top metal layer that creates the pathways between all the logic elements. This final masking stage is less costly than designing the chip from scratch.

Gate array chips usually contain nothing but two-input NAND gates. A NAND gate can be configured by itself or tied with other NAND gates to provide all the Boolean logic operators required for digital logic.

Logic arrays, programmable logic arrays (PLAs) and *uncommitted logic arrays* (ULAs) are all the same as gate arrays.

gateway

A *gateway* is a computer that connects two different communications networks together. The gateway will perform the protocol conversions necessary to go from one network to the other. For example, a gateway could connect a local area network of personal computers to a centralized mainframe network. Contrast with *bridge*, which connects two similar networks together.

gather write

See *scatter read/gather write*.

gauss

Gauss is a unit of measurement of magnetic energy.

Gaussian distribution

A *Gaussian dristribution* is a random distribution of events that is often graphed as a bell-shaped curve. It is used to represent a normal or statistically probable outcome.

Gaussian noise

In communications, *Gaussian noise*, also called *white noise*, is random interference generated by the movement of electricity in the line.

GCOS

GCOS is an operating system used in Honeywell minicomputers and mainframes.

GDDM

(Graphical Data Display Manager) GDDM is software that generates graphics images in the IBM mainframe environment. It contains routines to generate graphics on terminals, printers and plotters as well as accepting input from scanners. Programmers use GDDM for creating graphics, but users can employ the Interactive Chart Utility (ICU) within GDDM to create business graphics without programming.

GDDM/graPHIGS combines graphics capability with a user interface similar to the Presentation Manager in OS/2.

GDI

See *CGI*.

GDM

See CGM.

GE

(Greater than or Equal to) See *relational operators*.

gender changer

A *gender changer* is a coupling unit that reverses the gender of one of the connectors in order that two wires with male connectors or two wires with female connectors can be joined together.

general-purpose computer

Most digital computers are *general-purpose computers*, which means that they perform work according to the instructions that are fed into it. The tiny computers in toys, games and other hand-held devices may also be general-purpose computers. They can't perform any other functions, because the instructions have been permanently burned into thier read only memory (ROM); however, the computer circuitry is inherently general-purpose. In contrast, computer chips and computer systems can also be designed from scratch for special purposes. See *chip* and *database machine*.

general-purpose controller

A *general-purpose controller* is a peripheral control unit that can service more than one type of peripheral device, for example, a printer and a communications line.

general-purpose interface bus

See *GPIB*.

general-purpose language

A *general-purpose language* is a programming language that can be used to solve a wide variety of problems. FORTRAN, COBOL and BASIC are examples of general purpose languages. Contrast with *special-purpose language* such as

COGO, for solving problems in coordinate geometry, or GPSS for solving problems requiring simulation.

generalized routine

A *generalized routine* is a program routine that serves a changing environment by allowing different values to be used in the processing. Quick and dirty fixes to problems usually cause *hard coded* solutions that solve one set of conditions. By generalizing a routine and allowing variable data to be introduced, the routine can solve the same problem for different users or situations.

System software, such as operating systems and database management systems, are full of generalized routines that can serve a changing environment. One time this mix of programs is running, the next time another mix, and so forth.

generator

(1) A *generator* is a program that creates a program. See *application generator* and *macro generator*.

(2) A *generator* is a hardware device that creates electrical power or synchonization signals.

Generic CADD

Generic CADD is a full-featured computer-aided design and drafting package from Generic Software, Inc., that runs on IBM compatible pcs. Generic CADD offers three levels of implementation to fit the user's requirements. Level 1 is for the beginner, Level 2 for the intermediate user and Level 3 is aimed at the advanced CADD user. Level 1 is also available for the Macintosh personal computer.

Genifer

Genifer is an application generator from Bytel Corporation that generates dBASE III source code. An application is built by creating the actual menu, data entry and update screens that the user of the final application will see. After the characteristics of the screens are defined to Genifer, it generates traditional dBASE III source code that can always be modified by the programmer.

genlock

(**generator lock**) *Genlock* is the circuitry that synchronizes a video signal with another video signal in order to mix them. In a personal computer, a genlock display adapter converts screen output into a standard NTSC video signal, which it then synchronizes in order to mix with an external video source.

geostationary

Same as *geosynchronous*.

geosynchronous

Geosynchronous means aligned with the earth and refers to communications satellites that are placed 22,300 miles above the equator. The satellite travels at the same speed as the earth's rotation and thus appears to be stationary.

get

In programming, a *get* is a request for the next record in an input file. Contrast with *put*, which stores the current record in an output file.

ghost

(1) A *ghost* is a faint second image that appears close to the primary image on a display screen or printout. With regard to transmission, the ghost is a result of secondary signals that arrive ahead of or later than the primary signal. On a printout, the ghost is caused by bouncing print elements as the paper passes by.

(2) *Ghost* refers to displaying a menu option in a dimmed, fuzzy typeface in order to indicate that the option is not currently available. Pull-down menus typically ghost unavailable options.

giga

Giga means billion, and is abbreviated as "G." For example, 10 Gbytes is 10 billion bytes; 12 GHertz, or GHz, is 12 billion cycles per second. See *space/time*.

gigaflops

(giga FLoating point OPerations per Second) A *gigaflops* is one billion floating point operations per second.

GIGO

(Garbage In Garbage Out or Garbage In Gospel Out!) *GIGO* is what you get when you don't design a high level of data entry validation into your application.

GIS

(Generalized Information System) *GIS* is a query and data manipulation language from IBM that runs on IBM mainframes.

GKS

(Graphical Kernel System) GKS is a graphics system and language for creating 2-D, 3-D and raster graphics images. It is a device independent system that allows application programs to create and manipulate graphics on many varieties of display devices. GKS allows applications to be developed on one system and easily moved to another with minimal or no change. GKS is the first true standard for graphics applications programmers and has been adopted by both the American National Standards Institute (ANSI) and the International Standards Organization (ISO).

glare filter

A *glare filter* is a fine mesh screen that is placed over a CRT display screen to reduce glare from overhead and ambient light.

glitch

A *glitch* refers to any temporary or random malfunction in hardware. Contrast with *bug*, which is a permanent error. Sometimes a bug in a program may cause the hardware to appear as if it had a glitch in it (and vice versa). At times it can be extremely difficult to determine whether a problem lies within the hardware or the software.

global

Global pertains to an entire file, database, volume, program or system.

global variable

In programming, a *global variable* is a variable that is used by all modules in a program.

GO TO

(1) In a high-level programming language, *GO TO*, or *GOTO*, is a branching statement that directs the computer to go to some other part of the program. The equivalent in a low-level language is a *branch* or *jump* instruction.

(2) In dBASE, the *GOTO* command directs the user to a specific record in the database file.

(3) In word processing, *GO TO* directs the user to a specific page number.

GOTO-less programming

GOTO-less programming is the writing of a program without the use of GOTO instructions, which is an important rule in structured programming. A GOTO instruction points to a different part of the program without a guarantee of returning. Instead of using GOTOs, structures called subroutines or functions are used, which automatically return to the next instruction after the calling instruction when completed.

GPIB

(General Purpose Interface Bus) The *GPIB* (IEEE 488 standard) is a standard interface that connects peripheral devices to a computer and is often used for attaching sensors and programmable instruments. GPIB is a parallel interface that uses a special 24 pin connector.

Hewlett-Packard's version of the GPIB is the HPIB, or Hewlett-Packard Interface Bus.

GPSS

(General Purpose System Simulator) *GPSS* is a programming language that is used to build a model for simulation.

graceful degradation

Graceful degradation refers to a system that, after a failure of one of its components, can continue to perform at some reduced level of performance.

graceful exit

A *graceful exit* is the ability to get out of a problem situation with a program without having to turn the computer off.

grade

In communications, *grade* is the transmission capacity of a line and refers to a range or class of frequencies that it can handle, for example, telegraph grade, voice grade and broadband.

grandfather, father, son

Grandfather, father, son refers to the storing of previous generations of master file data, which is continuously being updated. The son is the current file, the father is a copy of the file from the previous cycle, and the grandfather is a copy of the file from the cycle before that one.

granularity

Granularity refers to the degree of modularity of a system. The more granularity (grains or granules), the more customizable or flexible the system.

graph

A *graph* is a pictorial representation of information. See *business graphics*.

graphic character

A *graphic character* is a printable symbol that includes numeric digits and alphabetic letters. A graphic character is not the same as *character graphics*, which are symbols, such as lines, corners and shaded blocks, that are used to create forms, boxes and primitive graphic images.

graphical interface

See *graphics interface*.

graphics

With regard to the computer, *graphics* is the creation and processing of picture images. Images can be drawn into the computer using graphics tablets, mice or light pens, and existing images on paper can be scanned into the computer using scanners or cameras. Once stored in the computer, images can be manipulated and copied in infinite ways. Colors can be changed, objects can be increased and decreased in size, slanted, squeezed and squashed. Frames of real pictures from video recordings can be combined with drawn objects. Text descriptions can be added to produce charts, reports, brochures and other kinds of presentation materials. Images can be printed on graphics printers and plotters, electronically transferred to high-resolution COM (computer output microfilm) machines, or they can be photographed with traditional cameras directly from the video display screen.

Known as *business graphics*, some software packages can generate graphic images, such as bar charts, scatter diagrams and pie charts directly from the data without human drawing efforts. These charts can often be enhanced by using graphics tools, such as paint programs.

A graphics computer system requires a graphics display screen, a graphics input device (tablet, mouse, scanner or camera), a graphics output device (dot matrix printer, laser printer, or plotter) and a graphics software package (CAD, draw or paint program). The higher the resolution of the graphics output device, the better the printed image will look. The higher the resolution of the display screen, the more realistic the images can be drawn and photographed.

Computer Graphics versus TV Realism

Although personal computers cost significantly more than a color TV, they can't produce animated pictures with the same quality as a TV, nor can they produce a still picture with the same visual quality. The reason is that a TV doesn't store the signal it receives from the broadcasting station; it simply transfers it directly to the screen. Images created in computers are generated and held in memory (working storage) and then copied to the screen. Personal computer memories haven't been large enough to represent all the dots in a single frame of TV, let alone been able to generate 30 frames per second to provide realistic animation.

Today, realistic (TV-like and better) graphics require high-powered CAD workstations or expensive add-ons to a personal computer. Animation of realistic images requires extremely powerful minicomputer workstations, and animation that can depict the intricate shading of human skin in a totally realistic fashion still challenges multi-million dollar supercomputers.

As chip technologies advance, memories and high-resolution graphics will become cheaper, and the personal computer of the 1990s will resemble the specialized CAD workstations of the 1980s.

Vector Graphics and Raster Graphics

Two methods are used for storing and maintaining pictures in a computer. The first method, called *vector graphics*, is used when objects are drawn into the computer. Vector graphics, also known as *object-oriented graphics*, maintains the image as a series of lines. The second method, called *raster graphics*, is used when objects are "painted" on screen or are scanned into the computer. Raster graphics is just like television, where the picture image is made up of dots.

Understanding these two methods and how they intertwine in today's graphics systems is essential for making sense out of computer graphics. When you create a picture on a video display screen, it may not be immediately obvious which method is being used. When you try to manipulate your image, it will become very clear which method has been used.

Vector Graphics for CAD and Drawing

Vector graphics is the method employed by CAD (computer-aided design) and drawing packages. As you draw, each line of the image is stored as a vector (two end points on an x-y matrix). For example, a square becomes four vectors, one for each side. A circle is turned into dozens or hundreds of tiny straight lines, the number of which is determined by the resolution of the system. The entire image is stored in the computer as a list of vectors, called a display list.

If the display screen used is a vector graphics screen, as is found in some specialized CAD systems, the image is also "drawn" on screen. If it's a raster graphics screen (made up of dots), as is the case with personal computers and most graphics systems today, the vectors are converted into dots in order to display the image on screen. This is called the *rasterization of vectors*.

Vector graphics is required when it is essential to have knowledge about the image created. Each part of the image can be isolated and identified from the other parts; for example, one vector is the roof, another vector is the floor and so on. This allows ultimate flexibility in changing the image. If you can select a part of an existing image and literally "lift" it out and away from the rest of the image, the software is using vector graphics.

Vector graphics can be transmitted directly to x-y plotters that "draw" the images from the list of vectors.

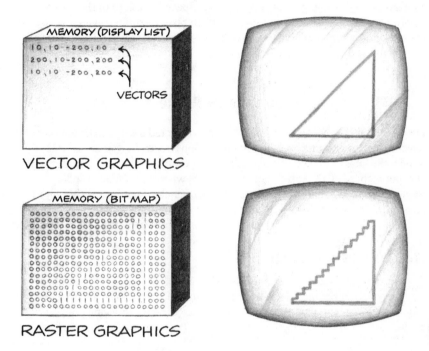

Raster Graphics for Painting

Raster graphics is the television-like method that uses dots to display an image on screen. Raster graphics images are created by scanners and cameras and are also generated by paint packages. A picture frame is divided into hundreds of horizontal rows, with each row containing hundreds of dots, called *pixels* (picture elements). Unlike television, which uses a single standard for the entire country (NTSC standard), there are dozens of raster graphics standards with new ones coming along all the time. Also unlike television, which records and displays the dots as infinitely variable shades and colors (analog method), computer graphics have a finite number of shades and colors (digital method) based on how much memory, or how large a number, is set aside for each dot within the computer.

When you scan an image or paint an object into the computer, the image is created by the computer in a reserved area of memory called a bit map, with some number of bits corresponding to each dot (pixel). In the simplest monochrome systems, one bit can represent a dot, either on or off. For gray scale (monochrome shades), several bits are required to hold the shade number for each dot. For color, more bits are required to hold a number for each intensity of red, green and blue in the dot. The image in the bit map is continuously transmitted to the video screen, dot for dot, a line at a time, over and over again. Any changes made to the bit map are instantly reflected on the screen.

Since colors are really numbers, changing red to green is simply searching for the red number and replacing it with the green number, just as in word processing. Animation is accomplished by continuously copying new sequences from other areas in memory into the bit map, one after the other.

Raster graphics images may take up more space on disk than their vector graphics counterpart, because storage for each pixel is required even if it's part of the background. A small object in vector graphics format will take up only a few vectors in the display list file.

Screens vs Printers

Desktop laser printers and graphics plotters connected to personal computers have higher resolutions than the standard graphics screens that are used to display the images. The resolution of contemporary desktop laser printers is 300 dots per inch, or 90,000 pixels per square inch, whereas common display resolutions are less than 5,000 pixels per square inch. That means the jagged lines on your display screen will print straight on your laser printer.

graphics engine

A *graphics engine* is specialized hardware that performs graphics processing independently of the main CPU. Graphics engines can perform a number of functions, including generating various graphic geometry (drawing lines and circles) as well as converting vectors to rasters (rasterization of vectors).

graphics interface

(1) A *graphics interface* is a user interface that displays pictures of objects rather than only names of objects. It typically refers to the interface developed by Xerox that has been popularized on the Apple Macintosh and is used in Digital Research's GEM, Microsoft's Windows and OS/2 Presentation Manager, and Hewlett-Packards's New Wave environments. See *Macintosh user interface* and *user interface*.

(2) *Graphics interface* refers to displaying graphics on screen.

Graphics Kernel System

See *GKS*.

graphics language

A *graphics language* is a set of instructions that let a programmer express a desired graphics image in a high-level language. The language is translated into graphics images by software or specialized hardware. See *graphics engine*.

graphics primitive

A *graphics primitive* is an elementary graphics building block, such as a dot, line and arc. In a solids modeling system, a cylinder, cube and sphere are examples of primitives.

graphics processor

Same as *graphics engine*.

graphics tablet

See *digitizer tablet*.

graphics terminal

A *graphics terminal* is an input/output device that is capable of accepting and displaying picture images. Graphics input is entered with a mouse or light pen, and the keyboard may have specialized function keys, wheels and dials. Graphics output on screen is displayed using raster graphics, vector graphics, combination raster and vector and direct view storage tube (DVST) technologies.

A graphics terminal may refer to one of the display standards available for IBM compatible pcs, such as MDA, CGA, EGA, VGA and Hercules.

graPHIGS

See GDDM.

gray scale

In computer graphics, *gray scale* is a series of shades from white to black. The more levels of gray scale that can be handled, the more realistic an image can be displayed, especially a photograph that has been scanned into the computer. Scanners can differentiate typically from 16 to 256 levels of gray scale. However, the amount of gray scale that can be created or entered into the computer depends on the memory and disk space that can be reserved. At 300 dots per inch, the resolution of contemporary desktop laser printers, each square inch is made up of 90,000 pixels. At 256 levels of gray scale, or one byte per pixel, it takes 90,000 bytes for one square inch of image. Although compression techiques help reduce the size of graphics files, high-resolution gray scale requires huge amounts of storage.

greeking

Greeking is the displaying of text in a representative form in which the actual letters are not discernible. For example, when previewing a finished document in desktop publishing, if the display screen is not large enough to handle the resoution, the text is greeked.

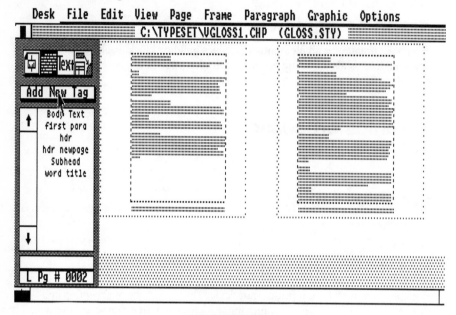

GREEKING

This Ventura Publisher example shows two facing pages of this book on a low-resolution screen, which cannot display the full characters.

GT

(Greater Than) See *relational operator*.

gulp

A *gulp* is an unspecified number of bytes!

gutter

In typography, a *gutter* is the space between two columns.

H&J

(Hyphenation and Justification) In word processing, *H&J* refers to the format of the right margin. Hyphenation breaks up words that exceed the margin, and justification aligns text uniformly at the right margin while spacing text evenly between both margins.

hacker

A *hacker* is a very technical person in the computer field, such as an assembly language programmer or systems progammer. However, hacker is often used in a derogatory manner to refer to people that use their technical knowledge to gain unauthorized access into computer systems and data banks.

half-adder

A *half-adder* is an elementary electronic circuit located within the arithmetic logic unit (ALU) that adds one bit to another, deriving a result bit and a carry bit.

half-duplex

In communications, *half-duplex* is the transmission of data in two directions, but in only one direction at a time. The technology has been around for years. Whenever you hear a two-way radio conversation in which each party speaks and then says "over," in order to hear from the other person, that's half-duplex transmission. Contrast with full-duplex transmission, which allows simultaneous transmission in both directions at the same time.

half height drive

A *half height drive* is a disk drive that takes up one half the vertical space of first-generation personal computer disk drives. The half height drive is 1 5/8" high by 5 3/4" wide.

halftone

In printing, a *halftone* is the simulation of a continuous-tone image, such as a shaded drawing or a photograph, with groups of dots. The dots are necessary, because all the printing processes, except for Mead's Cycolor process, print black dots or dots of color. The smaller the dots and the wider they're spaced apart, the lighter the resulting image. The denser the dots, the darker the image. If you look at any newspaper or magazine photograph through a magnifying glass, you'll see how the different dot densities simulate continuous shades.

In computer graphics, generating halftones is called *dithering*.

hammer

In a printer, a *hammer* is the mechanism that pushes the typeface onto the ribbon and paper or pushes the paper into the ribbon and typeface.

Hamming code

In communications, a *Hamming code* is an error correction code that is interspersed with the bits of each character. At the receiving station, the code is checked in order to detect missing bits, and one-bit errors can be corrected automatically.

handle

In computer graphics, a *handle* is a tiny square which is attached to a graphic image that is used for moving or reshaping the image. The handle is selected by moving the cursor onto it and pressing a key or mouse button.

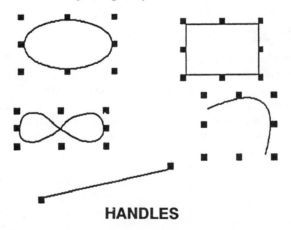

HANDLES

handler

A *handler* is a program routine that is dedicated to a particular task. For example, upon detection of an error, an error handler displays the appropriate messages and attempts to recover from the error condition.

handset

The *handset* is the part of the telephone that contains the speaker and the microphone.

handshaking

Handshaking are the signals transmitted back and forth over a communications network that establish a valid connection between two parties. Handshaking is part of the communications protocol that dictates the codes and electronic signalling required.

hanging paragraph

In typography, a *hanging paragraph* is a paragraph of text in which the first
line starts at the left margin, but the second and all
subsequent lines are indented some number of spaces, just
like this paragraph.

hard coded

Hard coded refers to a software program or program subroutine that is designed to perform a specific task and is not easily changed. Software can be designed in a generalized style that allows for future changes easily, or it can be designed to solve the immediate problem exactly as is. Hard coding a solution is the easiest and fastest way to program. It will also result in the least amount of machine time to run it. However, that machine time might mean 10 extra seconds per day, and when it comes time to change the program again, redoing the hard coded solution may take hours.

hard copy

Hard copy is printed output. Contrast with *soft copy*, which is spoken or displayed on screen.

hard disk

A *hard disk* is a magnetic disk made of metal and covered with a magnetic recording surface. Hard disks come in removable and fixed varieties that hold from five megabytes to hundreds of megabytes. Contrast with *floppy disk*, which uses a flexible disk made out the same material as magnetic tape.

hard return

In word processing, a *hard return* is a control code that is entered into a document by pressing the return, or enter, key. The standard ASCII file hard return is two characters, a CARRIAGE RETURN followed by a LINE FEED. However, this is not always followed; for example, WordPerfect uses only a LINE FEED as a hard return code. Hard returns may be invisible on screen, requiring that the codes be revealed in a special mode in order to see them; or they may appear on screen at all times as some special character such as the <D used in WordStar and WordStar-like programs.

Contrast with *soft return*, which is entered into the text automatically by the word processing program to mark the end of the line based on the current right margin.

hard sectored

Hard sectored is an organization technique that identifies the sectors on a disk by some physical mark or code. Hard sectored floppy disks have holes punched through them marking the beginning of each sector. Contrast with *soft sectored*, which uses identification numbers recorded on the disk by a *format* program.

Hardcard

The Hardcard is an add-on hard disk from Plus Development Corporation that plugs into an expansion slot in IBM and various compatible personal computers. Introduced in 1985, the Hardcard contains the control electronics and the hard disk on a printed circuit board that takes up only one slot, allowing full-length boards to be inserted on either side of it. It can be the first hard disk in a floppy-only system or additional hard disk storage in a hard disk system. Early BIOSs that make no provision for hard disks must be upgraded.

The Hardcard allows for the inclusion of hard disks in systems in which all the disk bays are currently filled. The Hardcard is noted for its high reliability.

hardware

Hardware is machinery or equipment, such as a CPU, video terminal, disk drive and printer. Any electronic, mechanical or electromechanical device is hardware. Contrast with *software*, which is the set of instructions that tell the computer what to do. Also contrast with *data*, which are the facts and figures that are stored in the hardware and are governed by the rules and regulations of both the hardware and the software.

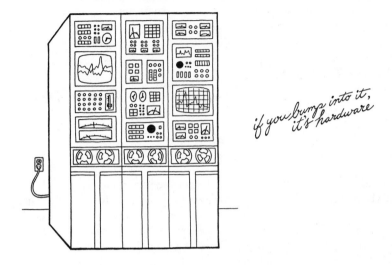

if you bump into it, it's hardware

Hardware vs Software

In operation, a computer system is both hardware and software. One is useless without the other, and each rules the other. The hardware dictates the instructions it can follow, and the instructions then tell it what to do.

As inseparable as hardware and software are in operation, they are quite different when they are being evaluated. Hardware is the world of storage and transmission. Software is the world of logic and language.

The more memory and disk storage a computer system has, the more work it can do. The faster the memory and disks transmit data and instructions between them and the CPU, the faster the work gets done. A user's problem can be translated into a hardware requirement based on the size of the files and databases that will be created and the number of concurrent users at terminals.

Software, on the other hand, is harder to specify. The programs must process the organization's business transactions properly, and even the smallest company's processing can be very complicated.

In addition, each program must be written in a programming language. The languages and software development tools used to develop the system will have a strong bearing on how responsive the system will be to changes in the future. In addition, each program designed for interaction with the user creates another language, the user interface, which is the way a person communicates with and commands the computer. The design of the user interface is critical to the success of the overall application.

Hardware always deals with the data processing problem in the same way. How much? How fast? But software deals with the tedious details of the problem that are always changing in an organization. It's much harder to analyze, design and develop the software solution than it is to specify the hardware.

hardware failure

A *hardware failure* is a malfunction within the electronic circuits or electromechanical components (disks, tapes) of a computer system. Contrast with *software failure*, which is an error due to improper logic within the program.

hardware monitor

A *hardware monitor* is a device that is connected to the circuits of a computer in order to analyze its performance.

hardwired

Hardwired is electronic circuitry that is designed to perform a specific task and is not easily changeable. It also refers to devices that are closely or tightly coupled together. For example, a hardwired terminal is a terminal directly connected to the CPU without going through a communications network or controller. Sometimes software is said to be hardwired, meaning that it is *hard coded* or set up to provide a solution to a fixed set of conditions.

harmonic distortion

In communications, *harmonic distortion* are frequencies that are generated as multiples of the original frequency due to irregularities in the transmission line.

Harvard Graphics

Harvard Graphics is a business graphics program from Software Publishing Company that runs on IBM compatible pcs. Harvard Graphics is an advanced program that turns existing data into graphs and charts for presentations in a wide variety of styles and formats. It also provides the ability to create columnar and free form text charts.

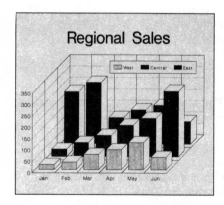
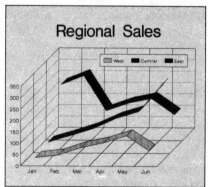

SAMPLE HARVARD GRAPHICS CHARTS
(Courtesy Software Publishing Corp.)

hash total

A *hash total* is a method of ensuring the accuracy of processed data. A hash total is a total of several fields of data in a file, even fields not normally used in calculations, such as account numbers. At various stages in the processing, the hash total is recalculated and compared with the original. If any data has been lost or changed, the mismatch will signal an error.

Hayes compatible

Hayes compatible is a modem that accepts the same command language as modems made by Hayes Microcomputer Products.

Hayes Smartmodem

The *Hayes Smartmodem* is a modem for personal computers from Hayes Microcomputer Products. Hayes Smartmodems were developed for first-generation personal computers and the command language that activates modem functions has become an industry standard.

Hayes V-series

The *Hayes V-series* is a family of modems with built-in error correction and compression. When two Hayes V-series modems communicate with each other, they automatically test for errors and compress and decompress the data, functions normally done by the protocol in the communications program and special compression programs. In addition, they switch from asynchronous to synchronous mode for improved transmission speed. A "Modem Enhancer" is also available that brings V-series capabilities to standard Hayes modems.

HDLC

(High-level Data Link Control) *HDLC* is an international communications protocol defined by ISO (International Standards Organization). HDLC is used in X.25 communications networks.

HDTV

See *high definition TV*.

head

See *read/write head*.

head crash

A head *crash* is the physical destruction of a hard disk. Due to head misalignment or contamination with dust and dirt particles, the read/write head collides with the disk's magnetic coated recording surface. The recorded data is destroyed, and both the disk platter and read/write head usually have to be replaced.

The read/write head actually touches the surface of a floppy disk, but on a hard disk, the read/write head hovers above its surface at a distance that is less the diameter of a human hair. It has been said that the read/write head flying over the disk surface is like trying to fly a jet plane six inches above the earth's surface. Fortunately, read/write heads fly better than jet planes under that condition.

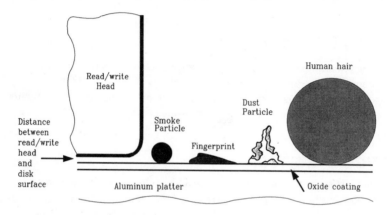

head-per-track disk

A *head-per-track disk* is a disk drive that has a read/write head positioned over each track, thus eliminating the access arm movement from track to track.

header

(1) In data processing, a *header* is the first record in a file that identifies the file. The name of the file, date of last update and various other status data are stored in the header.

(2) In a document or report, a *header* is common text that is printed at the top of every page. The header may also contain the page number.

(3) In communications, a *header* is the first part of the message that contains controlling data, such as originating and destination stations, message type and priority level.

(4) *Header* may refer to any caption or description used as a headline.

header label

A *header label* is the first record in a file that identifies the file.

heap

Same as *stack*.

heat sink

A *heat sink* is a material that absorbs heat.

help screen

A *help screen* is a screenful of instructions regarding the use of the program you're using. See *context sensitive help*.

Hercules Graphics Card

Hercules Graphics Card is a video display board from Hercules Computer Technology that provides both graphics and text on monochrome monitors for IBM compatible pcs. The Hercules resolution is 720x348 pixels. IBM's monochrome standard for its first-generation PCs, called *MDA* (monochrome display adapater), does not provide a graphics mode. In order to display graphics, a color video display board, such as the CGA or EGA, is required.

In order to fill this void, Hercules introduced its monochrome text/graphics board in 1982, and it has become an industry standard supported by most graphics software packages.

In 1986, Hercules introduced the Hercules Graphics Card Plus (HGC+), which can display customized fonts from memory.

In 1987, Hercules introduced the InColor Card, which is a color version of the Hercules Graphics Card Plus that provides 16 colors out of a palette of 64 and uses an EGA-compatible monitor. Another product from Hercules, called the Color Card, is a CGA board designed for dual monitor operation along with a Hercules' monochrome board. The Color Card and InColor Card are two distinct products.

Hertz

Hertz is the frequency of electrical vibrations (cycles) per second. One Hertz is equal to one cycle per second. In 1883, Heinrich Hertz detected electromagnetic waves. Hertz is abbreviated Hz.

heuristic

Heuristic is a method of solving a problem by exploration and trial and error in artificial intelligence applications. Heuristic program design provides a framework for solving the problem in contrast with a fixed set of rules (algorithmic) that cannot vary.

Hewlett-Packard Company

Hewlett-Packard Company, commonly known as "HP," was founded in 1939 by Bill Hewlett and Dave Packard in a garage behind the Packard's California home. Its first product, an audio oscillator for measuring sound, was the beginning of a line of electronics that made HP an international supplier of electronic test and measurement instruments. Walt Disney Studios, HP's first "big" customer, purchased eight oscillators to develop and test a new sound system for the movie "Fantasia."

HP entered the computer field in 1966 with the 2116A, the first of the HP 1000 series designed to gather and analyze the data produced by HP instruments. HP 1000 computers are used for CIM applications, such as process monitoring and control, alarm management and machine monitoring.

In 1972, HP branched into business computing with the 3000 series, a multiuser system that became well known for its

HEWLETT & PACKARD

(Courtesy Hewlett-Packard)

This photo of William R. Hewlett and David Packard was taken in 1964.

extremely high reliability, especially for that time. The successful 3000 family has continued to be HP's major computer series and has evolved into a full family of computers from micro to mainframe. Also in 1972, HP introduced the first scientific handheld calculator, the HP-35, obsoleting the slide rule and ushering in a new age of pocket-sized calculators. In 1982, the first HP 9000 workstation was introduced.

HP'S FIRST PRODUCT

(Courtesy Hewlett-Packard)

HP's first personal computer was the Touchscreen 150, an MS-DOS personal computer that gained only modest acceptance. In 1985, it introduced the Vectra, an 80286-based pc that was reasonably compatible with the IBM AT. In 1987, an expanded series of Vectras with greater compatibility was introduced, which has been well accepted within the HP community.

In 1984, HP revolutionized the printer market with its desktop LaserJet printer, which has set the standard for the industry.

In 1986, HP introduced a new internal design for its 3000 and 9000 families that will carry the company into the 1990s. The new HP "Precision Architecture" provides a significant increase in performance.

The Hewlett-Packard Company sells over 10,000 different products in the electronics and computer field, and it has gained a worldwide reputation for its rugged and reliable engineering.

2116A
(Courtesy Hewlett-Packard)

hexadecimal (hex)

Hexadecimal is a numbering system that uses 16 digits (hex=6, decimal=10). Hexadecimal is a shorthand method for representing binary numbers. Each four bits (half byte) is converted into a single hexadecimal digit.

Decimal	Binary	Hexadecimal
0	0000	0
1	0001	1
2	0010	2
3	0011	3
4	0100	4
5	0101	5
6	0110	6
7	0111	7
8	1000	8
9	1001	9
10	1010	A
11	1011	B
12	1100	C
13	1101	D
14	1110	E
15	1111	F

HGC

See *Hercules Graphics Card*.

hidden file

A *hidden file* is a disk file that has been given a status that prevents it from being viewed, changed or deleted. Hidden files are usually program files that are part of the system software; however, users can also hide files on disk to prevent unauthorized access.

hierarchical

Hierarchical refers to systems that have a structure made up of different levels like a company organization chart. The higher levels have control or precedence over the lower levels. Hierarchical structures are a one to many relationship; each item having one or more items below it.

    In communications, a hierarchical network refers to a single computer that has control over all the nodes connected to it.

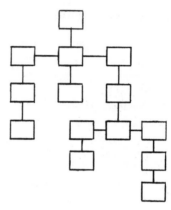

HIERARCHICAL

hierarchical file system

A *hierarchical file system* stores data in a top-to-bottom organization structure. All access to the data starts at the top and proceeds throughout the levels of the hierarchy. In IBM compatible pcs running Microsoft's DOS or OS/2 operating systems, the root directory is the starting point. Files can be stored in the root directory, or subdirectories can be created off the root directory that hold files and additional subdirectories. In the Macintosh, the disk window is the starting point. Files can be stored in the disk window, or folders can be created that can hold files and additional folders.

high definition TV

High definition TV is a television standard with a higher resolution than the current international standards. High definition TV will have in the order of 1,125 lines of resolution compared to the 525 lines for the present NTSC standard in the United States. Experimental systems are being tested in Japanese households, and tests will be set up in the United States in the 1990s. The major problem is trying to develop a transmission technique that will allow broadcasting in both regular and high definition standards at the same time.

high-level language

High-level languages are machine-independent programming languages, such as FORTRAN, COBOL, BASIC, PL/I, Pascal, dBASE and C. High-level languages let the programmer concentrate on the logic of the problem to be solved rather than the intricacies of the machine architecture, such as is required with low-level assembly languages. High-level languages are third and fourth-generation programming languages. Contrast with *low-level*, second-generation assembly languages.

high resolution

High resolution is high-quality imagery provided on a display screen or printed form. The more dots used per square inch, the higher the quality. To display totally realistic images including the shades of human skin requires about 1,000 x 1,000 pixels on a 12" diagonal screen. Desktop laser printers print very good text and graphics at 300 dots per linear inch, but typesetting machines can print over 1,200 dots per inch.

higher order software

See *HOS*.

HIPO

(Hierarchy plus Input-Process-Output) Pronounced "hy-po," *HIPO* is an IBM flow-charting technique that provides a graphical method for designing and documenting programs.

hi-res

(HIgh-RESolution) See *high resolution*.

HLLAPI

(High Level Language Application Program Interface) *HLLAPI* is a programming interface that allows an application program running in a pc to communicate with an application running in an IBM mainframe. The pc is hooked up to the mainframe via normal micro to mainframe 3270 emulation. HLLAPI tricks the mainframe into believing that a user is at a 3270 terminal, when, in fact, it's a program interacting with the mainframe.

hog

A *hog* is a program that uses an excessive amount of computer resources, such as memory or disk, or takes a long time to execute.

Hollerith tabulating machine

The *Hollerith tabulating machine* was the first automatic data processing system and was used to count the population of the United States in 1890. Developed by Herman Hollerith, a statistician who had worked for the Census Bureau, the system used cards to record the data as a series of punched holes. The Hollerith punched card was the size of an 1890 dollar bill in order that it could be conveniently stored in existing cabinets.

At the rate of growth in America, it was estimated that, with manual methods, the 1890 census wouldn't be completed until after 1900. With Hollerith's machines, it took only two years, and it saved the Census Bureau five million dollars.

Hollerith formed the Tabulating Machine Company and sold his machines throughout the world for census taking and various other purposes. His machines were even used in World War I. In 1911, his company was merged into the company that eventually became IBM.

HERMAN HOLLERITH
(Courtesy Library of Congress)

HOLLERITH TABULATING MACHINE
(Courtesy Smithsonian Institution)
These are replicas of the tabulating machine and sort box used in the 1890 census.

A UNIQUE CONCEPT IN 1891

This November 11, 1891 issue of The Electrical Engineer extols the virtues of using electricity as a means of counting.

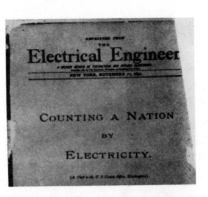

THE 1890 CENSUS

(Courtesy Scientific American)

home brew

Home brew refers to products that are developed at home by hobbyists.

home computer

A *home computer* is a personal computer that is used primarily for education and games. The Apple II series, Commodore 64 and 128, Tandy Color Computer and Atari ST are examples of home computers.

home key

The *home key* is a keyboard key that is used for cursor movement. It is used to move the cursor to the top left side of the screen or to the beginning of a list or file. It is sometimes used to move the cursor to the previous word or field. In icon-oriented environments, a picture of a house is used to represent a home key.

Honeywell Bull

Honeywell Bull was formed in March 1987, as a merger of Honeywell Information Systems, Groupe Bull of France and NEC of Japan. This is not the first time Honeywell and Bull were merged. In 1970, Honeywell took over General Electric's computer division, and GE's interest in Compagnie des Machines Bull was renamed Honeywell Bull.

Honeywell started out in Minneapolis in 1885, when Alfred Butz began making his patented temperature controls. In 1906, Mark C. Honeywell began making water heaters in Wabash, Indiana, and later got into temperature controls. In 1927, both companies merged to become the Minneapolis Honeywell Regulator Company.

Honeywell was one of the first computer manufacturers in the United States. In a joint venture with Ratheon, it launched the Datamatic 1000 in 1957, a monstrous, tube-driven machine. In 1959 and 1960, Honeywell introduced the Models 800 and 400, advanced second-generation computers that put Honeywell square into the computer business. In 1963, it introduced the Model 200, which was so successful at capturing IBM 1401 accounts, that IBM announced its new System/360 ahead of schedule. Honeywell provided a "Liberator" program to translate 1401 programs to the 200, which would run them five times faster.

In 1966, Honeywell acquired the Computer Control Company and incorporated its minicomputers into the Honeywell line. In 1970, it acquired the assets of GE's computer business and Honeywell's computer division was renamed Honeywell Information Systems, Inc.

Through Honeywell's association with Bull in Europe and Bull's association with NEC in Japan, research and development was mutually explored, and product lines were jointly developed throughout the 1970s and 1980s.

Honeywell offered a wide range of departmental minicomputers and mainframes to its customers throughout this time period.

In 1986, Honeywell-NEC Supercomputers Inc., a joint venture to market NEC supercomputers in the U. S. and Canada, was formed.

As of the March 1987 merger, Honeywell Bull is a privately-held company owned 42.5% by Bull, 42.5% by Honeywell and 15% by NEC.

DATAMATIC 1000
(Courtesy Honeywell Inc.)

hook

In programming, a *hook* is a place in the program that points to some other routine or program. It may refer to a program that is designed to be modifed later, the hooks in the program being where the expansion will take place.

hopper

A *hopper* is a tray, or chute, that accepts input to a mechanical reader such as a card reader.

horizonal scrolling

See *scrolling*.

horizontal synchronization frequency

See *scan rate*.

HOS

(Higher Order Software) *HOS* is a design and documentation technique that is used to break down an information system into a set of functions that are mathematically correct and error free. HOS uses a rigid set of rules for the decomposition of the total system into its elementary components. The resulting specifications are complete enough to have machine language programs generated directly from them.

host

A *host* is the central or controlling computer in a timesharing or distributed processing environment.

host-based

Host-based refers to a communications system that is controlled by a central computer system.

hot key

A *hot key* is a selected key or key combination that causes some function to occur in the computer, no matter what else is currently running. Hot keys are commonly used to activate a memory resident, or TSR, program.

housekeeping

Housekeeping refers to a set of instructions that are executed at the beginning of a program. Housekeeping sets all counters and flags to their starting values, may clear selected memory buffers and generally readies the program for proper execution.

HP

See *Hewlett-Packard Company.*

HP Precision Architecture

HP Precision Architecture is an internal architecture and machine language from Hewlett-Packard that is being incorporated into new models of its 3000 and 9000 families of computers and workstations. Introduced in 1986, it is an HP proprietary architecture based on reduced instruction set computer (RISC) design principles.

HP-UX

HP-UX is Hewlett-Packard's version of the UNIX operating system that runs on its 9000 family of workstations. It is based on the System V Interface Definition (SVID) and incorporates features from Berkeley 4.2 BSD (Berkeley Software Distribution) as well as several HP innovations.

HP 1000

The *HP 1000* is a family of minicomputers from Hewlett-Packard that are used in computer-integrated manufacturing (CIM) applications such as factory floor management. Introduced in 1966, HP 1000 machines are sensor-based computers that are used extensively in laboratory and manufacturing environments for collecting and analyzing data.

HP 3000

The *HP 3000* is a family of business-oriented computers from Hewlett-Packard. Introduced in 1972, the HP 3000 minicomputers set a standard for reliability and rugged engineering and have been HP's major computer line ever since. The HP 3000 has evolved into a complete line from micro versions to medium-scale mainframes. New models of the 3000 incorporate the HP Precision Architecture and also provide compatibility with the original 3000 machines.

HP 9000

The *HP 9000* is a family of high-performance UNIX workstations from Hewlett-Packard. Introduced in 1982, HP 9000 workstations are used extensively in computer-aided design (CAD) and engineering applications. The 9000 family is migrating to the HP Precision Architecture.

HPGL

(Hewlett-Packard Graphics Language) *HPGL* is a graphics file format from Hewlett-Packard. Developed as a standard plotter format, HPGL stores images in vector graphics format.

HPIB

(Hewlett-Packard Interface Bus) *HPIB* is Hewlett-Packard's version of the General Purpose Interface Bus (GPIB), which is the IEEE 488 standard.

hue

In computer graphics, a *hue* is a particular shade or tint of a given color.

hybrid circuit

See *hybrid microcircuit*.

hybrid computer

A *hybrid computer* is a digital computer that processes analog signals that have been converted into digital form. Hybrid computers are used extensively in process control and robotics.

hybrid microcircuit

A *hybrid microcircuit* is an electronic circuit composed of different types of integrated circuits and discrete components, which are mounted on a ceramic base. Hybrid microcircuits fall somewhere between printed circuit boards and integrated circuits and are used extensively in military and communications applications. Although used for digital circuits as well, hybrid microcircuits are especially suitable for building customized analog circuits, including analog to digital and digital to analog converters, amplifiers, modulators and integrators.

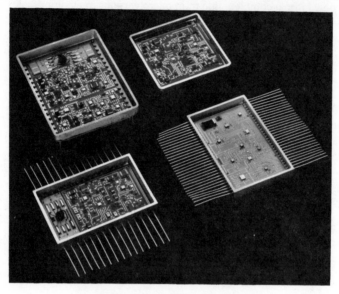

HYBRID MICROCIRCUITS
(Courtesy Circuit Technology Inc.)

hybrid network

In communications, a *hybrid network* is a network made up of equipment from multiple vendors.

Hyperaccess

Hyperaccess is a communications program from Hilgraeve, Inc., that runs on IBM compatible pcs. Version 3.2 handles transmission speeds from 50 to 19,200 bits per second, emulates nine different terminals and supports four protocols.

HyperCard

HyperCard is a database program from Apple that runs on the Macintosh personal computer. It lets users build databases that incorporate the graphical interface of the Macintosh. A file of records is called a stack of cards in HyperCard. A record is like a Rolodex card on screen, which can be customized with graphic images and button icons that, when clicked, can perform database operations. A button can be set up to run a HyperCard script (program) using the HyperTalk programming language, or a button can link a user with another associated record.

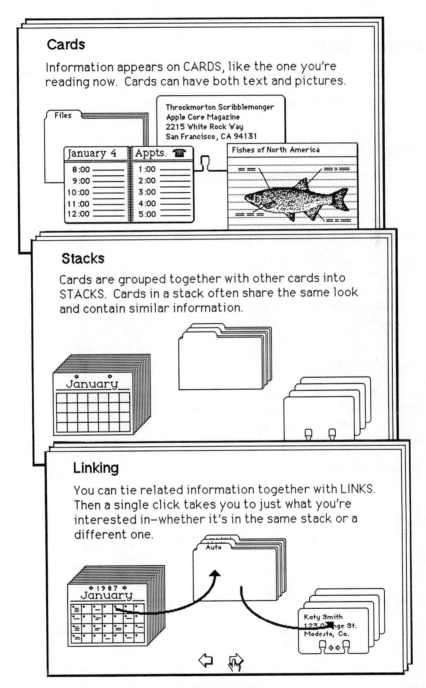

HYPERCARD

Sample Hypercard screens that explain basic functions.

Hypercube

A *Hypercube* is a parallel processing computer architecture that is made up of several processors.

hypermedia

Hypermedia refers to the use of data, text, graphics, video and voice as elements in a Hypertext system. All the various forms of information are linked together so that a user can easily move from one to another.

HyperTalk

HyperTalk is the programming language used in Apple's HyperCard database program.

Hypertext

Hypertext is a technique that links information together. Words are invisibly linked to other words or explanations. For example, by pointing to a key word in a sentence and selecting it, the linkage is activated and the associated information is revealed. The concept was developed by Ted Nelson as a way of accessing information in the computer the way a person thinks.

hyphenation

Hyphenation is the breaking of words that extend beyond the right margin. In word processing and desktop publishing programs, hyphenation is determined either by matching the words against a hyphenation dictionary, which is a disk file of words with the dashes in the proper locations, or by using a built-in set of rules, or both. Users can typically add their own words to the hyphenation dictionary, placing the hyphens where they want them. See *discretionary hyphen*.

hyphenation zone

The *hyphenation zone* is the distance from the right margin within which a word may be hyphenated.

hysteresis

Hysteresis is a lag between making a change, such as increasing or decreasing power, and the response or effect of that change.

Hz

(HertZ) See *hertz*.

I

IBM

(International Business Machines Corporation) *IBM* is and has almost always been the largest data processing and computer company in the world.

It started in 1911, in New York City, when the Computing-Tabulating-Recording Company (CTR) was created by merging The Tabulating Machine Company, Herman Hollerith's punched card machines company in Washington, D.C., with the International Time Recording Company, a time clock company with plants in upstate New York, the Computing Scale Company of America, a Dayton, Ohio maker of scales and meat and cheese slicers and Bundy Manufacturing, a small time clock maker in Poughkeepsie, New York. CTR had 1,200 employees and a capital value of $17.5 million.

THOMAS J. WATSON, SR.

(Courtesy IBM)

This photo of Watson, taken in 1920, was before his company was renamed IBM.

In 1914, Thomas J. Watson, Sr., became general manager. During the next 10 years, he dispensed with most of its non-tabulating business and turned it into an international enterprise that was renamed IBM in 1924.

IBM achieved spectacular success in the punched card data processing market by producing high-quality electromechanical machines and supplying the punched cards that went with them. From the 1920s through the 1960s, IBM developed a huge tabulating machines customer base that was ideal for conversion to computers.

The 701, introduced in 1953, launched IBM in the computer business; but the 650, announced a year later, put it well ahead of its competition. By the end of the 1950s, an estimated 1,800 650s were installed, making it the most widely used computer in the world.

IBM 701

(Courtesy Charles Babbage Institute, University of Minnesota)
Ronald Reagan and Herbert Grosch at a customer installation in 1957.

The 1401, announced in 1959, was IBM's second major computer success. By the mid 1960s, an estimated 18,000 of them were in use. The 1403 chain printer, introduced with the 1401, was the most highly praised printer of its time, once again demonstrating IBM's expertise in electromechanical systems.

In April 1964, IBM announced the System/360, the first time any company ever introduced a family of compatible computers. Using advanced circuitry for its time, the 360 series was enormously successful and set the standard for all the IBM mainframes to this day.

Although IBM achieved its greatest success with mainframe compatibility, it produced a very disparate line of minicomputers. Throughout the late 1970s,

IBM OFFICE, LONDON (1935)
(Courtesy IBM)

IBM introduced, among others, the System/3, System/32, System/38, Series 1 and 8100, each series incompatible with the others.

In 1981, IBM entered the bustling personal computer field and, once again, set the industry standard. There are now more IBM and IBM compatible personal computers than any other type of computer system in the world.

Throughout the 1990s, IBM's goal is to integrate its different products lines through a master plan called Systems Application Architecture. SAA is intended to provide common interfaces so that users will command and interact with all IBM machines in the same way and will be able to easily exchange information between IBM micros, minis and mainframes.

IBM compatible pc

IBM *compatible pc* is a personal computer that is compatible with the IBM standard. In this book, the term refers to IBM and IBM compatible personal computers. The term "pc" in lower case refers to all IBM personal computers, including both first-generation PCs and second-generation PS/2s. The term "PC" in upper case refers to first-generation PCs only, which includes PC, XT and AT type machines.

IBM PC

See IBM *personal computer*.

IBM personal computer

IBM *personal computers* and compatible models from other vendors are the most widely used computer systems in the world. They are typically single user personal computers, although they have been adapted into multiuser models for special applications. IBM personal computers use the Intel 8086 family of microprocessors, which provide a range from low to high-performance processing. The models of IBM's first-generation Personal Computer (PC) series have names: PC, XT, AT, Convertible, Portable, etc.; however, the models of its second generation, the Personal System/2 (PS/2), are known by model number: Model 25, Model 30, etc. Within each series, the models are also commonly referenced by their CPU size and speed.

All IBM personal computers are software compatible with each other in general, but not every program will work in every machine. Some programs are time sensitive to a particular speed class. Older programs may also not take advantage of newer higher-resolution display standards.

The PS/2 series introduced three advances over the PC series: (1) 3 1/2" 1.44 megabyte microfloppy disks, (2) VGA and 8514 graphics display standards, and (3) the Micro Channel bus architecture. The 3 1/2" disks and VGA can be easily installed on existing PCs and will become the standard for new compatible computers. The Micro Channel bus allows for multiprocessing and less aggravation, but cannot be retrofitted to existing PCs.

There are literally hundreds of models of IBM and IBM compatible computers to choose from; however, they all fall into one of the following categories.

Performance

The speed of the CPU (microprocessor) is the significant factor in machine performance. It is determined by its clock speed and the number of bits it can process internally. It is also determined by the number of bits it transfers across its data bus at one time (see chart on the bottom of the next page). The second major performance factor is the speed of the hard disk.

If the program takes advantage of it, CAD and other graphics applications can be speeded up with the addition of a math coprocessor, which is a chip that is plugged into a special socket available in almost all machines.

8086 & 8088-BASED COMPUTERS

The Intel 8088 is the CPU in the original IBM PC. The Intel 8086 is somewhat faster than the 8088. Both machines process 16 bits internally and are good for word processing and low-volume business applications. They can work with up to one megabyte of memory and require EMS (expanded memory) boards to go beyond that limit. All these machines run under DOS.

80286-BASED COMPUTERS

The Intel 80286 (commonly known as the 286) is the CPU in the original IBM PC AT. It is a full 16-bit computer that is good for high-volume data processing applications and has become the minimum standard for professional operations.

The 286 can intrinsically work with up to 16 megabytes of memory, but standard DOS applications cannot use more than one megabyte, unless special EMS (expanded memory) boards are installed. 286 machines running under OS/2 can work with the maximum memory.

IBM PS/2 Model 30

80386-BASED COMPUTERS

The Intel 80386 (commonly known as the 386) is the CPU that was first introduced by Compaq in its Compaq 386 model. It is the processor in high-end models of IBM's PS/2 series, HP's RS series and in models from many other vendors. It is a full 32-bit computer that is used for high-volume data processing, CAD and desktop publishing applications.

The 386 can work with four gigabytes of memory; however, 16 megabytes is typically the maximum limit. The 386 is inherently better designed than the 286 and allows multiple DOS applications to be run at the same time (when running under 386-specific operating systems). The 386 does not require special EMS memory boards to expand DOS memory limits. With the 386, the EMS standard can be simulated in normal extended memory, and all many DOS add-ons provide this "Expanded Memory Manager" feature.

80386SX-BASED COMPUTERS

The Intel 80386SX (commonly known as the 386SX) CPU is a lower-speed version of the 386. It uses a 16-bit data bus instead of a 32-bit data bus. It is faster than the 286, and more importantly, like the full-size 386, provides more flexibility in running existing DOS applications.

DISK SPEED

High speed disks have an access time of 28 milliseconds or less, and low-speed disks run 65 milliseconds or more. The higher speed disks also transfer their data faster than the slower speed units, resulting in significant improvements from fastest to slowest.

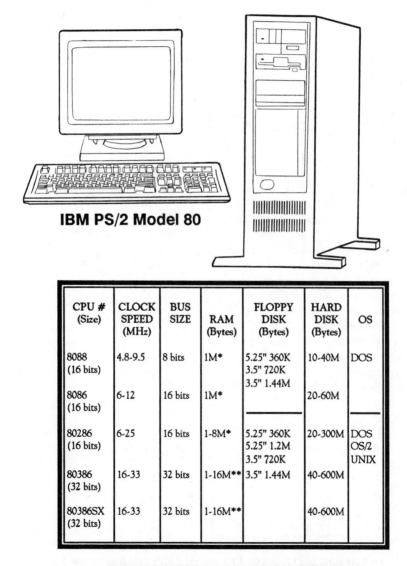

IBM PS/2 Model 80

CPU # (Size)	CLOCK SPEED (MHz)	BUS SIZE	RAM (Bytes)	FLOPPY DISK (Bytes)	HARD DISK (Bytes)	OS
8088 (16 bits)	4.8-9.5	8 bits	1M*	5.25" 360K 3.5" 720K 3.5" 1.44M	10-40M	DOS
8086 (16 bits)	6-12	16 bits	1M*		20-60M	
80286 (16 bits)	6-25	16 bits	1-8M*	5.25" 360K 5.25" 1.2M 3.5" 720K	20-300M	DOS OS/2 UNIX
80386 (32 bits)	16-33	32 bits	1-16M**	3.5" 1.44M	40-600M	
80386SX (32 bits)	16-33	32 bits	1-16M**		40-600M	

IBM COMPATIBLE PC SPECIFICATIONS
*Under DOS, RAM is expanded beyond 1M with EMS memory boards
**Under DOS, RAM is expanded beyond 1M with normal "extended" memory and a memory management program

Operating Systems

Almost all IBM personal computers use the DOS operating system from Microsoft Corporation, also commonly known as PC-DOS. MS-DOS, also known as DOS, is the version used in compatible computers. DOS is a single user operating system that runs one program at a time and is limited to working with one megabyte of memory, 640K of which is usable for the application program. Special add-in EMS memory boards break through the 1M barrier as long as the software package recognizes the EMS standard. Add-ons to DOS, such as Windows and DESQview, take advantage of EMS and allow multiple applications to be open at one time, thus enabling the user to switch back and forth between them without having to close one before opening another.

Microsoft's OS/2, an advanced multitasking operating system, is available for both 286 and 386-based machines. OS/2 is a single user operating system that works with up to 16 megabytes of memory and can run existing DOS applications one at a time. The eventual 386-specific version of OS/2 will trigger a special 386 "virtual mode" that will allow it to run multiple DOS applications

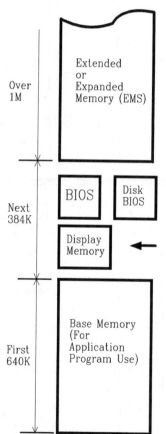

Extended memory is normal memory beyond 1M.

Expanded memory is a special memory beyond 1M created to increase the memory space for DOS applications.

This 384K "hole" is reserved for operating system use. It's made up of the main BIOS, as well as the BIOS's and memory on the various plug-in boards.

When the IBM PC was first developed, it used the Intel 8088 microprocessor, which could not address (work with) more than one megabyte of memory. The first 640K were reserved for the application, and the remainder for system use.

HOW MEMORY IS ALLOCATED IN AN IBM PC

at the same time. The 386 version of OS/2 will provide incentive for users to upgrade to the 386 and OS/2 at the same time.

BIOS COMPATIBILITY
The BIOS, or Basic Input/Output System, is the part of the operating system that contains the elementary instructions that activate the peripheral devices directly. The BIOS is stored in a permanent memory (ROM) chip in every IBM pc. In order to provide acceptable screen display performance, software vendors directly access the routines in this BIOS, even though they're supposed to communicate at a higher level through the operating system. Thus, the BIOS in the compatible machine must be 100% compatible with the IBM BIOS.

Display Standards

IBM has introduced several graphics and text display standards for its PC line. The standard is implemented by plugging in a video display board and connecting the appropriate monitor to it. With each new standard, the boards also incorporate the previous standards. For example, an EGA board has built-in CGA and MDA capability (see chart below).

With the PS/2, IBM introduced the VGA standard and built it into the main system board (motherboard). VGA is also available as a plug-in board for PCs from third-party vendors. Also with the PS/2, IBM introduced the 8514 high-resolution graphics standard. An 8514 adapter board plugs into the PS/2, providing a dual-monitor capability for CAD and graphics applications. The 8514 will be built into future models of the PS/2 line, as well.

In order to keep their programs competitive, vendors of graphics software packages have had to support the major graphics standards. In addition, there are many non-IBM, proprietary graphics standards for high-resolution displays. Either the software vendor provides the "driver" for the display, or the vendor of the display provides the driver for the software package. In either case, switching software or switching display systems is fraught with compatibility problems.

PC SERIES DISPLAY STANDARDS
MDA   720x350 text - monochrome
CGA   320x200 text and graphics (4 colors)*
EGA   640x350 text and graphics (16 colors)*
PGA   640x480 text and graphics (256 colors)
Hercules 729x348 text and graphics - monochrome (non-IBM)

PS/2 SERIES DISPLAY STANDARDS
MCGA   720x400 text, 320x200 graphics (256 colors)
VGA   720x400 text, 640x480 graphics (16 colors)*
8514   1,024x768 text and graphics (256 colors)

* More colors are available from third-party vendors.

REGISTER LEVEL COMPATIBILITY
Many application programs bypass the BIOS and address the screen hardware directly just as the BIOS does. Consequently, register level compatiblity is

required in the compatible's display electronics, which means that it must provide the same storage locations and identification as does the original IBM hardware.

Printers

Although IBM provides a number of printers that can connect to its line of personal computers, there are hundreds of printers that will also work with them. Like display screens, it has become the responsibility of the software vendor to support the wide variety of available printers on the market. When you purchase a word processing or desktop publishing package, you have to run an install program and select the appropriate printer driver for the printer you're using.

Keyboards

The keyboard introduced with the original IBM PC in 1981 was severely criticized by fast typists for its non-standard placement of the return and left shift keys. In 1984, IBM corrected this on its AT keyboard, but shortened the backspace key, making it harder to reach. In 1987, it introduced its Enhanced keyboard, which relocated all the function keys and placed the control key in an awkward location for touch typists. The escape key was relocated to the opposite side of the keyboard. By relocating the function keys, IBM made it impossible for software vendors to use them intelligently. What's easy to reach on one keyboard is difficult on the other, and vice versa. All this means nothing to the "hunt and peck" typist; however, to the fast touch typist, these deficiencies are maddening.

KEYBOARD COMPATIBILITY

A keyboard used in a compatible pc may not recognize every key combination, as does the IBM keyboard. For example, the shift key, pressed in combination with one of the cursor keys, is sometimes not recognized. In addition, the compatible vendors sometimes use proprietary keyboard interfaces, which means that if you don't like the keyboard you're using, you can't replace it with one from another vendor.

Floppy Disk Standards

The 360K floppy disk was introduced with the PC in 1981. In 1984, IBM introduced the 1.2 megabyte floppy disk along with its AT model. Although often used as backup storage, the high density floppy is not often used for interchangeability.

In 1986, IBM introduced the 720K 3 1/2" microfloppy disk on its Convertible laptop computer. It introduced the 1.44 megabyte double density version with the PS/2 line. These disk drives can be added to existing PCs, and due to their tremendous convenience over 5 1/4" disks, users are happy to migrate to them. The 1.44M storage capabity makes them quite useful as backup media.

PC FLOPPY DISK FORMATS
360K Minifloppy disk (double density 5 1/4" disk)
1.2M Minifloppy disk (high density 5 1/4" disk)
720K Microfloppy disk (double density 3 1/2" disk)

PS/2 FLOPPY DISK FORMATS
720K Microfloppy disk (double density 3 1/2" disk)
1.44M Microfloppy disk (high density 3 1/2" disk)

Hard Disk Standards

Fixed, non-removable, hard disks for IBM compatible pcs are available with storage capacities from 20 to over 600 megabytes. If a hard disk is added that is not compatible with the existing disk controller, a new controller board must be plugged in. However, one disk's internal standard does not conflict with another, since all programs and data must be copied onto it to begin with. Removable hard disks that hold at least 20 megabytes are gradually becoming available.

Bus Standards

When a new peripheral device, such as a monitor or scanner, is added to an IBM compatible pc, a corresponding, new controller board must be plugged into an expansion slot (in the bus) in order to electronically control its operation. In the first PCs (PC, XT, etc.), the bus was designed to handle 8-bits of data simultaneously; with the 16-bit AT model, the slot was extended to handle a 16-bit data path. 16-bit boards will not fit into 8-bit slots, but 8-bit boards will fit into 16-bit slots. 286 and 386 machines provide both 8-bit and 16-bit slots, while the 386s also have proprietary 32-bit slots for adding memory.

The bus in high-end models of the PS/2 line is called the "Micro Channel" and it is not compatible with the 8- and 16-bit PC buses. Boards that plug into these buses cannot be plugged into the Micro Channel. The Micro Channel is more advanced than the PC buses. It provides a 32-bit data pathway, is designed for multiprocessing and eliminates potential conflicts that arise when installing new peripheral devices (see *Micro Channel*).

In late 1988, IBM-compatible vendors announced the EISA bus (Extended Industry Standard Architecture) in order to extend the life of the PC bus and provide a non-Micro Channel (non-IBM) standard for future personal computers. EISA provides for 32 bits of data and, like the Micro Channel, allows for multiprocessing. EISA slots will accept the boards that plug into the PC bus.

MICRO CHANNEL COMPATIBILTY
As with the ROM BIOS in the first PCs, figuring out the Micro Channel's secrets has been an arduous task of reverse engineering since the PS/2 line was announced. As of the spring of 1989, a few companies have announced Micro Channel machines, and others have stated that they are licensing the architecture from IBM. It remains to be seen just how effective Micro Channel clones will be in the marketplace and how much EISA provides a meaningful alternative.

IBM PC & PS/2 Models

PC Model	Date of Introduction	CPU & Significance
PC	(Aug. 1981)	8088, Floppy disk system
XT	(Mar. 1983)	8088, Slow-speed hard disk system
XT 286	(Sep. 1986)	286, Slow-speed hard disk system
XT/370	(Oct. 1983)	8088 (with IBM 370 mainframe emulation)
AT	(Aug. 1984)	286, Medium-speed hard disk system
3270 PC	(Oct. 1983)	8088 (with 3270 mainframe terminal emulation)
PCjr	(Nov. 1983)	8088, Floppy-based home computer
PC Portable	(Feb. 1984)	8088, Floppy-based portable system
Convertible	(Apr. 1986)	8088, Microfloppy-based laptop portable

PS/2 Model		
Model 25	(Aug. 1987)	8086, PC bus (limited expansion)
Model 30	(Apr. 1987)	8086, PC bus
Model 30 286	(Sep. 1988)	286, PC bus
Model 50	(Apr. 1987)	286, Micro Channel bus
Model 50Z	(Jun. 1988)	Improved performance Model 50
Model 60	(Apr. 1987)	286, Micro Channel bus
Model 70	(Jun. 1988)	Desktop 386, Micro Channel bus
Model 80	(Apr. 1987)	Tower 386, Micro Channel bus

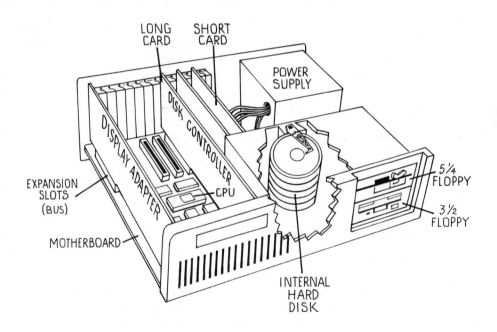

INTERNAL LAYOUT OF AN IBM PC

IBM Personal System/2

See *IBM personal computer*.

IBM PS/2

See *IBM personal computer*.

IC

See *integrated circuit*.

ICAS

(**I**ntel **C**ommunications **A**pplication **S**pecification) ICAS is a communications standard from Intel Corporation for a combination fax and modem board that allows personal computer users to exchange data more easily with fax machines. Introduced in 1988, Intel provides both the boards and the individual chips.

icon

An *icon* is a graphical representation of an object, such as a data file, text document or disk drive. Icons are used as a way of commanding the computer. Instead of typing in an object's name, the user points to the icon on screen by moving the cursor onto it with a mouse and then pressing one of the mouse's buttons. Once selected, icons can be moved or "dragged" across the screen. For example, in order to delete a file, the icon of that file is moved into the icon of a wastebasket.

UserPrep   General   Startup Device   DA Handler   Easy Access

ImageWriter   Key Layout   MultiFinder   Keyboard   Mouse

ICONS

These are examples of icons used in the Macintosh.

iconic interface

An *iconic interface* is a user interface that displays objects as tiny pictures (icons) on screen and employs a mouse to point to and select them.

I/E time

See *instruction cycle*.

IEC

(International Electrotechnical Commission) The IEC, founded in 1906, is an organization that sets international electrical standards. It is made up of national committees from a total of 44 countries.

IEEE

(Institute of Electrical and Electronic Engineers) IEEE is a membership organization that includes engineers, scientists and students in electronics and allied fields. Founded in 1963, the IEEE has over 290,000 members.

The Computer Society of the IEEE has over 90,000 members and holds numerous meetings and technical conferences on computers and local meetings cover current topics of interest. The IEEE is involved with setting standards for the computer and communications field. For more information, contact The Computer Society of the IEEE, 10662 Los Vaqueros Circle, Los Alamitos, CA 90720.

IEEE 488

See GPIB.

IEEE 802.1

IEEE 802.1 is a standard specification for local area networks from The Institute of Electrical and Electronics Engineers, Inc.

802.1
802.1 provides network management and internetwork standards.

802.2
802.2 is the standard for the data link layer (OSI layer 2) for the following three physical access methods.

802.3
802.3 is a standard for a local area network that uses the CSMA/CD access method (OSI layer 1). This standard has been popularized by the Ethernet local area network.

802.4
802.4 is a standard for a local area network that uses a token passing bus access method (OSI layer 1)

802.5
802.5 is a standard for a local area network that uses a token passing ring access method (OSI layer 1).

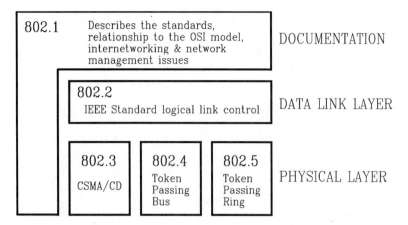

IEEE 802 LOCAL AREA NETWORK STANDARDS

IDMS

(Integrated Data Management System) *IDMS* is a database management system from Cullinet. IDMS/R (Relational) runs on IBM, Fujitsu and Siemens mainframes. IDMS/SQL (Structured Query Language) runs on Digital Equipment Corporation's VAX line of computers. Cullinet provides a number of products that complement IDMS, including expert system and CASE tools as well as a fourth-generation language.

if-then-else

If-then-else is a high-level programming language statement that compares two or more sets of data and tests the results. If the results are true, the THEN instructions are taken; if not, the ELSE instructions are taken. The following is a BASIC example:

```
10  IF ANSWER = "Y"  THEN PRINT "Yes"
20 ELSE PRINT "No"
```

In certain structured programming languages, the THEN is implied. All statements between the IF and the ELSE are carried out if the condition is true. All instructions between the ELSE and the ENDIF are carried out if the condition is not true. The following dBASE example tests the same condition:

```
IF ANSWER = "Y"
 ? "The Answer is Yes"
 ELSE
 ? "The Answer is No"
ENDIF
```

IGES

(Initial Graphics Exchange Specification) *IGES* is an ANSI standard graphics file format for 3-D wire frame models. The IGES format is designed to be independent of all computer-aided design and computer-aided manufacturing systems and is also intended for human interpretation.

IGES Organization

(Initial Graphics Exchange Specification Organization) The *IGES Organization* evolved out of the Air Force's Integrated Computer Automated Manufacturing (ICAM) program in 1979, which developed a method for data exchange that became known as the Initial Graphics Exchange Specification (IGES). The IGES Organization is involved with the IGES standard for graphics images and the PDES format for describing a complete product model. For more information, contact IGES Coordinator, National Bureau of Standards, Building 220, Room A-353, Gaithersburg, MD 20899, (301) 921-3691.

illustration program

Same as *drawing program*.

image processing

(1) *Image processing* analyzes the content of a picture using techniques that can identify levels of shades, colors and relationships that cannot be perceived by the human eye. Image processing works on images that are in raster graphics format, such as photographs that have been scanned into the computer or pictures of real objects that have been taken with video cameras. Image processing is used for solving myriads of identification problems, such as in forensic medicine or in creating weather maps from satellite pictures.

(2) *Image processing* may refer to a variety of image-oriented tasks that are not analyzed by machine, for example, scanning images, refining them in a paint program, accepting video images for touch up and so on. Image processing always refers to images in raster graphics format.

imaging

Imaging is the recording of graphic images on microfilm or videotape.

immediate access

Immediate access is the ability to read or write data without delay. Immediate access is *direct access* without delay or wait states.

immediate address

An *immediate address* is a machine instruction that contains a value to be used in the execution of the instruction. Most instructions contain only addresses that point to memory locations or peripheral devices where the data is actually stored.

IMOS

IMOS is the operating system used on NCR's I-9000 series of computers.

impact printer

An *impact printer* is a printer that uses a printing mechanism that bangs the character image into the ribbon and onto the paper. Line printers, dot matrix printers and daisy wheel printers are examples of impact printers. See *printer*.

impedance

Impedance is the resistance to the flow of alternating current in a circuit.

implementation

(1) Computer system *implementation* is the installation of new hardware and system software.

(2) Information system *implementation* is the installation of new databases and application programs and the adoption of new manual procedures.

IMS

(Information Management System) *IMS* is a hierarchical database management system from IBM that is used on large IBM mainframes. IMS is a first-generation database system that was widely used throughout the 1970s.

in hardware, in software

In hardware refers to logic that has been placed into the electronic circuits of the computer. Contrast with *in software*, which refers to the logic in a program.

incident light

In computer graphics, *incident light* is light that strikes an object. The color of the object is based on how the light is absorbed or reflected by the object.

InColor Card

See *Hercules Graphics Card*.

increment

Increment is to add a number to another number. Incrementing a counter means to add 1 or some other number to its current value.

indent

In word processing, *indent* is to align text some number of spaces to the right of the left margin. A *hanging paragraph* occurs when the first line of a paragraph starts at the left margin, but the second and all subsequent lines are indented.

index

(1) In data management, an *index* is a directory of the location of records and files on a disk. Indexing is the most common method used for keeping track of data on a disk or other direct access storage device, such as a drum or optical disk (CD ROM). An index of files contains an entry for each file name and its location. An index of records has an entry for each key field, for example, account number, and its location. The indexes are maintained by the operating system or database management system whenever data is retrieved or updated.

(2) In programming, an *indexed* instruction, called a subscript, is a relative instruction that can point to any one of the items in a table (array) of data stored within the program. See *indexed addressing*.

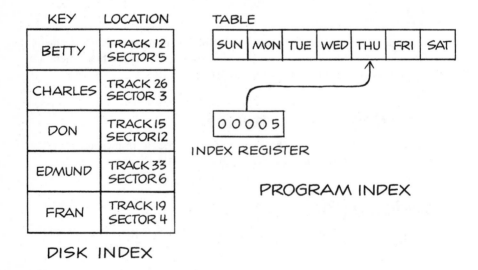

index hole

An *index hole* is a hole punched into a *hard sectored* floppy disk and its jacket that serves to mark the start of the sectors on each track.

index mark

An *index mark* is a physical hole or mark, or a recorded code or mark, on a disk that is used to identify a starting point for each track.

index register

An *index register* is a high-speed memory circuit that holds the current, relative position of an item in a table (array). At execution time, the index register value is added to the instructions that reference it.

indexed addressing

In programming, *indexed addressing* is a technique for referencing data in a table (array) with the use of an index register. For example, when an array is defined in a program, such as with a dimension statement, its assigned name references the beginning of the array. A specific item within the array is referenced in the program by adding a subscript to the array name. The subscript is a variable that is incremented by the program keeping track of the current item being worked on. This value is stored in an index register, and the index register adds it to the instructions that reference it at run time. In assembly language, the index register must be explicitly stored with the value. In high-level languages, the compiler takes care of it.

indexed sequential

See *ISAM*.

indexing

(1) *Indexing* is the creating of indexes based on key fields or key words.

(2) *Indexing* is the creating of timing signals based on detecting a mark, slot or hole in a moving medium.

indirect addressing

In programming, *indirect addressing* is a technique for addressing a relative location. The instruction references a location that, rather than containing the data, contains the address of the data. The data referenced by the second address is used for execution.

inductance

Inductance is the opposition to the changing flow of current in a circuit. Inductance is measured in units called "Henrys."

induction

Induction is the process of generating an electric current in a circuit from the magnetic influence of an adjacent circuit.

inference program

An *inference program* is the processing program in an expert system. It derives a conclusion from the facts and rules contained in the knowledge base using various artificial intelligence techniques.

infix notation

Infix notation is the common way arithmetic operators are used to reference numeric values. For example, $A + B / C$ is infix notation. Contrast with *Polish notation* and *reverse Polish notation*, which place the operators before and after the values.

information

Information is a summarization of data. Technically, data are raw facts and figures that are processed into information, such as summaries and totals. But since information can also be raw data for the next job or person, the two terms cannot be precisely defined. Both terms are used synonymously and interchangeably.

As office automation and traditional data processing merge, it may be more helpful to view information as the sum total of the different ways data is defined and stored, namely: data, text, spreadsheets, pictures, voice and video. Data are discretely defined fields in data records. Text is a collection of words in a field or word processing document. Spreadsheets are data in matrix (row and column) form. Pictures are lists of vectors or frames of bits. Voice is digitized sound waves. Video is a sequence of digitized frames.

In the future, information processing will have to integrate all these forms of information into common databases. Perhaps, then, the information age will have truly arrived.

information center

An *information center* is a section within an organization's information systems department that provides personal computer tools, assistance and training to end users. Information center personnel are trained in and provide assistance with such software packages as query languages, report writers, spreadsheets and financial planning systems. They are also available to provide ways of downloading data from the production databases maintained in the company's datacenter.

information management

Information management covers the definitions, uses, value and distribution of all data/information within an organization whether it is processed by the computer or not. Information management evaluates the kinds of data/information an organization requires in order to function and progress effectively.

Information is complex because the nature of business transactions is complex. It must be analyzed and understood before effective computer solutions can be developed. See *data administration*.

information processing

Same as *data processing*.

information resource management

See *information management*.

information science

Information science is the science that deals with the analysis of information as an organizational resource. See *information management*.

Information Services

Same as *Information Systems*.

information system

An *information system* is a business application of the computer that provides for the routine processing of the transactions and the periodic maintenance of the master files. It is made up of a database (master and transaction files), application programs and manual and machine procedures. The database stores the master files (subjects of the system) and the transactions (activities of the system). The application programs provide the data entry, updating, query and report processing of the system. The manual procedures document how to obtain the necessary data for input into the system and how to distribute the system's reports and forms. The machine procedures instruct the computer how to perform the system's batch processing activities, in which the output of one program is fed as input into the next program.

The daily processing of an information system is the interactive, realtime processing of the transactions that are entered on a first-come, first-served basis. At the end of the day or some other period, the batch processing programs update all master files that have not been updated since the last cycle. Reports are printed for the cycle's activities.

Periodic maintenance processing is the updating of the master files where customers, employees, vendors and inventory items are added, deleted and changed. This may done weekly, or more or less frequently depending on requirements. Disk maintenance is also periodically performed to maintain the efficiency of the system. Disks files are run through an optimizing program that resequences the fragmented disk files that have been updated many times.

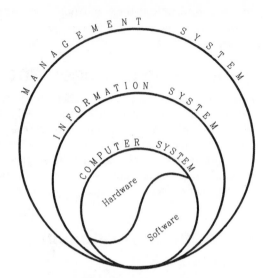

HOW SYSTEMS RELATE

Information Systems

Information Systems is the formal title for a data processing or MIS department within an organization. Other titles are Data Processing, Information Processing, Information Services, Management Information Systems and Management Information Services.

information utility

An *information utility* is an information service bureau that maintains and provides up-to-date data banks for public use.

infrared

Infrared is invisible light at the far, or high, end of the light spectrum. Contrast with *ultraviolet* light, which is at the low end of the light spectrum.

INGRES

(**IN**teractive **G**raphics and **RE**trieval System) *INGRES* is a relational database management system from Relational Technology Inc., that runs on Digital's VAX series and Motorola 68000-based microcomputers. INGRES includes an English-like fourth-generation language called "QUEL" and a query by example capability called "QBF," (query by form). Its forms management system lets the user create, edit and view the database as a series of forms.

Originally developed at the University of California at Berkeley in the early 1970s, Relational Technology was founded in 1980 to market a commercial version of the product, which first appeared in 1982.

inheritance

In object-oriented programming, *inheritance* refers to the ability of one class of objects to inherit properties from a higher class.

inhouse

Inhouse refers to any operation that takes place on the user's premises.

Initial Graphics Exchange Specification

See *IGES* and *IGES Organization*.

initial program load

See *IPL*.

ink jet

An *ink jet* is a printer mechanism that sprays one or more colors of ink onto paper. Ink jet technologies are maturing and producing high-quality printing approaching that of a laser printer.

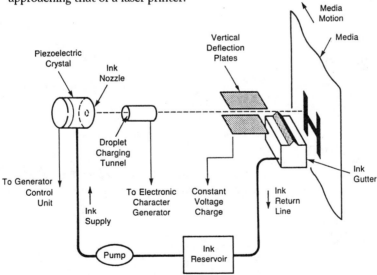

SINGLE NOZZLE INK JET PRINTING PROCESS

(Courtesy Dataquest)

INMARSAT

(INternational MARitime SATellite Organization) INMARSAT is an international organization that is involved in providing satellite communications to and from ships and offshore rigs. It is represented in the United States and partially owned by the Communications Satellite Corporation (COMSAT).

input

Input is any data entered into the computer or the act of entering data, either by keyboard, light pen, mouse, graphics tablet, magnetic disk or tape, communications channel or punched card. Whenever data is copied from one device to another, for example, from one disk to another, it must first be input into the computer's memory and then output to the destination device.

input area

An input area is a reserved segment of memory that is used to accept data or text from a peripheral device such as a keyboard, disk or tape. Same as buffer.

input device

An input device is a peripheral device that generates input for the computer such as a keyboard, scanner, mouse or digitizer tablet.

input program

Same as data entry program.

input queue

An input queue is a reserved segment of disk or memory that holds messages that have been received or job control statements describing work to be done.

input stream

An input stream is a collection of job control statements, which describe the work to be done, that have been entered into the computer system.

input/output

See I/O.

input/output area

See I/O area.

input/output bound

See *I/O bound*.

input/output bus

Same as *bus*.

input/output control unit

Same as *peripheral controller*.

input/output controller

Same as *peripheral controller*.

input/output processor

See *I/O processor*.

input/output statement

See *I/O statement*.

inquiry program

Same as *query program*.

Ins key

(**INS**ert key) The *Ins* key on a keyboard is used to switch between insert mode and overwrite mode. In insert mode, a typed-in text character will be inserted at the screen cursor location. In overwrite mode, the character will replace the current character at the cursor.

insert mode

The *insert mode* is a data entry mode that causes new data typed on the keyboard to be inserted at the current cursor location on screen. On many keyboards, there is an *Ins key* that is pressed to go back and forth between insert mode and overwrite mode.

install program

An *install program* customizes a software package for use in a particular computer system. Install programs perform a number of tasks, from requiring that the user type in a valid serial number for identification purposes to customizing the program for a particular monitor or printer. Personal computer software packages often bypass the operating system and drive the peripheral devices themselves, and the install program copies the required drivers into the program. The install program may also create a directory on the hard disk and copy all of the program modules from the floppies into that directory.

installation specification

An *installation specification* is the criteria defined by the original equipment manufacturer that indicates the proper physical installation for correct product performance.

instance variable

In object-oriented programming, an *instance variable* is the data in an object.

instantiate

In object-oriented programming, *instantiate* means to create an object of a specific class. Initializing the object's instance variables is commonly done at this time.

instruction

An *instruction* is a command to the computer. The term usually refers to machine language instructions that only the computer understands. However, it may also refer to a command statement in a programming language or software package.

Machine instructions are made up of two parts: the *op code* (operation code) and the *operands*. The op code specifies the type of instruction, or action to be taken, such as INPUT, ADD, COMPARE and GOTO. The operands are the references to data or peripheral devices. For example, in the instruction: ADD SUBTOTAL TO TOTAL, the op code is ADD, and the operands are SUBTOTAL and TOTAL.

Instructions are called *software*. Groups of instructions are called a *program*, or *software program*. Small sets of instructions are called *subroutines, program modules* or *functions*. See *machine language*.

instruction cycle

The *instruction cycle* is the time in which a single instruction is fetched from memory, decoded and executed. The first half of the cycle is transferring the instruction from memory to the instruction register and decoding it. The second half of the cycle is executing the instruction. An instruction cycle is also called I/E time.

instruction mix

An *instruction mix* is a selection of different kinds of instructions that has been chosen to write a program or to create a benchmark representing a typical class of programs.

instruction register

An *instruction register* is a high-speed memory circuit that holds an instruction for decoding and execution.

instruction repertoire

An *instruction repertoire* is the set of operation statements that make up a programming language.

instruction set

An *instruction set* is the entire group of machine language instructions that a computer can follow. Instruction sets are designed into the CPU and are one of the major components of its architecture. A set may contain from a handful (RISC) to several hundred instructions (CISC), depending on the complexity of the machine. Instructions in a computer are generally from one to four bytes long.

Instruction sets may be designed into read only memory chips, which contain the elementary operations required to activate the computer for each machine instruction. See *microcode*.

instruction time

The *instruction time*, or *I-time*, is the time in which an instruction is fetched from main memory and stored in the instruction register. It is the first half of the instruction cycle.

insulator

An *insulator* is a material that does not conduct electricity. Contrast with *conductor*, which is a material that lets current flow through it.

integer

An *integer* is a whole number; for example, 123 would be the integer of 123.232.

Integer BASIC

Integer BASIC is a version of the BASIC programming language that can handle only whole numbers and not fractions.

integral number

Same as *integer*.

integrated

Integrated refers to a collection of distinct elements or components that have been built into one unit.

integrated circuit

An *integrated circuit* is a collection of several electronic components on one chip. See *chip*.

integrated office systems

See *IOS*.

integrated services digital network

See *ISDN*.

integrated software package

An *integrated software package* is a software program that combines two or more applications together. In personal computers, the five major application areas are database management, word processing, spreadsheets, business graphics and communications. Integrated packages include two or more, or even all five, of these capabilities. Project management and slide show presentation capability are two more applications that may also be integrated. Programs such as Microsoft Works for the Macintosh, Apple Works for the Apple II series and Ashton-Tate's Framework for IBM and compatibles are examples of integrated packages.

The major advantage of an integrated package is that there's one common user interface, or method of interacting and commanding the computer. With IBM personal computers especially, integrated packages make it easier to copy and move data from one file structure to another, for example, from a spreadsheet to a word processing document. The disadvantage is that, thus far, no single integrated package provides all of the features and capabilities of stand-alone programs. In addition, windowing environments for IBM personal computers, such as Quarterdeck's DESQview, let data be transferred back and forth between individual, stand-alone programs.

integrated voice/data PABX

See *digital PABX*.

integrator

In electronics, an *integrator* is a device that combines an input with a variable, such as time, and provides an analog output. For example, a watt-hour meter provides a measurement of current over time.

integrity

See *data integrity*.

Intel Corporation

Intel Corporation is a leading semiconductor manufacturer that makes the 8086 family of microprocessors, which are the CPUs in IBM compatible pcs. See *8086/8088* and *80286/80386*.

Intellect

Intellect is a natural language query language from Artificial Intelligence, Inc., that runs on IBM mainframe and other computers. Intellect understands many questions that can be stated in the English language, for example: "Tell me the number of employees in the personnel department."

intelligence

Intelligence is simply processing capability. Thus, every computer is intelligent!

better watch out — intelligence is everywhere

intelligent cable

An *intelligent cable* is a multi-line cable that uses a built-in microprocessor for analyzing or converting signals.

intelligent controller

An *intelligent controller* is a peripheral control unit that uses a built-in microprocessor for controlling its operation.

intelligent database

An *intelligent database* is a database that contains knowledge about the content of the data stored in it. A complete set of validation criteria may be stored with each item of data, such as the minimum and maximum values that can be entered or a list of all the possible entires.

When validation criteria are left up to the individual programs, one program might allow input of one set of values, while the other allows another set of values. If the knowledge about the data is in the database itself, all programs entering and updating that data will automatically conform to that set of rules.

In advanced intelligent databases, conceptual views of the data can be implemented, which is how users naturally perceive the information that they work with. For example, although monthly salary is stored in the database, a user could query the database on annual salary. Even though only states are stored in each database record, the user could query on "Western States," "Midwest," or "New England."

intelligent form

An *intelligent form* is a data entry application that provides help screens and low levels of artificial intelligence in aiding the user to enter the correct data.

intelligent paper

See *intelligent form*.

intelligent terminal

An *intelligent terminal* is a terminal with built-in processing capability. It has memory, but no disk or tape storage. Intelligent terminals may use a general-purpose microprocessor or may have specialized circuitry as part of a distributed intelligence system. Contrast with *dumb terminal*, which is strictly an input/output device and has no processing capability.

INTELSAT

(**IN**ternational **TEL**ecommunications **SAT**ellite Corporation) *INTELSAT* is an international organization that is involved in launching and operating commercial satellites. INTELSAT was created in 1964 with only 11 countries participating. Today, 114 nations have ownership in it. INTELSAT is represented in the United States and partially owned by the Communications Satellite Corporation (COMSAT).

inter

Inter refers to crossing over boundaries; for example, interoffice means from office to office. Contrast with *intra*, which implies within a boundary, for example, intraoffice is within the office.

interactive cable TV

Interactive cable TV provides full television service combined with interactive capabilities. Viewers can respond to the actual TV program being viewed and take part in it by voting on issues or reacting to certain questions or situations. Interactive cable TV implies full television viewing, in contrast with videotext and teletext services, which provide limited graphics and animation. However, all services, including videotex and teletext, as well as time-sharing, may be provided over interactive cable TV channels. A decoder is required in the home between the cable and the TV that contains a keyboard or keypad for interactive use.

interactive session

An *interactive session* refers to a back-and-forth dialogue between the user and the computer. Contrast with *batch session*, typically in large computers, where the instructions for printing a report or updating a master file are entered and the job is processed as the computers resources become available to do so.

interactive video

Interactive video is the use of a videodisc or CD ROM that is controlled by a computer for an interactive education or entertainment program. See *videodisc* and *CD ROM*.

interblock gap

Same as *interrecord gap*.

interface

An *interface* is a connection between two devices. Hardware interfaces are the plugs, sockets and wires that carry electrical signals in a prescribed order. Software interfaces are the languages, codes and messages that programs use to communicate with each other, such as between an application program and the operating system. User interfaces are the keyboards, mice, joy sticks, light pens, tablets, dialogues, command languages, menus and display screens used for interactive communication between the user and the computer.

One of the biggest problems in this field is connecting one thing to another; thus, interfacing is a major part of what engineers, designers and consultants do. Users "talk to" the software. The software "talks to" the hardware, as well as to other software. Hardware "talks to" other hardware. All this "talking to" or "communicating to" is interfacing. It has to be designed, developed, tested and redesigned, and with each incarnation, a new standard is created. See *user interface, standards & compatibility* and *API*.

interface adapter

In communications, an *interface adapter* is a device that connects the computer or terminal to a network.

interlacing

Interlacing is a technique that refreshes a display screen by alternately displaying all the odd lines and then all the even lines. For example, television uses an interlaced signal that generates 60 half frames per second, or the equivalent of 30 full frames per second. Contrast with *non-interlaced*, which refreshes all the lines on the display sequentially from top to bottom. Interlaced methods require half as much signal information in the same time frame as non-interlaced methods.

interleaving

See *sector interleave*.

interlock

An *interlock* is a device that prohibits an action from taking place.

intermediate language

An *intermediate language* is a language that is halfway between the source language and machine language. The intermediate language cannot run by itself and must be run with a special interpreter for each CPU. Intermediate languages are used to make programming languages compatible with a number of computers. Since a large amount of the translation has already been done by the intermediate language compiler, it is faster to create an interpreter for a new CPU family than to create an entire new compiler over again.

intermittent error

An *intermittent error* is an error that occurs from time to time, but not consistently. Intermittent errors are extremely difficult to diagnose and repair.

internal font

An *internal font* is a set of characters for a particular typeface that is built into a printer. Contrast with *cartridge font* and *soft font*.

internal interrupt

An *internal interrupt* is an interrupt that is caused by processing, for example, a request for input or output or an arithmetic overflow error. Contrast with *external interrupt*, which is one caused by an event or action outside of the CPU.

internal sort

An *internal sort* is a sort that is accomplished entirely in main memory without having to use disks or tapes as temporary work files.

internal storage

Same as *memory*.

International Standards Organization

See *ISO*.

interpolate

Interpolate is to estimate values that lie between known values.

Interpress

Interpress is a page description language from Xerox that is used on the Xerox 2700 and 9700 page printers (medium to large-scale laser printers). Ventura Publisher, Xerox's desktop publishing program for IBM compatible pcs, outputs the Interpress language.

interpret

Interpret is to run a program one line at a time. Each line of source language is translated into machine language and then executed.

interpreter

An *interpreter* is a translator program for a high-level programming language that translates and runs the program at the same time. The program that is being interpreted is still in its original source language, the way the programmer wrote it. The interpreter translates one program statement into machine language and then causes the machine language to be executed. It then translates the next statement, and so on, until the program is finished.

Interpreted programs run more slowly than their compiler counterparts, because the compiler translates the entire program all at once before the program is run. However, it's convenient to write a program using an interpreter. Since a single line of code can be tested interactively, the programmer can test the results of a programming statement right away.

Programs that are interpreted are not stand-alone programs and must always be run with the interpreter in the computer. For example, in order to run a BASIC or dBASE source language program, the correct version of the BASIC or dBASE interpreter must be in the computer.

Often, a program is developed with an interpreter, and the final version is compiled for better run-time performance. For example, BASIC, the most commonly interpreted language, can also be compiled.

interpretive language

An *interpretive language* is a programming language that requires an interpreter in the computer in order to run it.

interprocess communication

Interprocess communication is the ability of one running program to get the attention of and communicate with another running program.

interrecord gap

An *interrecord gap* is the space generated between blocks of data on magnetic tape created by the starting and stopping of the reel of tape.

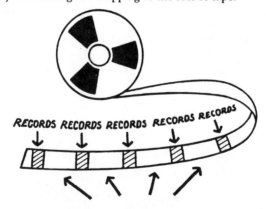

INTERRECORD (INTERBLOCK) GAPS

interrogate

(1) *Interrogate* is to search, sum or count records in a file.

(2) *Interrogate* is to test the condition or status of a terminal or computer system.

interrupt

An *interrupt* is a hardware feature that signals the CPU that an input or output is required. For example, keystrokes and mouse movement generate an interrupt. An instruction in the application program generates an interrupt when it's time to input or output some data. Networks also generate interrupt signals that the computer must respond to.

When an interrupt occurs, control is transferred to the operating system, which determines what action should be taken. All interrupts have a priority order in which they are taken. The higher the priority, the faster the interrupt will be serviced.

interrupt-driven

Interrupt-driven refers to a computer or communications network that uses interrupts.

interrupt mask

An *interrupt mask* is an internal switch setting that controls whether an interrupt can be processed or not. The mask is a bit that is turned on and off by the program.

interrupt priorities

Interrupt priorities are the sequence of importance assigned to the various interrupts in a computer system. If two interrupts occur at the same time, the interrupt with the highest priority is serviced first. In some systems, a higher-priority interrupt can gain control of the system while it's processing a lower-priority interrupt.

intra

Intra implies within a boundary; for example, intraoffice refers to operations that take place within the office. Contrast with *inter*, which crosses boundaries; for example, internetwork is from one communications network to another.

inverse video

Same as *reverse video*.

inverted file

In data management, an *inverted file* is a file that is indexed on many of the attributes of the data itself. For example, in an employee file, an index could be maintained for all secretaries, another for all clerks, another for managers, and so on. By maintaining attribute indexes, the indexes can be searched instead of the actual data. Boolean ANDs and ORs can be accomplished far faster than wading through the data in every record.

Inverted files take up a lot of disk space for the indexes, and updating can take appreciably longer.

inverted list

Same as *inverted file*.

inverter

An *inverter* is a logic gate that reverses the input to the opposite state. If a 1 is input, 0 is output, and vice versa. An inverter performs the Boolean logic NOT operation.

invoke

Invoke is to activate some routine or program that may be on disk and has to be loaded into memory, or it may be already in memory.

I/O

(Input/Output) An *I/O* is a transfer of data between the CPU and a peripheral device. Every transfer is an output from one device and an input into another.

I/O area

An *I/O area* is a reserved segment of computer memory that is used to accept data from an input device or to lay out data for transfer to an output device. Input/output areas may be physically located within the application program, operating system or database management system. Same as *buffer*.

I/O bound

I/O bound refers to an excessive amount of time getting data into and out of the computer in relation to the time it takes for processing within the computer. Faster I/O channels and disk drives will improve the performance of an I/O bound computer.

I/O channel

An *I/O channel* is a physical high-speed pathway between the computer and a peripheral device.

I/O interface

In large computers, an *I/O interface* is a channel between the CPU and a peripheral device. In small computers, it includes the controller and cable between the CPU and peripheral device.

I/O processor

An *I/O processor* is a hardware device or software program that is dedicated to handling only input and output operations. See *front end processor*.

I/O statement

An *I/O statement* is a programming language or command language statement that calls for data or stores data on a peripheral device.

IOCS

(Input Output Control System) Same as *BIOS*.

ion deposition

Ion deposition is a printing technology that is used in high-speed page printers. It is similar to the laser printer technique, except that instead of using light to create a charged image on a drum, it uses a printhead that deposits ions onto the drum. After toner is attracted to the ions on the drum, the paper is pressed directly against the drum causing the toner to be transferred and fused to it. The fusing is accomplished by pressure rather than by heat as in a laser printer. The quality of ion deposition is approaching that of a laser printer; however, the ink has not been embedded into the paper as deeply, and it can smear more readily.

IOS

(Integrated Office Systems) *IOS* is an IBM office automation system designed to integrate all models of IBM computers from micro to mainframe. IOS, which will be available in the 1990s, will provide office functions, such as electronic mail, appointment calendars and database query.

IPL

(Initial Program Load) *IPL* gets the computer started. Same as *bootstrapping*.

IR

(Industry Remarketer) *IR* is an term used by IBM for *VAR* or *VAD*.

IRG

(InterRecord Gap) See *interrecord gap*.

IRM

See *information resource management*.

IRMAboard

An *IRMAboard* is a micro to mainframe communications device from DCA associates that plugs into IBM and compatible, and Macintosh personal computers. The IRMAboard turns the personal computer into (emulates) an IBM 3278 (monochrome) or 3279 (color) mainframe terminal. IRMA is not an acronym; it is a real lady in DCA's marketing ads. The Macintosh version of the IRMAboard is called *MacIRMA*.

IRX

IRX is the operating system used on large models of NCR's I-9000 series of mainframes.

IS

See *information systems*.

ISAM

(Indexed Sequential Access Method) ISAM is a widely used disk access method that stores data sequentially, while also maintaining an index of key fields to all the records in the file for direct access capability. The sequential order of the file would be the one most commonly used for batch processing and printing, such as account number or name.

ISDN

(Integrated Services Digital Network) *ISDN* is an international telecommunications standard that allows a communications channel to simultaneously carry voice, video and data.

ISO

(International Standards Organization) *ISO*, founded in 1946, is involved with setting standards worldwide for all fields except electrotechnical, which is the responsibility of the International Electrotechnical Commission (IEC). ISO carries out its work through more than 160 technical committees and 2,100 subcommittees and working groups. ISO is made up of national standards organizations from more than 75 countries, each serving as secretariats for these technical bodies. ANSI (American National Standards Institute) is responsible for approximately 16 technical committees, 60 subcommittees and 190 working groups.

ISO developed the Open Systems Interconnection (OSI), a seven-layered model for communications processing.

For more information, contact Secretariat, International Standards Organization, American National Standards Institute, 1430 Broadway, New York, NY 10018, (212) 354-3300.

ISO/OSI

(International Standards Organization/Open Systems Interconnection) *ISO/OSI* is an international communications protocol for distributed processing. See *OSI*.

isometric view

In computer graphics, an *isometric view* is a picture of a 3-D object that shows all three dimensions in equal proportions. Isometric views do not show true perspective. Isometric means "equal measure."

Normal perspective   **Isometric view**

ISOMETRIC VIEW

(Courtesy Robo Systems Corporation)

isotropic

Isotropic refers to identical properties in all directions; for example, an isotropic antenna transmits and receives in all directions.

ISV

(Independent Software Vendor) An *ISV* is an individual or company that develops software. It typically refers to a third party application developer that uses programming languages and/or database programs of another vendor.

item

An *item* is one unit or member of a group. A *data item* is a unit of data that is equivalent to a field of data in a record.

iteration

An *iteration* is one repetition of a sequence of instructions or events. For example, in a program loop, one iteration is once through the instructions in the loop.

iterative operation

An *iterative operation* is an operation that requires successive executions of instructions or processes.

I-time

See *instruction time*.

Iverson notation

Iverson notation is a special set of symbols developed by Kenneth Iverson for writing statements in the APL programming language.

I^2L

(Integrated Injection Logic) I^2L is a type of bipolar transistor design known for its fast switching speeds.

I-9000

The *I-9000* is a series of minicomputers from NCR.

J

---

jack

A *jack* is a receptacle into which a plug is inserted.

Jacquard loom

The Jacquard loom, developed in 1801 by the French silk-weaver, Joseph-Marie Jacquard (1752-1834), used punched cards to control its operation. The punched card concept wasn't new; it had been used in earlier looms and music boxes. But, his loom was a vast improvement and allowed complex patterns to be created swiftly, literally transforming the textile industry within a decade. The loom was inspiration to Charles Babbage and, later, to Herman Hollerith.

JACQUARD LOOM
(Courtesy Smithsonian Institution)

jaggies

The *jaggies* are the stairstepped effect of diagonals and circles on a low-resolution graphics screen.

LOW RESOLUTION
GRAPHICS

HIGH RESOLUTION
GRAPHICS

Javelin Plus

Javelin Plus is a spreadsheet from Javelin Software Corporation that runs on IBM compatible pcs. Instead of the traditional row and column structure of spreadsheets, Javelin uses names to identify its cells, allowing users to consolidate data into unique spreadsheet models by using common cell names.

Jazz

Jazz is an integrated software package from Lotus Development Corporation that runs on Macintosh computers. Jazz combines file management, word processing, spreadsheet, graphics and communications into one package. Jazz is modeled after Lotus's Symphony, which runs on IBM personal computers.

JCL

(Job Control Language) *JCL* is a language that directs the operating system to run application programs in the computer. The JCL states the program size, priority and running sequence, as well as the files and databases used. Originally an IBM term, JCL has become a generic term for a job management language.

JES

(Job Entry Subsystem) *JES* is the part of IBM's MVS mainframe operating system which manages the job input. It accepts the jobs into the computer system, interprets the job control language, determines their order for execution and keeps track of them until they're finished.

jitter

A *jitter* is a flickering transmission signal or display image.

job

A *job* is a unit of work running in the computer. A job may be a single program or a group of programs that are required to work together, such as an application program and database management system.

job class

A *job class* is a descriptive category of a job that is based on the computer resources it requires when running.

job control language

See *JCL*.

job managment language

A *job management language* is a language used to direct the operating system to run a particular mix of application programs. See *JCL*.

job processing

Job processing is the handling and processing of jobs in the computer.

job queue

A *job queue* is the lineup of programs ready to be executed.

job stream

A *job stream* is a series of related programs that are run in a prescribed order. The output of one program is the input to the next program, and so on.

join

In relational database management, a *join* is the matching of one file against another based on some condition, and the creation of a third file containing

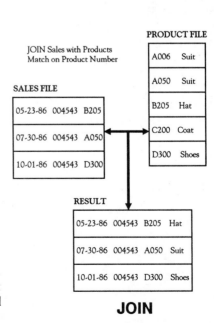

data from the matching files. For example, a customer file can be joined with an order file creating a file of records for all customers who purchased a particular product.

Josephson junction

The *Josephson junction* is a microelectronic circuit technology that employs superconductor materials. Josephson junction circuits are immersed in a liquid helium refrigeration unit to obtain the near-absolute zero temperatures required for operation. Named after Brian Josephson, who developed the original theory behind it, the Josephson junction is noted for its ultra-fast switching speeds in the 5 to 20 picosecond (trillionths of a second) range.

journaling

Journaling is the recording of transactions or processes for accounting or backup and recovery purposes.

JOVIAL

(Jule's Own Version of the International Algebraic Language) JOVIAL is a high-level programming languaged developed by Systems Development Corporation (SDC) in the early 1960s. JOVIAL was similar to ALGOL and was widely used for military applications in the U. S. throughout the 1960s and 1970s. The J in JOVIAL's name is for Jules Schwartz, one of the key architects of the language. After naming the language OVIAL, for Our Version of the International Algebraic Language, it was decided that JOVIAL sounded better.

joy stick

A *joy stick* is an omnidirectional lever that is used to move the cursor on screen more rapidly than it can be moved with the directional arrow keys. The joy stick is used extensively in video games, but is also used as an input device in CAD systems.

JOY STICK

Julian date

A *Julian date* is the representation of a month and day by the consecutive number of the day starting with January 1. For example, February 1 is 32. Normal dates are converted into Julian dates for calculation purposes.

jump

A *jump* is another term for a BRANCH or GOTO instruction, which directs the computer to some other place in the program.

jumper

A *jumper* is a metal bridge that is used to close a circuit. It can be a short length of wire or a plastic-covered metal block that is pushed onto two pins. Jumpers are often used in place of toggle switches (DIP switches) on a printed circuit board.

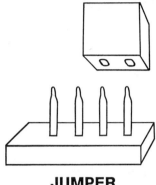

JUMPER

junction

A *junction* is the point at which two elements make contact. In a transistor, a junction is the point where an N-type material makes contact with a P-type material.

justification

In typography, *justification* refers to laying out text evenly between the left and right margins. The text in this paragraph is justified; however, all the other definitions in this book are set *ragged right*, which means that the right margin in not uniformly aligned. Justified text is often considered more formal than unjustified text.

K

(Kilo) *K* stands for kilo, and kilo means one thousand. However, K may stand for 1,000 or, more precisely, 1,024. Since computers use the binary numbering system, most specifications are in binary numbers, which start with 1 and double: 1, 2, 4, 8, 16, 32, 64, 128, 256, 512, 1024. For example, 64K means 65,536 bytes when it refers to memory and storage devices (64x1024), but a 64K salary does mean $64,000.00.

According to the IEEE, upper case "K" stands for 1,024, and lower case "k" stands for 1,000.

KB

KiloByte or KiloBit) *KB* stands for one thousand bytes or bits. See *K* and *space/time*.

Kermit

Kermit is an asynchronous communications protocol for personal computers developed at Columbia University and used in several public-domain communications programs. Kermit is a slow protocol but is noted for its transmission accuracy over noisy telephone lines, because it checks for errors in the commands it sends as well as the data. Kermit can also communicate effectively with IBM mainframes.

kernel

A *kernel* is the fundamental part of a program, such as an operating system, that resides in memory at all times.

kerning

In typography, *kerning* is the spacing of certain combinations of letters, such as WA, MW and TA, where each character overlaps into some of the space of the other character for an improved appearance. Kerning is provided with typesetting and desktop publishing systems.

Fixed
Spacing

Proportional
Spacing

Kerned
Letters

KERNING

key

(1) A *key* is a button on the keyboard.

(2) A *key* is the data that identifies a record. For example, account number, product code, employee number and customer name are typical keys, or key fields, used to identify a record in a file or database. As an identifier, each key value must be unique for each record. Sort keys are all the fields in the record that will be used to sort the file. The values in sort keys do not have to be unique.

(3) A *key* is a numeric code that is used by an algorithm to create a code for encrypting data for security purposes.

key cap

A *key cap* is the outer cover of a keyboard key. Key caps can be replaced with new ones in order to display references to commonly used codes used in a program.

key click

Key click is the audible feedback provided when a key is pressed. Key click is often adjustable by the user.

key-driven

Key-driven refers to any device that is activated by pressing keys.

key entry

Key entry is the data entry of information using a keyboard.

key field

See *key (2)*.

key in

Key in refers to entering data into a computer by typing on a keyboard.

key rollover

See *n-key rollover*.

key-to-disk machine

A *key-to-disk machine* is a stand-alone data entry machine that stores the keyboarded input on a magnetic disk for processing by a computer.

key-to-tape machine

A *key-to-tape machine* is a stand-alone data entry machine that stores the keyboarded input on a magnetic tape for processing by a computer. The key-to-tape machine was introduced by Mohawk Data Sciences in the mid 1960s and was the first advancement in batch-oriented data entry since the keypunch machine. The key-to-tape machine revolutionized data entry, and Mohawk Data Sciences stock soared from $2 to over $200 within a few short years.

key word

(1) A *key word* is a word used in a text search.

(2) A *key word* is a word in a text document that accurately identifies the contents of the document and is used in an index.

(3) A *key word* is a reserved word in a programming or command language.

keyboard

A *keyboard* is a set of input keys. Keyboards on terminals and personal computers contain the standard typewriter keys in addition to a number of specialized keys and features outlined below.

ENTER OR RETURN KEY
The enter key, also called the return key, works similar to the carriage return key on a typewriter. In text processing applications, it ends a paragraph or a short line. In data entry applications, pressing return signals the end of the input for that field or line.

CURSOR KEYS

The four arrow keys move the cursor in the corresponding direction on the screen. Cursor keys are used in conjunction with the shift, alt and control keys to move the cursor in bigger jumps; for example, CONTROL UP ARROW might scroll the keyboard. Some terminals and first-generation personal computers do not have all four cursor keys. In these cases, the control or alt keys are used in conjunction with some other letter key to move the cursor.

CONTROL AND ALT KEYS

The control and alt keys are used like a shift key. They are held down while another key is pressed. Control and alt key combinations are used to command the computer.

ESCAPE KEY

The escape key is commonly used to exit the mode or menu you're currently working in. It is also used in several other ways; for example, it may call up a menu, or it could delete an entry. It is sometimes used to command the computer; for example, the escape key is pressed first, and then another key is pressed to cause some action to happen.

NUMERIC LOCK

The numeric lock key locks a combination number/cursor keypad into numeric mode only.

HOME AND END KEYS

In word processing, the home key usually moves the cursor to the top left side of the current screen, and the end key moves the cursor to the bottom right side of the screen. Both keys are often used in conjunction with the shift, control and alt keys for various cursor movements; for example, CONTROL HOME may move the cursor to the beginning of a file, and CONTROL END may move the cursor to the end of the file.

PG UP AND PG DOWN KEYS

The page up and page down keys move the cursor up and down a page, screen or frame. Like the home and end keys, they are used in combination with the shift, control and alt keys for various cursor movement.

FUNCTION KEYS

Function keys, usually labeled f1, f2, etc., are additional keys used to command the computer. Their use depends entirely on the application program running in the computer.

BACKSPACE KEY

The backspace key deletes the character to the left of the cursor when pressed. Backspace is used to quickly erase typos.

DELETE KEY

The delete key eliminates the character at the current cursor location. Used in conjunction with the shift, control and alt keys, the delete key may erase a segment of text, such as a word, sentence or paragraph.

INSERT KEY

The insert key usually toggles back and forth between insert mode and overwrite mode. It is also used to "paste" a segment of text or graphics into the document at the current cursor location.

REPEATING KEYS

Most computer keyboard keys repeat when held down. This is something first-time computer users must learn quickly. If you hold a key down that is used to command the computer, you'll be entering the command several times.

AUDIBLE FEEDBACK

Some keyboards cause a clicking or beeping sound to be heard from the computer when keys are pressed. This is done to acknowledge that the character has been entered and is very useful when the typist types faster than the characters appear on screen. Audible feedback is often adjustable for personal preference.

All Keyboards Are Not Equal

The keyboard is an important part of a terminal or personal computer system, and, for experienced typists, the keyboard is critical. The amount of tension and springiness varies greatly from keyboard to keyboard, and the "feel" of a keyboard is entirely personal.

Key placement varies on keyboards. Fast, experienced typists should be aware that some keyboards have awkward return and shift key placements, such as the keyboards on first-generation IBM compatible pcs. Fast typists should be sure that a keyboard has N-key rollover, which allows subsequent keys to be pressed while other keys are still held down. For example, if you press a s d and f without lifting your fingers from any of the keys, all four letters should be entered and displayed on screen. If not, the keyboard will not be responsive to fast typing.

keyboard enhancer

A *keyboard enhancer* is a software program that allows a user to input a predefined segment of text with one keystroke. Same as *macro processor* or *keyboard macro processor*.

keyboard macro processor

See *keyboard enhancer*.

keyboard processor

(1) A *keyboard processor* is the circuit in the keyboard that converts keystrokes into the appropriate character codes.

(2) See *keyboard enhancer*.

keyboard template

A *keyboard template* is a plastic card that fits over the function keys on the keyboard and is used to identify the use of these keys for a particular software program.

keypad

A *keypad* is a small set or supplementary set of keyboard keys. Keypad refers to the number keys on a calculator or touch-tone telephone. It often refers to the number only or number and cursor key cluster on the right hand side of a computer keyboard.

CALCULATOR KEYPAD

TELEPHONE KEYPAD

keypunch

Keypunch refers to punching holes in a punched card. The term is sometimes used to refer to typing on a computer keyboard.

keypunch department

Same as *data entry department*.

keypunch machine

A *keypunch machine* is a punched-card data entry machine. A deck of blank cards is placed into a hopper, and, upon operator command, the machine feeds one card to a punch station. As characters are typed, a series of dies at the punch station punch the appropriate holes in the selected card column.

Khornerstones

Khornerstones is a benchmark test provided by Workstation Laboratories that measures CPU, input/output and floating point performance.

kicks

See *CICS*.

kilo

See K.

knowledge base

A *knowledge base* is a database of rules about a subject that is used in artificial intelligence applications. See *expert system*.

knowledge based system

A *knowledge based system* is an artificial intelligence application that uses a database of knowledge about a subject, such as in an expert system.

knowledge engineer

A *knowledge engineer* is an individual who translates the knowlege of an expert into the knowledge base of an expert system.

KSR terminal

(Keyboard Send Receive terminal) A *KSR terminal* is a terminal that uses a keyboard for entering and transmitting data. Contrast with *RO terminal* (receive only), which does not have a keyboard.

label

(1) In data management, a *label* is a made-up name that is assigned to a file, field or other data structure. With regard to tape files, a *label* is the first or last record in the file and is used for identification purposes.

(2) In spreadsheets, a *label* is any descriptive text that is entered into a cell.

(3) In programming, a *label* is a made-up name used to identify a variable or the beginning of a subroutine.

(4) In computer operations, a *label* is a small, self-sticking form that is attached to the outside of a disk or tape to identify it.

LAN

See *local area network*.

LAN Manager

LAN Manager is local area network management software jointly developed by Microsoft and 3Com that runs on IBM compatible pcs. LAN Manager runs as an application under OS/2 and supports both DOS and OS/2 workstations. It also supports Microsoft's NetBIOS standard, which is a detailed, low-level protocol introduced in 1985 with IBM's PC Net.

LAN Manager provides a "named pipes" capability, which allows programs in one workstation to exchange data with programs in different workstations.

IBM's version of LAN Manager is called LAN Server.

landscape

Landscape is a printing orientation where the data is printed across the wider side of the form. Contrast with *portrait* orientation, which is the common layout of a printed page.

language

See *machine language, programming language, graphics language, page description language, fourth-generation language, standards & compatibility* and *user interface.*

language statement

See *statement.*

laptop computer

A laptop computer is a portable computer that usually weighs less than a dozen pounds and has a self-contained power supply. Popularized by Radio Shack's Model 100, which was introduced in 1984, laptops are quite popular for people constantly on the road. They use common flashlight batteries or rechargeable batteries, and when power is available, they can be plugged into a common AC outlet. Laptop computers use flat screen technologies for compactness and light weight.

Radio Shack Model 100

Toshiba T-1000

large scale integration

See *LSI.*

laser

(Light Amplification from the Stimulated Emission of Radiation) *Lasers* generate a very uniform light that can be precisely focused. They are used in a wide variety of applications, such as communications, electrophotographic printing and optical disk (CD ROM) storage. Lasers are used to transmit light pulses over optical fibers which, unlike their electrical counterpart, are not affected by nearby electrical interferences.

In 1957, the laser was conceived and named by Gordon Gould, a graduate student in physics at Columbia University. When Gould filed for patents in 1959, he found that Charles Townes, a Columbia professor, and Arthur Schawlow, who was working for AT&T Bell Laboratories, had already filed for them. The year before, AT&T had, in fact, demonstrated a working laser at Bell Labs. In 1977, after years of litigation, a court awarded Gould rights to the first of three patents and by the end of the 1980s, he owned the rights to all three. After almost 30 years of court battles, Gould finally reaped millions of dollars in royalties, but spent much of his life without the recognition he deserved.

DEVELOPING THE LASER
(Courtesy AT&T)

This photo of the development of the helium-neon laser
was taken at AT&T's Bell Laboratories in 1964.

laser printer

A *laser printer* is a printer that uses the electrophotographic method used in copy machines to print a page at a time. A laser is used to "paint" the dots of light onto a photographic drum or belt. The toner is applied to the drum or belt and then transferred onto the paper. Desktop laser printers use cut sheets of paper as in a copy machine, and large laser printers use either cut sheets or rolls of paper.

In 1975, IBM introduced the first laser printer, called the 3800, which was designed for high-speed printing. In 1978, Siemens introduced the ND 2 and Xerox introduced the 9700. These self-contained printing presses are either online to the mainframe or offline, accepting data in print image format on reels of tape or disk packs. Large-scale machines offer features such as printing on both sides of the page and collating. Since laser printers use dot matrix technology, an infinite variety of fonts can be printed, as well as graphics. In addition, the form can be printed along with the data.

In 1984, Hewlett-Packard announced the first desktop laser printer, called the LaserJet, which has revolutionized personal computer printing and has spawned desktop publishing. Laser printers now compete directly with high-end daisy wheel and dot matrix printers.

Although high-resolution color laser printers are also available, less expensive desktop versions are on the horizon and may become widely used throughout the 1990s.

Note: All medium to large-scale printers that print a page at a time do not use a laser. Some use ion deposition, which creates the image with electricity rather than light. See *electrophotographic*.

LaserJet

The *LaserJet* is a series of desktop laser printers from Hewlett-Packard. Introduced in 1984 at a retail price of $3,000, it quickly became a huge success and set the standard for the desktop laser printer market. The LaserJet prints up to 8 pages per minute with a resolution of up to 300 dots per linear inch. The courier font is built in, and it accepts additional fonts from plug-in ROM cartridges.

The LaserJet PLUS, introduced in 1985, accepts soft fonts from the computer, prints more graphics on a page and is more flexible. The LaserJet and LaserJet PLUS both have a limited-capacity 100- sheet input tray, and both units reverse the pages on output. The LaserJet PLUS 500 has two 250-sheet input trays with correct order output.

The LaserJet Series II, introduced in 1987, has six built-in fonts, two slots for cartridges, accepts soft fonts and has one 250 sheet input tray maintaining correct order output. Fonts and features are also selectable from a keypad on the front panel. The Series II uses the Canon SX laser printer engine rather than the CX engine as on previous models, providing a better quality and darker printed image.

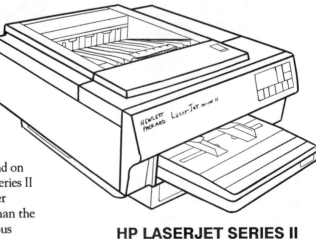

HP LASERJET SERIES II

LaserWriter

The *LaserWriter* is a series of desktop laser printers from Apple Computer. Introduced in 1985, the LaserWriter uses the built-in Postscript page description language, which means that the printer does a great deal of the actual graphics and text creation internally.

In late 1987, Apple introduced the LaserWriter II series, which, like the HP LaserJet Series II printers, also uses the newer Canon SX laser printing system. The bottom end of the LaserWriter II series is the SC, a non-Postscript printer which uses bit mapped fonts that must be downloaded into the system. The NT and NTX models are both Postscript printers with higher speeds and more memory that are built for connection into an AppleTalk network.

last-in, first-out

See *LIFO*.

LATA

(Local Access and Transport Area) A *LATA* is a geographic region that has been set up to differentiate local and long distance telephone calls. Any telephone call between parties within an individual LATA are handled by the local telephone company.

latch

A *latch* is an electronic circuit, such as a flip-flop, that maintains one of two states. It is set and then reset.

latency

Latency is the time between initiating a request for data and the beginning of the actual data transfer. On a rotating medium, such as a disk, latency is the time it takes for the selected sector to come around and be positioned under the read/write head. Channel latency is the time it takes for a computer channel to become unoccupied in order to transfer data.

latent image

A *latent image* is an invisible image that is typically made up of electrical charges. For example, in a Xerographic copy machine process, a latent image of the page to be copied is created on a plate or drum as an electrical charge.

layout setting

A *layout setting* is a value that is used to format a printed page. Margins, tabs, indents, headers, footers and column widths are examples of layout settings.

LCD

(Liquid Crystal Display) *LCD* is a display technology that is commonly used in digital watches and laptop computers. Because they use less power, LCDs replaced LEDs (light emitting diodes) in digital watches years ago. Power is used only to move molecules rather than to energize a light-emitting substance.

Liquid crystals are rod-shaped molecules that flow like liquid, and are used to direct light between two polarizing filters. In their normal state, the crystals direct the light through the polarizers, allowing a natural light gray background color to show. When energized, they redirect the light to be absorbed in one of the polarizers, causing the dark appearance of crossed polarizers to show.

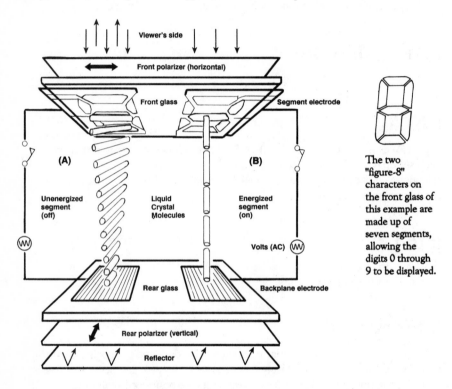

The two "figure-8" characters on the front glass of this example are made up of seven segments, allowing the digits 0 through 9 to be displayed.

TWISTED-NEMATIC LIQUID CRYSTAL DISPLAY
(Courtesy LXD Inc.)

Side A shows a light gray segment (background). The light source from the viewer's side shines through the front polarizer, through the front glass, down the liquid crystals, through the rear glass and through the rear polarizer. It bounces off the reflector, back through the rear polarizer and rear glass, back up the liquid crystals, back through the front glass and front polarizer to the viewer. In the normal state, the liquid crystals are induced to lay parallel with their polarizing plates.

Side B shows a dark segment (crossed polarizers). When the segment is energized, the liquid crystal molecules turn perpendicular to the polarizing plates. Light shines through the front polarizer and glass, down the molecules and through the rear glass. It is then absorbed in the rear polarizer.

The layer of liquid crystals (between the bottom of the front glass and the top of the rear glass) is only 3/10,000ths of an inch thick.

Backlit displays use a translucent reflector and shine a light source behind it. This "transflective" type of display helps make the background brighter, thus making the characters appear sharper.

LE

(Less than or Equal to) See *relational operators*.

leader

(1) A *leader* is the beginning length of unrecorded tape that is used to thread the tape onto the tape drive.

(2) A *leader* is the first record in a file that is used for identification purposes. See *header label*.

(3) *Leaders* are the dots or dashes used to draw the eye across the printed page, such as in a table of contents.

leading

Leading is the vertical spacing between lines of type. The name is derived from the early days of typesetting when the space was achieved with thin bars of lead. Today, leading refers to the vertical space between baselines. See *typeface* for an illustration.

leading edge

(1) A *leading edge* is the edge of a punched card or document that enters the reading station first.

(2) In digital electronics, the *leading edge* is a pulse as it changes from a 0 to a 1.

(3) In programming, a *leading edge* is a loop that tests a condition before the loop is entered.

leading zeros

Leading zeros are zeros used to fill in a field to the left of the actual number and do not increase the numerical value of the data. For example, all the zeros in the number 0000006588 are leading zeros.

leaf

In database management, a *leaf* is the last node of a tree.

leapfrog test

A *leapfrog test* is a storage diagnostic routine that replicates itself throughout the storage medium.

leased line

A *leased line* is a dedicated communications channel that is leased from a common carrier. Leased lines can usually handle greater transmission speeds than the dial-up telephone system. Leased lines from the telephone company can be conditioned, or electronically fine tuned, to reduce the transmission error rate.

least significant bit

The *least significant bit* is the binary digit in the rightmost position of the byte, word or field.

least significant digit

The *least significant digit* is the digit in the rightmost position of the number.

LED

(Light Emitting Diode) *LED* is a display technology that uses a particular variety of semiconductor diode that emits light when charged with electricity. LEDs usually give off a red glow, although other colors can be generated as well. LEDs were the digit displays on the earliest digital watches. Their higher power requirement caused them to give way to the LCD (liquid crystal display), which is always visible and does not require the wearer to press a button to activate it. LEDs are used for the drive-in-use lights found on floppy and hard disk drives, as well as in display panels for countless electronic products.

left justify

In typography, *left justify* is the same as *flush left*, in which all text is aligned to the left margin. All the text in this book is left justified.

LEN

(Low Entry Networking) *LEN* refers to networking IBM System/3x mid-range office computers into IBM's SNA communications environment. LEN is based on IBM's PU 2.1 peer-to-peer communications capability.

letter quality

Letter quality is the print quality of an electric typewriter, which is produced on a variety of printers. A laser printer produces the best quality. All daisy wheel printers and some ink jet printers produce letter quality printing. Dot matrix printers that use a 24-pin print head provide a near letter quality (NLQ) image, but the characters are not as dark and crisp as on the other printers mentioned.

lexicographic sort

A *lexicographic sort* arranges items in alphabetic order without regard to upper and lower case letters, such as the way terms are listed in this book. Normal personal computer sorting (ASCII code) puts words starting with lower case letters after all words starting with upper case letters, because that's the normal sequence assigned to these characters. For example, a word starting with "a" would come after a word starting with "Z."

LF key

See *line feed key*.

librarian

A *librarian* is an individual who works in the data library.

library

(1) A *library* is a collection of programs or data files for a particular purpose.

(2) A *library* is a collection of prewritten subroutines which provides processing functions that don't have to be written by the programmer. The programmer provides a call (reference) in the program to a particular subroutine in order to use it.

(3) A *library* is the physical location where tapes, disks and copies of reports are maintained. See *data library*.

library routine

A *library routine* is a prewritten subroutine that is part of a macro or function library.

LIFO

(Last In First Out) *LIFO* is a queueing method in which the next item to be retrieved is the item most recently placed in the queue.

light bar

A *light bar* is the use of color or a reverse video image to highlight a selected option in an on-screen menu. For example, if the display is normally white on black, the selected item might be displayed as black on white. The reverse display, or even a different color, gives the impression that the word or line is "lighted" up.

Light bar menus are available to programmers within the programming language itself, such as in Paradox's PAL language, or in separate utility programs that work with many programming languages, such as Flash-Up Windows.

light emitting diode

See *LED*.

light guide

A *light guide* is a transmission channel that contains a number of optical fibers packaged together.

light pen

A *light pen* is an input device that uses a light-sensitive stylus connected by a wire to a video terminal. The user brings the light pen to the desired point on the screen surface and presses a button, causing it to identify the location on the screen. Light pens are used to select options from a menu displayed on screen or to draw images in graphics systems by "dragging" the cursor around the screen.

The pixels (dots) on a display screen are constantly being refreshed (re-illuminated) over and over again. When the user presses the light pen button, allowing the pen to sense light, the pixel being illuminated at that moment identifies the location on the screen.

LIGHT PEN

lightwave

Light wave refers to light in the infrared, visible and ultraviolet ranges, which falls between x-rays and microwaves. Wavelengths in this range are between 10 nanometers and one millimeter.

lightwave system

A *lightwave system* refers to an optical system that transmits light pulses over optical fibers; for example, the intercity trunks of the telephone companies are rapidly being converted to lightwave systems. Lightwave systems now in production can transmit over a billion light pulses per second.

LIGHTWAVE SYSTEM

(Courtesy Rockwell International)

Although this looks like a city of the future, it is actually a 10" square circuit board containing an advanced lightwave transmission system. This model LTS-21130, from Rockwell's Lightwave Systems Division, is capable of transmitting 1.13 billion bits per second. That means 16,000 digitized voice conversations can be transmitted simultaneously over one hair-thin optical fiber.

LIM EMS

(Lotus/Intel/Microsoft Expanded Memory Specification) Same as *EMS.*

limited distance modem

Same as *short-haul modem.*

line

(1) For text-based printers or display terminals, a *line* is a row of printed or displayed characters. For graphics-based systems, a line is a row of dots.

(2) In communications, a *line* is a pathway between two terminals or computers over which data, text, pictures, voice and video is transmitted.

LINES

(Courtesy AT&T)

The exploding communications field in 1883. This photo was taken at Broadway and Courtlandt Streets in New York City.

line adapter

In communications, a *line adapter* is a device, like a modem, that converts an internal digital signal into a form suitable for transmission over a communications line and vice versa. It provides such functions as parallel to serial and serial to parallel conversion and modulation and demodulation.

line analyzer

A *line analyzer* is a device that monitors the transmission of a communications line.

line concentration

See *concentrator*.

line conditioning

See *conditioning*.

line dot matrix printer

A *line dot matrix printer* is a line printer that uses the dot matrix printing method. See *printer*.

line drawing

A *line drawing* is a graphic image outlined by solid lines, where the mass of the drawing is imagined by the viewer. See *wire frame*.

line driver

In communications, a *line driver* is a hardware device that is used to extend the transmission distance between terminals and computers that are directly connected. Line drivers are used for digital transmission and are required at both ends of the private line. They transmit signals up to several miles.

line editor

A *line editor* is a simple editing program that allows text to be changed one line at a time. For example, EDLIN is the line editor that comes with Microsoft's DOS operating system.

line feed

A *line feed* is a character code that advances the cursor on screen or the paper in the printer to the next line. It is character 10 in the ASCII character set. A line feed button on the printer will advance the paper one line if pressed.

line frequency

A *line frequency* is the number of times within each second in which a wave or some repeatable set of signals is transmitted over some cable or channel. See *scan rate*.

line level

In communications, the *line level* is the signal strength within a transmission channel. Line levels are measured in decibels or nepers.

line load

(1) In communications, the *line load* is the percentage of time a communications channel is used.

(2) In electronics, the *line load* is the amount of current that is carried in a circuit.

line number

(1) In BASIC, a *line number* refers to a specific language statement. All lines of source code are numbered in BASIC.

(2) On display screens, a *line number* is a specific row of text characters or row of dots.

(3) In communications, a *line number* is a specific communications channel.

line of code

A *line of code* is a statement in a programming language. A line of code in assembly language is usually equal to only one machine instruction, but a line of code in a high-level programming language may represent a single or complex series of instructions to the computer. Lines of code are used to measure the complexity of a program. However, comparisons are misleading if the programs are not in the same language or category. For example, eight lines of code in a report writer may be equivalent to 100 lines of code in a COBOL program.

line printer

A *line printer* is a printer that prints a line at a time. Line printers are usually connected to mainframes and minicomputers. See *printer*.

line segment

In vector graphics, a *line segment* is a vector.

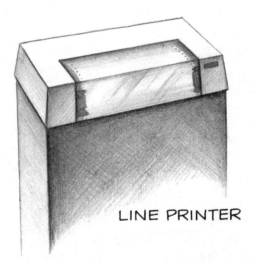

LINE PRINTER

line speed

See *data rate*.

line squeeze

In a mail merge operation, a *line squeeze* is the vertical adjustment of the body of text when a blank line is encountered in the name and address. Instead of printing a blank name and address line, the blank line is moved to the end of the letter. In the following example, if a company field is blank, a blank line is printed with the name on the left. The name on the right is printed with line squeeze and a blank field is relocated to the end of the page.

```
    Pat Smith                Pat Smith
                             10 South Main
    10 South Main            Bearcat, OR 80901
    Bearcat, OR 80901
```

linear

Linear is an arrangement along one line, one axis or one dimension and implies a sequential nature. Linear operations imply uniformity, equality and regularity; for example, the outputs of a linear system are uniformly based on the inputs. An increase in the input provides an equal increase in output.

linear programming

Linear programming is a mathematical technique that is used to obtain an optimum solution in resource allocation problems, such as production planning.

link

(1) In communications, a *link* is the line, channel or circuit over which data is transmitted.

(2) In data management, a *link* is a pointer embedded within a record that refers to data or the location of data in another record.

(3) In programming, a *link* is a call to another program or subroutine.

link edit

Link edit is the act of using a linkage editor.

linkage editor

A *linkage editor* is a utility program which adapts a program that has just been assembled or compiled into a particular computer environment. It formally links cross references between separate program modules, and it links the program to various libraries containing prewritten subroutines. The output of a linkage editor is a load module, a program ready to run in the computer.

linked list

In data management, a *linked list* is a group of items, each of which points to the next item. A linked list allows for the organization of a sequential set of data in noncontiguous storage locations.

linker

See *linkage editor*.

Linpack

Linpack is a benchmark program for testing a computer's performance. Linpack is a FORTRAN program that executes 100 equations with 100 unknowns. The results of the test depend on the computer's floating point, CPU and memory speed as well as the compiler's efficiency.

LIPS

(Logical Inferences Per Second) *LIPS* are used to measure the "thinking" speed of artificial intelligence applications. Humans can do about 2 LIPS. In the computer, 1 LIPS equals from 100 to 1,000 instructions.

liquid crystal display

See *LCD*.

liquid crystal shutters

Liquid crystal shutters are a set of LCD shutters that are used to control the image on electrophotographic page printers. The liquid crystal dots function as gates that open and close, allowing light to pass through and paint a photosensitive drum or belt. Liquid crystal shutters provide an alternative to the laser mechanism in desktop laser printers.

Lisa

The *Lisa*, introduced in 1983 by Apple Computer, was the first personal computer offered with integrated software. It was also the first personal

computer that
incorporated Xerox's
user interface which
uses icons (graphic
representations) and a
mouse to select them.
The Lisa was ahead of
its time, but due to a
high price tag of
$10,000, sluggish
performance and lack of
commitment by Apple,
it was a commercial
failure. The Lisa,
renamed the Mac XL,
lived out the rest of its
days as a Macintosh.

LISA

LISP

(**LIS**t Processing) *LISP* is a high-level programming language used extensively in
non-numeric programming (also called list processing), in which objects, rather
than numbers, are manipulated. Developed in 1960 by John McCarthy, LISP is
very different in syntax and structure than common languages like BASIC and
COBOL. For example, in LISP there is no syntactic difference between data and
instructions as there is in most other languages.

LISP is used extensively in artificial intelligence applications, as well as in
compiler creation, and is available in both interpreted and compiled versions.
LISP automatically handles more program activities than conventional
languages, such as dynamic memory management, and lets the programmer
concentrate on manipulating the objects. The language itself can be modified
and expanded by the user.

Many varieties of LISP have been developed, including versions that perform
calculations efficiently. The following Common LISP example converts
fahrenheit to centigrade:

```
(defun convert ()
  (format t "Enter fahrenheit ")
  (let ((fahr (read)))
   (format t "Centigrade is ~D"
        (truncate (*(-fahr 32)
            (/ 5 9))))))
```

list

(1) A *list* is any arranged set of data.

(2) *List* is to display or print a group of selected records.

list processing

List processing is the processing of non-numeric data and refers to languages that provide functions that aid in the programming of such data, such as LISP, Prolog and Logo. List processing languages provide special commands and functions that work with lists of data, such as names, words and objects. For example, a single command might select the first or last object in the list, or next to first or next to last. Some languages have a command to reverse the order of all the elements in the list. Although all these functions can be performed in traditional programming languages, the list processing languages make it much easier to do so. In addition, recursion is provided in list processing languages, which allows a subroutine to call itself over and over again, thus allowing objects in a list to be repetitively analyzed until an answer is found.

listing

A *listing* may be any printed output generated from the computer, but often refers to a source language program printout.

literal

In programming, a *literal* is an unchanging item written into the program, such as a message that will be displayed on screen. Literals are translated into machine language without conversion.

liveware

Liveware is a category of objects known as human beings.

load

(1) In computer operations, *load* is to transfer something into the computer's memory or onto a peripheral device. To load a program is to copy the program from a disk or tape into memory for execution. To load a disk is to fill it up with programs or data. Load also means to physically mount a storage medium, such as a disk or tape, into or onto the drive.

(2) In programming, to *load* a register is to store data in a register.

(3) In performance measurement, a *load* is the current use of a system as a percentage of total capacity.

(4) In electronics, a *load* is the flow of current through a circuit.

load module

A *load module* is a program in machine language form ready to run in the computer. A load module is the output of a link editor.

loaded line

In communications, a *loaded line* is a telephone line that uses loading coils to reduce distortion. The loading coils are used to restore high-end voice frequencies but can interfere with data transmission.

loader

A *loader* is a program routine that brings a program into memory for execution.

loader routine

Same as *loader*.

loading coils

See *loaded line*.

local area network

A *local area network* is a communications network that serves several users within a confined geographical area. Although the term may refer to any communications network within a building or plant, it typically refers to the interconnection of personal computers.

   Personal computer local area networks function as distributed processing systems in which each computer, or node, in the network does its own processing and manages some of its data. Shared data

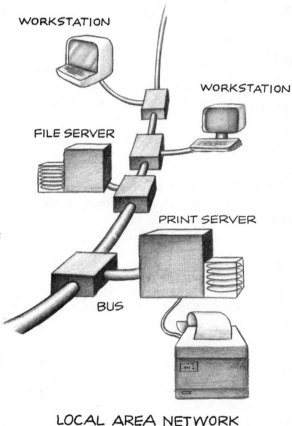

LOCAL AREA NETWORK

is stored in a high-performance pc in the network, called a *file server* or *network server*, which acts as a remote disk drive to all the users in the network.

The printers that are attached to the network can function on a first-come, first-served basis, or they can be connected to a computer, called a *print server*, which collects the print output and feeds it to the printer one job at a time.

A   local area network is the backbone of office automation and allows electronic mail and other information to be communicated between all users of the system. Local area networks are becoming essential for small work groups that enter, share and exchange the same information.

With the use of a *gateway*, local area network can connect to minicomputer and mainframe networks.

BASEBAND NETWORKS
Baseband networks are all digital networks that require information in digital form. Examples are ARCNET, Token Ring, Ethernet and Starlan. All of these networks are driven by network management software that resides in the file servers and the workstations. Examples of network software are Microsoft's NetBIOS and LAN Manager, AppleTalk, TPC/IP and Novell's NetWare.

BROADBAND NETWORKS
Broadband networks use carrier frequencies and can handle voice and video transmission as well, for example, Wang Computer's WangNET.

local bypass

A *local bypass* is where an organization connects two or more of its own business locations within the same city and bypasses the local telephone company.

local loop

A *local loop* is a communications line between a telephone customer and the telephone company's central switching exchange. Local loops have traditionally been strictly analog; however, some of these lines are being adapted to digital transmission. See *DTS*.

local variable

In programming, a *local variable* is a variable that is used only within the routine or function it is defined in. A variable with the same name used elsewhere will have no affect on a local variable.

log

A *log* is a record of computer processing that contains statistics about all machine operations taking place. Logs are used for statistical purposes as well as backup and recovery.

log-on/log-off

Log-on/log-off is making a connection and breaking a connection between a user and the computer. The log-on requires users to sign in and identify themselves. The log-off breaks the connection. Service bureaus charge their customers from the time they log-on until the time they log-off.

logic

Logic refers to a sequence of operations that is performed by the hardware or the software. Hardware logic is the circuits and chips that perform the computing and controlling operations of the computer. Software logic, or program logic, is the sequence of instructions in a program.

   Note: Logic is not the same as logical. Logical refers to the design of a system, rather than its physical implementation. See *logical vs physical*.

logic analyzer

(1) A *logic analyzer* is a device that monitors the performance of a computer by timing various segments of the running programs. The total running time and the time spent in selected progam modules is analyzed and displayed in order to isolate the code that is the least efficient.

(2) A *logic analyzer* is a device that is used to test and diagnose an electronic system, which includes an oscilloscope for displaying various digital states.

logic array

Same as *gate array* or PLA.

logic bomb

A *logic bomb* is a program that destroys data; for example, it may reformat the hard disk or randomly insert garbage into data files. A logic bomb may be brought into a personal computer by downloading a public-domain program that has been tampered with. Once executed, the logic bomb usually does its damage right away, whereas a software virus slowly invades a system and attaches itself to other programs.

logic chip

A *logic chip* is a chip that performs logic functions, such as processing and controlling. Contrast with *memory chip*, which functions as internal working storage.

logic circuit

A *logic circuit* is a circuit that performs logic functions. See *logic chip*.

logic gate

A *logic gate* is a collection of transistors and other electronic components that make up a Boolean logical operation, such as AND, NAND, OR and NOR. Transistors make up logic gates. Logic gates make up circuits. Circuits make up electronic systems.

logic operation

A *logic operation* is an operation that analyzes one or more inputs and generates a particular output based on a set of rules. See *AND, OR and NOT* and *Boolean logic*.

logic operator

A *logic operator* is one of the Boolean logical operation, such as AND, OR and NOT.

logic-seeking printer

A *logic-seeking printer* is a printer that analyzes the content of each line to be printed and skips over blank spaces at high speeds.

logical

(1) *Logical* refers to a reasonable solution to a problem.

(2) *Logical* refers to the symbolic representation of data or of a computer resource, such as a peripheral device. It implies the user's view of the object rather than the computer's view of it.

logical field

A *logical field* is a data field that contains a yes/no, true/false condition only.

logical vs physical

Logical vs physical is the user's view vs the computer's view. Logical implies a higher level than the physical. The following examples show logical to physical relationship:

Users relate to data logically by data element name; however, the actual fields of data are physically located in sectors on a disk. For example, if you want to know which customers ordered how many of a particular product this week, your logical view of this data is customer name and quantity. The physical organization of this data might have customer name in a customer file and quantity in an order file cross referenced by customer number. The physical sequence of the customer file could be indexed, while the sequence of the order file could be sequential.

A message transmitted from Phoenix to Boston is logically going between the two cities; however, the physical circuit could be Phoenix to Chicago New York to Boston.

When you command your program to change the output from the video screen to the printer, that's a logical request. The program will perform the physical change of address from, say, device number 02 to device number 04.

logical record

A *logical record* is a data record that is independent of its physical location. It may be physically stored in two or more locations.

logical unit

See *LU*.

Logo

Logo is a high-level programming language that is designed for first-time programmers and is noted for its ease of use, list processing and graphics capabilities. Logo is a recursive language that contains many list processing functions that are in the LISP programming language, although Logo's syntax is less cryptic and, as a result, more understandable for novices.

Logo's graphics language is called turtle graphics, which allows complex graphics images to be created with a minimum of coding. The turtle is a triangular-shaped cursor, which is moved on the screen with Logo commands that activate the turtle as if you were driving it, for example, go forward 100 units, turn right 45 degrees, turn left 20 degrees.

Stemming originally from a National Science Foundation research project, Logo was created by Seymour Papert in the mid- 1960s along with colleagues at Massachusetts Institute of Technology (MIT) and members of Bolt Beranek & Newman Inc. Originally developed on large computers, Logo has been adapted to most personal computers.

The following Object Logo example converts fahrenheit to centigrade:

```
to convert
local [fahr]
print "|Enter fahrenheit |
make "fahr ReadWord
print "|Centigrade is |
print (:fahr - 32) * 5 / 9
end
```

long card

In IBM compatible pcs, a *long card* is a full-length controller board that plugs into an expansion slot on the computer's bus. Contrast with *short card*, which takes up half the length. In order to shorten the overall size of the computer's cabinet, some designs do not permit long cards in every slot.

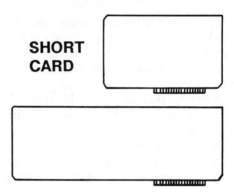

SHORT CARD

LONG CARD

long-haul

In communications, *long-haul* refers to modems or communications devices that are capable of transmitting over long distances.

long lines

In communications, *long lines* are communications circuits that are capable of handling transmissions over long distances.

longitudinal redundancy check

See *LRC*.

look up

A *look up* is a search for data within a table stored in memory or in a data file.

loop

In programming, a *loop* is the repetition of some function within the program. Whenever any process must be repeated, a loop is set up to handle it. A program usually has a main loop that allows it to work on more than one set of data. It also contains a series of minor loops for each repeating process. For example, in an invoice program, the main loop reads the order record and prints the invoice and repeats this over and over until there are no more orders to read. After printing today's date, bill-to and ship-to addresses, the program will usually print some number of line items. Since there's more than one line item, and since it's a variable number, the code that handles this process is put into a loop. The line item loop is said to be nested within the main loop. Loops are at the very heart of programming, and learning how to set up loops is what programming technique is all about.

Loops are accomplished by various programming structures, each one having a beginning, body and end of the loop. For example, a FOR NEXT loop repeats all statements between the FOR and the NEXT for a fixed number of times. A DO loop repeats all statements between the DO and the END until a condition, which is tested at the beginning of the loop, is satisfied. For example, DO WHILE NOT EOF (end of file) repeats a process until there are no more records to read.

The end of the loop is a GOTO instruction that points back to the beginning of the loop. In assembly language programming, the programmer writes the GOTO. In high-level languages, the end part of the loop is the GOTO. For example, the following assembly language routine counts to 10 by 1.

```
            MOVE      "0" TO COUNTER
LOOP        ADD       "1" TO COUNTER
            COMPARE  COUNTER TO "10"
GOTO        LOOP IF UNEQUAL
            STOP
```

The same routine using a DO loop:

```
            COUNTER = 0
            DO WHILE COUNTER  10
              COUNTER = COUNTER + 1
            ENDDO
            STOP
```

loopback

Loopback refers to a diagnositc procedure in which a transmitted message or signal is sent back from the receiving end to the sending end for comparison with the original data.

loosely coupled

Loosely coupled refers to stand-alone computers that are interconnected via a communications network. Loosely coupled computers can process on their own and are not dependent on other computers for their routine operation. They can exchange data on demand by requesting a transfer from another machine in the network. Contrast with *tightly coupled*, which implies two or more machines that are entirely dependent on each other, such as with a database machine, or that work very closely together, such as in a multiprocessing environment.

lo-res

See *low resolution*.

lost cluster

A *lost cluster* is a set of disk records that are not associated with any file name in a disk directory. Lost clusters can occur when a file is not closed properly, which can happen if an application program is not formally exited before turning the computer off. In Microsoft's DOS operating systems, the CHKDSK /f command will recover lost clusters and turn them into files starting with the name FILE0000.CHK. If the files contain text, they can then be viewed with a word processor or text editor.

Lotus 1-2-3

Lotus 1-2-3 is a spreadsheet from Lotus Development Corporation that runs on IBM compatible pcs, DEC minicomputers and IBM mainframes. Introduced in 1982, it was the first, new and innovative spreadsheet developed for the IBM PC. Lotus 1-2-3 was the first spreadsheet to include graphics, file management and limited word processing along with traditional spreadsheet capabilities. Its ability to quickly and easily convert numeric data into a business graph was one of its most dazzling features at the time. The program also incoporated a user interface that was easy to learn and easy to use. New features combined with a very well- organized marketing campaign made Lotus 1-2-3 a huge success.

In 1987, HAL was introduced as an add-on product that lets users type in English-like commands and queries instead of wading through several levels of menus or entering precise expressions.

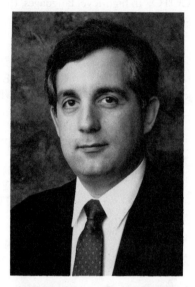

MITCHELL D. KAPOR

(Courtesy ON Technology, Inc.)

Mitch Kapor was co-programmer of Lotus 1-2-3 and founder of Lotus Development Corporation. He currently heads a new company called ON Technology.

Lotus menu

The *Lotus menu* is the user interface that is designed into Lotus 1-2-3. It has set a standard that is easy to learn and easy to use. Improving on the Multiplan spreadsheet from Microsoft, which displayed a row of menu options and allowed the user to select one by typing the first letter of its name, the Lotus menu added a line of explanation. The explanation line is displayed when the cursor is moved onto the command. For example, in Lotus, the following explanation is displayed by highlighting RETRIEVE in the FILE menu. Experienced users wouldn't need the explanation; they would just type "R."

Erase the current worksheet and display the selected worksheet

The Lotus menu has been used in countless other software packages, as it is an extremely simple and effective user interface.

low entry networking

See LEN.

low frequency

Low frequency is an electromagnetic wave that vibrates in the range from 30 to 300,000 Hertz (cycles per second).

low-level language

A *low-level language* is a programming language that is very close to machine language. All assembly languages are low-level languages. Contrast with *high-level language*.

low resolution

Low resolution is a low-grade image quality that is displayed or printed. Low resolution is due to a limited number of dots or lines per inch of image area.

LPM

(Lines Per Minute) *LPM* measures the print speed of a printer.

LRC

(Longitudinal Redundancy Check) *LRC* is an error checking method that generates a parity bit from a specified string of bits on a longitudinal track. When bits are recorded in a row and column format, such as on a magnetic tape, the LRC method is often used in conjunction with the VRC method (vertical redundancy check), which creates a parity bit for each character.

LSI

(Large Scale Integration) *LSI* refers to the large numbers of electronic components built on a chip. LSI ranges approximately from 3,000 to 100,000 transistors on a chip.

LSI-11

LSI-11 is a family of board-level computers from Digital Equipment Corporation that uses the micro version of the PDP-11 architecture. Introduced in 1974, it was the first implementation of Digital's Q-bus product line.

LT

(Less Than) See *relational operators*.

LU

(Logical Unit) In an IBM SNA network, an *LU* is one end, or one point of connection, in a communications session. A user at a terminal, a user at a personal computer and a printer are examples of an LU.

The complete session, or LU-LU session, is defined by session type. IBM has defined LU types 0 through 7 with type 5 undefined as yet. For example, a type 2 session is between an application program in the mainframe and a single 3270 terminal. A type 3 session is between an application program and a printer. A type 6 session is between two application programs, such as two CICS programs communicating with each other.

LU 6.2

(Logical Unit Type 6.2) *LU 6.2* provides peer-to-peer communications in an IBM SNA environment. It is a special type 6 LU session which is supported by software called "Advanced-Program-to-Program Communications" (APPC).

Before LU 6.2, all communications traffic was managed as a master-slave relationship. With LU 6.2, both sides have equal responsibility for initiating and managing the session.

Associated with an LU 6.2 session is IBM's PU (physical unit) 2.1, which provides the software necessary to support LU 6.2.

lumen

A *lumen* is a unit of measurement of the flow, or rate of emission, of light. An ordinary wax candle generates 13 lumens while a 100 watt bulb generates 1,200 lumens. The intensity of light is measured in *candelas*. The same wax candle generates one candela of intensity.

Lumena

Lumena is a paint program from Time Arts, Inc., that runs on IBM compatible pcs. Lumena is an advanced program that is designed for artists and illustrators who require a variety of sophisticated special effects. It accepts video and scanned input and generates standard NTSC video output as well as hard copy. Lumena requires a special video graphics board, such as the Targa board from TrueVision or the Vision 16 board from Everex.

luminance

In computer graphics, *luminance* is the amount of brightness, measured in lumens, that is given off by a pixel or area on a screen.

machine

A *machine* is any electronic or electromechanical unit of equipment. A machine always refers to hardware; however, the term "engine" is used to refer to both hardware and software.

machine address

Same as *absolute address*.

machine cycle

A *machine cycle* is the shortest interval in which an elementary operation can take place within the processor. Machine cycles are made up of some number of clock cycles.

machine-dependent

(1) *Machine-dependent* refers to a program, such as an assembly language program, that runs on one particular family of computers.

(2) *Machine-dependent* refers to programs that reference specific features of a computer or peripheral device.

machine-independent

(1) *Machine-independent* refers to a program that can be readily converted to run on two or more different families of computers.

(2) *Machine-independent* refers to programs that can run in computers with different types of peripheral devices.

machine instruction

A *machine instruction* is an instruction that the computer understands directly. Contrast with an instruction in a low-level assembly language or a statement in a high-level programming language.

machine language

Machine language is the computer's native language and is the only language the computer understands. In order for a computer to run a program, the program must be in the same machine language of the computer that is executing it, unless the computer is capable of emulating or simulating a foreign machine language.

Although programmers may modify machine language in order to make a quick fix to a running program, they do not create machine language. It is created by software programs called *assemblers, compilers* and *interpreters*, which take the language the programmer writes and translate it into machine language. When programmers write in low-level assembly language, which is very close to machine language, they're still not writing machine language.

If a program runs under an interpreter, the program remains in its original source language form just as the programmer wrote it. It is translated by the interpreter into machine language a line at a time when the program is run.

The machine language tells the computer not only what to do, but where to do it. When a programmer writes the statement, TOTAL = TOTAL + SUBTOTAL, the + must be turned into machine code that tells the computer to add, and TOTAL and SUBTOTAL must be converted into memory locations where that data is temporarily stored. A programmer deals with data logically, "add this, subtract that," but the computer must be fed machine language that tells it precisely where this and that are located.

All computers have machine language that cause it to INPUT from and provide OUTPUT to peripheral devices and communication channels. All computers have machine instructions to process data by CALCULATING, COMPARING and COPYING it, and all computers have a GO TO capability that directs the computer back to the beginning of a routine or to another routine in the program. In addition, there are instructions that test and control peripheral devices. For example, an instruction can check the status of a disk to see if it is ready to read or write. Another instruction causes the access arm to go to (seek) a specific track.

Machine languages differ substantially between micros, minis and mainframes. What may take one instruction in a mainframe, can take 15 instructions in a microcomputer. See *assembly language, compiler* and *instruction*.

machine readable

Machine readable is any paper form or storage medium that can be automatically read by the computer. For example, various typewritten and printed fonts can be scanned in and recognized by the computer. Punched cards can be read into the computer. Data or programs on magnetic disk or tape can be read by the computer.

Macintosh

Macintosh is a series of single user, 32-bit personal computers from Apple Computer, initially introduced in 1984. The Macintosh is very popular because of its simulated on-screen desktop environment which is easy to learn and easy to use. In addition, this method of commanding the computer is used with almost all application programs that run in the Macintosh. See *Macintosh user interface*.

The Macintosh uses the Motorola 68000 family of microprocessors and runs under its own proprietary operating system. The part of the operating system that simulates the desktop is called "Finder." The multitasking version of Finder is called "MultiFinder."

The Macintosh series provides medium-high-resolution graphics and a built-in graphics languages, called "QuickDraw," which provides a standard for software developers.

Except for the Mac II, all models of the Macintosh have a 9" diagonal monochrome (black on white) screen.

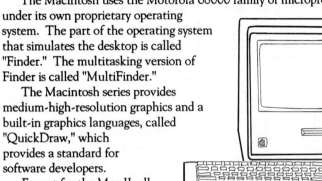

MACINTOSH

MAC AND MAC PLUS

Introduced in January 1984, the first Macintosh had 128K of memory, one built-in floppy disk drive with an external slot for one more, two serial ports and a four-voice sound generator. When more memory was available later in the year, a 512K Macintosh was nicknamed the "Fat Mac."

The Mac Plus, introduced in January 1986, added expandability by providing an external SCSI (Small Computer Systems Interface) port that connects hard disks, tape backups and other high-speed devices.

MAC SE

The SE, introduced in March 1987, provides more memory (from one to four megabytes), an optional built-in 20 megabyte hard disk and contains one internal expansion slot for connecting a third-party device.

MAC II

The Mac II, introduced in March 1987, uses the faster 68020 CPU, which runs at a

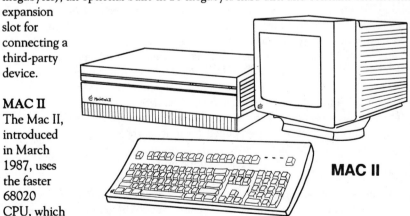

MAC II

higher clock speed and has a full 32-bit data bus instead of a 16-bit bus. Mac II models have built-in hard disks with 40 to 160 megabyte capacities and memory capacity up to eight megabytes (and more as denser memory chips arive).

The Mac II is the first Macintosh to provide a color graphics option, which produces up to 256 colors on screen at a 640x480 resolution. Mac II models are designed for expandability with three (IIcx) or six (II & IIx) built-in NuBus expansion slots for additional peripheral and coprocessor boards.

MODEL	CPU # (32 bits)	CLOCK SPEED (MHz)	BUS SIZE	RAM (Bytes)	FLOPPY DISK (Bytes)	HARD DISK (Bytes)	SCREEN RESOLUTION
Mac	68000	7.8	16 bits	128-512K	3.5" 400K	20M	512x342
Mac Plus	68000	7.8	16 bits	1-4M	3.5" 400/800K	20-160M	Black on white 9" diagonal
Mac SE	68000	7.8	16 bits	1-4M	3.5" 400/800K	20-160M	
Mac SE 30	68030	15.7	32 bits	1-8M*	3.5" FDHD "SuperDrive"	20-160M	
Mac II	68020	15.7	32 bits	1-8M*	400/800/1400K Mac formats;	20-160M	640x480, 12" 256 cols. or B/w
Mac IIx	68030	15.7	32 bits	1-8M*	Also MS-DOS, OS/2 &	20-160M	640x870. 15" & 1152x870, 21"
Mac IIcx	68030	15.7	32 bits	1-8M*	ProDOS disks	20-160M	Black on white

MACINTOSH SPECIFICATIONS
*Memory limit will increase to 32 Mbytes with 4 Mbit chips

Macintosh user interface

The *Macintosh user interface* has become a very popular method for commanding the computer. Originally developed at Xerox's Palo Alto Research Center and commercially introduced on the Xerox Star computer in 1981, Apple later built a very similar version. This style of user interface uses a graphical metaphor based on familiar office objects positioned on a two-dimensional "desktop" workspace.

Programs and data files are represented on screen by tiny pictures (icons) that look like the actual objects. An object is selected by moving a mouse over the real desktop which correspondingly moves the cursor on screen. When the cursor is over an icon on screen, it is selected by pressing the mouse's button.

A hierarchical file system is provided that lets a user "drag" a document icon into and out of a folder icon. Folders can also contain other folders and so on. To delete a document, its icon is literally dragged into a trash can icon. For people that are not computer enthusiasts, managing files on the Macintosh is a breeze compared to the DOS command line in the IBM pc world.

The Macintosh always displays a row of menu titles at the top of the screen. The full menu appears as if it were "pulled down" from the top of the screen when selected. With the mouse button held down, the option within the menu is selected by pointing to it and then releasing the button.

Unlike the IBM pc world, which leaves the design of the user interface up to the software vendor, Macintosh developers almost always conform to the Macintosh interface. As a result, users are comfortable with a new program from

The Computer Glossary

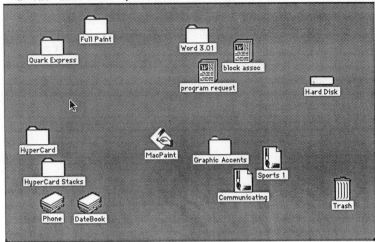

MACINTOSH DESKTOP

the start even if it takes a while to learn all the rest of it. They know there will be a row of menu options at the top of the screen, and basic tasks are always performed the same. In operation, the operating system and application programs are almost indistinguishable, providing a uniform environment for the user. Apple also keeps technical jargon down to a minimum.

Although the Macintosh user interface provides consistency; it does not make up for an application program that is not designed well. Not only must the application's menus be clear and understandable, but the locations on screen that

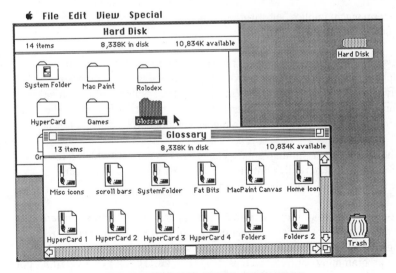

MACINTOSH FILE SYSTEM

The HARD DISK window at the top shows a series of folders with the GLOSSARY folder selected. The GLOSSARY window shows the series of documents contained within the folder.

a user points to must be considered. Since the mouse is the major selecting method on a Macintosh, mouse movement should be kept to a minimum. In addition, for experienced typists, the mouse is a cumbersome substitute for well-designed keyboard commands, especially for intensive text editing.

Pull-down menus have been adapted to many IBM, Commodore and Amiga personal computer software applications. Microsoft's Windows and OS/2 Presentation Manager, Digital Research's GEM, Hewlett-Packard's New Wave, X Window and countless other programs and operating environments also incorporate some or all of the desktop/mouse/icon features.

MacIRMA

MacIRMA is an emulation board from DCA that turns the Macintosh personal computer into an IBM mainframe terminal. See *IRMAboard*.

MacPaint

MacPaint is a paint program from Apple Computer that comes with the Macintosh personal computer. In addition to normal painting capabilities, MacPaint is integrated into the Macintosh system for providing screen dumps of the entire screen no matter what application is running. At any time, the user can press a particular key combination, and the contents of the current screen are stored in a MacPaint file for later retrieval and printing. The Macintosh screens used in this book were created with MacPaint.

macro

(1) The term *macro* implies "substitution," and refers to a number of different techniques.

(2) In assembly language, a *macro* is a prewritten subroutine, such as an input/output routine, that is called upon at various places in the program. At assembly time, the macro statements (macro calls) are "substituted" with either the complete macro subroutine or a series of instructions that branch to the subroutine. The macro equivalent in a high-level language is called a *function*.

(3) In the dBASE programming language, a *macro* is a variable which references another variable that actually contains the data. At run time, the macro variable is "substituted" with the data variable.

(4) In spreadsheets, word processors and other application programs, a *macro* is a small program, or script, which automates operations normally activated by selecting menus. In addition to menu selections, macro languages may include common programming controls, such as IF THEN, GOTO and DO WHILE. For execution, the macro is assigned a key command. When the keys are pressed, the macro is activated; in other words, the macro is "substituted" for the keystroke.

macro assembler

A *macro assembler* is an assembler that substitutes the macro subroutines for the macro calls.

macro generator

See *macro recorder*.

macro language

(1) A *macro language* is an assembly language that uses macro subroutines.

(2) A *macro language* is a language that is used to create a macro program, or script.

macro processor

(1) In assembly language programming, a *macro processor* is the part of the assembly program that substitutes the macro subroutines for the macro calls.

(2) In personal computers, a *macro processor* allows for the creation of a macro and the execution of a macro from a keyboard command.

macro recorder

A *macro recorder* is the ability of a program to convert a user's keystrokes into a macro that can be stored on disk and then called for and executed later.

mag disk

See *magnetic disk*.

mag tape

See *magnetic tape*.

magnetic card

A *magnetic card* is a plastic card coated with a magnetizable recording surface that is used for data storage in earlier computer and word processing systems. The magnetic cards are usually contained in magazines that hold several cards, and an individual magnetic card is moved onto and wrapped around a drum for reading and writing. See *magnetic stripe*.

magnetic core

See *core storage*.

magnetic disk

Magnetic disks are direct access storage devices that are the primary storage medium used with computers for fast access to programs and data. Disks are analogous to phonograph records and turntables. The flat sides of the disk platter are the recording surfaces, the tone arm is the access arm, and the stylus (needle) is the read/write head. The major difference is that phonograph records are permanently recorded; whereas magnetic disks can be recorded, erased and recorded over again just like magnetic tape.

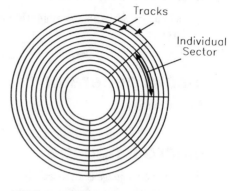

SECTORS ON A DISK

TRACKS AND SECTORS

The disk surface is divided up into several circular tracks that are concentric (circles within circles). The greater number of tracks, the more storage capacity of the disk. The digital data (bits) are recorded as tiny spots on these tracks. The tinier the spot, the more bits per inch and the greater the storage capacity. Most disks hold the same number of bits on each track, even though the outer tracks are physically longer than the inner ones. However, some disks do hold more data in the outer tracks.

The circular tracks are further divided into segments, called sectors, which determine the least amount of data that can be read or written (recorded) at one time. In order to update the disk, a sector is read into the computer, changed and written back to the disk. A sector can contain several records, or one record can span several sectors. The access methods in the operating system figure out how to fit the data into these fixed sectors, which is one of the main purposes of having a disk operating system (DOS).

HARD AND SOFT SECTORS

Hard sectored disks identify the sectors with some mark or hole that is physically part of the disk. Soft sectored disks contain the sector identification within the recording tracks. Soft sectored disks, fresh out of the box, must be processed once

LARGE CAPACITY
REMOVABLE HARD DISK

by a format program, which records the identification in the tracks.

HARD DISKS

Hard disks on personal computers hold from five to over 300 million bytes of data. Minicomputer and mainframe hard disks hold from several million to billions of bytes. Fixed hard disks are permanently sealed and cannot be removed from the drive, whereas removable hard disks are encased in modules called disk packs or disk cartridges and can be moved from one computer to another.

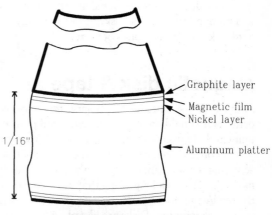

SIDE VIEW OF HARD DISK PLATTER

Graphite layer
Magnetic film
Nickel layer
Aluminum platter
1/16"

Hard disks provide fast access to any location on the disk because they rotate typically from 2,400 to 3,600 revolutions per minute and are constantly spinning after being turned on. Hard disks are made up of one or more aluminum platters of the same size, from 3 1/2 to 14 inches in diameter, each side coated with the same type of ferromagnetic material used on magnetic tape.

Ultra-fast hard disks can be designed with a separate read/write head over each track. Since these fixed head disks have no access arm to move, the only delay experienced is a couple of milliseconds of latency time, the time it takes for the disk to spin around to the beginning of the requested sector.

FLOPPY DISKS

Floppy disks are a removable medium that hold approximately from 150,000 to two million bytes of data per disk. They are considerably slower than hard disks,

HARD DISK

FLOPPY DISK

since the disk does not spin until a data transfer is requested, and then they only reach a rotation speed of typically 300 revolutions per minute, 10 times as slow as hard disks. Floppy disks are single plastic platters with magnetic coating on one or both sides. They are encased in either a stiff, but bendable, plastic envelope (8" and 5 1/4" disks) or in a rigid plastic shell (3 1/2" disks).

MEASUREMENTS

Disk storage capacities are measured in bytes (characters) per disk, although bytes per sector is useful information for systems programmers. The speed of a disk drive is measured in access times, the average time it takes to get to a random track on the disk. A fast hard disk is 18 milliseconds or less, a slow hard disk is 85 milliseconds or more.

magnetic disk & tape

Magnetic disk & tape are the primary storage media used in computer systems to permanently hold programs and data until purposefully erased. Each disk or tape unit can hold from hundreds of thousands to hundreds of millions of bytes. When both media are available, the choice of disk versus tape depends on the accessing requirements. Tape is a sequential medium; disk is a direct access medium. Tape is a long string that must be moved forward and backward across the read/write head. Locating a program or data on tape can take from several seconds to minutes. Disks are like phonograph turntables with rotating platters and a mechanical arm that moves the read/write head between the outer and inner edges. Any part of the disk surface can be located for reading and writing (recording) within a time frame from as slow as one second on a floppy disk to as fast as 1/100th of a second on a hard disk.

Disks are almost always used for the daily processing of transactions, and tapes are used for backup and historical purposes. On mainframes and minis, disk packs are considerably more expensive than reels of tape. As a result, transactions that were originally stored on disks are often transferred to tape after they are no longer needed for routine processing or inquiries. The larger the organization, the more economical tape becomes for archival storage. In addition, reels of tape are easier and safer to transport than large disk packs. For personal computers, disks are used for all interactive processing, and both floppy disks and tapes are used for backup. Since 1986, Bernoulli disks have provided a removable option for both processing and backup for personal computers, and removable hard disk cartridges, which emerged in the late 1980s, will become a very popular storage alternative for both processing and backup in the 1990s.

In time, magnetic disks and tapes may become as obsolete as the punched card. Erasable optical disks are beginning to emerge that hold billions of bytes of data. And, if erasable optical disks don't obsolete magnetic media, some solid state storage device might emerge after the turn of the century that will. After all, we're still using electric motors to whirl disks and tapes around, a rather incongruous contrast to the unbelievable magic that takes place within the chip.

magnetic drum

Magnetic drums are direct access storage devices that are used for high-speed, immediate access to data. A magnetic drum is a cylinder that spins around a central hub, like a roll of paper towels. The external surface of the cylinder is the magnetic recording surface, which is divided into band-like tracks that run around the circumference. Since there is a read/write head fixed over each track, there's no mechanical arm movement. Magnetic drums used to provide the fastest retrieval speed; however, fixed head disk drives have achieved and surpassed the speed of magnetic drums.

magnetic field

A *magnetic field* is the invisible, electrical energy field that is emitted by a magnet. Same as *flux*.

magnetic ink

Magnetic ink is an ink containing magnetic particles that can be detected by magnetic sensors. Magnetic ink is used to print the MICR (magnetic ink character recognition) characters that encode the account numbers on bank checks.

magnetic ink character recognition

See *MICR*.

magnetic oxide

A *magnetic oxide* is an oxide (acid) that is capable of being magnetized (ferromagnetic) and is used to coat the recording surfaces of magnetic disks and tapes.

magnetic recording

Magnetic recording is the technique used to record digital data on disks and tapes. Writing (recording) is accomplished by passing the recording surface on or near a read/write head that discharges an electric impulse onto the surface at the appropriate time. Although various electromagnetic signalling techniques are used, the concept is simple. A tiny spot with either a positive or negative polarity, representing a 0 or 1 bit, is deposited on the disk or tape surface. When tapes are recorded, an erase head clears the surface first, since blocks of data are not fixed in size as they are with disks. Reading is accomplished by passing the surface by the read/write head and sensing the polarity of the bit or the changes of polarity.

Note that bubble memory is also a form of magnetic recording; however, unlike tapes and disks, the surface is not moved. The bubbles (bits) are electromagnetically moved inside the thin film of magnetic material.

magnetic stripe

A *magnetic stripe* is a small length of magnetic tape that is adhered to ledger cards, badges and credit cards. Magnetic stripes are read by specialized readers that are sometimes incorporated into accounting machines and terminals. Due to heavy wear, the digital data recorded on the magnetic stripe is of a low-density format, or it is written several times.

magnetic tape

Magnetic tapes are sequential storage devices that are primarily used for data collection, backup and historical purposes. Just like the tape used in an audio tape recorder or video cassette recorder (VCR), computer tape is made of flexible plastic with one side coated with a ferromagnetic material. Magnetic tapes come in reels, cartridges and cassettes of many sizes and shapes.

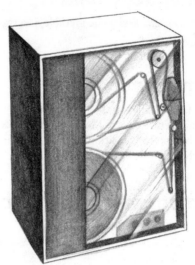

½"REEL-TO-REEL TAPE

As with any tape mechanism, locating a specific item on the tape requires reading everything in front of it. There is no way to fast forward to a particular record. All the data on the tape must be input into the computer until the required data is found. In order to add and delete records on a tape, the current tape is input to the computer and a blank tape is used for output. If data on tape is only changed and the physical number of records is not altered, some tape drives can update in place by reading a block of data and writing back over it in the same place.

Data bits are usually recorded on a number of parallel recording tracks that run the length of the tape. For example, 9-track tape holds one byte of data across the tape's width, 8 bits for each byte, plus a parity bit generated for self-checking purposes. Data is recorded in blocks of contiguous bytes, separated by a space, called an interrecord or interblock gap, created during the start-up and stop-down time of the tape mechanism.

Tape is often used as an interchange medium between different mainframes and minicomputers, since there are common standards for 1/2" wide open-reel tape that are widely used. Magnetic tape is also less expensive than disk packs and disk cartridges and provides a very economical way of storing large amounts of historical data. However, when tapes are used for archival storage, they must be periodically recopied. If the tape is not used for several years, the magnetic bits can contaminate each other, since the tape surfaces are tightly coiled together.

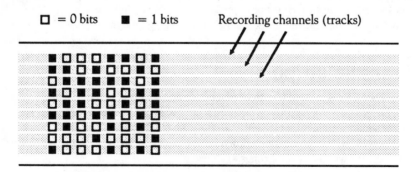

RECORDED BITS ON MAGNETIC TAPE

Storage capacities are measured in bits per inch (BPI); however, since tape is laid out in parallel tracks, bits per inch is equivalent to bytes per inch. Typical recording densities for tapes used in mainframes

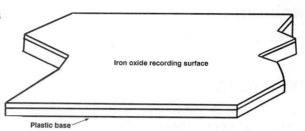

Iron oxide recording surface

Plastic base

CROSS SECTION OF MAGNETIC TAPE

and minis are 200, 556, 800, 1600 and 6250 BPI. Tape drive speed is measured in inches per second (IPS). Drive speed times recording density determines the transfer rate of a tape drive.

magneto-optic recording

Magneto-optic recording combines laser and magnetic technologies to create high-density erasable storage disks. The recording surface is made of a magnetic recording material, such as a turbium iron alloy, that records magnetic spots (bits) in the typical positive and negative orientation as with regular magnetic disks and tapes. The difference is that the bits are much smaller, because a laser is used to pinpoint the bit. The laser heats the bit to approximately 300 degrees centigrade, at which temperature the bit is realigned when subjected to a magnetic field. In order to record new bits on the surface, the existing bits have to be reset, or prealigned, in one direction first. See *optical disk*.

mail box

A *mail box* is the computer storage assigned to a user for electronically transmitted mail and messages.

mail merge

A *mail merge* is the printing of a standard letter that has been individualized with names and address from a list. Usually part of a word processing or database management program, a mail merge can merge any data from a list or file into the letter in order to customize it. For example, in the sentence: "Dear XXX, you have ordered XXX on XXX, and we hope you enjoy it," all the XXXs represent data that will be merged from the list. A field squeeze is provided with the mail merge so that data of varying lengths can be merged and the text squeezed around it. A line squeeze is also necessary in order to allow for a varying number of lines in the name and address. The mail merge is accomplished by typing a letter and inserting merge points that identify the particular line or field of data that is to be merged from the list.

main line

See *main loop*.

main loop

In programming, the *main loop* is the set of instructions that constitute the primary structure of the program. For example, in an invoicing print program, the main loop reads the next order and prints the invoice. It repeats itself until there are no more orders to print. In a batch update program, the main loop reads the transaction, updates the master record and repeats itself until all the transactions have been processed. See *modular programming*.

main memory

Main memory is the computer's primary working storage. It is also called *main storage*, RAM or just plain *memory*. Main memory is the memory that is directly addressable by the CPU. See *memory*.

main storage

See *main memory*.

mainframe

A *mainframe* is a large computer. In the mid 1960s, the ancient days of computers, all computers were mainframes, since the term referred to the cabinet that held the CPU (central processing unit). Although, technically, mainframe still means main housing, it usually refers to a large computer system and all the associated expertise that goes along with it.

There are small, medium and large-scale mainframes, handling as few as fifty and as many as several thousands of online terminals. Large-scale mainframes can handle hundreds of millions of bytes of main memory and hundreds of billions of bytes of disk storage. Medium and large-scale mainframes use smaller computers as front end processors that connect directly to the communications networks. Small-scale mainframes and superminis overlap in capabilities, the term used to describe the model depending on the vendor that makes it.

The original mainframe vendors were Burroughs, Control Data, GE, Honeywell, IBM, NCR, RCA and Univac, otherwise known as IBM and the seven dwarfs. After GE's computer division was absorbed by Honeywell and RCA's computer division was absorbed by Univac, the mainframe vendors were known as IBM and the BUNCH. Since Burroughs and Univac merged into Unisys, the BUNCH is now also history. All of the original mainframe vendors have developed at least one series of minicomputers, and Honeywell Bull, NCR and Unisys have also introduced IBM compatible pcs.

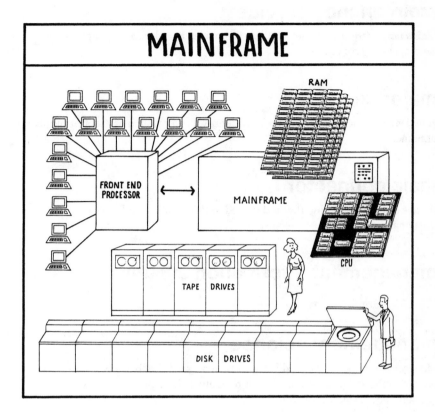

maintenance

(1) Hardware *maintenance* is the testing and cleaning of equipment in order to prevent problems in the future.

(2) Information system *maintenance* is the routine updating of master files, such as adding and deleting employees in a payroll file, changing credit limits in a customer file and changing prices in an inventory file.

(3) Software or program *maintenance* is the updating of application programs in order to meet an organization's changing information requirements.

(4) Disk or file *maintenance* is the periodic reorganizing of online disk files that have undergone fragmentation due to continuous updating.

maintenance credits

Maintenance credits are monetary credits that are issued to a customer by the vendor for qualified periods during which the vendor's products are not functioning properly.

maintenance service

Maintenance service is the service that is provided in order to keep a product in good operating condition.

major key

A *major key* is the primary key used to identify a record, such as account number or name.

male connector

A *male connector* is a plug that is designed to fit into a particular socket, which is the female counterpart.

management information system

See *MIS*.

management science

Management science is the study of statistical methods, such as linear programming and simulation, in order to analyze and solve organizational problems. Same as *operations research*.

management support systems

See *decision support system*.

management system

A *management system* is the structure and function of leadership and control within an organization. The management system is how people interact with other people and with machines. Together, they set the goals and objectives for the organization, outline the strategy and tactics, and develop the plans, schedules and necessary controls to run it.

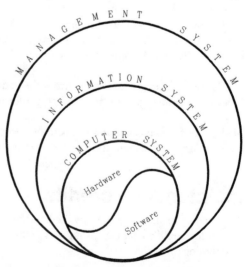

HOW SYSTEMS RELATE

Manchester coding

See *phase encoding*.

MANTIS

MANTIS is an application development language from Cincom Systems, Inc., that runs on IBM mainframes, Digital's VAX series, Wang, Honeywell, NCR, ICL and Siemens computers. MANTIS provides both a procedural and non-procedural language for developing prototypes and applications. MANTIS creates its own internal file and database structures and it works with Cincom's SUPRA database, as well as DB2, IMS and other database managers.

mantissa

A *mantissa* is the numeric value in a floating point number. See *floating point*.

manufacturing automation protocol

See *MAP*.

map

A *map* is a printed or machine-coded list of data or objects that are currently stored in memory or on disk. A bit map is a list of bits in memory that represent the pixels on a video screen or a series of other objects. See *mapping*.

MAP

(Manufacturing Automation Protocol) *MAP* is a communications protocol introduced by General Motors Corporation in 1982. MAP's goal is to provide common standards for the interconnection of computers and programmable machine tools used in factory automation. At the lowest physical level, MAP uses the IEEE 802.3 token bus protocol. Although MAP has provided vitally needed consolidation of standards, it continues to be in a constant state of revision.

MAP is often used in conjunction with *TOP*, an office protocol developed by Boeing Computer Services. TOP is used in the front office and MAP is used on the factory floor.

MAPPER

(MAintaining, Preparing and Processing Executive Reports) *MAPPER* is a fourth-generation language from Unisys that runs on Unisys mainframes. In 1980, MAPPER was introduced as a high-level report writer for use by non-technical personnel. It was later turned into a full-featured, programming system. MAPPER has been used very successfully by many users.

mapping

Mapping is the transfer of a set of data or codes from one place to another. For example, program modules on disk are mapped into memory. A graphic image in memory is mapped onto the video screen. A logical database structure is mapped onto the physical database. Mapping is often used to refer to laying out anything.

mark

(1) A *mark* is a small blip that is printed on or manufactured into various storage media and is used for timing or counting purposes.

(2) A tape *mark* is a special character recorded at the end of a magnetic tape.

(3) A *mark* is a special bit or symbol used to identify the beginning or end of various data structures, such as a word mark, record mark or group mark.

(4) In digital electronics, a *mark* refers to a 1 bit; a space to a 0 bit.

(5) In optical recognition and mark sensing, a *mark* is a pencil line in a preprinted box.

Mark I

The *Mark I* was an electromechanical calculating machine that was the brainchild of Harvard University Professor Howard Aiken. It was built in IBM's Endicott, New York plant and assembled at Harvard in 1943. The Mark I was 51 feet long and weighed five tons. Its input/output devices included two card readers, one card punch and two typewriters, all standard IBM equipment of that era. Made of over 75,000 relays, switches, wheels and cams, its clicking sound was like a "thousand pairs of knitting needles" according to Captain Grace Hopper, one of the machine's original users. Yet it could barely do three calculations per second.

Although its successors, the Mark II, III and IV were more sophisticated, the Mark I was more advanced for its time. It provided IBM engineers with the experience necessary to develop their own computers in the late 1940s.

MARK I
(Courtesy Smithsonian Institution)

MARK IV, MARK V

MARK IV is an application generator from the Answer Systems Division of Sterling Software, Inc., that runs on IBM mainframes. MARK IV was one of the first program generators that used fill-in-the-blank forms for describing the problem instead of programming it. MARK V is an online version of MARK IV.

mark sensing

Mark sensing is the detection of pencil lines in predefined boxes on paper forms or punched cards. The form must be laid out with boundaries for each pencil stroke that represents a yes, no, single digit or letter, providing all the possible answers to each question. A mark sense reader detects the presence or absence of the marks and converts them into the appropriate digital code, or in the case of punched cards, punches holes in the card for punched card entry into the computer.

mask

(1) A *mask* is a pattern that is used to transfer a design onto an object. See *photomask*.

(2) A *mask* is a pattern of bits that is used to accept or reject bit patterns in another set of data. For example, the Boolean AND operation can be used to match a mask of 0s and 1s with a string of data bits. When a 1 occurs in both the mask and the data, the result bit will contain a 1 in that position.

Hardware interrupts are often enabled and disabled in this manner with each interrupt assigned a bit position in a mask register.

mask bit

A *mask bit* is a 1 bit in a mask used to control the corresponding bit found in data.

maskable interrupts

Maskable interrupts are hardware interrupts that can be enabled and disabled by software.

masked

Masked refers to being disabled or cut off such as with regard to an interrupt that has been masked.

mass storage

Mass storage is a high-capacity storage device, such as a disk or tape. The term is used to refer to any external peripheral storage device, in contrast with the computer's internal memory.

massage

Massage is to process data.

master card

A *master card* is a master record in punched card format.

master clock

A *master clock* provides the primary source of internal timing for a processor or stand-alone control unit.

master console

A *master console* is the primary terminal used by the computer operator or systems programmer to command the computer system.

master control program

See *operating system*.

master file

A *master file* is a collection of records pertaining to one of the main subjects of an information system, such as customers, employees, products and vendors. Master files contain descriptive data, such as name and address, as well as summary information, such as amount due and year-to-date gross sales. Contrast with *transaction file*, which contains data about the activities of the subjects, such as orders, payments, time cards and purchases.

master record

A *master record* is a set of data for an individual subject, such as a customer, employee or vendor. See *master file*.

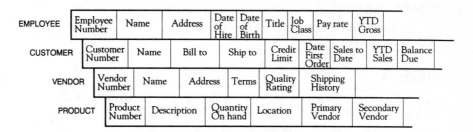

EMPLOYEE	Employee Number	Name	Address	Date of Hire	Date of Birth	Title	Job Class	Pay rate	YTD Gross	
CUSTOMER	Customer Number	Name	Bill to	Ship to		Credit Limit	Date First Order	Sales to Date	YTD Sales	Balance Due
VENDOR		Vendor Number	Name	Address	Terms	Quality Rating	Shipping History			
PRODUCT			Product Number	Description	Quantity On hand	Location	Primary Vendor	Secondary Vendor		

MASTER RECORDS

(Typical Subjects Within an Organization)

math coprocessor

A *math coprocessor* is a mathematical circuit that performs floating point operations at high speed. In a personal computer, it's a single chip that plugs into a special receptacle on the motherboard.

For CAD and desktop publishing operations, it improves the performance of the system dramatically. However, the program must be written to activate the math coprocessor; otherwise it will not improve its performance. See *array processor* and *vector processor*.

mathematical expression

A *mathematical expression* is an arithmetic formula or algorithm that states the relationship between two or more variables. For example, **A + (B*C)** is a mathematical, or arithmetic, expression.

mathematical function

See *mathematical expression*.

matrix

A *matrix* is an array of rows and columns. See *x-y matrix*.

matrix printer

See *dot matrix* and *printer*.

MB, Mb

See *megabyte* and *megabit*.

MCA

(Micro Channel Architecture) See *Micro Channel*.

MCGA

(Multi Color Graphics Array) MCGA is a video display standard that is built into low-end models of the IBM PS/2 series. MCGA enhances the CGA standard by adding 64 gray scale shades and increasing the number of colors from four to 256 at 320x200 pixels. It provides standard EGA resolution of 640x350 with 16 colors, but does not support the higher 640x480 VGA resolution.

MCI decision

The *MCI decision*, made by the Federal Communications Commission (FCC) in 1969, granted Microwave Communications Corporation (MCI) the right to provide private, intercity telecommunications services in competition with the Bell telephone system.

MC68000

See 68000.

MDA

(Monochrome Display Adapter) *MDA* is a video display board from IBM that is available as a plug-in board for IBM PC and compatible personal computers. MDA generates high-resolution monochrome text, but does not provide for graphics. Resolution is 720x350 pixels, with each character occupying a cell of 9x14 dots.

Monochrome text and graphics is available on IBM and compatible PCs with the use of the Hercules Graphics display adapter. MDA was superseded by the VGA (video graphics array) in IBM's PS/2 series.

mean time between failure

See *MTBF*.

media

Media, the plural of medium, refers to storage devices, such as disk and tape.

media conversion

Media conversion is the converting of data from one storage medium to another, such as from disk to tape, from tape to disk and from floppy disk to hard disk.

media failure

A *media failure* is the condition of not being able to read from or write to a storage device, such as a disk or tape, due to a defect in the magnetic recording surface.

medium frequency

Medium frequency is an electromagnetic wave that vibrates, or oscillates, in the range from 300,000 to 3,000,000 Hertz (cycles per second). See *electromagnetic spectrum*.

medium scale integration

See *MSI*.

meg

Meg is an abbreviation for mega, which stands for one million.

mega

Mega stands for one million; however, it may refer more precisely to the value 1,048,576 when the number is derived from binary notation.

MEGA

The MEGA is a personal computer series from Atari Corporation that is used in homes and small businesses. The MEGA uses a Motorola 68000 CPU and comes with an operating system (TOS) built into ROM. The GEM operating environment is also included which provides a Macintosh-like interface for applications. The MEGA comes with two or four megabytes of RAM, and display resolution is 640x200 with 16 colors on a 12" screen. A built-in 720K microfloppy disk is standard, and a 20 megabyte hard drive is

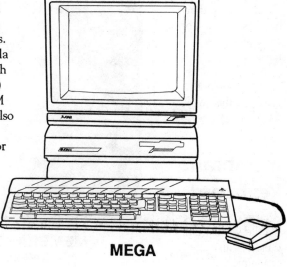

MEGA

optional. Also included is a MIDI interface and a three-voice sound chip with a range from 30 to beyond 20,000 Hertz. The MEGA series is compatible with the Atari ST series, and IBM pc compatibility is optional.

megabit

A *megabit* is 1,000,000 or 1,048,576 bits. It is also written as MB, Mb, Mbit and M-bit. See *space/time*.

megabyte

A *megabyte* is 1,000,000 or 1,048,576 bytes or characters. It is also written as MB, Mb, Mbyte and M-byte. See *space/time*.

megaflop

A *megaflop* is one million floating point operations per second.

megahertz

A *megahertz* is one million cycles per second.

megapel display

In computer graphics, a *megapel display* is a display system that handles a million or more pixels. A resolution of 1,000 lines by 1,000 dots requires a million pixels for the full screen image.

membrane keyboard

A *membrane keyboard* is a flat keyboard that is used as an economical alternative to a standard keyboard or

MEMBRANE KEYBOARD
(Courtesy Polytel Computer Products Corp.)

This Polytel KEYPORT 300 membrane keyboard is used with an overlay for many different applications.

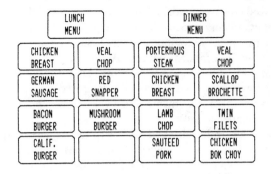

Typical overlay for restaurant management

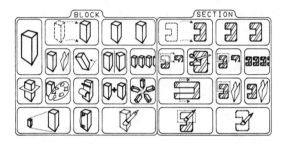

Overlay for DesignCAD software package

as a dustproof and dirtproof keyboard for hazardous environments. A membrane keyboard is constructed of two thin plastic sheets (membranes) that contain printed circuits made of electrically conductive ink so that they can be flexible. The circuits oppose each other in the middle. Covering the top membrane is a printed keyboard panel, and sandwiched between the two membranes is a spacer sheet with holes corresponding to the keys on the keyboard. When a user presses a simulated key on the flat panel, the top membrane is pushed through the hole in the spacer, making contact with the bottom membrane and completing the circuit.

memo field

A *memo field* is a text field in a data record that can contain a variable amount of text (words). In dBASE, any number of fields, up to the maximum field limit, can be defined as memo fields. The text can be entered or edited in the memo fields using dBASE's own text editor or any word processor. Although the physical text is stored in a companion file with a DBT extension, the memo fields are displayed and controlled within dBASE as if they were physically part of the data record.

memory

Memory is the computer's working storage, which is constructed of RAM chips. It is one of the most important parts of the computer, as it determines the size and number of programs that can be held within the computer at the same time, as well as the amount of data that can be processed immediately.

All program execution and data processing takes place in memory. The instructions in a program are copied into memory from a disk or tape, and the instructions are extracted out of memory into an electronic circuit for analysis and execution. The instructions direct the computer to input data into memory from a keyboard, disk, tape or communications channel. As data is entered into memory, the previous contents of that memory space are lost. Once the data has been brought into memory, it can be processed (calculated, compared and copied). Then the results can be output from memory to a video screen, printer, disk, tape or communications channel.

Memory can be viewed as an electronic checkerboard, with each square on the board holding one byte of data or instruction. Since each square has a separate address like a post office box, the individual character within the square can be manipulated independently from all the rest of the squares. Because of this, the computer can break apart programs into instructions and records into fields, all of which are stored as large blocks on disks and tapes.

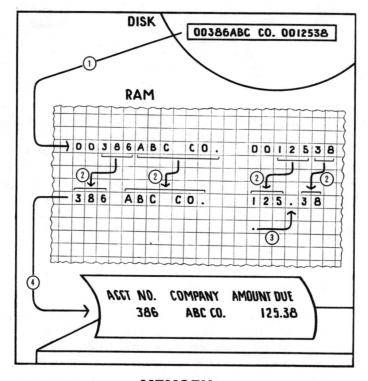

MEMORY

Memory allows data to be broken apart and rearranged in any prescribed manner.

(1) An entire data record is read from the disk and written into memory.

(2) The individual characters are copied from the input buffer to the output buffer. Numeric data is stripped of preceding zeros by a special format instructions that filters out the unwanted zeros.

(3) The decimal point also comes from a format instruction, which copies it into the specified location.

(4) The formatted line is read from memory and transmitted to the printer.

Memory Doesn't Usually Remember

Oddly enough, the computer's main memory doesn't remember anything when the power is turned off. That's why you have to be sure to save your files before you quit your program. Although there are memory chips that do hold their content permanently, such as ROMs, PROMs and EPROMs, they're used for internal control purposes and not for the user's data.

The "remembering" memory in a computer system is its disks and tapes, and they're usually called storage devices in order not to confuse them with the computer's working memory.

Terms synonomous with the computer's working memory are RAM, *main memory, main storage, primary storage, read/write memory, core* and *core storage.*

memory bank

A *memory bank* is a physical section of computer memory. Computers can be designed with multiple memory banks, such that data transfers can take place within each of the memory banks at the same time. Memory bank is often used to generally refer to the computer's remembering capability, which also implies its disks and tapes.

memory cache

See *cache memory.*

memory cell

A *memory cell* is one bit of memory. In dynamic RAM memory, a memory cell is made up of one transistor and one capacitor. In static RAM memory, a memory cell is made up of about five transistors.

memory chip

A *memory chip* is a chip that holds programs and data either temporarily or permanently. The major categories of memory chips are RAMs and ROMs.

memory cycle

A *memory cycle* is the series of operations that take place when a bit of memory is read or written. For destructive memories, it includes the regeneration of the bits.

memory cycle time

Memory cycle time is the time between the start of one read or write operation and the next.

memory dump

A *memory dump* is the display or printout of the contents of memory. When a program abends (abnormally ends), a memory dump can be taken in order to examine the status of the program at the time of the crash. The programmer looks into the buffers to see which data items were being worked on when it failed. Counters, switches and flags in the program can also be inspected.

memory management

Memory management is the way a computer deals with its memory, which includes memory protection and any virtual memory or memory swapping techniques. See *virtual memory*, EMS and EMM.

memory protection

Memory protection prohibits one program from accidentally destroying or stopping another program that is also active in memory. Protective boundaries are created around the program and each program is allowed to access data only within its boundary.

An example of a memory protection technique is the subdivision of all memory into small blocks of, say, 2,048 bytes. An index to all the blocks is maintained in which each entry becomes a key to that block. When a program is brought into memory, it is assigned a number, and all the blocks it occupies are assigned the same number in the key index. Before the computer executes an instruction, it matches the memory block number with the program number, and if it doesn't match, it prohibits the operation by interrupting the computer.

memory sniffing

Memory sniffing is a diagnostic routine that continually tests memory while the computer is processing data. The processor uses cycle stealing techniques that allow it to perform its memory test during unused machine cycles. An entire memory bank can be "sniffed" every few minutes.

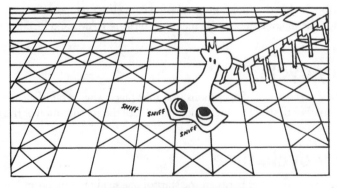

MEMORY SNIFFING

memory typewriter

A *memory typewriter* is an enhanced typewriter and limited-function word processing machine. Memory typewriters hold a limited number of pages of text in their memories, and, with a display of one or two lines, allow for text editing. Memory typewriters provide various word processing functions, such as headers, footers, page numbering, centering, underline, boldface and italics.

A memory typewriter with disk storage provides expanded document management like a word processor; however, the small displays make cut & paste and search & replace operations tedious, and scrolling through a text document is slow and cumbersome.

menu

A *menu* is a list of available options and commands displayed on screen in an interactive program. Selection of a menu option is accomplished by entering the number or letter assigned to it, by pressing the letter key of the first letter of the word (see *Lotus menu*) or by highlighting the option and pressing the return key, a mouse button or some other key (see *Macintosh user interface*). Menu-driven programs are easier to learn than command-driven systems, which require the user to learn a language.

Menu

Menu is a software subsidiary of the Black Box Corporation that offers the world's most complete listing of software information for local area networks and IBM compatible, Apple II, Macintosh and Commodore personal computers.

menu-driven

Menu-driven refers to a program that is commanded by selecting options from a list displayed on screen.

mesa

Mesa is a semiconductor process used in the 1960s for creating the sublayers in a transistor. The deep etching of the Mesa process gave way to the planar process that creates sublayers by implanting chemicals into the substrate.

mesh network

A *mesh network* is a net-like communications network whereby there are at least two pathways to each node. The term network means net-like as well as communications

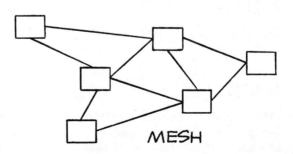

network. Thus, the term mesh is used to avoid saying network communications network.

message

In communications, a *message* is a set of data that is transmitted over a communications line. Just as a program becomes a "job" when it's running in the computer, data becomes a message when it's transmitted over a network.

message queue

See *queue*.

message switch

A *message switch* is a computer that is used to switch data from one point to another. Computers have always been ideal message switches due to their input/output and compare capabilities. When a computer acts as a message switch, it inputs the message, compares its destination with a set of stored destinations and then outputs it to a selected communications channel.

metal oxide semiconductor

See *MOS*.

meter

A *meter* is about 33 inches or 9/10ths of the length of one yard (32.9184 inches or 0.9144 of a yard).

MFM

(Modified Frequency Modulation) *MFM* is a recording technique commonly used for magnetic disks. MFM reduces the number of synchronization bits required on the disk from earlier FM recording methods.

MHz

(MegaHertZ) A *MHz* stands for one million cycles per second.

MICR

(Magnetic Ink Character Recognition) *MICR* refers to the special encoded characters on bank checks and deposit

⑂ 1 2 3 4 5 6 7 8 9 0

⑂ ⑃ ⑄ ⑅

MICR CHARACTERS

slips. MICR readers detect the encoded characters and convert them into digital data for the computer.

micro

(1) A *micro* is a microcomputer or personal computer.

(2) A *micro* is a microprocessor.

(3) *Micro* means one millionth, such as in *microsecond*.

(4) *Micro* means very small, such as in *microchip*.

(5) In CDC assembly language programming, a *micro* is a macro call which is substituted with a single variable.

Micro Channel

The *Micro Channel* is a 32-bit bus used in high-end models of IBM's PS/2 personal computer series. It is designed for multiprocessing, which is when two or more CPUs are working in parallel within the computer at the same time.

The boards that plug into the Micro Channel are designed with built-in identification that is interrogated by the operating system, thus eliminating the manual switch settings that are sometimes required and the conflicts that may arise when installing boards in the PC bus used in non-Micro Channel IBM compatible pcs.

The boards that plug into the Micro Channel are also not interchangeable with boards for the PC bus. See IBM *personal computer*.

micro disk

See *microfloppy disk*.

micro manager

A *micro manager* is an individual that manages the personal computer operations within an organization. A micro manager is responsible for the analysis, selection, installation, training and maintenance of personal computer hardware and software. See *information center*.

Micro PDP-11

A *Micro PDP-11* is a microcomputer version of the PDP-11 minicomputer from Digital Equipment Corporation. Introduced in 1975, it uses the Q-bus architecture and serves as a stand-alone computer or is built into other equipment.

micro to mainframe

Micro to mainframe refers to the interconnection of personal computers with large mainframe networks. Micro to mainframe communications allows the personal computer to emulate (look like) a mainframe terminal and have an interactive session with the mainframe like other mainframe users at terminals. Micro to mainframe links also can be used to extract copies of the organization's database from the mainframe into the personal computer for analysis and manipulation, using personal computer software packages.

microchip

A *microchip* is a miniaturized, electronic integrated circuit. See *chip*.

microcircuit

A *microcircuit* is a miniaturized, electronic circuit, such as is found on an integrated circuit. See *chip*.

microcode

Microcode is a translation layer between the machine instructions and the elementary operations of the computer. Stored in ROM chips, microcode enables the computer architect to add new machine instructions to the computer without having to design them into the electronic circuits from scratch. The microcode contains each machine instruction and the elementary circuit operations that must be performed to carry out that instruction at the very lowest machine level. The process of developing microcode is called *microprogramming*.

Microcom Networking Protocol

See *MNP*.

microcomputer

A *microcomputer* is a computer that uses a microprocessor as its central processing unit (CPU). In 1977, Apple Computer, Radio Shack and Commodore Business Machines introduced the first microcomputers that could be purchased off the shelf like a consumer appliance. Although microcomputers were available in kit form before that, these three companies really started the personal computer revolution. The terms microcomputer and *personal computer* are synonymous.

microelectronics

Microelectronics is the miniaturization of electronic circuits. See *chip*.

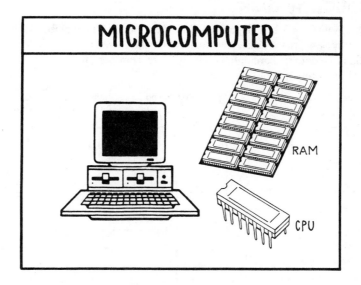

MICROCOMPUTER

RAM

CPU

microfiche & microfilm

Microfiche & microfilm are films that contain miniaturized documents. A *microfiche*, pronounced "micro-feesh," is a 4x6" sheet of film that holds several hundred document pages. A *microfilm* is a continuous film strip that can hold several thousand document pages. The documents are magnified for human viewing by specialized readers, some of which can automatically locate a particular page using various indexing techniques.

Microfiche & microfilm are generated by devices that take pictures of paper documents, or by COM (computer output microfilm) units that accept output directly from the computer.

Microfiche & microfilm have always been an economical alternative for high-volume data and picture storage. However, optical disks are beginning to compete with film-based systems and, in time, they may become the preferred storage medium.

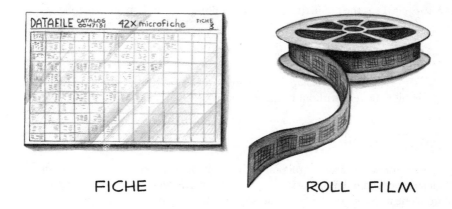

FICHE ROLL FILM

microfloppy disk

A *microfloppy disk* is a 3 1/2" floppy disk that is encased in a rigid plastic shell. Developed by Sony, these disks have quickly become the medium of choice. They hold more data and are much easier to store, transport and handle than their 5 1/4" counterparts.

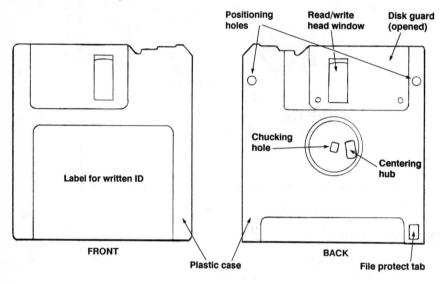

MICROFLOPPY DISK

microform

In micrographics, a *microform* is a medium that contains microminiaturized images such as microfiche and microfilm.

micrographics

Micrographics is the production, handling and use of microfilm and microfiche.

microimage

In micrographics, a *microimage* is any photographic image of information that is too small to be read without magnification.

microinstruction

A *microinstruction* is an instruction in the computer's microcode. It is the most elementary computer operation that can take place, for example, moving a bit from one register to another. It takes several microinstructions to carry out one machine instruction. See *microprogramming*.

microjacket

In micrographics, a *microjacket* is two sheets of transparent plastic that are bonded together to create channels into which strips of microfilm are inserted and stored.

micromainframe

A *micromainframe* refers to a personal computer with mainframe or near mainframe speed.

micromini

A *micromini* refers to a personal computer with minicomputer or near minicomputer speed.

micron

A *micron* is one millionth of a meter, which is approximately 1/25,000 of an inch. The tiny elements that make up a transistor on a chip are measured in microns. Measurements below the micron level are made in Angstroms, in which 10,000 Angstroms equals one micron.

The following photograph, magnified 1,000 times, shows the surface of a memory chip. The lines, which are the outer, current-carrying pathways, are approximately three microns wide.

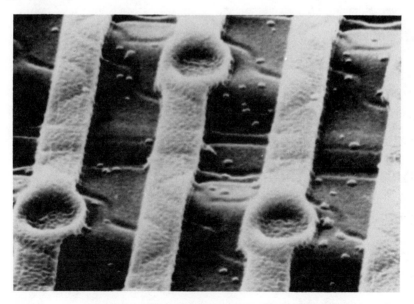

A MICROSCOPIC VIEW OF A CHIP
(Courtesy AT&T)

microprocessor

A *microprocessor* is a CPU on a single chip. The first microprocessor, a 4-bit unit called the 4004, was developed by Ted Hoff, Jr., of Intel Corporation in 1971.

A microprocessor requires a power supply, clock and memory in order to function as a complete computer. A computer on a chip also has a built-in clock and memory requiring only an external power supply and data to make it work.

Microprocessors spawned the personal computer revolution and have dramatically influenced every other field of endeavor.

First-generation microprocessors used in personal computers were Intel's 8080, Zilog's Z80, Motorola's 6800 and Rockwell International's 6502.

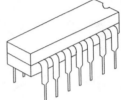

MICROPROCESSOR

microprogram

Same as *microcode*.

microprogramming

Microprogramming is the programming of microcode, which is the translation layer between a machine instruction and the elementary operations (microinstructions) necessary to carry out the instruction.

micropublishing

In micrographics, *micropublishing* is the issuing of new or reformatted information on microfilm for sale or distribution.

microrepublishing

In micrographics, *microrepublishing* is to issue microfilm that has been previously or is simultaneously published in hardcopy for sale or distribution.

microsecond

A *microsecond* is one millionth of a second. See *space/time*.

Microsoft Corporation

Microsoft Corporation was founded in 1975 by Paul Allen and Bill Gates, two college students who wrote the first BASIC interpreter for the Intel 8080 microprocessor. They licensed it to Micro Instrumentation and Telemetry Systems (MITS) to accompany its Altair 8800 microcomputer kit. By the end of 1976, more than 10,000 Altairs were sold with Microsoft's BASIC.

Versions of MBASIC were licensed to Radio Shack, Apple Computer and myriads of other hardware vendors. Eventually, a version called GW-BASIC ("Gee Whiz BASIC") was developed for 16-bit personal computers. Although Microsoft quickly became a leader in microcomputer programming languages, its outstanding success is due to supplying IBM with its DOS operating system and the compatible companies with the MS-DOS version.

Microsoft's position as the major operating system supplier to the world's largest computer base allows it to have considerable influence over the future of the personal computer industry. Paul Allen has since left Microsoft and now heads up his own personal computer software company called Asymetrix.

PAUL G. ALLEN
(Courtesy Asymetrix Corporation)

WILLIAM H. GATES
(Courtesy Microsoft Corporation)

Microsoft DOS

In this book, *Microsoft DOS* refers to the DOS (also called PC-DOS) operating system from Microsoft Corporation that runs in IBM personal computers, as well as to the MS-DOS operating system from Microsoft that runs in IBM compatible personal computers.

Microsoft Word

Microsoft Word is a full-featured word processing program from Microsoft Corporation that runs on Macintosh and IBM compatible pcs. The IBM version provides a graphics-based WYSIWYG display. Version 3.1 provides up to eight windows for working on multiple documents at the same time.

Microsoft Works

Microsoft Works is an integrated software program from Microsoft Corporation that runs on Macintosh computers. It provides file management with relational-like capabilities, word processing, spreadsheet, business graphics and communications capabilities in one package.

MicroStation

MicroStation is a full-featured, computer-aided design and drafting system (CADD) from Intergraph Corporation that runs on IBM compatible pcs. MicroStation is a major subset of and fully compatible with Interactive Graphics Design System (IGDS), the core software of all Intergraph VAX-based systems. Microstation provides 3-D capabilities, dual screens, a powerful user command language, an interface to dBASE III, excellent performance and many powerful drafting features.

MicroVAX

A *MicroVAX* is the smallest model of the VAX computer series from Digital Equipment Corporation. Both the MicroVAX I, introduced in 1983, and the MicroVAX II, introduced in 1984, were deskside models, but in 1986, the first desktop model was introduced, the MicroVAX 2000. MicroVAXs run under the same VMS operating system as the larger VAX computers and also run under Ultrix, Digital's version of the UNIX operating system. MicroVAXs use the same Q-bus architecture as the earlier Micro PDP-11 minicomputers.

microwave

A *microwave* is an electromagnetic wave that vibrates at one billion Hertz (cycles per second) and above. Microwaves are the transmission frequencies used in communications satellites, as well as in earth-based systems that transmit radio waves between stations that have line-of-sight of each other.

MICROWAVE TOWER
(Courtesy AT&T)

This early microwave radio relay station was installed in 1968 at Boulder Junction Colorado.

MIDI

(Musical Instrument Digital Interface) *MIDI* is a standard protocol for the interchange of musical information between musical instruments, synthesizers and computers. MIDI defines the codes for a musical event, which includes the start of a note, its pitch, length, volume and musical attributes, such as vibrato. It also defines codes for various button, dial and pedal adjustments used on synthesizers. MIDI is commonly used to synchronize notes produced on several synthesizers. MIDI control messages can orchestrate a series of synthesizers, each playing a part of the musical score.

A computer with a MIDI interface can be used to record a musical session, but instead of recording the analog sound waves as in a tape recorder, the computer stores the music as keystroke and control codes. The recording can be edited in an entirely different manner than with conventional recording, for example, the rhythm can be changed by editing the timing codes in the MIDI messages. In addition, the computer can easily transpose a performance from B major into D major.

The original objective of MIDI was to allow the keyboard of one synthesizer to play notes generated by another synthesizer. However, since Version 1.0 of MIDI in August 1983, the standard has synthesized more than just music; it has brought the world of electronic control of music to virtually everybody and has benefitted musicians and teachers alike.

MIDI devices require a special plug and connector (port) that is built into the musical instruments and synthesizers. The MIDI port is standard on Atari ST personal computers and can be adapted to other personal computers. The Macintosh personal computer is also popular among MIDI enthusiasts, since its graphics-based video screen produces a crisp image for musical notation.

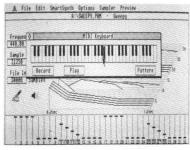

SOFTSYNTH™ Digidesign

Digidesign's Softsynth program, which runs on Atari and Macintosh computers, is an Additive Synthesis program that lets users create sounds and mix waveforms together. The keyboard on screen simulates a MIDI keyboard that is attached to the system and allows users to play the keyboard from the computer.

THE COPYIST™ Dr. T's™ Music Software

Dr. T's Music Software program, The Copyist, which runs on Atari, Amiga and IBM compatible pcs, is a musical scoring program. It lets users create scores from scratch, or take MIDI recorded music and transcribe it into traditional musical notation.

MIDI SOFTWARE

(Courtesy Digidesign and Dr. T's Music Software)

midicomputer

A *midicomputer* is a computer that has a performance and capacity somewhere between a minicomputer and a mainframe.

mill

Mill is sometimes used to refer to the processor in the context of number crunching.

millimeter

A *millimeter* is one thousandth of a meter or 1/25th of an inch.

million

A *million* is one thousand times one thousand. In computer specifications, a million is represented by *mega*; for example, one megabyte is one million bytes. One millionth is represented by *micro*; for example, one microsecond is one millionth of a second.

millisecond

A *millisecond* is one thousandth of a second. See *space/time*.

mini

See *minicomputer*.

mini-supercomputer

A *mini-supercomputer* is a supercomputer that is about a quarter to half as fast in vector processing as a full-scale supercomputer, but costs about one tenth as much. Major vendors in the mini-supercomputer arena are Convex Computer, Alliant Computer Systems and Multiflow Computer. Note: A mini-supercomputer is not the same as a supermini.

minicomputer

A *minicomputer* is a small to medium-scale computer that is the midrange between a microcomputer and a mainframe. Minicomputers can support from a handful up to several hundred user terminals, the latter systems often being called superminis. Unlike microcomputers and mainframes, minicomputers are intrinsically designed as multiuser systems and are relatively easy to install and operate in a multi-terminal environment. A minicomputer system costs roughly from $20,000 to $200,000.

In 1959, Digital Equipment Corporation launched the minicomputer industry with the introduction of the PDP-1. Soon after, Data General and Hewlett-Packard introduced minicomputers, and eventually Wang, Tandem, Datapoint and Prime joined the ranks. IBM introduced several minicomputer series, such as the System 34, System 36, System 38, Series 1 and 8100.

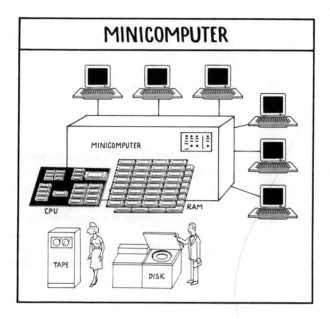

minifloppy

A *minifloppy* is a 5 1/4" floppy disk, introduced by Shugart in 1978, that is used extensively in personal computers. The minifloppy superseded the 8" floppy disk developed by IBM, and it, too, is quickly being superseded by the 3 1/2" microfloppy disk developed by Sony. See *floppy disk*.

minor key

A *minor key* is a secondary key used to identify a record. For example, if transactions are sorted by account number and date, account number is the major key and date is the minor key.

MIPS

(Million Instructions Per Second) *MIPS* is used to measure the execution rate of a computer; for example, .5 MIPS means 500,000 instructions per second. A large mainframe can perform 10 to 50 MIPS, whereas an inexpensive microprocessor might be in the .05 MIPS range. However, MIPS specifications are not uniform across all vendors' lines. Some MIPS rates are best-case mixes, some are averages and the rare few are worst-case ratings. As a result, MIPS has been referred to as "MisInformation to Promote Sales."

MIPS rate, which is tied to the computer's clock speed, is only one factor in overall performance. Bus and channel speed and bandwidth (8-bit, 16-bit, 32-bit), disk and memory speed, memory management techniques and system software also determine total throughput of a computer system.

Mirror II

Mirror II is a communications program from Softklone Distributing Corporation that runs on IBM compatible pcs. Version 1.0 handles transmission speeds from 75 to 115,200 bits per second, emulates 11 different terminals, supports six protocols and uses the Crosstalk XVI command language

MIS

(1) (Management Information System) An *MIS* is an information system that has integrated all the data for the departments it serves and implies a system that provides operations and management with all levels of information required. MIS was the buzzword of the mid to late 1970s, when online systems were being implemented within all large organizations. See *decision support system*.

(2) (Management Information Systems or Management Information Services) *MIS* is a formal name for the information processing department within an organization.

mnemonic

A *mnemonic*, pronounced "nih-monic," and meaning memory aid, is a name or symbol used for some code or function. All computer languages are made up of mnemonics, except for the machine language itself. Names used to reference instructions, variables and subroutines are mnemonics. For example, BRANCHEQ could be the mnemonic for a BRANCH ON EQUAL instruction.

MNP

(Microcom Networking Protocol) *MNP* is a communications protocol from Microcom that is used in high-speed asynchronous modems. MNP is layered into classes, each class providing the same functions of the previous class. Class 4 MNP monitors the condition of the line and changes the speed according to the current quality of the line. Class 5 compresses data and provides a higher transmission throughput. Class 6 tries to find the highest transmission speed of the modem at the other end and transmits accordingly.

Mockingboard

A *Mockingboard* is a sound synthesizer from Sweet Micro Systems that runs on the Apple II series of personal computers. The Mockingboard is a printed circuit board that is inserted into the computer and allows for the creation of stereo music, sound effects and synthetic speech. A text-to-speech program comes with the board that converts typed text to speech output.

mode

A *mode* is a state of operation within which a system has been placed. There are countless modes for hardware and software. For example, *protected mode* is an operating state where one program cannot accidentally contaminate another. *Burst mode* is when a channel jumps from low speed to high speed for a short period of time. *Insert mode* allows text to be inserted into existing text. Mode implies that the condition, status, or state that it refers to can be changed to a different mode.

model

(1) A *model* is a particular style or type of hardware device.

(2) A *model* is a mathematical representation of some device or process that is used for analysis and planning purposes. Models are sets of equations that represent some condition or set of operations in the real world. A model differs from an ordinary list of descriptions, in that it also describes the interrelationships of all the components. For example, *data models*, which indicate how data is perceived by different departments, can be used to forecast likely bottlenecks if users request certain kinds of information.

   Models used in planning for marketing, distribution and manufacturing functions are a series of equations into which variables can be plugged in order to test the impact of various decisions. Whereas business models are often simple equations such as NET INCOME = GROSS REVENUES - EXPENSES, scientific models require elaborate formulas to represent such things as airplanes, rivers and planets. Scientific models are used to simulate the actual movement and change of real-world objects.

model-based expert system

A *model-based expert system* is used in such areas as diagnosing equipment problems. It is an expert system that is based on the knowledge of the structure and function of the object the system is designed for. Contrast with *rule-based expert system*, which follows the path a human expert would take in diagnosing the situation.

modeling

Modeling is the simulation of a condition or activity by performing a set of equations on a set of data. See *model*, *financial planning system* and *spreadsheet*.

modem

(MOdulator-DEModulator) A *modem* is a device that adapts a terminal or computer to a communications network. Modems turn digital pulses from the computer into frequencies (modulate) within the audio range of the telephone system and convert the frequencies back into digital pulses (demodulate) on the receiving side. Specialized modems are used to connect personal computers to a broadband local area network, which, similar to the telephone system, use electromagnetic waves for transmission signals, but at different frequencies. The telephone industry also refers to a modem as a *dataset*.

The modem handles the dialing and answering of the call and also generates the speed of the transmission, which is measured in bits per second. Modems used on telephone lines transmit at speeds of 300, 1,200, 2,400, 4,800, 9,600 and 19,200 bits per second. The effective data rate is 10% of the bit rate; thus, 300 bits per second (bps) is equivalent to 30 characters per second (cps). It would take a full minute to fill up a video screen at that rate; 15 seconds at 1,200 bps and about seven seconds at 2,400 bps. Due to noisy lines in the dial-up telephone system, the higher speeds can be problematic, and private lines may be required.

In order to have a personal computer dial up and communicate with another computer or public information service, more than a modem is required. The computer must have a serial port available into which the modem is connected. In addition, a communications program must be used in order to direct the computer to do the transmitting and receiving.

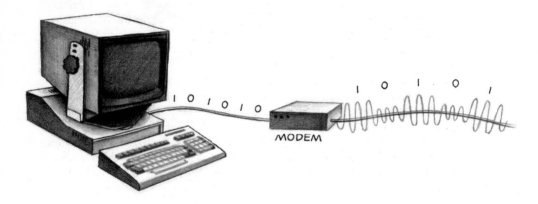

modem eliminator

In communications, a *modem eliminator* is a device that allows two computers in close proximity to be hooked up without modems. In asynchronous systems, such as when the serial ports of two personal computers are connected together, a modem eliminator crosses over the send and receive lines. In this case, a modem eliminator is the same as a *null modem cable*.

In synchronous systems, the modem eliminator provides active intelligence with regard to synchronizing the lines.

modified frequency modulation

See *MFM*.

modify structure

Modify structure is a statement in a database language that allows the user to change the structure of the records in the file. For example, field lengths and field names can be changed, and fields can be added or deleted. Modify structure statements also usually convert the old data file into the new structure without the loss of data unless, of course, fields have been truncated or deleted.

Modula-2

(MODUlar LAnguage-2) *Modula-2* is a high-level programming language developed by the Swiss professor Nicklaus Wirth, creator of Pascal. Modula-2 was introduced in 1979 and is an enhanced version of the Pascal language. Modula-2 supports separate compilation of modules, whereas Pascal does not.

The following example changes fahrenheit to centigrade in Modula-2:

```
  MODULE FahrToCent;
FROM InOut IMPORT ReadReal,WriteReal,
WriteString,WriteLn;
VAR Fahr:REAL;
  BEGIN
WriteString("Enter fahrenheit ");
ReadReal(Fahr);
WriteLn;
WriteString("Centigrade is ");
WriteReal((Fahr - 32) * 5 / 9);
  END  FahrToCent
```

modular programming

Modular programming breaks down the design of a problem into separate components or modules, each of which can be programmed as a single unit. Modular programming allows different programmers to develop parts of the program so that each part can be tested separately and then merged together. It imposes a structure onto the design of the program that aids in documenting and maintaining the program.

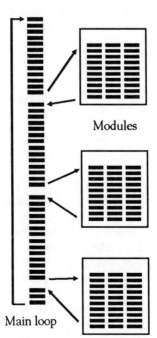

Modules

Main loop

modulate

Modulate is to mix a voice or data signal onto a carrier for transmission in a communications network. A carrier is a electromagnetic wave that vibrates at a fixed frequency. Data is modulated onto the carrier by various methods, including *amplitude modulation*, in which the height of the wave is changed; or *frequency modulation*, in which the frequency is changed; or *phase modulation*, in which the phase (polarity) of the wave is changed. The data is filtered out of the carrier by the reverse process called *demodulation*.

module

A *module* is a hardware or software component that is a self-contained system that interacts with a larger system. Hardware modules are often made to plug into a main system. Program modules are designed to handle a specific task within a larger program.

modulo

Modulo is a mathematical operation in which the result is the remainder. For example, 20 modulo-3 generates a remainder of 2, 20 modulo-2 results in a 0.

molecular beam epitaxy

Molecular beam epitaxy is a technique used in fabricating chips that builds up the tiny layers of a chip at the atomic level. Layers as thin as two atoms can be deposited on the chip in extremely precise locations. Molecular beam epitaxy may replace the traditional chip-making process, which creates layers by implanting materials into an existing substrate. See *chip*.

monadic

Monadic means one and refers to a single item or an operation that deals with one item or operand.

monitor

(1) A *monitor* is a display screen that is used to show the output of a computer, video cassette recorder or other video-generating device. Monitors are available in monochrome or color, and in analog or digital varieties. Analog monitors are the traditional video monitors that have been used for high-quality display in video and TV recording studios. Analog monitors accept RGB (red, green, blue) signals and/or composite (mixed) signals. Digital monitors accept specific digital signals and convert them into analog signals internally. See *video display board*.

(2) A *monitor* is a control program that often resides in a ROM chip and provides diagnostic routines upon startup as well as various control functions, such as setting bit rates for communications and serial devices. The monitor may also

contain the autostart routine that calls for and loads the operating system into memory.

(3) A *monitor* is a software program that monitors the progress of activities within a computer system.

(4) A *monitor* is a device that is attached to various printed circuit boards within the processor and is used to monitor hardware activities at the lowest hardware level.

monochrome

Monochrome means single color and refers to monitors that display only one color along with black, such as white on black, black on white, green on black and amber on black.

monolithic integrated circuit

A *monolithic integrated circuit* is an integrated circuit in which the base material, or substrate, not only holds the circuit, but contains active elements that take part in the operation of the circuit. This is the most common form of chip fabrication.

monospacing

Monospacing refers to a set of font characters that have uniform horizontal spacing, such as 10 characters per inch. Contrast with *proportional spacing*, which provides varying widths depending on the character. Even with proportional spacing however, numeric digits are usually monospaced in order to provide uniform alignment within columns.

Monte Carlo method

The *Monte Carlo method* is a set of techniques which provides approximate solutions to problems that can be expressed mathematically. Using random numbers and trial and error, the Monte Carlo method repeatedly calculates the equations to obtain an optimum solution.

Morse code

Morse code, developed by Samuel Morse in the mid-19th century, is a data code represented by dots and dashes. A dot can be a voltage, carrier wave or light beam of one duration, while a dash is a longer duration. Morse code was commonly used to send telegraph messages until the telephone system superseded it. Morse code was frequently used for line-of-sight signalling with a light beam throughout World War II.

MOS

(Metal Oxide Semiconductor) Pronounced "moss," MOS is one of two major categories of designing and fabricating logic and memory chips (the other is bipolar). MOS technology derives its name from its use of metal, oxide and semiconductor layers. There are several varieties of MOS technologies, including PMOS, NMOS and CMOS.

MOSFET

(Metal Oxide Semiconductor Field Effect Transistor) A MOSFET is a common type of transistor fabricated as a discrete component or into MOS integrated circuits.

most significant bit

The *most significant bit* is the leftmost 1 bit in a byte, word or field. It is the bit with the greatest value in the number or item.

most significant digit

The *most significant digit* is the digit, other than 0, that is in the leftmost position of the number. It is the digit with the greatest value in the number.

motherboard

A *motherboard* is the main printed circuit board in an electronic device which contains sockets that accept additional printed circuit boards. In a personal computer, the motherboard contains the bus, the microprocessor and all the chips used for controlling the peripherals that are considered standard with the system, such as the keyboard, text and graphics display, serial and parallel ports and joystick and mouse interfaces.

Motorola, Inc.

Motorola, Inc. is a leading semiconductor manufacturer that makes the 68000 family of microprocessors which are used in Apple's Macintosh series and Sun workstations. See *68000, 68020, 68030.*

mouse

A *mouse* is a puck-like object that is used as a pointing and drawing device. As it is rolled across the desktop in any direction, the cursor moves correspondingly on the screen. A serial mouse is one that is connected to the computer via a cable that plugs into a standard serial port. A bus mouse is one that connects to a printed circuit board that is inserted into one of the computer's internal expansion slots. All mice have at least one button that can be pressed. Most have two, and some have three.

A mechanical mouse has a rubber ball on its bottom and can be moved across any desktop surface. An optical mouse uses an optical sensor instead of a rotating ball, and it is rolled over a special pad that contains a grid for the sensor to calibrate the incremental movements of the mouse.

MOUSE

A mouse is similar to the pen-like or puck-like device on a digitizer tablet, called the *tablet cursor*. However, the tablet cursor makes contact with the digitizer tablet with absolute reference. Placing the tablet cursor on the upper left part of the tablet moves the screen cursor to that exact same location on screen. With a mouse, the movement is relative. When the mouse is moved, the screen cursor moves in the corresponding direction. The mouse could be moved across your arm, for example, and the screen cursor would move as well.

USER WITH MOUSE

(Courtesy Xerox Corporation)

move

(1) In programming, *move* is to copy data from one place in memory to another. At the end of the move, the source and destination data are identical.

(2) In word processing and graphics, *move* is to relocate text and objects to another part of the document or drawing.

MPE

(MultiProgramming Executive) MPE is a multitasking operating system that runs on the Hewlett-Packard 3000 series of minicomputers.

MPU

(MicroProcessor Unit) Same as *microprocessor*.

ms

(MilliSecond) A *millisecond* is a thousandth of a second. See *space/time*.

MS-DOS

(MicroSoft-Disk Operating System) MS-DOS is the operating system from
Microsoft Corporation that runs in IBM compatible personal computers. It is
almost identical to the operating system that is used on the IBM personal
computers, called *DOS*, or *PC-DOS*, except that MS-DOS works with a version
of BASIC called GW-BASIC, and IBM's DOS works with a version of BASIC
called BASICA.

There are also machine-specific versions of MS-DOS for IBM compatible
computers that are not 100% compatible with the IBM PC series, such as the
Tandy 2000 and the HP 150.

MS-DOS is a single user system that normally runs one program at a time.
With windows environments added on to it, such as MS-Windows or DESQview,
it can be made to run a second program in background mode. MS-DOS can
address up to one megabyte of RAM, although only 640K is usable for
application programs. The remaining 384K is used by the operating system.
MS-DOS can handle up to 32 megabytes per disk drive. The one megabyte
memory limit has been increased to 32 megabytes with the addition of an
expanded memory board (EMS); however, software programs must be written to
support the EMS standard.

Most programs written to run under MS-DOS will run under Microsoft's OS/2
operating system without conversion; however, like MS-DOS, only one program
can be run at a time, and only 640K of memory can be managed when running in
the compatibility mode.

In this book, DOS refers to both DOS (PC-DOS) and MS-DOS versions of the
program.

MS-Windows

See *Windows*.

MSI

(Medium Scale Integration) *MSI* refers to the relatively small number of
electronic components that are built onto a single chip. MSI ranges
approximately from 100 to 3,000 transistors on a chip.

MTBF

(Mean Time Between Failure) MTBF is the average time a component works without failure. It is the number of failures that occur divided into the total number of hours under observation.

Multi Color Graphics Array

See MCGA.

Multibus

Multibus is a bus architecture from Intel Corporation. Multibus is the IEEE 796 standard.

multidrop line

See *multipoint line*.

MultiFinder

See *Finder*.

Multimate

Multimate is a word processing program from Ashton-Tate that runs on IBM compatible pcs. Multimate is noted for its Wang-like user interface.

MultiPlan

MultiPlan is a spreadsheet from Microsoft that runs on CP/M and IBM compatible pcs. MultiPlan was one of the first spreadsheets for personal computers and came out soon after SuperCalc. MultiPlan has been superseded by Microsoft's Excel spreadsheet.

multiplexing

Multiplexing is the transmission of multiple signals over a single communications line or computer channel. The two common multiplexing techniques are *frequency division multiplexing*, which separates signals by using different carrier frequencies to hold them in, and *time division multiplexing*, which separates signals by interleaving them one after the other.

multiplexor

In communications, a *multiplexor* brings together several low-speed
communications lines, transforms them into one high-speed channel and reverses
the operation at the other end. See multiplexing.

multiplexor channel

A *multiplexor channel* is a computer channel that interchanges signals between
the CPU and several low-speed peripheral devices, such as terminals and printers.
Some multiplexor channels have an optional burst mode that can provide a
high-speed transfer of data to only one peripheral device at a time.

multipoint line

In communications, a *multipoint line* is a single line that interconnects three or
more devices.

multiported memory

Multiported memory is a memory that provides more than one access path to its
contents. It allows the same bank of memory to be read and written
simultaneously, but not the exact same bit location.

multiprocessing

Multiprocessing is simultaneous processing with two or more processors in one
computer, or two or more computers that are processing together. When two or
more computers are used, they are tied together with a high-speed channel and
share the general workload between them. In the event one fails to operate, the
other takes over. In fault tolerant systems, two or more processors are built into
the same cabinet. Multiprocessing is also accomplished in special-purpose
computers, such as array processors, which provide concurrent mathematical
processing on sets of data.

Although computers are built with various overlapping features, such as
executing instructions while inputting and outputting data, multiprocessing refers
specifically to concurrent instruction executions.

multiprogramming

Same as *multitasking*.

multisync monitor

A *multisync monitor* is a display monitor that adjusts automatically to the
synchronization frequency of the video display board that's sending signals to it.

Multisync monitors can adjust to a range of frequencies, but not all of them. The multisync monitor was popularized by the NEC MultiSync monitor.

NEC MULTISYNC MONITOR

multitasking

Multitasking is the running of two or more programs in one computer at the same time. Multitasking is controlled by the operating system, which loads the programs and manages them until finished. The number of programs that can be effectively multitasked depends on the amount of memory available, CPU speed, capacity and speeds of peripheral resources, as well as the efficiency of the operating system.

Multitasking is accomplished due to the differences in input/output and processing speed. While one program is waiting for input, instructions in another program can be executed. With interactive programs, the seconds of delay between keyboard entries are used to execute instructions in other programs. In batch processing systems, the milliseconds of delay getting data into and out of the computer are used to execute instructions in other programs.

Traditionally, multitasking meant running two or more tasks within the same program at the same time, and *multiprogramming* meant running two or more programs within the same computer at the same time. Today, multitasking means multiprogramming, and *multithreading* is sometimes used to refer to multitasking. The reason for all this confusion is simple. The personal computer industry thinks it invented computers, and it rarely looks back on the 30 years that preceded it. Considering how revolutionary personal computers have been, it's also no wonder. However, in the 1970s, the same thing happened with the minicomputer industry. You would have thought they invented computers, too. It's a shame we don't learn from history. We'd make less mistakes, and we'd also keep the terminology straight!

multithreading

Multithreading is the concurrent processing of transactions. It implies that transactions, or messages, can be worked on in parallel, and that one transaction may not be completely processed before another is started. Multithreaded programs are often written in *reentrant code*.

multiuser

Multiuser is two or more users sharing a single computer.

MVS/ESA

(Multiple Virtual Storage/Enterprise Systems Architecture) MVS/ESA is an operating system from IBM which runs on IBM mainframes that have been upgraded to the ESA/370 architecture. Introduced in 1988, MVS/ESA increases virtual memory capability to 16 terabytes (trillion bytes).

MVS/XA

(Multiple Virtual Storage/eXtended Architecture) MVS/XA is one of the two major operating systems (the other is VM) that runs on large IBM mainframes. MVS/XA is primarily a batch processing-oriented operating system that manages large amounts of memory and disk space. Online operations are provided with CICS, TSO and other system software.

The original MVS was introduced in 1974, and in 1981, the XA version increased its virtual memory capability to two gigabytes (billion bytes).

MYCIN

MYCIN is an expert system for diagnoising blood infections developed at Stanford University in the early 1970s by Bruce Buchanan and Edward Shortliffe.

NAK

(Negative AcKnowledgement) In communications, a *NAK* is the code which is used to indicate that a message was not received, or that a terminal does not wish to transmit.

NAND

(Not AND) A *NAND* is a Boolean logic operation that states that if both inputs are true (1), then there's no output (0). If any single input is false (0), then there is output (1). Two-input NAND gates are often used as the sole logic element on gate array chips, because every logical operation can be created out of NAND gates.

nanometer

A *nanometer* is one billionth of a meter.

nanosecond

A *nanosecond* is a billionth of a second and is used to measure the speed of logic and memory chips. A nanosecond seems unbelievably fast, but it can be brought down to earth a bit by converting it to travel distance. In one nanosecond, electricity travels about a foot; thus, it can be visualized as a one-foot length of wire.

The advantage of the tiny chip is the decreased time electricity has to travel between circuits and logic elements. Electricity travels at the speed of light (186,000 miles per second); yet, it's never fast enough for the hardware designer who will worry over an extra few inches of circuit path. The slightest delay is multiplied millions of times, since millions of pulses are sent through a wire in a single second. See *space/time*.

NAPLPS

(North American Presentation-Level Protocol Syntax) *NAPLPS* is a text and graphics transmission format that was originally developed for videotex and teletext systems. NAPLPS uses a coded system to transmit large amounts of information over narrow bandwidth transmission lines and requires that the receiving devices have processing capability to expand the code into actual images. NAPLPS was first developed through the Canadian Standards Association and later modified and enhanced by AT&T. It became an ANSI standard in 1983.

narrowband

In communications, *narrowband* refers to voice-grade or low-speed transmission of approximately 2,400 bits per second or less.

NAS

(Network Application Support) NAS, introduced in 1988, is a set of proprietary and industry standards adopted by Digital Equipment Corporation that allow for the interconnection between Digital's computers and IBM, IBM compatible and Macintosh computers within the DECnet environment. NAS also includes the X.400 electronic mail protocol, the X Windows display standard, Adobe's PostScript page description language and SQL for database manipulation.

National Computer Graphics Association

See *NCGA*.

National Software Testing Laboratory

The *National Software Testing Laboratory* is an independent organization in Philadelphia that evaluates personal computer hardware and software. NSTL adheres to controlled testing methodologies in order to ensure accurate and objective results. NSTL publishes its results in Software Digest Ratings Report and PC Digest.

native language

Same as *machine language*. See *native mode*.

native mode

Native mode refers to a computer that is running a program in its native machine language. Contrast with *emulation mode*, which is when a computer has the built-in capability of running a foreign language.

Natural

Natural is a fourth-generation language from Software AG.

natural langauge

Natural language is the language you speak. Any computer language that lets you express your request in normal English language is a natural language program. However, the term is used for programs that can accept a large degree of English, but not all of it. Few programs on the market today are entirely natural language programs. However, by the turn of the century, this will change dramatically. You will be able to phrase a question any way you'd like, and the program will understand it.

NC

See *numerical control*.

NCGA

(National Computer Graphics Association) The NCGA is an organization of individuals and major corporations dedicated to developing and promoting the computer graphics industry and improving graphics applications in business, industry, government, science and the arts.

NCGA strives to encourage communication among computer graphics users, consultants, educators and vendors; increase general awareness of potential computer graphics applications; raise national productivity and encourage the effective use of existing resources; and maintain a clearinghouse for industry information. For more information, contact NCGA, 2722 Merrilee Drive, Suite 200, Fairfax, VA 22031.

JOHN H. PATTERSON
(Courtesy NCR)

NCR Corporation

In 1884, John Henry Patterson purchased the National Manufacturing Company of Dayton, Ohio, and renamed it National Cash Register. NCR became the leading cash register company in the country and, by 1911, had sold its one millionth cash register.

Throughout the 1930s and 1940s, NCR gained a reputation in the banking and retail industries as a maker of accounting machines that were used for posting customer accounts. NCR has specialized in both industries ever since.

In 1952, it acquired the Computer Research Corporation, a fledgling electronics firm, which, by, 1955 had created and sold 30 CRC 102 scientific-oriented data processing systems. Turning its new acquisition towards the business world and bypassing the vacuum tube age, NCR introduced a transistorized computer system in 1957, called the 304. It accepted data from NCR cash registers and banking terminals via paper tape. Due to its high reliability, it was widely accepted in the retail and banking industries.

EARLY CASH REGISTER

(Courtesy NCR)

One of NCR's more novel devices was its CRAM (Card Random Access Memory) storage unit, introduced in 1961. It held removable cartridges containing strips of magnetic tape offering large amounts of peripheral storage for its time. CRAM units were more reliable than other vendors' magnetic strip offerings.

From its Century series of the 1960s, the Criterion series of the 1970s, to the 9300 mainframes of the 1980s, NCR has kept abreast of the times, providing a complete line of integrated point-of-sale and financial computer systems.

NCR paper

(No Carbon Required paper) NCR paper is a multiple-part paper form that does not contain sheets of carbon paper between the forms. The ink for the second and subsequent sheets is adhered to the reverse side of the previous sheet.

NE

(Not Equal to) See *relational operator*.

negative logic

Negative logic is the use of a high voltage for a 0 bit and a low voltage for a 1 bit. Contrast with *positive logic*, which uses a low voltage for a 0 bit and a high voltage for a 1 bit.

neper

A *neper* is a unit of measurement that is based on Napierian logarithms and represents the ratio between two values, such as current or voltage.

nesting

In programming, *nesting* is locating a loop within a loop. The fundamental structure of all programs is a series of loops, which are sets of instructions repeated some number of times. When an if-then or do loop is placed within the beginning and end of another loop, it is said to be nested. The number of loops that can be nested may be limited by the programming language.

NetBIOS

NetBIOS is an applications programming interface (API) which activates network operations on IBM compatible pcs running under Microsoft's DOS operating system. It is a set of network commands that the application program issues in order to transmit and receive data to another station on the network. The commands are interpreted by a network control program or network operating system that is NetBIOS compatible.

Netview

Netview is network management software from IBM that runs on its large mainframes in an SNA environment. It is made up of several network monitoring and control programs. NetView controls SNA as well as non-SNA and non-IBM devices. As is typical with SNA environments, NetView provides host-based, central control over the network.

NetView/PC is a product that interconnects NetView with Token Ring local area networks, Rolm CBXs and non-IBM modems, while maintaining control in the host.

NetWare

NetWare is a family of local area network operating systems from Novell Inc., that run on IBM compatible pcs, Macintosh computers and Digital's VAX series. As of mid-1988, there were over 200,000 file servers using NetWare software. Advanced NetWare supports up to 100 users per file server. ELS NetWare, an entry level system, supports four or eight users, and SFT NetWare (System Fault Tolerant), provides automatic recovery from network hardware malfunctions.

Novell's NetWare software supports a large number of LAN topologies, including Token Ring, Ethernet, ARCNET and Starlan.

network

(1) In communications, a *network* is the communication path between terminals and computers.

(2) In database management, a *network* is a database design technique. See *network database*.

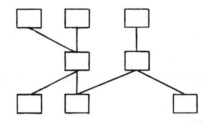

NETWORK

network administrator

A *network administrator* is an individual who is responsible for the operation of a local area network. The network administrator ensures that all users of the system have enough disk capacity on the file and database servers and is generally responsible for the smooth operation of the network.

network architecture

A *network architecture* is the overall design of a communications system, which includes the hardware, software, access methods and protocols used. It also defines the method of control, for example, whether computers can act independently or whether they are controlled by other computers that are constantly monitoring the network. Network architectures determine how other networks can be interconnected to the system and how expandable and flexible the system can be. A network architecture usually defines a complete set of rules and standards that may be implemented in stages as the organization grows.

IBM's SNA (System Network Architecture), Digital Equipment Corporation's DNA (Digital Network Architecture) and Unisys' DCA (Distributed Communications Architecture) are examples of network architectures.

With regard to local area networks (LANs), network architecture refers to the various topologies, for example, bus, ring, star and tree configurations.

network control program

A *network control program* is a software program that controls the traffic between multiple terminals and a mainframe. It typically resides in a front end processor and performs such operations as polling the terminals one after the other.

network database

A *network database* is a database organization method that allows for data relationships to be designed in a net-like form. A single data element can point to multiple data elements and can itself be pointed to by other data elements. Both network databases and hierarchical databases imply a fixed pathway for "navigating" through the database to speed up processing. Contrast with *relational database*.

network operating system

A *network operating system* is a control program that resides in a file server within a local area network. It handles the requests for data from all the users (workstations) on the network.

network server

Same as *file server*.

neural network

A *neural network* is a modeling technique that is used to learn how to mimic the performance of a system. Neural networks consist of a set of elements that start out connected in a random pattern, and, based upon operational feedback, are molded into the complex pattern required to generate the required results.

NewWave

NewWave is an operating environment from Hewlett-Packard that runs with Microsoft's DOS operating system. Based on Version 2.0 of Microsoft's Windows, NewWave provides the ability to integrate data files and activate tasks within the system.

NewWave's "object-management" facility allows data from various different applications to be merged together to create a compound document. In addition, "hot connects" can be created that automatically update the document if data in one of the source files is updated.

NewWave allows for the creation of automatic procedures, called "agents," which can be activated on a prescribed timetable or when other events occur in the computer. For example, at the end of the month, an agent can be set up to extract data out of the corporate mainframe and prepare a report using two or more application programs.

Major software vendors are modifying application programs to run in the NewWave environment.

NFS

(Network File System) *NFS* is a distributed file system from Sun Microsystems that allows data to be shared with many users in a network. NFS allows users to share data regardless of processor type, operating system, network architecture or protocol.

nibble

A *nibble* is one half a byte, or four bits.

N-key rollover

N-key rollover is a keyboard feature that allows a typist to press a series of keys in fast sequence. Each subsequent key can be pressed without having to raise the finger off the last key.

NLQ

(Near Letter Quality) *NLQ* printing is almost as good as, but not quite as clear and crisp as, a typewriter. The highest quality (slowest speed) print mode of a dot matrix printer is often called NLQ printing.

NMOS

(N-Channel Metal Oxide Semiconductor) Pronounced "en-moss," *NMOS* is a type of microelectronic circuit design that is used for logic and memory and chips. NMOS transistors are faster than their PMOS counterpart and more of them can be put on a single chip. NMOS transistors are also used in CMOS technology.

node

(1) In communications, a *node* is a computer system used as a junction or connection point in a communications network. It also refers to a terminal connected to the network.

(2) In database management, a *node* is an item of data that can be accessed by two or more routes.

(3) In computer graphics, a *node* is an endpoint of a graphical element.

noise

Noise is any extraneous signal that invades the transmission of electrical pulses or frequencies. Noise can come from strong electrical or magnetic signals in nearby lines, from poorly fitting electrical contacts, and from power line spikes.

NOMAD

NOMAD is a relational database management system from National CSS that runs on IBM mainframes. NOMAD was one of the first database systems that provided a non-procedural language for data manipulation.

non-impact printer

A *non-impact printer* is a printer that prints without banging a ribbon onto paper, such as a thermal or ink jet printer. See *printer*.

non-interlaced

See *interlaced*.

non-numeric programming

Non-numeric programming deals with objects, such as words, board game pieces and people, rather than numbers. See *list processing*.

non-procedural language

A *non-procedural language* is a computer language that does not require traditional programming logic to be stated. For example, a command, such as LIST, might display all the records in a file on screen, separating fields with a blank space. In a procedural language, such as COBOL, all the logic for inputting each record in the file, testing for end of file and separating the data on the screen has to be implicitly programmed. Query languages, report writers and interactive database programs provide non-procedural languages for user operation.

non-return-to-zero

See *NRZ*.

NonStop

NonStop is a family of fault tolerant computer systems from Tandem Computers Inc. NonStop systems are used for online transaction processing applications that demand 100% availability, such as in the financial community.

non-trivial

Non-trivial is a favorite word among some programmers for any task that is difficult to do.

non-volatile memory

Non-volatile memory is memory that holds its content without power. Firmware chips, such as ROMs, PROMs, EPROMs and EEPROMs are examples of non-volatile memory. Magnetic disks and tapes may also be classified as non-volatile memory; however, technically they are peripheral storage units, not memory devices.

NOR

(Not OR) *NOR* is a Boolean logical condition that states that if both inputs are false (0), then the output is true (1), and if any input is true (1), then the output is false (0). An *exclusive NOR* is a condition in which the output is true if both inputs are false or if both inputs are true, and the output is false if one input is true and the other false.

normal wear

Normal wear is the deterioration due to the natural forces that act upon a product while it is being operated within proper specifications and for the purpose for which it was intended.

normalize

See *third normal form*.

Norton SI

(Norton System Information) The *Norton SI* is one of the programs in the Norton Utilties that analyzes the performance of the computer. The Norton SI provides a computing index (CI) that measures CPU speed, a disk index (DI) that measures disk speed and a performance index (PI) that is a composite of the computing and disk indexes. It uses the IBM PC XT as a base reference, which is 1.0. For example, the CI for the original 8 Mhz HP Vectra is 7.7, which means it is almost eight times as fast as the XT internally. The DI is 1.1, which means the Vectra disks are only slightly faster than the XT's. The PI is 5.5 indicating that the Vectra is five and one half times as "powerful" as the XT.

Norton Utilities

The *Norton Utilities* is a package of programs from Peter Norton Computing that assists the user with running an IBM compatible pc. The programs allow the user to restore deleted files on the disk, search and edit disk files no matter what format they are in and list and manage disk directories, among other things. Programs such as these provide an invaluable aid to both the novice and the advanced personal computer user. See *Norton SI*.

NOS

(Network Operating System) *NOS* is the operating system that runs on Control Data's CYBER series of large mainframes.

NOS/VE

(Network Operating System/Virtual Environment) *NOS/VE* is a multitasking, virtual memory operating system from Control Data Corporation that runs on CDC's medium to large-scale mainframes.

NOT

NOT is a Boolean logic condition that reverses the state of the input pulse. If a 0 bit is entered, a 1 is output. If a 1 bit is entered, a 0 is output. See *AND, OR & NOT*.

Nota Bene

Nota Bene is a word processing system from Dragonfly Software that runs on IBM compatible pcs. Using the XyWrite word processing program as its foundation, Nota Bene adds a considerable number of features to it, including menus, a different keyboard layout and much more sophisticated handling of foreign characters and laser printers. It also integrates a free-form text retrieval system that allows instant retrieval of text, correspondence, notes and random jottings from thousands of pages of unstructured notes.

notation

Notation is the way a system of numbers, phrases, words or quantities is written or expressed. Positional notation is the location and value of digits in a numbering system, such as the decimal or binary system.

Nova

Nova is a series of minicomputers from Data General. When introduced in 1969, the Nova was the first 16-bit minicomputer that used four accumulators in its CPU, an advanced technology for its time. Novas, running under its RDOS operating system, were used extensively in the OEM marketplace; for example, as controllers for cat scanners.

Novell network

A *Novell network* is a local area network that uses one of Novell's NetWare operating system programs to manage the network. See *NetWare*.

NRZ

(Non-Return-To-Zero) *NRZ* is a signalling method used both in magnetic recording and communications that does not automatically return to a neutral state after each bit is transmitted.

ns

(NanoSecond) See *nanosecond*.

NSTL

See *National Software Testing Laboratory*.

NTSC

(National Television Standards Committee) The *NTSC* governs the standard for television and video playback and recording in the United States. The NTSC standard is 525 lines of resolution and is transmitted at 60 half frames (interlaced) per second. The signal is generated as a composite of red, green and blue signals for color and also includes an FM frequency for audio and an MTSC signal for stereo.

null character

A *null character* is a character that has all bits set to 0. It prints as a blank, but it is not the same as a space character. It is used for special purposes, such as padding and filling fields and communications blocks, and as a delimiter character. Filling a data entry field with null characters would allow the program to determine if any keystrokes, even blanks, were entered at the keyboard.

null modem cable

A *null modem cable* is an RS-232-C cable that is used to connect two personal computers together that are in close proximity. The cable connects to the serial ports of each computer, and, since telephone lines are not used, no modems are required. The cable crosses the connections so that the sending wire on one end becomes the receiving wire on the other end.

number crunching

Number crunching is the calculating of numbers and usually refers to computers running mathematical, scientific or CAD applications in which large amounts of calculations are required.

numbers

Numbers in a computer can be stored in several forms. Although they are all coded as binary digits (bits), some methods retain the decimal nature of a number while others convert the number entirely into binary.

BINARY CODED DECIMAL
This method encodes each decimal digit in a single byte. A variation of this, called *packed decimal*, encodes two decimal digits in one byte.

BINARY FIXED POINT
With this method, the entire number is converted into a binary number and stored in a fixed unit of storage based on the architecture of the computer. For example, 16 bits, or two bytes, can hold values from zero up to 65,535. In 32 bits, a number up to 4,294,967,295 can be held. Binary numbers are calculated faster than binary coded decimal numbers.

BINARY FLOATING POINT
With floating point numbers, very small fractions and very large numbers can be maintained and calculated very quickly. Both the significant digits of the number, called the *mantissa*, and the *exponent*, which is the power to which the number is raised, are converted to binary numbers. See *floating point*.

numerical control (NC)

Numerical control is a category of automated machine tools, such as drills and lathes, that operate from instructions in a program. Numerical control machines are used in manufacturing tasks, such as milling, turning, punching and drilling.

First-generation numerical control machines were either hardwired to perform a specific set of tasks or programmed in a very low-level machine language. Today, numerical control machines are controlled by their own microcomputers and are programmed in high-level languages, such as APT and COMPACT II, which automatically generate the tool path, the physical motions of the machine required to perform the operation.

The term numerical control was coined in the 1950s when the instructions to the machine tool were numeric codes. Just like the computer industry, symbolic languages were soon developed, but the original term remained.

OA

See *office automation*.

object code

Same as *machine language*.

object computer

An *object computer* is the computer a program will eventually run in. The term is used to distinguish between the computer the program is intended for and the computer it is created on. See *cross assembler/compiler*.

object language

(1) Same as *object program*.

(2) An *object language* is the translated language that is derived from a cross assembler or cross compiler.

object module

An *object module* is the direct output of an assembler or compiler. Object modules cannot execute in the computer until after they have been link edited, which ties the cross references between modules together and creates an executable format.

object program

An *object program* is a machine language program that is ready to run in a particular operating environment. It has been assembled, or compiled, and link edited. Contrast with *object module*, which cannot execute because it has not been link edited.

object-oriented graphics

Same as *vector graphics*.

object-oriented interface

An *object-oriented interface* refers to the type of graphical interface that was developed by Xerox which uses icons and a mouse. The Macintosh, Microsoft Windows and GEM are examples of object-oriented interfaces.

object-oriented programming

Object-oriented programming is a technology for creating programs that are more responsive to future changes. Object-oriented programs are made up of self-sufficient modules that contain all of the information needed to manipulate a given data structure. The modules are created in class hierarchies, and the methods or code in one class can be passed down the hierarchy or inherited. New and powerful objects can be created quickly by inheriting their characteristics from existing classes. For example, the object MACINTOSH could be one instance of the class PERSONAL COMPUTER, which could inherit properties from the class COMPUTER SYSTEM. Adding a new computer requires entering only what makes it different from other computers, while all the general characteristics of personal computers can be inherited.

Smalltalk, from Xerox's Palo Alto Research Center (PARC), was the first object-oriented programming language.

Objective-C

Objective-C is an object-oriented C programming language from The Stepstone Corporation that runs on many popular workstations and IBM compatible pcs. It was the first commercial object-oriented extension of the C language. It includes packages sets of classes, called "ICpaks" for both general-purpose data structure manipulation and iconic user interface construction.

OCO

(Object Code Only) *OCO* is a policy announced by IBM in 1983 that withholds source code and provides only object code (machine language) to its customers. Large mainframe customers often want to get into the source code in order to customize the programs for their own use. Without the source code, they cannot make modifications, at least not without a lot of difficulty. It is customary for all vendors to provide only the object code of their "canned" software packages.

OCR

(Optical Character Recognition) OCR refers to the machine recognition of printed characters. OCR systems can recognize many different kinds of special OCR fonts, as in the examples below, as well as typewriter and computer-printed characters. Advanced OCR systems can recognize hand printing. The characters are converted into ASCII or EBCDIC code by the OCR software.

OCR-A (FULL ALPHA)
NUMERIC	0123456789
ALPHA	ABCDEFGHIJKLMNOPQRSTUVWXYZ
SYMBOLS	>$/-+-#"

OCR-A (NRMA/EURO BANKING)
NUMERIC	0123456789
ALPHA	ACDMNPRUXY
SYMBOLS	>$/+#"♩ЧH

OCR-B(SUBSET 1, ECMA 11 and ANSI X3.49-1975)
NUMERIC	00123456789
ALPHA	ACENPSTVX
SYMBOLS	<+>-¥

OCR MULTIFONT
OCR-B	¥00123456789><++#
12L/12F	¥0123456789+#
1403-OCR	00123456789><+#
407-1	0123456789

SAMPLE OCR FONTS

(Courtesy Recognition Equipment Corporation)

octal

Octal is a numbering system that uses eight digits. It is used as a shorthand method for representing binary numbers that use six-bit characters. Each three bits (half a character) is converted into a single octal digit. Okta is Greek for 8.

Decimal	Binary	Octal
0	000	0
1	001	1
2	010	2
3	011	3
4	100	4
5	101	5
6	110	6
7	111	7

OEM

(Original Equipment Manufacturer) An *OEM* is a manufacturer that sells equipment to a reseller. The term is also used to refer to the reseller, as well. OEM customers typically purchase hardware from a manufacturer and resell it under their own brand names. They may combine units from several vendors as well as add software. The terms OEM and VAR are often used synonymously.

off-hook

Off-hook is the state of a telephone line that allows dialing and transmission but prohibits incoming calls from being answered. The term goes back to the days when a telephone handset was lifted off of the hook that held it. Contrast with *on-hook*.

off-the-shelf

Off-the-shelf refers to products that are packaged and available for sale.

office automation

Office automation is the integration of all information functions in the office, which include word processing, data processing, electronic mail, graphics and desktop publishing.

The backbone of office automation is a local area network, which serves as a pathway between all users and computers. Users can create, store and retrieve any form of information (message, mail, data, voice, etc.) and transmit it to any other user within the organization.

All traditional office functions, such as dictation, typing, filing, copying, TWX and Telex operation, microfilm and records management and telephone and telephone switchboard operations, are candidates for integration into an office automation system.

Office automation often refers to the word processing operation, and although word processing is often the first approach taken, office automation implies many new ways of looking at work in the office. While it is viewed as a solution to bottlenecks and backlogs in office operations, its implementation will eventually change the way people perform their jobs.

The irony of the so-called "Office of the Future" is that once we have all the technology to implement it properly, we probably won't need the office. If people can access all the information required to do a job from a terminal, and through video conferencing can interact with whomever they're talking to as if they were in the same room, then, in time, the concept of the central office as a workplace will undergo dramatic change.

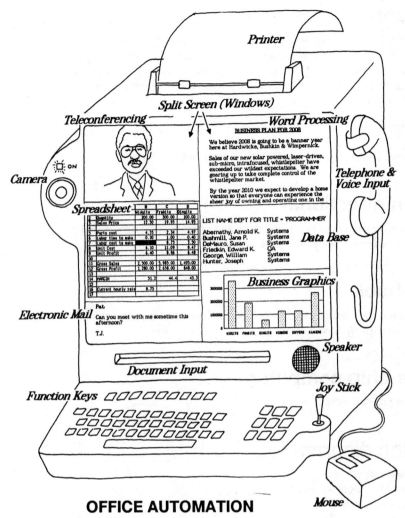

OFFICE AUTOMATION

This terminal depicts the various paper and electronic functions of an integrated office system.

offline

Offline means not connected to or not mounted in the computer. Even if a terminal, printer or other device is physically connected to the computer, it is still offline if it is not turned on, or not in ready mode. Disks and tapes that have been demounted and stored in the data library are considered offline. Contrast with *online*, which means connected or mounted and ready to go.

offline storage

Offline storage refers to disks and tapes that are kept in a data library.

offset

An *offset* is a value that is added to a base value in order to derive the actual value. For example, a relative address is the offset value added to each machine instruction when the program is executing. In word processing, an offset is the amount of space the document will be printed from the left margin.

OLTP

(OnLine Transaction Processing) See *transaction processing*.

omnidirectional

Omnidirectional means in all directions and refers to radio signals that are transmitted and received in all directions.

on-hook

On-hook is the state of a telephone line that can receive an incoming call. Contrast with *off-hook*.

one-chip computer

See *computer on a chip*.

onion diagram

An *onion diagram* is a graphical representation of a system that is made up of concentric circles. The innermost circle is the core, and all outer layers are dependent on the core.

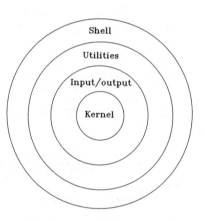

ONION DIAGRAM OF AN OPERATING SYSTEM

online

Online refers to a peripheral device, such as a terminal or printer, that is ready to operate. A personal computer printer can be attached and turned on, yet still not online, if the ONLINE or SEL light is out. Pressing the ONLINE button will usually turn it back online.

An online computer system refers to a system with terminals, but does not imply how the system operates. For example, a *data collection* system is an online system that accepts and stores data from several terminals, but does not update any other files. An *interactive* system is an online system that implies data entry and updating. A *transaction processing* system is an online system that updates the necessary files as the work comes in, such as in an order processing system. A *realtime* system is an online system that provides an immediate response to a question. Although often said of a business system, realtime is more applicable to scientific and process control applications.

Although complete overkill, it is not incorrect to say that one has an online, realtime, interactive, transaction processing system, especially if you're trying to impress someone, but, hopefully, not a systems person.

on-line means happiness!

OOPS

(Object Oriented Programming System) See *object-oriented programming*.

op code

See *operation code*.

open architecture

Open architecture refers to a system in which the specifications are made public in order to encourage third-party vendors to develop add-on products for it. For example, much of Apple Computer's early success was due to the open architecture philosophy of the Apple II. IBM followed Apple's lead in making the PC series an open architecture one as well.

open shop

An *open shop* is a computing environment that allows users to program and run their own programs. Contrast with *closed shop*, in which only the data processing staff is allowed access to the computer.

Open Software Foundation

The *Open Software Foundation* was formed in May of 1988 to develop a new operating system environment based on the UNIX standard. Initial funding is provided by Apollo Computer, Groupe Bull, Digital, Hewlett-Packard, IBM, Nixdorf Computer and Siemens. The foundation was created in response to an earlier announcement that AT&T and Sun Microsystems would jointly create a new standard.

open system

In communications, an *open system* is a network that allows the interconnecting of a wide variety of terminals and user devices. See *OSI*.

Open System Interconnection

See *OSI*

operand

An *operand* is the part of a machine instruction that references the data or a peripheral device. In the instruction, ADD A to B, A and B are the operands, or nouns, and ADD is the operation code, or verb. In the instruction READ DRIVE A, TRACK 9, SECTOR 32, the drive, track and sector references are the operands.

operating system

An *operating system* is a master control program that runs the computer and acts as a scheduler and traffic cop. It is the first program loaded (copied) into the computer's memory after the computer is turned on, and the central core, or kernel, of the operating system must reside in memory at all times. The operating system may be developed by the vendor of the hardware it's running in or by an independent software house.

The operating system is an important component of the computer system, because it sets the standards for the application programs that run in it. All programs must be written to "talk to" the operating system.

Also called an executive or supervisor, the operating system performs the following functions.

JOB MANAGEMENT
In small computers, the operating system responds to commands from the user and loads the requested application program into memory for execution. In large computers, the operating system carries out its job control instructions (JCL), which can describe the mix of programs that must be run for an entire shift.

TASK MANAGEMENT
In single tasking computers, the operating system has virtually no task management to do, but in multitasking computers, it is responsible for the concurrent operation of one or more programs (jobs). Advanced operating systems have the ability to prioritize programs so that one job gets done before the other. In order to provide users at terminals with the fastest response time, batch programs can be put on lowest priority and interactive programs can be given highest priority. Advanced operating systems have more fine-tuning capabilities so that a specific job can be speeded up or slowed down by commands from the computer operator.

Multitasking is accomplished by designing the computer to allow instructions to be executed during the same time data is coming into or going out of the computer. In the seconds it takes one user to type in data, millions of instructions can be executed for dozens, or even hundreds, of other users. In the milliseconds it takes for data to come in from or go out to the disk, thousands of instructions can be performed for some other task.

DATA MANAGEMENT

One of the major functions of an operating systems is to keep track of the data on the disk; hence the term DOS, or disk operating system. The application program does not know where the data is actually stored or how to get it. That knowledge is contained in the operating system's access method, or device driver, routines. When a program is ready to accept data, it signals the operating system with a coded message. The operating system finds the data and delivers it to the program. Conversely, when the program is ready to output, the operating system transfers the data from the program onto the next available space on the disk.

In theory, the operating system is supposed to handle every kind of input and output request, including the ones to the display screen and the printer. By keeping the details of the peripheral device within the operating system, a device can be replaced with a newer model, and only the routine in the operating system that deals with that device needs to be replaced.

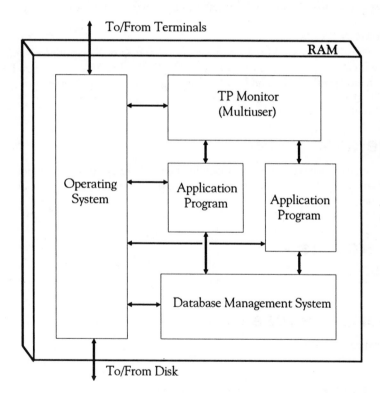

OPERATING SYSTEM

This chart depicts the interaction of the operating system with other system and application programs within the computer. The actual storage and retrieval of data on disk and transmission and receipt of data at the terminals is provided by program routines, called *access methods*, which are components of the operating sytem.

Within the Microsoft DOS/IBM compatible pc world, however, it's a different story. All the different display and printer standards were never built into DOS. As a result, each application program is responsible for providing its own drivers, making the installation more tedious and adding considerable extra work for the software vendors.

SECURITY
Multiuser operating systems maintain a list of authorized users and provide password protection to unauthorized users who may try to gain access to the system. Large operating systems also maintain activity logs and accounting of the user's time for billing purposes. They also provide backup and recovery routines to start over again in the event of a system failure.

HISTORY
Operating systems became coincident with timesharing and multitasking computers in the mid-1960s. Before then, programmers either wrote their own input/output routines or used canned subroutines that were added to each program. Even today, an operating system is not used in all computer applications. For example, when single chip computers are used in appliances, games or toys, the program written for the chip drives the hardware directly.

COMMON EXAMPLES
IBM compatible pcs use Microsoft's DOS, OS/2 and XENIX operating systems. Apple II computers use Apple's DOS and PRODOS. The Macintosh uses the System along with Finder and Multifinder. Digital uses the VMS and Ultrix operating systems. IBM mainframes use MVS, VM or DOS/VSE.

operation code

The *operation code* is the part of a machine instruction that tells the computer what to do, such as input, add or branch. The operation code is the verb, and the operands are the nouns.

operations

See *datacenter*.

operations research

See *management science*.

operator

An *operator* is an individual who operates the computer and performs such activities as commanding the operating system, mounting disks and tapes and placing paper in the printer. Operators may also write the job control language (JCL), which schedules the daily work for the computer.

optical character recognition.

See *OCR*.

optical disk

An *optical disk* is a disk that is written (recorded) and read by light. Videodiscs, compact discs (CDs) and CD ROM disks are optical disks that, like phonograph records, are recorded at the time of manufacture and cannot be erased. WORM (write once read many) disks are optical disks that are recorded in the user's environment, but they cannot be erased either.

Erasable optical disks function like magnetic disk drives and can be erased and rerecorded over and over again. As of the late 1980s, a number of erasable optical disks are emerging that use a number of recording technologies, such as magneto-optic, dye polymer and phase change.

Throughout the 1990s, erasable optical disks may become increasingly viable as alternatives to magnetic disk. The storage capacity of an optical disk is considerably greater than its magnetic disk counterpart for the same amount of disk surface. As the technology matures and prices come down, optical disks could eventually replace magnetic media. In addition, lasers can be moved electronically and don't have to be physically moved as do the read/write heads on magnetic disks and tapes. This could have a large impact on random access retrieval times in the future.

The huge storage capacities of optical disks let an organization keep its transaction history online in the computer system rather than offline in a data library. Thus, data from past activities is immediately available for analysis.

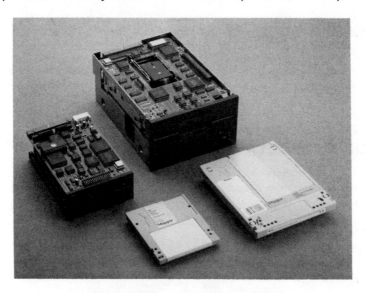

ERASABLE OPTICAL DISKS

(Courtesy Maxtor Corporation)

The small 3 1/2" Fiji I drive holds 160-megabyte removable cartridges and has an average seek time of 100 milliseconds. The large 5 1/4" Tahiti I drive holds one-gigabyte removable cartridges and has seek times of less than 30 milliseconds.

optical fiber

An *optical fiber* is a very thin glass wire designed for the transmission of light. Optical fibers have enormous transmission capacities (bandwidths), capable of carrying billions of bits per second. In addition, unlike electrical pulses, light pulses are not affected by interference caused by random radiation in the environment.

When the telephone companies finally get around to replacing the copper wire that extends from their central stations into everyone's home (local loops) with optical fiber, all varieties of information services will be interactively available to the consumer. In addition, high definition TV will be easily transmitted into the home. At the present time, the telephone companies are busy replacing their main intercity trunk lines with optical fibers. In time, the local loops are next.

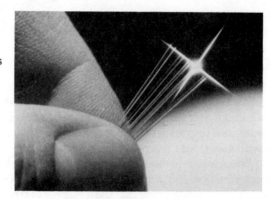

OPTICAL FIBERS

(Courtesy AT&T)

Each of these hair-thin optical fibers can carry thousands of digitized voice conversations at the same time.

optical mouse

An *optical mouse* is a mouse that uses light to get its bearings. It is rolled over a small desktop pad that contains a reflective grid. The mouse emits a light and senses its reflection as it is moved. Contrast with *mechanical mouse*, which uses a moving rubber ball.

optical reader

An *optical reader* is an input device that recognizes typewritten or printed characters and bar codes and converts them into their corresponding digital codes.

optical recognition

See *OCR*.

optical scanner

An *optical scanner* is an input device that reads characters and images into the computer that are printed or painted on a paper form. An optical scanner may or may not recognize the data it's reading. For example, OCR scanners are recognition devices that convert printed and typewritten characters into their corresponding digital codes. Bar code scanners convert the bars into the digital digits they represent. However, graphics scanners do not recognize what they see; they merely convert it into a matrix of dots like a television screen. Any analysis of the graphics images they send to the computer must be performed by humans or image processing software.

optoelectronics

Optoelectronics is the merging of light and electronics technologies, such as in optical fiber communications systems.

OR

OR is a Boolean logical condition that states that if either one of the two inputs is true (1) then the output is true (1). See *AND, OR & NOT*. An *exclusive* OR is an OR in which the output is true if only one of the inputs is true, but not both inputs.

Oracle

Oracle is a broadcast television text-message service.

ORACLE

ORACLE is a relational database management system from Oracle Corporation that runs on a wide variety of microcomputers, minicomputers and mainframes. ORACLE was the first database management system to incorporate the SQL database language.

ordinal number

An *ordinal number* is a number that identifies the sequence of an item, for example, record #34. Contrast with *cardinal number*, which shows how many, for example, 34 records in the file.

orphan

See *widow & orphan*.

OS

(1) (Operating System) OS is an abbreviation for operating system.

(2) OS may refer to Microsoft's OS/2 operating system.

OS 1100

OS 1100 is an operating system from Unisys that runs on its 1100 Series of mainframes.

OS/2

OS/2 is a single user, multitasking operating system from Microsoft that runs on 286 and 386-based IBM compatible pcs. OS/2 can address up to 16 megabytes of main memory and up to one gigabyte of virtual memory. It can run multiple OS/2 programs concurrently in "protected mode," which prevents one application program from interfering with another application program if it should crash (abnormally end).

OS/2 is a much more sophisticated program than DOS and requires significantly more memory to operate properly. Many OS/2 commands are the same as in DOS, and many new commands have been added.

OS/2's Presentation Manager provides a graphics-based user interface for commanding the computer similar to Microsoft's Windows environment for DOS. OS/2's Extended Edition, available only through IBM, provides built-in communications and database management.

OS/2 can run one DOS application program at a time in "real mode." A special version of OS/2 specifically for the 386, when available, will allow multiple DOS applications to be run concurrently by triggering a special "virtual mode" in the 386.

OS/3

OS/3 is an operating system from Unisys that runs on the System 80 family of IBM 370 compatible mainframes.

OS/8

OS/8 is a single user, multitasking operating system from Digital Equipment Corporation that runs on its PDP-8 series of minicomputers. Variants of OS/8 run on Digital's DECstation and DECmate systems.

oscillate

Oscillate is to swing or move back and forth between the minimum and maximum values of a range. An oscillation is one cycle, typically one complete wave in an alternating frequency.

oscillator

An *oscillator* is an electronic circuit that is used to generate high-frequency pulses. See *clock*.

oscilloscope

An *oscilloscope* is a test instrument that displays electronic signals (waves and pulses) on a screen. It creates its own time base against which the signals can be measured, and the display frames can be frozen for visual inspection.

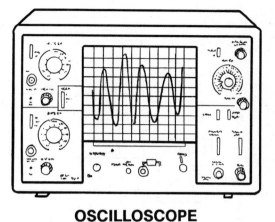

OSCILLOSCOPE

OSF

See *Open Software Foundation*.

OSI

(Open System Interconnection) The *OSI* is a communications reference model that has been defined by the International Standards Organization (ISO). It is a seven-layer communications protocol intended as a standard for the development of communications systems worldwide. OSI has only recently been completed. It is similar to IBM's SNA protocol layers, but not identical. Most vendors have agreed to support OSI in one form or another; however, adherance to this standard is vital in order to achieve universal communications. See *Corporation for Open Systems*.

Layers 1 and 2 are mandatory in order to transmit and receive in any communications system. Layers 3, 4 and 5 are provided by the controlling network software (network control programs and network operating systems) and have typically been treated as one layer by vendors. Layers 4, 5 and 6 are often combined into one or two layers in existing communications systems.

Control is passed from one layer to the next, starting at the application layer in one station, proceeding to the bottom layer, over the communications channel to the next station and back up the hierarchy.

From top to bottom, the layers of the OSI model are:

LAYER 7 - APPLICATION LAYER
Layer 7 is the set of messages that application programs use to request data and services from each other. Electronic mail and query languages are examples of this layer.

LAYER 6 - PRESENTATION LAYER
Layer 6 is used to convert one data format to another, for example, one word processor format to another or one database format to another.

LAYER 5 - SESSION LAYER
Layer 5 establishes and terminates the session, queues the incoming messages and is responsible for recovering from an abnormally terminated session.

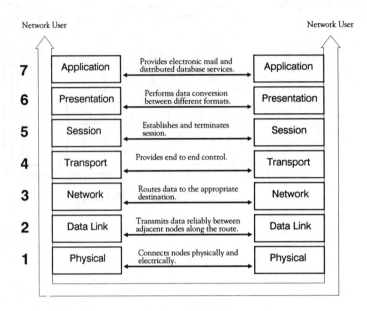

Network User   Network User

7	Application	Provides electronic mail and distributed database services.	Application
6	Presentation	Performs data conversion between different formats.	Presentation
5	Session	Establishes and terminates session.	Session
4	Transport	Provides end to end control.	Transport
3	Network	Routes data to the appropriate destination.	Network
2	Data Link	Transmits data reliably between adjacent nodes along the route.	Data Link
1	Physical	Connects nodes physically and electrically.	Physical

OSI MODEL

LAYER 4 - TRANSPORT LAYER
Layer 4 is responsible for converting messages into the structures required for transmission over the network. A high level of error recovery is also provided in this layer.

LAYER 3 - NETWORK LAYER
The network layer establishes the connection between two parties that are not directly connected together. For example, this layer is the common function of the telephone system. When an X.25 packet switching network performs this function, the route that has been established from one device to another is called a virtual circuit.

LAYER 2 - DATA LINK LAYER
The data link layer is responsible for gaining access to the network and transmitting the physical block of data from one device to another. It includes the error checking necessary to ensure an accurate transmission. This layer is the communications protocol that is most commonly referenced and often implies the specifications for Layer 1 as well. See "Categories of Data Link Protocols" on the following page.

LAYER 1 - PHYSICAL LAYER
The physical layer defines the actual set of wires, plugs and electrical signals that connect the sending and receiving devices to the network. The RS-422 interface is a common standard in this layer, and the RS-232 interface is a common standard for personal computers.

Categories of Data Link Protocols

The data link layer (layer 2 of the OSI model) is the most commonly referenced in communications because it is responsible for packaging the data for transmission and transmitting it. Packaging refers to breaking up the data into blocks of a specified length and appending codes to it for identification and error checking. The data link protocol often includes the electrical and physical specifications (layer 1 of the OSI model) as well.

Following are the major categories of data link protocols:

ASYNCHRONOUS TRANSMISSION

Originating from mechanical teletypewriters, asynchronous transmission sends one character at a time out on the communications line with start and stop bits appended to each character. It is the common form of personal computer communications outside of local area networks, and it is widely used for connecting terminals to minicomputers and timesharing services. The most elementary asynchronous protocols, called *ASCII* or *teletype* protocols, provide little or no error checking and are only acceptable for text messages. The serial port on a personal computer is an asynchronous transmission channel, and Xmodem, Ymodem and Kermit are typical error checking protocols.

SYNCHRONOUS TRANSMISSION

Developed for higher speeds and higher volumes of transmission than asynchronous protocols, synchronous transmission sends a block of data out on the line at one time, with both the sending and receiving stations synchronized to each other. Synchronous protocols have extensive error checking. Examples are IBM's SDLC, Digital's DDCMP, and the international standard, HDLC.

LOCAL AREA NETWORK PROTOCOLS

Developed for medium transmission speeds between personal computers, local area networks interconnect up to thousands of users. The networks typically use collision detection (CSMA/CD) or token passing methods for gaining access to the network. Examples are IBM's Token Ring, Datapoint's ARCNET, Xerox's Ethernet and AT&T's Starlan. In time, fiber optic local area networks will provide the capacity to handle large volumes of high-resolution graphics as well as voice and video.

THE CONCEPT

Imagine two computers "talking" to each other in this simulated data link protocol:

Are you there? **Yes, I am.** Are you ready to receive? **Yes, I am.** Here comes the message--bla, bla, bla-- did you get it? **Yes, I did.** Here comes the next part--bla, bla, bla-- did you get it? **No, I didn't.** Here it comes again-- bla, bla, bla-- did you get it? **Yes, I did.** There is no more. Goodbye. **Goodbye.**

outline font

An *outline font* is a set of outlines for each character. The outline characters are converted into bit maps (dots) before printing. See *scalable fonts*.

outline processor

An *outline processor* is a software program that allows the user to type in thoughts and organize them into an outline form.

output

Output is any computer-generated information in printed hard copy, video display or machine readable form, such as disk and tape.

output area

An *output area* is a reserved segment of memory that is used to lay out data or text in order to be transferred to an output device such as a disk or tape. Same as *buffer*.

output bound

Output bound refers to a computer that is slowed down by its output functions, typically to slow-speed communications lines or to printers. See *print buffer*.

output device

An *output device* is any peripheral device that receives output from the computer, such as a video display screen, printer, card punch or COM unit. Although disk and tape drives receive output from the computer, they are considered storage devices.

overflow error

An *overflow error* occurs when calculated data cannot fit within the designated field. The result field is usually left blank or is filled with some special character in order to flag the error condition.

overhead

Overhead is the amount of processing time taken up by system software, such as the operating system, teleprocessing monitor or database manager.

overlay

(1) An *overlay* is any preprinted and precut form that is placed over a screen, keys or tablet to identify the various parts of it, such as a keyboard template that identifies the function keys.

(2) An *overlay* is a program segment that is called into memory when required. When a program exceeds the memory capacity of the machine it's running in, the parts of the program that are not continuously used can be set up as overlays. Each time an overlay is called in, the instructions and associated user functions in the previous overlay are lost. The associated delays from calling in overlays are only noticeable on a floppy disk computer.

overstrike

(1) *Overstrike* is to type over an existing character.

(2) An *overstrike* is a character with a line through it.

overwrite mode

Overwrite mode is an entry mode that "writes over" existing characters when the cursor is on existing text and keys are pressed. Contrast with *insert mode*, which adds new text into existing text.

PABX

(Private Automatic Branch eXchange) A *PABX* is an inhouse telephone switching machine that electronically interconnects one telephone extension to another, as well as to the outside telephone system.

Modern PABXs are controlled by computers that perform various telephone management functions, such as least cost routing for outside calls, call forwarding and conference calling, as well as elaborate accounting of the telephone calls handled. When PABXs are adapted or designed for digital traffic as well as voice traffic, they are called digital PABXs. The term PABX is used synonymously with *PBX*.

pack/unpack

(1) *Pack/unpack* is to compress/decompress data on a storage device.

(2) *Pack/unpack* are instructions that convert a decimal number into packed decimal format and vice versa.

package

See *software package*.

packaged software

See *software package*.

packed decimal

Packed decimal is a storage mode for decimal numbers that places two decimal digits into a single byte. Each digit occupies four bits of the byte, thereby reducing the storage space by half. The sign bit occupies four bits in the least significant byte.

packet switching

Packet switching is a technique for handling high-volume traffic in a communications network. Packet switching breaks apart all messages to be transmitted into fixed length units called packets. The packets are routed to their destination through the most expedient route, and all the packets in a single message may not travel the same route. The destination computer reassembles the packets into their appropriate sequence. This method is used to efficiently handle messages of different lengths and priorities in a single network. X.25 is an international standard for a packet switching network.

packing density

Packing density is the number of bits or tracks per inch of recording surface. The packing density determines how much storage is available on a storage unit, such as a magnetic disk. Packing density also refers to the number of memory bits or other electronic components on a chip.

padding

Padding is any character used to fill up the unused portion of a data structure, such as a field. For example, if an item of data does not take up the full length of a fixed length field, the rest of the field is padded with blanks or zeros.

paddle

A *paddle* is an input device that has a dial and controls the cursor on screen in a back-and-forth motion. Used primarily in video games, paddles are used to hit balls, move missiles, and steer objects such as automobiles or rockets. The paddle usually has one or more buttons that can be used to start and stop the game or fire a missile. Objects on screen that can be moved in all directions are controlled more easily with a joy stick than a paddle.

page

(1) In virtual memory systems, a *page* is a segment of the program that is transferred into memory.

(2) In videotex systems, a *page* is a transmitted frame.

(3) In word processing, a *page* is a printed page.

page break

In printing, a *page break* marks the end of a page. A hard page break is one that is inserted by the user, and the page will always break at that location. A soft page break is one that is created by a word processing or report program based on current settings. The soft page break will change if the page length setting is changed or more data is added.

page description language

A *page description language* (PDL) is a high-level language for defining printer output. If an application program outputs a page description language instead of the specific codes required by the printer, that output can be printed on any printer that supports that page description language.

With a page description language, much of the character and graphics shaping is done within the printer rather than within the user's computer. Instead of downloading an entire font from the computer to the printer, which includes the design of each character, a command to build a particular font with a specific point size is sent, and the printer creates the characters of the font from basic design elements for that particular font style. Likewise, a command to draw a circle is sent to the printer rather than sending the actual bits of the circle image.

page makeup

Page makeup is the setting up, or formatting, of a printed page, which includes the layout of headers, footers, columns, page numbers, graphics, rules and borders.

page printer

A *page printer* is a printer that prints a page at a time. See *laser printer* and *ion deposition*.

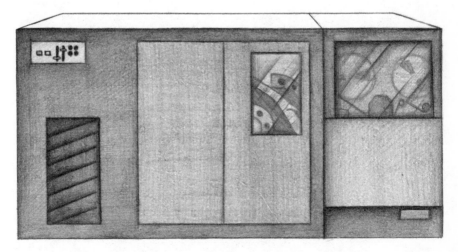

PAGE PRINTER

PageMaker

PageMaker is a desktop publishing program from Aldus Corporation. Originally introduced for the Macintosh in 1985, PageMaker and the Macintosh set the standard for desktop publishing. In fact, Paul Brainerd, president of Aldus, coined the term "desktop publishing." An IBM compatible pc version of PageMaker was introduced in 1987, which has also been widely accepted.

pagination

(1) *Pagination* is the numbering of pages.

(2) *Pagination* refers to the laying out of printed pages, which includes the setting up and printing of columns, rules and borders. Although pagination is used synonymously with *page makeup*, the term often refers to the printing of long manuscripts rather than the laying out of graphics and text for brochures.

paging

Paging is the transfer of program segments into and out of memory in a virtual memory environment.

paint

Paint is to fill an area with a shade, color or image. In computer graphics, paint means to literally "paint" the screen, using a graphics tablet or mouse to simulate a paintbrush. It also refers to pointing to a specific area on the screen and filling it with color. Paint refers to the transfer of any dot matrix image, such as in the expression, "The laser printer paints the image onto a photosensitive drum." It also refers to the free-form ability of designing a screen layout by typing anywhere on the screen, for example, "To paint the screen with text."

paint program

A *paint program* is a graphics program that allows the user to simulate painting on the screen with the use of a graphics tablet or mouse. Paint programs create raster graphics images.

PAL

(1) (Programmable Array Logic) Same as *programmable logic array*. See *gate array*.

(2) (Paradox Application Language) *PAL* is the programming language in the Paradox relational database management system.

(3) *PAL* is the European television standard that uses 625 lines of resolution, 100 more lines than the NTSC standard in the United States.

palette

In computer graphics, a *palette* is the total range of colors that can be used for display, although typically only a smaller number can be used at one time. Palette may also refer to a list of functions or modes.

paper tape

Paper tape is a storage medium that holds data as patterns of punched holes. It is a slow, low-capacity storage medium that, although extremely popular in the first half of the century, is used in limited applications today. A paper tape machine, like magnetic tape, is a sequential access storage device.

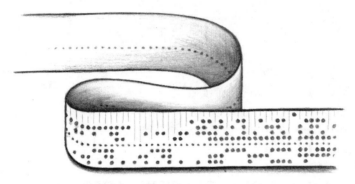

PAPER TAPE

paperless office

The *paperless office* is an office in which all information is stored in electronic form. Long predicted since the beginning of computer systems, the paperless office is still somewhat of a myth. Although paper usage has been reduced in many organizations, it has also increased in many others. Today's personal computers make it easy to spit out any number of copies of a document.

However, in time, laptop computers with immense amounts of storage and ultra-high-resolution screens will become commonplace, and will serve to replace paper when a person is travelling. In the future, optical fiber networks will allow anyone at home or in the office to send data, text, pictures, voice and video anywhere in the world electronically. Also, people will eventually get used to the idea that a paper source document is no longer better proof of a transaction than its electronic form. As laser printers improve, especially color laser printers, it will be very easy for everyone to reproduce any document, no matter how complicated it is. As a result, paper proof will have less validity. As these events begin to coincide, the paperless office will indeed become a reality.

paradigm

A *paradigm*, pronounced "para-dime," means model, example or pattern. The term is gaining popularity in general and is being used more frequently within the computer industry.

Paradox

Paradox is a relational database management system from Ansa/Borland that runs on IBM compatible pcs. Paradox is a full-featured program that uses a Lotus menu for its interactive processing and has a complete programming language, called "PAL," for application development. Paradox is known for its well-designed user interface and ease of use; especially its query by example method for asking questions. Paradox allows users to ask complicated questions and select data from multiple files quickly and easily compared with other database systems.

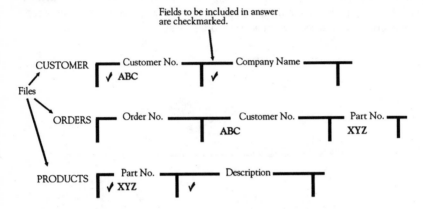

A RELATIONAL QUERY IN PARADOX

This example links three files together for a query. The ABC links the customer file with the orders file by customer number. The XYZ links the orders file with the products file by part number. The ABC and XYZ are arbitrary examples. The user can type in any words or letters to be used as matching examples as long as they are the same in both records.

parallel interface

A *parallel interface* is a multi-line channel that transfers one or more bytes simultaneously. For example, personal computers often connect printers via a Centronics 36-pin parallel interface, which transfers one byte at a time over eight wires. Additional wires are used for other electronic signalling. Larger computers use parallel interfaces that transfer more than one byte at a time. Contrast with *serial interface*, which uses only one line for data and transfers one bit after the other over that line.

parallel port

A *parallel port* is an external interface to a printer or other peripheral device. On IBM compatible pcs, the parallel port typically uses a DB-25 connector at the computer side and a Centronics 36-pin connector at the printer side. See *serial and parallel port* and *plugs & sockets*.

parallel processing

Parallel processing is simultaneous processing of more than one event or task within a computer. It usually refers to various internal design techniques that provide overlapped processing within a single computer, such as with vector processors or database machines, but it may be used to refer to a coprocessor or multiprocessing environment where two or more CPUs are working together. See *vector processor*, *pipeline processing* and *DMA*.

parameter

A *parameter* is a value that is entered by the user in order to customize the program for the user's needs. Parameters are any information needed by the program, such as file names, coordinates, limitations, exceptions and ranges of values. If a parameter is optional, and the user does not enter a value for it, then the default setting is used.

parameter-driven

Parameter-driven is a program that requires parameters for its use. It implies that the program solves a problem that has to be entirely or partially described with values (parameters) from the user.

PARC

(Palo Alto Research Center) PARC is Xerox Corporation's research and development center. The Smalltalk programming language and the icon-oriented interface, which is so popular on Apple's Macintosh series, were invented and developed at PARC. Established in 1970, it occupies a 200,000 square foot facility in the Stanford University Industrial Park in Palo Alto, California.

parent-child

In database management, a *parent* is a record or file that contains required data about a subject, such as employees and customers. The parent data must exist before it can have children; for example, the *child* of a customer file may be the order file. Parent-child relationships are used to express how data is related and accessed.

PARENT-CHILD

parity bit

A *parity bit* is an extra bit attached to the byte, character or word used to detect errors in transmission.

parity checking

Parity checking is an error detection technique that checks for the accurate transmission of digital data either internally within the computer system or externally over a network. Parity checking uses the parity bit, for example, the ninth bit of each byte, to hold a 0 or a 1 depending on the content of the byte. For even parity systems, the parity bit is made a 1 when there are an even number of bits in the byte. In odd parity systems, the parity bit is a 1 when the byte contains an odd number of bits.

Each time the byte is transmitted from one place to another, the destination byte is checked for correct parity. If a bit was lost during transmission, parity checking will detect it.

parity error

A *parity error* is an error condition that occurs when the parity bit of a character is found to be incorrect.

parser

A *parser* is the program module that performs parsing operations in a computer language.

parsing

Parsing is the analysis of a sentence or language statement that breaks down the words into basic units that can be converted into machine language. For example, in the dBASE expression, SUM SALARY FOR TITLE = "MANAGER", the parsing must identify the word SUM as the primary command, the word FOR as a conditional search, the word TITLE as a field name and the word MANAGER as the data to be searched for.

Parsing may also be used to break down a natural language statement, such as GIVE ME A TOTAL OF ALL THE MANAGERS' SALARIES into the commands required by a high-level language, such as in the example above.

partition

A *partition* is a reserved portion of main memory that is used to hold a program while it's being executed. Older mainframe operating systems required that the amount of memory be specified by the systems programmer before the programs were run. Modern operating systems dynamically create the necessary partitions for multitasking.

Pascal

Pascal is a high-level programming language developed by Niklaus Wirth (Swiss) in the early 1970s. Pascal is noted for its structured programming design, which caused it to achieve popularity in the academic communities in both Europe and the United States. Pascal is available in both interpreter and compiler form.

Pascal has unique ways for defining variables. For example, a range of values or set of unique values can be stated and applied to any variable. If any other type of data is stored in the variable, the program will generate an error at run time. This automatic error trapping is very helpful in program development. Another feature, called a set, is an array-like structure that can hold a varying number of predefined values. Sets can be matched and manipulated providing the programmer with powerful non-numeric programming capabilities.

Pascal set a unique standard, which has had strong influence on programming languages that followed it, such as ADA, dBASE and PAL, although most of them have not implemented all the features. Pascal was named after the French mathematician, Blaise Pascal. See *Pascaline* below.

The following example in Turbo Pascal converts fahenheit to centigrade:

```
program convert;
var
fahr, cent : integer;
begin
 write('Enter fahrenheit ');
 readln(fahr);
 cent := (fahr - 32) * 5 / 9;
 writeln('Centigrade is ',cent)
end.
```

THE PASCALINE

(Courtesy The Computer Museum, Boston)

Pascaline

The *Pascaline* was a calculating machine that was developed in 1642 by Blaise Pascal, a French mathematician and philosopher. The Pascaline could perform only addition and subtraction, and it was not the most advanced machine of its time. However, it received a lot of attention because 50 of them were built and placed in prominent locations throughout Europe. Although the device was expensive to repair, accountants of the era expressed concern that they might be displaced by this technological advancement.

password

A *password* is a word or code used to identify an authorized user. Passwords are usually managed by the operating system or database management system. Passwords serve as a security measure against unauthorized use of the computer or access to data; however, the computer can compare the password only with a stored set of passwords and has no way of knowing whether the person using the system is really legitimate or not.

paste

Paste refers to inserting data into a file or document. See *cut & paste*.

patch

Patch refers to making a temporary or quick fix to a program that doesn't work. Eventually, too many patches in a program render it inefficient from a machine-processing standpoint and difficult to understand by either the original or another programmer. Patch also refers to changing the machine code instead of the source code when there is no time to change and recompile the source language program.

path

(1) In communications, a *path* is the route between any two nodes. Same as line, channel, link or circuit.

(2) In database management, a *path* is the route from one set of data to another, for example, from customers to orders.

(3) In programming, a *path* is the set route taken by the program to process a set of data.

(4) In IBM compatible pcs running Microsoft's DOS or OS/2, a *path* is the hierarchical route to a file directory on the disk. For example, if a file named MYLIFE is located in a subdirectory called STORIES within a directory called JOE, the path entered at the operating system prompt to retrieve that file would be: \JOE\STORIES\MYLIFE.

PBX

(Private Branch eXchange) A *PBX* was an inhouse telephone switching system that required manual operation to get an outside line. PBXs were replaced with electronic systems called PABXs (private automatic branch exchanges); however, the two terms are used synonymously.

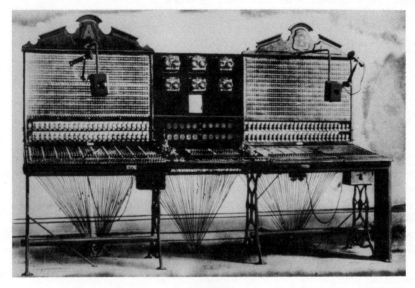

PBX

(Courtesy AT&T)

This PBX was installed in Bangor, Maine in 1883.

PC, pc

(1) (Personal Computer) A *PC* is a first-generation IBM personal computer, which includes the PC, PCjr, XT, AT, Portable and Convertible models. The term may be used to explicitly exclude the second-generation Personal System/2 series, or it may refer to all IBM personal computers. In this book, upper case "PC" refers to IBM's first-generation computer series, and lower case "pc" refers to all IBM personal computers, including the PS/2 series.

(2) (Personal Computer) *PC* is used loosely to refer to any personal computer.

(3) (Printed Circuit) Before personal computers, *PC* always referred to printed circuits.

PC board

See *printed circuit board*.

PC bus

The *PC bus* is the bus architecture used in first-generation IBM compatible pcs. The PC bus comes in two versions: an 8-bit bus and a 16-bit bus, the latter also known as the AT bus. 8-bit boards will fit into both 8-bit and 16-bit buses, but 16-bit boards will fit only in the 16-bit bus. None of the PC bus boards will plug into the Micro Channel bus used in the PS/2 series.

PC compatibility

See *IBM personal computer*.

PC keyboard

The *PC keyboard* is the keyboard that was introduced on the original IBM PC in 1981. Often criticized for its non-standard placement of the return and left shift keys, it set a standard which was followed by countless other compatible vendors. The PC keyboard provides a keypad that contains both numeric keys and cursor keys. When the NUM LOCK (numeric lock) is depressed, the keypad serves as a numeric data entry keyboard. In normal mode, the keys become arrow keys and move the cursor. Regardless of key placement, a lot of people like the feel of IBM keyboards.

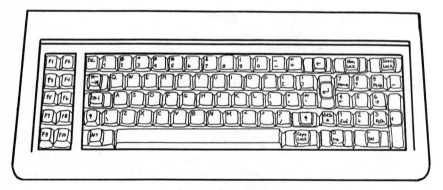

PC KEYBOARD

PC Paintbrush

PC Paintbrush is a paint program from ZSoft Corporation that runs on IBM compatible pcs. PC Paintbrush is a very popular program that has set an industry standard graphics file format. The PCX raster graphics format is generated and accepted by many graphics, word processing and desktop publishing programs.

PCB

See *printed circuit board*.

PC-DOS

PC-DOS is another term for Microsoft's DOS operating system that runs on IBM personal computers. The term is often used to differentiate between the DOS operating system supplied with an IBM machine and the MS-DOS version supplied with an IBM compatible machine. PC-DOS and MS-DOS are usually identical except for the way they deal with the BASIC programming language, and IBM compatible computers are often tested with PC-DOS to find out how compatible they truly are.

PCL

(Printer Control Language) *PCL* is the printer language from Hewlett-Packard that activates the HP LaserJet printers. PCL has become an industry standard that is provided on many different brands of laser printers and typesetters. If a machine supports the PCL language, it accepts the same printer files that are sent to LaserJet printers.

PCM

(1) (Pulse Code Modulation) *PCM* is a technique for digitizing speech by sampling the sound waves and converting each sample into a binary number. The PCM algorithms are implemented within the chip.

(2) (Plug Compatible Manufacturer) A *PCM* is an organization that makes a computer or electronic device that is compatible with an existing machine.

p-code

See *UCSD P-system*.

PDES

(Product Data Exchange Specification) *PDES* is a standard format for the exchange of data between advanced computer-aided design (CAD) and computer-aided manufacturing (CAM) programs. PDES describes a complete product, including the geometric aspects of the images as well as manufacturing features, tolerance specifications, material properties and finish specifications. See *IGES Organization*.

PDL

See *page description language*.

PDP

(Programmed Data Processor) *PDP* is a series of minicomputers manufactured by Digital Equipment Corporation. The first PDP machine was the PDP-1, an 18-bit computer that was introduced in late 1959. Its $120,000 price tag was considerably less than the million dollar machines of the time, and 50 of them were built. In 1962, the PDP-4 cost half as much as the PDP-1, and 65 of them were built. The PDP-7, 9 and 15 were 18-bit successors to the PDP-1, and were introduced throughout the 1960s and early 1970s.

PDP-8

(Courtesy Charles Babbage Institute, University of Minnesota)

In 1963, Digital introduced the PDP-5, a 12-bit computer. Following it in 1965 was the PDP-8, Digital's first machine designed for mass production and its first major success. Starting at around $20,000 in 1965, the PDP-8 legitimized the minicomputer industry. By the late 1970s, with its processor on a single chip, the PDP-8 was available for under $3,000 and found its way into the DECmate workstations used primarily for word processing.

In 1963, Digital introduced its largest PDP model, the 36-bit PDP-6. It was followed by various PDP-10 models during the 1970s, and eventually this series evolved into the DECsystem 10 and DECsystem 20.

In 1970, Digital introduced the 16-bit PDP-11, which would become the most widely used minicomputer in the world. Over 50,000 systems were sold during the 1970s.

The PDP series was followed by the VAX series in 1977; however, PDP-11s are still in production.

peek-a-boo

Peek-a-boo refers to checking for the same character code in the same column of two or more punched cards by placing them on top of each other and looking through them.

peek/poke

Peek/poke are instructions that view and alter a single byte of memory. *Peek* displays the contents of the byte specified, and *poke* changes it to a specific value. These instructions are used to alter specifically known memory locations.

peer

In communications, a *peer* is a functional unit that is on the same protocol layer as another.

peer-to-peer communications

Peer-to-peer communications is the communicating from one user to another user in the network. It implies the ability to initiate the session at the user's discretion.

pel

Same as *pixel*.

pen plotter

See *plotter*.

people/machine interface

See *user interface*.

PEPPER board

PEPPER boards are graphics display boards for IBM compatible pcs from Number Nine Computer Corporation. PEPPER boards provide the extremely high-resolution images that are required in computer-aided design (CAD), high-end graphics and certain desktop publishing applications.

peripheral

A *peripheral* is any hardware device connected to a computer, such as monitors, keyboards, printers, plotters, disk and tape drives, graphics tablets, scanners, joy sticks, game paddles and mice.

peripheral controller

A *peripheral controller* is a set of electronic circuits that control the operation of a peripheral device such as a screen, printer, disk or tape. The peripheral controller, or control unit, receives electronic signals from the CPU, and, in turn, sends the appropriate electronic signals to the peripheral unit to perform actual positioning, reading and writing functions. In a personal computer, a peripheral controller is usually contained on one printed circuit board. In large computers, peripheral controllers can be stand-alone units.

permanent memory

Same as *non-volatile memory*.

permutation

A *permutation* is one possible combination of items out of a larger group of items. For example, with the group of numbers 1, 2 and 3, there are six possible permutations of any two numbers: 12, 21, 13, 31, 23 and 32.

perpendicular recording

See *vertical recording*.

persistence

In a CRT, *persistence* is the length of time a phosphor dot will remain illuminated after it has been energized. Long-persistence phosphors reduce flicker, but generate ghost-like images that linger on screen for a fraction of a second.

personal computer

A *personal computer* is a computer that is designed for an individual user. The personal computer is functionally identical to larger computers that serve multiple users and have greater storage capacities.

Personal computers are typically used for applications, such as word processing, spreadsheets, database management and various graphics-based programs, such as computer-aided design (CAD) and desktop publishing. They are also used to handle traditional business applications, such as invoicing, payroll and general ledger. At home, personal computers are primarily used for games, education and word processing.

With the addition of a modem and the use of a telephone line, a personal computer becomes a terminal to the outside world, capable of retrieving information from any data bank or information service that provides public information.

There are a wide variety of personal computers on the market, priced from $100 to over $10,000. The size of the computer is based on its memory and disk capacity. Its speed is based on the microprocessor that runs it. Its visual quality is based on the resolution of its display screen and printer.

Most personal computers run one program at a time, but multitasking machines, which run more than one program concurrently, will become commonplace in the 1990s.

Major Suppliers of Personal Computers

The personal computer world is overwhelmingly dominated by IBM and IBM compatible pcs. There are dozens of vendors and hundreds of models to choose from, although all available models fall into a handful of categories (see *IBM personal computers*).

The next largest supplier is Apple Computer, which provides the Apple II and Macintosh families. The Apple II series is the most widely used computer in elementary and high schools as well as at home. The Macintoshes are popular in small businesses and in the home, and they are also used in large corporations, being especially popular for graphics-based applications, such as desktop publishing, illustration and computer-aided design (CAD).

Both Atari and Commodore continue to carve out a niche for their personal computer lines, which are popular as home and small business computers. Each of them has support from software vendors providing a well rounded supply of applications as is found in the IBM and Apple worlds.

The History of Personal Computers

The personal computer has revolutionized the computer industry and brought millions of non-computer people face to face with a computer. Although Xerox had been working on advanced personal computer concepts in the mid-1970s with its Alto computer, the commerical business of personal computing began in 1977, when Apple Computer, Radio Shack and Commodore introduced the first

THE FIRST PERSONAL COMPUTER

(Courtesy Xerox Corporation)

In the mid 1970s, Xerox developed the Alto computer, which was the forerunner of its Star workstation and the inspiration for Apple's Lisa and Macintosh computers.

off-the-shelf computers that could be purchased like any other electric appliance in a retail store. Before these three companies offered their wares, computers were seen only in professional sales offices and showrooms.

The first generation of personal computers used an 8-bit microprocessor with a maximum memory capacity of 64K and floppy disks for storage. The Apple II, Atari 500, and Commodore 64 became popular home computers. Apple was also successful in the business market after VisiCalc, the first spreadsheet, was introduced. However, the business world was soon dominated by the Z80 microprocessor and CP/M operating system used by countless vendors in the early 1980s, such as Vector Graphic, NorthStar, Osborne and Kaypro. By 1983, hard disks were beginning to show up on these machines, but the CP/M world was soon to be history.

In 1981, IBM introduced the PC, an Intel 8088-based machine, which was slightly faster than the genre, but had 10 times the memory of existing machines. It was floppy-based, and its DOS operating system was provided by Microsoft, which also provided a compatible version (MS-DOS) for the clone makers. CP/M vendors converted to the IBM camp virtually overnight, and it became the standard for the industry. The IBM PC was successfully cloned by Compaq and unsuccessfully cloned by most others. However, by the time IBM announced its AT (advanced technology) model in 1983, the compatible manufacturers finally suceeded in making very compatible computers and eventually succeeded in collectively grabbing the majority of the IBM personal computer market.

IBM's AT set a performance standard with the 80286 chip, but although the hardware can work with up to 16 megabytes of memory, its DOS operating system can't handle more than one megabyte, and only 640K of it is usable for applications. In order to use more memory, users have to plug in special EMS memory boards or use add-on environments, such as DESQview.

In 1983, Apple announced the Lisa, which was a Motorola 68000-based machine that included integrated applications, in which, for example, you could move data out of a spreadsheet and into a word processing document. The Lisa used a redesigned version of the Xerox Star, which simulates a user's desktop by displaying graphical objects (icons) on screen and providing a mouse to point to them. The Lisa was ahead of its time, but its $10,000 price tag and sluggish performance made it a flop. Apple all but abandoned it in favor of the Macintosh, an abbreviated version of the Lisa introduced in 1984. The Macintosh caught on immediately and has had a steady following ever since, although it's captured only a fraction of the business market compared to the IBM compatible pc world.

In 1986, Compaq ushered in the next generation of personal computers with the Compaq 386, an Intel 80386-based machine, which handles huge amounts of memory and disk space. The 80386 machines will become the dominant processor in the 1990s, since they are not only more powerful than the 80286 (IBM AT), but they are capable of multitasking existing applications more effectively.

In 1987, IBM announced a new series of personal computers called the PS/2, providing improved graphics, a new bus architecture and 3 1/2" microfloppy disks. The PS/2 Model 80, IBM's first 80386-based system was introduced. The OS/2 operating system, jointly developed by IBM and Microsoft, was also introduced to take advantage of the larger capacities of the new series. Although, in order to use OS/2 effectively, all applications must be upgraded to work with it. In the same year, more powerful Macintoshes were announced by Apple, including the

Mac SE and Mac II, the latter a Motorola 68020-based system that is capable of running a certain amount of IBM pc software when a coprocessor board is plugged in. The Mac II has opened up new doors for Apple and has become a very competitive graphics-based workstation.

Personal computers at the 80386 and 68020 performance levels are starting to compete with minicomputer workstations for high-end graphics and CAD applications, which require large amounts of calculating power. These high-performance workstations will encourage the development of more artificial intelligence and high-resolution graphics applications that are the backbone of the next generation.

In order to tie together all the personal computers that exist within an organization, networking has become an important issue, and, throughout the 1990s, will be the major issue. The personal computer industry sprang up without any cohesive planning. All of a sudden, it was there, and individual machines were bought to solve individual problems, such as automating a budget, typing a letter or searching a file. However, the real data in an organization exists in the mainframe database, and it doesn't serve the organization well to have an employee retype the reports from the mainframe into the micro in order to analyze and manipulate it. The personal computer, originally, out of the control of MIS professionals, is now squarely back in their hands. Personal computers can serve as invaluable processing and communications tools for the user when they are designed into the fabric of the organization along with all the other computer systems.

As stand-alone machines, personal computers place creative capacity into the hands of an individual that would have cost millions of dollars less than 20 years ago. The use of personal computers is slowly but surely shifting the balance of power from the large company to the small company, from the elite to the masses, from the wealthy to individuals of modest means. In 10 years, the personal computer field has revolutionized the computer industry, and no matter how hard it is to believe, this is just the beginning!

Personal System/2

See IBM *personal computer*.

PET computer

(Personal Electronic Transaction computer) The PET *computer*, manufactured by Commodore Business Machines, was one of the first three personal computers introduced in the late 1970s. It used the CP/M operating system and provided floppy disks for storage.

PFS:Professional Write

PFS:Professional Write is a word processing program from Software Publishing Corporation that runs on IBM compatible pcs. Professional Write is a program that is very easy to learn and use and meets the needs of many people who write uncomplicated letters and memos. Softwar Publishing provides an entire series of PFS programs for database, spreadsheets and other applications.

PGA

(1) (Professional Graphics Adapter) *PGA* is a video display board from IBM that is available as a plug-in board for IBM PC and compatible personal computers. PGA generates medium-resolution color text and graphics at 640x480 pixels with 256 colors. The PGA is a video coprocessor that provides 3-D drawing functions. Although supported by CAD programs, PGA was rarely supported by general business applications.

(2) (Pin Grid Array) A *PGA* is a housing for a chip that contains a high density of pins. For example, a 1.5" square PGA can have nearly 200 pins. PGAs are used when large amounts of input and output are required.

phase change recording

Phase change recording is an optical recording technique that uses a laser to alter the crystalline structure of a metallic surface. The crystal structure is altered to create a bit that reflects or absorbs light when the bits are read. See *optical disk*.

phase encoding

Phase encoding is a magnetic recording technique used for high-speed devices that records a 0 bit as a split negative-positive sequence and a 1 bit as a positive-negative sequence.

phase locked

Phase locked is a technique for maintaining synchronization in an electronic circuit. The circuit receives its timing from input signals, but also provides a feedback circuit for synchronization.

phase modulation

In communications, *phase modulation* is a transmission technique that modulates (merges) a data signal into a fixed carrier frequency by modifying the phase of the carrier wave. Contrast with *frequency modulation* (FM) and *amplitude modulation* (AM), which are the two other major techniques for modulating a carrier.

phase modulation recording

Same as *phase encoding*.

phase shift keying

Phase shift keying is a method of modulating data onto a carrier by modifying the phase of the waves. Contrast with *frequency shift keying*, which modifies the frequency of the carrier.

PHIGS

(**P**rogrammer's **H**ierarchical **I**nteractive **G**raphics **S**tandard) *PHIGS* is a graphics system and language that is used to create 2-D and 3-D graphics images. Like the GKS standard, PHIGS is a device independent interface between the application program and the graphics subsystem. PHIGS manages graphics objects in a hierarchical manner so that a complete assembly can be specified with all of its subassemblies. PHIGS is a very comprehensive standard requiring high-performance workstations and host processing.

phone connector

A *phone connector* is a plug and socket for a two or three-wire coaxial cable that is commonly used to plug microphones and other audio equipment into amplifiers. Contrast with *phono connector*, which is also used with audio as well as video cables.

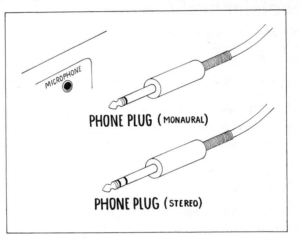

phoneme

A *phoneme* is an utterance of speech, such as "k," "ch," and "sh," that is used in synthetic speech systems to compose words for audio output.

phono connector

A *phono connector*, also called an *RCA connector*, is a plug and socket for a two-wire coaxial cable that is used for audio and video signals. It is commonly used to interconnect high fidelity components as well as the composite

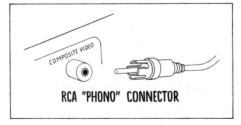

video output from a computer to a television, such as on the Apple II computer series. Contrast with *phone connector*, which is typically used for microphones and similar audio interconnections. See *F connector* and *plugs & sockets*.

phosphor

Phosphor is a rare earth material that is used to coat the inside face of a cathode ray tube (CRT). When struck by an electron beam, the phosphor emits a visible light for a few milliseconds. In color displays, red, green and blue phosphor dots are grouped as a cluster.

photocomposition

Photocomposition is the composition of a printed page using electrophotographic machines, such as phototypesetters and laser printers. See *page makeup* and *pagination*.

photolithography

Photolithography is a technique that uses a photomask to imprint a design onto an object. For example, the design of the circuit paths and electronic elements on a chip are transferred onto a wafer's surface using this method. A photomask is created with the design for each layer of the chip. The wafer is coated with a light-sensitive film and is exposed to light shining through the photomask. The light reaching the wafer hardens the film, and when the wafer is exposed to an acid bath (wet processing) or hot ions (dry processing), the unhardened areas are etched away.

photomask

A *photomask* is an opaque image on a transluscent plate that is used as a light filter to transfer an image from one device to another. See *chip*.

photomicrography

Photomicrography is the photographing of microscopic images.

photooptic memory

Photooptic memory is a storage device that uses a laser beam to record data onto a photosensitive film. See *optical disk* and *CD ROM*.

photorealistic image synthesis

In computer graphics, *photorealistic image synthesis* is a format for describing a picture that depicts the realism of the actual image. It includes such attributes as surface texture, light sources, motion blur and reflectivity.

photoresist

Photoresist is the light-sensitive film used in photolithography that temporarily holds the pattern to be etched away.

photosensor

A *photosensor* is a light-sensitive device that is used in optical scanning machinery.

phototypesetter

A *phototypesetter* is a device that creates professional-quality text. Input to the phototypesetter comes from the keyboard, over a communications channel or via disk or tape. The output is a paper-like or transparent film that is processed into a camera-ready master for printing. Advanced industrial machines generate the actual printing plates.

Phototypesetters employ various light technologies for the creation of the characters. Older machines use a spinning film strip that is used as a photomask for a particular font. Light passing through the film strip is enlarged by lenses to the appropriate type size, exposing the film. Other machines create images on CRTs that are used to expose the film, and the latest units use lasers to generate the image directly onto the film like a laser printer.

The phototypesetter has always been used to print books, magazines and all commercially printed materials. They were originally the only machines that could handle multiple fonts and text composition capabilities, such as kerning, where space is tightened between letter combinations, such as WA and AV.

Today, low-cost desktop laser printers are being used to typeset text, and although they can't produce the ultra-fine lines of the high-resolution (1,200 dots per inch and more) phototypesetters, they can produce excellent printed matter.

physical

Physical implies dealing with the computer at its lowest or most basic level. For example, a physical address is the machine address built into a peripheral device or storage location. A physical interface, or physical level interface, is the plug and socket used to interconnect two hardware devices. A physical link layer interconnects two communications devices. A physical link is a pointer embedded in data that points to other data. Contrast with *logical*, which implies a symbolic reference to something. Eventually, the logical must wind up being physical in order to get anything done. See *logical & physical*.

Physical Unit 2.1

See *PU 2.1*.

pica

(1) In word processing, *pica* is a font that prints at 10 characters per linear inch.

(2) In typography, a *pica* is approximately 1/6th of an inch.

Pick operating system

The *Pick operating system* is an operating environment from Pick Systems that runs on IBM compatible pcs and a variety of minicomputers and mainframes. It includes a multiuser, multitasking, virtual memory operating system and a relational database management system.

The Pick system was originally developed by Dick Pick, who created a system for the U. S. Army while working at TRW Corporation. He later transformed it into the Reality operating system for Microdata. Eventually, Pick obtained the right to license the system to other vendors.

The Pick operating environment is highly praised for its ease of use and flexibility and is used by a number of different vendors that provide multiuser computer systems.

picosecond

A *picosecond*, pronounced "pee-co-second," is one trillionth of a second.

picture

In programming, a *picture* defines the type of data allowed entry into a field or the way a data field is to be printed. A special character is used to represent each character in the field; for example, 9999 represents four numeric digits. XXX999 represents three alphanumeric digits followed by three numeric digits. A picture for a telephone number could be (999) 999-9999. Characters used for pictures are similar but not identical in all programming languages.

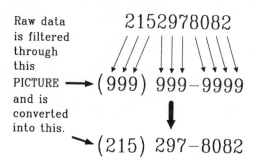

PICTURE FIELD

picture element

See *pixel*.

Picturephone

Picturephone is a video communications service from AT&T that lets users see the individuals that they are talking to. Although many people thought the Picturephone was going to be a reality by the end of the 1980s, it will not become prevalent until after the turn of the century.

PicturePower

PicturePower is a picture database from PictureWare, Inc., that runs on IBM compatible pcs. It is a self-contained database system for text and pictures that is also fully compatible with dBASE III. PicturePower accepts scanned images and provides facilities for editing them. It lets the user build a screen form and place the images in the form along with text.

When used with dBASE, PicturePower links dBASE records to its picture database, and a RAM resident routine allows users to display PicturePower images while working within dBASE.

PicturePower-HC is a High-Compression version that includes an add-in board for compressing images as much as 20 to 1.

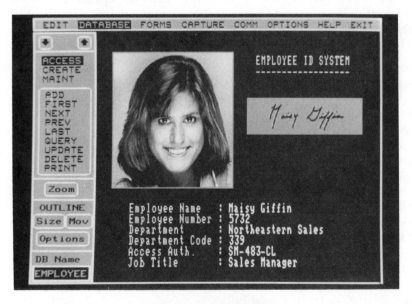

PICTUREPOWER

(Courtesy PictureWare, Inc.)

pie chart

A *pie chart* is a graphical representation of information in which each unit of data is represented as a pie-shaped piece of a circle. See *business graphics*.

piezoelectric

Piezoelectric refers to the electricity generated from a crystal that is subjected to pressure. Certain crystal oscillators and microphones are piezoelectric devices.

PIF file

A *PIF file* is a program description file that is used in Microsoft Windows. It is created with the Windows PIF Editor program, and it holds information that Windows needs to know about the program, such as how much memory it uses and if it bypasses the operating system and writes directly to the screen or takes over the keyboard.

piggyback board

A *piggyback board* is a small printed circuit board that plugs into another printed circuit board in order to enhance its capabilities. Piggyback boards do not plug into the motherboard, but would plug into the boards that plug into the motherboard.

PILOT

(Programmed Inquiry Learning Or Teaching) *PILOT* is a high-level programming language used to generate CAI (computer assisted instruction) programs. PILOT generates question-and-answer types of courseware. A version of PILOT that incorporates turtle graphics runs on Atari personal computers.

PIM

(Personal Information Manager) A *PIM* is a combination word processor, database and desktop accessory program that organizes a variety of information. It allows the user to tie together more loosely structured information than traditional programs. PIMs vary widely, but all of them attempt to provide methods for managing information the way people think about their jobs and functions. Apple's HyperCard is an example of a PIM.

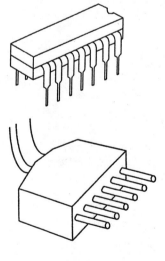

PINS

pin

A *pin* is one of the male leads on a multiple line plug, such as an RS-232 connector. Each pin is connected with its female counterpart to close a circuit. A pin is also one of the footlike leads on a chip that plugs into a socket on the printed circuit board.

PIN

(Personal Identification Number) A *PIN* is a number chosen by the user as a personal password for identification purposes.

pin feed

A *pin feed* is a paper movement method that contains a set of pins on a platen or tractor. The pins engage the paper through perforated holes in its left and right borders.

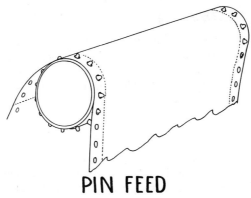

PIN FEED

pinch roller

A *pinch roller* is a small, freely-turning wheel that pushes the magnetic tape against a motor-driven wheel in order to move the tape in a tape drive.

ping-pong

In communications, *ping-pong* refers to switching the transmission to the opposite direction. This is also known as "turning the line around."

ping-pong buffer

See *double buffer*.

pinouts

Pinouts are the description of the function of electronic signals transmitted through each pin in a connector.

PIP

(**P**eripheral **I**nterchange **P**rogram) *PIP* is a utility program in the CP/M operating system that is used to copy and transfer files.

pipe

In an operating system, a *pipe* is a command that directs the output of one function or program into another function or program. In Microsoft DOS and OS/2 operating systems, the pipe symbol is a split vertical line (|). The statement, **dir | sort newlist**, directs the output of the directory list to be sorted and then stored in a file called NEWLIST.

pipeline processing

Pipeline processing is a category of techniques that provide simultaneous, or parallel, processing within the computer It refers to overlapping operations by moving data or instructions into a conceptual pipe with all stages of the pipe processing simultaneously. For example, while one instruction is being executed, the computer is decoding the next instruction.

pitch

The *pitch* is the number of printed characters per inch. For example, pica is 10 characters per inch, and elite is 12 characters per inch. With proportionally spaced characters, the pitch is variable and must be measured as an average.

pixel

(**PIX** [picture] **EL**ement) A *pixel* is the smallest display element on a video display screen. A screen is broken up into thousands of tiny dots, and a pixel is one or more dots that are treated as a unit. A pixel can be one dot on a monochrome screen, three dots (red, green and blue) on color screens, or clusters of these dots.

For monochrome screens, the pixel, normally dark, is energized to different light intensities, creating a range from dark to light. For color, each red, green and blue dot is energized to different intensities, creating a range of colors perceived as the mixture of these dots. Black is all three dots off, white is all three dots on, and grays are even intensities of each color.

The number of memory bits assigned to each pixel determines the number of shades and colors that can be represented. The most economical system is a monochrome display in which one bit is used for one pixel, either on or off. In the most elaborate color display, which uses one full byte for each of the red, green and blue dots, each dot can display 256 different shades, or up to 16,777,216 color combinations per pixel. Considering a high-resolution screen uses about a million pixels, three million bytes of memory must be reserved to hold such a high-resolution screen image.

pixel graphics

Same as *raster graphics*.

PLA

(Programmable Logic Array) See *gate array*.

planar

Planar is the technique developed by Fairchild Instrument that is used to create the sublayers of a transistor in a chip by forcing chemicals under pressure into the exposed areas. The planar process was a major step in the creation of the microchip. Contrast with the earlier *mesa* process, which created more deeply etched channels in the semiconductor material.

planar area

In computer graphics, a *planar area* is an object that has boundaries, such as a square, circle or polygon.

planning system

See *spreadsheet* and *financial planning system*.

plasma display

A *plasma display* is a flat-screen technology that contains an inert ionized gas sandwiched between an x-axis panel and a y-axis panel. An individual dot (pixel) is selectable by charging an x-wire on one panel and a y-wire on the other panel. When the x-y coordinate is charged, the gas in that vicinity glows a bright orange color. A plasma display is also called a gas discharge display.

platen

A *platen* is the long, thin cylinder in a typewriter or printer that guides the paper through it and serves as a backstop for the printing mechanism to bang into. In small desktop printers, the platen has a sprocket on each side of it containing pins that grab the perforated holes in the paper. The sprockets may also be attached to a tractor feed mechanism, which can be adjusted to any paper size. The platen in this type of printer may also be adjusted to pressure feed a single cut sheet of paper as in a typewriter.

platform

A *platform* is the hardware architecture of a particular model or family of computers. The platform is the standard to which software developers write their programs. A platform may also refer to the system software, such as the operating system, network management software and database management system.

PLATO

(Programmed Logic for Automatic Teaching Operations) *PLATO* is an educational system developed by Donald Bitzer and marketed by CDC (Control Data Corporation). PLATO was the first system to use graphics combined with specially developed touch-sensitive screens for interactive use. PLATO users can develop their own courseware or use courseware developed by CDC. PLATO is available on CDC's timesharing computers and requires a special terminal for its use. PLATO has also been adapted to a personal computer for customer use.

platter

A *platter* is one of the disks in a disk pack or hard disk drive. Resembling a small phonograph record covered with magnetic tape, each platter provides a top and bottom recording surface. There are usually from two to eight platters in a hard disk and up to a couple of dozen in large disk packs for minicomputers and mainframes. Sizes vary from three to five inches in diameter for small computers, and up to about 15 inches for large computers.

PL/I

(Programming Language 1) IBM introduced *PL/I* in 1964, along with its new family of 360 computers. PL/I was developed as a general-purpose language combining features from both COBOL and FORTRAN, the two high-level languages then in use. IBM hoped that PL/I would supplant both languages and it would have to support only one language in the future; however, this never came to pass, as PL/I usage has dwindled over the years.

A PL/I program is made up of blocks of code called procedures that can be compiled independently of the main program. In a PL/I program, there is always a main procedure and zero or more additional procedures, each of which can be nested within the main procedure or be placed external to it. Functions, which are procedures that pass arguments back and forth, are also provided in PL/I. PL/I syntax is free-form and requires a semicolon at the end of the statement.

PL/M

(Programming Language for Microprocessors) *PL/M* is a dialect of PL/I developed by Intel as a high-level language for their microprocessors. PL/M+ is an extended version of PL/M, developed by National Semiconductor for its microprocessors.

plot

Plot is to create an image by drawing a series of lines. In programming, a plot statement creates a single vector (line) or a complete circle or box that is made up of several vectors.

plotter

A *plotter* is a graphics printer that draws images with ink pens. Plotters require data in vector graphics format, which makes up an image as a series of point-to-point lines.

Flatbed plotters limit the overall size of the drawing to the fixed height and width of the "bed," onto which the paper is placed for drawing. Flatbed plotters draw by moving the pen in both horizontal and vertical axes.

Drum plotters limit one side of the drawing to the width of the drum, but not the other side, since the paper is continuously moved through it like a standard printer. Drum plotters draw by moving the pen along one axis and the paper along the other.

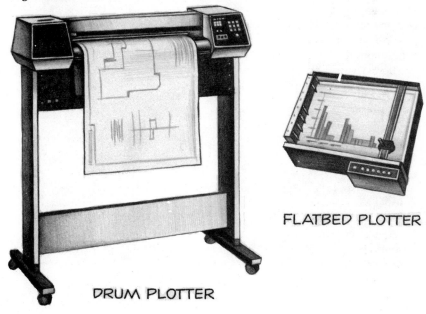

FLATBED PLOTTER

DRUM PLOTTER

PLP

(Presentation Level Protocol) *PLP* is the North American standard protocol for videotex transmission.

plug compatible

A *plug compatible* device is hardware that is designed to perform exactly like another vendor's product. For example, a plug compatible CPU is a computer that runs the exact same software as the machine it's compatible with. A plug compatible peripheral device is one that can plug into the computer and work exactly the same as the device it's replacing.

plugboard

A *plugboard* is a board with holes in it that is used for programming a machine. Each hole is a socket for an input or an output signal. One end of a wire is inserted into an output socket, and the other end is inserted into an input socket, which closes a circuit and activates a particular function.

Plugboards were used to program tabulating machines in the days of punched cards. The mound of "spaghetti" on the plugboard in the following picture wasn't easy to create. Programming plugboards was often more difficult than programming today's computers, since timing was a consideration. As the punched card moved at a constant rate of speed from one station to the next, the processing steps had to be completed within a fixed amount of time.

THE AUTHOR HARD AT WORK (1962)

In those days, "Tabulating Technicians" were the lucky ones. Instead of standing all day at their sorters and tabulators, they were allowed to sit down in order to wire their plugboards.

plugs & sockets

Plugs & sockets are the physical connectors that are used to link together all variety of electronic devices. The plugs and sockets on the following three pages are the most commonly used for interconnecting computers to peripheral devices and communications networks. F connectors, phono (RCA) connectors and phone connectors, which are used to connect TVs, VCRs, and other audio and video components, are listed under their respective terms in this book.

If your equipment has this connector type	For this interface
DB25 (4-, 12- or 24-pin)	RS-232 (V.24), IBM® Parallel, RS-530
DB37	RS-449, 442, 423; Bernoulli®
DB50	Dataproducts® Datapoint®, UNIVAC® and others
DB15	Texas Instruments®, NCR® POS; Ethernet
DB9	449 Secondary, ATARI®, DAA and Video interfaces
5-Pin Din	IBM PC Keyboard
36-pin	Parallel printers: Centronics®, EPSON®, Gemini®
Mate-N-Lok®	Current Loop, Telephone
IEEE-488	GPIB, HPIB
M/34	V.35
M/50	Dataproducts, UNIVAC, DEC™ and others
BNC	Coaxial
BNC and TNC	WANG®, Dual Coaxial
Twinaxial	IBM Systems 34, 36, 38, 5520 and others
Telco	Telephone
RJ-11	Voice Telephone
RJ-45	Data Telephone
Barrier Block	Utility current loop, and other 2- or 4-wires

DB-25

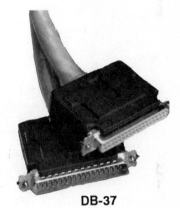

DB-37

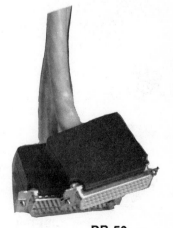

DB-50

PLUGS & SOCKETS

(Chart and photos courtesy Black Box Corporation)

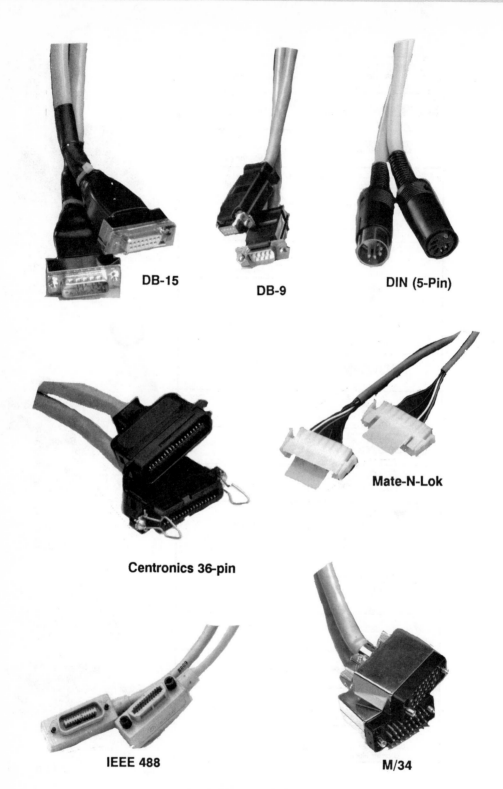

DB-15

DB-9

DIN (5-Pin)

Centronics 36-pin

Mate-N-Lok

IEEE 488

M/34

PLUGS & SOCKETS

(All photos courtesy Black Box Corporation)

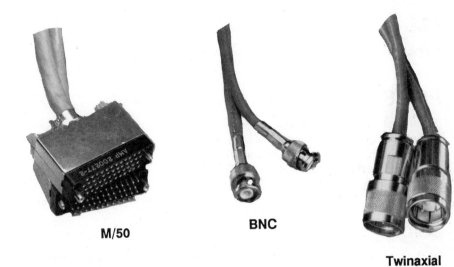

M/50

BNC

Twinaxial

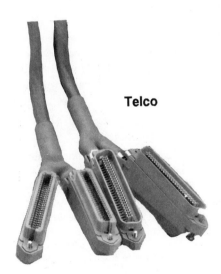

Telco

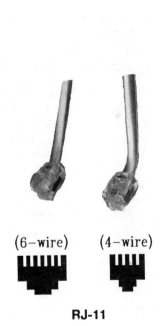

(6-wire)   (4-wire)

RJ-11

RJ-45

PLUGS & SOCKETS

(All photos courtesy Black Box Corporation)

PM

See *preventive maintenance* and *Presentation Manager*.

PMOS

(Positive channel Metal Oxide Semiconductor) Pronounced "pee-moss," PMOS is a type of microelectronic circuit design in which the substrate, or base material, is positively charged. PMOS transistors were used in the first microprocessors and are still used in CMOS fabrication. They are also used in low-cost products, such as calculators and digital watches.

point

(1) *Point* is to move the cursor onto a line or graphic image (icon) on screen by rolling a mouse across the desk or by pressing the arrow keys.

(2) In typography, a *point* is equal to 1/72nd of an inch and is used to measure the vertical height of a printed character. The characters you're reading now are printed in a 10 point Goudy Old Style font, and the large boldface words used as headers are printed in a 16 point Helvetica font. See *typeface* for an illustration.

point of sale

Point of sale is the capture of data at the time and place of sale. Point of sale systems use standard display terminals or specialized terminals with features, such as optical scanning for reading specialized OCR characters or bar codes, or magnetic card readers for reading the magnetic strip on the back of credit cards. Specialized point of sale terminals may also include a cash register as well, in order to combine several functions into a space-saving unit.

Point of sale systems may be online to a central computer for credit checking and immediate inventory updating, or they may use stand-alone terminals or microcomputers that hold the transactions until the end of a period, such as the end of the day, when they are sent to a main computer for second or third shift batch processing.

BAR CODE

POINT OF SALE

The concept of a point of sale system is that the transaction is recorded when it occurs, and not afterwards. Point of sale dramatically reduces data entry errors associated with retail systems, in which the data is entered after the fact.

pointer

(1) In database management, a *pointer* is an address embedded within the data that specifies the location of data in another record or file.

(2) In programming, a *pointer* is a variable that is used as a reference to the current item in a table (array) or to some other object, such as the current row or column the cursor is on.

(3) A *pointer* is a device, such as a mouse, tablet cursor or stylus, that moves the cursor on the screen.

(4) In the Macintosh, a *pointer* is the on-screen cursor.

pointing device

A *pointing device* is an input unit that is used to move the cursor on the screen, such as a mouse or graphics tablet. Pointing devices are also used for drawing on the computer.

Poisson distribution

Poisson distribution is a statistical method developed by 18th century French mathematician S. D. Poisson, which is used for predicting the probable distribution of a series of events. For example, when the average transaction volume in a communications system can be estimated, Poisson distribution is used to determine the probable minimum and maximum number of transactions that can occur within a given time period.

poke

See *peek/poke*.

polarity

(1) In electronics, *polarity* refers to being positively or negatively charged. Electricity is considered to be negatively charged and flows naturally toward a mass of opposite, positive charges.

(2) In micrographics, *polarity* refers to the change in the light to dark relationship of an image when copies are made. Positive polarity is dark characters on a light background, while negative polarity is light characters on a dark background.

polarized

Polarized refers to the one-way direction of a signal or the molecules within a material pointing in one direction.

Polish notation

Polish notation, developed by the Polish logician Jan Lukasiewicz in 1929, is a way of stating a mathematical expression without using group symbols. The expression A(b+c) would be expressed in Polish notation as +bc*A. In reverse Polish notation, it would be expressed as bc+A*.

polling

Polling is the continuous interrogation from a computer to the devices attached to it to determine if a device wishes to transmit. If a terminal or computer is ready to transmit, it sends back an acknowledgement code (ACK), and the transmission sequence begins. The polling software resides in the main computer or in the communications front end.

An alternate technique is an interrupt-driven system, in which the device that's ready to transmit sends a signal to the destination computer indicating it has a message to send.

polling cycle

A *polling cycle* is one round in which each and every terminal connected to the computer or controller has been polled once.

polygon

In computer graphics, a *polygon* is a multi-sided object that can be filled with color or moved around as a single entity.

POLYGON

polyline

In computer graphics, a *polyline* is a single entity that is made up of a series of connected lines.

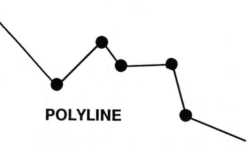

POLYLINE

pop

See *push/pop*.

populate

Populate is to fill a printed circuit board, typically a memory board, with chips. A fully populated board is one that contains all the chips it has sockets to hold.

port

A *port* is an interface (connector) between the computer and the outside world. The number of ports on a communications controller or front end processor determine the number of communications channels that can be connected to it. The number of ports on a computer determine the number of peripheral devices that can be attached to it.

The number of ports that are typically specified on a personal computer, such as two serial ports and one parallel port, refer only to the external connectors available to hook up devices, such as printers and modems. However the computer has many more internal ports that are used to connect disk drives, display screens and other peripherals. See also *porting*.

port expander

A *port expander* is a device that connects several lines to one port in the computer. A line is given access to the port either by a hardware switch or through software selection.

portable computer

A *portable computer* is a personal computer that can be easily transported. The first portable computer was the Osborne I, a CP/M-based 8-bit machine, that was soon followed by many others, such as the Kaypro, Hyperion and Attache. In 1982, Compaq Computer introduced the first IBM compatible portable computer, which, at 30 pounds, may have been borderline portable, but nevertheless became an enormous success. Today, lighter-weight portable computers use flat-panel display screens and weigh from six to 20 pounds.

A portable computer can be just as powerful as a desktop model, its limitations often being the number of expansion slots or disk drives that it has room for. If a portable computer is small and has a self-contained battery, it is considered a *laptop* computer.

porting

Porting refers to converting software to run in a different computer environment.

portrait

Portrait is a printing orientation in which the data is printed across the narrow side of the form, as in a standard page or letter. This book is printed in portrait orientation. Contrast with *landscape* orientation, which prints data across the wider side of the form.

POS

See *point of sale*.

positive logic

Positive logic is the use of a low voltage for a 0 bit and a high voltage for a 1 bit. Contrast with *negative logic*, which uses a high voltage for a 0 bit and a low voltage for a 1 bit.

POSIX

(Portable Operating System Interface for uniX) *POSIX* is an IEEE standard that defines the language interface between application programs and the UNIX operating system. Adherence to the standard by all UNIX vendors will ensure compatibility when programs are moved from one UNIX computer to another.

postfix notation

See *reverse Polish notation*.

postprocessor

A *postprocessor* is a software program that provides some final processing to data, such as formatting it for display or printing.

PostScript

PostScript is a page description language from Adobe Corporation that was initially used in Apple's LaserWriter laser printer and is now supported by many other printer manufacturers. PostScript provides a language that an application program can use to describe text fonts and graphics images for printing. PostScript requires a PostScript printer and a word processing, desktop publishing or other program that generates printer output in PostScript format.

   PostScript printers have built-in CPUs and memory and perform the graphics and font creation internally.

pot

See *potentiometer*.

potentiometer

A *potentiometer* is a device that provides variable resistance to electrical current and is used to control the amount of current that flows through a circuit. A volume switch is a common use of a potentiometer.

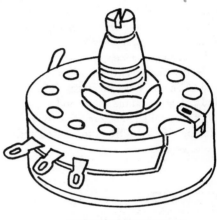

POTENTIOMETER

power

See *computer power*.

power down

Power down is to turn off the computer in an orderly manner, for example, removing floppy and hard disk cartridges before turning the power switch to zero.

power supply

A *power supply* is an electrical system that converts the AC current from the wall outlet into the DC currents required by the computer circuitry.

power up

Power up is to turn the computer on in an orderly manner.

power user

A *power user* is an individual that is very proficient at using a personal computer. It implies that the person can install and learn new software packages and is also comfortable with installing new hardware features. Power users within an organization are the ones that can help others learn about and use personal computers.

precedence

Precedence is the order in which a programming language calculates the individual numbers in an arithmetic expression or compares the individual items in a logical expression. The mathematical precedence is typically (1) Unary + and - signs, (2) Exponentiation, (3) Multiplication and division, (4) Addition and subtraction. Logical precedence is typically (1) NOT, (2) AND, (3) OR.

For example, since multiplication is evaluated before addition, the expression: B * A + B, yields an entirely different answer than the expression: B * (A + B). In the dBASE query: **list for item="Shirt" .AND. color="Gray" .OR. color = "Red"**, all gray and red shirts, and any item that's red, will be selected, since ANDs are evaluated before ORs. By putting parentheses around the colors, such as **(color="Gray" .OR. color="Red")**, the ORs are evaluated as a group by themselves.

precision

Precision is the number of digits used to express the fractional part of a number. The more digits, the more precision. *Single precision* implies using a single computer word to hold a number, for example, in a 16-bit computer, 16 bits would be used to hold and process the entire number. *Double precision* is the use of two computer words.

predicate

In programming, a *predicate* is a statement that evaluates an expression and provides a true or false answer based on the condition of the data.

prefix notation

See *Polish notation*.

prepress

In typography and printing, *prepress* refers to the preparation of camera-ready materials up to the actual printing stage, which includes typesetting, manual and automated page makeup.

preprocessor

A *preprocessor* is a software program that performs some preliminary processing on the input before it is processed by the main program.

presentation graphics

Presentation graphics are business graphics, such as bar charts and graphs, that are used as presentation material in meetings and lectures. Presentation graphics implies a highly designed set of business graphics that employs artistic type fonts and stylized graphics, such as 3-dimensional charts.

Presentation Manager

Presentation Manager is a windows environment from Microsoft Corporation that runs under the OS/2 operating system. It is very similar to Version 2 of Microsoft's Windows for its DOS operating system. It allows users to create multiple windows on screen and command the computer with icons and a mouse, which is the user interface developed by Xerox at their Palo Alto Research Center (PARC) in the mid 1970s.

Prestel

Prestel is a commercial videotex service of British Telecom (formerly part of the British Post Office). Prestel services are offered in the United States through British Videotex and Teletext (BVT).

preventive maintenance

Preventive maintenance is the routine checking of hardware that is performed by a field engineer on a regularly scheduled basis. Contrast with *remedial maintenance*, which is service that is required due to a malfunction.

primary storage

Primary storage is the computer's internal memory (RAM). Contrast with *secondary storage*, such as disk and tape.

Prime Computer

Prime Computer was founded in 1972 by seven engineers from Honeywell and one venture capitalist. Their goal was to create a minicomputer that was twice as fast as existing minicomputers. By the end of its first year, Prime introduced its 200 system, the first to use metal oxide semiconductor (MOS) memory.

With the introduction of innovative technology throughout the 1970s, Prime's revenues quickly accelerated. In 1980, its stock climbed 273%, the single greatest appreciation of any stock on the New York exchange at that time.

Prime has been a successful computer vendor in the scientific and engineering community as well as in commercial data processing. It has done well in foreign markets, and sales outside of the United States account for almost half of the company's revenues.

primitive

(1) In computer graphics, a *primitive* is a graphics element, such as a dot, line or arc, that is used as a building block for creating images.

(2) In programming, a *primitive* is a fundamental instruction, statement or operation.

(3) In microprogramming, a *primitive* is a microinstruction, which is an elementary machine operation.

print buffer

See *printer buffer*.

print image format

Print image format refers to a document that has been prepared for the printer. The layout codes for the particular printer being used have been embedded into the document at the appropriate places.

print server

A *print server* is a computer in a network that controls one or more printers. It stores the print image output from all the users of the system and feeds it to the printer as the printer becomes available.

print spooler

See *printer spooling*.

printed circuit board

A *printed circuit board* is a flat board that holds chips and other electronic components. The back side of the printed circuit board is printed with electrically conductive

PRINTED CIRCUIT BOARD

(Courtesy Rockwell International)

This printed circuit board is a 9,600 bps modem.

pathways between the components. The printed circuit board of the 1960s connected elementary discrete components together. The printed circuit board of the 1980s connects chips together, each chip containing hundreds of thousands of elementary components.

printer

A *printer* is a device that converts computer output into printed images. The following is an overview of printer types.

SERIAL PRINTERS
Serial printers print a character at a time from approximately 10 to 400 characters per second (CPS), which is equivalent to about 6 to 240 lines per minute (LPM). Serial printers use dot matrix and character printer technologies. Serial printers are referred to as character printers regardless of the printing technology employed.

LINE PRINTERS
Line printers print a line at a time from approximately 100 to 5,000 LPM and are the standard impact printers found in the datacenter. Line printers use drum, chain, train and band technologies.

PAGE PRINTERS
Page printers, also called *laser printers*, print a page at time from approximately 6 to 215 pages per minute (400 to 14,000 LPM), and primarily employ the electrophotographic technique used in copy machines. High-speed page printers are widely used in large datacenters. See *laser printer*.

GRAPHICS PRINTERS
Graphics printers ues impact serial dot matrix, impact line dot matrix, electrostatic, thermal, ink jet and electrophotographic technologies.

COLOR PRINTERS
Color printers use impact dot matrix with multiple color ribbons, electrophotographic with multiple color toners, electrostatic plotters with multiple color toners, printers using the Cycolor technology, ink jet with multiple color inks and thermal-transfer with multiple colors.

Impact Printers

BAND, CHAIN & TRAIN PRINTERS
A continuous loop of several character sets connected together spins horizontally around a set of hammers. When the desired character is in front of the selected print location, that particular hammer hits the paper forcing the shaped character image on the band, chain, or train into the ribbon and onto the paper. Since the chain, band, or train moves so fast, it appears to print a line at a time. A band is a solid loop, while the chain is individual character images (type slugs) chained together. The train is individual character images (type slugs) revolving in a track, one pushing the other. See *band printer* and *chain printer*.

DRUM PRINTER

A rotating drum (cylinder) contains the character set carved around it for each print location, like an odometer. When the desired character for the selected print location has rotated around to the hammer line, the appropriate hammer hits the paper from behind, forcing it against the ribbon that is between the paper and the drum. Since the drum rotates so fast, it appears to print a line at a time. See *drum printer*.

CHARACTER PRINTERS

Character printers are similar to Selectric typewriters, printing one character at a time. A daisy wheel or similar mechanism is moved serially across the paper. At the selected print location, a hammer hits the shaped character image on the wheel into the ribbon and onto the paper.

SERIAL DOT MATRIX

A vertical set of printing wires moves serially across the paper, formulating characters by impacting a ribbon and transferring dots of ink onto the paper. The clarity of the character is determined by how close the dots print together.

LINE DOT MATRIX

A stationary or oscillating line of printing wires generate images by impacting a ribbon and transferring dots of ink onto the paper a line at a time.

Non-impact Printers

ELECTROPHOTOGRAPHIC

A drum is charged with a high voltage and an image source paints a negative light copy of the image to be printed onto the drum. Where the light falls onto the drum, the drum is discharged. A toner (ink) is allowed to adhere to the charged portion of the drum. The drum then fuses the image onto the paper by pressure and heat. See *electrophotographic*.

ELECTROSENSITIVE

Dots are charged onto specially coated silver-colored paper, usually in a serial fashion. The charge removes the alumnimum coating, leaving a black image.

ELECTROSTATIC

Dots are charged onto specially coated paper, usually a line at a time. An ink adheres to the charges that become embedded into the paper by pressure or by heat.

INK JET

Continuous streams of ink are sprayed onto paper, or droplets of ink generate a dot matrix image, usually in a serial fashion. Another technique uses ink in a solid form, which is melted just before it is ejected.

THERMAL

Dots are burned onto specially coated paper that turns black or blue when heat is applied to it. A line of heat elements forms a dot matrix image as the paper is passed across it, or a serial head with heating elements is passed across the paper.

THERMAL WAX TRANSFER

Dots of ink are transferred from a mylar ribbon onto paper by passing the ribbon and the paper across a line of heat elements, or by passing a serial head with heating element across the paper. See *thermal wax transfer*.

printer buffer

A *printer buffer* is a memory device that accepts printer output from one or more computers and transmits it to the printer. It lets the computer rid itself of its printer output at high speed and be used for another task while the printer is printing. Printer buffers with automatic switching are connected to two or more computers and accept their output on a first-come, first-served basis.

printer driver

A *printer driver* is a program routine that converts an application program's request to print into the language the printer understands.

printer file

(1) A *printer file* contains the information required by a printer driver in order to turn a program's request to print into the codes, or language, required by the printer. The printer file contains the codes to perform such functions as turning on and off underline and boldface and changing fonts. Width tables that contain the horizontal width of every character in each represented font are also included.

(2) A *printer file* is a document in print image format ready to be printed. Printer files are created by a PRINT TO DISK option in a program.

printer spooling

Printer spooling is the printing of documents in a background mode while other tasks are being performed in the computer.

printout

(PRINTer OUTput) Same as *hardcopy*.

privacy

Privacy refers to the authorized distribution of information (who has a right to know?). Contrast with *security*, which deals with unauthorized access to data.

private line

(1) A *private line* is a dedicated line leased from a common carrier.

(2) A *private line* is a line owned and installed by the user.

problem-oriented language

A *problem-oriented language* is a computer language designed to handle a particular class of problems. For example, COBOL was designed for business applications. FORTRAN, ALGOL and APL were designed for scientific and mathematical problems. GPSS and SIMSCRIPT were designed for simulation problems. Query languages are designed for phrasing questions (interrogation problems).

procedural language

A *procedural language* is a programming language that requires programming discipline, such as COBOL, FORTRAN, BASIC, C, Pascal and dBASE. Programmers writing in procedural languages must develop a proper order of actions in order to solve the problem, based on a knowledge of data processing operations and programming techniques.

Contrast with *non-procedural language*, which generates the necessary program logic for the computer directly from a user's description of the problem. Today's fourth-generation database languages provide both procedural code for customized programs and non-procedural code for interactive use.

The following dBASE example shows code required to display data in a file in both its procedural programming language and its non-procedural interactive language:

```
        Procedural                    Non-procedural

        USE FILEX                     USE FILEX
         DO WHILE .NOT. EOF           LIST NAME, AMOUNTDUE
         ? NAME, AMOUNTDUE
         SKIP
        ENDDO
```

procedure

(1) A manual *procedure* is a series of human tasks.

(2) A machine *procedure* is a list of routines or programs to be executed, such as described by the job control language (JCL) in a minicomputer or mainframe, or the batch processing language in a personal computer.

(3) In programming, a *procedure* is another term for a subroutine or function.

(4) In COBOL, the *procedure* division is the section of the program that describes the processing.

process

Process refers to manipulating data and pertains to any action taken by the computer. When data is processed, its content may be changed, or it may simply be transferred intact, for example, a file transmitted from one computer to another. When data is displayed only on a screen, it is still said to be processed, since the data record is processed into a special screen format for readability. It also takes hundreds, if not thousands, of machine instructions to accomplish such a task.

In order to evaluate a system's performance, the time it takes for the computer to process data internally is reviewed separately from the time it takes to read and write the data. It usually takes far more time to get the data into and out of the computer than it does to process it internally. See *computer (The 3 C's)*.

process-bound

Process-bound is an excessive amount of processing taking place and implies an imbalance between input/output and processing operations on a large computer. Process-bound may also imply that an application program that requires extensive processing has slowed down other users of the system.

In a personal computer, process-bound is a common occurrence when a spreadsheet is being recalculated or a CAD image is being redrawn.

process control

Process control is the automated control of a process, such as a manufacturing process or assembly line. Process control is used extensively in industrial operations, such as oil refining, chemical processing and electrical generation. Process control systems employ hybrid computers that use analog systems to monitor real-world signals and digital computers to do the analysis and controlling. Process control systems make extensive use of analog to digital and digital to analog conversion.

processing

Processing is the manipulation of data within the computer. However, the term is used to define a variety of computer functions and methods. See *centralized processing, distributed processing, batch processing, transaction processing, multiprocessing* and *computer (The 3 C's)*.

processor

(1) Same as *CPU*.

(2) *Processor* refers to categories of software; for example, assemblers and compilers are *language processors*. A program that handles words is called a *word processor*.

processor unit

Same as *computer*.

Procomm

Procomm is a shareware communications program from Datastorm, that runs on IBM compatible pcs. Version 2.4.2 handles transmission speeds from 300 to 19,200 bits per second, emulates 10 different terminals and supports eight protocols. Procomm is available on many electronic bulletin boards where you are encouraged to download it into your computer and pay for it if you use it.

production database

A *production database* is a central database containing an organization's master files and daily transaction files.

production system

A *production system* is a computer system that is used to process an organization's daily work. Contrast with a computer system that is used only for development and testing or for ad hoc inquiries and analysis.

Professional Yam

Professional Yam (Professional Yet another modem) is a communications program from Omen Technology that runs on IBM compatible pcs. Professional Yam is a powerful, flexible, full-featured program for the serious communications user. Version 16.92 emulates 11 different terminals and supports 10 protocols.

Professional 300

The *Professional 300* was a desktop computer from Digital Equipment Corporation that incorporated the PDP-11 chip set. Introduced along with the DECmate II and Rainbow 100 in 1982, Professional 300s were used as desktop versions of the PDP-11.

PROFS

(**PR**ofessional **OF**fice System) *PROFS* is an office automation program from IBM that runs in a VM mainframe environment. It provides an electronic mail facility for text and graphics, a library service for centrally storing text, electronic calendars and appointment scheduling, and it allows document interchange with DISOSS users. IBM personal computer users can access PROF connected to the mainframe.

program

A *program* is a collection of instructions that tell the computer what to do. A program is called *software*; hence, program, software and instructions are synonymous. A program is written in a programming language and is converted into the computer's machine language by software called assemblers and compilers.

A program is made up of (1) instructions, (2) buffers and (3) constants. Instructions are the directions that the computer will follow, and a particular sequence of instructions is called the program's *logic*. Buffers are reserved spaces in the program that will accept and hold the data while it's being processed. Constants are fixed values within the program that are used for comparing.

The program calls for data in an input-process-output sequence. After data has been input into one of the program's buffers from a peripheral device, such as a keyboard or disk, it is processed. The results are then output to a peripheral device such as a display terminal or printer. If data has been updated, it is output back onto the disk.

The application program, the program that does the organization's data processing, does not instruct the computer to do everything. When the program needs input or is ready to output some data, it sends a request to the operating

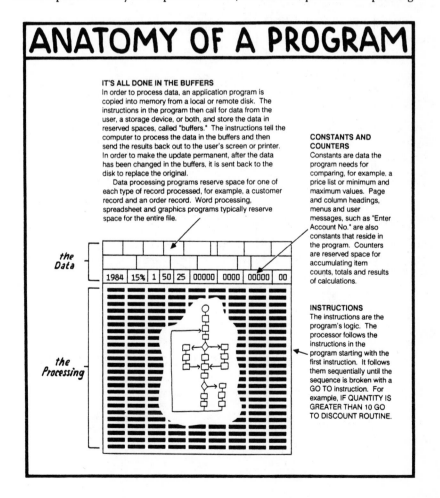

ANATOMY OF A PROGRAM

IT'S ALL DONE IN THE BUFFERS
In order to process data, an application program is copied into memory from a local or remote disk. The instructions in the program then call for data from the user, a storage device, or both, and store the data in reserved spaces, called "buffers." The instructions tell the computer to process the data in the buffers and then send the results back out to the user's screen or printer. In order to make the update permanent, after the data has been changed in the buffers, it is sent back to the disk to replace the original.

Data processing programs reserve space for one of each type of record processed, for example, a customer record and an order record. Word processing, spreadsheet and graphics programs typically reserve space for the entire file.

CONSTANTS AND COUNTERS
Constants are data the program needs for comparing, for example, a price list or minimum and maximum values. Page and column headings, menus and user messages, such as "Enter Account No." are also constants that reside in the program. Counters are reserved space for accumulating item counts, totals and results of calculations.

the Data

| 1984 | 15% | 1 | 50 | 25 | 00000 | 0000 | 00000 | 00 |

INSTRUCTIONS
The instructions are the program's logic. The processor follows the instructions in the program starting with the first instruction. It follows them sequentially until the sequence is broken with a GO TO instruction. For example, IF QUANTITY IS GREATER THAN 10 GO TO DISCOUNT ROUTINE.

the Processing

system, which contains the actual instructions to perform input and output activities. The operating system performs the activity and turns control back to the application program.

program generator

See *application generator*.

program logic

Program logic is the sequence of instructions in a program. There are many logical solutions to the same problem. One way may get the job done a lot faster than another, but if the program logic correctly solves the problem, the results will be the same. Give a complicated problem to ten programmers, and each programmer may create program logic that is slightly different from all the others.

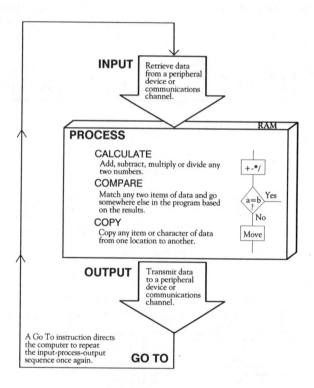

PROGRAM LOGIC

INPUT, PROCESS, OUTPUT and GO TO operations are the primary instructions built into every computer. Although program logic becomes quite complicated in actual practice, it is all based on inputting data into the computer, processing it and outputting the results. The main loop of many data processing programs performs this sequence over and over again.

program maintenance

Program maintenance is the changing of programs in order to bring them up to date with the organization's requirements. Changes in program logic are made when the program must process the data differently. Changes in constants are made when their fixed values have changed, for example, a message must say something differently. Changes in buffers are made when the data record has been structurally modified in order to increase the size of a fixed length field or to add another field to the record. If a database management system is used to control the data, then there may be no buffer changes required in the program, because either the buffers aren't affected or the program contains no buffers.

program state

A *program state* is the mode of operation, or status of a computer, when instructions in an application program are being executed. Contrast with *supervisor state*, which occurs when instructions in the operating system are being executed.

program statement

A *program statement* is a sentence or line of instruction in a high-level programming language. One program statement may result in several machine instructions when the program is compiled.

program step

A *program step* is an elementary instruction, such as a machine language instruction or an assembly language instruction. Contrast with *program statement*, which is an instructional sequence in a high-level programming language.

programmable

Programmable is capable of following instructions. What sets the computer apart from all other electronic devices is its programmability.

programmable calculator

A *programmable calculator* is a calculator that can be programmed. A programmable calculator is a limited-function computer, usually only capable of working with numbers and not alphanumeric data.

programmable logic array

See *PLA*.

programmatic interface

Same as *application program interface*.

programmer

A *programmer* is an individual who designs the logic for and writes the lines of codes of a computer program. See *application programmer* and *systems programmer*.

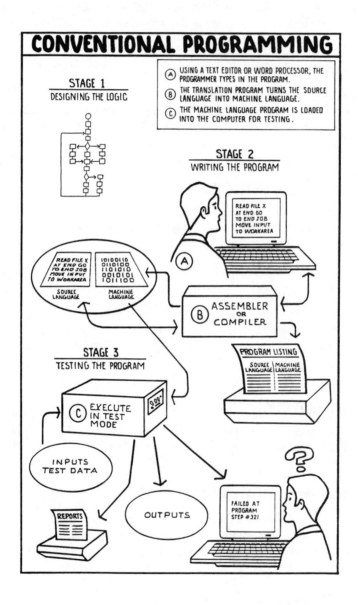

programmer analyst

A *programmer analyst* is an individual who analyzes and designs information systems and designs and writes the application programs for the system. A programmer analyst is both systems analyst and applications programmer.

programming

Programming is the creation of a computer program. The steps in programming are (1) developing the program logic to solve the particular problem, (2) writing the program logic in the form of a specific programming language (coding the program), (3) assembling or compiling the program to turn it into machine language form, (4) testing and debugging the program, and (5) preparing the necessary documentation.

The program logic is the most difficult part of programming. Writing the actual language statements is comparatively easy once the solution has been developed. However, regardless of how difficult the design of the program may be, documenting the program is considered to be the most annoying activity by many programmers. Consequently, it is often not done with the same enthusiasm as the design and writing of the program.

programming language

A *programming language* is a language used to write instructions for the computer. The purpose of a programming language is to allow the programmer to express data processing activities in a symbolic manner without regard to the details that the machine has to know. For example, when a programmer writes MULTIPLY HOURS TIMES RATE, these words are meaningless to the machine. MULTIPLY must be turned into a code that means multiply. HOURS and RATE must be turned into memory locations where those items of data are actually located. The programming statements that are written by the programmer are called *source language*, and they are turned into the computer's *machine language* by translator programs called *assemblers, compilers* and *interpreters*.

Like human languages, each programming language has its own grammar and syntax. There are many dialects of the same language; however, unlike human languages in which different dialects can be understood, programming language dialects cannot. Standards have been set up by the American National Standards Institute (ANSI) for many programming languages, and any language said to be conforming to the ANSI standard is, therefore, a dialect-free language. However, it can take years for new features to be included in the ANSI standards, and new dialects will always spring up as a result.

Programming languages fall into two major categories: low-level assembly languages and high-level languages. Assembly languages are available for every CPU family, and they translate one line of code into one machine language instruction. High-level languages translate programming statements into several machine instructions.

The traditional high-level programming languages are ALGOL, FORTRAN, COBOL, PL/I, APL, RPG II & III and BASIC. ALGOL was never widely used in the United States, and APL and PL/I usage has diminished over the years.

Languages such as Pascal, dBASE and C have gained enormous popularity in recent years, and Logo, LISP and Prolog are used for artificial intelligence applications. FORTH is used in process control and artificial intelligence, and object-oriented languages, originating with Smalltalk, are providing another new programming wave.

Programming languages are made up of three classes of instructions, or statements: (1) sequential processing, (2) selection, and (3) iteration. Sequential processing is a series of steps that are taken one after the other. Selection is a test in which two or more sets of data are compared, and, based on the results, control is passed to the part of the program that handles it. In high-level languages, IF THEN ELSE and CASE statements provide selection. Iteration is a series of steps that must be repeated some number of times. Iteration is accomplished with DO LOOPS and FOR NEXT LOOPS in high-level languages and GOTOs in low-level languages.

Prokey

Prokey is a keyboard macro processor from RoseSoft Inc., that runs on IBM compatible pcs. Prokey allows users to eliminate repetitive typing by setting up an occurrence of text or a series of commands as a macro. The contents of the macro are automatically typed in when one or more special keys are pressed.

Prolog

(PROgramming in LOGic) *Prolog*, developed in France in 1973, is a programming language used in the development of artificial intelligence applications, such as natural language, expert systems and abstract problem solving. Used throughout Europe and Japan, Prolog has recently gained popularity in the United States for use on personal computers. Prolog is very similar to the LISP programming language. Like LISP, Prolog is designed to deal with symbolic representations of objects.

The following example, written in University of Edinburgh Prolog, converts farhrenheit to centigrade:

```
convert:- write('Enter fahrenheit'),
  read(Fahr),
  write('Centigrade is '),
  Cent is (5 * (Fahr - 32)) / 9,
  write(Cent),nl.
```

PROM

(Programmable Read Only Memory) A *PROM* is a permanent memory chip that is programmed, or filled, by the customer rather than by the manufacturer of the chip. PROMS are programmed in a PROM programmer unit that holds several chips at the same time. Contrast with *ROM* (read only memory) chips, which are programmed at the time of manufacture.

PROM blaster (blower)

Same as PROM *programmer*.

PROM programmer

A PROM *programmer* is a device that writes (records) instructions and data into PROM chips. The PROM programmer transfers data or a program in machine language form into the PROM chips that have been inserted into its sockets. PROM programmers hold from a handful to several hundred chips. The bits in a new PROM chip are all 1s, which are simply continuous lines. The PROM programmer essentially only creates 0s by "blowing" the middle out of the 1s.

PROM PROGRAMMER

PROM programmers are available for programming only PROMs, only EPROMs or both types of chips. The bits in EPROMs, which are not permanently "blown," can be erased in a separate ultraviolet light unit and reprogrammed over again in the PROM programmer.

prompt

A *prompt* is a message from the software that requests some action by the user, for example, "Type ? for Help" or "Enter employee name."

property list

In a list programming language, a *property list* is an object that is assigned a descriptive attribute (property) and a value. For example, in Logo, **PUTPROP "KAREN "LANGUAGE "PARADOX** assigns the value PARADOX to the property LANGUAGE for the person named KAREN. To find out what language Karen speaks, the Logo statement **PRINT GETPROP "KAREN "LANGUAGE** will generate PARADOX as the answer.

proportional spacing

Proportional spacing is the spacing of characters according to the width of each character. For example, an I takes up less horizontal width than an M. In a fixed-spacing printer, the I and M take up the same amount of space, causing an uneven appearance on the page.

The next step beyond proportional spacing is kerning, where character combinations, such as WA and FA are squeezed together so that one character overlaps the space of another; thus, providing an improved appearance. See *kerning*.

Proportional spacing

Now is the

Fixed spacing (Monospacing)

Now is the

PROPORTIONAL SPACING

protected mode
See *memory protection*.

protocol
See *communications protocol*.

prototyping
Prototyping is the creation of a system on a trial basis for testing and approval. With regard to information systems development, prototyping has become a valuable asset for clarifying information requirements. In the traditional approach, the functional specs, which are the blueprint and design of the information system, must be finalized and frozen before the system can be built. This places a large burden on managers to know what information they want now and in the future. While the analytically-oriented person may have a clear picture of information requirements, the average manager may not.

Using the fourth-generation capabilities of a database management system as a   prototyping tool, systems analysts and users can formulate and develop the new system together. Databases can be created and manipulated at a mainframe terminal or on a personal computer while the user monitors the progress. Once users see tangible output on a display screen or printed report, they can figure out what's missing or what the next question might be if this were a production system. If prototyping is carefully done, the end result can be a working system. Even if the final system must be reprogrammed from scratch using conventional languages for departmental standardization or machine efficiency, the prototyping has served to provide specifications for a working system rather than a theoretical one. In addition, the active participation on the part of the users will help them define their requirements far more effectively, and everyone will wind up with a better system.

PR/SM

(Processor Resources/Systems Manager) PR/SM is a hardware upgrade from IBM that turns a large-scale 3090 mainframe into as many as four logical processors, each capable of running a different operating system and set of application programs.

PS

(Personal Services) PS is a series of office automation programs that run on IBM personal computers, minis and mainframes, which includes word processing, electronic mail and library services.

p-System

See *UCSD P-System*.

PS/2 bus

Same as *Micro Channel*.

PTT

(Postal, Telegraph & Telephone) The PTT is the national governmental agency responsible for combined postal, telegraph and telephone services in many European countries.

PU

(Physical Unit) In an IBM SNA environment, a PU refers to a particular type of hardware device and the associated software that manages the communications within it. IBM has defined four types of PUs. Types 1 and 2 are communications control units. Type 3 is currently undefined. Type 4 is a front end processor. Type 5 is a mainframe.

PU 2.1

(Physical Unit 2.1) In an IBM SNA environment, PU 2.1 refers to a class of hardware and associated software that can exchange data with another type 2.1 device without having to route the data through a host computer. PU 2.1 software is used to support an LU 6.2 session. As with all PU Type 2 devices, a PU 2.1 device may also exchange data with the mainframe.

public domain software

Public domain software is software that is freely distributed to anyone who desires to use it.

pull-down menu

A *pull-down menu* is a menu that appears to be pulled downward from the top line of the screen when selected. A pull-down menu is selected by pointing to one of the titles (displayed at the top of the screen) with a mouse. In the Macintosh, the menu remains displayed as long as the mouse button is held down. In other systems, the menu remains pulled down automatically. An item within the menu is selected by pointing to it with the mouse and releasing the mouse button or pressing the button, depending on the system. In the following Macintosh example, the Paste option is selected in the Edit menu. In this case, when the mouse button is released, the Paste function will be performed. In some systems, keyboard commands can also cause pull-down menus to be displayed.

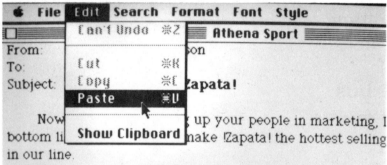

PULL-DOWN MENU
(Courtesy Apple Computer, Inc.)

pulse code modulation

See *PCM*.

punched card

A *punched card* is a storage medium made of card stock that holds data in the form of patterns of punched holes. Punched cards usually have 80 or 96 columns, each capable of storing one character of data. The holes are punched into the card by a keypunch machine or card punch peripheral device connected to a computer. Punched cards are read into the machine by a card reader.

Although punched cards are still used as turnaround documents for invoicing and inventory, the punched card has long since seen its heyday. From 1890 until the early 1960s, punched cards were synonymous with data processing. In those days, concepts were very simple, the database was the file cabinet, and a record was a single punched card. Each processing activity was performed on a separate machine, the collective group of which was called *unit record equipment, tabulating equipment* or *electronic accounting machines* (EAM).

PUNCHED CARDS (CIRCA 1900)

(Courtesy IBM)

The keypunch machine and punched cards in
this photo were the ones used in the 1890 census.

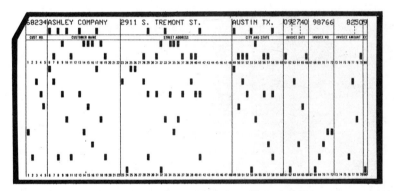

80-COLUMN PUNCHED CARD

(Courtesy IBM)

push/pop

Push/pop is to store/retrieve an item on a stack. *Push* enters a new item on the
stack, and *pop* retrieves an item from the stack, moving the rest of the items in
the stack up one level. See *stack*.

P9

Same as *80386-SX*.

Q&A

Q&A is an integrated file manager and word processor from Symantec Corporation that runs on IBM compatible pcs. Q&A also includes a mail merge capability as well as a programming language for customizing data entry forms and reports. A feature called the "Intelligent Assistant" provides a natural language query capability that can learn new words from the user. Although Q&A works only with single files and has no relational capability, it is a powerful and easy-to-use program for the beginner.

QBE

(Query By Example) *QBE*, originally developed by IBM for its mainframe systems, has become a popular method for stating a query to a database on many computers. For example, Paradox, a database management system from Ansa/Borland, has taken QBE to its limits with the ability to do a relational query on screen to any number of data tables.

The QBE format displays a replica of an empty record on screen, requiring the user to type in the search condition by filling in the field columns. The following example selects all customers in Pennsylvania that have balances of $5,000 or more.

CUSTOMER FILE

NAME	ADDRESS	CITY	STATE	ZIP	BALANCE
			PA		>=5000

"Select all Pennsylvania customers with balances of $5000 or more"

QUERY BY EXAMPLE

Q-bus

The *Q-bus* is a bus architecture from Digital Equipment Corporation that is used in its PDP-11 series of minicomputers as well as in its MicroVAX versions of the VAX series.

QMF

(Query Management Facility) *QMF* is a fourth-generation language from IBM intended for end-user interaction with IBM's DB2 database system.

Quark Xpress

Quark Xpress is a desktop publishing program from Quark, Inc., that runs on the Macintosh personal computer. It is one of the few programs that integrates a comprehensive word processing capability into a desktop publishing system so that text can be created, edited and published within the same program. Quark Xpress is noted for its precise typographic control over text. In addition, it contains sophisticated graphics features, such as the ability to create a custom border, pixel by pixel, that is used to frame text and graphics. The actual image of the new design is automatically displayed in the standard frame menu. The example below shows the frame editor. The left side of the screen zooms in on the selected portion of the frame, which, in this case, is the upper left hand side. The pattern is created or modified a dot (pixel) at a time.

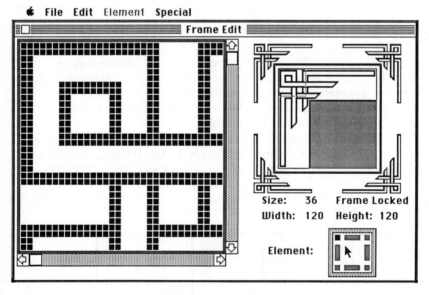

QUARK EXPRESS

quartz crystal

A *quartz crystal* is a slice of quartz used to generate the frequencies necessary to control a computer or communications system. The quartz is cut and ground to a prescribed thickness, which will cause it to vibrate at a specific frequency when power is applied to it.

Quattro

Quattro is a spreadsheet program from Borland International that runs on IBM compatible pcs. Quattro is similar in operation to Lotus 1-2-3, Release 2, but provides enhanced graphics as well as macro generation capabilities that are easier to use.

query

A *query* is an interrogation of a file or database that allows users to count, sum and list selected records contained in it. A query program allows the user to select data and display it on a display screen or print it. A query generates a total or listing, whereas a report implies a more elaborate printout with page headings, page numbers and subtotals. A query is plain; a report is fancy.

query by example

See *QBE*.

query language

A *query language* is a generalized language that allows a user to interrogate a database. Query languages provide either a command language, a menu-driven method or a query by example (QBE) format for expressing the question and allow users to count, sum and list selected records in a database.

Query languages are routinely provided in contemporary database managment systems, but stand-alone packages are also available for interrogating files created by traditional programming languages, such as COBOL and BASIC. A query language is different from a query program that is part of an existing application. The query langauge implies that any condition existing in the database can be selected, whereas a custom-developed query program may allow only specific search conditions, such as the retrieval of a customer record or employee record by account number. A query language could be used to select which customers purchased a certain kind of product, or which employees speak Spanish.

queue

Pronounced "Q," a *queue* is a temporary holding place for data either in memory or on a disk. For example, message queues hold data sent in from terminals until the computer can get around to process it. A *print queue* stores output directed for the printer until the printer is free to print it.

Quickdraw

Quickdraw is a graphics display system that is built into Apple's Macintosh computer line. Quickdraw accepts commands from the application program and draws the corresponding objects on the screen. This built-in graphics capability is one of the main reasons that Macintosh computers have been so successful as computer-aided design (CAD), illustration and desktop publishing systems. The Quickdraw language provides a consistent interface that software developers can work with.

Quicksilver

Quicksilver is a dBASE compiler from WordTech Systems Inc., that allows dBASE programs to be developed and run without the requirement of having the dBASE program in the computer. Quicksilver does not support all the interactive dBASE commands, but does add a windowing capability to the language, allowing programmers to display multiple windows on screen.

quit

Quit is to get out of the program you're currently in. It's a good habit to quit a program before turning the computer off. Some programs don't close all the files properly until the user formally quits the program.

qwerty keyboard

The *qwerty keyboard* is the standard English language keyboard layout found on every typewriter and computer keyboard. Q, w, e, r, t and y are the first six letters starting at the top left, alphabetic row of the keyboard. Originally developed for mechanical typewriters, the placement of the keys was designed to eliminate jamming by separating various common letter combinations in English.

STANDARD TYPEWRITER KEYBOARD

RACE

(Randon Access Card Equipment) A *RACE* unit was a mass storage device from RCA that stored data on magnetic cards. The cards were released from their cartridge and made to pass down a raceway after which they were wrapped around a read/write head. The magnetic cards would often jam and damage all the data contained on them.

rack

A *rack* is a frame or cabinet into which components are mounted.

rack mounted

Rack mounted refers to components that are built to fit in a metal frame. Electronic devices, such as testing equipment and tape drives, are typically made as rack mounted units.

radio

Radio is the transmission of electromagnetic energy (radiation) over the air or through a hollow tube called a waveguide. Although radio is often thought of as only AM or FM, all through-the-air transmission, including satellite transmission and microwave transmission between line-of-sight towers, is radio. The alternative to radio transmission is metal cable, such as twisted wire pairs and coaxial cable, or optical fibers made of glass. See *RF*.

radio frequency

See *RF*.

Radio Shack

See *Tandy Corporation.*

radix

A *radix* is the base value in a numbering system. For example, in the decimal numbering system, the radix is 10.

radix point

A *radix point* is the location in a number that separates the integral part from the fractional part. For example, in the decimal numbering system, the radix point is the same as the decimal point.

ragged right

In typography, *ragged right* refers to the uneven appearance of text at the right margin. Ragged right implies that text is uniformly aligned to the left margin (flush left). In this book, all the text in the definitions is set ragged right, as is this paragraph.

RAM

(Random Access Memory) *RAM* is the computer's primary working memory. It's called random access because each byte of memory can be accessed at random without regard to the adjacent byte or bytes. Most RAM chips require power to keep their content, although, in the future, non-volatile RAM may become economical and viable. See *memory.*

RAM disk

A *RAM disk* is a disk drive that is simulated in memory (RAM). The computer thinks the RAM disk is just another disk drive. In order to use a RAM disk, program and data files are copied from the disk into the RAM disk's memory, and all inputs and outputs that normally go to the disk go instead to the RAM disk. The program's processing is speeded up, because there's no mechanical disk action, only memory transfers. However, if the power fails, all the updated data in the RAM disk will be lost. *E-disk, emulated disk, virtual disk* and *pseudo disk* are synonymous terms.

RAM refresh

RAM refresh is the recharging of dynamic RAM chips many times per second in order to keep the bit patterns valid.

RAM resident program

A *RAM resident program* is a program that stays in memory at all times. The advantage of a RAM resident program is that it's immediately usable without having to call it in from the disk. For example, for IBM compatible pcs, Sidekick provides a calculator, calendar and notepad, among others, and is instantly available when a particular "hot key" is pressed. RAM resident programs may also be used to trap the output of another program and modify or enhance it while the other program is running. For example, Ram-Resident PrintMerge modifies printer output before it goes to the laser printer. RAM resident programs are also called *TSR* (terminate and stay resident) programs.

RAMAC

(**R**andom **A**ccess **M**ethod of **A**ccounting and **C**ontrol) The *RAMAC*, introduced by IBM in 1956, was the first data processing system to use a disk drive. Each of it's 24 inch diameter platters held 100,000 characters of data. All 50 platters held a "whopping" five million characters. The RAMAC was half computer, half tabulating machine. It had a limited internal drum memory for program storage, but still required plugboard wiring for its input and output.

RAMAC 305 COMPUTER
(Courtesy IBM)

RAMIS II

RAMIS II is a database management and decision support system from Mathematica Products Group that runs on IBM mainframes. The earlier version of RAMIS II was one of the first database packages with a non-procedural language.

random access

Same as *direct access*.

random noise

Same as *Gaussian noise*.

random number generation

Random number generation is a programming function that produces a random number upon request. Random numbers can be created very easily in a computer, since there are many random events that take place, for example, the duration between depressions of keys on the keyboard. Only a few milliseconds' difference is enough to seed a random number generation routine with a different number each time. Once started, an algorithm can be used to compute different numbers throughout the session.

range

A *range* is a group of values from a minimum to a maximum. For example, when data is entered, it may be valid only if it falls within a certain from and to range. When working with a spreadsheet, an entire range of cells can be moved or copied to another part of the spreadsheet. The range may refer to a row of cells, a column of cells or a rectangular block of cells, in which case the range specifies a rectangle starting at the upper left cell and ending with the lower right cell.

raster display

A *raster display* is a graphics monitor that generates dots line by line on the screen. Contrast with *vector display*, which actually draws the lines on the screen.

raster graphics

Raster graphics is the technique, such as used in television, for representing a picture image as a matrix of dots. Unlike television, which conforms to a national standard, there are many varieties of raster graphics standards used in computer graphics. Contrast with *vector graphics*, which stores objects as collections of lines.

raster scan

Raster scan is the line by line displaying or recording of a video image.

rasterization of vectors

Rasterization of vectors refers to the conversion of graphic objects made up of vectors, or line segments, into dots for output to raster graphics screens, dot matrix and laser printers. Unless vector graphics terminals and plotters are used, all object-oriented graphics must be converted to raster images for display and printing.

raw data

Raw data is data that has not been processed.

ray tracing

In computer graphics, *ray tracing* is the creation of reflections, refractions and shadows on a graphics image. Ray tracing follows a series of rays from a specific light source and computes each pixel in the image to determine the effect of the light. Ray tracing is an enormously process-intensive operation.

RAY TRACING
(Courtesy Computer Sciences Department, University of Utah

R:BASE

R:BASE is a relational database management system from Microrim, Inc., that runs on IBM compatible pcs. R:BASE was the first database management system to compete with dBASE II back in the early 1980s. R:BASE provides interactive data processing, a complete programming language and an application generator for fast development of programs without traditional programming.

RBOC

(Regional Bell Operating Company) An *RBOC* is one of the seven regional telephone companies that were created on January 1, 1984, when AT&T divested itself of its local telephone business. Nynex, Bell Atlantic, BellSouth, Southwestern Bell, US West, Pacific Telesis and Ameritech are the seven RBOCs.

RCA connector

Same as *phono connector*.

RCS

(Remote Computer Service) *RCS* is synonomous with remote timesharing services.

RDBMS

(Relational Database Management System) See *relational database*.

read

Read is to input into the computer from a peripheral device, such as a disk or tape. Like reading a book or playing an audio tape, reading does not destroy the content of the object being read.

A read is technically an input and an output (I/O), since data is being output from the peripheral device and input into the computer. Memory is also said to be read when it is accessed to transfer data out to a peripheral device or to somewhere else in memory. Every peripheral or internal transfer of data is a read from somewhere and a write to somewhere else.

read error

A *read error* is a failure to read the data on a storage or memory device. If a magnetic or optical recording surface becomes contaminated with dust or dirt, or is physically damaged, the bits may become indecipherable. If there is a malfunction of one of the electronic components in a memory chip, the contents may be unretrievable.

A well-designed program will provide alternate ways of recovering from a read error, such as allowing you to bypass it, or try again. A permanent read error in a file on disk or tape may prevent the rest of the file from being accessed. In these cases, a utility program or special recovery program must be used to retrieve the remaining data in the file.

read only

Read only pertains to any storage media that permanently holds its content, such as a ROM, PROM, CD ROM, compact disc, videodisc or phonograph record.

reader

A *reader* is a peripheral input device, such as a punched card reader, magnetic card reader or optical character recognition (OCR) reader. A microfiche or microfilm reader reads the film and displays its contents and is, therefore, an input and output device.

readme file

A *readme file* is a text file placed onto software distribution disks that contain last-minute updates or errata that have not been printed in the documentation manual.

read/write channel

Same as *I/O channel*.

read/write head

A *read/write head* is a device that reads (senses) and writes (records) data on a magnetic disk or tape. For writing, the surface of the disk or tape is moved past the read/write head, and by discharging electrical impulses at the appropriate times, bits are recorded as tiny, magnetized spots of positive or negative polarity. For reading, the surface is moved past the read/write head, and the bits that are present induce an electrical current across the gap. Unlike a laser beam, which can be electronically moved, all magnetic media (disks and tapes) require movement of the recording surface past the read/write head in order to function.

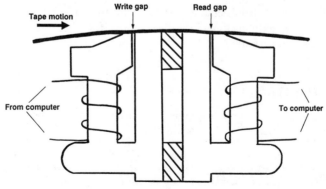

TAPE DRIVE READ/WRITE HEAD

read/write memory

Same as *RAM*.

real address

Same as *absolute address*.

real mode

See *OS/2*.

real storage

In a virtual memory system, *real storage* refers to actual, physical main memory.

realtime

Realtime implies immediate processing and refers to online computer systems that can respond to questions by providing fast answers or can respond to transactions by updating the corresponding master files right away. Although the term is used to refer to business applications, it is more appropriately used in process control and scientific processing. For example, in avionics (electronic airplane instrumentation), a realtime computer must respond to signals immediately in order to fly the airplane. The same goes for space vehicle operations, where embedded realtime computer systems are specialized for every detail of the flight.

Realtime also refers to simulated operations that are performed in the same timeframe as the real operation. For example, in computer graphics animation, it takes a very fast computer to simulate objects moving across the screen in realtime, at the same rate they would move in real life.

realtime clock

A *realtime clock* is an electronic circuit that maintains the time of day. A realtime clock may also provide timing signals for the computer for other timing operations, such as timesharing.

realtime image

In computer graphics, a *realtime image* is a graphics image that can be animated on screen in the same time frame as in real life.

realtime information system

A *realtime information system* is a computer system that can respond to transactions by immediately updating the appropriate master files and/or generating a response in a time frame fast enough to keep an operation moving at its required speed. See *transaction processing*.

realtime operating system

A *realtime operating system* is a master control program that can provide immediate response to input signals and transactions and application program requests.

realtime system

A *realtime system* is a computer system that can respond to input signals fast enough to keep an operation moving at its required speed. See *realtime information system*.

reasonable test

A *reasonable test* is a test of a value to determine if it falls within a range considered normal or logical. Reasonable tests can be made on electronic signals to detect unwanted, extraneous noise as well as on data to determine possible input errors.

reboot

Reboot refers to reloading the operating system and restarting the computer system. See *boot*.

record

A *record* is a group of related fields that are used to store data about a subject, such as an employee, customer or vendor, or a transaction, such as an order or payment. A collection of records is called a file, and a collection of files is called a database.

Master records contain fixed data, such as account number, and variable data, such as balance due. Transaction records contain only fixed data, such as quantity and product code. The number of records in a file is synonymous with the number of subjects or transactions in the file.

In data management, record may also refer to a block of data that is read and written (recorded) on the disk at one time and may have no relationship to data records in a data processing system.

record format

Same as *record layout*.

record head

A *record head* is the device that records a signal on a disk or tape. In computer devices, the *record head* is called the read/write head.

record layout

A *record layout* is the format of a data record, which includes the name, type and size of each field in the record.

NAME	ADDRESS	CITY	STATE	ZIP
Conrad, James R.	809 Garibaldi Lane	Benton Falls	TN	37255-0265

RECORD LAYOUT

record locking

See *file and record locking*.

record mark

A *record mark* is a symbol used to identify the end of a record.

record number

A *record number* may refer to the sequential number assigned to the record in a file, or to a key field, such as an account number. The physical record number will vary when the file is updated or sorted, but the logical record number, such as the account number, will always remain with the record.

records management

Records management deals with the creation, retention and scheduled destruction of an organization's paper and film documents. Computer-generated reports and documents fall into the records management domain, but traditional data processing files do not.

rectifier

A *rectifier* is an electrical circuit that converts AC current into DC current with the use of diodes that act as one-way valves.

recursion

In programming, *recursion* is the ability of a subroutine or program module to call itself. Recursion is helpful for writing routines that solve problems by repeatedly processing the output of the same process.

redundancy check

In communications, a *redundancy check* is a method for detecting transmission errors by appending calculated bits onto the end of each segment of data. See *cyclical redundancy check*.

reentrant code

Reentrant code is a program that can be used by multiple users simultaneously. When a program is written in reentrant style, only one copy of the machine code is loaded into memory, and the code is shared among any number of users on the system.

Reentrant code is written without keeping track of the progress of the processing it's performing. The progress, in the form of counters, flags and other indicators, is maintained within the calling program in order to keep the reentrant program from being modified.

Reentrant processing is analogous to several people each baking their own cake from a single recipe on the wall. Everyone keeps track of their own progress on the master recipe by jotting down the step number they're at on their own sheets of paper.

Reentrant code is used in system software, such as operating systems and teleprocessing monitors. It also lends itself to multithreading operations, where concurrent events are taking place within the computer.

reflective spot

A *reflective spot* is a metallic foil that is placed on each end of a magnetic tape. The tape drive shines light on the tape, and when the light is reflected back to a photosensor, the end of tape is signalled.

reformat

(1) *Reformat* refers to changing the record layout of a file or database.

(2) *Reformat* refers to initializing a disk over again.

refraction

Refraction is the bending of a ray of light, heat or sound as it passes through different materials.

refresh

Refresh is to continously charge a device that cannot hold its content. For example, CRTs (cathode ray tubes) must be constantly refreshed, because the color phosphors hold their glow for only a few thousandths of a second. Dynamic memory chips (DRAMs) require constant refreshing to maintain their charged bit patterns.

refresh rate

In computer graphics, the *refresh rate* is the time it takes to redraw or redisplay an image on screen.

regenerator

(1) In communications, a *regenerator* is the same as a *repeater*.

(2) In electronics, a *regenerator* is a circuit that repeatedly supplies current to a memory or display device that continuously loses its charges or content.

register

A *register* is a small, high-speed memory circuit that holds addresses and values of internal operations. For example, registers keep track of the address of the instruction being executed and the data being processed. When a program crashes, the contents of the registers are often displayed in order to help isolate the problem. The registers will tell the programmer what was happening at the moment of failure.

In microcomputer assembly language programming, the programmer constantly references registers for routine functions, such as moving data from one place to another.

register level compatibility

Register level compatibility refers to a hardware component that is 100% compatible with another device. Registers are small, high-speed memory circuits that hold instructions, addresses and data and are the physical places wherein processing takes place. Register level compatiblity requires that the same type, size and names of registers be used in the device.

relational capability

Relational capability implies that two or more data files can be linked together for viewing, editing or the creation of reports. For example, a customer file and an order file can be treated as one file in order to ask a question that relates to information in both files, such as the names of the customers that purchased a particular product. Many routine business queries involve more than one data file.

relational database

Relational database is a method for organizing files in a database that specifically prohibits linking one file to another. In hierarchical and network databases, records in one file point to the locations of records in another file, such as customers to orders and vendors to purchases. These relationships are linked within the system to provide for fast processing. In a relational database, relationships between files are strictly logical through matching account numbers and names, for example. However, the replication of account numbers or other matching criteria must be considered and included in the design of the records.

The objective of a relational database, introduced in 1970 by Edgar Codd, is that ad hoc requests for data can be easily accommodated. A relational system can take any two or more files, and, based on any matching conditions between them, can generate a new file containing the records that meet the matching criteria. In practice, a pure relational query can be extremely slow. In order to speed up the process, indexes are typically built and maintained on the key fields used for matching, thus violating the principle of "ad hoc" capability. In addition, relational capability existed long before the term came into existence, and the same database design criteria have always been a consideration.

Most personal computer database management systems use the relational method. Mainframe and minicomputer databases provide relational capability along with traditional hierarchical, network and other structures. Most database systems today claim relational capability as long as any ad hoc request can be accommodated.

relational operator

A *relational operator* specifies a comparison between two values.

Relational Operator		Symbol
EQ	Equal to	=
NE	Not equal to	< > (or #)
GT	Greater than	>
GE	Greater than or equal to	> =
LT	Less than	<
LE	Less than or equal to	< =

relational spreadsheet

See *spreadsheet*.

relative address

A *relative address* is an address that is relative to the first location of the program rather than a fixed location of memory. The relative address is added to the base address in order to derive the absolute address, the actual current location of the data. See *relocatable code* and *base/displacement*.

relative vector

In computer graphics, a *relative vector* is a vector with end points designated in relative coordinates. Contrast with *absolute vector*.

relay

A *relay* is an electrical switch that is used to allow a small current to control a larger one. The small current energizes the relay, which then closes a gate, allowing the large current to flow through.

Relay Silver

Relay Silver is a communications program from VM Personal Computing that runs on IBM compatible pcs. Version 1.0 handles transmission speeds from 50 to 9,600 bits per second, emulates four different terminals and supports four protocols. Relay Silver can be controlled by programming languages, such as BASIC, Pascal and 8086 assembly language.

relocatable code

Relocatable code refers to a machine language program that can reside in any portion of memory. Relocatable code is required in a multitasking environment in which more than one program is run at the same time and there's no fixed location for a program at any given time. For example, in Microsoft's DOS and OS/2 systems, COM files are machine language programs that must reside in a fixed location of memory, whereas EXE files are relocatable code files that can be placed anywhere in memory.

Relocatable code is accomplished with a relative addressing scheme in which the hardware increments the addresses of the machine instructions at run time. The increment is based on where the program currently resides in memory.

REM statement

A *REM statement* is a remarks statement that is used to document the program and contains no executable code.

remedial maintenance

Remedial maintenance is a service that is required due to a malfunction of the product. Contrast with *preventive maintenance*, which is regularly scheduled maintenance.

remote batch

Same as *remote job entry*.

remote communications

Remote communications is a category of software that allows a personal computer to control or duplicate the operation of another personal computer in a remote location using the standard dial-up telephone system. Technical support personnel can view a duplicate of the user's screen while the user is performing an operation. The remote communications software resides in both computers, and it allows a remote user to be an interactive participant in the other computer.

remote job entry

See *RJE*.

removable disk

A *removable disk* is a disk that is inserted into its respective disk drive for reading and writing and removed when not required. Floppy disks and disk cartridges are removable disk media.

Renderman interface

The *Renderman interface* is a graphics format from Pixar Corporation that uses the photorealistic image synthesis method for capturing the description of a real image.

repeater

In communications, a *repeater* is a device that amplifies or regenerates the data signal in order to extend the distance of the transmission. Repeaters are available for both analog and digital signals. Repeaters are used extensively in long distance transmission systems to keep the signals from losing their strength. Repeaters are used in local area networks to extend the normal distance limitations of the network.

report

A *report* is a printed or microfilmed collection of facts and figures with page numbers and page headings. In a database program, the report option is typically used to prepare any kind of printed output, including complex reports as well as mailing labels. See *query*.

report generator

Same as *report writer*.

report writer

A *report writer* is a program that prints a report from a set of layout descriptions entered by the user. A report writer is typically part of a database management system, but may also be a stand-alone program that works with an organization's existing files. Input to a report writer is the name of the file, the data to be printed in each print column, page headings, subheadings, totals and any special calculations that are to be made with the data. Once a report has been described, most report writers can store the description for future use. Report writers can usually select records from the file and sort them into a new sequence before printing.

reproducer

A *reproducer* is a tabulating machine that copies the holes from one set of punched cards and punches them into a deck of blank cards.

reprographics

Reprographics is the duplicating of printed materials using various kinds of printing presses and high-speed copiers.

reserved word

A *reserved word* is a word that is part of a programming or command language that describes some action or function. Reserved words cannot be used to name user-defined objects, such as fields and files.

reset button

A *reset button* is a button, or special key, on a computer that restarts (reboots) the computer. All current screen activities are cleared, and any data within the internal memory of the computer is erased. The reset button on a printer clears the printer's memory and readies it to accept new data from the computer.

resident module

A *resident module* is the part of a program that must remain in memory at all times. Instructions and data that stay in memory can be accessed much faster than on disk.

resistor

A *resistor* is an electronic component that resists the flow of current in an electronic circuit.

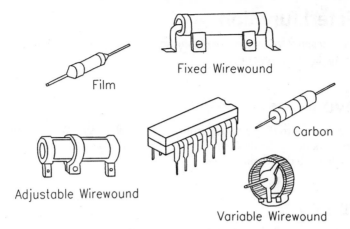

Film

Fixed Wirewound

Adjustable Wirewound

Carbon

Variable Wirewound

RESISTORS

resolution

Resolution is the degree of sharpness of a displayed or printed character or image. On a display screen, resolution is expressed as the number of horizontal dots (columns) by the number of vertical lines (rows). For example, a 680x400 resolution means 680 dots across each of 400 lines. For printers, resolution is expressed as the number of dots per linear inch. For example, a desktop laser printer prints at 300 dpi (dots per inch), which means that it prints 300 dots across and 300 dots down, or 90,000 dots per square inch.

COLUMNS OF RESOLUTION

640 x 480

ROWS OF RESOLUTION

response time

Response time is the time it takes for the computer to answer a question or accept a line of input.

restart

Restart is to resume computer opertion after a planned or unplanned termination. See *checkpoint/restart*.

restricted function

A *restricted function* is a computer or operating system function that cannot be used by an application program.

retrieve

Retrieve is to input into the computer from a peripheral device. When a user interrogates (queries) a database, the data is retrieved into the computer first and then transmitted to the terminal screen.

return key

The *return key* , also called the *enter key*, is a keyboard key that ends a line or paragraph. In data processing applications, pressing the return key ends the line of input. In word processing, pressing the return key inserts a return character into the document, which may be displayed on screen as a special character or may be invisible until purposefully revealed. In word processing, the return key is not used exactly like the carriage return key on a typewriter. The return key is pressed only to end a short line or at the end of a paragraph. It is not pressed to end lines within a paragraph, because the word processing software automatically wraps the words to the next line. On a computer keyboard, the return key is typically marked "Enter."

reverse engineering

Reverse engineering is the analysis of a completed system in order to isolate its individual components or building blocks. For example, when a chip is reverse engineered, all the individual circuits that make up the chip are isolated and identified.

reverse polish notation

Reverse polish notation is a method for expressing mathematical expressions in certain programming languages, such as FORTH. In reverse Polish notation, the numbers precede the operation. For example, 2 + 2 would be expressed as 2 2 +, and 10 - 3 * 4 would be 10 3 - 4 /.

reverse video

Reverse video is a display mode that is used for highlighting characters on the screen. For example, if the normal display is green characters on a black background, the reverse video would be black characters on a green background.

revision level

See *version number*.

RF

(Radio Frequency) *RF* is the range of electromagnetic frequencies above the audio range and below visible light. All broadcast transmission, from AM radio to satellites, falls into this range, which is between 30 thousand and 300 billion Hertz (cycles per second).

RF modulation

RF modulation refers to the transmitting of a signal through a carrier frequency. For example, when a computer, VCR or other device produces video display output to a television set via a fictitious television channel, such as Channel 3 or Channel 4, it is providing *RF modulation*.

RF shielding

RF shielding is a material that prohibits electromagnetic radiation from penetrating it. Personal computers and electronic devices that are used in the home must meet certain U. S. government standards for electromagnetic interference.

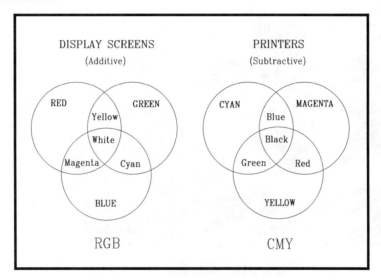

RGB AND CMY COLOR MIXING

RGB

(Red Green Blue) RGB refers to the method of recording and generating colors in a video system. On a television or color monitor, colors are displayed as varying intensities of red, green and blue dots. When red, green and blue are all turned on high, white is produced. As the intensities are equally lowered, shades of gray are produced. When all dots are turned off, the base color of the screen appears.

Color printing uses the CMY, or cyan, magenta, yellow system for mixing colors. In RGB, colors are added to create white. In CMY, colors are subtracted to create white. See *colors*.

RGB monitor

An *RGB monitor* is a video display screen that requires separate red, green and blue video signals from the computer. RGB monitors generate a higher-quality display image than display screens that use a composite signal in which all the colors are mixed together, such as in a standard TV set. RGB monitors come in both analog and digital varieties.

ribbon cable

A *ribbon cable* is a thin, flat, multiconductor cable that is widely used in electronic systems, for example, to interconnect peripheral devices to the computer internally and externally.

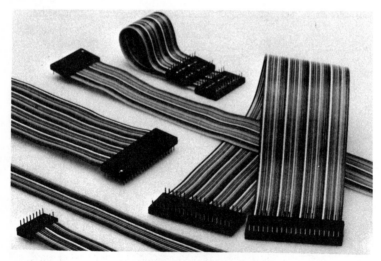

RIBBON CABLES
(Courtesy 3M Company)

right justify

In typography, *right justify* aligns text to the right margin. Same as *flush right*.

rigid disk

Same as *hard disk*.

ring network

A *ring network* is a communications network that connects terminals and computers in a circular fashion.

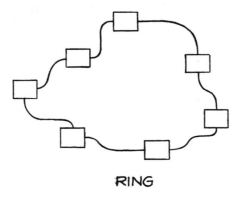

RING

RISC architecture

(Reduced Instruction Set Computer) *RISC architecture* is a computer architecture that has a limited number of instructions that it can perform. The concept is that most data processing programs use only a few instructions most of the time, and if those basic instructions are made to execute faster, there's an increase in performance most of the time. RISC architecture typically eliminates the microcode layer, which has been traditionally used to make it easier to implement new and complex instructions., but which adds processing time to all the instructions. Instead, a smaller number of instructions are designed in right down at the circuit level to begin with. Since complex instructions are removed from the computer, RISC computers require that the assemblers and compilers generate a series of simple instructions to perform complex functions.

Although RISC computers are only from 15% to 50% faster than their counterpart CICS (complex instruction set computer) computers, RISC chips are considerably less expensive to produce. Therefore, the dollars per MIPS (million instructions per second) is decidedly in favor of the RISC computer.

There's controversy over RISC architecture. Its proponents claim its increased speed and lower cost is an extreme advantage. Its opponents claim its improvements are not worth proliferating the world with new machine languages and that far greater performance improvements will be coming anyway.

In the early days, we didn't have multiply and divide instructions. The operations were performed in software with repetitive additions and subtractions. Then multiply and divide were built into the hardware. Eventually, all sorts of fancy instructions were created to do such things as table lookups (search for an item in a group of items). Now, we're heading back full circle.

Once the ties get wider and the hemlines get higher, the only other choice is to make the ties thinner and the hemlines lower.

RJE

(Remote Job Entry) *RJE* is the transmission of batches of transactions from a remote terminal or computer. The receiving computer processes the data and may transmit the results back to the RJE site for printing. RJE hardware at remote sites can employ teleprinters with disk or tape storage, or complete micro or minicomputer systems.

RLL

(Run Length Limited) *RLL* is a technique used for encoding data on a magnetic disk that requires less bits than the common MFM method. See *ST506 RLL interface*.

RO terminal

(Receive Only terminal) *RO terminals* are teleprinters, or printing terminals without keyboards. Constrast with *KSR terminal* (keyboard send receive), which have keyboards for input.

RoboCAD 4

RoboCAD 4 is a computer-aided design (CAD) program from Robo Systems that runs on IBM compatible pcs. It provides up to 256 colors and layers, has two drawing pages and a scratch pad, and can transfer data to RoboSOLID, a solids modeling program. In addition to standard drawing capabilities, it features user-definable multiple parallel lines, four mathematical curve types, ellipse, intelligent hatch, full insert transforms including squash and skew, a visual library, radial and rectangular repeat copy functions, text balloons and a variety of text functions.

robot

A *robot* is a stand-alone hybrid computer system that performs physical and computational activities. Robots can be designed similar to human form, although most industrial robots don't resemble people at all. They have one or more arms and joints designed for specific activities. The advantage of a robot is that it is a multiple-motion device, capable of performing many different tasks like a person can.

Robots are used extensively in manufacturing, performing such functions as welding, riveting, scraping and painting. Office and consumer applications are also being developed. Robots are being designed with artificial intelligence so they can respond more effectively to unstructured situations. For example, specialized robots can identify objects in a pile, select the objects in the appropriate sequence and assemble them into a unit.

Robots use analog sensors for recognizing objects in the real world and digital computers for their direction. Analog to digital converters convert temperature, motion, pressure, sound and images into binary code for the robot's computer.

The outputs of the computers direct the physical actions of the arms and joints by pulsing their motors.

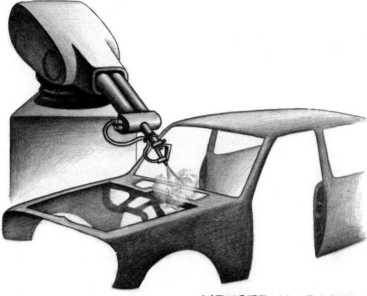

INDUSTRIAL ROBOT

robotics

Robotics is the art and science of the creation and use of robots.

robustness

Robustness refers to the quality and capability of a program. When a program is said to be robust, it works well and doesn't fall apart when some unusual condition occurs.

roll in/roll out

Roll out/roll in is a memory managment technique for freeing up memory temporarily in order to perform another task. The current program or program segment is stored (rolled out) on disk, and another program is brought in (rolled in) that memory space.

rollover

See *n-key rollover*.

ROM

(Read Only Memory) A *ROM* is a memory chip that permanently stores instructions and data. Its contents are placed into the ROM at the time of manufacture and cannot be altered. ROMs are used extensively to hold codes and programs that are reasonably permanent.

ROMs are used in the cartridges that plug into calculators, game computers and laser printers. ROMs are used in laptop computers to hold operating systems and application programs; however, if there is an update to any of the programs, the ROM chip has to be replaced with a new one.

A variation of the ROM, called a PROM, or programmable ROM, is also widely used. Unlike ROMs, PROMs are purchased empty and are filled by the customer.

ROM BIOS

(Read Only Memory Basic Input Output System) A *ROM BIOS* is the part of an operating system that contains the machine instructions necessary to activate the peripheral devices. The ROM indicates that it is permanently stored in a read only memory chip. See *BIOS*.

root directory

In hierarchical file systems, the *root directory* is the starting point in the hierarchy. When the system is first started, the root directory is made the current directory.

Access to directories in the hierarchy requires naming the directories that are in its path. In Microsoft's DOS and OS/2 operating systems, going down the hierarchy requires naming the directories in the path from the current directory to the destination directory, but going back up or sideways requires naming the entire path starting from the root directory.

rotational delay

The *rotational delay* is the amount of time it takes for the disk to rotate until the required location on the disk reaches the read/write head.

round robin

Round robin is a continuously repeating sequence, such as the polling of a series of terminals, one after the other, over and over again.

router

In communications, a *router* is a device that selects an appropriate travel path and routes a message accordingly. Routers are used in complex networks where there are many pathways between users in the network. The router examines the destination address of the message and determine the most effective route. See *bridge, gateway* and *brouter*.

routine

A *routine* is a set of instructions that perform a task. Same as *subroutine, subprogram, module, procedure* and *function*.

row

A *row* is a horizontal set of data or components that is also called the *x-axis*. Contrast with *column*, which is a vertical set of data or components.

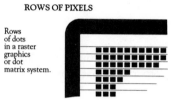

ROWS OF PIXELS

Rows of dots in a raster graphics or dot matrix system.

ROWS OF TEXT

Rows, or lines, of text in a character-based system.

A
AB
ABC

ROWS OF DATA

Rows, lines or records in a spreadsheet, text or database file.

NAME	STREET	BALANCE
Jones, Jennifer A.	10 West Main Ave.	0000208.49
Russo, George C.	23 East Benton St.	0000107.49
Morrison, Emil T.	1240 Parkway East	0001005.77
Fernandez, Joseph R.	39 Gate Drive	0003484.49

ROWS

RPG

(Report Program Generator) *RPG*, developed by IBM in 1964, was one of the first program generators designed for business reports. RPG II, introduced in 1970, was an advanced version that has been widely used as a programming language to develop business applications for small computers. The RPG statements are written on preprinted forms that provide fixed columns for writing each part of the statement. Programs like these were the forerunner of today's fourth-generation languages that allow users to process data without having to learn how to be a programmer.

RPN

See *reverse polish notation*.

RPQ

(Request for Price Quotation) An *RPQ* is a document created by a customer and delivered to a vendor, which requests a price for specifically designated hardware, software or services.

RSTS/E

RSTS/E is an operating system from Digital Equipment Corporation that is used on the PDP-11 series of minicomputers.

RSX-11

(Resource Sharing eXtension-PDP 11) *RSX-11* is a multiuser, multitasking operating system from Digital Equipment Corporation that runs on the PDP-11 series of minicomputers.

RS-232, RS-232-C

RS-232 is a widely used interface between a computer and a peripheral device, such as a modem, mouse, drawing tablet or printer. RS-232 is an EIA standard for serial transmission and typically uses the 25-pin DB-25 or the 9-pin DB-9 connector. It has a normal cable limitation of 50 feet, but with high-quality cable, it can be extended to several hundred feet.

The RS-232 standard defines the purposes, electrical characteristics and timing of the signals in the cable. However, all 25 wires in the cable are not used all the time. Many applications use less than a dozen.

Note: The same DB-25 plug and socket used in RS-232 serial cables is also used as a connector for parallel printer cables. See *DB-25*.

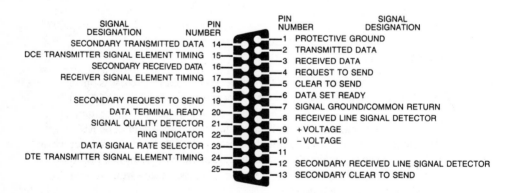

RS-232 INTERFACE

(Courtesy Black Box Corporation)

RS-422, RS-423, RS-449

RS-422 and *RS-423* are EIA standards for serial transmission that extend the distances and speeds beyond the RS-232 standard. Both interfaces typically use a DB-37 connector, but may be implemented with a variety of other connectors. RS-422 is a balanced system requiring more wire pairs than RS-423 and is intended for use in multidrop, or multipoint, lines.

RS-449 specifies the pin definitions for RS-422 and 423. RS-422 and 423 are subsets of RS-449, each specifying the electrical and timing characteristics of the lines.

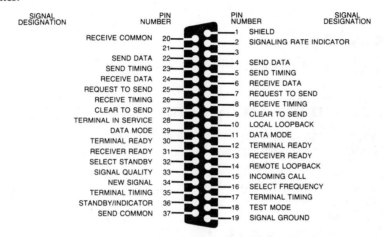

RS-449 INTERFACE

(Courtesy Black Box Corporation)

RS-485

RS-485 is an EIA standard for multidrop, or multipoint, communications lines. It can be implemented with as little as a wire block with four screws or with DB-9 or DB-37 connectors. By using lower impedance drivers and receivers, RS-485 allows more nodes on a multidrop line than RS-422.

RT

The *RT* is a personal computer from IBM that uses a reduced instruction set computer (RISC) architecture. Introduced in 1986, the RT was designed for high-performance workstation and computer-aided design applications. Its proprietary microprocessor is not compatible with the Intel-based IBM PC or PS/2 series.

RTS

(Request To Send) In RS-232 signalling, *RTS* is the signal on pin 4 that is sent from the computer to the modem which indicates that it is ready to send data.

RT-11

RT-11 is a single user, multitasking operating system from Digital Equipment Corporation that runs on its PDP-11 series of minicomputers.

rubber banding

In computer graphics, *rubber banding* is the moving of a line or object where one end stays fixed in position.

rubout key

The *rubout key* on a terminal keyboard deletes the last character that was entered.

rule-based expert system

A *rule-based expert system* is an expert system based on a set of rules that a human expert would follow in diagnosing a problem. Contrast with *model-based expert system*.

ruler line

A *ruler line* is a graphic representation of a ruler on screen that is used for laying out text and graphics.

rules

(1) *Rules* are a set of conditions or standards which have been agreed upon.

(2) In printing, *rules* are horizontal and vertical lines which are used between columns or at the top and bottom of a page in order to enhance the appearance of the printed page.

run

(1) *Run* is to execute a program.

(2) A *run* is a single program that is to be executed, or a group of programs that are to be executed sequentially.

run around

In desktop publishing, *run around* is the flowing of text around a graphic image.

run length limited

See *RLL*.

run time

Run time refers to the actual execution of a program.

run time version

Run time version refers to software that enables another program to work with its special features, but restricts the use of all the features of the original program. For example, in personal computers, a run time version of a database management system allows a program written in its programming language to run without requiring the full DBMS in the computer. However, the user would not be able to access all the interactive features of the full DBMS. A run time version of a windowing environment, such as Microsoft Windows or Digital Research's GEM, may accompany a program in order to provide it with a Xerox/Macintosh interface without requiring the user to have the complete windowing package in the computer.

SAA

(System Application Architecture) Introduced in 1987, *SAA* is a set of standards from IBM that provide consistent interconnections among all of IBM's computers. SAA is a collection of user interfaces, software interfaces, communications protocols and other conventions that will bring together the 370 mainframe line, System/36 and System/38 minicomputers, and PS/2 personal computer series into a coherent product line.

SAM

See *sequential access method*.

Samna

Samna is a series of word processing programs from Samna Corporation that run on IBM compatible pcs and UNIX minicomputers. Introduced in 1983, Samna was one of the first full-featured word processors for personal computers. In 1986, Samna integrated desktop publishing features into its Word IV and Plus IV programs, providing integration of graphs and text and the ability to edit columns and equations on screen. Samna Plus IV also provides an integrated spreadsheet and text retrieval system, and Release 2.0 (1988) adds a thesaurus and graphics preview mode.

Samna Word IV was the first word processing program to be approved by the Legal Technology Advisory Council of the American Bar Association.

sampling

(1) In statistics, *sampling* is the analysis of a group by determining the characteristics of a significant percentage of its members chosen at random.

(2) In digitizing operations, *sampling* is the conversion of real-world signals or movements at regular intervals into digital code.

sampling rate

In digitizing operations, the *sampling rate* is the frequency with which samples are taken and converted. The higher the *sample rate*, the closer real-world objects are represented in digital form.

sans-serif

Sans-serif is a modern style of typeface without the serifs, the added horizontal lines added at the tops and bottoms of the vertical member of the letter. For example, the boldface headers for each term in this book are sans-serif, while the text you're reading now is a typeface with serifs.

AAA   AAA

SAS

(Statistical Analysis System) *SAS* is an integrated data management, analysis and presentation system from SAS Institute Inc., that runs on IBM mainframes, IBM compatible pcs and a variety of minicomputers. SAS is widely used for data analysis on IBM mainframes and Digital VAX minicomputers. SAS is a modular system that includes software for data entry, updating, queries and report writing, spreadsheets, computer-based training, presentation graphics, project management, operations research, scheduling, linear programming, statistical quality control, econometric and time series analysis, mathematical, engineering and statistical applications as well as full application development.

satellite

See *communications satellite*

satellite channel

A *satellite channel* is a particular carrier frequency for the radio transmission of data.

satellite computer

A *satellite computer* is a computer in a separate location that is available to communicate with the host computer or is under the control of the host. A satellite computer can function as a slave to the master computer or perform off-line auxiliary tasks.

satellite link

A *satellite link* is a signal that travels from the earth to a communications satellite and back down again. Contrast with *terrestrial link*, which is a line that travels across the earth.

saturation

(1) On magnetic disks and tapes, *saturation* occurs when the magnetizable particles are completely aligned and a more powerful writing signal will not improve the reading back.

(2) In a bipolar transistor, *saturation* occurs when the current on the gate (the trigger) is equal to or greater than what is necessary to close the switch.

(3) In a diode, *saturation* occurs when the diode is fully conducting.

save

Save is to write the contents of memory to disk or tape. Since memory (RAM chips) lose their content when the power is turned off, it is prudent to save work that has been changed at periodic intervals. Some database and word processing programs save data automatically as memory fills up, or at regular intervals, say, every five minutes. However many programs, especially spreadsheet programs, require that the user specifically save the data. Even with programs that provide automatic saving, it is still necessary to inform the program that you're finished before you turn the power off, since the last set of data updated only in memory, may still be in memory.

SBS

(Satellite Business Systems) *SBS* was developed to offer satellite communications services to business using rooftop antennas on customer's premises. SBS is currently part of the MCI Corporation.

scalable fonts

Scalable fonts are type fonts that can be automatically sized from a base font. Also called *outline fonts*, scalable fonts are found in page description languages, such as Postscript, in which the outlines of the font are maintained, but the actual font size is computed as needed. Contrast with *bit mapped fonts*, which are a set of predefined dot patterns of each letter and digit for each font size. Thus, if 10-point and 16-point fonts are required, all the dot patterns for the 10-point font and all the dot patterns for the 16-point font must be sent to the printer. With scalable fonts, only codes designating the style of font and font size are sent to the printer, or to a special graphics controller board that generates the actual patterns.

scalar

A *scalar* is a single item or value. Contrast with *vector* and *array*, which are made up of multiple values.

scalar processor

A *scalar processor* is a computer that performs arithmetic computations on one number at a time. Contrast with *vector processor*, which performs several calculations simultaneously.

scalar variable

In programming, a *scalar variable* is a variable that contains only one value.

scale

(1) In computer graphics and printing, *scale* is to resize an object, making it smaller or larger.

(2) *Scale* is to change the representation of a quantity in order to bring it into prescribed limits of another range. For example, values such as 1249, 876, 523, -101 and -234 might need to be scaled into a range from -5 to +5.

(3) *Scale* is to designate the position of the decimal point in a fixed or floating point number.

scan

(1) In graphics and video display functions, *scan* is to move across a picture frame a line at a time, either to detect the image, as in an analog or digital camera, or to refresh a CRT-based video screen.

(2) In optical technologies, *scan* is to view a printed form a line at a time in order to convert an image into a bit mapped representation, or to recognize printed characters and convert them into a digital data code, such as ASCII.

scan head

A *scan head* is an optical sensing device in an optical scanner or facsimile machine that is moved across the image to be scanned.

scan line

A *scan line* is one of many horizontal lines in a graphics frame.

scan rate

(1) *Scan rate* is the total number of lines that are illuminated on a video display screen in one second. For example, a resolution of 400 lines that is refreshed 60 times per second requires a scan rate of 24kHz (24,000 cyles per second). The scan rate is called the *horizontal synchronization frequency* in the television industry.

(2) The *scan rate* is the number of times per second a scanning device samples its field of vision.

scanner

A *scanner* is a hardware device that reads text, images and bar code. Text and bar code scanners recognize printed fonts and bar codes and convert them into a digital code, such as ASCII. Graphics scanners convert a printed image into a video image (raster graphics) without recognizing the actual content of the text or pictures.

scatter diagram

A *scatter diagram* is a graph that is plotted with dots or some other symbol at each data point. A scatter diagram is also called a scatter plot or dot chart.

scatter plot

Same as *scatter diagram*.

scatter read/gather write

Scatter read/gather write is an input/output capability that inputs data into two or more noncontiguous locations of memory with one read operation. It also outputs data from two or more noncontiguous memory locations with one write operation.

SCERT

(Systems and Computers Evaluation and Review Technique) Pronounced "skirt," *SCERT* is a program that measures the performance of a running system by modeling the computer environment and the kinds of programs that run in it.

scheduler

A *scheduler* is the part of the operating system that initiates and terminates jobs (programs) in the computer. Also called a dispatcher, the scheduler maintains a list of jobs to be run and allocates appropriate computer resources as required.

scheduling algorithm

A *scheduling algorithm* states the criteria examined and their order of importance for the operating system to put a job into execution. Such things as priority, length of time in the job queue and available resources are part of a scheduling algorithm.

schema

A *schema* is the definition of an entire database. A subschema is the definition of a user's partial view of the database.

Schottky

Schottky is a category of bipolar transistors that is known for its fast switching speeds in the three-nanosecond range. *Schottky II* devices have switching speeds in the range of a single nanosecond.

scientific applications

Scientific applications simulate real-world activities using mathematics. Real-world objects are turned into numbers (mathematical models), and their actions are simulated by manipulating these models using mathematical formulas.

For example, an airplane can be described mathematically, and some of its flight characteristics can be simulated in the computer. Rivers, lakes and mountains can also be simulated. Virtually any objects with known characteristics can be modeled and simulated.

Scientific applications require enormous calculations and often require supercomputers to perform the simulations. As personal computers become more powerful, more laboratory experiments will be converted into computer models that can then be interactively examined by students without the risk and cost of the actual experiments.

scientific computer

A *scientific computer* is a computer that is specialized for high-speed mathematic processing. See *array processor* and *floating point processor*.

scientific language

A *scientific language* is a programming language that is designed for mathematical formulas and matrices, such as ALGOL, FORTRAN and APL. Although all programming languages allow for this kind of processing, statements in a scientific language make it easier or simpler to express these actions.

scientific notation

Scientific notation is the displaying of a number in floating point form; for example, 2345E3 is equivalent to 2,345,000, where the number following the E represents the number of zeros or the power to which the preceding number should be raised.

scissoring

In computer graphics, *scissoring*, also called *clipping*, is the deleting of any parts of an image which fall outside of a window that has been sized and laid over the original image.

SCO XENIX

SCO XENIX is a version of Microsoft's XENIX operating system that runs on IBM compatible pcs from the Santa Cruz Operation (SCO). SCO XENIX is very similar to UNIX System V, with additional enhancements made by SCO. It is also capable of coexisting on the same computer with Microsoft's DOS operating system.

scrambler

A *scrambler* is a hardware device or software program that encodes data.

scrambling

Scrambling is encoding data to make it indecipherable. See *encryption* and *DES*.

Scrapbook

In the Macintosh, the *Scrapbook* is a disk file that holds frequently-used text and graphics objects, such as a company letterhead.

scratch tape

A *scratch tape* is a magnetic tape that contains data that is no longer needed and can be erased and reused.

scratchpad

A *scratchpad* is a special register or a reserved section of memory or disk that is used for temporary storage.

screen

(1) A *screen* is the display area of a video terminal that is physically a cathode ray tube (CRT) or one of the flat screen technologies, such as electroluminescent or LCD.

(2) A *screen* refers to the purpose or the kind of information being displayed, for example, a menu screen, data entry screen or graphics screen.

screen dump

A *screen dump* is the ability to print the entire contents of the current display screen. With IBM compatible pcs, pressing the Prt Sc (Print Screen) key with the Shift key held down may or may not print the current screen. If not, a screen dump program, compatible with your particular graphics display system, must be loaded and then activated at the appropriate time. In the Macintosh, pressing the "3" key with the Apple and Shift keys held down creates a MacPaint file of the current screen no matter what application you're running.

screen overlay

(1) A *screen overlay* is a clear, fine-mesh screen that reduces the glare on a video screen.

(2) A *screen overlay* is a clear touch panel that allows the user to command the computer by touching displayed buttons on screen.

(3) A *screen overlay* is a window of data displayed on screen temporarily. The part of the screen that was overlaid is saved and restored when the screen overlay is removed.

script

(1) *Script* is a typeface that looks like handwriting or calligraphy.

(2) A *script* is a program or macro.

scroll arrow, scroll bar

A *scroll arrow* is an icon that points either up, down, left or right and is clicked in order to scroll the screen in the corresponding direction. The screen moves one line, or increment, with each click of the mouse.

A *scroll bar* is a horizontal or vertical bar that contains a box. The box is clicked and dragged either up or down, or left or right, in order to scroll the screen. The box functions like an elevator in a shaft.

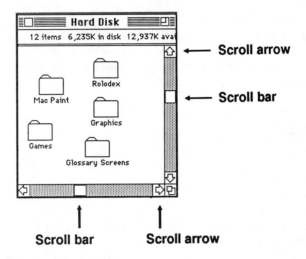

← **Scroll arrow**

← **Scroll bar**

↑ **Scroll bar**   ↑ **Scroll arrow**

scrolling

Scrolling is the ability to continuously move forward, backward and sideways through the images in a window (video screen). Vertical scrolling is moving forward and backward, and horizontal scrolling is moving sideways. Scrolling implies continuous and smooth movement, a line, character or pixel at a time, as if the data were on a paper scroll being rolled behind the screen. However, scrolling isn't always smooth. The screen may be bumped a few rows or columns all at once, especially in database programs that move from one column (field) to another. Scrolling also refers to only a single field of data, in which a long phrase can be typed into a small box on screen.

VERTICAL SCROLLING

SCSI

(Small Computer System Interface) Often pronounced "scuzzy," the *SCSI* is an interface standard for a personal computer that connects up to seven peripheral devices. SCSI is standard on the Macintosh series starting with the Macintosh Plus and is available for IBM personal computers by inserting an SCSI printed circuit board in one of its expansion slots. The SCSI provides a high-speed, parallel data transfer of up to four megabytes per second and has the advantage of connecting multiple peripheral units while taking up only one slot in the computer.

scuzzy

See *SCSI*.

SDLC

(Synchronous Data Link Control) *SDLC* is the primary data link protocol used in IBM's SNA (System Network Architecture) communications networks. SDLC is a bit-oriented, synchronous protocol, which is similar to the international HDLC protocol. SDLC is representative of layer 2 in the OSI model.

SE

See *systems engineer*.

seamless integration

Seamless integration refers to the addition of a new program or routine that works smoothly with the existing system. It implies that the new feature can be activated and used as if it had been built in from scratch. Contrast with *transparent* installation, which implies that there is no discernible change in the system after installation.

search & replace

In word processing, *search & replace* looks for occurrences of text and replaces them with other text.

search key

A *search key* is the data being looked up in a search routine.

second-generation computer

A *second-generation computer* is a computer that is made of discrete transistors and electronic components. In the early 1960s, the IBM 1401 and Honeywell 400 were examples of second-generation computers.

second source

A *second source* is an alternative supplier of an identical product. A *second source* manufacturer is one that holds a license to produce an original product from another manufacturer.

secondary channel

In communications, a *secondary channel* is a subchannel that is derived from the main channel. It is used for diagnostic or supervisory purposes, but does not carry data messages.

secondary storage

Secondary storage is external storage, such as disk and tape, as contrasted with the computer's main memory.

sector

A *sector* is the smallest unit of storage read or written by a disk. Sectors are fixed in length, and the same number of sectors usually reside in one track. However, the hardware may vary the disk speed to fit more sectors into tracks located on the outer edges of the disk platter. The sector is the physical unit called for by an instruction, for example, READ TRACK 17 SECTOR 23.

sector interleave

The *sector interleave*, or sector map, is how sectors are numbered on a hard disk. The interleave can be sequential (0,1,2,3...) or staggered, for example, 0,3,6,1,4,7,2,5,8. In sequential numbering, if data in sector 1 is read, by the time the access to 2 is given, the beginning of sector 2 has passed the head and must rotate around to come under the head again. The staggering of sectors optimizes sequential reads and writes to a disk.

sector map

See *sector interleave*.

security

Security is the protection of data against unauthorized access. Programs and data can be secured by issuing identification numbers and passwords to all authorized users of the system. However, the systems programmer, or other technically competent individuals, will ultimately have access to these codes.

Passwords can be checked by the operating system to prevent users from logging onto the system in the first place, or they can be checked in software, such as database management systems, where each user can be assigned an individual view (subschema) of the database. Any application program running in the computer can also be designed to check for passwords.

Data transmitted over communications networks can be secured by encryption to prevent successful eavesdropping.

Although precautions can be taken to detect an unauthorized user, it is extremely difficult to determine if a valid user is performing unauthorized tasks. Effective security measures are a balance of technology and personnel management.

security kernel

A *security kernel* is the part of the operating system that grants access to users of the computer system.

seed

A *seed* is a starting value that is used by a random number generation routine to create random numbers.

seek

(1) A *seek* is the moving of the access arm to the requested track on a disk.

(2) *Seek* is an instruction in a low-level assembly language that activates a seek operation on the disk.

(3) *Seek* is a command in a high-level programming language that is used to select a record by key field.

seek time

Seek time is the time it takes to move the read/write head to a particular track on a disk after the instruction has been executed. The average seek time is also called the access time.

segment

(1) *Segment* may refer to any partition, reserved area, partial component or piece of a larger structure. For example, a program segment is one part of a larger program that may be called in separately or programmed separately.

(2) A *segment* is one of the bars that make up a single character in an LED or LCD display.

selection sort

A *selection sort* is a search for specific data, starting at the beginning of a file or list. It copies each matching item to a new file so that the selected items are in the same sequence as the original data.

selective calling

In communications, *selective calling* is the ability of the transmitting station to indicate which station in the network is to receive the message.

selector channel

A *selector channel* is a high-speed computer channel that connects a peripheral device, such as a disk or tape, to the computer's memory.

selector pen

Same as *light pen*.

Selectric typewriter

The *Selectric typewriter*, introduced in 1961 by IBM, was the first typewriter to use a golf-ball-like print head that moved across the paper, rather than moving the paper carriage across the print mechanism. The Selectric typewriter rapidly became one of the world's most popular typewriters. IBM has always excelled in the creation and production of electromechanical devices.

self-checking digit

See *check digit*.

self-clocking

Self-clocking is the recording of digital data on a magnetic medium such that the clock pulses are intrinsically part of the recorded signal, and a separate timer clock is not required. Phase encoding is a self-clocking recording technique that is commonly used.

self-documenting code

Self-documenting code refers to programming statements that are simple and obvious and that can be easily interpreted by another programmer.

semantic gap

The *semantic gap* is the amount of difference between a data or language structure and the real world. For example, in an order processing system that uses a hierarchical database, a company cannot be both customer and supplier within the database. Since there is no way to model this real-world possibility, the semantic gap is said to be large. A network database could handle this condition, resulting in a smaller semantic gap. See *object-oriented database*.

semantics

Semantics is the study of the meanings of words. As applied to computer languages, semantics governs the basic rules of the language. For example, a reserved word, such as DISPLAY or LIST, should not be used as the name of a data file or field so that you don't wind up with LIST LIST. Contrast with *syntax*, which deals with the correct order or symbols used in combining words in a command phrase.

semaphore

A *semaphore* is a hardware or software flag that is used to indicate the status of some activity.

semiconductor

A *semiconductor* is a solid state substance that can be electrically altered. Certain elements in nature, such as silicon, perform like semiconductors when they are chemically combined with other elements. A semiconductor is halfway between a conductor, a material that conducts electricity, and an insulator, a material that resists electricity. When charged with electricity or light, semiconductors change their state from nonconductive to conductive or vice versa. The most significant semiconductor is the transistor, which simply acts like an on/off switch, allowing current to pass or not to pass through it.

semiconductor device

A *semiconductor device* is an elementary component, such as a transistor, or a larger unit of electronic equipment comprised of chips.

sensor

A *sensor* is a hardware device that measures or detects a real world condition, such as motion, heat or light and converts the condition into an analog or digital representation of it. An optical sensor detects the intensity or brightness of light, or the intensity of red, green and blue for color systems.

sequel

See *SQL*.

sequence check

A *sequence check* is the testing of a list of items or file of records for correct ascending or descending sequence based on the item or key fields in the records.

sequential access method

The *sequential access method* is the organization of data in a prescribed ascending or descending sequence. Data stored in this fashion must be searched for by reading and comparing each record, starting from the beginning or end of the file.

serial

Serial implies one after the other. Sequential also implies one after the other, but in a consecutive order, such as by account number or name.

serial and parallel port

A *serial and parallel port* is one serial and one parallel connector for connecting peripheral devices to your personal computer. Personal computers are often advertised as having a serial and parallel port. Although more than one of each may be necessary for a particular requirement, the serial port allows you to hook up a modem, mouse or printer, and the parallel port lets you hook up to a printer.

For minicomputers and mainframes, there are myriads of connectors that are referenced by many designations. See *plugs & sockets*.

serial interface

See *serial port*.

serial mouse

A *serial mouse* is a mouse that connects to a computer's serial port. See *bus mouse*.

serial number

(1) A *serial number* is a manufacturer-assigned number that is printed on the equipment. It is also a number assigned to a software package by the software vendor and is displayed when a program is loaded.

(2) A *serial number* is a number that indicates the position of an item in a list.

serial port

A *serial port* is a receptacle that is used to attach a serial device, such as a modem, mouse or printer, to a personal computer. The typical serial port is the RS-232 25-pin variety, although 9-pin connectors are also used for serial devices. A serial port implies that the data is transmitted over the lines one bit at a time. Contrast with *parallel port*, which transmits data one byte at a time over eight wires.

serial printer

A *serial printer* is a printer that prints one character at a time, in contrast to a line or page at a time. The term serial in this context has no relationship to a serial or parallel interface that is used to attach the printer to the computer. See *printer*.

serial transmission

Serial transmission is the transmission of data one bit at a time, one bit following the next. Contrast with *parallel transmission*, which transmits one or more bytes (8, 16 bits, etc.) at the same time.

serialize

Serialize is to convert a parallel signal that is made up of one or more bytes into a serial signal that is one bit after the other.

Series/1

The *Series/1* is a series of minicomputers from IBM that was introduced in 1976. Series/1 machines are used in a variety of ways, including general business computing, as communications processors and as data collection and analysis systems in process control applications.

serif

Serifs are the horizontal lines that are added to the tops and bottoms of traditional typefaces, such as the one you're reading now. See *sans-serif*.

service

Service is another term for the functionality derived from a particular software program. For example, "network services" refers to a series of communications control programs that provide for the transmission, receiving and routing of data within a network. "Database services" provides for the storage and retrieval of data in a database.

service bureau

A *service bureau* is an organization that provides data processing and timesharing services to its customers. Service bureaus offer a wide variety of software packages, as well as customized programming. Customers pay for their processing, which is calculated from their actual use of the computer. Service bureaus also charge a monthly rental for each byte of online disk storage reserved for customers' programs and databases.

Connection is made to a service bureau through dial-up terminals, private lines, or other networks, such as Telenet or Tymnet.

In addition, service bureaus can offer or specialize in batch processing services, such as data entry or COM (computer output microfilm) processing.

servo

A *servo* is an electromechanical device that uses feedback to provide precise starts and stops for such functions as the motors on a tape drive or the moving of an access arm on a disk.

session

(1) In communications, a *session* is the active connection and transmission of data between two users at terminals, between two computers or between a user and the computer.

(2) A *session* is the time between starting up and ending an application program.

seven-segment display

A *seven-segment display* is a common display that is found on digital watches and readouts and looks like a series of 8s. Each digit or alphabetic letter is formed by the selective illumination of up to seven separately addressable bars.

sex changer

See *gender changer*.

shadow batch

A *shadow batch* system is an online data collection system that simulates a transaction processing environment. Instead of updating master files, such as customer and inventory files, when orders or shipments are initiated, the transactions are only stored in the computer system for reference. When a user makes a query, the master record from the previous update cycle is retrieved; but before it's displayed, it's updated in memory with any transactions that may affect it. The up-to-date master record is then displayed for the user. At the end of the day or period, the transactions are then actually batch processed against the master file.

shared DASD

(shared Direct Access Storage Device) A *shared DASD* is a disk that is accessed by two or more computers within a single datacenter. When disks are shared in personal computer networks, they are called file servers or database servers.

shared logic

Shared logic is the use of a single computer that provides processing for two or more terminals. Contrast with *shared resource*.

shared resource

A *shared resource* is a peripheral device, such as a disk or printer, that is shared by multiple users. For example, a file server and laser printer in a local area network are shared resources. Contrast with *shared logic*.

shareware

Shareware is personal computer software that is distributed free of charge to users. Shareware programs ask you to pay a nominal charge for the program if you use it and like it. In that way, you'll be registered with the company and be able to receive additional support and notifications of updates. Shareware is usually available on electronic bulletin boards, where you can dial up the service and download the program directly into your computer.

sheet feeder

A *sheet feeder* is a mechanical device that feeds stacks of standard cut forms, such as letterheads and legal paper, into a printer.

shell

A *shell* is an outer layer of a program that provides the user interface, or way of commanding the computer. Shells are typically add-on programs created for command-driven operating systems, such as UNIX and Microsoft's DOS. The shell provides a menu-driven or graphical icon-oriented interface to the system in order to make it easier to use.

shift register

A *shift register* is a high-speed memory circuit that holds some number of bits for the purpose of shifting them left or right. It is used internally within the processor for multiplication and division, serial/parallel conversion and various timing considerations.

short card

In IBM compatible pcs, a *short card* is a plug-in printed circuit board that is half the length of a full-size board. See *long card*.

short-haul modem

In communications, a *short-haul modem* is the same as a *line driver*, except that it transmits signals up to about a mile. The line driver can transmit signals up to several miles.

SI

See *Norton SI*.

sideband

In communications, a *sideband* is either the upper or lower half of a carrier wave. Since both sidebands are normally mirror images of each other, one of the halves can be used for a second channel to increase the data-carrying capacity of the line or for diagnostic or control purposes.

Sidekick

Sidekick is a desktop utility program from Borland International that runs on IBM compatible pcs. Introduced in 1984, Sidekick was the first memory resident desktop program for IBM personal computers. It provides the user with a calculator, WordStar-compatible notepad, appointment calendar, phone dialer and ASCII conversion table at any time by pressing a specific key (hot key) no matter what application program is currently running.

An enhanced version of Sidekick, called *Sidekick Plus*, was introduced in 1988. It provides additional WordStar commands for the notepad, the ability to set alarms in the calendar, new scientific and programming calculators, some limited file management capabilities and an outliner that includes table-of-contents generation.

Sieve of Eratosthenes

A *Sieve of Eratosthenes* is a benchmark program that is used to test the pure mathematical speed of a computer. The program calculates prime numbers based on Eratosthenes's algorithm.

SIG

(Special Interest Group) A *SIG* is a group within the Association of Computing Machinery (ACM) that meet and share information about a particular topic of interest.

SIGGRAPH

SIGGRAPH is a special interest group on computer graphics that is part of the Association of Computing Machinery (ACM).

sign

A *sign* is a symbol that identifies a positive or negative number. In digital code, a sign is either a separate character or part of the byte. For example, in ASCII code on micros and minis, the sign is kept in a separate character typically transmitted in front of the number it represents (ASCII 45 is minus, ASCII 43 is plus). In EBCDIC code on IBM mainframes, the minus sign can be stored as a separate byte (hex 60), or, more commonly, as half a byte (+ = hex C, - = hex D), which is stored in the high-order bits of the least significant byte. For packed decimal, it is stored in the low-order bits of the least significant byte.

sign on/sign off

Same as *log-on/log-off*.

signal

A *signal* is the physical form of transmitted data, such as electrical pulses and frequencies, or light pulses and frequencies. Signal may refer to the transmission of only data, only control codes or both.

signal converter

A *signal converter* is a device that changes the electrical or light characteristics of a signal.

signal processing

See *digital signal processing*.

signal to noise ratio

The *signal to noise ratio* is the ratio of the amplitude (power, volume) of a data signal to the amount of noise (interference) in the line. Usually measured in decibels, the signal to noise ratio measures the clarity or quality of a transmission channel or electronic device.

signaling in band

In communications, *signaling in band* is sending control signals within the same frequency range as the data signal.

signaling out of band

In communications, *signaling out of band* is the sending of control signals outside of the frequency range of the data signal.

significant digits

The *significant digits* are the digits in the number that add value to the number. For example, in the number 00006508, 6508 are the significant digits.

silica

Same as *silicon dioxide*.

silica gel

Silica gel is a highly absorbent form of silicon dioxide that is often wrapped in small bags and packed in with equipment to absorb moisture during shipping and storage.

silicon

Silicon (Si) is the base material for fabricating microelectronic circuits (chips). Next to oxygen, silicon is the most abundant element in nature and is found in a natural state in the majority of rocks and sand on earth. The silicon used in chips is mined from rocks and then purified.

Its atomic structure and abundance make it an ideal semiconductor material. Pure silicon is obtained by putting it through a chemical process at high temperatures. In its molten state, the silicon is mixed (doped) with other chemicals to alter its electrical nature. See *semiconductor* and *chip*.

silicon dioxide

Silicon dioxide (SiO^2) is a hard, glassy mineral found in such materials as rock, quartz, sand and opal. In MOS chip fabrication, silicon dioxide is used to create the insulation layer between the metal gates of the top layer and the silicon elements below it.

silicon foundry

A *silicon foundry* is a company that fabricates chips for another chip company that designs the chips but doesn't have its own manufacturing facility. A silicon foundry is typically a large chip maker that uses its excess manufacturing capacity in this manner.

silicon nitride

Silicon nitride (Si^3N^4) is a silicon compound that is capable of holding a static electric charge and is used as a gate element on some MOS transistors.

silicon on sapphire

See *SOS*.

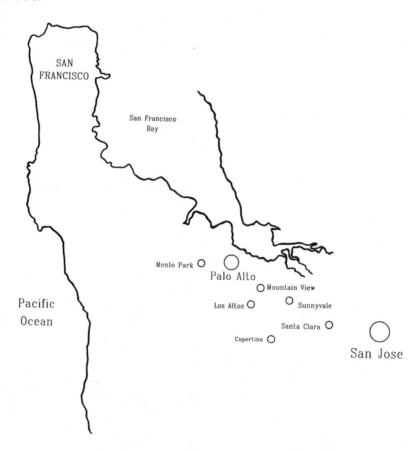

SILICON VALLEY

Silicon Valley

Silicon Valley is an area around Palo Alto and Sunnyvale in the Santa Clara Valley of California, (south of San Francisco) that is noted for its large number of high-technology companies.

SIM

(Society for Information Management) Founded in 1968 as the Society for Management Information Systems, *SIM* is an organization of MIS professionals. SIM members can use the society as an exchange or marketplace for technical information. SIM offers educational and research programs, competitions and awards to its members. For more information, contact SIM, 111 East Wacker Drive, Suite 600, Chicago, IL 60601 (312) 644-6610

SIMM

(Single Inline Memory Module) A *SIMM* is a small printed circuit board that holds a handful of memory chips.

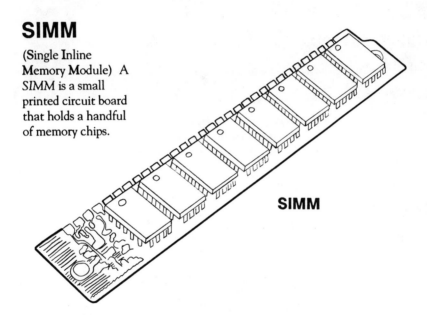

SIMM

simplex

Simplex is one way transmission. See *half-duplex* and *full-duplex*.

SIMSCRIPT

SIMSCRIPT is a programming language that is used for discrete simulations.

simulation

(1) *Simulation* is the mathematical representation of the interaction of real-world objects. See *scientific applications*.

(2) *Simulation* is the execution of a machine language program designed to run in a foreign computer.

THE NETWORK ANALYZER

(Courtesy The MIT Museum)

This high-tech machine was used to simulate electrical power grids during the 1930s.

sine wave

A *sine wave* is a uniform wave that is generated by a single frequency.

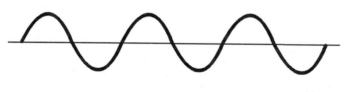

SINE WAVE

single board computer

A *single board computer* contains the processor and memory on a single printed circuit board.

single density disk

A *single density disk* is a first-generation disk.

single precision

Single precision is the use of one computer word to hold a numeric value for calculation.

single sided disk

A *single sided disk* is a floppy disk that stores data on only one side.

single threading

Single threading is the processing of one transaction to completion before processing another transaction.

sink

A *sink* is a device or place that accepts something. For example, a heat sink accepts heat in an electronic circuit in order to dissipate it. A message or data sink stores messages or data temporarily, such as in a communications system.

skew

(1) *Skew* is the misalignment of a document or punched card in the feed tray or hopper that prohibits it from being scanned or read properly.

(2) In facsimile, *skew* is the difference in rectangularity between the received and transmitted page.

(3) In communications, *skew* is a change of timing or phases in a transmission signal.

sky wave

A *sky wave* is a radio signal that is transmitted into the sky and is reflected back down to earth from the ionosphere.

slave

A *slave* is a computer or peripheral device that is controlled by another computer. For example, a terminal or printer in a remote location that only receives data is a slave. When two personal computers are hooked up via their serial or parallel ports for transmission, the file transfer program may make one computer the master and the other the slave.

slave tube

A *slave tube* is a display monitor (CRT) connected to another monitor in order to provide an additional viewing station.

sleep

(1) In programming, *sleep* is an inactive state due to an endless loop or programmed delay. A sleep statement in a programming language creates a delay for some specified amount of time.

(2) *Sleep* refers to the inactive status of a terminal, device or program that is "awakened" by sending a code to it.

slot

(1) A *slot* is a receptacle for additional printed circuit boards.

(2) A *slot* is a receptacle for the insertion and removal of a disk or tape cartridge.

(3) In communications, a *slot* is a narrow band of frequencies.

(4) A time *slot* is a continuously repeating interval of time or a time period in which two devices are able to interconnect.

(5) A *slot* can refer to any reserved space for the temporary or permanent storage of instructions, data or codes.

slow scan TV

Slow scan TV is the transmission of individual video frames over ordinary telephone lines. Slow scan TV is not a realtime transmission; it takes several seconds to transmit one frame.

SLSI

(Super Large Scale Integration) *SLSI* refers to ultra-high-density chips that contain 10 million or more transistors and electronic components. SLSI chips should materialize by the mid-1990s.

slug

A *slug* is a metal bar containing the carved image of a letter or digit that is used in a printing mechanism.

Small Computer System Interface

See *SCSI*.

Smalltalk

Smalltalk is an operating system and object-oriented programming language that was developed at Xerox's Palo Alto Research Center (PARC). As an integrated environment, Smalltalk eliminates the distinction between programming language and operating system. It also allows the programmer to customize the user interface and behavior of the system.

Smalltalk was the first object-oriented programming language and it was used on Xerox's Alto computer, which was expressly designed for it. Smalltalk was originally used to create prototypes of simpler programming languages and the windows-oriented graphical interfaces that are so popular today.

Smalltalk/V

Smalltalk/V is a version of the Smalltalk programming language from Digitalk, Inc., that runs on IBM compatible pcs.

smart card

A *smart card* is a credit card with a built-in computer. Smart cards can be used as identification cards or as financial transaction cards. It contains a microprocessor and memory that, when inserted into a specialized reader, can exchange financial and/or identification data about the card holder with a computer system. The smart card is more secure than a magnetic card (magnetic strip on the back of a credit card), since it cannot be tampered with. The computer inside the smart card may be programmed to self-destruct if the wrong password is entered too many times. As a financial transaction card, the smart card can permanently store many transactions and actually maintain a bank balance within the card.

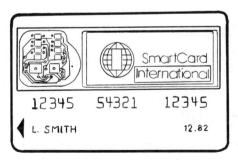

SMART CARD

smart terminal

A *smart terminal* is a video terminal with various display characteristics, such as blinking characters, reverse imaging (dark on light), underlines and boldface. Smart terminals may also contain built-in communications protocols to connect to minicomputers and mainframes. Sometimes smart terminal is used to refer to intelligent terminal. See *intelligent terminal* and *dumb terminal*.

Smartcom III

Smartcom III is a communications program from Hayes Microcomputer Products that runs on IBM compatible pcs. Smartcom III will work with any modem, but is naturally suited for Hayes modems and has a special protocol for error checking modems, such as the Hayes V-series. Version 1.0 emulates three different terminals, supports four protocols and can run two communications sessions concurrently if two modems are attached to the computer. The program also contains its own script language, called "SCOPE," that lets users automate communications activities. In "learn mode," Smartcom III will convert a routine log-on operation into a script.

SmartKey

SmartKey is a keyboard macro processor from Software Research Technologies that runs on IBM compatible pcs. SmartKey was one of the first macro processors allowing users to eliminate repetitive typing by setting up an occurrence of text or a series of commands as a macro. As of Version 5.2, SmartKey can be programmed to initiate actions based on time, date and keyboard input.

smoke test

A *smoke test* is connecting power to a brand new or newly repaired device in order to see if it works. If there's smoke, it doesn't work.

smoothed data

Smoothed data is statistical data that has been averaged such that the curves on a graph are smooth and free of irregularities.

smoothing circuit

A *smoothing circuit* is an electronic filtering circuit in a DC power supply that removes the ripples that come from the AC power lines.

SNA

(Systems Network Architecture) *SNA* is IBM's network architecture for its mainframe communications networks. SNA is a seven-layered protocol from which the OSI model was originally developed; however, the seven layers are not identical to OSI.

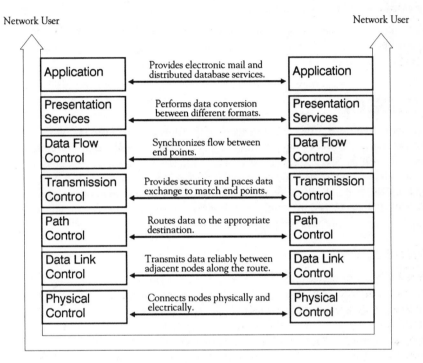

SNA LAYERS

SNADS

(SNA Distribution Services) *SNADS* is network software from IBM that routes documents and mail throughout the network to the appropriate destination. It also provides store and forward capabilities if a user or user's machine is unavailable to receive a transmission.

snapshot

A *snapshot* is the storing of the entire contents of memory including all hardware registers and status indicators. Snapshots are periodically taken to be used to restore the system in the event of a failure.

snapshot dump

A *snapshot dump* is a memory dump of selection portions of memory.

snapshot program

A *snapshot program* is a trace program that provides selected dumps of memory when specific instructions are executed or when certain conditions are met.

sneaker net

A *sneaker net* is a human alternative to a local area network. The sneaker net is made up of human beings running from one machine to another, floppy disk in hand.

SNOBOL

(StriNg Oriented symBOlic Language) *SNOBOL* was one of the first string processing, or list processing programming languages. Developed at Bell Labs in the early 1960s, SNOBOL was used for text processing, algebraic expressions, graph analysis and to develop compilers for other languages. SNOBOL, SNOBOL2 and SNOBOL3 versions dealt primarily with string manipulation. SNOBOL4, developed in 1966, was a more powerful version of the language used for general-purpose programming.

soft

Soft means flexible and changeable. Software implies instructions that can be rearranged to produce different results. The computer's soft nature was and still is its biggest virtue. The reason it takes so long to get new systems developed from inhouse information systems departments has little to do with the soft concept. It's based on the software tools that existing systems were developed under (file systems vs database management systems), which programming languages they were written in (assembly language vs high-level languages), combined with the current skill level of the technical staff, compounded by the organization's bureaucracy, red tape and politics.

soft copy

Soft copy is data temporarily displayed on a video screen. Contrast with *hard copy*, which is printed output from the computer.

soft font

A *soft font* is a set of characters for a particular typeface that is stored in the computer system and downloaded (transmitted) to the printer before printing. Contrast with *internal font* or *cartridge font*.

soft hyphen

See *discretionary hyphen*.

soft key

Same as *function key*.

soft patch

A *soft patch* is a quick fix to the machine language currently in memory, but lasts only as long as the program is running.

soft return

A *soft return* is a control code inserted into a text document to mark the end of the line according to the current right margin. Soft returns are automatically changed when the right margin is changed and the document is reformatted for printing. The soft return tells the printer to drop down one line and go back to the left margin.

The actual codes used for soft returns differ among word processors. For example, WordPerfect uses a return code (ASCII 13) for soft returns, while WordStar Professional uses a line feed code (ASCII 10). Some word processors, such as XyWrite, do not insert a soft return in the document, allowing the text to fit within the current margins from one word processor to another.

Contrast with *hard return*, which is the code inserted when the user presses the return key.

soft sectored

Soft sectored refers to the identification of sectors on a disk by recording the sector numbers in the track itself. The sector identification is accomplished when a fresh disk out of the box is run through a format program. Contrast with *hard sectored*, which uses physical markers or holes in the disk to identify the beginning of the sectors.

Softstrip

Softstrip is an optical scanning system from Cauzin Systems, Inc., that runs on IBM compatible pcs, Apple II and Macintosh computers. The Softstrip is a specially encoded pattern that holds from 50 to 600 bytes of data per inch, depending on the printer that is used. It is scanned into the computer by a Softstrip reader that connects to the personal computer's serial port.

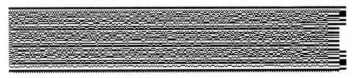

SOFTSTRIP

(Courtesy Cauzin Systems, Inc.)

SoftSwitch

SoftSwitch is a family of conversion programs from SoftSwitch, Inc., that allows electronic mail to be transmitted between IBM mainframes and a variety of other vendor's electronic mail systems.

software

Software is instructions to the computer. A series of instructions that performs a particular task is called a program or software program. The two major categories of software are *system software* and *application software*. System software is made up of control programs, such as operating systems, database management systems and network control programs. Application software is any program that processes data for the user. For example, inventory, payroll and accounts receivable programs as well as spreadsheets and word processors, all fall into the application software category.

Software Carousel

Software Carousel is a switching program from SoftLogic Solutions, Inc., that runs on IBM compatible pcs. It allows the user to activate several application programs at the same time and switch back and forth between them.

software engineering

Software engineering is the design, documentation and development of software.

software failure

A *software failure* is the inability of a program to continue processing due to erroneous logic. Same as *crash, bomb* and *abend*.

software house

A *software house* is an organization that develops customized software for a customer. Contrast with *software publisher*, which develops and markets software packages.

Software-IC

A *Software-IC* is an object-oriented programming class that has been packaged for sale from The Stepstone Corporation. It is based on the Objective-C programming language from Stepstone.

software interface

Same as *API*.

software package

A *software package* is an application program that has been developed for sale to the general public. Although a set of programs developed and written for only one organization may be called a package, package usually refers to an off-the-shelf program.

software programmer

Same as *systems programmer*.

software protection

See *copy protection*.

software publishing

Software publishing is the developing and marketing of software products. Just like book publishers, software publishers either must find software that has been written or contract for the development of it, analyze its potential viability in the marketplace, develop the documentation for it, and handle the marketing and distribution of the product.

software stack

A *software stack* is a stack that is implemented in memory. See *stack*.

software tools

Software tools are programs that aid in the development of other software programs. Software tools may assist the programmer in the design, coding, compiling, link editing or debugging phases.

solder mask

A *solder mask* is an insulating pattern applied to a printed circuit board that exposes only the areas to be soldered.

solenoid

A *solenoid* is a magnetic switch that closes a circuit and is very often used as a relay.

solid logic

Same as *solid state*.

solid state

Solid state refers to an electronic component or circuit that is made of solid materials. For example, transistors, chips and bubble memories are solid state devices. There is no mechanical action in a solid state device, that is, no visible moving parts. However, there is an unbelievable amount of electromagnetic action going on inside the semiconductor and thin film materials.

Solid state devices for storage of data are much faster and more reliable than mechanical disks and tapes. If all data were stored in solid state form, it could be accessed very quickly. However, solid state memories that hold their content without power are far more costly than ordinary RAM memory chips. And there is still a large cost difference between RAM memories and disks and tapes. Even though solid state costs continually drop, disks, tapes and optical disks also continue to improve their cost/performance ratio. It appears that there will always be a hierarchy of storage environments, ranging from slower mass storage devices to the highest speed solid state devices.

The first solid state device was the "cat's whisker" of the 1930s, in which a whisker-like wire was moved around on a solid crystal in order to detect a radio signal.

solid state memory

Solid state memory is any transistorized, semiconductor or thin film memory that contains no mechanical parts. Disks, tapes and vacuum tube memories are specifically not in this category.

solid state relay

A *solid state relay* is a relay that contains no mechanical parts, and all switching mechanisms are semiconductor or thin film components.

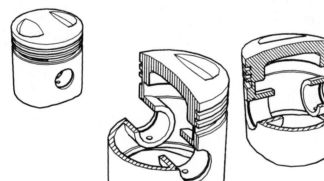

SOLIDS MODELING

(Courtesy Robo Systems Corporation)

solids modeling

In computer-aided design (CAD) *solids modeling* is a mathematical technique for representing solid objects. Solids modeling is the most advanced form of computer-aided design. Unlike wire frame and surface modeling, solids modeling systems ensure that all surfaces meet properly and that the object is geometrically correct.

When certain attributes are included in a solids model, interference checking can be accomplished, which tests whether two objects are trying to occupy the same space at the same time.

To show its internal functions, a solids object can be sectioned; It can be sliced into two halves (cross section), and other sections can be sliced out of it.

sort

A *sort* is the reordering of data into a new sequence. Sorting capabilities are provided within the operating system and many application programs, such as word processing and database management programs. In word processing programs, sorting allows for all the text in the document or a marked block of text to be resequenced into either an ascending (normal) or descending sequence. In database programs, sorting resequences all the records in the file by one or more fields and often generates an entirely new copy of the file. The operating system typically has a sort capability that allows users to resequence lists of file names on their disks.

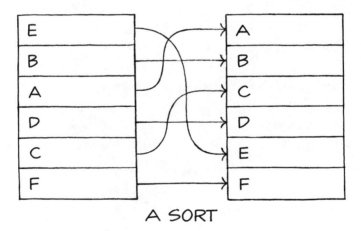

A SORT

sort algorithm

A *sort algorithm* is the formula used to reorder data into a new sequence. Like all complicated problems, there are many solutions that can achieve the same results. One sort algorithm can resequence data significantly faster than another. In the early 1960s, when tape was the primary storage medium, the sale of a computer system may have hinged on the sort algorithm, since without random access capability, every transaction had to be sorted into the sequence of the master file.

sort field

Same as *sort key*.

sort key

The *sort key* is the field or fields in the record that dictate the sequence of the file. For example, the sort keys STATE and CUSTOMER NAME mean that the file will be arranged alphabetically by customer name within an alphabetical order of states. State is the major sort key and customer name is the minor sort key.

sorter

(1) A *sorter* is a sort program.

(2) A *sorter* is an individual who manually puts data into a specific sequence.

(3) A *sorter* is a punched card machine that distributes punched cards into separate stackers based on the contents of one column, or character, in the card. The complete operation requires passing the cards through the machine once for each column being sorted.

SORTER
(Courtesy IBM)

This Model 083 Sorter could read 1,000 punched cards per minute and distribute them into their respective stackers. These kinds of machines were used extensively throughout the 1950s and 1960s.

SOS

(1) (Silicon On Sapphire) *SOS* is a MOS chip-fabrication method that places a thin layer of silicon over a sapphire substrate (base).

(2) (Sophisticated Operating System) *SOS* was the operating system used on the Apple III personal computer.

sound bandwidth

The *sound bandwidth* is the range of frequencies that can be heard by a human being (from 20 to 20,000 Hertz). However, the range of human voice is substantially less than the human ear and is typically confined to a bandwidth from 300 to 3,300 Hertz for voice grade transmission.

source

The *source* is the source of current in a metal oxide semiconductor (MOS) transistor. Same as *emitter* in a bipolar transistor.

source code

The *source code* is the language a program is written in by the programmer. Source code is translated into object code all at once by assemblers and compilers, or a line a time by an interpreter when the program is running. In some cases, source code may be automatically converted into another dialect or language by a conversion program. Source code is not executable by the computer directly. It must be converted into machine language first.

source computer

A *source computer* is the computer in which a program is being assembled or compiled. Contrast with *object computer*, which is the computer that the program will eventually run in.

source data

Source data is original data that is handwritten or printed on a source document or typed into the computer system from a keyboard or terminal.

source data acquisition

Same as *source data capture*.

source data capture

Source data capture is the capturing of data electronically when a transaction actually occurs, for example, at the time of sale.

source document

A *source document* is a paper form onto which data is written. Order forms and employment applications are examples of source documents.

source language

Same as *source code*.

source program

A *source program* is a program in its original form, as written by the programmer.

source statement

A *source statement* is an instructional phrase in a programming language (source language).

space/time

The following units of measure are used to define storage and transmission capacities.

S P A C E		Bytes or bits	T I M E		Fraction of second
Kilobyte	(KB)	1,000 (or 1,024)	Millisecond	(MS)	1/1,000th
Megabyte	(MB)	1,000,000	Microsecond	(μS)	1/1,000,000th
Gigabyte	(GB)	1,000,000,000	Nanosecond	(NS)	1/1,000,000,000th
Terabyte	(TB)	1,000,000,000,000	Picosecond	(PS)	1/1,000,000,000,000th

Storage capacities are usually measured in:

Disk, tape, memory	Bytes
CPU and memory chips	Bits

Transmission speeds are usually measured in:

Disk access time	Milliseconds
Memory access time	Nanoseconds
Machine cycle	Microseconds/Nanoseconds
Instruction execution	Microseconds/Nanoseconds
Transistor switching	Nanoseconds/Picoseconds

spaghetti code

Spaghetti code is a program that is written without a coherent structure. Each decision point in a program (if this, do that) directs the computer to branch to some other part of the program. If the programmer uses an excessive number of GOTO instructions, the result is spaghetti code. A GOTO instruction directs the computer elsewhere in the program with no assurance of returning. If, after branching to another routine, another GOTO instruction branches somewhere else, the logic of the program can become very hard to follow and maintain.

However, if a branch is made to a function or subroutine that, after accomplishing its task, automatically returns to the place in the program that called it, the logic in the program is straighforward and understandable. See *structured programming*.

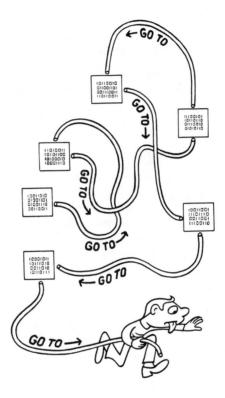

SPAGHETTI CODE

SPARC

(Scalable Performance ARChitecture) SPARC is a 32-bit reduced instruction set (RISC) computer from Sun Microsystems.

spatial data management

Spatial data management is a technique for accessing both static data and animated video sequences by physically pointing or "steering" through the data, much like a player at an arcade game.

spec

See *specification*.

special character

A *special character* is any character that is not a digit from 0 through 9 or an upper or lowercase letter from A to Z. For example, @, #, $, %, &, * and + are all special characters.

special-purpose computer

A *special-purpose computer* is a computer designed from scratch to perform a specific function. Contrast with the *general-purpose computer*, which is the predominant type of computer built.

special-purpose language

A *special-purpose language* is a programming language that is designed to solve a specific problem or class of problems. For example, LISP and Prolog are designed to solve non-numeric problems and are used extensively in artificial intelligence applications. Even more specialized are languages, such as COGO (Coordinate Geometry), for solving civil engineering problems, and APT (Automatic Programmed Tools), for directing machine tools.

specification

A *specification* is a definition of a data structure or processing routine in a program. Functional specifications for an information system include the database structure and the detailed processing for each data entry, update, query and report function in the system.

spectral color

In computer graphics, a *spectral color* is the color of a single wavelength of light, starting with violet at the low end and proceeding through indigo, blue, green, yellow and orange and ending with red.

spectral response

Spectral response is the variable output of a light-sensitive device that is based on the color of the light it perceives.

spectrum

A *spectrum* is a range of electromagnetic frequencies.

speech recognition

Same as *voice recognition*.

speech synthesis

Speech synthesis is the generation of machine voice by arranging phonemes (speech utterances, such as "k," "ch," and "sh") into words. Speech synthesis is used in text to speech applications, where text input must be turned into the spoken word in applications for the deaf or handicapped. Although words spoken by a person can be digitized and stored in the computer, it would require a much larger database of words compared to speech synthesis methods.

speed of electricity/light

The *speed of electricity*, which is the same as the *speed of light*, is approximately 186,000 miles per second. Electricity and light travel around the equator over seven times in one second. This inherent speed of Mother Nature is why computers are so fast. Within the tiny chip, electricity has to flow only a couple of millimeters, and, within an entire CPU, perhaps only a few feet. Yet, as fast as that is, it's never fast enough. There is resistance in the lines, and it does take time to cause an electronic switch to open and close. Even though switching speeds are in the billionths and trillionths of a second, the application of computers, especially in the areas of graphics, CAD, image processing and scientific exploration, is always exhausting the fastest computers.

spelling checker

A *spelling checker* is a separate program or capability within a word processing program that checks the correct spelling of words in a text file (document). Features of a spelling checker are checking spelling as the user types, checking only a marked block within the document, or checking the entire document or group of documents. In addition, an advanced spelling checker can correct common typos and misspellings, as well as any peculiar misspellings of an individual user once they have been corrected.

spike

A *spike*, also called a transient, is an extremely short burst of extra voltage in a power line. A spike lasts only a fraction of a second, whereas a surge is an oversupply of voltage lasting up to several seconds.

spindle

A *spindle* is a central shaft onto which hard disk platters are stacked. The spindle is attached to a motor that spins the disks.

SpinRite

SpinRite is a special formatting program from Gibson Research Corporation that runs on IBM compatible pcs. It reformats the hard disk without erasing the existing data. SpinRite rewrites only the sector identification data on the disk in order to reestablish the alignment, which may have drifted over time.

SPL

(Systems Programming Language) *SPL* is an assembly language from Hewlett-Packard that runs on the HP 3000 series of minicomputers. See *assembly language* for an SPL program example.

split screen

Split screen refers to the display of two or more sets of data on screen at the same time. A split screen implies that one set of data can be manipulated independently of the other. Split screens, or windows, are usually created by the operating system or application program software, rather than the hardware.

spooling

(Simultaneous Peripheral Operations On Line) With personal computers, *spooling* refers to printing a document or file in the background while allowing the user to work on something else.

Spooling originated with mainframe operations in which data on low-speed peripheral devices, such as a card reader, was transferred to disk first and then fed to the computer at high speed. Conversely, output from the computer to a low-speed device, such as a printer, was stored on disk and then fed to the printer. Spooling is also used to transmit to and receive from remote batch terminals that transmit at low speeds. Spooling programs monitor the activity of shared peripherals and schedule their tasks based on the priority of the data that is being stored.

spreadsheet

A *spreadsheet* is a software program that simulates a paper spreadsheet, or worksheet, in which columns of numbers are summed for budgets and plans. A spreadsheet appears on screen as a matrix of rows and columns in which the intersection of each row and column is identified as a cell with a unique row/column number or letter. Since the spreadsheet is much larger than the viewing area of the screen, the spreadsheet can be scrolled (moved) horizontally and vertically. The user fills in the cells with (1) descriptions, (2) numbers or (3) formulas. The descriptions, also called *labels*, can be any text, for example, RENT, GAS, PHONE or GROSS SALES. The numbers, also called *values*, are the actual data. The formulas command the spreadsheet to do the calculations, for example, SUM CELLS A5 TO A10. Formulas are reasonably easy to create, since most spreadsheets allow the user to point to each cell and type in the arithmetic operation that affects it. Roughly speaking, a formula is created by saying "this cell + that cell * that cell."

The formulas are the magic of a spreadsheet. After numbers are added or changed, the formulas will recalculate the data either automatically or with the press of a key. Since the contents of any cell can be calculated with or copied to any other cell, a total of one column can be used as a detail item in another column. For example, in a budget, the total from a column of detailed expense items can be carried over to a summary column showing all expenses. If data in the detail column changes, its column total changes, which is then copied to the summary column, and the total in the summary column changes as a result. If this were done manually on paper, each change of data would require recalculating, erasing and changing the totals of each column. This automatic "ripple" effect allows users to create a plan, plug in different assumptions and immediately see the impact on the bottom line. This "what if?" capability has made the spreadsheet an indispensable tool for budgets, planning, forecasting, financial statements and many other equation-based tasks.

The spreadsheet concept originated with VisiCalc in 1978 for the Apple II, and was followed by SuperCalc, Multiplan and a host of others. Eventually Lotus 1-2-3 for the IBM PC became a huge success and is the most widely used personal computer spreadsheet program today. Microsoft Excel became the standard for the Macintosh and is now available for IBM compatible pcs.

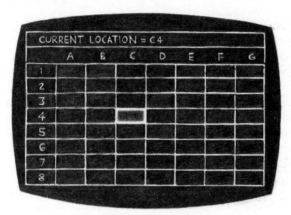

SPREADSHEET

Classes of Spreadsheets

STANDARD
Every spreadsheet has the capability of creating a two-dimensional matrix of rows and columns. In order to summarize data, totals from various parts of the spreadsheet can be summed to another part of the spreadsheet.

DYNAMIC LINKING
Dynamic linking allows data in one spreadsheet file to automatically update another spreadsheet file. Although often referred to as 3-D spreadsheets, dynamic linking creates the effect of a third dimension in a separate file. For example, several detail files can be summarized into one summary file. Excessive linking is difficult to manage, since the relationships span several physical files.

3-DIMENSIONAL
3-D spreadsheets make summarizing data easy, because each cell in the spreadsheet has an X, Y and Z reference. For example, a spreadsheet of expense

items by month uses two dimensions, but expense items by month by department requires three dimensions.

While the 3-D method is superior for consolidating data, it lacks some of the flexibility inherent in the dynamic linking approach, since all pages must have essentially the same structure. In addition, all data must reside in one file as with a standard 2-D spreadsheet.

RELATIONAL SPREADSHEETS

Relational spreadsheets provide an optional method for storing the data separate and apart from the formulas. The data is stored in a central database and the formulas are stored in the spreadsheet. When the spreadsheet is called up, the data from the database is copied into it, thus ensuring that everyone's spreadsheet always contains the most current data.

Relational spreadsheets reference data by name rather than by row and column number. With name references, data can be used in multiple spreadsheets with greater accuracy, and new spreadsheets can be created more easily. A spreadsheet that analyzes the budget for one department can analyze the budget for any department simply by changing the department name and recalculating.

Name references make it possible to analyze data from multiple perspectives. Since data isn't tied to cell references as with 3-D spreadsheets, more than three dimensions can be created. For example, in a corporate budget, numbers are kept for every combination of accounts, time periods and departments in both forecast and actual versions. A view of accounts by department by period can be automatically switched to a view of accounts by period by version. Instead of requiring inordinately complicated spreadsheet programming by the user, the relational spreadsheet prepares the views and consolidations automatically.

spreadsheet compiler

A *spreadsheet compiler* is a program that translates spreadsheets into programs that run by themselves without having to have the original spreadsheet program in the computer to use them.

sprocket feed

Same as *pin feed*.

SPSS

SPSS is a statistical package from SPSS, Inc., that runs on over 40 mainframes and minicomputers, as well as on IBM compatible pcs. SPSS provides over 50 statistical processes, including regression analysis, correlation and analysis of variance, and is used extensively in the marketing research field. SPSS, originally named "Statistical Package for the Social Sciences," was written by Norman Nie, a professor at Stanford University, in 1968. In 1976, Nie formed SPSS, Inc., to market the product.

SQL

(Structured Query Language) *SQL*, pronounced "S Q L " or "see qwill," is a language designed to interrogate and process data in a relational database. There are many varieties of SQL incorporated into a large number of software packages. SQL, originally developed by IBM for their mainframes, has been implemented for mini and microcomputer applications. SQL can be used to interactively work with a database on screen, or SQL commands can be embedded within a traditional programming language as the interface between the program and an SQL database.

SQL engine

An *SQL engine* is a program that accepts an SQL command and accesses the database to obtain the requested data. Users' requests in a query language or database language must be translated into an SQL request before the SQL engine can process it.

SQL Server

SQL Server is a database engine, or SQL engine, from Sybase, Inc., that is jointly marketed by Microsoft and Ashton-Tate. It runs on IBM compatible file servers and uses the SQL language as its primary interface.

square wave

A *square wave* is the graphic image of a digital pulse as visualized on an oscilloscope. It looks square because it rises very quickly to a particular amplitude, stays constant for the duration of the pulse and drops quickly at the end of it.

0   1   0   1   0   1   0   1

SQUARE WAVE

SQUID

(Superconducting Quantum Interference Device) A *SQUID* is an electronic detection system that uses Josephson junctions circuits. A SQUID is an extremely sensitive device and is capable of detecting the most minute signals.

SRAM

See *static* RAM.

SSCP

(System Services Control Point) An *SSCP* is a central switching point, or node, in an IBM SNA communications network. Contrast with *LU*, which is an end user node. Often referred to as the "brain" of the SNA network, SSCP resides within IBM's VTAM software and is responsible for controlling the flow of data to designated users.

SSI

(Small Scale Integration) *SSI* is the manufacture of chips with approximately two to 100 electronic components (transistors, etc.).

SSP

(System Support Program) *SSP* is a multiuser, multitasking operating system from IBM that is the primary control program for System/34 and System/36 minicomputers.

ST

The *ST* is a personal computer series from Atari Corporation that is used in homes and small businesses. The ST uses a Motorola 68000 CPU and comes with an operating system (TOS) built into ROM. The GEM operating environment is also included which provides a Macintosh-like interface for applications. The 520ST comes with 512K of RAM, and the 1040ST comes with one megabyte. Display resolution is 640x200 with 16 colors on a 12" screen. A built-in 720K

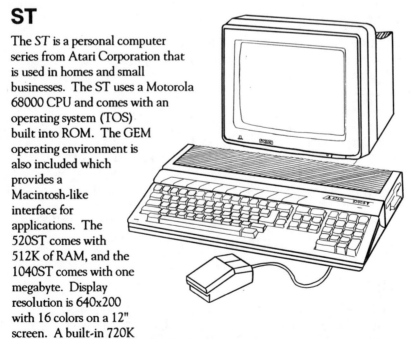

microfloppy disk is standard, and a 20 megabyte hard drive is optional for the 1040ST. Also included is a MIDI interface and a three-voice sound chip with a range from 30 to beyond 20,000 Hertz.

stack

(1) A *stack* is a set of hardware registers or a reserved amount of main memory that is used for arithmetic calculations or for keeping track of internal operations. Stacks are used to keep track of the sequence of routines that are called in a program. For example, one routine calls another, which calls another and so on. As each routine is completed, the computer must return control to the calling routine all the way back to the first routine that started the sequence. Stacks usually work on a last-in-first-out basis in order to accomplish this. The last item, or address, placed (pushed) onto the stack is the first item removed (popped) from the stack.

(2) A *stack* is a file in Apple Computer's HyperCard software.

stack pointer

A *stack pointer* is the address that identifies the location of the most recent item placed on the stack.

stacker

A *stacker* is an output bin in a document feeding or punched card machine. Contrast with *hopper*, which holds the items on the input side.

stair stepping

Same as *jaggies*.

STAIRS

(STorage And Information Retrieval System) *STAIRS* is a text document management system from IBM that runs on IBM mainframes. STAIRS allows users to search for documents based on key words or word combinations.

standard deviation

In statistics, the *standard deviation* is the average amount a number varies from the average number in a series of numbers.

standards & compatibilty

Standards & compatibility is the most important issue in the computer field. As an unregulated industry, we have wound up with literally thousands of data formats and processing languages, but very few standards that are universally used. This subject is as heated as politics and religion to hardware and software vendors and industry planners.

No matter how much the industry talks about compatibility, new formats and languages appear routinely without regard to anyone's standard. The standards makers are always trying to cast a standard in concrete, while the innovators are trying to create a new one. Even when standards are created, they are violated as soon as a new feature is added by the vendor.

If a format or language is used extensively and others copy it, it becomes a defacto standard and may become as widely used as official standards from such organizations as the American National Standards Institute (ANSI) or the Institute of Electrical and Electronic Engineers (IEEE). When defacto standards are sanctioned by these organizations, they become stable, at least, for a while.

In order to truly understand this industry, it is essential to understand the categories for which standards are created.

Machine Languages

Machine language is the computer's native language. It defines the instructions that the computer can execute, and it is designed into the electronic circuits of its processor (CPU). For example, the Apple II uses a 6502 microprocessor, and it understands only 6502 machine language. The BASIC interpreter program that resides in read only memory chips within the Apple II turns BASIC language statements into 6502 machine language.

Machine language is the fundamental standard for hardware compatibility. Vendors have several families of computers, each with different machine languages. For example, although the IBM 370, 30xx and 43xx series computers all use the same machine language as the older 360 series, the IBM Series/1, System/38 and 8100 series are each different.

After a program is written, it must be assembled, compiled or interpreted (translated) into the machine language the computer understands. In order to run in a different machine, the program must be reassembled or recompiled into a different machine language, which may or may not be possible, depending on the type and version of the original language.

Since the late 1960s, companies seeking a chunk of the IBM market have designed computers that run the same machine language as the IBM computers.

MACHINE LANGUAGES

RCA's Spectra 70 was the first IBM compatible mainframe, and companies, such as Amdahl, Itel, National Advanced Systems, Hitachi and Fujitsu have introduced IBM compatible mainframes at one time or another.

IBM pc machine language compatibility is achieved by using the same Intel 8086 family of microprocessors that IBM uses.

Machine language compatibility can also be achieved by simulation or emulation. A simulator is a software program that translates and executes a program in a foreign machine language. An emulator is hardware that executes the machine language of another computer and is used to encourage customers to buy a new series of computers. For example, in the 1960s, IBM provided an optional emulator in its System/360 series that executed most of the customer's existing 1401 programs.

Data Codes

The data code is built into the computer and determines how each character of data, a letter, digit or special character is represented in binary code. Fortunately, there are only two major data codes in wide use today, EBCDIC and ASCII. That means data stored in one code can easily be converted to the other. IBM mainframes and minicomputers use EBCDIC, and so do other mainframes. ASCII is used by all personal computers, most minicomputers and some mainframes.

Other codes are used in various different machines, but all data codes can be converted from one to another with one possible exception. If numbers are stored in floating point and the new machine can't handle as many digits as the old machine, a loss of precision may occur.

When data is moved to a different computers, data code conversion is often only one small part of the conversion process. Data, text and graphics formats must also be converted if different programs are going to process them.

The following is a small sample of the ASCII and EBCDIC data codes:

Character	ASCII	EBCDIC
space	01000000	00100000
period	01001011	00101110
less than sign	01001100	00111100
plus sign	01001110	00101011
dollar sign	01011011	00100100
A	11000001	01000001
B	11000010	01000010
C	11000011	01000011
D	11000100	01000100
a	10000001	01100001
b	10000010	01100010
c	10000011	01100011
d	10000100	01100100

Hardware Interfaces

The hardware interface specifies the plugs, sockets, cables and electrical signals that pass through each line between the CPU and a peripheral device or communications network.

Common hardware interfaces for personal computers are the Centronics parallel interface, typically used for printers, and the RS-232-C interface, typically used for modems, graphics tablets, mice and printers. In addition, the SCSI (Small Computer System Interface) is used for high-speed peripherals, such as disks and tapes, and the GPIB (General Purpose Interface Bus) IEEE 488 standard is used to connect instruments in process control applications.

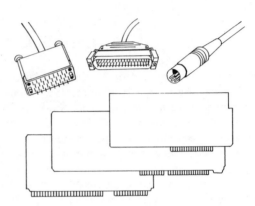

The bus in a computer's motherboard, into which additional printed circuit boards are inserted, is a hardware interface. For example, the Micro Channel in IBM's PS/2 series accepts a physically different board than the original PC bus.

Local area networks (LANs), such as ARCNET and Ethernet, also dictate the hardware interface as part of their specifications.

Storage Media

There are many varieties of disk packs, disk cartridges, floppy disks, reel-to-reel tapes, tape cartridges and tape cassettes. Each one has its own unique shape and size and can only be inserted into a storage drive especially made for it. With removable media, the physical standard is half the compatibility issue. The other half is the recording patterns, which are invisible to the human eye. Magnetic tapes and disks fresh out of the box are blank recording surfaces. The actual

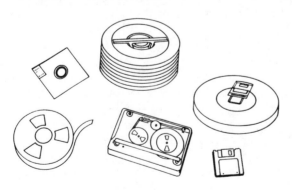

recording tracks are placed onto the surface by the read/write head of the storage drive. Thus, the same floppy disk that stores 720,000 bytes in one disk drive, can hold 800,000 bytes if formatted for another. If the computer reads an incompatible tape or reads and writes and incompatible disk, it will signal a read/write error.

For minicomputers and mainframes, the half-inch magnetic tape reel is a common interchangeable storage medium. For personal computers, the 5 1/4" minifloppy and the 3 1/2" microfloppy disks are commonly used.

Operating Systems

An operating system is a master control program that manages the running of the computer system. In all environments, except for specialized scientific and process control applications, the operating system is a separate program that interacts with all the application programs. The application programs must be set up to "talk" to the operating system.

If application programs are moved to a different computing environment, they have to be converted to interface with a different operating system. If a new operating system is installed that is not compatible with the old operating system, all the application programs have to be converted to the new operating system.

In large organizations, thousands of programs have been converted from one operating system to another over the years. For the first time on a large scale, users will finally understand exactly what has been going on behind the glass-enclosed datacenters. Microsoft's OS/2 operating system is not compatible with its DOS operating system. In order to fully migrate to OS/2, all copies of software packages have to be upgraded to OS/2 versions.

With IBM personal computers, a translation function within the operating system, called the BIOS, is stored in read only memory chips that are plugged into the motherboard. A compatible BIOS is required in order to have operating system compatibility with IBM personal computers.

OPERATING SYSTEMS

Communications

Transmitting between two personal computers or between a personal computer and a timesharing or information service is relatively simple. All that's required is a modem for each computer, the dial-up telephone system and a communications program in each computer that uses the same error checking protocol to ensure that data has not been lost. Several error checking protocols usually accompany a personal computer communications program. If data is not critical, an ASCII protocol without error checking can be used, which is found in every communications program.

Transmitting in a network is another story. Traditional minicomputer and mainframe networks allow multiple users to have access to central databases via terminals. The control is typically in the main, or host, computer. Personal computer local area networks have evolved to share information within a small work group. The major communications problem most large organizations have is to tie independent networks together so that each user's workstation can communicate with any other user's workstation within the company.

Since each type of network uses different protocols, conversion from one protocol to another is required. In today's multivendor environment, protocol conversion can be performed by black boxes, gateways, digital PABXs or via interconnection to value added communication services.

The Open Systems Interconnection (OSI) is a seven-layer reference model for worldwide communications that has been defined by the International Standards Organization (ISO). Although most vendors have committed to support OSI in one form or another, it will take a long time before universal communications is ever achieved. Computers were originally developed for computations, not communications. Who could have realized the implications back then? However, it's still too bad that computer communications was not standardized in the early days as was the telephone industry. Had we had the foresight to do so, right now, every computer user in the world would be able to communicate with every other. See *OSI* and *Corporation for Open Systems*.

COMMUNICATIONS

Programming Languages

Every software program is written in a programming language, and there is at least one programming language for every major CPU series. There is typically an assembly language and a number of high-level languages for each series or family. Assembly languages are machine specific, and the machine language they generate runs on only one CPU family. Unless the machine languages are very similar, it is very difficult to translate an assembly language program from one CPU series into another.

The high-level programming language was created to eliminate this machine dependency. Programming languages, such as COBOL, FORTRAN and BASIC are supposed to be able to run on many different computers. However, due to many dialects of each language, compatibility is still a major issue. Each compiler vendor keeps adding new features to its language thereby making it incompatible with previous or other versions. By the time a new feature becomes a standard, a dozen new features have been already implemented. For example, dBASE has become a defacto standard business programming language. Since 1981, dBASE has spawned competitive products, such as Clipper, QuickSilver, Force III, dbXL and Foxbase, all of which are incomplete versions of dBASE. None of them provides every command in dBASE, and many of them provide features not found in dBASE.

There's no rule of thumb for translating one dialect of a programming language into another. The job may be very difficult or very easy. At times, software programs are written to translate one dialect into another, as well as one programming language into another. If the translation program cannot translate the program entirely, then manual tailoring is necessary. In these cases, it is sometimes easier to rewrite the program from scratch.

Compatibility can be achieved when a programming language conforms to the ANSI (American National Standards Institute) standard for that language. If the same version of an ANSI COBOL compiler is available for two different CPUs, a program written in ANSI COBOL will run on both machines.

PROGRAMMING LANGUAGES

File Management Systems

In its simplest form, a data file uses fields of the same length for each item of data, for example, a plain EBCDIC or ASCII file would look like:

Chris Smith	3443 Main Street	Bangor	ME	18567
Pat Jones	10 West 45 St.	New York	NY	10002

A common format created by BASIC programming languages is an ASCII comma delimited file; for example, the data above would look as follows:

"Chris Smith","3443 Main Street","Bangor","ME","18567"
"Pat Jones","10 West 45 St.","New York","NY","10002"

Both file formats above are simple, contain only data (except for the quotes and commas) and can be easily manipulated by a word processing program. However, data files may also contain special codes that identify the way the data is structured within the file. For example, variable length records require a code in each field that indicates the size of the field.

Whether fixed length or variable length fields, the data in non-DBMS systems is linked directly to the processing. The program must know the sequential order of fields in each record that it processes, and it cannot accept records in a different format. If a program is to process a different file format, either it must be changed or the file format must be changed. Incompatible file formats can exist within the same organization as a result of systems being developed for different purposes at different times.

The access methods within the operating system perform the actual storage and retrieval of data. When data is converted from one computer environment to another, either special conversion programs must be written that can retrieve from one access method and store in another, or data is converted into a plain ASCII or EBCDIC format to be used as a common denominator for entry into the new system.

NAME	ADDRESS	CITY	ST	ZIP

NAME	ADDRESS	CITY	ST	ZIP

RECORD FORMATS

These two fixed length record layouts are incompatible even though they contain the same kinds of data. The same program can't process them unless it's designed to input both record formats. In order to process a different file, the program has to be changed or the file structure (record layout) has to be changed.

Database Management Systems

Database management systems typically have their own proprietary formats for storing data. For example, a header record with a unique format that contains identification data is typically placed at the beginning of each file. Codes may also be embedded throughout each record. Many database programs have an importing and exporting capability that automatically converts common database formats into their proprietary format. If not, the program usually can import and export a plain EBCDIC or ASCII file, which is stripped of all proprietary codes and can be used as a common denominator between both systems. If conversion facilities cannot be found, a custom program can be written to convert one database format into another providing documentation describing the old format is available.

The application program interface (API), or language used by the application program to "talk" to the database, is typically a proprietary

DATABASES

language in every DBMS. SQL (Structured Query Language) has recently become popular as a standard language and has been implemented in many DBMSs. That means any application program requesting data in the SQL language would work with any database management system that supports SQL.

Text Systems

Although the basic structure of an English-language text file is standard throughout the world: word, sentence, paragraph, page; every word processing, desktop publishing and typesetting program uses its own codes to set up the layout within a document. For example, the code that turns on boldface in WordPerfect Version 5.0 is [BOLD]; in WordStar, it's ^PB.

The codes that define a header, footer, footnote, page number, margin, tab setting, indent and font change are unique to the word processing program in which the document was created or the desktop publishing program into which the text file is converted. Believe it or not, even the codes to end a line or paragraph are not the same and vary all over the place.

Document conversion is accomplished with black boxes or special conversion programs. Although every word processing program has a search & replace capability, it may not be effective for converting embedded layout codes from one format to another. In some programs, the search & replace simply does not work for layout codes. In addition, while some systems use one code to turn a function on and another code to turn it off, other systems use the same code for on and off, requiring manual verification and tailoring when using the search & replace function.

WORD PROCESSING

Graphics Systems

There are many formats for storing a picture in a computer; but, unlike text and data files, which are primarily made up of alphanumeric characters, graphics formats are much more complex.

To begin with, there are the two major categories of graphics: vector graphics (objects made up of lines) and raster graphics (television-like dots). Images stored in vector format can be moved to another vector system typically without loss of resolution. However, there are "2-D only" vector formats as well as 3-D vector formats. A true 3-D image cannot be created from a 2-D format.

There are many raster formats; each one dictating and thus limiting the number of dots of resolution. Raster images can be moved to another raster format without loss of resolution as long as the new format has the same or higher resolution as the older one.

Standard graphics formats allow graphics data to be moved from machine to machine, while standard graphics languages let graphics programs be moved from machine to machine. For example, GKS and PHIGS are major graphics languages that have been adopted by many high-performance workstation and computer-aided design (CAD) vendors. Apple's consistent use of its QuickDraw language has helped the Macintosh become very popular in graphics-oriented applications.

GRAPHICS

High-resolution graphics has typically been expensive to implement due to its large storage and fast processing requirements. However, as personal computers become more powerful, graphics will become more widely used in business applications. The ability to see a person's face or a product's appearance on screen will eventually become as commonplace as text and data. In the meantime, it will be important for business consultants and database designers to begin to familiarize themselves with graphics standards.

Standards Organizations

The following organizations set standards for computers, communications and related products throughout the world.

ANSI (American National Standards Institute)
CCITT (Consultative Committee for International Telephony & Telegraphy)
EIA (Electronic Industries Association - U. S.)
IEEE (Institute of Electrical and Electronics Engineers - U. S.)
ISO (International Standards Organization)
NBS (National Bureau of Standards - U. S.)
VENDORS - When a vendor's product is widely used, it becomes a defacto standard. Apple, Ashton-Tate, Control Data, Digital, HP, IBM, Intel, Lotus, Microsoft, Motorola, Unisys and many other hardware and software vendors have set defacto standards.

The Future

It would seem that the problem of standards and compatibility is a never ending dilemma, and perhaps it is. However, the fact is that standards could be created that would embrace the future and allow for expandability far more than they currently do. Ironically, in a field that is on the very forefront of the future, it seems as if this industry has a very myopic view of it.

Some day, a standard for defining the standard will have to be implemented in order that one program can ask another what language it speaks. A program could also interrogate a data file and determine its format as well. If the program can't understand the other program's language or the file's format, the interfacing problem would still exist as it does today. However, as programs become more multi-lingual, a standard identification protocol would go a long way to establishing an artificial intelligence link between all software in the future.

Star

In 1981, Xerox introduced the *Star* workstation, which incorporated the desktop environment that uses icons and a mouse. This user interface, or way of commanding the computer, was later used by Apple in its Lisa and Macintosh computers. The Star workstation was introduced at $15,000 per unit and was never a great success. Neither was Apple's Lisa with its $10,000 price tag. However, the less expensive Macintosh has become a major success, and Apple is often given credit for inventing the whole idea. See *Alto*.

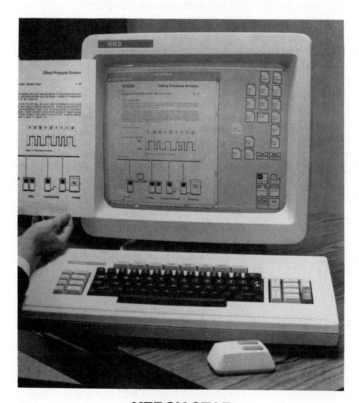

XEROX STAR
(Courtesy Xerox Corporation)

star-dot-star

Star-dot-star refers to the asterisk-dot-asterisk (***.***) code that designates all files stored in a Microsoft DOS or OS/2 disk directory. File names are made up of a name from one to eight characters long and an optional extension of up three characters. If the extension is used, it is connected to the name with a dot, for example, **chap.nov**.

There are many standard extensions used by various software vendors. For example, EXE is a software program that is ready to run in the computer, DBF is a dBASE file, and WKS is a Lotus 1-2-3 file. BAK is used for backup files. See *extension*.

You can create your own filing system by using the file extension to classify the different kinds of files that you create. For example, if your word processor doesn't require a particular extension (most don't), you could use **nov** for your novel and name your chapters **chap1.nov**, **chap2.nov**, and so forth. To get a directory listing of only the **nov** files, you would enter **dir *.nov** at the A or C prompt. The asterisk acts as a wild card and takes on any name. To copy all the nov files to the B disk, you would enter **copy *.nov b:**. You can selectively delete files this way; for example: **del *.bak** erases all the BAK files in the current disk directory. To select all files beginning with M, you would enter **dir m*.***.

The **?** is a single character wild card. If you named your files **1chap.nov** and **2chap.nov**, you would select the **chap** files with **dir ?chap.nov**.

star network

A *star network* is a communications network in which all the terminals are connected to a central computer. Private Automatic Branch Exchanges (PABXs) are prime examples of a star network. Local area networks, such as IBM's Token Ring and AT&T's Starlan are also examples of a star network.

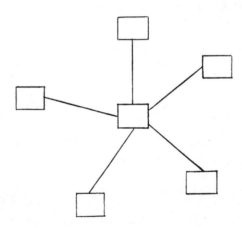

Starlan

Starlan is a local area network developed by AT&T that interconnects personal computers via two twisted wire pairs. It uses the CSMA/CD access method and transmits at one megabit per second. Starlan uses both a star topology in which all personal computers connect to a central hub, as well as a bus topology in which up to 10 computers can be daisy chained each to the other. The Starlan network is provided by plugging a Starlan printed circuit board into each personal computer.

In 1988, Starlan was renamed Starlan 1, and Starlan 10 was introduced, a 10 megabit Ethernet version of Starlan that uses twisted wire pairs or optical fibers.

start bit

In communications, a *start bit* is the first bit transmitted before each character in ansynchronous (start/stop) transmission.

start/stop transmission

Same as *asynchronous communications*.

STARTUP.CMD

(startup CoMmanD) *STARTUP.CMD* is a Microsoft OS/2 file that, if present on disk, is executed immediately when the computer is started (booted). The file contains OS/2 instructions that can initialize operating system settings and/or automatically call in a specific application program. The equivalent file in DOS is the *AUTOEXEC.BAT* file; however, in OS/2, the AUTOEXEC.BAT file is also executed when the computer is switched to DOS mode (real mode).

stat mux

(STATistical MUltipleXor) See *statistical multiplexor*.

state-of-the-art

State-of-the-art is the most current technique or method applied to designing and developing hardware and software.

statement

In a high-level programming language, a *statement* is a descriptive phrase that generates one or more machine language instructions in the computer. In a low-level assembly language, programmers write instructions rather than statements, since each source language instruction is translated into one machine language instruction.

static electricity

Static electricity is a stationary electrical charge that is the result of intentional charging or of friction in low-humidity environments.

static RAM

(static Random Access Memory) *Static RAMs* are memory chips that require power in order to hold their content. A static RAM bit is made up of a pretzel-like circuit called a flip-flop that allows current to flow through one side or the other. The bits in static RAM change their state from 0 to 1 and 1 to 0 by transistor switching only, and are faster than dynamic RAMs (DRAMs), which take more time to charge a tiny storage cell called a capacitor. In addition, static RAMs don't need to be continuously refreshed hundreds of times per second as do dynamic RAMs.

Static RAM chips have access times in the 10 to 30-nanosecond range, whereas dynamic RAM memories are usually above 30, and Bipolar and ECL memories are under 10 nanoseconds.

statistical multiplexor

In communications, a *statistical multiplexor* combines several low-speed channels into a single high-speed channel and vice versa. Whereas the normal multiplexor is set to a fixed interleaving pattern, the statistical multiplexor can analyze the traffic load and dynamically switch to different channel patterns to speed up the transmission.

stepper motor

A *stepper motor* is a motor that turns in small, fixed increments and is used to control the movement of the access arm on a disk drive. Contrast with *voice coil* motors, which allow smaller movements than a stepper motor.

stop bit

In communications, a *stop bit* is a bit transmitted after each character in asynchronous (start/stop) transmission.

storage device

A *storage device* is a hardware device that can hold data. In this book, storage device refers only to external peripheral equipment, such as disk and tape, in order to contrast it with internal main memory (RAM).

storage hierarchy

Storage hierarchy is the range of speeds of all memory and storage devices within the computer system. The following list starts with low-speed devices and goes up the highest speed.

Punched cards
Punched paper tape
Removable cartridge mass storage devices (non-disk)

Magnetic tape
Floppy disks
CD ROM and optical disks
Magnetic disks with movable read/write heads
Magnetic disks with fixed read/write heads
Bubble memory
Low-speed bulk memory
Main memory
Cache memory
Microcode
Registers and stacks

storage media

Storage media are disks, tapes and bubble memory cartridges.

store & forward

In communications, *store & forward* refers to the temporary storage of a message for transmission to its destination at a later time. Store & forward techniques allow for routing over networks that are not accessible at all times; for example, messages headed for different time zones can be stored & forwarded when daytime has arrived at the destination location. Routine messages can be stored & forwarded at night in order to take advantage of off-peak rates.

stored program concept

The *stored program concept* is the following of instructions from a program that has been temporarily stored in an internal memory. See *von Neumann architecture*.

stream-oriented file

A *stream-oriented file* is a file, such as a text document or digital voice file, that is more openly structured than a data file. Text and voice are continuous streams of characters, whereas database records are repeating structures with a fixed or reasonably rigid format.

streaming tape

A *streaming tape* is a high-speed magnetic tape drive that is frequently used to make a backup copy of an entire hard disk.

STRETCH

STRETCH was the code name for IBM's first "supercomputer," the 7030, which was started in 1955 and completed in 1961. The first of eight units was delivered to the Los Alamos Scientific Laboratory and was in use for 10 years. STRETCH was IBM's first attempt at building transistorized computers and was designed to "stretch" the speed of its current vacuum tube models by a factor of 100. The machine was very sophisticated for its time, providing simultaneous execution of instructions, and parallel floating point arithmetic as well as business instructions. It is estimated that IBM lost over 40 million dollars in developing STRETCH, but that it learned an enormous amount about building second-generation computers which it applied to subsequent models that were quite profitable.

STRETCH
(Courtesy Charles Babbage Institute, University of Minnesota)

string

(1) In programming, a *string* is any contiguous set of alphanumeric characters that does not contain numbers used for calculations. Strings are data, such as names, addresses, descriptions, words and sentences. Contrast with *numeric* data, which contains amounts, such as quantity and amount due, that will be used in calculations. Most programming languages differentiate strongly between string and numeric data and will not allow a numeric operation to be performed on a string and vice versa.

(2) *String* is used loosely to refer to any collection of structures, such as a string of bits, fields or records.

Stringy Floppy

Stringy Floppy was a brand name of Exatron, Inc., for a continuous loop cartridge of 1/16" wide magnetic tape.

stroke

(1) In printing, the *stroke* is the weight, or thickness, of a character. For example, in the HP LaserJet printer, one of the specifications of the font description is the stroke weight from -3 to +3.

(2) In computer graphics, *stroke* may refer to a pen or brush stroke, or it may refer to a *vector* in a vector graphics image.

stroke writer

Same as *vector display*.

structured programming

Structured programming is a variety of design techniques that impose a logical structure on the writing of a program. For example, the logic starts at the beginning of the program and preceeds to the end of the program in the same order as the processing takes place. Large routines are broken down into smaller, modular routines. The use of the GOTO statement is discouraged, which prevents the programmer from branching to a routine that does not return to the place in the program that called it.

For documentation purposes, certain statements in the source program are indented, so that the beginnings and endings of loops are more visible when reviewing the logic of the program. In addition, structured walkthroughs, which invite criticism from peer programmers, are also part of the structured programming environment.

Programming languages such as Pascal, Ada, C and dBASE are inherently structured programming languages and force a discipline onto the programmer. However, languages such as FORTRAN, COBOL and BASIC don't force good habits and require discipline on the part of the programmer.

Structured programming techniques require more preparation in the beginning and cannot be developed as quickly "on-the-fly." However, making changes in structured programs is easier as a result. See *spaghetti code* and CASE.

style sheet

In word processing and desktop publishing, a *style sheet* is a file that contains layout settings for a particular document format. Style sheets include such settings as margins, tabs, headers and footers, columns and fonts. The style sheet contains the default settings for a particular category of document.

stylus

A *stylus* is a pen-shaped instrument that is used to "draw" images or point to menus. When used with a CRT, a stylus is a light-sensitive pen. When used with a digitizer tablet, it generates an electrical or magnetic field that is picked up by the tablet.

ST506 interface

The *ST506 interface* is a standard disk controller that is used to connect a hard disk to an IBM compatible pc. The ST506 transfers data at approximately 500 kilobytes per second and can manage two disk drives each holding up to 127.5

megabytes. The ST506 RLL, ESDI and SCSI interfaces are examples of disk drive standards with higher performance than the ST506.

ST506 RLL interface

(ST506 Run-Length Limited interface) The *ST506 RLL interface* is a standard disk controller that is used to connect a hard disk to an IBM compatible pc. The ST506 RLL standard transfers data at approximately 750 kilobytes per second and can manage two disk drives, each holding up to 200 megabytes. The ESDI and SCSI interfaces are examples of disk drive standards with higher performance than the ST506 RLL.

subroutine

A *subroutine* is a group of instructions that perform a specific processing function. Program modules, macros, functions and procedures are all subroutines.

subschema

In database management, a *subschema* is an individual user's partial view of the database. The schema is the entire logical view of the database.

subscript

(1) In word processing and mathematical notation, a *subscript* is a digit or symbol that appears below the line. Contrast with *superscript* which is a symbol that appears above the line.

(2) In programming, a *subscript* is an expression that references data stored in a memory table (array). For example, in a pricing table called **PRICETABL**, the programming statement to reference a particular price in the table might look like **PRICETABLE (ITEM)**, the "item" being the subscript variable. In a two-dimensional pricing table that includes a discount structure, the programming statement **PRICETABLE (ITEM,DISCOUNT)** could reference a discounted price. In this case, the relative locations of the current ITEM and DISCOUNT are kept in two separate index registers.

substrate

A *substrate* is the base supporting material upon which integrated circuits are built. Silicon is the most widely used substrate for the manufacturing of chips.

substring

A *substring* is a specific subset of an alphanumeric field or variable. A substring function in a programming language or application program, such as a spreadsheet or database management system, extracts the subset out of an alphanumeric field or variable. For example, **SUBSTR(PRODCODE,4,3)** extracts characters 4, 5 and 6 out of a product code field.

Summit

Summit is a Lotus 1-2-3 add-in program from Migent, Inc., that runs on IBM compatible pcs and allows Lotus users access to the Emerald Bay database engine.

Sun Microsystems

Sun Microsystems, founded in 1982, is a manufacturer of network-based, high-performance workstations. The Sun-3, Sun-4 and Sun386i product lines include stand-alone and networked systems, diskless workstations and file servers. The Sun-4 family is based on the SPARC microprocessor, and the Sun 386i is based on the Intel 80386 microprocessor.

Sun supports an open systems model of computing throughout its product line which allows it to interact in networks of computer systems from other vendors. Its Open Network Computing software is supported by over 100 vendors, including Apple, Digital and Hewlett-Packard. Sun's Network File System (NFS) software, which allows data sharing across the network, has become an industry standard.

Super VGA

See *VGA*.

SuperCalc

SuperCalc is a spreadsheet program from Computer Associates International Inc., that runs on IBM compatible pcs. SuperCalc was one of the first major electronic spreadsheets following in VisiCalc's footsteps in the early 1980s. SuperCalc5, introduced in 1988, is an advanced version that provides enhanced graphics and the ability to link up to 256 spreadsheets. It can also display three spreadsheets on screen at one time.

supercomputer

A *supercomputer* is the fastest computer available and is typically used for scientific simulations or animated graphics requiring enormous numbers of realtime calculations. Supercomputers are also used for petroleum exploration and production, structural analysis, computational fluid dynamics, physics and chemistry, electronic design, nuclear energy research and meteorology.

superconductor

A *superconductor* is a material that has almost no resistance to the flow of electricity, but must be bathed in liquid helium in order to operate in a temperature of absolute zero, or minus 459 degrees Fahrenheit. So far, the major use for superconductors, made of alloys of niobium, is for making high-powered magnets used in medical imaging machines that use magnetic fields instead of x-rays to see inside the human body.

Using experimental materials, such as copper oxides, barium, lanthanum and yttrium, breakthroughs at IBM's Zurich research lab in 1986 and at the University of Houston in 1987 raised the temperature of superconductivity to -59 degrees Fahrenheit.

These research activities may foretell the next generation of computers and other electronic systems, because if superconductors can be made to work at reasonable temperatures, they will have a dramatic impact on the future. The Josephson junction, an ultra-high-speed superconductor transistor, which is used today only in very specialized applications, can provide computers with a thousand-fold increase in processing speed if it can be economically produced.

supercontroller

Same as *digital* PABX.

SuperKey

SuperKey is a keyboard macro processor from Borland, International that runs on IBM compatible pcs. SuperKey lets users create keyboard macros, partially or completely rearrange the keyboard and also encrypt data and program files.

supermini

A *supermini* is a large-scale minicomputer that overlaps in processing capability with a small-scale mainframe. The difference in terminology is point of view. If you're a mini maker, your largest machine is "super." If you're a mainframe maker, your smallest machine isn't worth talking about! Note: Supermini is not the same as mini-supercomputer.

superscript

Superscript is any letter, digit or symbol that appears above the line. Contrast with *subscript*, which is below the line.

supervisor

Supervisor is another term for an operating system. It may also refer only to the part of the operating system that always stays in memory.

supervisor call

A *supervisor call* is the instruction in an application program that interrupts the computer and changes it to the supervisory state. The operating system then analyzes the call and directs the appropriate routine to handle it.

supervisor control program

A *supervisor control program* is the part of the operation system that always resides in memory. Same as *kernel*.

supervisor state

The *supervisor state* is the mode a computer is in when it is executing instructions from the operating system. In this mode, the computer can execute privileged instructions that are not normally available to the application program, such as input/output instructions. Contrast with *program state*, which occurs when the computer is executing instructions within an application program. These conditions are normally associated with large computers.

support

(1) *Support* is the assistance provided by a hardware or software vendor in installing and maintaining its product in the customer's environment.

(2) *Support* refers to software or hardware that is designed to work with some other software or hardware product. When a device is said to support X, Y and Z, it means that is designed to interconnect with X, Y or Z. When software is said to support X, Y and Z, it means that the program has been written or converted to communicate with X, Y or Z and use the features of those devices or programs.

SUPRA

SUPRA is a relational database management system from Cincom Systems, Inc., that runs on IBM mainframes and Digital's VAX series. SUPRA includes a user-oriented query language, called "SPECTRA," and a program that automates the database design process, called "NORMAL."

surface

A *surface* is a language that interfaces to a database engine, as coined by Wayne Ratliff, creator of dBASE II. See *Emerald Bay*.

surface modeling

In computer-aided design, *surface modeling* is a mathematical technique for representing solid-appearing objects in a computer-aided design (CAD) system.

Surface modeling is a more complex method for representing objects than wire frame modeling, but not as sophisticated as solids modeling. Although surface and solids models appear the same on screen, they are quite different. Surface models cannot be sliced open as can solids models. In addition, in surface modeling, the object can be geometrically incorrect; whereas, in solids modeling in must be correct.

surface mount technology

Surface mount technology is a printed circuit board packaging technique that mounts the chips directly onto the board rather than into receptacles that have been previously soldered onto the board. Boards can be built faster and smaller using surface mount technology.

surge

A *surge* is an oversupply of voltage from the power company that can last up to several seconds.

surge protector, surge suppressor

A *surge protector*, or *surge suppressor*, is a device that protects a computer from surges and spikes in the power line voltage. Surge protectors plug into the electric wall outlet and contain receptacles for plugging in the computer and other peripheral devices. Surge protectors prohibit increased voltages from reaching the computer, but not decreased voltages due to brownouts. Line or voltage regulators are required to keep an even flow of current at all times, and UPS (uninterruptible power supply) systems are required to keep the system running in the event of a power failure.

swapping

In virtual memory systems, *swapping*, also called paging, is the transfer of program pages or segments into memory as required.

switch

(1) A *switch* is a mechanical or electronic device that directs the flow of electricity.

(2) In programming, a *switch* is any bit or byte used to keep track of

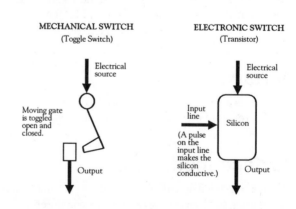

MECHANICAL SWITCH
(Toggle Switch)

Electrical source

Moving gate is toggled open and closed.

Output

ELECTRONIC SWITCH
(Transistor)

Electrical source

Input line

Silicon

(A pulse on the input line makes the silicon conductive.)

Output

some function. Switch sometimes refers to a branch in a program.

(3) A *switch* is a parameter in a language that modifies the command. For example, in Microsoft's DOS operating system, the switch /S, used in the command **FORMAT A:** /S, formats a disk and also copies the operating system to the newly formatted disk.

switched line

In communications, a *switched line* is a link that was established by dialing.

switched network

(1) The *switched network* is the international dial-up telephone system.
(2) A *switched network* is a network in which any user can send a message to any other user.

SYLK file

(**SY**mbolic **LinK** file) A *SYLK file* is a file format that is compatible with Microsoft's Multiplan spreadsheets.

symbol set

In printing, a *symbol set* is a group of symbols that are extensions to the standard character code for use in a particular country or specific application. Symbol sets provide the standards for the codes in the upper half of the ASCII character set that are not part of the ASCII standard.

symbolic language

(1) A *symbolic language* is a programming language that uses symbols, or mnemonics, for expressing operations and operands. All modern programming languages are symbolic languages.

(2) A *symbolic language* primarily manipulates symbols rather than numbers. See *list processing*.

Symphony

Symphony is an integrated software package from Lotus Development Corporation that runs on IBM compatible pcs. Symphony combines word processing, database management, speadsheet, business graphics and communications into one software package. Symphony contains its own macro language. Its counterpart for the Macintosh is Jazz.

sync character

In synchronous communications systems, a *sync character* is a special character that is transmitted to synchronize timing.

sync generator

A *sync generator* is a device that supplies synchronization signals to a series of cameras to keep them all in phase.

synchronous communications

Synchronous communications is a high-speed transmission mode used extensively in mainframe networks that transmits fixed blocks of data. Special characters are used to synchronize both the sending and receiving stations so that start and stop bits for each character are not required to be transmitted.

The two major categories of synchronous protocols are byte-oriented and bit-oriented. Byte-oriented, or character-oriented, protocols use control codes made up of full bytes, such as the common bisynchronous (BSC) protocols used by IBM and other vendors. Bit-oriented protocols use miscellaneous bit patterns as control codes rather than full bytes, for example, IBM's SDLC and the international HDLC protocol. Contrast with *asynchronous communications*, which transmits one character at a time.

synchronous data link control

See *SDLC*.

synchronous protocol

See *synchronous communications*.

syntax

Syntax is a set of rules governing the structure of and relationship between symbols, words and phrases in a language statement.

syntax error

A *syntax error* occurs when a program cannot understand the command that has been entered.

sysgen

(SYStem GENeration) A *sysgen* is the installation of a new or revised operating system. It includes selecting the appropriate utility programs and identifying the peripheral devices and storage capacities of the system the operating system will be controlling.

sysop

(**SYS**tem **OP**erator) Pronounced "siss-op," it is the person who runs an online communications system or bulletin board.

system

(1) A *system* is group of related components that interact to form a task.

(2) A *computer system* is made up of the CPU, operating system and peripheral devices.

(3) An *information system* is made up of the database, all the data entry, update, query and report programs and manual and machine procedures.

(4) *System* often refers to the operating system.

system development cycle

The *system development cycle* is the sequence of events in the development of an information system (application), which requires mutual effort on the part of user and technical staff.

    I. SYSTEMS ANALYSIS & DESIGN
        feasibility study
        general design
        prototyping
        detail design
        functional specifications

    II. USER SIGN OFF

    III. PROGRAMMING
        design
        coding
        testing

    IV. IMPLEMENTATION
        training
        conversion
        installation

    V. USER ACCEPTANCE

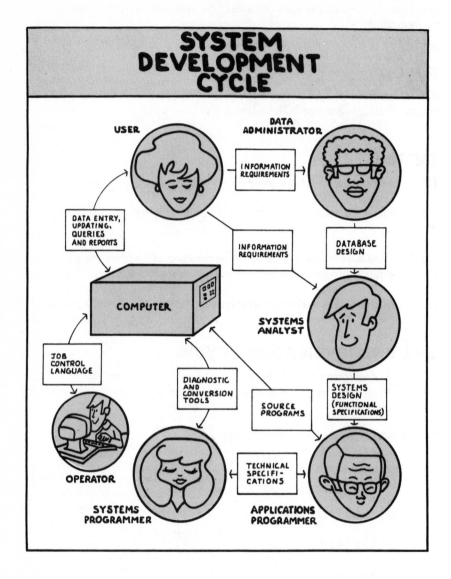

system development methodology

A *system development methodology* formalizes and codifies a series of phases for the system development cycle. It defines the precise objectives for each phase and the results required from each phase before the next one can commence. A systems development methodology may provide specialized forms for the preparation of the documentation throughout each phase.

system failure

A *system failure* is a hardware or software malfunction. System failure often refers specifically to a problem within the operating system.

system life cycle

The *system life cycle* is the useful life of an information system. The length of the system life cycle depends on the nature and volatility of the business, as well as the software development tools used to generate the databases and application programs. Eventually, an information system that is patched over and over no longer is structurally sound enough to continue to be expanded. Natural changes in business over the years affect the duration of the system, no matter how well it is designed.

Tools like database management systems allow for changes more readily, but increased transaction volumes can negate the effectiveness of the original selection and design later.

system software

System software is a major category of programs that are used to control the computer and run an organizations application programs, such as operating systems, communications control programs and database managers. Contrast with *application software*, which comprise the data entry, update, query and report programs that process the organization's data.

system test

A *system test* is a the running of a complete system for testing purposes.

System/3

The *System/3* is a batch-oriented minicomputer from IBM that was used in small businesses. Introduced in 1969, the System/3 used a new, small punched card, about half the size of previous punched cards. With the addition of the Communications Control Program (CCP), the System/3 handled up to several dozen online, interactive user terminals.

System/7

The *System/7* is a sensor-based minicomputer from IBM that was introduced in 1970 and used in process control applications. The System/7 has been superseded by the Series/1 family.

System/32

The *System/32* is a batch-oriented, single task minicomputer from IBM. Introduced in 1975, the System/32 provides a single terminal for operator use. It was superseded by the System/34, which could run System/32 applications in a special System/32 mode.

System/34

The *System/34* is a multiuser, multitasking minicomputer from IBM that was introduced in 1977. The System/34 supports several dozen terminals, and the typical system uses from a handful to a dozen terminals. The System/34 is capable of running System/32 programs in a special System/32 mode, which runs one program at a time. Most large System/34 users have migrated to the System/38, while small System/34 users have migrated to the System/36.

System/36

The *System/36* is a multiuser, multitasking minicomputer from IBM that was introduced in 1983. It superseded the System/34 and is almost entirely compatible with it. System/34 programs run in the System/36 after recompilation. The typical System/36 supports from a handful to a couple of dozen terminals. The System/36 has been superseded by the AS/400 series introduced in 1988.

System/360, System/370

See *360, 370 series.*

System/38

The *System/38* is a minicomputer from IBM that includes an operating system with an integrated relational database management system. Introduced in 1978, the System/38 was an advanced departure from previous System/3x minicomputers. The typical System/38 handles from a dozen to several dozen terminals. The System/38 has been superseded by the AS/400 series introduced in 1988.

SYSTEM 2000

SYSTEM 2000 is a hierarchical, network and relational database management system from the SAS Institute that runs on IBM, CDC and Unisys computers. SYSTEM 2000 has been integrated into the SAS System.

systems

Systems is a general term for the department, the people or the work involved in systems analysis & design activities.

systems analysis & design

Systems analysis & design is the examination of a problem and the creation of a solution to the problem. Systems analysis is effective when all sides of the problem can be reviewed. Systems design is most effective when more than one solution can be proposed, for example, a manual alternative, or a second automated alternative.

Systems are solutions to problems, but in and of themselves, they create other problems. They have a life of their own, and the plans for the care and feeding of any new system are as important as the problems they solve. When systems are considered as solutions only and not problems themselves, there is a good chance that they will not perform as expected.

systems analyst

A *systems analyst* is an individual who is responsible for the development of a business information system. Systems analysts design and modify information systems by turning user requirements into a set of functional specifications, which are the blueprint and design of the system. They design the database or help design it if data administrators are available. They develop the manual and machine procedures and the detailed processing specs for each data entry, update, query and report program in the system.

Systems analysts are the architects, as well as the project leaders, of an information system. It is their job to develop information solutions to user's problems, determine the technical and operational feasibility of their solutions, as well as estimate the costs to develop and implement them. In today's environment, systems analysts develop prototypes of the system along with the users, so that the final specifications are examples of screens and reports that have been carefully reviewed by the users. Experienced systems analysts should leave no doubt in users' minds as to the kind of system that's being developed for them, and they should insist that all responsible users review and sign off on every detail.

Systems analysts require a balanced mix of business and technical knowledge, interviewing and analytical skills, as well as a good understanding of human behavior.

systems disk

A *systems disk* is a disk pack or disk drive reserved only for system software, which includes the operating system, assemblers, compilers and other utility and control programs.

systems engineer

A *systems engineer* is a professional title often used by hardware vendors for individuals who perform systems related tasks, such as analysis, design and programming. Systems engineers are also often involved in pre-sales activities.

systems house

A *systems house* is an organization that develops customized software and/or turnkey systems for customers. Contrast with *software house*, which develops software packages for sale to the general public. Systems house and software house are often used synonymously.

systems integrator

Same as *OEM* or *VAR*.

Systems Network Architecture

See *SNA*.

systems program

A *systems program* is a control program, such as an operating system, network control program or database manager. Contrast with *application program*, which provides data entry, updating, query and report functions for the daily operation of the business.

systems programmer

A *systems programmer* is an individual who is a technical expert on some or all of the computer's system software, such as the operating system, network control program and database management system. In a company with large mainframe operations, systems programmers are responsible for the efficient performance of all the computer systems.

In a user organization, systems programmers don't actually program the computer; rather they act as technical advisors to systems analysts, application programmers and operations personnel. For example, they would know the processing capacity of the computer and whether additional tasks can be added. They would review and recommend conversion to a new operating system or database management system in order to optimize computer performance.

In large mainframe environments, there is one systems programmer for approximately 10 or more application programmers. In small minicomputer and personal computer environments, users rely on their vendors or consultants for systems programming assistance.

In a hardware or software vendor's organization, a systems programmer designs and writes system software, such as operating systems, communications control programs, database managers, assemblers, compilers and interpreters, all of which are usually far more complex than the typical business application program.

S-100 bus

The *S-100 bus* is the IEEE 696 standard for a bus architecture primarily used in personal computers. The S-100 bus was used extensively in first generation CP/M machines.

tab character

A *tab character* is the special character that is inserted into a word processing or text document to indicate one tab movement. In ASCII code, the horizontal tab character is an ASCII 9, and the vertical tab character is an ASCII 11.

tab key

A *tab key* is a key on the keyboard that moves the cursor to the next tab stop.

tabbing

Tabbing is the moving of a cursor on a video display screen or the print head on a printer to a specified column.

table

(1) In programming, a *table* is a collection of adjacent fields. Also called an *array*, a table contains data that is either constant within the program or is called in when the program is run. See *decision table*.

(2) In relational database management, a *table* is the same as a database file, a collection of records.

table look-up

A *table look-up* is the act of searching for data in a table. Table look-ups are commonly used in data entry validation to check for valid codes.

tablet

See *digitizer tablet*.

tabulate

(1) *Tabulate* is arrange data into a columnar format.

(2) *Tabulate* is to sum and print totals.

tabulating equipment

Tabulating equipment refers to a variety of punched card data processing machines including keypunches, sorters, collators, interpreters, reproducers, calculators and tabulators.

TABULATING EQUIPMENT

(Courtesy IBM)

The photo of this early sorter was taken in 1918. The cards were placed in the hopper at the top and distributed into the stackers below. Apparently, gravity must have helped.

tabulator

A *tabulator* is a punched card accounting machine that prints and calculates totals.

tag

(1) A *tag* is a set of bits or characters that identifies various conditions about data in a file and is often found in the header records of such files.

(2) A *tag* is a name (label, mnemonic) assigned to a data structure, such as a field, file, paragraph or other object.

(3) A *tag* is a key field in a record.

(4) A *tag* is a brass pin on a terminal block that is connected to a wire by soldering or wire wrapping.

tag sort

A *tag sort* is a sorting procedure in which the key fields are sorted first to create the correct order, and then the actual data records are placed into that order.

tagged image file format

See *TIFF*.

Tandem Computers

Tandem Computers was founded in 1974 to address the needs of the online transaction processing (OLTP) market that was becoming dependent on computers for applications such as inventory changes, reservations and stock and money transfers. In 1976, Tandem introduced the first commercially available computer that was based on a multiprocessor, fault tolerant architecture.

The Tandem "NonStop" computer series is built around multiple parallel processors rather than redundant processors. All the processors are used to process data, but if one fails, the system is capable of distributing the workload to the remaining processors. Tandem's architecture allows for expansion even when the computer is running. Most systems can be expanded to 16 processors, or to as many as 224 processors using a fiber optic link. With its network software, up to 4,080 processors can be tied together.

James G. Treybig is the principal founder of Tandem Computers and has been president of the company since its formation.

tandem processors

Tandem processors are two processors hooked together in a multiprocessor environment.

Tandy Corporation

Tandy Corporation grew out of a family leather business that traces its roots back to 1919. In 1963, it acquired the Radio Shack chain which was made up of nine electronics stores in the Boston area. Radio Shack originally started in 1921 when the most amazing electronic marvel of the times was the radio. After acquiring Radio Shack, Tandy began to devote itself to the consumer electronics business and eventually spun off all unrelated products.

Tandy introduced one of the first off-the-shelf personal computers in 1977, the TRS-80 Model I. Since then, it has introduced a number of different models to meet the needs of home computer enthusiasts and small businesses. Tandy's Model 100 and 200 lap-size portable computers have been extremely popular. Initially, Tandy's personal computers adhered to their own standards, but starting with the Model 1000 in 1984, Tandy has changed its policy and builds in a high degree of IBM pc compatibility.

During the past 10 whirlwind years in which countless computer manufacturers and dealers have come and gone, Tandy's built-in, stable distrubution channel of Radio Shack stores and dealers has obviously accounted for its huge success in personal computers. Today, Tandy has over 7,000 company-owned stores and dealer franchises.

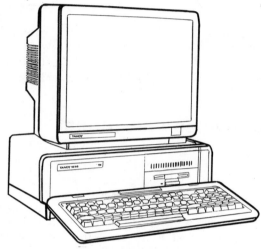

TANDY 1000TX

tap

In communications, a
tap is a connection onto the main transmission medium of a local area network.
See *transceiver*.

tape

See *magnetic tape & disk*.

tape drive

A *tape drive* is the physical unit that holds, reads and writes the magnetic tape.
See *magnetic tape & disk*.

tape mark

A *tape mark* is a special character code used to indicate the end of a tape file.

tape transport

A *tape transport* is the mechanical part of a tape drive.

target computer

Same as *object computer*.

target language

Same as *object language*.

tariff

A *tariff* is a schedule of rates for common carrier services.

task

A *task* is a program that is run as an independent unit. The instructions being executed in the task can be a complete, single application program or a program module that is part of a larger system. See *multitasking*.

task management

Task management is the part of the operating system that controls the running of one or more programs (tasks) within the computer at the same time.

T-carrier

A *T-carrier* is a digital transmission service from a common carrier or telephone company. Introduced by AT&T in 1983 as a voice transmission service, its use for data transmission has grown steadily. T1 service provides a 1.544 megabit per second line that can be used for up to 24 voice or data channels at 64 kilobits per second each or any mix thereof. T3 service provides a 44.6 megabits per second line that can handle up to 28 T1 lines or 672 voice or data channels.

T-carrier service requires multiplexors at both ends that merge (multiplex) the various signals together for transmission and decode (demultiplex) them at the destination. Multiplexors can analyze the traffic load and vary the speeds of the channels for optimum transmission. T1 and T3, originally developed for copper wire transmission, may refer to all forms of fiber optic, microwave and satellite transmissions at 1.544 and 44.6 megabits respectively.

TCAM

(TeleCommunications Access Method) TCAM is a communications program that is widely used to transfer data between IBM mainframes and 3270 terminals. See *access method*.

TCP/IP

(Transmission Control Protocol/Internet Protocol) TCP/IP is a communications protocol that is designed to interconnect a wide variety of different computer equipment. TCP/IP was originally developed by the Department of Defense's Advanced Research Projects Agency (ARPA) and later adapted for the Ethernet local area network. It is used with many Digital VAX computers running UNIX and is supported by a large number of hardware vendors, especially in the scientific and technical environments. One of the important features of TCP/IP is its TELNET virtual terminal service, which allows users to log onto and interact with different types of host computers in the network.

TCU

(Transmission Control Unit) A TCU is a communications control unit that is controlled by the computer and does not execute internally stored programs. Contrast with *front end processor*, which executes its own instructions.

TDM

(Time Division Multiplexing) TDM is a technique that weaves several low-speed signals into one high-speed transmission. For example, if A, B & C are three digital signals of 1,000 bits per second each, they can be interwoven into one higher-speed channel (3,000 bits per second) as follows: AABBCCAABBCCAABBCC. At the receiving end, the different signals are divided out and merged back into single streams.

tech writer

A *tech writer* is an individual who is responsible for writing documentation for a hardware or software product.

telco

(TELephone COmpany) A *telco* is a company that provides telephone services.

telecommunications

Telecommunications refers to the communication of all forms of information, including voice and video. See *communications*.

telecommunity

A *telecommunity* is a society in which information can be transmitted or received freely between all members without technical incompatibilities.

telecommuting

Telecommuting is working at home and communicating with the office.

teleconferencing

(1) Video *teleconferencing* is a video conference among several users that is provided by video cameras and monitors set up in the customer's premises or in a public conferencing center. Video teleconferencing requires its own communications network that uses coaxial cable, optical fibers, microwave or satellite transmission, since conventional computer networks can't handle video.

Video conferencing is very slowly being integrated into data networks. In time, all data networks will provide this capability.

(2) Audio *teleconferencing* is a telephone conference among several users that is provided internally by an organization's PABX (private automatic branch exchange) and externally by the telephone companies.

(1) Computer *teleconferencing* is a keyboard conference among several users at their terminals or personal computers that is provided by specialized communications software in a host computer. Users type their messages on their keyboards and view the commentary on their display screens.

telecopying

Telecopying (long distance copying) is the formal term for facsimile.

telegraph

Telegraph refers to low-speed communications at up to approximately 150 bits per second. Telegraph grade lines, stemming from the days of the telegraph key and morse code, are not capable of transmitting a voice conversation.

THE FIRST "DIGITAL" COMMUNICATIONS
Telegraph keys and receivers like these were used to tap out morse code.

telemarketing

Telemarketing is selling over the telephone.

Telematics

Telematics is the convergence of telecommunications and information processing.

telemetry

Telemetry is the transmitting of data sensed by instrumentation and measuring devices to a remote station where it is recorded and analyzed. For example, data from a weather satellite is telemetered to the earth.

Telenet

Telenet is a domestic communications service provided by GTE. Telenet is a value-added, packet switching network that enables many varieties of terminals and computers to exchange data.

telephony

Telephony is the science of converting sound into electrical signals that can be transmitted within cables or via radio and be reconverted back into sound.

teleprinter

A *teleprinter* is a terminal that includes a keyboard for input and a printer for output. Contrast with *video display terminal*, which provides output on a display screen. Teleprinters provide *hard copy*, display terminals provide *soft copy*.

TELEPRINTER

teleprocessing

Teleprocessing, which stands for "long distance processing," is an early IBM term for data communications.

teleprocessing monitor

See *TP monitor*.

Teletex

Teletex is an international electronic mail network that is an enhanced version of the Telex network. Teletex provides both upper and lowercase tranmission at faster speeds than the Telex network and also provides interconnection with the Telex network.

teletext

Teletext is a broadcasting service that transmits information, such as news, weather and advertising, directly to a subscriber's television set. Teletext transmission uses the unused portion of the TV signal called the vertical blanking interval, which is the black line between frames on a TV when the vertical hold is not properly adjusted. Only about a hundred frames can be transmitted this way; however, thousands of frames can be offered to the customer when dedicated TV channels are used.

A special decoder that contains a keypad for interactive use is necessary for adapting the teletext signal to the TV. Teletext frames are broadcast in a consecutive sequence that repeats over and over. When the user selects a frame from the keypad, the frame is stored in the decoder and displayed on the TV as soon as it is repeated from the broadcasting station. See *videotex*.

Teletype

Teletype is a trademark of the Teletype Corporation and refers to a variety of teleprinter devices used for communications. The Teletype machine was one of the first communications terminals in the United States.

teletypewriter

A *teletypewriter* is a low-speed teleprinter, often abbreviated TTY.

Telex

Telex is an international dial-up communications service that uses teleprinters for terminals and transmits Baudot code at 50 bits per second, or 66 words per minute. In the United States, Telex is administered by Western Union, which in 1971 purchased the Bell System's TWX service and connected it to the Telex network. In the early 1980s, a new service called Teletex was initiated that provides higher speeds and upper and lowercase text transmission to subscribers using intelligent terminals and personal computers.

template

(1) A *template* is a plastic or stiff paper form that is placed over the function keys on a keyboard to identify their use.

(2) A *template* is an empty spreadsheet without the user data. It contains only descriptions and formulas. Templates are available for popular spreadsheets from independent software vendors for various business analysis applications. For example, a tax return template can be plugged into a spreadsheet providing the user with automated tax preparation just like a canned tax software package.

terminal

(1) A *terminal* is an input/output device for a computer that usually has a keyboard for input and a video screen or printer for output.

(2) A *terminal* is an input device to a computer or telecommunications network, such as an optical scanner, video camera, telephone or punched card reader. A terminal is also an output device, such as a monitor, printer or card punch.

(3) A *terminal* is a connector used to attach a wire.

terminal session

A *terminal session* is the time in which a user is working with at a terminal.

terminal strip

A *terminal strip* is an insulated bar that contains a set of screws to which wires are attached.

terminate and stay resident

See *TSR*.

terrestrial link

A *terrestrial link* is a communications line that travels on, near or below ground. Contrast with *satellite link*, which travels from the earth to a satellite and back down again.

test data

Test data is a set of data created for testing new or revised programs. Test data is developed by the programmer and the user and must contain a sample of every category of valid data as well as as many invalid conditions as possible. The test data should be kept intact for testing future revisions. When new routines are

added, new test data should be created and added to the old test data, but the
original set should always be used unless the data conditions change.

testing

Testing is the running of new or revised programs to determine if they process
properly. See *test data*.

text

Text is words, sentences and paragraphs. The contents of a word processing
document is called text. Contrast with *data*, which is a precisely defined unit of
information, such as name, address and amount due. Although any numeric
digit or alphabetic letter is all the same to a computer, the software has to deal
with its structure according to the way humans deal with it. Text-based systems
must be able to handle words, which, to the software, are any group of non-blank
characters surrounded by blanks.

text editing

Text editing is the ability to change text by adding, deleting and rearranging
letters, words, sentences and paragraphs.

text editor

A *text editor* is a software program that creates and manages text files. Text
editors are used to create and edit source language programs, data and text files.
Unlike word processors, text editors do not have elaborate formatting and
printing features. For example, there's usually no automatic word wrap or
underline, boldface and italics printing in text editors.

text mode

(1) *Text mode* refers to displaying only text and not graphics.

(2) *Text mode* refers to entering and manipulating text.

texture mapping

In computer graphics, *texture mapping* is the creation of a special surface on a
graphics image. Through the use of algorithms, all varieties of textures can be
produced, for example, the rough skin of an orange, the metallic surface of a can
and the irregularity of a brick.

The BUNCH

The BUNCH stood for IBM's main competitors in the mainframe business after RCA and GE got out of the business. The BUNCH included Burroughs, UNIVAC, NCR, CDC and Honeywell.

thermal printer

A *thermal printer* is a non-impact printer that uses a print head of electrically heated pins and special heat-sensitive paper. The pins are pushed against the paper, and, when selectively heated, the paper darkens upon contact. Thermal printers are quiet, low-cost devices that provide a low-resolution print image.

thermal wax transfer

Thermal wax transfer is a printing process that transfers a waxlike ink onto paper. For example, in a color printer, a mylar ribbon is used that contains several hundred repeating sets of full pages of black, cyan, magenta and yellow ink. A sheet of paper is pressed against each color and passed by a line of heating elements that transfers the dots, or pixels, of ink onto the paper.

thick film

Thick film refers to a layer of magnetic, semiconductor or metallic material that is thicker than the microscopic layers, called *thin films*, of the transistors on a chip. For example, metallic thick films are silk screened onto the ceramic base of hybrid microcircuits.

thimble printer

A *thimble printer* is a letter quality impact printer similar to a daisy wheel printer, except that, instead of a daisy wheel, the characters are formed facing out and around the rim of a thimble-shaped cup. The NEC Spinwriter printers are examples of thimble printers.

thin Ethernet

Thin Ethernet is an Ethernet network that uses a small diameter coaxial cable for interconnecting computers over limited distances.

thin film

Thin film refers to a microscopically thin layer of semiconductor or magnetic material that is deposited onto a metal, ceramic or semiconductor base. For example, the layers of materials that make up a chip and the surface coating on magnetic storage media are called thin films.

third normal form

In database management, *third normal form* is the final result of a process which breaks down data into record groups that are more efficiently processed in a relational database. Data stored in third normal form relates only to the key field in the record. For example, data in order records relate only to the order number (key field) in the record. Data in customer records relate only to the customer number (key field).

third-generation computer

A *third-generation computer* is one that uses integrated circuits, disk storage and online terminals. The third generation started roughly in 1964 with the advent of the IBM System/360 series.

THOR

(Tandy High-intensity Optical Recorder) *THOR* is a compact disc recorder and player from Tandy Corporation that uses an erasable optical technology. The first model to be released in 1989 will record audio signals on a special compact disc that can be played back, erased and rerecorded. The audio disc can also be played back on any standard CD player. Models for recording data will be forthcoming at a later date.

thrashing

Thrashing is excessive paging in a virtual memory computer. If programs are not written to run in a virtual memory environment, the operating system may spend excessive amounts of time swapping program pages in and out of the disk.

throughput

Throughput is the speed with which a computer can process data. A computer's throughput is a combination of its peripheral input and output speeds, its internal processing speed, and the efficiency of its operating system and other system software all working together.

TI

(Texas Instruments, Inc.) *TI* is one of the largest semiconductor manufacturers in the U. S. TI also makes a large variety of calculators. In the early 1980s, TI sold a large number of 99/4a home computers. Although it later offered a couple of high-quality IBM compatible pcs, it has since gotten out of the personal computer business.

TIFF

(Tagged Image File Format) *TIFF* is a standard file format used to capture graphic images. TIFF stores images in bit mapped (raster graphics) format.

tightly coupled

Tightly coupled implies that two computers are linked together and are dependent on each other. One computer may control the other, or both computers may monitor each other. For example, a database machine is tightly coupled to the main processor. Two computers tied together for multiprocessing are tightly coupled. Contrast with *loosely coupled*, such as personal computers in a local area network.

time base generator

A *time base generator* is an electronic clock that creates its own timing signals for synchronization and measurement purposes.

time-division multiplexing

See *TDM*.

time slice

A *time slice* is a fixed interval of time that is allotted to each user or program in a multitasking or timesharing system.

timesharing

Timesharing is a computer that serves multiple users at the same time. The term usually refers to service bureaus; however, timesharing can be implemented on in-house systems as well. Timesharing allows users access to authorized programs and databases from their terminals.

Timesharing implies that authorized users can initiate the running of selected programs whenever they wish. However, a computer system can serve multiple users without timesharing. In this case, scheduled programs are run, and every user interacts with same programs and screens, such as in an online data collection system in which several data entry operators feed transactions into the computer. In today's multitasking computers, timesharing is implicit, and the term is often not used to define the operation.

timing clock

See *clock*.

timing signals

Timing signals are electrical pulses that are generated in the processor or in external devices in order to synchronize computer operations. The main timing signals come from the computer's clock, which provides a frequency that can be divided into many slower cycles. Other internal timing signals may come from a timesharing or realtime clock.

In disk drives, timing signals for reading and writing are generated by holes or marks on one of the platters, or by the way the digital data is actually recorded. In synchronous communications systems, timing signals are generated by sending special sync characters to the destination device in order to synchronize both sending and receiving stations.

Tiny BASIC

Tiny BASIC is a subset of the BASIC programming language that has been used in first generation personal computers with limited memory.

TM/1

(Tables Manager/1) *TM/1* is a relational spreadsheet program from Sinper Corporation that runs on IBM compatible and Wang personal computers. Although TM/1 uses the common matrix layout of a spreadsheet, it stores the data in a separate database and links the data to the spreadsheet by names, such as JAN, FEB and GROSS SALES, instead of cell references (row x, column y). When the database is updated, all the spreadsheet models are automatically updated.

In addition, the database itself can be viewed in up to eight dimensions. For example, a table of products by period can be instantly switched to products by location, categories by location and categories by period.

```
            A              B               C                D
1        YEARS           LOCS           EXPENSES          MONTHS
2         1988         NEW ENGLAND        *LIN*           *COL*
3    1986          CONNECTICUT    OFFICERS SALARIES    JAN
4    1987          MAINE          OFFICE SALARIES      FEB
5    1988          MASSACHUSETTS  ADVERTISING          MAR
6    1988 FORECAST  NEW HAMPSHIRE AUTOMOBILE EXPENSE   1ST-QTR
7    1988 VARIANCE  RHODE ISLAND  BAD DEBT EXPENSE     APR
8                   VERMONT       BANK SERVICE CHARGE  MAY
9                   NEW JERSEY    CLEANING             JUN
10                  NEW YORK      COLLECTION EXPENSE   2ND-QTR
11                  PENNSYLVANIA  COMMISSIONS          JUL
12                  NEW ENGLAND   CONTRIBUTIONS        AUG
13                  MID ATLANTIC  DELIVERY EXPENSE     SEP
14                  ALL LOCATIONS DEPRECIATION         3RD-QTR
15                                DUES & SUBSCRIPTIONS OCT
16                                EMPLOYEE BENEFITS    NOV
17                                ENTERTAINMENT        DEC
18                                FREIGHT              4TH-QTR
19                                HEAT POWER & LIGHT   YEAR
20                                INSURANCE
21                                INSURANCE OFFICER LIFE

TABLE: BUDGET                                           371/1765k
  1vudata 2positn 3lines  4colmns 5dbsave 6vutabl 7print
```

SAMPLE TM/1 STRUCTURE

(Courtesy Sinper Corporation)

From this four-dimensional structure, the user can
select any slice such as the one on the next page.

```
              A              C            D            E           F
 1                         1987         1988      1988 FORECAS  1988 VARIANC
 2   OFFICERS SALARIES    7,227,235    7,551,668    8,044,544   ( 492,876)
 3   OFFICE SALARIES     10,080,505   11,146,052   11,687,114   ( 541,062)
 4   ADVERTISING          1,032,194    1,088,082    1,145,724   (  57,642)
 5   AUTOMOBILE EXPENSE      516,319      562,698      589,021   (  26,323)
 6   BAD DEBT EXPENSE        104,402      115,026      115,431   (     405)
 7   BANK SERVICE CHARGE     105,506      111,421      121,065   (   9,644)
 8   CLEANING               214,029      224,177      231,724   (   7,547)
 9   COLLECTION EXPENSE      311,353      347,897      342,771       5,126
10   COMMISSIONS          1,540,364    1,665,071    1,744,908   (  79,837)
11   CONTRIBUTIONS           53,946       59,509       60,675   (   1,166)
12   DELIVERY EXPENSE        53,021       60,764       61,173   (     409)
13   DEPRECIATION         1,561,434    1,682,673    1,762,323   (  79,650)
14   DUES & SUBSCRIPTIONS    308,235      327,300      347,703   (  20,403)
15   EMPLOYEE BENEFITS    1,516,213    1,699,308    1,695,326       3,982
16   ENTERTAINMENT          207,399      223,045      234,888   (  11,843)
17   FREIGHT                405,362      444,283      464,805   (  20,522)
18   HEAT POWER & LIGHT   1,035,314    1,119,713    1,173,805   (  54,092)
19   INSURANCE            1,726,455    1,910,275    1,952,562   (  42,287)
20   INSURANCE OFFICER LIFE  54,255       58,336       62,103   (   3,767)
21   INTEREST               928,142    1,015,396    1,058,734   (  43,338)
     YEARS LOCS         EXPENSES MONTHS
    *COL* NEW ENGLAND *LIN*     YEAR      TABLE: BUDGET                371/1765k
    1           2in/out  3modify 4disply 5graph  6jmp w  7recalc 8goto  9edit   0help
```

SAMPLE TM/1 SLICE

(Courtesy Sinper Corporation)

This slice of year-end totals across years for each expense was derived
with a few keystrokes from the model on the previous page.

TOF

(Top Of Form) *TOF* is the beginning of a physical paper form. In order to
position paper in some printers, the printer is turned off-line, the forms are
aligned properly and the TOF button is pressed.

token passing

In communications, *token passing* is a network access method that uses a
continuously repeating frame (the token) that is transmitted onto the network by
the controlling computer. When a terminal or computer wants to send a
message on the network, it waits for an empty token. When it finds one, it fills it
with the address of the destination station and some or all of its message.

Every computer and terminal on the network constantly monitors all the
passing tokens to determine if it is a recipient of a message from another device.
It it is, it "grabs" the message and resets the token to empty status. Token passing
is used in bus-type and ring-type networks.

token ring network

(1) A *token ring network* is a communications network that uses the token passing
technology in a sequential manner. Each station in the network passes the token
on to the station next to it.

(2) *Token Ring network* is a local area network developed by IBM that
interconnects personal computers via a special cable containing twisted wire
pairs. It uses the token passing access method and transmits at four megabits per
second. Token Ring uses a star topology in which all computers connect to a

central wiring hub, but passes tokens to each of up to 255 stations in a sequential, ring-like sequence. Token Ring conforms to the IEEE 802.5 standard and is a part of IBM's SAA strategy to interconnect all of its various computer lines.

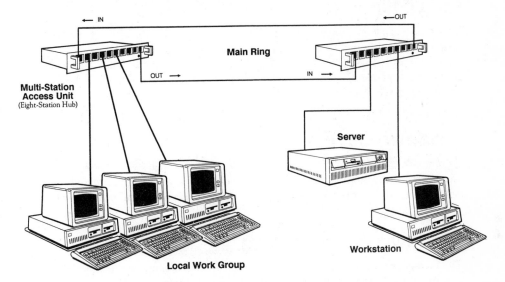

TOKEN RING NETWORK
(Courtesy Black Box Corporation)

toner

Toner is an electrically charged ink that is used in copy machines and laser printers. The toner adheres to an invisible image that has been charged with the opposite polarity onto a plate or drum or onto the paper itself.

toolbox

See *toolkit*.

toolkit

A *toolkit* is a series of program modules that aid a programmer in the development of software. Toolkits provide routines that are called upon by the program to perform various functions, for example, the "Macintosh Toolbox" lets programmers create Macintosh-style pull-down menus and icons.

TOP

(Technical Office Protocol) *TOP* is a communications protocol for office systems from Boeing Computer Services. At the bottom layer or physical level, TOP uses the IEEE 802.3 CSMA/CD Ethernet-style protocol. TOP is often used in conjunction with MAP, the factory automation protocol developed by General Motors. TOP is used in the front office, and MAP is used on the factory floor.

top of file

Top of file is the beginning of a file. In a word processing file, top of file is the first character of text in the document. In a data file, top of file is either the first physical record in the file or the first logical record in the file if the file is indexed. For example, in dBASE, GOTO TOP could go to physical record 6,508 if the file is indexed on name and the name in record 6,508 is AARDVARK.

topdown design

Topdown design is a design technique that starts with the highest level of an idea and works its way down to the lowest level of detail. Contrast with *bottom-up design*, which starts at the lowest (detail) level and works up to the highest level.

topdown programming

Topdown programming is a programming design and documentation technique that imposes a hierarchical structure on the design of the program. See *structured programming*.

topology

In communications networks, a *topology* is the pattern of interconnection between terminals and computers. For example, a *star* topology connects all nodes to a central system. A *bus* topology connects all devices to a single line. A *ring* topology connects devices in a circle.

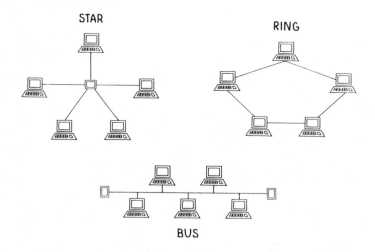

TOPOLOGY

TOPS

(1) *TOPS* is a multiuser, multitasking, timesharing, virtual memory operating system from Digital Equipment Corporation that runs on its PDP-6, DECsystem 10 and DECsystem 20 minicomputers.

(2) (**T**ransparent **OP**erating **S**ystem) *TOPS* is a local area network from TOPS, a subsidiary of Sun Microsystems. TOPS uses the AppleTalk protocol and interconnects Apple computers, IBM compatible pcs and Sun 3 workstations. A plug-in network board called the "Flashcard" adds Appletalk hardware to IBM compatible pcs. TOPS provides a peer-to-peer networking capability in which each user on the network can gain access to authorized files from any workstation in the network. A single, dedicated file server is not required in the TOPS network.

TOPVIEW

TOPVIEW is a windowing environment for the IBM personal computer from IBM, which enhances the DOS operating system and enables users to view and run more than one program at a time. As a first-generation windowing program, TOPVIEW was never widely accepted.

TOTAL

TOTAL is a network database management system from Cincom Systems, Inc., that runs on a wide variety of mainframes and minicomputers.

total bypass

Total bypass is the bypassing of both local and long distance telephone lines by using satellite communications.

touch screen

A *touch screen* is an input method for a video terminal that uses a clear panel overlaid on the screen. The panel is designed as a matrix of cells, each cell about a half an inch square to accommodate the end of a person's finger. The program displays the options on screen in the form of graphic buttons, and the user touches one of the buttons.

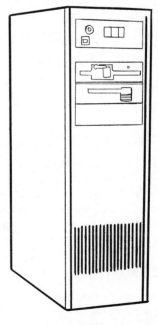

TOWER

tower configuration

A *tower configuration* is a floor-standing cabinet that is taller than it is wide. Desktop computers are sometimes turned on their side and placed into a set of feet that creates a tower configuration.

TP monitor

(TeleProcessing monitor) A *TP monitor* is a communications control program that manages the transfer of data between multiple local and remote terminals and the application programs that serve them. The TP monitor may also include programs that format the terminal screens and validate the data entered. CICS is an example of a TP monitor in the IBM mainframe environment.

TPI

(Tracks Per Inch) *TPI* measures the density of tracks recorded on a disk or drum.

track

A *track* is a storage channel on a disk or tape. Tracks are a series of concentric circles on disks or parallel lines on tape. They are designated by the disk or tape drive that records them. When tracks are written (recorded) on a particular disk or tape, only that model of disk drive or tape drive can read them. Tracks are not physical grooves as they are in phonograph records; they are a continuous stream of bits, recorded one after the other.

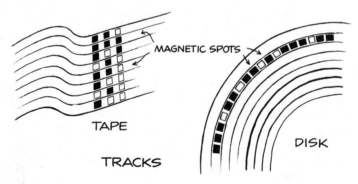

trackball

A *trackball* is an input device on a video terminal. The trackball is moved with the palm of the hand and, correspondingly, moves the cursor on the screen. Trackballs are used in various graphics applications as well as arcade games. Variations of trackballs are made to replace mice, since the trackball is stationary and takes up less desktop room than a mouse.

tractor feed

A *tractor feed* is a mechanism that moves continuous paper forms through the printer with the use of sprocket wheels. The continuous forms must have sprocket holes prepunched on both the left and right sides. Tractor feeds provide uniform, high-speed paper movement. Contrast with *sheet feeder*, which feeds single sheets of paper into the printer.

trailer

(1) In data processing, a *trailer* is the last record in a file, which usually contains the number of records in the file and hash totals.

(2) In communications, a *trailer* is a code or set of codes that make up the last part of a transmitted message.

trailer label

A *trailer label* is the last record in a file and contains identification data about the file.

train printer

A *train printer* is a line printer that uses type slugs that ride around in a track as its printing mechanism. It is similar to a chain printer, but the type slugs are not connected together; they are pushed around the track by engaging with a drive gear at one end of the mechanism. The slugs and track are usually assembled as a cartridge and can be replaced with new cartridges when the type faces wear out or fonts need to be changed. See *chain printer*.

training

(1) *Training* is the teaching of the details of a particular subject. With regard to software packages, training provides instruction about each command and keystroke used in the application. Contrast with *education*, which provides concepts about a subject. Education about software packages includes explanations of how programs are loaded and executed in the computer.

(2) In communications, *training* is the process by which two modems determine the correct protocols and transmission speeds to use.

(3) In voice recognition systems, *training* is the recording of the user's voice in order to provide samples and patterns for recognizing that same user's voice in the future.

transaction

A *transaction* is any business activity or request that is entered into the computer system. Orders, purchases, changes, additions and deletions are examples of transactions in an information system. Queries and other requests are also transactions to the computer, but are usually just acted upon and not recorded in the system. Transaction volume is a major factor in determining the size and speed of a computer system.

transaction file

A *transaction file* is a collection of records that record the activity of an organization. The data in transaction files is used to update the data in master files, which contain the subjects of the organization. Transaction files also serve as audit trails and, after some period of time, are converted from online disk to offline tape for future statistical and historical processing. Eventually, with the advent of optical disks, transaction files will remain online in the computer system so that an organization's entire history will always be immediately available for ad hoc queries. See *information system*.

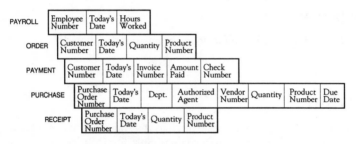

PAYROLL	Employee Number	Today's Date	Hours Worked					

ORDER	Customer Number	Today's Date	Quantity	Product Number				

PAYMENT	Customer Number	Today's Date	Invoice Number	Amount Paid	Check Number			

PURCHASE	Purchase Order Number	Today's Date	Dept.	Authorized Agent	Vendor Number	Quantity	Product Number	Due Date

RECEIPT	Purchase Order Number	Today's Date	Quantity	Product Number				

OPERATIONS TRANSACTIONS
(Typical Daily Activities)

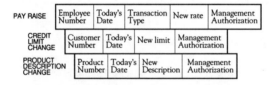

PAY RAISE	Employee Number	Today's Date	Transaction Type	New rate	Management Authorization

CREDIT LIMIT CHANGE	Customer Number	Today's Date	New limit	Management Authorization

PRODUCT DESCRIPTION CHANGE	Product Number	Today's Date	New Description	Management Authorization

MAINTENANCE TRANSACTIONS
(Typical Periodic Activities)

transaction processing

Transaction processing is the processing of transactions as they are received by the system. Transaction processing systems, also called *online* or *realtime* systems, are systems that process transactions as soon as they are entered at terminals or arrive over communications lines. Transaction processing implies that master files are being updated throughout the day the moment that they are affected. Contrast with *batch processing*, in which transactions are stored in the computer and the updating of master files is performed later, at the end of a cycle (day, week or other period).

If you buy something and throw the receipt in a box waiting for the end of the year to add them together for tax purposes, that's batch processing. However, if you document your transaction at the moment of purchase and add the new amount to the previous total, that's transaction processing.

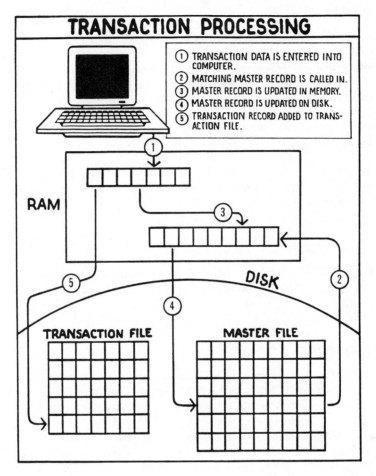

TRANSACTION PROCESSING

1. TRANSACTION DATA IS ENTERED INTO COMPUTER.
2. MATCHING MASTER RECORD IS CALLED IN.
3. MASTER RECORD IS UPDATED IN MEMORY.
4. MASTER RECORD IS UPDATED ON DISK.
5. TRANSACTION RECORD ADDED TO TRANS-ACTION FILE.

RAM

DISK

TRANSACTION FILE

MASTER FILE

transceiver

A *transceiver* is a transmitter and receiver of analog or digital signals that comes in many forms. For example, a transponder on a communications satellite is a transceiver. The interfacing unit or printed circuit board that adapts a personal computer to a local area network is a transceiver.

transcribe

Transcribe is to copy data from one medium to another, for example, from one source document to another, or from a source document to the computer. Transcribe often implies a change of format or codes, as well.

transducer

A *transducer* is a device that converts one energy into another; for example, a read/write head converts magnetic energy into electrical energy and vice versa. In process control applications, a transducer is used to convert pressure into an electrical reading.

transfer

Transfer is the transmission of data between remote stations in a network, between memory and peripheral devices in a computer system, or from one place in memory to another. Transfers within the computer are actually copies, since the data is in both locations at the end of the transfer. Input, output and move instructions activate data transfers in the computer.

transfer rate

The *transfer rate*, also called the *data rate*, is the transmission speed of a communications channel or computer channel. Transfer rates are measured in bits or bytes per second.

transfer time

Transfer time is the time it takes to transmit or move data from one place to another. It is the time interval between starting the transfer and the completion of the transfer.

transformer

A *transformer* is an electromagnetic device that changes the voltage of alternating current (AC). It is made up of a number of steel laminations that are wrapped with two coils of wire; the primary coil on the input side and the secondary coil on the output side. The voltage change is derived from the number of windings in each coil. For example, if the input is 120 volts, the primary coil has 1,000 windings, and the secondary coil has 100 windings, the output voltage will be 12 volts. In order to create direct current (DC), the output of the secondary coil is passed through a rectifier.

transient

A *transient* is a malfunction that occurs at random intervals, for example, a rapid fluctuation of voltage in a power line or a memory cell that intermittently fails.

transient area

A *transient area* is the area in memory that is used to hold programs while they are processing data. The bulk of a computer's main memory is used as a transient area.

transient state

A *transient state* is the exact point at which a device changes modes, for example, from transmit to receive or from 0 to 1.

transistor

A *transistor* is semiconductor device that is the building block of digital logic and memory circuits. Transistors are also used to amplify signals; however, in digital computers, the transistor acts as an electric switch similar to a light switch on the wall. When you toggle a light switch, you bridge the gap between two wires, and current flows from the electrical source to the light. Now, instead of a real gap, imagine a piece of semiconductor material in the gap that normally resists the flow of current. When the semiconductor material is charged, it allows the current to flow through it. Transistors, along with resistors, capacitors and diodes, make up logic gates. Logic gates make up circuits, and circuits make up electronic systems. See *Boolean logic*.

THE FIRST TRANSISTOR (1947)
(Courtesy AT&T)

MOSFET TRANSISTOR

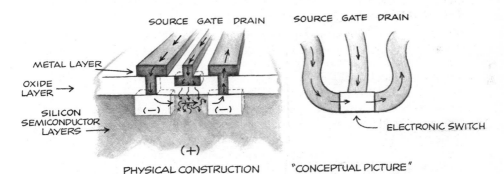

SOURCE GATE DRAIN   SOURCE GATE DRAIN

METAL LAYER

OXIDE LAYER →

SILICON SEMICONDUCTOR LAYERS →

(−)   (−)

(+)

ELECTRONIC SWITCH

PHYSICAL CONSTRUCTION   "CONCEPTUAL PICTURE"

A PULSE ON THE GATE TEMPORARILY ALLOWS
CURRENT TO FLOW FROM ONE SIDE TO THE OTHER

translate

(1) *Translate* is to change one language into another; for example, assemblers, compilers and interpreters translate source language into machine language.

(2) In computer graphics, *translate* is to move an image on screen without rotating it.

(3) In telecommunictions, *translate* is to change the frequencies of a band of signals.

TransLISP PLUS

TransLISP PLUS is a version of the LISP programming language from Solution Systems that runs on IBM compatible pcs. TransLISP PLUS provides an interface to Microsoft C that allows the programmer to write a C program and easily add it to the LISP library as a function.

transmission

A *transmission* is the transfer of data over a communications channel.

transmission channel

A *transmission channel* is the path between two nodes in a network. It may refer to the physical type of cable being used or to the signal being transmitted within the cable, for example, a subchannel within a carrier frequency. In a radio transmission, transmission channel refers to the signals being generated as the carrier frequency or subchannel within a carrier frequency.

transmission control unit

See *TCU*.

transmit

Transmit is to output data onto a communications channel.

transmitter

A *transmitter* is a device that can generate signals. Essentially, all control units within the computer generate signals that are output to the respective peripheral devices they control. When data is transferred from memory to disk, it is actually being transmitted over a cable to the disk, not unlike transmission within a network. However, in these cases, the term *transfer* is used. In this book, the term transmit is confined to communications networks.

transparent

Transparent implies a function that is invisible to the user. If a change in hardware or software is called transparent, it will have no visible effect on the user and/or the programs currently running in the computer.

transponder

A *transponder* is a receiver and transmitter in a communications satellite. The transponder receives a transmitted microwave signal from earth, amplifies it and retransmits it back to earth at a different frequency. There are several transponders on a communications satellite.

transport layer

The *transport layer* is the fourth level of a communications protocol. See *OSI*.

trapdoor

A *trapdoor* is a built-in interface within a program that allows access to the program. Trapdoor implies an ad hoc or emergency entrance or exit within the program that can be used when necessary.

trapping

Trapping is the testing for a particular condition. Error trapping is the testing for error conditions in a program, which provides error messages or alternatives for dealing with them. In programming, trapping refers to comparing for certain data and dealing with it. When debugging a program, trapping refers to catching the offending data, program value or instruction.

tree structure

A *tree structure* is a hierarchical structure with many branches.

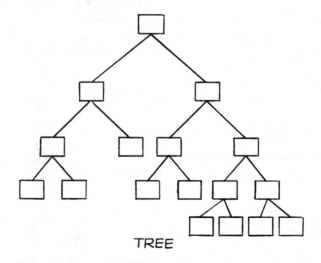

TREE

trichromatic

In computer graphics, *trichromatic* refers to the use of red, green and blue to create all the colors in the spectrum.

trillion

A *trillion* is one thousand times one billion. In computer specifications, a trillion is represented by *tera*; for example, one terabyte is one trillion bytes. One trillionth is represented by *pico*; for example, one picosecond is one trillionth of a second.

Trilogy

Trilogy was founded in 1979 by Gene Amdahl, chief architect of the IBM System/360 and founder of Amdahl Corporation. The purpose of the company was to create chips using wafer scale integration and use them to build a large IBM compatible supercomputer. The company was funded with over a quarter of a billion dollars of venture capital, the largest funding for a startup in history.

Trilogy came close to success, but never quite made it. By 1984, it dropped the supercomputer project and soon after, the entire "superchip" project. In October 1985, Trilogy acquired Elxsi Corporation, a manufacturer of multiprocessor systems compatible with Digital Equipment's VAX series. Eventually Trilogy merged itself into Elxsi.

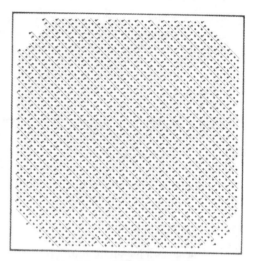

THE TRILOGY SUPERCHIP
(Courtesy Elxsi Corporation)

This is the actual size of the chip Trilogy had tried to develop using wafer scale integration.

triple precision

Triple precision is the use of three computer words instead of one to hold a number used for calculation, thus allowing three times as large a number for more arithmetic precision.

Trojan horse

A *Trojan horse* is a program routine that invades a computer system by being secretly attached to a valid program that will be downloaded into the computer. It may be used to locate password information, or it may alter an existing program to make it easier to gain access to it. A *virus* is a Trojan horse that continues to infect programs over and over again.

TRS

(Text Retrieval System) TRS is a text processing software from Software AG of North America that adds text handling features to its ADABAS database management system.

TRS-80

(Tandy Radio Shack-80) TRS-80 was the first family of personal computers from Tandy Corporation introduced in 1977.

TRS-80

truncate

Truncate is to cut off leading or trailing digits or characters from an item of data without regard to the accuracy of the remaining characters. Truncation occurs when data is converted into a new record with smaller field lengths than the original.

trunk

A trunk is a communications channel between two points. The term is typically used with telephone systems and often refers to large bandwidth channels between major switching centers, which are capable of transmitting many simultaneous voice conversations or data signals.

truth table

A truth table defines all the input and outputs of a logical condition. The following example is a truth table for the Boolean AND operation.

Inputs	Output
1 AND 1	1
1 AND 0	0
0 AND 1	0
0 AND 0	0

TSO

(Time Sharing Option) TSO is system software from IBM that provides time sharing on an IBM mainframe running in an MVS environment. Time sharing allows a user or programmer to activate and run a program from a terminal.

TSR

(Terminate and Stay Resident) *TSR* programs are RAM resident programs that remain in memory at all times so that they can be instantly activated. In IBM compatible pcs running under DOS, desktop accessory TSR programs have become popular in order to have instant access to a calculator or calendar. However, these TSR programs often conflict with each other, each one fighting for the right to exist within the computer, and various combinations of programs will not work together.

OS/2, which is a more advanced operating system than DOS, is designed to keep several programs active in memory (multitasking) at all times. Consequently, any program can function as a TSR program. In addition, windows environments for DOS, such as Windows or DESQview, also provide the ability to switch back and forth quickly between multiple applications.

TTL

(Transistor Transistor Logic) *TTL* is a digital circuit in which the output is derived from two transistors. Although true TTL technology is a very specific design method, the term is used generically to refer to any digital input or circuit.

TTY

(TeleTYpewriter) See *teletypewriter*.

TTY protocol

A *TTY protocol* is a low-speed asynchronous communications protocol with limited or no error checking.

tube

See CRT and *vacuum tube*.

tuner

A *tuner* is the electronic part of a radio or television that locks on to a selected carrier frequency (station, channel) and filters out the audio and video signals for amplification and display.

tuple

In relational database management, a record, or row, is called a *tuple*; however, the term is not often used. In relational database, a column is called an *attribute*, and a file is called a *table* or a *relation*.

turbo

Turbo is used in trade names of hardware and software to imply high speed. It often refers to fast clock rates in personal computers. Borland International, Inc. has popularized its use in its language products, for example, "Turbo C" and "Turbo Pascal."

Turbo Mouse

A *Turbo Mouse* is a mouse alternative from Kensington Microware Ltd,. that works with a Macintosh computer. The Turbo Mouse is a trackball that is moved with the fingers while the hand remains stationary. If the ball is moved slowly, the cursor moves slowly across the screen, but if the ball is moved quickly, the same amount of ball movement moves the cursor a greater distance on the screen. The Turbo Mouse provides a much more comfortable alternative to the mouse for many people.

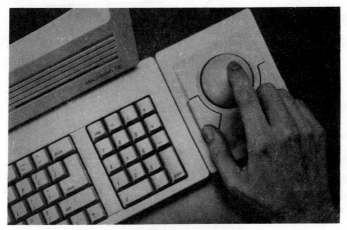

TURBO MOUSE
(Courtesy Kensington Microware)

turnaround document

A *turnaround document* is a paper document or punched card that is prepared for re-entry into the computer system. Paper documents are printed with special fonts for optical scanning, and punched cards are punched with appropriate codes. Invoices and inventory stock cards are examples of turnaround documents.

turnaround time

(1) In a batch processing environment, *turnaround time* is the time it takes to receive the reports after submission of documents or files for processing. In an online environment, turnaround time is called *response time*.

(2) In half-duplex transmission systems, *turnaround time* is the time it takes to change from transmit to receive and vice versa.

turnkey system

A *turnkey system* is a complete system of hardware and software delivered to the customer in a ready-to-run condition. Turnkey systems typically have all software installed and ready to go.

turnpike effect

In communications, the *turnpike effect* is when everything "locks up" due to increased traffic conditions and bottlenecks in the system.

turtle graphics

Turtle graphics is a method used for creating graphic images in the Logo programming language. The turtle is an imaginary pen that is given drawing commands, such as "go forward" and "turn right." On screen, the turtle is shaped like a triangle. See *Logo*.

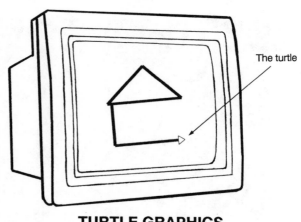

The turtle

TURTLE GRAPHICS
Go forward 100 units.
Turn left 90 degrees.

tutorial

A *tutorial* is an instructional book or program that takes the user through a prescribed sequence of steps in order to learn a product. Contrast with *documentation*, which, although instructional in nature, tends to group features and functions according to category.

tweak

Tweak is to make minor adjustments in an electronic system or in a software program in order to improve performance.

twinaxial

Twinaxial is a cable that is similar to coaxial cable, but with two inner conductors instead of only one. Twinaxial cables are used in IBM System 34, 36 and 38 communications environments. See *plugs & sockets*.

twisted pair

A *twisted pair* is a pair of small insulated wires that are commonly used in telephone cables. The wires are twisted around each other to minimize interference from other wires in the cable. Cables containing from one to several hundred twisted pairs are used in myriads of electronic and telephone interconnections. Twisted pair wires have limited bandwidths compared to coaxial cable or optical fiber.

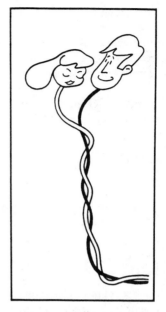

TWISTED PAIR

two-out-of-five code

Two-out-of-five code is a numeric code that stores one decimal digit in five binary digits in which two of the bits are always 0 or 1, and the other three bits are always in the opposite state.

TWX

(TeletypeWriter eXchange Service) *TWX* is a dial-up communications service within the United States and Canada, which uses teleprinters for terminals and can transmit 5-bit Murray code or 7-bit ASCII code at up to 150 bits per second. Originally part of the Bell Telephone System, the TWX network was sold to Western Union in 1971 and was interconnected with Western Union's Telex network.

Tymnet

Tymnet is a domestic communications service from Tymshare Corporation. Tymnet is a value-added, packet switching communications network that enables many varieties of terminals and computers to exchange information.

type

(1) In data or text entry, *type* refers to pressing the keys on the keyboard.

(2) In programming, a *type* is a category of variable that is determined by the kind of data stored in it. For example, integer, floating point, string, logical, date and binary are common data types.

(3) In Microsoft's DOS and OS/2 operating systems, *type* is a command that displays the contents of a text file.

type ball

A *type ball* is a golf ball-sized printing element that contains all the print characters on its outside surface and is used in typewriters and low-speed teleprinters. The type ball was introduced with IBM's Selectric typewriter.

type font

A *type font* is a set of print characters of a particular design (typeface), size (point size) and weight (light, medium, heavy). See *font*.

typeface

A *typeface* is the design of a set of printed characters, such as Courier, Helvetica and Times Roman. The text you're reading now is printed in the Goudy Old Style typeface. The word headers are in the Helvetica typeface.

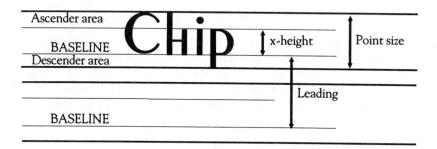

TYPEFACE MEASUREMENTS

typeover mode

In word processing and other data entry applications, *typeover mode* is a state in which each character typed on the keyboard replaces the character at the current cursor location. Contrast with *insert mode*, in which each typed-in character is inserted into the text.

U

UART

(Universal Asynchronous Receiver Transmitter) A *UART* is an electronic circuit that converts parallel bits to serial bits and vice versa. Inside the computer, data is worked on in parallel, 8 or more bits at a time, whereas transmission over a communications channel is usually serial (one bit following the other). The serial transmission is asyncronous, which means the UART is responsible for generating and detecting the start and stop bits that accompany each character transmitted.

UCSD p-System

(University of California at San Diego p-System) The *UCSD p-System* is a software development system that is designed for transportability across different computers. Programs written in the UCSD p-System can run on several computers without change. The programs are written in traditional languages, such as BASIC and Pascal, but UCSD p-System compilers are used to translate the language into an interim language called *p-code*. The p-code is executed by an interpreter program in the target machine.

UHF

(Ultra High Frequency) *UHF* is a range of electromagnetic frequencies from 300 million to 3 billion Hertz (cycles per second).

ULA

(Uncommitted Logic Array) Same as *gate array* or *PLA*.

ultimate wafer

The *ultimate wafer* is a semiconductor wafer that contains an integrated set of circuits throughout its entire surface. See *wafer scale integration*.

ultra high frequency

See *UHF*.

ultrafiche

Ultrafiche, pronounced "ultra feesh," is a microfiche that holds up to 1,000 document pages per 4x6" sheet of film. Normal microfiche stores around 270 pages per sheet.

ultraviolet

Ultraviolet is a band of invisible radiation within the light spectrum, but just before visible light. Ultraviolet light is used to erase EPROM (erasable PROM) chips, which are fully erased in about 10 minutes.

Ultrix

Ultrix is a version of the UNIX operating system from Digital Equipment Corporation that runs on its VAX and PDP-11 line of computers.

unary

Unary is a single entity or operation on only one object.

unbundled

Unbundled refers to separate prices for hardware and software.

uncommited logic array

Same as *gate array* and PLA.

unconditional branch

In programming, an *unconditional branch* is an instruction or statement that passes control to a different part of or to another program. Constrast with *conditional branch*, which passes control based on the results of comparing sets of data.

undelete

Undelete refers to restoring the last delete operation that has taken place. In word processing programs, there may be several levels of undelete capability allowing any or all of several previous deletions to be restored. In order to undelete a file that has been deleted in Microsoft's DOS operating system, a separate utility program is required. In order to salvage the file completely, the undelete feature of the utility must be used before any other data has been recorded on the disk.

underflow

(1) An *underflow* occurs when the result of a computation is smaller than the smallest quantity the computer can store.

(2) An *underflow* occurs when an item is called for in an empty stack.

undo

Undo refers to restoring the last editing operation that has taken place. For example, if a line of text has been deleted, performing an undo will restore the line back in its original place. Some programs have several levels of undo, for example, the last and next to last editing operation can be restored.

Unibus

Unibus is a bus architecture from Digital Equipment Corporation that was introduced in 1970 along with its PDP-11 computers. Unibus peripherals can be connected to a VAX computer through Unibus attachments on the VAXs.

unidirectional

Unidirectional is the transfer or transmission of data in a channel in one direction only.

uninterruptible power supply

See *UPS*.

Unisys

Unisys was created in 1986 as a merger of the Burroughs Corporation and the Sperry Corporation, the largest merger ever in the computer field and one of the largest industrial mergers in history. However, this was not the first merger or name change for the Sperry Corporation. In 1955, it merged with Remington Rand to become Sperry Rand. In 1973, the computer division of Sperry became

Sperry Univac, and, again in 1984, it became the Computer Systems division of the Sperry Corporation.

Throughout the 1960s and 1970s, Sperry became known for its large-scale mainframes in commercial and government installations. Sperry has been heavily involved in large defense contracts providing communications and realtime systems for the military and for NASA.

In 1971, Sperry absorbed responsibility for the RCA Spectra 70 computer line when RCA decided to get out of the computer

BURROUGHS ADDING MACHINE (CIRCA 1895)
(Courtesy Smithsonian Institution)

business. Sperry provided customer support and maintenance of the product line until it slowly became phased out due to obsolescence.

Burroughs started out as a maker of calculating machines and cash registers. It was first involved with computers by supplying memory for the ENIAC in 1952. A decade later, it introduced the B5000 computer system, which quickly became known for its advanced operating systems featuring timesharing and virtual memory capabilities. Burroughs B series computers became firmly entrenched in the banking and financial industries thoughout the 1960s and 1970s.

As a new company, Unisys will continue to emphasize both product lines in their respective niches. Large Burroughs mainframes have been renamed the Unisys A Series while the smaller mainframes have been renamed the Unisys V Series. Sperry product lines are now the Unisys 1100 Series and the System 80 series.

Unisys also offers the 5000, 6000 and 7000 Series of minicomputers as well as Intel microprocessor-based personal computers. Unisys supports the UNIX operating system from micro to mainframe.

unit record equipment

Same as *tabulating equipment*.

UNIVAC I

The *UNIVAC I*, introduced in 1951 by Remington Rand, was the first computer manufactured in quantity. Over 40 UNIVAC Is were sold to government and private industry, making it the first major computer success story. Its memory was made of mercury-filled acoustic delay lines, which held 1,000 12-digit numbers, and it used magnetic tapes for storage, which held one million characters at a density of 128 characters per inch.

In the early 1950s, UNIVAC was synonymous with "computer." In 1952, it was used to predict Eisenhower's victory over Stevenson in the presidential election. But in the mid 1950s, UNIVAC gave up that recognition and its lead to IBM's 650 computer series. Other UNIVAC models were introduced in 1957 and 1960 to compete with IBM, but UNIVAC never again held the lead in mainframe computers. The UNIVAC name was used for many subsequent computers from Remington Rand, Sperry Rand and, eventually the Sperry Corporation. In 1982, the Sperry Univac division was renamed the Computer Systems division of Sperry.

UNIVAC I
(Courtesy Unisys)

universal product code

The *universal product code* is the standard bar code that is printed on retail merchandise. It contains the vendor's identification number and the product number, which is read into the terminal by passing the bar code over a scanner.

UNIVERSAL PRODUCT CODE

UNIX

UNIX is a multiuser, multitasking operating system from AT&T that runs on a wide variety of computer systems from micro to mainframe. UNIX was written in the C programming language, which was also developed at AT&T's Bell Laboratories. Hence, UNIX was written in a language that was designed to create operating systems in the first place. It is C's transportability that allows UNIX to run on different computers.

UNIX is made up of the "kernel," the heart of the operating system, the "file system," a hierarchical directory method for organizing files on the disk and the "shell," the user interface which provides the way the user commands the system. Normal UNIX commands are very cryptic but they can be replaced with shells that are easier to use. The following list shows typical UNIX commands with their Microsoft DOS counterparts:

Command	UNIX	DOS
List directory	ls	dir
Copy a file	cp	copy
Delete a file	rm	del
Rename a file	mv	rename
Display contents	cat	type
Print a file	lpr	print
Check disk space	df	chkdsk

UNIX was started in 1969 by Ken Thompson and originally developed for the PDP-7 minicomputer. Additional work was done by Dennis Ritchie, and, by 1974, UNIX had matured into a state-of-the-art operating system primarily running on PDP computers. UNIX became very popular in scientific and academic environments. For example, considerable enhancements were made to UNIX at the University of California in Berkeley, and versions of UNIX include the "Berkeley extensions," which became widely used on Digital's VAX systems. By the late 1970s, commercial versions of UNIX, such as Interactive System One (IS/1) and then XENIX, became available.

In 1981, in order to provide an acceptable product for the commercial world, AT&T began to consolidate the many versions of UNIX that were in use into new standards which evolved into UNIX System III and then UNIX System V. In 1984, System V was established as a major standard that incorporated all of the important characteristics of previous versions. AT&T's System V Interface Definition (SVID) specifies the minimum requirements for UNIX compatibility.

unpack

Unpack is to convert a packed decimal number into a normal numeric format, or to return encrypted or compressed data into its original format.

UPC

See *universal product code*.

update

Update is to change data in a file or database. Update and *edit* are often uses synonymously. However edit implies changing existing data, whereas update also implies file maintainance, in which records are added and deleted as well as changed.

The steps in updating a disk record are: (1) reading the old record into memory, (2) copying the new data on top of the old data in memory, and (3) writing (recording) the modified record back on the disk, either overlaying the original or writing to a new location and then deleting the old record.

The steps in updating a tape record are: (1) reading the old record into memory, (2) copying the new data on top of the old data in memory, and (3) writing the modified record onto a different tape.

upload

Upload is to transmit data from a personal computer or workstation to a central computer or file server. Upload typically refers to the transmission of an entire file rather than a single record. Contrast with *download*.

UPS

(Uninterruptible Power Supply) A UPS provides backup power for a computer system when the electrical power fails or drops to an unacceptable voltage level. Small UPS systems provide battery power for only a few minutes; enough to power down the computer in an orderly manner. Sophisticated systems are tied to electrical generators and can provide power for days. A UPS system can be interconnected with a file server in a local area network so that, in the event of a problem, all users in the network can be alerted to save files and shut down immediately.

"Online UPS," provide a constant source of electrical power. "Offline UPS," also known as "standby power systems (SPS)," take a couple of milliseconds to switch to battery after detecting a power failure.

A *surge suppressor* filters out surges and spikes, and a *voltage regulator* maintains uniform voltage during a brownout, but a UPS is the only device that will keep a computer running when there is no electrical power. UPS systems typically provide surge suppression and may also provide voltage regulation.

uptime

Uptime is the time during which a system is working without failure. Contrast with *downtime*.

upward compatible

Upward compatible refers to software that will run without modification on larger or later models of a computer system. Contrast with *downward compatible*, which is software that will run on smaller or earlier models of a computer system.

user

A *user* is any individual who interacts with the computer at an application program level. Programmers, operators and other technical personnel are not users when they're working in a professional capacity on the computer.

user area

A *user area* is a reserved part of a disk or memory for user data.

user-friendly

User-friendly implies a system that is easy to learn and use. However, this term has been so abused that many people in the trade are now very reluctant to use it.

user group

A *user group* is an organization of users of a particular hardware or software product. User groups share experiences and ideas to improve their understanding and use of a particular product. User groups are often responsible for influencing vendors to change or enhance their products.

user interface

A *user interface* is a combination of menus, screen design, keyboard commands and language, which together create the way a user interacts with a computer. Hardware, such as a mouse and touch screen, are also part of it. The user interface is probably the most important aspect to the success of a software packages. In time, interactive video, voice recognition and natural language understanding will dramatically change current day user interfaces. See *Macintosh user interface* and *Lotus menu*.

USRT

(Universal Synchronous Receiver Transmitter) A *USRT* is an electronic circuit that converts parallel bits to serial bits and vice versa. Inside the computer, data is worked on in parallel (8 or more bits at a time), whereas transmission over a communications channel is serial (one bit following the other). The USRT is also responsible for generating timing for synchronous transmission.

utility program

A *utility program* is a program that supports the operation of the computer. Utility programs, or simply "utilities," provide file management capabilities, such as sorting, copying, comparing, listing and searching, as well as diagnostic routines that check the "health" of the computer system.

V

V Series

(1) The *V Series* is a line of small to medium-scale mainframes from Unisys Corporation. The V Series is a new name for the B2500 and B3500 product lines from Burroughs that were originally introduced in 1966.

(2) See *Hayes V-series*.

VAC

(Volts Alternating Current) See *volts* and *alternating current*.

vacuum tube

A *vacuum tube* is an electronic component that is used as a switch, amplifier or display screen by controlling the flow of electrons in a vacuum. Vacuum tubes were used as on/off switches in first-generation computers and were replaced with transistors in second-generation systems. Today, the primary use of a vacuum tube is the cathode ray tube (CRT) used for

VACUUM TUBE (1915)

(Courtesy AT&T)

---

video display screens in monitors and television sets. In time, it, too, will be replaced by flat screen technologies.

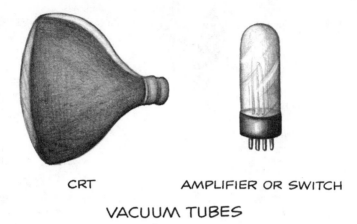

CRT   AMPLIFIER OR SWITCH

VACUUM TUBES

VAD

(Value Added Dealer) Same as VAR (*value added reseller*).

Valdocs

(VALuable DOCumentS) *Valdocs* is an extended word processor program from Epson Corporation that runs on its QX-10 personal computers and provides text, calculation, drawing and calendar functions. Introduced in 1982, Valdocs was originally designed for Epson's HASCI (Human Applications Standard Computer Interface) keyboard, which provided a series of dedicated function keys for common tasks.

validity checking

Validity checking is a set of routines in a data entry program that tests the input for correct and reasonable conditions, such as numbers falling within a range and correct spelling, if possible.

value

(1) In programming, a *value* is any actual data, for example, numeric quantities, such as .02, 5, 35.95 and 65,089, or alphanumeric items, such as "North Region," "Red Shirt" and "December 11, 1988." In the expression, **state = "PA"**, the value PA is stored in the variable called STATE.

(2) In spreadsheets, a *value* is the numeric data within the cell.

value-added network

A *value-added network* is a communications network that provides services beyond normal transmission, such as automatic error detection and correction, protocol conversion and message storing & forwarding. Telenet and Tymnet are examples of value-added networks.

VAN

See *value-added network*.

vaporware

Vaporware is software that does not exist. It usually refers to products that are advertised, but that are not ready for delivery to customers.

VAR

(Value Added Reseller) A *VAR* is an organization that adds value to a system and resells it. For example, a VAR could purchase a computer and various peripherals from different vendors and a graphics software package from another vendor and package it all together as a specialized CAD system. See *OEM*.

variable

In programming, a *variable* is a structure in memory which holds the data that has been assigned to it. It holds the value until a new value is assigned to it or the program is finished. Variables are equivalent to a field in a record, which holds one item of data. Variables are used to hold control values, for example, a number that is used to repeat a process. Variables are used to store the data typed in from the keyboard. Variables are also used to hold messages, such as "printer is not responding." Variables may hold up to several hundred bytes, but they usually contain compact values that are held only temporarily until a routine is completed. For example, in a data entry program, they act as an interim holding place for the data on screen, and then they are copied to an output record that is written to the disk.

Variables are usually assigned with an equal sign; for example, **city** = **"Chicago"**, assigns the value **Chicago** to a variable named **city**. In some programming languages, such as BASIC and dBASE, the type of the variable is automatically created by the syntax of the expression. For example, numeric data is unquoted, **counter = 1**, and string (character oriented) data is quoted, **product = "ABC4344"**. In other languages, the type must be declared; for example, in C, the statement, **int counter = 1**, specifies that only integers will be allowed in the variable.

A *local variable* is a variable that can be referenced only within the subprogram, function or procedure it was defined. A *global variable* can be used by all modules in the program.

variable length field

A *variable length field* is a record structure that holds fields of varying lengths. When fields are fixed in length, alphanumeric data, such as names and addresses, waste a lot of storage space, since the same amount of space is reserved for PAT SMITH as it is for GEORGINA WILSON BARTHOLOMEW.

Variable length fields are created with a size code at the beginning of each field that identifies the length of the subsequent field. There's considerably more programming involved in variable length fields, because every record has to be separated into fixed length fields when it is brought into memory. Conversely, each record has to be coded into the variable length format before it is written to disk.

The same storage savings can be achieved by other means, for example, compressing data on its way to the disk, and uncompressing it when it comes back. All the blank spaces in fixed length fields will be filtered out with this technique; however, unless these methods are integrated into the operating system, they may provide unacceptable performance.

Each data field is preceded by an identification field that indicates its length.

ID	Williams, James T.	ID	5 Main St.	ID	Harrisburg	ID	PA
ID	Maloney, Pat	ID	75 Arbor Lane	ID	Rye	ID	NY

VARIABLE LENGTH FIELDS/RECORDS

variable length record

A *variable length record* is a record that contains one or more variable length fields.

VAX

(Virtual Address eXtension) VAX is a family of 32-bit computers ranging from desktop personal computers to large-scale mainframes from Digital Equipment Corporation. Large VAX computers can be clustered together to provide a multiprocessing environment serving thousands of online users.

All VAX computers share the same VMS operating system, and programs running on one VAX machine can run on any other. VAX systems provide a compatibility mode for running software written for Digital's earlier PDP computers.

In 1977, the VAX-11/780 was the first model introduced, and over 20 models have followed. In 1984, Digital introduced the VAX/8600, and subsequent models have used the 8000 series designation.

Due to its compatible architecture, the VAX series has achieved outstanding success during the 1980s.

VAXcluster

A *VAXcluster* is a group of VAX computers from Digital Equipment Corporation that are coupled together in a multiprocessing environment.

VAXmate

The *VAXmate* is an AT-compatible personal computer from Digital Equipment Corporation that was introduced in 1986.

VCR

(Video Cassette Recorder) A *VCR* is a videotape recording and playback machine that comes in several formats for commercial and home use. The Sony Umatic format (3/4" tape cassette) is widely used in companies for instructional use. The VHS and Beta formats (1/2" tape cassette), first used extensively in the home for entertainment, are now widely used in industry for instructional video courses.

Although VCRs are analog recording machines, they have been used to store digital data with the use of an adapter.

VDI

(Virtual Device Interface) *VDI* is an ANSI standard format for creating device drivers. For example, if a vendor sells a screen display and adapter board with a proprietary resolution, and also includes a driver written in the VDI format, software packages that support VDI will be able to use the new monitor.

The VDI standard has been incorporated into the CGI standard. When CGI is officially endorsed by ANSI, it may supersede VDI.

VDM

See CGM.

VDT

(Video Display Terminal) A *VDT* is a terminal with a keyboard and a video display screen.

VDU

(Video Display Unit) Same as *VDU*.

vector

(1) In computer graphics, a *vector* is a line designated by its end points (x-y or x-y-z coordinates). When a circle is drawn, it is made up of hundreds of small vectors.

(2) In matrix algebra, a *vector* is a one-row matrix.

vector display

A *vector display* is a display terminal that draws vectors on the screen. Contrast with *raster display*, which generates dots on the screen.

vector graphics

(1) *Vector graphics* is a method of coding a graphic image as straight lines. Contrast with *raster graphics*, which codes images as patterns of dots. See *vector* and *graphics*.

(2) *Vector Graphic, Inc.*, was a well-known microcomputer vendor during the early 1980s.

vector processor

A *vector processor* is a computer that performs simultaneous calculations on numerical elements. For example, in object-oriented computer graphics (vector graphics), a line is represented by its end points (coordinates). To move that line to a different place on the screen requires adding or subtracting the same number to both end points. If both ends are calculated simultaneously, the relocation computation is performed in half the time. If the entire picture image is relocated, then hundreds, or even thousands, of coordinates must be calculated with the same number. If all the end points can all be calculated fast enough, realtime motion can be simulated on screen. See *array processor* and *math coprocessor*.

Vectra

Vectra is a series of IBM compatible personal computers

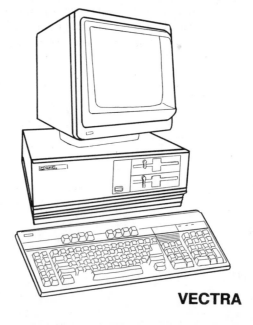

VECTRA

from Hewlett-Packard. The first Vectra, an AT compatible personal computer, was introduced in late 1985. In 1987, an entire series of Vectras, from 8086 to 80386 models, was introduced. The Vectras are known for their extreme ruggedness and reliability, which is what Hewlett-Packard is famous for.

Ventura Publisher

Ventura Publisher is a desktop publishing program from Xerox Corporation that runs on IBM compatible pcs. Ventura Publisher is a full-featured program that duplicates almost all of the capabilities of pagination systems that run on larger computers. Although it is capable of creating short four and eight-page brochures, it is known for its ability to print large text files, such as long chapters in a magazine or book.

   Ventura Publisher is designed to accept text and graphics from most major word processor and graphics programs. It has built-in, although limited, text and graphics capabilities, which can be used to edit text and add simple drawings. Ventura includes a run time version of GEM (Graphics Environment Manager) from Digital Research, which provides it with a mouse-driven user interface.

verify

In data entry operations, *verify* is to compare the keystrokes of a second operator with the files created by the first operator.

VersaCAD DESIGN

VersaCAD DESIGN is a high-performance, general-purpose CAD system for IBM compatible pcs. Utilizing a logical command structure and easy-to-learn approach, VersaCAD DESIGN is the first fully integrated system that features powerful 2D geometric and construction drafting, 3D modeling and 16 multiple viewports, light source color shading, mass properties calculations, bill of materials with report generation, presentation graphics output, complete programmability and universal CAD communications.

   VersaCAD is also available for the Macintosh and features a wide variety of detail design objects, attributes and geometric construction tools in a fully interactive system accurate to 16 decimal digits. It provides 3D capabilities, CAD oriented HyperCard stacks including bill of materials and full support of the Macintosh user interface.

version number

The *version number* of a software program identifies the evolution of the program. The difference between version 2.2 and 2.3 can be night and day, since new releases of software not only add new features to the package, but more often than not correct the bugs in the previous version. That means the problem that's been driving you crazy may have been fixed. Version number 1.0 drives terror into the hearts of experienced users, since it means that the program has just been released, and bugs are still to be uncovered after extensive customer use.

Version numbers, such as 3.1a or 3.11, indicate a follow-up release only to fix a bug in the previous version, whereas 3.1 and 3.2 usually indicate enhancements in the product.

vertical recording

Vertical recording is a magnetic recording method that records the bits vertically instead of horizontally, taking up less space and providing greater storage capacity. The vertical recording method uses a specialized material for the construction of the disk.

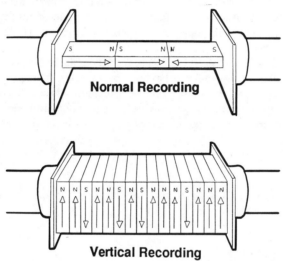

Normal Recording

Vertical Recording

vertical redundancy checking

See VRC.

vertical synchronization frequency

The *vertical synchronization frequency* is the number of times per second a frame is transmitted to a video display screen. The typical frequency is 60 times per second in non-interlaced mode, in which all the lines are displayed for each frame, or 30 frames per second when odd and even lines are alternately displayed.

very large scale integration

See VLSI.

vesicular film

Vesicular film is a film that is used to make copies of microfilm or microfiche. It contains its own developer and creates a pink negative or positive copy when exposed to a negative master through ultraviolet light.

VGA

(Video Graphics Array) VGA is a display system that is built into various models of the PS/2, IBM's second-generation personal computer series. VGA boards are also available for plugging into first-generation IBM compatible pcs. VGA supports previous IBM display standards; thus software written for MDA, CGA and EGA display modes will also run under VGA. The text mode (720x400 pixels) has 50 more lines of resolution than EGA, and the graphics mode has 130 more lines of resolution (640x480). In low-resolution mode (equivalent to the CGA 320x200 mode), on-screen colors have been increased from 4 to 256. VGA generates analog signals and requires an analog RGB montor.

Although VGA, as originally defined by IBM, has only 16 colors in its 640x480 mode, third-party vendors of VGA boards have boosted the colors to 256. They have also added a higher-resolution "Super VGA" 800x600 mode that will further improve the visibility of graphics-based applications. See *8514/A*.

VHF

(Very High Frequency) *VHF* is a range of electromagnetic frequencies from 30 million to 300 million Hertz (cycles per second).

VHSIC

(Very High Speed Integrated Circuit) Pronounced "vizik," *VHSIC* refers to ultra-high-speed chips employing LSI and VLSI technologies.

video

Video refers to the audio/visual playback and recording technology used in the television industry that has been standardized by the National Television Standards Committee (NTSC). Since most computer screens use the same tubes and technology (raster graphics) that are found in televisions, the term video also refers to computer display screens and computer terminals. However, there is only one television/video standard in the United States, while there are hundreds of computer/video display standards.

video adapter

Same as *video display board*.

video board

Same as *video display board*.

video camera

A *video camera* is a camera that takes continuous pictures and generates a signal for display on a monitor or for permanent recording. Signals generated by video cameras are traditionally analog, but digital video cameras are available that convert the analog signals into a digital format.

A video camera captures images by breaking down the image into a series of lines. Each line is scanned one at a time, and the continuously varying intensities of red, green and blue light across the line are filtered out and converted into a continuously variable (analog) signal. The standard video signal of 525 scan lines used throughout the United States and Canada is governed by the National Television Standards Committee (NTSC).

VIDEO
(Courtesy RCA)

In the late 1920s, Felix the Cat was one of the first video recording stars. These photos depict one of the earliest video cameras and the resulting image it displayed.

video card

Same as *video display board*.

video display board

A *video display board* is a printed circuit board that plugs into a personal computer and generates the text and graphics images on a monitor (display screen). It is responsible for the resolution quality and number of colors that can appear on screen. It converts the characters or graphic patterns (bit map) within a reserved segment of the computer's memory into signals that refresh the display screen. In digital display systems, the video display board generates digital signals for the monitor. The monitor then does the conversion from digital to analog. In analog display systems, the video display board does the digital to analog conversion and sends analog signals to the monitor.

The monitor must be capable of handling the frequency range of the video display board (number of lines per second). Multisync monitors can accept a range of frequencies and work with more than one type of display board. The major classes of video output that can be generated by display boards are described in the following list. There are many standards within each class. Video display boards may be capable of generating one or more standards within one or more classes.

Monochrome Display Systems

Digital
Analog

Color Display Systems

Digital RGB
Analog composite
Analog RGB
Analog RGB with NTSC video input and output (see *video graphics board*)

video display card

Same as *video display board*.

video display terminal/unit

Same as *video terminal*.

video graphics board

A *video graphics board* is a printed circuit board that is plugged into the computer and connected to a monitor in order to display text and graphics on screen as well as to accept standard television video signals (NTSC) from a camera or video cassette player. For example, the Targa board from Truevision and the Vision board from Vision Technologies are video graphics boards that plug into personal computers.

Since the common display board used in personal computers generates graphics, and since the computer's CRT screen is also called a video display, the term video graphics board may be used to refer to a video display board that does not accept true NTSC video signals.

video RAM

Video RAM is a specially designed memory that is used to hold and transfer an image onto the video screen. The video RAM contains a certain amount of processing logic that converts the pixel data onto the screen in the required format.

video teleconferencing

See *teleconferencing*.

video terminal

A *video terminal* is a common term for a data entry and display device that uses a keyboard for input and a display screen for output. Although the display screen of a video terminal resembles a television set, it usually does not accept standard video signals; rather, it accepts a proprietary display signal developed by computer vendors, which provides for the display of text or graphics or both. See *video*.

videodisc

A *videodisc* is a read-only optical disc that holds up to two hours of video data. Like a phonograph record or compact disc player, many videodisc players provide random access capability to any location on the disc. Various videodisc systems were introduced during the 1970s, but only the LaserVision optical disc technology has survived. By the end of the 1980s, videodiscs have barely made a dent in the home video market, where videotape recorders dominate. It appears that videotapes will continue to be the major video recording and playback medium until such time as an erasable optical system can be economically mass produced. Videodiscs will be used for interactive instructional training courses.

Videodiscs used for movies use a constant linear velocity (CLV) format that records the signal on a continuous, spiraling track, as does a phonograph record. In addition, the signal density is uniform, and the player increases or decreases the speed of rotation depending on which part of the disc is being played. Videodiscs used for interactive purposes use a constant angular velocity (CAV) format like that of a magnetic disk, in which the tracks are concentric circles, each one containing one frame of video. Each side of a CAV videodisc holds 54,000 frames, which is 30 minutes of continuous video at 30 frames per second. Videodiscs are recorded in an analog format unlike that of a videotape recorder.

videotex

Videotex is an interactive information and transaction service that includes such services as shopping, banking, news, weather reports and electronic mail. Videotex services can also provide a gateway to other timesharing and electronic publishing services.

Videotex is delivered over a telephone line to a decoder, which contains a keyboard and is attached to the subscriber's TV set. Videotex information is stored in the decoder and is displayed as predefined screens, or frames, which can be retrieved by number or by menu selection. Due to the limited bandwidth of telephone lines, videotex cannot deliver fully animated TV-like pictures, but can deliver simple graphics, including limited animation. The decoder stores the transmitted frames in its memory and continuously refreshes the TV screen from its memory.

Although videotex experiments have been tried in various parts of the United States, it has yet to catch on as a commercial medium.

view

(1) *View* refers to displaying data on screen.

(2) In relational database management, a *view* is a special display of data that is created as needed. A view temporarily ties two or more files together so that the combined files can be displayed, printed or queried. For example, customers and orders or vendors and purchases can be linked. All the fields to be included are specified by the user. The original files are not permanently linked or altered; however, if the system allows the viewed data to be directly edited, the data in the original files will be changed.

Viewdata

Viewdata is the British term for videotex.

VINES

(VIrtual NEtwork operating System) *VINES* is a UNIX System V-based network operating system from Banyan Systems Inc., that runs on Banyan's own network servers or other 80286, 80386 and 68000-based personal computers. VINES incorporates a naming and addressing system that allows users to locate any resouce on the network without having to know the network topology. An optional electronic mail system is also available.

VINES integrates multiple local area networks (LANs), IBM compatible pcs, minicomputers and mainframes into comprehensive information networks that can be incrementally upgraded as an organization's requirements grow.

virtual

Virtual refers to a simulated or conceptual environment and, as a result, may refer to "virtually" anything.

virtual circuit

A *virtual circuit* is the resulting pathway that is created between two devices communicating with each other in a packet switching system. A message being transmitted from New York to Los Angeles may actually start from New York and go through Atlanta, St. Louis, Denver and Phoenix before it winds up in Los Angeles.

virtual device

Same as *virtual peripheral*.

virtual disk

A *virtual disk* is a disk that is simulated in memory. See *RAM disk*.

virtual image

In graphics, a *virtual image* is the complete graphic image stored in memory, not just the part of it that is displayed at the current time.

virtual machine

(1) A *virtual machine* is a computer that runs multiple operating systems with each operating system running its own programs; for example, an IBM mainframe running under VM or an 80386-based IBM compatible pc running under VM/386.

(2) A *virtual machine* is one operating system and its associated application programs running within a virtual machine environment.

(3) *Virtual machine* may refer to a computer that uses virtual memory in contrast with one that does not.

virtual memory

Virtual memory is a technique that simulates more memory than actually exists and allows the computer to run several programs concurrently regardless of their size. The virtual memory system breaks up a program into segments, called *pages*. Instead of bringing the entire program into memory, it brings as many pages into memory as it can fit based on the current mix of programs, and leaves the remaining pages on disk. When instructions are called for that are not in memory, the appropriate disk page is called in, overlaying the page in memory. If a memory page contains variables or other data that are altered by the running of the program, then the page is temporarily stored on disk when room is needed for new pages. The input and output of program pages is called *paging* or *swapping*.

In order to take total advantage of virtual memory techniques, programs should not contain a lot of "spaghetti code," in which the logic of the program points back and forth to all ends of the program. If they do, *thrashing* will result, which is an excessive amount of disk accesses to bring in program segments. Disk access should be reserved for calling in the next set of data, not the same instructions over and over again.

Although virtual memory can be implemented in software only, for efficient operation, virtual memory requires specialized hardware features. Application programs sometimes claim virtual memory capability, but that often refers to internal techniques that allow for working on large files, not true virtual memory capability.

virtual networking

As defined by Banyan Systems Inc., *virtual networking* is the ability for users to transparently communicate locally and remotely across similar and dissimilar networks through a simple and consistent user interface.

virtual peripheral

A *virtual peripheral* is a peripheral device that is simulated by the operating system. For example, if a program is ready to output data to the printer, but the printer is not available, the operating system will transfer the printer output to disk and keep it there until a printer becomes available.

virtual route

Same as *virtual circuit*.

virtual storage

Same as *virtual memory*.

virus

A *virus* is a program that is used to infect the operation of a computer system. After the virus code is written, it is buried within an existing program, and, once that program is loaded into the computer, the virus replicates by attaching copies of itself to other programs in the system. The purpose of the virus can range from a simple prank that pops up a strange message on the

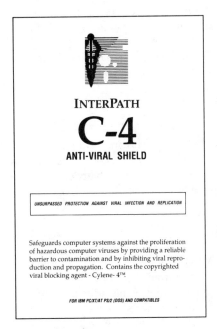

INTERPATH

C-4

ANTI-VIRAL SHIELD

UNSURPASSED PROTECTION AGAINST VIRAL INFECTION AND REPLICATION

Safeguards computer systems against the proliferation of hazardous computer viruses by providing a reliable barrier to contamination and by inhibiting viral reproduction and propagation. Contains the copyrighted viral blocking agent - Cylene- 4™.

FOR IBM PC/XT/AT PS/2 (DOS) AND COMPATIBLES

VIRUS PROTECTION

(Courtesy InterPath)

Users are very happy to install a software package such as this one in order to protect themselves from "disease."

screen out of the blue, to the actual destruction of programs and data that may be set to occur at any time in the future.

A virus cannot be brought into the computer by downloading or transmitting data into it; it can be brought in only by downloading or installing an executable program, which then has to be run in the computer at least one time. A virus is similar to a *worm*, which is also a destructive program; however, the virus always attaches itself to other programs, whereas the worm may not.

VisiCalc

VisiCalc was the first electronic spreadsheet. It was introduced in 1978 for the Apple II computer. Conceived by Dan Bricklin, a student at Harvard Business School, and programmed by a friend named Bob Frankston, VisiCalc became a major success. VisiCalc launched an industry and was almost entirely responsible for having the Apple II be used in business. Thousands of $3,000 Apples were purchased just to run the $150 VisiCalc program.

VisiCalc was a command-driven program that was soon followed by SuperCalc, MultiPlan and a host of others, each one improving on the user interface. Eventually Lotus 1-2-3 dominated the spreadsheet market for IBM compatible pcs, and Microsoft Excel for the Macintosh. Spreadsheets have also been implemented on minicomputers and mainframes, and it all started with VisiCalc.

VLSI

(1) (Very Large Scale Integration) *VLSI* refers to the very large number of electronic transistors and other components that are built onto a single chip. VLSI is in the range of approximately 100,000 to 1,000,000 components per chip.

(2) *VLSI Technology, Inc.*, is a designer and manufacturer of customized computer chips.

VM

(Virtual Machine) *VM* is an operating system that runs on IBM mainframes. Originally developed by IBM customers, VM has been adopted by IBM as a major system product. VM has the ability of running multiple operating systems within the computer at the same time, each operating system running its own programs.

VMS

(Virtual Memory System) *VMS* is a multiuser, multitasking, virtual memory operating system from Digital Equipment Corporation which runs on its VAX line of computers. Any application program running under VMS will run on any VAX computer from the smallest MicroVAX to the largest model in the VAX line.

VM/386

(Virtual Machine/386) VM/386 is a multitasking operating environment from IGC Corporation that runs in 80386-based IBM compatible pcs. VM/386 uses the 386's virtual mode and allows multiple copies of DOS to run in the machine, each running an individual application program.

voice answer back

Voice answer back is a voice message system that generates audio responses in order to provide feedback for the human operator who is performing some function.

voice channel

A *voice channel* is a transmission channel or subchannel that carries human voice.

voice coil

A *voice coil* is a type of motor that is used to move the access arm of a disk drive in very small increments. Like the voice coil of a speaker, the amount of current determines the amount of movement. Contrast with *stepper motor*, which is commonly used for access arm movement, but moves in fixed increments.

voice grade

Voice grade refers to the bandwidth required to transmit human voice, which is approximately 3,000 Hertz.

voice recognition

Voice recognition is the understanding of spoken words by a machine. The spoken words are digitized (turned into digital code) as they are in digital telephone systems, but the digital codes are matched against coded dictionaries in order to identify the words. The recognized words are stored in the computer just as if they were typed in on the keyboard.

Today, most systems must be "trained," requiring samples of all the actual words that will be spoken by the user of the system. The sample words are digitized, stored in the computer and used to match against future words. More sophisticated systems require voice samples, but not of every word. The system uses the voice samples in conjunction with dictionaries of larger vocabularies to match the incoming words.

In the future, voice recognition systems will be able to understand just about anybody. There's a feeling among many that typing will be an obsolete skill in the future. Although this may happen eventually, it won't be soon. Unless major breakthroughs occur within the next 10 years, it may be well after the turn of the century before voice recognition is economical enough to be part of everybody's terminal or personal computer. We will need improved performance in the order of 1,000 times what we have today to make universal voice recognition feasible.

voice response

Voice response is voice output from the computer. Voice response units can make up sentences from stored words, which were originally recorded by a person and stored in analog or digital form, or they can create the sounds from scratch using synthetic voice techniques.

volatile memory

Volatile memory is memory that does not hold its contents without power. A computer's main memory, made up of dynamic RAM or static RAM chips, loses its content immediately upon loss of power.

volt

A *volt* is the unit of measurement of force, or pressure, in an electrical circuit. The common voltage of an AC power line is 120 volts of alternating current (alternating directions). Common voltages within a computer are from 5 to 12 volts of direct current (one direction only).

volt-amps

Volt-amps is the measurement of electrical usage that is computed by multiplying volts times amps. See *watts*.

voltage regulator

A *voltage regulator* is a device that is used to maintain a level amount of voltage in the electrical line. Contrast with *surge suppressor*, which filters out excessive amounts of current, and contrast with *UPS*, which provides backup power in the event of a power failure.

volume

A *volume* is a peripheral storage unit, such as a hard disk, floppy disk, disk cartridge, disk pack or reel of tape.

von Neumann architecture

Von Neumann architecture refers to the stored program concept in which instructions are temporarily stored in a memory while being executed. John von Neumann (1903-1957), a Hungarian-born, internationally renowned mathematician, was the first person to publicly promote this kind of architecture.

The term is often used to refer to the sequential nature of this design concept. In a von Neumann machine, an instruction is analyzed, then the data is processed, then the next instruction is analyzed and the next set of data is processed.

VP-Planner Plus

VP-Planner Plus is a spreadsheet and data analysis program from Paperback Software that runs on IBM compatible pcs. The program is keystroke, file and macro compatible with all versions of Lotus 1-2-3, while providing additional features, such as background recalculation, the ability to manipulate a variety of disk-based database files, and a built-in word processor and report generator.

VP-Planner Plus also includes a multi-dimensional database that stores categories of data in up to five dimensions. The spreadsheet program is used as an interface to both enter and retrieve data from the multi-dimensional file.

VRAM

See *video* RAM.

VRC

(Vertical Redundancy Check) VRC is an error checking method that generates and tests a parity bit for each character (byte) of data that is moved or transmitted.

VRX

VRX is the operating system used on NCR's V8500 and V8600 mainframes.

VS

(1) (Virtual Storage) Same as *virtual memory*.

(2) VS is a series of minicomputers manufactured by Wang Laboratories that use virtual storage techniques.

VSAM

(Virtual Storage Access Method) VSAM is a widely used IBM access method for storing data, which is used in large IBM mainframes.

VSAT

(Very Small Aperture satellite Terminals) VSATs are small earth stations for satellite transmission that handle up to 56,000 bits of digital transmission per second. VSATs that can handle the T1 data rate of up to 1.544 megabits per second are called *TSATs*.

VT 100, 200, 300

(Video Terminal) *VT* refers to a series of display terminals from Digital Equipment Corporation that are used on its PDP and VAX minicomputers. VTs are asynchronous terminals that are available in text and graphics models in both monochrome and color.

VTAM

(Virtual Telecommunications Access Method) *VTAM* is a commonly used communications program from IBM. It controls communication and the flow of data in an SNA network. IBM's NetView is a VTAM application program.

VTR

(Video Tape Recorder) A *VTR* is a video recording and playback machine that records standard NTSC analog video signals on reels of magnetic tape. Contrast with VCR, which uses tape cassettes as the recording medium.

V.21

V.21 is the CCITT standard for 300 bps full-duplex modems for use in the switched telephone network.

V.22

V.22 is the CCITT standard for 1,200 bps full-duplex modems for use in the switched telephone network.

V.22 bis

V.22 bis is the CCITT standard for 2,400 bps full-duplex modems for use in the switched telephone network.

V.23

V.23 is the CCITT standard for 600 and 1,200 bps half-duplex modems for use in the switched telephone network.

V.24

V.24 is the CCITT standard that is operationally compatible with the RS-232 standard.

V.25, V.25 bis

V.25 and V.25 bis are the CCITT standards for automatic dial commands. Due to the popularity of the Hayes Smartmodem command set, V.25 is not often used in the United States.

V.26

V.26 is the CCITT standard for 2,400 bps full-duplex modems for use in four-wire leased lines.

V.26 bis

V.26 bis is the CCITT standard for 1,200 and 2,400 bps full-duplex modems for use in the switched telephone network.

V.27

V.27 is the CCITT standard for 4,800 bps full-duplex modems for use in leased lines.

V.27 bis

V.27 bis is the CCITT standard for 2,400 and 4,800 bps full-duplex modems for use in leased lines.

V.27 ter

V.27 ter is the CCITT standard for 4,800 bps full-duplex modems for use in the switched telephone network.

V.29

V.29 is the CCITT standard for 9,600 bps half-duplex modems that is commonly used in facsimile machines.

V.32

V.32 is the CCITT standard for 9,600 bps full-duplex modems for use in the switched telephone network.

V8500, V8600

The V8500 and V8600 are series of mainframes manufactured by NCR.

wafer

(1) A *wafer* is a round slice of silicon approximately 1/30th of an inch thick and from three to six inches in diameter that is the base unit upon which hundreds of chips are created through a series of photomasking, etching and implantation steps. See *chip*.

(2) A *wafer* is a small, continuous-loop magnetic tape cartridge that is used for the storage of data.

TAPE WAFER

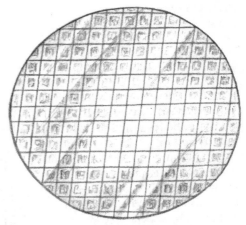

SILICON WAFER

wafer scale integration

Wafer scale integration is a semiconductor wafer that contains an integrated set of circuits throughout its entire surface. It is the next evolutionary step in microminiaturizing electronic circuits, but it is a difficult one. Trilogy, Inc., formed in 1980 by the famous computer designer Gene Amdahl, was funded with the largest amount of venture capital in the history of the world, yet it failed to achieve wafer scale integration.

Just as the integrated circuit interconnects hundreds of thousands of transistors today, some day in the future, wafer scale integration will interconnect several hundred integrated circuits, eliminating the need to cut the chips out of the wafer and package them, only to have to reconnect them again later.

wait state

A *wait state* is an amount of time spent waiting for some operation to take place. It can refer to a variable length of time a program has to wait before it can be processed, or it may refer to a specific duration of time, such as a machine cycle.

wand

A *wand* is a hand-held optical reader that is used to read typewritten fonts, printed fonts, optical character recognition (OCR) fonts and bar codes. The wand is waved over each line of characters or codes in a single pass.

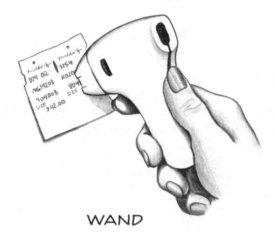

WAND

Wang Laboratories

Wang Laboratories was founded in 1951 by Dr. An Wang, who came to the United States from China in 1945 to study applied physics at Harvard University. In Wang's first decade in business, the company produced specialized electronic devices which included electronic counters, machine tool controls, block-tape readers, encoders and telecoder generators.

In 1965, Wang introduced its first electronic scientific desk calculator that generated a natural logarithm with one keystroke. By 1969, Wang programmable calculators became an industry standard.

In 1971, Wang introduced its first word processing product, a dual cassette typing system called the

DR. AN WANG
(Courtesy Wang Laboratories)

1200. In 1972, it introduced the 2200 series of small business computers. In 1976, came a CRT-based word processing system called the WPS, and in 1977, Wang introduced its VS (Virtual Storage) line of minicomputers. By 1978, Wang was the largest supplier of small business computers in North America and the largest worlwide supplier of CRT-based word processing systems.

WANG CALCULATOR (1965)
(Courtesy Wang Laboratories)

Throughout the 1980s, Wang has continually enhanced its computer line and word processing products. By introducing such products as the Wang Integrated Office Solution in 1986, a voice/data network for office systems, Wang has made a strong commitment to office automation and continues to integrate and develop its product line accordingly.

On March 27, 1988, Dr. Wang was inducted into the National Inventors Hall of Fame for his 1948 invention of a pulse transfer device that enabled magnetic core memories to be used in computers. The Hall of Fame has recognized the achievements of an elite group of 68 inventors which includes Thomas Edison, Louis Pasteur and Alexander Graham Bell.

Wangnet

Wangnet is a broadband local area network from Wang Laboratories.

warm boot

A *warm boot* is a bootstrap operation that is performed after the system has been running.

watts

Watts are a measurement of electrical usage that is obtained by multiplying volts, amps and the power factor (VOLTS x AMPS x POWER FACTOR). The power factor is a number between 0 and 1, which represents 0 to 100% of the useful energy. In electric heaters or incandescent light bulbs, the power factor is 1, or 100%. Because of the switching nature of the power supplies used, computers have a power factor of approximately 60 to 70%, or .6 to .7. Thus, watt ratings for personal computers are less than the traditional computation for watts, which is VOLTS x AMPS.

wave

A *wave* is the shape of radiated energy. All radio signals, light rays, x-rays, and cosmic rays radiate an energy that looks likes rippling waves. Try to visualize this wavelike energy yourself. Take a piece of paper and start drawing an up and down line very fast while pulling the paper slowly in a direction perpendicular to the line. You should wind up with a bunch of waves on the paper. Another way to visualize a wave is to move your right hand up and even with your eye level with the palm facing down, and holding your fingers together, begin to vibrate them up and down. If you focus on your finger tips while you move your hand to the right, you will be able to catch a glimpse of the wave.

waveguide

A *waveguide* is a rectangular, circular or elliptical tube through which radio waves are transmitted.

Weitek coprocessor

A *Weitek coprocessor* is a math coprocessor for micro and minicomputers from Weitek Corporation. Weitek has been making coprocessors since 1981 that run on high-performance CAD and graphics workstations from companies such as Sun and Apollo. Weitek coprocessors for Intel-based machines run faster than the 80287 and 80387 coprocessors from Intel. In order to use the Weitek coprocessor, the software must be written to activate it.

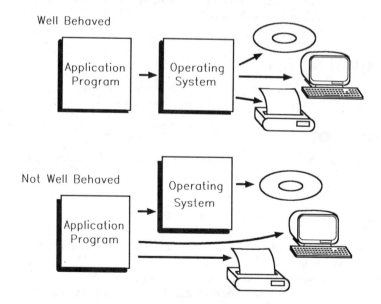

well behaved, well mannered

Well behaved or *well mannered* programs are application programs that don't deviate from a standard. For example, many programs written for Microsoft's DOS operating systems bypass the normal interaction with the operating system and directly activate the hardware. Since these programs are not well behaved, they will not run in all IBM compatible computers unless the hardware is 100% compatible with the IBM machines. On the other hand, well behaved programs will run in all IBM compatible computers.

what if?

What if? is one of the fundamental concepts behind the use of a spreadsheet as a planning tool. When new data is entered into the spreadsheet, results are calculated based upon the formulas in the spreadsheet. Assumptions can be plugged in that ripple through to the bottom line. For example, "if the hourly labor rate is increased by $2, how much does it affect the profit for this product line?"

Whetstones

Whetstones is a benchmark program that tests floating point operations. The results of the program are expressed in Whetstones per second. Whetstone I tests 32-bit, and Whetstone II tests 64-bit floating point operations. Contrast with *Dhrystones*, which tests a general mix of instructions.

WHIRLWIND I
(Courtesy The MIT Museum)

WHIRLWIND

WHIRLWIND was the first electronic digital computer with realtime capability and the first to use magnetic core memory. Developed at the Massachusetts Institute of Technology (MIT) throughout the 1940s, it became operational in the early 1950s. The machine was continually enhanced eventually using over 12,000 vacuum tubes and 20,000 diodes and occupying two floors of a building on the MIT campus. It wound up with 2K of 16-bit magnetic core memory and used a magnetic drum as well as magnetic tape for auxiliary storage.

WHIRLWIND made many contributions towards the making of future computers, including circuit design, the use of CRTs and realtime communications. Project members later worked on IBM's 700 series, and one in particular named Kenneth Olson, founded Digital Equipment Corporation.

white noise

Same as *Gaussian noise*.

wide area network

In communications, a *wide area network* is a network that interconnects geographical boundaries such as cities and states.

widow & orphan

A *widow* is the last line of a paragraph that appears alone at the top of the next page, and an *orphan* is the first line of a paragraph that appears alone at the bottom of a page. Widow and orphan settings in word processing and desktop publishing programs are usually set for a minimum of two lines, but can changed by the user.

wild cards

Wild cards are symbols that are used to represent any value when naming files. For example, in Microsoft's DOS and OS/2 operating systems, the symbol * stands for any name of up to eight characters, and the symbol ? stands for any single character. The description *.WK1 references all files with a WK1 extension. The description **CR*.*** references all files that start with CR no matter what their extension.

Winchester disk

A *Winchester disk* is a sealed disk technology that was developed by IBM, which incorporates the access arm, read/write heads and disk platters into a sealed unit. By aligning the read/write heads to their own set of disks, greater storage capacities and accessing speeds are obtainable than with removable disk cartridges. The Winchester disk was originally designed as a dual 30-megabyte configuration, and its 30-30 specification, the same as a Winchester rifle, gave rise to its name. Although originally a self-contained, removable module, the term is used today to refer to any fixed hard disk.

window

(1) A *window* is a separate viewing
area on a display screen as provided
by the software. Operating systems
can provide multiple windows on
screen, allowing the user to keep
several application programs active
and visible at the same time.
Individual application programs can
provide multiple windows as well,
providing a viewing capability into
more than one document,
spreadsheet or data file.

WINDOWS

(2) A *window* is a reserved area of
main memory. Same as *buffer*.

(3) A *window* is a period of time in which an event can or must occur.

windowing software

Same as *windows program*.

Windows

Windows is a windows program from Microsoft Corporation that runs in IBM
compatible pcs under Microsoft's DOS operating system. With Windows, two or
more applications can be open at the same time and users can switch back and
forth between them. If the applications are written to run under Windows, data
and graphics can be copied and moved from one application program to the
other. Data and graphics from normal DOS applications can be copied and
moved into Windows applications. Windows also provides print spooling, which
allows printing to take place in the background.

Windows provides a desktop environment similar, although not identical, to the
Macintosh. Multiple application programs, or multiple copies of the same
application program, can be opened into windows that can be sized and located
anywhere on screen. The applications can be also converted into icons and
placed on the desktop when not used. Windows makes it easier to work with
subdirectories than normal DOS, but it does not create folders into which
documents are placed as does the Macintosh.

Several desktop application programs are provided with Windows, including a
clock, calculator, card file, calendar and notepad.

windows environment

A *windows environment* is a computer that is running under an operating system
that provides multiple windows on screen. DESQview, Microsoft Windows,

Presentation Manager, Finder, MultiFinder and X Window are examples of windows environments.

windows program

(1) A *windows program* is software that adds a windows capability to an existing operating system.

(2) A *Windows program* is an application program that is written to run under Microsoft Windows.

Windows/386

Windows/386 is a special version of Windows from Microsoft Corporation that runs under Microsoft's DOS operating system only on IBM compatible pcs using the 80386 CPU. Windows/386 takes advantage of the 80386's virtual mode and allows multiple DOS applications to run in a multitasking environment with memory protection. Memory protection prevents the entire computer from stopping if a single application program crashes. Windows also simulates the EMS 4.0 memory standard in normal extended memory without requiring special EMS boards.

wire frame modeling

In computer-aided design (CAD), *wire frame modeling* is a technique for representing 3-D objects, in which all surfaces are visibly outlined in lines, including the opposite sides and all internal components that are normally hidden from view. Compared to surface and solid modeling, wire frame modeling is the least complex method for representing 3-D images.

WIREFRAME
(Courtesy CADKEY, INC.)

wire wrapped

Wire wrapped refers to electrical connections that are wired together by wrapping the bare end of a wire around a metal prong. Wire wrapping techniques used to be the most common form of interconnection between components.

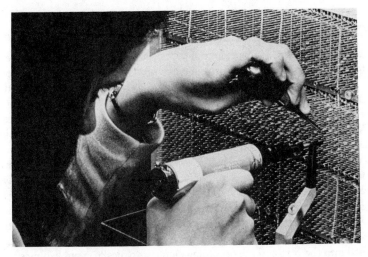

WIRE WRAPPING
(Courtesy Digital)

wireless

Same as *radio*.

wizzywig

See *WYSIWYG*.

WKS file, WK1 file

A *WKS file* is a worksheet file created from Lotus 1-2-3, version 1A. A *WK1 file* is a version 2.0 file.

word

(1) A *word* is the computer's internal storage unit and refers to the amount of data it can hold in its registers and process as a single unit. For example, a 16-bit computer processes two bytes in the same time it takes an 8-bit computer to process one byte, providing the timing clocks are of equal speed.

(2) In word processing, a *word* is the primary text structure. It is identified by a blank space before and after a group of characters.

word addressable

Word addressable refers to a computer that can address memory only on word boundaries. Contrast with *byte addressable*, which is memory that can be addressed by each individual byte.

word processing

Word processing is the management of text documents and replaces all the operations normally associated with a typewriter. The advantage over typing is that documents are permanently stored in the computer and can be called back for editing. However, the many additional features of word processing have made the typewriter obsolete for all functions except typing labels and envelopes.

Word processing lets you type anything you want on your computer's keyboard and see the words appear on screen. The text you create is called a *document*, and the document is stored on a disk as a text file. Text files are quite common among all personal computers and have the most interchangeability of any file produced on the computer. Underlines, boldface and other layout settings may not show up correctly, but the words will appear the same.

After you create the document, you can print it with an infinite variety of type fonts if you have a laser printer. Advanced word processors allow graphics to be merged into the text and are becoming elementary desktop publishing systems.

Word processing can be performed on any personal computer, minicomputer or mainframe network. Word processing is often the first step towards office automation.

Standard Features of a
Full-Featured Word Processor

WORD WRAP AND CENTERING
Word processors wrap a word around to the next line when it extends over the right margin. They also provide for centering text and returning to the left margin.

TEXT EDITING
You can always change existing text by deleting it, typing over it or inserting text into it.

SEARCH & REPLACE, MOVE & COPY
You can search for any occurrence of text and replace it with any other. You can mark a block of text and move it elsewhere in the document or copy it throughout the document.

LAYOUT SETTINGS
A word processor lets you reset margins, tabs, line spacing, indents and fonts anywhere in the document, as well as print underlined or boldface text.

HEADERS, FOOTERS AND PAGE NUMBERING
Headers and footers are common text on the top and bottom of every page. Page numbering can be selected as a separate entity or as part of a header or footer. Page numbering in letters, digits and Roman numerals is also common.

MAIL MERGE
Mail merge lets you write a letter and print it with different names from a list of names and addresses.

MATH AND SORTING
Math capability lets you add up columns of numbers and compute arithmetic expressions within the document. Sorting reorders lines of text in the document into ascending (low to high) or descending (high to low) sequence.

PREVIEW, PRINT AND GROUP PRINT
A document can be previewed before it is printed to show any layout change that is not normally shown, such as page breaks, headers, footers and footnotes. Documents can be printed as individual documents or as groups of documents with page numbers consecutively numbered from the first to the last document.

FOOTNOTES
Footnote entries can be made at any place in the document, and the footnotes printed at the end of a page or document.

SPELLING CHECKER AND THESAURUS
Spelling for an individual word, marked block of text or an entire document can be checked. When words are in doubt, possible corrections are suggested. Advanced systems can correct the misspellings automatically the next time around.

FILE MANAGEMENT
Documents can be copied, renamed and deleted, and directories, or folders, can be created and deleted from within the program. Advanced systems set up a purge list of names or glimpses of document contents in order to allow a user to easily rid the disk of unwanted files periodically.

Advanced Features

WINDOWS
Windows lets you work with two or more documents at the same time.

COLUMNS
All word processors let you create columns by tabbing to a tab stop. However, true columns wrap the words within each column. This is very useful, for example, when writing a resume with employer name on the left and work history on the right, or for script writing.

Magazine-style columns are another variety of columns that wrap words from the bottom of one column to the top of the next column.

TABLES OF CONTENTS AND INDEXES

Tables of contents and indexes can be generated from entries typed throughout the document.

DESKTOP PUBLISHING

Graphics can be merged into the text and displayed on screen either normally or in a special preview mode and printed. A graphic object can be resized (scaled), rotated and anchored so that it remains with a particular segment of text. Rules and borders can also be printed with the text.

Graphics-based versus Text-based

Graphics-based word processing programs, such as Microsoft Word on IBM pcs or all the Macintosh word processing programs, show you a reasonable facsimile on screen of the typeface that will be printed. Text-based programs always show the same type size on screen.

Graphics-based systems are superior for preparing newsletters or brochures that contain a lot of fancy typesetting and font changes. Text-based screens are fine for standard office typing or for documents that use a limited number of fonts.

Format Standards

Almost every word processing program generates its own proprietary codes for layout settings. For example, in WordStar, ^PB turns on and off boldface, but in Version 5.0 of WordPerfect, [BOLD] turns boldface on, and [bold] turns it off.

There are conversion programs that convert documents from one format to another. If a conversion program doesn't exist, multiple search & replace commands will have to be performed. However, if the same code turns a mode on as well as off, as in the WordStar example above, then each search & replace has to be verified manually to ensure that the right code is being changed.

The User Interface

Word processing is a keyboard-intensive application often involving long hours in front of a computer's display screen. In addition, many word processing users are touch typists and appreciate the advantage of being able to type and edit text quickly.

As straightforward as the design criteria are, the actual interaction with a word processing program runs from the ridiculous to the sublime. Some of the most awkward programs have sold well due to clever marketing.

As a novice, it's very difficult to tell a good user interface from a bad one. It takes months to discover the nuances. In addition, what's good for the occasional user might be horrid for the user who types eight hours a day.

Changing margins, tabs and indents should be easy, but centering text, changing to boldface and underline, the functions that are done over and over again, should be accomplished with a couple of simple keystrokes at the most. Changing to a different font should be just as simple.

Fast typists should avoid the use of a mouse-driven program. Mice impede fast typing and editing.

The two most important features of a word processing system are its keyboard and display screen. The feel of a keyboard is personal, and only you can judge it, and only after hours of typing. Display screens should have the highest resolution possible, and color screens are far better than monochrome as long as the program allows the user to change colors. Color preference is individual, and after hours at a screen, it's easy to figure out which color combination is the most restful to your eyes.

word processing machine

A *word processing machine* is a computer that is specialized for only word processing functions. Same as *word processor*.

word processor

(1) A *word processor* is a word processing software program that provides word processing functions on a computer.

(2) A *word processor* is a computer that has been specialized for word processing functions. Until the late 1970s, word processors were always dedicated machines. However, since a personal computer can do word processing as well as any other kind of processing, personal computers have rapidly replaced the dedicated word processor.

word publishing

Word publishing refers to word processing programs that provide a certain number of desktop publishing features such as merging, displaying and printing graphics with text.

word wrap

Word wrap is a feature of all word processing and other text handling systems that aligns text automatically within the preset margins. Unlike a typewriter, in which you have to press the carriage return key to move to the beginning of the next line, word wrap keeps track of the characters being typed and performs the operation automatically. In some word processing programs, word wrap is a feature that can be switched off for writing programming source code.

WordPerfect

WordPerfect, introduced in 1980, is a word processing program from WordPerfect Corporation (formerly Satellite Software International), that runs on IBM compatible pcs, the Apple II series, Macintosh, Amiga and Atari personal computers. WordPerfect is a full-featured program that is extremely popular.

Version 5.0, introduced in 1988, is a significantly improved program that includes many desktop publishing features and enhancements for using a laser printer. Graphics can be merged into the document and then resized and rotated, and a WYSIWIG preview mode allows users to see the finished document before printing.

WordStar

WordStar is a series of word processing programs from MicroPro International that run on IBM compatible pcs. The original WordStar, introduced in 1978 for CP/M machines, was the first full-featured word processing program for microcomputers. It gave sophisticated word processing capabilities to personal computer users at significantly less cost than the dedicated word processing machines of the time.

In late 1984, MicroPro introduced WordStar 2000, an elaborate and sluggish word processing program that was not readily accepted by existing WordStar users. Later versions were significantly improved, and, in late 1987, Version 3.0 featured desktop publishing capabilities.

MicroPro has sold over 3,000,000 copies of its WordStar programs, and the original WordStar has been renamed "WordStar Professional." The original WordStar commands have become an industry standard and are used in many text editors and notepads that are integrated into larger systems.

work group

A *work group* is two or more individuals who need to share the same files and databases. Local area networks are designed around work groups to provide for the electronic sharing of the required data.

worksheet

Same as *spreadsheet*.

worksheet compiler

Same as *spreadsheet compiler*.

workstation

(1) A *workstation* is a high-performance, single user microcomputer or minicomputer that has been specialized for graphics, computer-aided design (CAD), computer-aided engineering (CAE) or scientific applications. Today, high-end personal computers, such as 80386-based machines and the Macintosh II, are also competing in the market traditionally served by workstation vendors, such as Digital, Hewlett-Packard, Sun and Apollo.

(2) *Workstation* is used to refer to any terminal or personal computer.

worm

(1) (Write Once Read Many) A *WORM* device is a storage device, such as an optical disk, that can be written (recorded) once. Although it can be erased by writing 1 bits onto the data, it cannot be rewritten.

(2) A *worm* is a destructive routine in a program that is designed to adulterate a program or database either all at once or over a period of time. Same as *logic bomb*.

WP

See *word processing*.

write

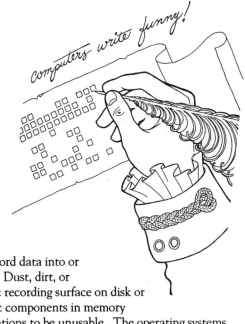

Write is to record data into or onto a memory or storage device, such as disk, tape, memory and firmware. Read and write is analogous to play and record on an audio tape recorder.

write error

A *write error* is the inability to record data into or onto a memory or storage device. Dust, dirt, or damaged portions of the magnetic recording surface on disk or tape, or malfunctioning electronic components in memory devices will cause the storage locations to be unusable. The operating systems may be able to flag the damaged portions of the storage device and keep processing.

write protect

Write protect prohibits the erasing or changing of a disk file. See *file protection*.

write protect notch

A *write protect notch* is a small, square cutout on the side of a floppy disk that is used to render the disk read only. When the notch is covered on 5 1/4" floppy disks, the files on the disk cannot be erased or changed. See *floppy disk*.

WXmodem

(Window Xmodem) *WXmodem* is a faster version of the Xmodem communications protocol that allows the sending system to transmit data without waiting for the receiving system to acknowledge the transfer.

WYSIWYG

(What You See Is What You Get) Pronounced "wizzy-wig," it refers to graphics-based display screens that show graphics and text on screen the way the printer will print them. WYSIWYG screens show different sizes and styles of typefaces on screen similar to the way they will print. Although a 24-point font will show up on screen in a proper ratio to a 10-point font, if the screen and printer fonts are not matched, there will be either slight or obvious differences between the screen characters and the printed characters. In addition, a desktop laser printer, at 300 dots per inch, has a much higher resolution than almost any display screen. In such cases, the screen and printout cannot truly be 100% the same.

WYSIWYG

X

x-axis

See *x-y matrix*.

x-height

In typography, the *x-height* is the height of the letter x in lower case. Point size includes the x-height, the height of the ascender and the height of the descender. See *typeface* for an illustration.

X Window

X *Window* is a windowing environment for graphics workstations that was developed at the Massachusetts Institute of Technology (MIT) with participation from Digital Equipment Corporation and IBM. X Window differs from traditional windowing programs that work on a single computer system. It is designed to allow graphics generated in one computer system to be displayed on another workstation in the network. X Window, designed to run under any operating system, is supported by all major graphics workstation vendors.

xcopy

Xcopy is a copy program that comes with Microsoft's DOS and OS/2 operating systems. It allows all subdirectories within a directory to be copied at one time. The following example copies all files and subdirectories in the current directory to the XYZ directory. New subdirectories will be created in the XYZ directory if they do not already exist. The /S copies the subdirectories, and the /E says to copy subdirectories even if they're empty (no files).

```
xcopy *.* \xyz /s /e
```

XDOS

XDOS is a program from Hunter Systems that takes executable code for Intel-based microprocessors and converts it into executable Motorola 68020 code ready to run under UNIX. That means a program that runs on an IBM compatible pc can be translated into a running program on a UNIX-based 68020 computer.

XENIX

XENIX is a version of the UNIX operating system from Microsoft Corporation that runs on IBM compatible pcs. XENIX conforms to AT&T's System V Interface Definition (SVID) with additional enhancements such as file and record locking, graphics and networking. XENIX was originally developed for the Tandy Radio Shack Model 16 multiuser business computer.

In February 1987, AT&T, Microsoft, Interactive Systems Corp., and The Santa Cruz Operation joined to create a single standard for the 80386 and future Intel microprocessors. Developed by Microsoft, the new UNIX standard will be upward compatible from UNIX System V, Version 5.3, and XENIX System V, Version 2.2.

XLISP

XLISP is a microcomputer version of the LISP programming language that has been in the public domain for a number of years.

Xmodem

Xmodem is a simple asynchronous communications protocol for personal computers that can detect most transmission errors, but not all. Xmodem was originally developed by Ward Christensen to transfer data between first-generation personal computers using CP/M.

Xmodem-CRC

Xmodem-CRC is an advanced Xmodem protocol that uses a cyclic redundancy check (CRC) to detect all transmission errors.

XMT

In communications, XMT is an abbreviation for transmit.

XNS/ITP

(Xerox Network Systems/Internet TransPort) XNS/ITP was the main protocol used in early Ethernet networks. Although widely used, it is now often being replaced with TCP/IP.

xon-xoff

In communications, *xon-xoff* is a simple asynchronous protocol that keeps the receiving device in synchronization with the sending device. When the buffer in the receiving device is full, it sends an *x-off* signal (transmit off) to the sending device, telling it to stop transmitting. When the receiving device is ready to accept more, it sends the sending device an *x-on* signal (transmit on) to start again.

x-y matrix

An *x-y matrix* is a group of rows and columns. The x-axis is the horizontal row, and the y-axis is the vertical column. An x-y matrix is the framework of two-dimensional structures, such as mathematical tables, display screens, digitizer tablets, dot matrix printers and 2-D graphics images.

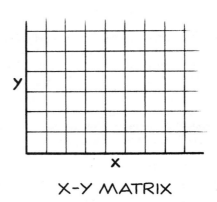

X-Y MATRIX

x-y monitor

In graphics, an *x-y monitor* is the screen portion of a vector display terminal. The entire vector display would be the monitor combined with the vector graphics controller.

x-y plotter

Same as *plotter*.

x-y-z matrix

An *x-y-z* matrix is a three-dimensional structure. The x and y axes are the first two dimensions, and the z axis is the third dimension. In a graphic image, the x and y provide width and height, and the z provides depth.

XyWrite

XyWrite, pronounced "zy-write," is a word processing program from XyQuest, Inc., that runs on IBM compatible pcs. It is noted for its large number of features, speed and flexibility. XyWrite is a command-driven word processing system; however, its entire user interface can be customized by the user, including the keyboard, command menus and help screens. Designed after the Atex minicomputer typesetting system, it offers the user extensive control over the printing of a document. XyWrite includes a programming language for advanced, programmer-oriented users.

X.12

X.12 is a standard international communications protocol for electronic data interchange (EDI).

X.21

X.21 is a standard international communications protocol that is used in a circuit switching network.

X.25

X.25 is a standard international communications protocol that is used in packet switching networks.

X.25 Pad

An X.25 Pad is a hardware adapter that allows non-X.25 devices to communicate in an X.25 network.

X.400

X.400 is an OSI standard mail and messaging protocol.

X.500

X.500 is an OSI standard mail and messaging protocol that includes the capability of maintaining directories of users.

y-axis

See *x-y matrix*.

Ymodem

Ymodem is an asynchronous communications protocol for personal computers that is identical to the Xmodem-CRC protocol, with the addition of batch file transfer.

z-axis

A *z-axis* provides the third dimension to a graphics image. The width dimension is the x-axis and the height dimension is the y-axis.

zap

Zap is a command that typically deletes the data within a file but leaves the file structure intact so that new data can be entered. Commands such as ERASE and DEL remove the file name from the disk requiring that it be created again.

zero wait state

Zero wait state refers to a memory that begins to transfer its data immediately upon being accessed without waiting one or more machine cycles in order to respond.

Zmodem

Zmodem is an asynchronous communications protocol for personal computers that can handle larger transfers of data without error than its Xmodem-CRC predecessor. Zmodem is especially effective in satellite transmission, where end-to-end delays can be several seconds long.

Z80, Z8000

The *Z80* is an 8-bit microprocessor from Zilog Corporation that was the successor to the Intel 8080. The Z80 was widely used in first-generation personal computers that used the CP/M operating system. The Z8000 is the 16-bit successor to the Z80.

1.2M

1.2M may refer to the high-density floppy disk used on IBM AT and compatible personal computers that holds 1.2 megabytes.

1.44M

1.44M may refer to the high-density microfloppy disk used in IBM compatible pcs that holds 1.44 megabytes.

1401

The *1401* was a second-generation computer system from IBM that was introduced in 1959 and used up until the late 1960s. It used magnetic cores for

IBM 1401
(Courtesy IBM)

memory (up to 16K) and magnetic tapes (up to six drives) for storage. Punched cards were the primary input medium. The 1401 was an outstanding success for IBM; an estimated 18,000 units were installed. As competition from Honeywell's 200 series started to get serious, IBM announced the System/360, a family of third-generation computers. 360 models provided 1401 emulation so that customers could migrate to the 360 right away.

16-bit

See *8-bit, 16-bit, 32-bit.*

286

See *80286, 80386.*

2780, 3780

2780 and 3780 are standard communications protocols for transmitting batch data (non-interactive). The numbers originated with early IBM remote job entry (RJE) terminals that included a card reader and a printer.

32-bit

See *8-bit, 16-bit, 32-bit.*

360K

360K may refer to the 5 1/4" minifloppy disk used with IBM compatible pcs that holds 360 kilobytes.

360, 370 series

The System/360 series, announced by IBM in 1964, was the first time a hardware vendor every introduced a family of compatible computer systems. It's ironic that IBM's biggest problems today are incompatibility, when it invented the concept.

IBM 360 "SOLID LOGIC"
(Courtesy IBM)

The three transistors on this module used in the 360 series were a sign of advanced technology of the day.

The machine language and architecture of the 360s has been carried into all the models in all the series that followed it, although there have been many subsequent enhancements. And, as is typical in migration, programs written for newer models often won't run in older models. In 1970, IBM upgraded the line to the System/370 series. Later series in order of introduction include the 303x, 43xx, 308x and 309x. In 1983, IBM introduced the PC XT/370, a personal computer that runs 370 programs. In 1987, the 9370 was introduced, the first small-scale departmental computer that uses the 370 architecture.

370 architecture

370 architecture refers to any IBM machine that is part of the mainframe line stemming from the original System/360 series back in the mid-1960s. See *360*, *370 series*.

386

See *80386*.

386^{Max}

386 "to the Max" is a memory management program from Qualitas, Inc., that runs in 80386-based IBM compatible pcs. It converts normal extended memory in the 386 into expanded memory and fits multiple RAM resident (TSR) programs into unused portions of memory above 640K.

386SX

See *80386SX*.

303x

The *303x* is a series of medium to large-scale IBM mainframes initially introduced in 1977, which includes the 3031, 3032 and 3033 models. See *360*, *370 series*.

308x

The *308x* is a series of large-scale IBM mainframes initially introduced in 1980, which includes the 3081, 3081 Model Group K and 3084. See *370 series*.

309x

The *309x* is a series of large-scale IBM mainframes initially introduced in 1986. See *370 series*.

3270

3270 is the communications protocol for interactive terminals connected to IBM mainframes, which includes the 3278 monochrome terminal and the 3279 color version. In order to interconnect to IBM mainframes, the 3270 protocol is commonly used in other devices; for example, hardware and software can be added to personal computers and minicomputers that allows them to emulate the 3270. The IBM mainframe thinks it's interacting with a regular user terminal, but it could be communicating with a VAX mini or a Macintosh.

3770

3770 is a standard communications protocol for batch transmission (non-interactive) in an IBM SNA environment.

3780

See *2780, 3780*.

4GL

See *fourth-generation language*.

43xx

The *43xx* is a series of medium-scale IBM mainframes initially introduced in 1979, which include the 4300, 4321, 4331, 4341, 4361 and 4381. See *360, 370 series*.

486

See *80486*.

5100

The *5100* was the first desktop computer from IBM. Introduced in 1974, it came with up to 64K of memory and a built-in tape drive, and APL and BASIC were the available programming languages. Although called a portable computer, it weighed almost 50 pounds. Eight inch floppy disks became available on the model 5110 in 1976.

6502

The *6502* is an 8-bit microprocessor chip from Rockwell International that is used in the Apple II series and earlier models of the Atari and Commodore personal computers.

650

The 650, introduced in 1954, was IBM's first major computer system success. It used a magnetic drum for memory, magnetic tape for storage and punched cards for input. By the end of the 1950s, there were an estimated 1,800 650s installed, making it the most widely used computer in the world.

IBM 650
(Courtesy IBM)

6800

The 6800 is an 8-bit microprocessor chip from Motorola, Inc. The 6801 is a computer on a chip version of the 6800, which also contains RAM, ROM, an input/output control unit and a timing clock.

68000, 68020, 68030

The 68000 is a 32-bit microprocessor from Motorola, Inc., that uses a 16-bit data bus and can address up to 16 megabytes of memory. It is used in the Macintosh and in a variety of other workstations. The 68020 is a full 32-bit version of the 68000, and the 68030 is an enhanced model that runs at higher clock speeds.

7-track, 9-track

7-track and 9-track are magnetic tape coding schemes that indicate the number of parallel tracks that follow the length of the tape. 7-track tape holds a 6-bit character plus parity, and 9-track tapes hold an 8-bit byte plus parity.

720K

720K may refer to the 720 kilobyte microfloppy disk used in IBM compatible pcs.

8-bit, 16-bit, 32-bit

The *8-bit, 16-bit* and *32-bit* specifications are the computer's internal word size, which is the amount of data the processor can hold in its registers and work on at the same time. Large-scale supercomputers hold 64 bits. All things being equal, a 16-bit computer works twice as fast as an 8-bit computer; however, this specification measures only one aspect of a computer'performance.

Traditionally, this bit designation held true not only for the word size, but also for the width of the internal data bus, the pathway over which data is transferred from memory to the processor. However, in some cases word and bus size are different. For example, the Intel 8088 used in first-generation IBM PCs uses a 16-bit word, but only an 8-bit bus. The Motorola 68000, used in various Macintosh models, processes a 32-bit word, but uses only a 16-bit bus.

Bit specifications are also used to designate the amount of memory the processor can address, or work with. For example, an 8/16-bit computer uses an 8-bit word size, but its address register holds 16 bits and can address 65,536 memory locations. A 16/24-bit computer uses a 16-bit word and data bus, but has a 24-bit address bus that can address 16,772,216 memory locations.

802.1, 802.2, 802.3, 802.4, 802.5

See *IEEE 802.1.*

8080

The *8080* is an 8-bit microprocessor chip from Intel that was introduced in 1974. It was the successor to the 8008, the first commercial 8-bit microprocessor. The 8080 was the precursor to the 8086/8088 microprocessors.

8086/8088

The 8086/8088 are 16-bit microprocessor chips from Intel introduced in 1978. The 8088 was the first microprocessor used in the IBM PC. The 8088 uses an 8-bit data bus, while the 8086 uses a 16-bit data bus. Both the 8086 and the 8088 address 20 bits, or up to 1,048,576 bytes of memory.

80286, 80386

The 80286 and 80386, commonly known as the 286 and 386, are microprocessors from Intel Corporation that are higher-performance models of the 8086 and 8088. The 286 and 386 are upward compatible from the 8086/8088. Except for programs that utilize enhanced features of the 286 and 386, most software packages run in all three CPUs (8086/8088, 286, 386).

The 286, introduced in 1984, is from five to 20 times faster (depending on clock speed) internally than the 8088. It is a multitasking, 16-bit CPU that can address 16 megabytes of memory (24-bit address bus). The 386, introduced in 1986, is from 20 to 35 times faster internally (depending on clock speed) than the 8088. It is a multitasking, 32-bit CPU that can address up to four gigabytes of physical memory (32-bit address bus) and up to 64 terabytes of virtual memory.

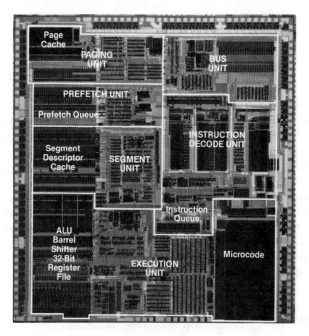

80386 CPU

(Courtesy Intel Corporation)

The 386 is a significantly more advanced CPU than the 286. It has a "virtual mode" that allows it to run multiple DOS applications at the same time. This mode is triggered by programs such as VM/386 and, eventually, the 386-specific version of OS/2.

80386SX

The 80386SX, commonly known as the 386SX, is a slower version of the 386 microprocessor from Intel Corporation. It provides the same internal 32 bit processing, but uses a 16-bit data bus instead of a 32-bit data bus. With the addition of an adapter board, the 386SX can be installed in existing 286 machines. The 386SX is also known as the "P9," its original code name. The 386 provides the advanced features of the full-size 386 at less speed and less cost.

80486

The 80486, commonly known as the 486, is a high-speed version of the 386 microprocessor expected to be in production in 1989.

8100

The 8100 is a minicomputer from IBM that was introduced in 1978. The 8100 was designed for departmental computing and uses the DPPX/SP operating system. A DPPX/SP system for the 9370 series is being developed so that 8100 users can migrate to the 370 architecture.

8514/A

The *8514/A* is a high-resolution video display adapter from IBM for Micro Channel models of the PS/2 personal computer series. It provides a resolution of 1024x768 pixels, with up to 256 colors or 64 shades of gray. The 8514/A board plugs into the PS/2 bus and coexists with the built-in VGA display standard. It is designed for high-resolution, dual-monitor CAD and graphics applications.

The 8514/A is more than a video controller as are the medium-resolution IBM EGA and VGA standards. It provides a video coprocessor that performs 2-D graphics functions internally, thus relieving the CPU of graphics tasks and improving the performance of computer-aided design applications. The 8514/A is about three times as fast as VGA and requires about a tenth of the microprocessor's time to perform graphics functions.

As the 8514/A catches on, 8514 boards that plug into the AT bus will most likely become available from third-party vendors, as graphics-based Windows and Presentation Manager applications will take full advantage of the high resolution.

88000

The *88000* is a family of 32-bit RISC microprocessors from Motorola, Inc.

88100

The *88100* is the first processor in the 88000 family of 32-bit RISC microprocessors from Motorola, Inc. Introduced in 1988, it incorporates four built-in execution units that allow up to five operations to be performed in parallel.

9-track

See *7-track, 9-track.*

9370

The *9370* is a series of small-scale IBM mainframes initially introduced in 1986. The 9370 uses the same machine language and architecture as the larger 4381 and 3090 mainframes. See *370 series.*

.

See *star-dot-star.*